Peru, Bolivia & Ecuador

Ben Box, Robert and Daisy Kunstaetter,
Julius Honnor, Geoffrey Groesbeck

We need the tonic of wildness... At the same
time that we are earnest to explore and learn all
things, we require that all things be mysterious
and unexplorable, that land and sea be
infinitely wild, unsurveyed and unfathomed by
us because unfathomable. We can never have
enough of nature.

Henry David Thoreau, Walden

To Galápagos Islands

Pacific Ocean

COLOMBIA

8 · Otavalo
9 · QUITO
Guayaquil · Riobamba · Baños
Tumbes · Puyo
Cuenca
Macará · **ECUADOR**
Piura · Loja
Vilcabamba

Chiclayo · Jaén
Chachapoyas · Iquitos
Trujillo

3 · Huaraz

PERU · **BRAZIL**

LIMA
La Oroya
Huancayo
Pisco
Ica · Ayacucho · *Manu Biosphere Reserve*
Nasca · Abancay · 1 *Machu Picchu* · 4
Cusco
Puerto Maldonado

Arequipa · 2 · Juliaca
Puno · 5
Lake Titicaca · Rurrenabaque
Copacabana
LA PAZ · Coroico · Trinidad
BOLIVIA
Oruro · Cochabamba
7 · San Javier · Concepción
Salar de Uyuni · Potosí · Sucre · Santa Cruz · San Ignacio de Velasco
CHILE · Uyuni · 6 · San Rafael
Tupiza · San José de Chiquitos
Tarija

ARGENTINA · **PARAGUAY**

Galápagos Islands

Charles Darwin
Teodoro Wolf
10 · Pinta
Marchena
Genovesa
Santiago
Fernandina · Santa Cruz
San Cristóbal
Isabela · Floreana · Española

200 km
200 miles

Think Peru, Bolivia and Ecuador and you automatically think of the Andes, the long, sinuous mountain chain that runs the full length of all three countries and forms the geographical and cultural spine of South America. Here, at over 12,000 feet, the first Incas rose from the freezing waters of Lake Titicaca. They named their capital Cusco, 'Navel of the World', and built an empire that lasted until the Spanish came, saw, conquered and converted the natives. But old habits die hard and today indigenous customs and beliefs are very much in evidence: in the beautiful and skillful *artesanía* (handicrafts); the spectacular festival costumes; the sacred temples and pyramids; or in the burying of a llama foetus under a new house to repel evil spirits. Often these ancient traditions were subsumed into the 'new' religion of the colonial masters. It is the synthesis of ancient America and medieval Europe that is the essence of these countries. Thousands of years of empire-building, natural disasters, conquest, occupation and independence have all been played out, against the backdrop of those mighty mountains, the one constant in a continent of constant change.

$\rightarrow$

Contents

4

GALAPAGOS
ISLANDS

QUITO
ECUADOR

PERU

LIMA

LA PAZ
BOLIVIA

- Lima & the South Coast
- Cusco & Southern Peru
- Northern Peru
- Peruvian Amazon
- La Paz & around
- Southern & Central Highlands
- Eastern Bolivia
- Quito & the Highlands
- Oriente
- Galápagos Islands

Essentials 8

Lima & the South Coast 66

Cusco & Southern Peru 98

Northern Peru 172

About the guide

Until recently, backpacking was the preserve of the impecunious student, stretching their pesos/baht/rupees as far as possible, sleeping in cockroach-infested, cell-like rooms and risking food poisoning by eating at the cheapest market stalls they could find. Today's backpackers, however, are different. They still have the same adventurous spirit but they probably don't have endless months to swan around the globe; they're interested in the people, culture, wildlife and history of a region and they're willing to splash out occasionally to ensure that their trip is truly memorable.

Footprint's Backpacker guides are designed precisely for this new breed of traveller. We've selected the best sights, sleeping options, restaurants and a range of adventure activities so that you can have the experience of a lifetime. With over 80 years' experience of writing about Latin America, we hope that you find this guide easy to use, enjoyable to read and good to look at.

Essentials, the first chapter, deals with practicalities: introducing the region and suggesting where and when to go, what to do and how to get around; we give the lowdown on visas, money, health and transport, and provide overviews of history, culture and wildlife. The rest of the guide is divided into area-based chapters, colour-coded for convenience. At the start of each chapter, a highlights map gives an instant overview of the area and its attractions. A star rating system also gives each area marks out of five for Landscape, Activities, Culture etc. The Costs category refers to value for money in relation to Europe and North America, where $$$$$ is expensive and $ is very cheap. Follow the cross references to the district that interests you to find a more detailed map, together with a snapshot of the area, showing the amount of time you will need, how to get there and move around, and what to expect in terms of weather, accommodation and restaurants. **Special features** include expert tips, inspiring travellers' tales, suggestions for busting your budget and ideas for going that little bit further.

We use a range of symbols throughout the guide to indicate the following information:
- Sleeping
- Eating
- Entertainment
- Festivals
- Shopping
- Activities and tours
- Transport
- Directory

Please note that hotel and restaurant codes, pages 26 and 30, should only be used as a guide to the prices and facilities offered by the establishment. It is at the discretion of the owners to vary them from time to time.

Footprint feedback We try as hard as we can to make each Footprint guide as up to date as possible but, of course, things always change. If you want to let us know about your experiences – good, bad or ugly – then don't delay, go to www.footprintbooks.com and send in your comments.

Essentials

Aymara woman in Puno.

Where to go

The variety which Peru, Bolivia and Ecuador can offer the visitor is enormous. The obvious attractions in Peru are Machu Picchu, the Nasca Lines and the jungle reserves of Manu and Tambopata, while in Ecuador the colonial heritage of the capital, Quito, and the wildlife extravaganza that is the Galápagos Islands are the major draws. Bolivia's major attraction for tourists, meanwhile, is its wild natural beauty. Much of the country lies off the beaten track; a vast wilderness waiting to be explored and appreciated. The problem is, if you're on a tight schedule, how to fit it all in. Seeing a lot of these countries by bus in the space of a few weeks is a forlorn hope. Flying offers a relatively cheap alternative and an opportunity to see more.

Two weeks

The best option for a two week visit is to limit yourself to one or two countries. As Peru is sandwiched in the middle, it is logical to combine it with a visit to either Bolivia or Ecuador. In Peru there are certain places that fit neatly into seven days of travelling. **Southern Peru** offers a very rewarding short circuit covering the most important and popular sites in this part of the country. **Cusco** and **Machu Picchu**, the crown jewels of the Inca Empire, require at least four days, more if you plan to hike the **Inca Trail**. Beautiful **Titicaca**, the highest navigable lake in the world, the elegant colonial city of **Arequipa** and nearby **Colca Canyon**, and the incredible **Nasca Lines** could all be combined with Cusco into a 9-10 day tour using air, rail and road travel.

You could then head from Lake Titicaca across the border to the Bolivian capital, **La Paz**, which is fairly small and manageable and easy to explore on foot in a couple of days. Several interesting trips can be made from La Paz, including the ruins of the great pre-Inca city of **Tiahuanaco**. From La Paz you can mountain bike down the 'world's most dangerous road' to the little town of **Coroico**, a popular resort in the sub-tropical valleys of the **Yungas**.

An alternative to Bolivia would be to fly from Lima to the beautiful colonial city of **Quito**, in Ecuador. You could easily spend a few weeks in and around Quito without exhausting all possibilities. One of Ecuador's great attractions is its relative compactness and much of what you want to see is only a few hours by road from the capital. Only two hours north is **Otavalo**, home to one of the finest craft markets in all of Latin America and a few hours' south is the spectacular **Cotopaxi National Park**, the stunning **Quilotoa circuit** and **Baños**, a very popular spa town at the foot of an active volcano.

If you don't arrange a trip to the **Amazon jungle** from Cusco (see below), it's realtively cheap and easy to arrange one from Quito to one of Ecuador's many jungle lodges. The alternative is to travel under your own steam to one of the main jungle towns and arrange a tour from there with a local agency. Tours can be arranged from Puyo, Tena, Misahuallí, Coca and Baños, which is on the road from the highlands to the Oriente. And then there's the **Galápagos Islands**, Ecuador's famed wildlife showcase. It's expensive to visit but well worth it. Galápagos tours range from four days up to 14 days, but seven days would be optimal, if you can afford it, to fully appreciate this once-in-a-lifetime experience.

From top to bottom: Lake Titicaca; Laguna Colorada; Galápagos Islands; Inca Trail.

One month

A month allows you the luxury of several further options for exploring more of Peru, Bolivia and Ecuador. With this amount of time to spare you really should visit **Manu National Park** or the **Tambopata National Reserve** in Peru's southeastern jungle. These provide wonderful opportunities for watchers of birds, butterflies and animals and for plant lovers. Trips to the southeastern jungle can be booked in Cusco, which is the jumping off-point for flights or the 24-hour overland journey.

Another option in Peru is to head for **Huaraz**, in the **Cordillera Blanca**, only seven hours by road from Lima and one of the world's top climbing and trekking destinations. A week spent exploring the Cordillera and neighbouring areas can easily be linked with the coastal archaeological sites near the colonial city of **Trujillo** and further north, around **Chiclayo**. From Chiclayo you could venture to the more remote **Chachapoyas** region, which contains a bewildering number of prehispanic archaeological sites. A week minimum here would be a

Top tips

How big is your footprint?

During the past decade there has been a phenomenal growth in tourism that promotes and supports the conservation of natural environments and is also fair and equitable to local communities. This 'eco-tourism' segment is probably the fastest growing sector of the travel industry in all of South America. Amongst the best known examples in the region are the Kapawi lodge in southern Oriente (p400) and Chalalán Eco Lodge in Bolivia (p264).

Tourism Concern ⓘ *Stapleton House, 277-281 Holloway Rd, London N7 8HN, UK T0207-753 3330, www.tourismconcern.org.uk*, aims to promote a greater understanding of the impact of tourism on host communities and environments. **Centre for Responsible Tourism (CRT)** ⓘ *PO Box 827, San Anselmo, California 94979, USA*, co-ordinates a North American network and advises on North American sources of information on responsible tourism. **Centre for the Advancement of Responsive Travel (CART)** ⓘ *UK T01732-352757*, has a range of publications available as well as information on alternative holiday destinations. **CARE International UK** ⓘ *10-13 Rushworth St, London SE1 0RB, T0207-934 9334, www.careinternational.org.uk*, works to impove the economic conditions of people living in developing countries. They are currently involved in the development of the Che Guevara Trail in Bolivia.

✅ Choose a destination, tour operator or hotel with a proven ethical and environmental commitment; if in doubt ask.
✅ Spend money on locally produced (rather than imported) goods and services and use common sense when bargaining.
✅ Stay in local, rather than foreign-owned, accommodation; the economic benefits for host communities are far greater.
✅ Use water and electricity carefully; travellers may receive preferential supply while local communities are overlooked.
✅ Learn about local etiquette and culture; consider local norms of behaviour and dress appropriately.
✅ Protect wildlife and other natural resources.
✅ Always ask before taking photographs or videos of people.
❌ Don't give money or sweets to children – it encourages begging – instead give to a recognized project, charity or school.

good idea. North of Peru, there are several border crossings to the south of Ecuador. The easiest, from Piura to Loja, goes via **Vilcabamba**, once a fabled fountain of youth, today the southern terminus of Ecuador's 'gringo trail'. Only six hours north of here is **Cuenca**, a lovely colonial city and also a great place to buy Panama hats (yes, they're made in Ecuador!).

Alternatively, you could spend more time in Bolvia instead of visiting northern Peru. Those visiting during the dry season – April to October – would be strongly advised not to miss a trip to **Rurrenabaque**, from where you can take a jungle or pampas tour and experience the country's amazing diversity of wildlife. Rurre is also the starting point for the fantastic **Chalalán Eco-lodge**. Ecotourism with a capital 'E', it stands in the **Madidi National Park**, one of Bolivia's newest protected areas, and one which boasts a greater biodiversity than anywhere else on earth. The **Southern Altiplano** is one of the most remote corners of Bolivia and also one of the most fascinating. Old colonial **Potosí** is probably the most interesting of all Bolivia's cities and a visit to its former silver mines is a must. Nearby is the country's official capital, **Sucre**, a real gem of colonial architecture. Southwest from Potosí is **Uyuni**, the starting point for a three- to four-day tour to the **Salar de Uyuni**, a vast, blindingly white salt lake and one of the most spectacular sights in the entire country. South of the Salar, near the Chilean border, are deserts, volcanoes and multi-coloured soda lakes teeming with flamingos.

When to go

Ecuador's climate is so varied and variable that any time of the year is good for a visit. In the highlands, temperatures vary more with altitude than they do with the seasons (which mainly reflect changes in rainfall). To the west of the Andes, June to September are dry and October to May are wet (but there is sometimes a short dry spell in December or January). To the east, October to February are dry and March through September are wet. There is also variation in annual rainfall from north to south, with the southern highlands being drier. In the Oriente, as in the rest of the Amazon basin, heavy rain can fall at any time, but it is usually wettest from March to September. The Galápagos are hot from January to April, when heavy but brief showers are likely. From May through December is the cooler misty season.

Peru's high season in the highlands is from May to September. At this time the days are generally clear and sunny, though nights can be very cold at high altitude. During the wettest months in the highlands, November to April, some roads become impassable. April and May, at the tail end of the highland rainy season, is a beautiful time to see the Peruvian Andes. On the coast, high seasons are September and Christmas to February. The summer months are from December to April, but from approximately May to October much of this area is covered with *la garúa*, a blanket of cloud and mist.

The best time to visit the jungle in **Peru** and **Bolivia** is during the dry season, from April to October. During the wet season, November to April, it is oppressively hot (40° C and above) and while it only rains for a few hours at a time, it is enough to make some roads virtually impassable.

These are also the months when mosquitos and other biting insects are at their worst, so this is not a good time to visit the jungle. As for the rest of **Bolivia**, the Altiplano does not receive much rain, so timing is not so crucial here, although hiking trails can get very muddy during the wet season. During the winter months of June and July, nights tend to be clearer but even colder than at other times. These are the best months to visit the Salar de Uyuni, as the salt lake is even more impressive under clear blue skies.

Overall June-September offers the best weather conditions, but this is also the high season when prices rise and accommodation and bus tickets are hard to come by. If you know when you will be travelling it's best to buy your ticket in advance and book hotel rooms, especially in the more expensive categories.

Sport and activities

The region has an incredibly varied climate and landscape, making it perfect for a multitude of outdoor activities. This is one of the very best parts of the world for a number of adventure sports, including trekking and climbing, whitewater rafting, mountain biking and surfing. Facilities for adventure tourism tend to develop in correlation with general tourist services so always make sure the infrastructure and equipment is adequate before signing up for a potential dangerous activity. Also check the experience and qualifications of operators and guides. Peru, Bolivia and Ecuador also offer probably the greatest wildlife viewing opportunities on the planet and Peru is unmatched anywhere for the sheer scale of its ancient ruins.

Birdwatching

Peru has nearly 20% of all bird species in the world and 45% of all neotropical birds. Birdwatching is possible all year round and the range to be seen is hugely rewarding for beginners and the more experienced. Ecuador is also one of the richest places in the world for birds.

★ **Head for**
Manu Biosphere Reserve ▸▸ *p208*
Tambopata-Candamo Reserved Zone ▸▸
p211 **Paracas ▸▸** *p88* **Colca Canyon ▸▸**
p160 **Mindo ▸▸** *p329* **Ambaró ▸▸** *p305* **Río**
Napo lodges ▸▸ *p398*

Climbing

There is excellent climbing throughout the region, with over a thousand peaks above 5,000 m and several more above 6,000 m. Peru has fantastic ice climbing while Ecuador has something to offer for both beginners and experts, with the magical opportunity to climb an active volcano by moonlight. Bolivia has some

of the best mountaineering in the world but the infrastructure is not very developed, so do not expect to be rescued if you get into trouble. The climbing season runs from May to September, with the best months being June-August. Proper technical equipment, experience and/or a competent guide are essential to cross

5 best

Ancient ruins

Machu Picchu ➤➤ *p114*
Huaca de la Luna ➤➤ *p178*
Tiahuanaco ➤➤ *p229*
Choquequirao ➤➤ *p146*
Kuelap ➤➤ *p190*

glaciers and climb snow and ice safely. A number of summits are achievable by acclimatized beginners with a competent guide and the correct high-altitude climbing equipment.

⭐ **Head for**
La Paz ➤➤ *p237* Cotopaxi ➤➤ *p357* Chimborazo ➤➤ *p360* Sorata ➤➤ *p254* Cordillera Blanca ➤➤ *p201*

ⓘ **Peruvian Mountain Guide Association** (AGMP), Casa de Guías, Huaraz, see p201.
Asocación Ecuatoriana de Guías de Montaña (Aseguim), Pinto 416 y JL Mera, p 2, Quito, T02-223 4109. They can be very hard to contact in an emergency, it is best to contact them through **Safari Tours** (p340) or **Compañia de Guías de Montaña**, p339). **Club Andino Boliviano**, C Mexico 1638, La Paz, T/F02-2324682, is the national mountaineering club in Bolivia.

Cultural tourism

Cultural tourism is a rapidly growing niche market and covers more esoteric pursuits such as archaeology and mystical tourism. Several tour operators in Peru offer customized packages for special interest groups. Local operators offering these more specialized tours are listed in the travelling text under the relevant location. Under the umbrella heading **Al-Tur, PromPerú** has 31 interesting community-based tourism projects in archaeology, agro-tourism, education,

jungle trips, llama trekking, nature tourism and traditional medicine. See p44 for contact details.

⭐ **Head for**
Cusco ➤➤ *p135* Chiclayo ➤➤ *p180* Trujillo ➤➤ *p177*

Cycling/mountain biking

Although the area is blessed with fantastic routes, views and a generally stable climate, cycling is yet to really take off. It is best to take a guide or join a tour group as most routes and trails remain unmapped. There are more and more operators specializing in biking, many of the 'gravity assisted' type, with good equipment and back-up. One of the most thrilling rides in the entire continent is in Bolivia, down the 'world's most dangerous road', but there are also many places for novices.

⭐ **Head for**
Cordillera Blanca ➤➤ *p200* Chimborazo ➤➤ *p360* Baños ➤➤ *p357* La Paz to Coroico ➤➤ *p237* Chacaltaya ➤➤ *p236*

Diving and snorkelling

The Galápagos Islands are well known for their distinctive marine environments and offer more than 20 dive sites. Each island contains its own unique environment and many are home to underwater life forms found nowhere else. There are several tour operators in Quito which feature diving and full instruction on their programmes.

You should note that diving in the Galápagos is for experienced divers only due to difficult conditions. Snorkelling is highly recommended, however, and you will come face-to-face with all manner of marine animals. A safer and easier option for novice divers is Machalilla National Park, on the coast of Ecuador.

⭐ **Head for**
Parque Nacional Machalilla ▸▸ *p384*
Galápagos ▸▸ *p422*

Parapenting/hang gliding

Vuelo Libre (parapenting) is just taking off in Peru. Flying from the coastal cliffs is easy and the thermals are good. The area with the greatest potential is the Sacred Valley of Cusco which has excellent launch sites, thermals and reasonable landing sites. The season in the Sierra is May to October, with the best months being August and September. Some flights in Peru have exceeded 6,500 m.

⭐ **Head for**
Cusco ▸▸ *p135* **Huaraz** ▸▸ *p193*

Rafting and kayaking

Peru and Ecuador are perfect for rafting and kayaking of all classes and skill levels. At the height of the Andes expect to find routes for only the most experienced, while lower down, the rivers calm to provide great conditions for beginners and those who are content to drift and admire some of the magnificent, untouched scenery. The Río Blanco, In Ecuador, is possibly the best of all, with 47 km of non-stop grade III-IV rapids and is offered by agencies in Quito.

⭐ **Head for**
Cusco ▸▸ *p135* **Quito** ▸▸ *p339*
Baños ▸▸ *p356* **Tena** ▸▸ *p392*

Sandboarding

If you've always fancied tearing down a massive sand dune on a wooden board, then southern coastal desert in Peru is the place for you. As much fun as snowboarding but without the cold or required technical expertise, sandboarding is a growing sport amongst warm weather thrill-seekers.

⭐ **Head for**
Huacachina ▸▸ *p90* **Nasca** ▸▸ *p90*

Skiing

Without the aid of lifts, skiing in Peru is largely for the high altitude enthusiast. Pastoruri, at 5,000 m, has the only piste and holds a championship during *Semana del Andinismo* at the end of the November to June season. The extreme ski descent craze has hit the Cordillera Blanca in a big way and no peak is considered off limits.

Bolivia boasts the world's highest ski run, at Chacaltaya (5,345 m), but facilities are limited and you can only ski immediately after a fresh snowfall.

★ **Head for**
Cordillera Blanca ▸ *p193*
Chacaltaya ▸ *p236*

ⓘ **Club Andino Boliviano** (see above under Climbing) arranges trips to Chacaltaya.

Surfing and bodyboarding

Peru is internationally renowned for its surf spots. Point Break, Left and Right Reef breaks and waves up to 6 m high can be found. September to February is best on the north coast and March to December south of Lima. Ecuador also has excellent beaches for beginners and experts. Waves are generally best from December to March.

★ **Head for**
Huanchaco ▸ *p178* **Montañita**
(south of Puerto López) ▸ *p384*

ⓘ *Tablista* is a bimonthly surfing mag in Peru. Also look out for *X3*. www.wannasurf.com is a good site for surfing information in Peru and Ecuador.

Trekking

The whole region has wonderful trekking opportunites, from easy one day hikes to more challenging treks through mountain ranges and jungle habitats. It is also possible to combine hikes and treks with visits to ancient ruins, the prime example being the 4 day hike to Machu Picchu. Bolivia is endowed with many excellent treks, some of them on existing Inca roads. Most of the popular treks begin around La Paz and cross the Cordillera Real, finishing in the sub-tropical Yungas, but

Essentials Travelling Sport & activities

5 best

Adventure highs

Whitewater rafting on the Río Blanco ▸▸ *p339*
Climbing in the Cordillera Blanca ▸▸ *p201*
Mountain biking down the near-perfect volcanic cones
of Chimborazo ▸▸ *p360*
Exploring the reefs and sea life of the Galápagos Islands ▸▸ *p422*
Sandboarding down the world's highest sand dune ▸▸ *p90*

many other parts of the country also offer excellent possibilities. Intrepid hikers could find themselves in isolation for days with only the occasional llama for company, passing through campesino villages, where the inhabitants may have never seen a fleece jacket or pair of hiking boots.

★ **Head for**
Cordillera Blanca ▸▸ *p201* Cusco and Sacred Valley ▸▸ *p117* Vilcabamba ▸▸ *p376* Quilotoa ▸▸ *p354* La Paz ▸▸ *p236* Sorata ▸▸ *p254*

ⓘ Check out trekkinginecuador.com. Good trekking guidebooks are *Trekking in Ecuador* by Robert & Daisy Kunstaetter (Mountaineers, Seattle, 2002) and *Trekking in Bolivia* by Yossi Brain by the same publisher. Also *The Andes A Trekking Guide* by John & Cathy Biggar (Andes).

Wildlife watching

Peru, Ecuador and Bolivia have a huge range of diverse habitats that can now be easily visited through a number of good tour companies. The Galápagos is the outstanding area for seeing wildlife but this is a very expensive option. The southern Peruvian Amazon offers fantastic wildlife opportunities - jaguar, giant river otters, over a dozen species of monkey and huge black caiman to name but a few - while in Bolivia, jungle or pampas tours from Rurrenabaque, are much cheaper and

very popular, though nothing can match the sheer splendour of Madidi, Amboró or Noel Kempff Mercado.

★ **Head for**
Manu Biosphere Reserve ▸▸ *p208* Tambopata ▸▸ *p210* Noel Kempff Mercado ▸▸ *p307* Amboró ▸▸ *p305* Madidi ▸▸ *p258* Cuyabeno ▸▸ *p395* Galápagos ▸▸ *p404* Parque Nacional Machalilla ▸▸ *p384*

Discover trekking...

...in Ecuador!

www.trekkinginecuador.com

Arriving by air

The majority of international flights to the region arrive at **Quito** (UIO, page 320), **Lima** (LIM, page 71) or **La Paz** (LPB, page 222), with the first two receiving by far the majority of flights. One way and return flights are available to all of these destinations. Also inquire about 'Open Jaws' (flying into one point and returning from another). Most airlines offer different fare types such as fixed return, yearly return or student (under 26) fares. While student fares are often the most flexible they may not necessarily be the cheapest. Airpasses for North, Central and South America are often bought in conjunction with International flights so ask when booking if you plan to use internal flights.

From the UK flights to Quito start at between £400-500 (in low season). Lima is more expensive (£500-600), higher still in July and at Christmas. **From the USA**, flights to Lima and Quito cost around US$325-510. Most airlines offer discounted fares on scheduled flights through agencies who specialize in this type of fare. For a list of these agencies see below. The busy seasons are 7 December-15 January and 10 July-10 September. If you intend travelling during those times, book as far ahead as possible. Between February-May and September-November special offers may be available.

Flights from Europe

It is only possible to get regular flights direct to **Lima** or **Quito**, making these destinations the most useful entry/exit points with the widest range of options and prices. Direct flights are available from Madrid or Barcelona with **Iberia** and from Amtsterdam with **KLM**. Most connecting flights in Europe are through these cities although it is possible to fly to the US and get a connecting flight with one of the carriers shown below. It is also possible to fly direct to South American cities and then get a connecting flight onward to Lima, La Paz or Quito with carriers such as **Varig**. Direct flights to **La Paz** from Europe are not offered by any airline, the best option here is to fly direct to Lima, Rio de Janeiro or São Paulo and catch a connecting flight. Alternatively, you can fly to Miami and connect from there.

From the USA and Canada

Lima is the best served destination from the USA with Miami serving as the main gateway, together with Atlanta, Dallas, Houston, Los Angeles and New York. The main carriers

Essentials Travelling Getting there & flying around

Top tips

Transport

Bus

✓ For international service, it's cheaper to take a bus to the border, cross and then take another to your final destination.

✓ Make sure you see your gear being stored on the correct bus, especially at busy terminals. 'Mistakes', intentional or innocent, are not uncommon.

✓ In general, try to reserve, and pay for, a seat as far as possible in advance and arrive in good time, as buses often depart when full. Confirm that the bus leaves from same place that the ticket was purchased.

✓ In the Highlands, don't just rely on buses to get from A to B. Ask where the *colectivos* leave from. They may be a bit more expensive, but they are quicker.

✓ In the wet season, bus travel is subject to long delays and detours.

✓ It is always possible to buy food on the roadside, as buses stop frequently, but make sure you have very small-denomination notes.

✓ Always carry your valuables with you, even when leaving the bus at a meal stop.

✓ On overnight trips, especially in the Andes, you will appreciate extra clothing or a blanket as many buses do not have any form of heating.

✓ On all journeys take toilet paper. Toilet facilities on cheaper buses are almost non-existent but bus drivers are generally happy to stop anywhere.

✗ If your bus has a VCR, don't expect to see any scenery by day, and don't expect to get any sleep at night.

✗ Avoid the back seats at all costs. On unpaved roads you will spend more time airborne than seated, and the windows will be jammed open, causing you to cough your lungs up from the exhaust fumes and clouds of choking dust, as well as freeze to death at night in the mountains.

Car

✓ When hiring a car check exactly what the insurance policy covers. In many cases it will only protect you against minor bumps and scrapes and not major accidents. Ask if extra cover is available. Beware of being billed for scratches which were on the vehicle before you hired it.

✗ Never leave a car unattended except in a locked garage or guarded parking space. Street children will generally protect your car fiercely in exchange for a tip. Lock the clutch or accelerator to the steering wheel with a heavy, obvious chain or lock.

✗ You cannot take a hire car across the border from Peru.

available from these destinations are **Aero Continente, American Airlines, Lan Chile/Lan Perú, Continental, Delta, Copa, Lacsa** and **AeroMéxico**. From Canada, there are only direct flights from Toronto with **Air Canada** which flies three times a week. Flights from all other Canadian cities must fly via one of the above gateways.

Quito can be reached directly from Miami, Houston and New York with **American Airlines, Lan Chile** and **Continental Airlines**. Flights from all other US cities must go via these destination. Cheaper fares may be available from **Copa Airlines** and **TACA**, although these go via Panama City and San José, Costa Rica.

There are daily direct flights from Miami to **La Paz** with **American Airlines** and **LAB**. **Continental Airways** also has a direct service from Miami to **Santa Cruz** three times a week.

Discount flight agents

In the UK
Journey Latin America, 12-13 Heathfield Terr, London, W4 4JE, T020-8747 8315; 12 St Ann's Square, Manchester, M2 7HW, T0161-832 1441, www.journeylatinamerica.co.uk
STA Travel, 86 Old Brompton Rd, London, SW7 3LQ, T0870 160 0599, www.statravel.co.uk. They have 65 other branches in the UK, including many University campuses. Specialists in low-cost student/youth flights and tours, also good for student Ids and insurance.
Trailfinders, 194 Kensington High St, London, W8 7RG, T020-7938 3939, www.trailfinders.com. They also have other branches in London, as well as in Birmingham, Bristol, Cambridge, Glasgow, Manchester, Newcastle, Dublin and Belfast.
Trips Worldwide, 14 Frederick Pl, Clifton, Bristol BS8 1JT, T0117-311 4400, www.tripsworldwide.co.uk.

North America
Air Brokers International, 685 Market Street, Suite 400, San Francisco, CA94105, T01-800-883 3273, www.airbrokers.com. Consolidator and specialist on RTW and Circle Pacific tickets.
Discount Airfares Worldwide On-Line, www.etn.nl/discount.htm. A hub of consolidator and discount agent links.
Exito Latin American Travel Specialists, 108 Rutgers St, Fort Collins, CO 80525, T1800-655-4053; worldwide T970-482-3019, www.exito-travel.com
STA Travel, 5900 Wiltshire Blvd, Suite 2110, Los Angeles, CA 90036, 1-800-781-4040, www.sta-travel.com. Also branches in New York, San Francisco, Boston, Miami, Chicago, Seattle and Washington DC.
Travel CUTS, in all major Canadian cities and on university and college campuses, T1-866-246-9762, www.travelcuts.com. Specialist in

Essentials Travelling Getting there & flying around

student discount fares, IDs and other travel services. Branches in other Canadian cities as well as California, USA.

Australia and New Zealand
Flight Centre, T133133, www.flightcentre.com.au. With offices throughout Australia and other countries.
STA Travel, T1300-360960, www.sta travel.com.au; 208 Swanston St,

Melbourne, VIC 3000, T03-9639 0599. In NZ: 130 Cuba Street, PO Box 6604, Wellington, T04-385 0561, cuba@statravel.co.nz. Also in major towns and university campuses.
Travel.com.au, T02 9249 6000, outside Sydney: T1300 130 482, www.travel.com.au.
Trailfinders, 8 Spring St, Sydney, NSW 2000, T1300-780212, www.trailfinders.com.au

...and leaving again

When you buy your ticket, always check whether departure tax is included in the price. International departure tax is US$28 in **Peru**, payable in dollars or soles, US$25 in **Ecuador**, and US$25 in **Bolivia**, payable in dollars or bolivianos but cash only. You will not be allowed to board the plane without proof of payment

Regional flights

Peru Two main national carriers serve the major routes in Peru, these are AeroContinente, www.aerocontiente.com.pe, and Tans, www.tans.com.pe. Note that the Peruvian government has suspended Aero Continente flights until further notice. Prices range from US$63 to US176 for a one-way trip anywhere from Lima. Prices rise during holiday times and elections so try to book early to guarantee flights. Both **Lan Perú**, www.lanperu.com, and **Grupo Taca**, www.grupotaca.com, also offer flights along the major routes. For the more remote highland and jungle areas try **Aero Cóndor**, www.aerocondor.com.pe, and **LC Busre**, www.lcbusre.com.pe. Be aware that these areas are prone to long delays and constant timetable revision due to unpredictable weather. All internal flight prices are in US dollars and are subject to 19% tax. Flights must be reconfirmed in the departure town at least 24 hours in advance.

Ecuador The main internal airline is **TAME** (Quito, T02-290 9900, www.tame.com.ec). All major airports and the Galápagos are served but be wary of constantly changing routes and timetables. In addition **Aerogal**, www.aerogal.com.ec, and **Icaro**, www.icaro.com.ec, both offer services on a smaller number of routes.

Bolivia The main internal carriers are **Lloyd Aéreo Boliviano** (LAB), www.labairlines.com and **Aero Sur**, www.aerosur.com although the military air service, **TAM**, also has occasional flights. **LAB** has a 30 day domestic airpass for US$296 for five flights to all destinations although many flights radiate from La Paz, Santa Cruz or Cochabamba. **LAB** also offer 5% discount to family members if travelling together and 5% discount to students under 26. **Aero Sur** also give 5% discount to students under 26 as well as offering a 20% discount to those over 65. Insure your bags heavily as there can be long delays and possible loss of luggage.

Getting around by road and rail

Peru

Bus Services along the coast to the north and south as well as inland are good. There are varying degrees of comfort offered, ranging from the relative luxury of first class to packed, uncomfortable second class. Direct first class (*ejecutivo*) service buses to major centres. Many buses have bathrooms, movies and reclining seats (*bus cama*) but there are varying classes and the price and quality of the journey will change accordingly. The companies thought to have the best services and the most routes are **Ormeño** (www.ascinsa.com/ORMENO), **Cruz del Sur** (www.cruzdelsur.com.pe) and **CIVA**. In addition, smaller *Combis* operate between most small towns on 1-3-hour journeys. Prices of bus tickets are raised by 60-100%, 2-3 days before Semana Santa, 28 July (Independence Day) and Christmas. Tickets are sold out 2-3 days in advance at this time and transport is hard to come by.

Car You must have an international driving licence to drive in Peru, but if renting a car, your home driving licence will be accepted for up to six months You must also be over 21. Car hire rates tend to be very expensive but ask tourist offices, and hotels should know of the cheapest companies. Always check that the vehicle comes with spare wheels etc. You must be over 25 to hire a car

Gasoline varies in availability around the country and the price depends on the octane rating. Unleaded is widely available along the Pan American Highway and in large cities. Diesel is referred to as 'petróleo'. Prices range from US$3.55-4.55 per gallon for gasoline and US$2.90 for diesel. There are some toll roads in Peru but these will cost little more than US$1.50 for use.

Bolivia

Bus Going by bus in Bolivia may be the cheapest way to get around but it can also be dirty, uncomfortable, extremely time-consuming and, at times, downright scary. As a rule of thumb, the newer carriers have the best amenities. Actually catching a bus can present serious problems. La Paz and the other major cities have central bus terminals, but not all buses leave from them and finding out when and where the others leave from can take as long as the journey. On top of this, bus times are regularly changed to take account of local, regional and national festivals, elections and soccer matches. During the wet season journey times can be increased by hours, even days, as roads get washed out and vehicles get stuck in the mud. Interurban buses are called *flotas*, urban ones *micros*, and there are also minibuses and *trufis* (shared taxis).

Ecuador's main towns are linked by a network of paved roads.

Essentials Travelling Getting around by road & rail

❝ Travellers' tales

Bus travel in the Bolivian Andes

Bolivian road warning signs take the shape of crosses, which line the side of the road to indicate where vehicles have gone over the edge. Most of the crosses appear on particularly dangerous bends and many drivers, being devout Catholics, will cross themselves on seeing one. This, of course means that many of the sharpest bends on the road are negotiated with one hand on the steering wheel.

Similarly, many of the buses do little to inspire confidence. For a start, they are usually packed to suffocation point with people, luggage and livestock. Overcrowded, it seems, is not a word familiar to Bolivian bus company employees. And secondly, they tend to break down a lot. But don't worry – seemingly anything can be repaired at the side of the road, given time. The driver and his ayudante (helper) will disappear under, or into, the engine, hit things, tie bits together with wire and probably pray a lot. Magically, the bus starts and the journey continues.

Probably the worst bus journey in all of Bolivia is the trip from La Paz to Pelechuco in the Cordillera Apolobamba – around 18-24 hours of dust-filled torture crossing the Altiplano in some battered old hulk that should have been consigned to the scrapheap years ago. Anyone over 172 cm tall will spend the entire trip smashing their kneecaps into the back of the seat in front and arrive in need of major surgery and a good night's rest. The pain, cold and tedium is only alleviated by the need to get out and push the bus every so often. All males of working age get off and push with all their might until it becomes obvious that the combined weight of the female passengers still on board is preventing any significant movement. So, off they get and the bus can then be pushed out of the mud/sand/hole.

But it's not all discomfort and near-death experiences. There's no better way to see the country, meet the people, sit on their chickens, sleep on their sheep, or be kept awake all night by their screaming children. Just look on it as cultural interaction. *Yossi Brain*

Car The awful condition of the roads, tolls, high altitudes, behaviour of other drivers who almost never dip their headlights, drive drunk, or fall asleep at the wheel, and even people sleeping at the roadside, all conspire to make driving in Bolivia a very bad idead. Furthermore, regulations are tight and police checks frequent. Always carry your passport, a driving licence and an International Driving Permit. You can be fined or imprisoned for not doing so, even though car rental companies only require your national driving licence. The minimum age for renting a car is 25 and hire rates are prohibitively high. Check with **Autómovil Club Boliviano** (T/F02-237 2139), for any special documents which may be required.

There are two types of gasoline: 85 and 92 octane, the prices range from US$1.76 to US$2.24 per gallon; diesel costs US$2 per litre. Road **tolls** vary from US$0.50 to US$2.50.

Train Trains run from Oruro south to Uyuni and to the Argentine border. The only other public railway of significance runs from Santa Cruz to the Brazil border and southward. The new Santa Cruz terminal is amazingly efficient, and has connections with bus lines as well. For train information in La Paz T02-241 6545/6. Always check departure times in advance.

Ecuador

Bus A good network of paved roads runs throughout the coast and highlands. Several companies use comfortable air-conditioned buses on their longer routes and most have regular, frequent timetables. Fares for the better services are higher and some companies have their own stations, away from the main bus terminals. Some of the better companies are **Flota Imbabura**, **Transportes Ecuador** and **Transportes Esmeraldas**.

Car If driving your own vehicle, obtaining temporary admission can be complex and time-consuming. A *carnet de passages* is an official requirement, but this rule is not consistently applied. Ask the motoring organization in your home country about the availability of the *carnet*. You must be 21 and have an international credit card to hire a car in Ecuador. Surcharges may apply to clients between age 21 and 25. An authorization for a charge of as much as US$5,000 may be requested against your credit card account. Rental rates are expensive, a small car costs about US$500 per week including all taxes and insurance. A sturdier 4WD (recommended for the Oriente and unpaved roads) can be more than twice as much.

There are two grades of gasoline, 'Extra' (82 octane, US$1.48 per US gallon) and 'Super' (92 Octane, US$1.98). Both are unleaded. Diesel fuel (US$1.03) is notoriously dirty and available everywhere.

Train The only train services running in the country are really for tourists only. One runs from the capital to Cotopaxi National Park (see page 328), another is the highly-acclaimed rail journey from Riobabamba down to the lowlands, via the famous 'Devil's Nose' (see page 360). A third runs from Ibarra part of the way to the coast, but is not covered in this guidebook.

A bed for the night

This guide focuses on the best accommodation in the mid-range categories (AL-D). Bottom-end budget accommodation (E-F) is only included if it represents excellent value for money or is the only option in a certain area. 'Budget buster' boxes highlight more expensive options (LL-L) that offer a really unique or special experience.

LL (over US$150) to A (US$46-65) Hotels in these categories can be found in most of the large cities but especially where there is a strong concentration of tourists or business travellers. They should offer extensive leisure and business facilities (including email), plus restaurants and bars. Credit cards are usually accepted and dollars cash changed typically at poor rates.

B (US$31-45) Hotels in this category should provide more than the standard facilities and a fair degree of comfort. Many include a good breakfast and offer extras such as a TV, minibar, air conditioning and a swimming pool. They may also provide tourist information and airport pick-ups. Most accept credit cards.

C (US$21-30) and D (US$12-20) Hotels in these categories range from very comfortable to functional and there are some real bargains to be had. You should expect your own bathroom, constant hot water, a towel, soap and toilet paper. There is sometimes a restaurant and a communal sitting area. Hotels used to catering for foreign tourists and backpackers often have luggage storage, money exchange and kitchen facilities.

E (US$7-11) and F (under US$6) Hotels in these categories are often extremely simple with bedside or ceiling fans, shared bathrooms and little in the way of furniture.

Sleeping

Peru

Accommodation is plentiful throughout the price ranges and finding a hotel room to suit your budget should not present any problems, especially in the main tourist areas and larger towns and cities. The exception to this is during the Christmas and Easter holiday periods, Carnival, Cusco in June and Independence celebrations at the end of July, when all hotels seem to be crowded. It's advisable to book in advance at these times and during school holidays and local festivals, see page 41. By law there are now four types of accommodation, each will have a plaque outside defining its status: Hotel (H), Hostal (HS), Hostal Residencial (HR) or Pensión (P). Foreigners do not pay the 19% IVA (sales tax) but luxury and first class hotels also add a 10% service charge which is not included in our prices. Student discounts are rare but for information on youth hostels and student accommodation consult **Intej**, www.intej.org or the **Asociación Peruana de Albergues Turísticos Juveniles**, Lima (T01-446 5488).

Top tips

Room service

There is no regulated terminology for categories of accommodation in South America, but you should be aware of the generally accepted meanings for the following. Hotel is the generic term, much as it is in English. *Hospedaje* means accommodation, of any kind. *Pensión* and *residencial* usually refer to more modest and economical establishments. A *posada* (inn) or *hostal* may be an elegant expensive place, while *hosterías* or *haciendas* usually offer upmarket rural lodgings.

- Always take a look at the room before checking in. Hotel owners will often attempt to rent out the worst rooms first - feel free to ask for a better room or bargain politely for a reduced rate if you are not happy.
- In cities, remember that rooms away from the main street will be less noisy.
- Air conditioning is only required in the lowlands and jungle. If you want an air conditioned room it will add approximately 30% to the price.
- The electric showers in cheaper places should be treated with respect. Always wear rubber sandals to avoid an unwelcome morning shock.
- Taller travellers (over 180 cm) should check out the length of beds, especially in the highland areas.
- A torch or candles is advisable in establishments in more remote areas, where electricity may only be supplied during certain hours.
- More upmarket hotels will usually have their own restaurant, while more modest places may only serve a simple breakfast.
- Some hotels charge per room and not per bed, so if travelling alone, it may be cheaper to share a room with others.
- The cheaest and nastiest hotels are found near bus and train stations and markets. In small towns, better accommodation can often be found around the main plaza.
- And finally, be sure that taxi drivers take you to the hotel you want rather than the one they think is best.

Bolivia

Away from the main cities, high-class hotels are few and far between. Getting off the beaten track usually means sacrificing creature comforts, but not necessarily standards of hygiene. Many of the hotels we recommend are not luxurious but conform to certain basic standards of cleanliness and are popular with travellers, which is often the best sign of an establishment's pedigree. Prices are low in Bolivia, but not uniformly so. The eastern part of the country tends to be a bit more expensive, especially the city of Santa Cruz, which is geared more towards commerce than tourism and therefore has few good budget places to stay. Smaller places which see plenty of tourists, such as Coroico, Rurrenabaque, Sorata or Copacabana, on the other hand, are full of good-value budget accommodation. Even in La Paz, it is quite easy to find a clean, comfortable hotel room, without a private bathroom,

Background

→ **How the other half lived**

The great *haciendas* of Ecuador were founded shortly after the Spanish Conquest, either as Jesuit *obrajes* (slave workshops) or land grants to the conquistadors. When the Jesuits fell from favour and were expelled from South America, these huge land holdings passed to important families close to the Spanish royalty; notables such as the Marqués de Solanda and Marqués de Maenza, to name just two. They were enormous properties covering entire watersheds and most of the owners never even laid eyes on all their land. The earliest visitors to Ecuador, people like La Condamine and Humbolt, were guests at these haciendas.

The *hacienda* system lasted until agrarian reform in the 1960s. The much reduced land holdings which remained in the hands of wealthy families, frequently surrounding beautiful historic homes, were then gradually converted to receive paying guests. **Cusín**, by Lago San Pablo, **La Ciénega**, near Lasso, and **Andaluza**, outside Riobamba, were among the first to take in tourists. They have since become successful upscale *hosterías* and are listed under the corresponding geographic locations in the text. They are no longer working haciendas but are nonetheless pleasant and comfortable places to stay. Prices are usually in our L range and up. See www.hacienda-ecuador.com.

Essentials Travelling Sleeping

for around US$4-5 per person. For those on a tight budget, a cheaper room can be found in a *hospedaje*, *pensión*, *casa familial* or *residencial*; they are normally to be found in abundance near bus and railway stations and markets. Note that there are often great seasonal variations in hotel prices in resorts, and prices can rise substantially during public holidays and festivals.

Hotels must list their prices by law and are also subject to a relatively accurate assessment of quality as shown by the number of stars shown. The full range of accomodation is available although the mid-range to cheaper places are the most common with the cheapest options offered for as little as US$5. All hotels charge a 20% tax which has been included in the listings in this book. Some hotels run a curfew which is strictly kept to, in La Paz this is often at midnight but can be 2130 in Copacabana so check.

Ecuador

There are over 1200 hotels in Ecuador, with something to suit every taste and budget. The greatest selection and most upscale establishments are found in the largest cities and more popular resorts. In less visited places the choice of better class hotels may be limited, but friendly and functional family-run lodgings can be had almost everywhere. At New Year, Easter and Carnival accommodation can sometimes be hard to find and prices are likely to rise. It is advisable to book in advance at these times and during school holidays and local festivals. Many (even the cheaper places) now add a service of 10% and a tax of 12% to rates but check if this is included in the price quoted.

Eating and drinking

Peru

Peruvian cuisine differs around the country. Along the **coast** the best dishes are seafood based with the most popular being *ceviche* which is a white fish marinated in lemon juice, onion and hot peppers. The staples of corm and potatoes are prevalent in **highland** cooking and can be found in a large and varied range of dishes. There is also an array of meat dishes with *lomo saltado* (stir-fried beef) always found on the menu and guinea pig (*cuy*) featuring as a regional delicacy. **Tropical cuisine** revolves around fish and the common yucca and fried bananas.

Lunch is considered the main meal throughout Peru and most restaurants will serve one or two set lunches called the *menú ejecutivo* (US$2 or more for a three-course meal) or *menú económico* (US$1.50-2.50). A la carté meals normally cost US$5-8 but in the top class restaurants it can be up to US$80. There are many Chinese restaurants (*chifas*) all over the country which offer good reasonably priced food.

The traditional favourite **beers** such as *Cusqueña* and *Arequipeña* (both lager) have recently been taken over by the giant *Bavaria* brewery and many connoisseurs claim that they have lost much of their distinctive taste. *Trujillo Malta* is probably the best dark beer, a sweetish 'maltina' brown ale . The best wines are from Ica, Tacama and Ocucaje. *Gran Tinto Reserva Especial* and *Viña Santo Tomas* are reasonable and cheap. The most famous local drink is *pisco* which is a strong, clear brandy and forms the basis of the deliciously renowned *pisco sour*.

Bolivia

Standard international meals can be found at most good hotels and restaurants but local cuisine is normally extremely tasty and very hot. Among the most popular are, hot spicy chicken (*sajta de pollo*), fried breaded meat (*silpancho*) and ox-tongue with chillis (*ají de lengua*). Also worth trying are the many meat and vegetable soups as well as meat or chicken pasties (*salteñas*) which are a national institution and eaten for elevenses. In the lowland regions, most meals come with yucca and cooked banana and it is common to find wild meats on the menu.

In any restaurant the *comida del día* is the best value meal and the cheaper restaurants normally offer a basic set luch and dinner. Many restaurants do not open for breakfast but the markets in most towns provide good, cheap meals at this time of day.

Tropical fruits make excellent juices.

Anyone for cuy?

Top tips

Restaurant price codes

The following price codes are used for restaurants and other eateries in this guide. Prices refer to the cost of a meal for one person, with a drink.

†††	over US$12
††	US$6-12
†	under US$6

Local beers are predominantly lager based but good, *Paceña* and *Ducal* are the most popular and *El Inca* offers something a little different (it is like a stout). The best wine producing area is near Tarija at the La Concepción vineyard. The national spirit, *singani*, is distilled from grapes and is strong and cheap. It is usually drunk with *Sprite* and known as a *chuflay*. There are many brands of bottled water. Do not drink tap water unless it has been sterilized and never take ice in drinks, even in the most expensive restaurants.

Ecuador

As with much of South America, cuisine here changes with the region. In the **highlands** potato and cheese soup (*locro de papas*), fried potato and cheese patties (*llapingachos*), roast guinea pig (*cuy*) and tender ground corn steamed in corn leaves (*humitas*) are some of the most typical dishes. Seafood plays an important role on the **coast**, particularly in fried snacks (*empanadas de verde*) and dishes that are also prepared in coconut milk (*encocadas*). Dishes in the **Oriente** usually consist of yucca and a range of river fish. Popular throughout the country is *ceviche* which is generally safe although *ceviche de pescado* (fish) and *ceviche de concha* (clams) can be hazardous as they are marinated raw. Most Ecuadorean food is not overly spicy but many restaurants accompany dishes with a small bowl of hot pepper sauce (*ají*).

The main beers available are *Pilsener*, *Club* and *Biela* and in the major cities good Argentine and Chilean wines can be found. The most popular spirit is unmatured rum, called *aguardiente* (literally 'fire water'). With such an outstanding number of different **fruits** avaiable, there are a number of excellent fruit drinks on offer. The best are passion fruit (*maracuyá*), pineapple (*piña*) and blackberry (*mora*).

Shopping

Handicrafts (*artesenía*), like food, enjoy regional distinctiveness, especially in items such as textiles. Each region, village even, has its own characteristic pattern or style of cloth, so the choice is enormous. Throughout the Andes, weaving has spiritual significance as well as a practical side. Reproductions of pre-Columbian designs can be found in pottery and jewellery and many people throughout the continent make delightful items in gold and silver. Musical instruments from Bolivia, Panama Hats from Ecuador and all manner of ceramics are just some of the things you can bring home with you. Remember that handicrafts can almost invariably be bought more cheaply away from the capital, though the choice may be less wide. **Bargaining** is expected when you are shopping for handicrafts and souvenirs. Remember that most items are made by hand, so ask yourself if it is worth taking advantage of the piteous state of the people you are buying from; they are trying to make a living, not playing a game. You want a fair price, not the lowest one.

Peruvian crafts

Good items to buy are **textiles**, especially in Lima, Cusco and Lake Titicaca. Equally common but well made are llama and alpaca wool products that include ponchos, rugs, hats, gloves, sweaters and coats. The engraved gourd (*mate burilado*) is one of the most genuine images of folk art in Peru. Interesting items are bags for coca leaves, belts and knitted conical hats which can be found around Lake Titcaca. For gold and silver jewellery, Lima is the best place to look.

Bolivian crafts

All but the most hardened anti-shopping visitors to Bolivia should arrive with plenty of space in their rucksacks. Llama- and alpaca-wool knitted and woven items are at least as good as those from Peru and much cheaper. Among the many items you can buy are *mantas* (ponchos), bags, *chullos* (bonnets), gold and silverware and musical instruments such as the *charango* (a mandolin traditionally with armadillo-shell sound-box, now usually of wood) and the *quena* (Inca flute), and other assorted wooden items. Rurrenabaque is a good place to buy well made (and colourful) hammocks for around US$5.

Ecuadorean crafts

The huge markets at **Otavalo** and **Saquisilí** are the best places to head for to find wall-hangings, sweaters, blankets and shawls. Authentic Panama hats can be found at the coast and at Cuenca and are sold at a fraction of the prices in Europe. Silver jewellery, ceramics and brightly painted carvings are all excellently made and there is even the opportunity to promote the conservation of the rainforest throught buying some of the beautiful items made from *tagua*, or vegetable ivory. Quito has a raft of *artesenías* and buying goods in any of the shops can often be a good option as it will be packaged to ensure that in returns home in one piece.

All manner of handicrafts can be found in Peru, Bolivia and Ecuador.

Essentials Travelling Shopping

Accident & emergency

Contact the relevant emergency service and your embassy (p34). Make sure you obtain police/medical reports in order to file insurance claims.

Emergency services
Peru Police T01-475 2995, Ambulance (Lima) T01-225 4040, Fire T116
Bolivia T911, Police T110, Ambulance T118, Fire T119
Ecuador Police T911 in Quito and Cuenca, T101 elsewhere, Ambulance T131

Children

Travel with children can bring you into closer contact with South American families and, generally, presents no special problems – in fact the path is often smoother for family groups. Officials tend to be more amenable where children are concerned and even thieves and pickpockets seem to have some traditional respect for families, and may leave you alone because of it!

People contemplating overland travel in South America with children should remember that a lot of time can be spent waiting for public transport. Even then, buses can often be delayed during the journey due to bad weather.

All civil airlines charge half fare for children under 12. Children's fares on **Lloyd Aéreo Boliviano** are considerably more than half, and there is only a 7 kg baggage allowance. (LAB also checks children's ages on passports.) Note that a child travelling free on a long excursion is not always covered by the operator's travel insurance; it is advisable to pay a small premium to arrange cover.

Food can be a problem if the children are not adaptable. It is easier to take food such as biscuits, drinks and bread with you on longer trips.

In all **hotels**, try to negotiate family rates. If charges are per person, always insist that two children will occupy one bed only, therefore counting as one tariff. If rates are per bed, the same applies.

Customs & duty free

Peru
Those entering Peru are allowed 400 cigarettes or 50 cigars or 500g of tobacco as well as three litres of alcoholic drink. You are only allowed new items or gifts up to the value of US$300. On no account should any object of archaeological interest be removed and taken out of Peru.

Bolivia
The import allowance consists of 200 cigarettes, 50 cigars and 450g of tobacco. In addition one unopened bottle of alcohol.

Ecuador
Free of import duty are 300 cigarettes or 50 cigars or 250g of tobacco, one litre of spirits and a reasonable amount of perfume and gifts amounting to no more than US$200. If you are planning to bring unusual or valuable items (for example video equipment), obtain special permits or be prepared to pay duty on those items. Reasonable amounts of climbing gear and a used laptop should not be a problem. Your luggage will always be sniffed by dogs when leaving and may also be inspected by security personnel. Do not attempt to take any archaeology, wild plants or animals or certain works of art out of Ecuador without a special permit.

Top tips

Don't forget your toothbrush...

✓ Take as little as possible. Clothes that are quick and easy to wash and dry are a good idea. Loose-fitting clothes are more comfortable in hot climates and can be layered if it gets cooler.

✓ You can easily, and cheaply, buy things en route, but five musts are: good walking shoes, a sun hat, sunglasses, flip-flops and a mosquito net.

✓ Keep a stash of toilet paper and tissues on your person.

✓ Other useful items are a Swiss Army knife (with corkscrew), a money belt, a headtorch/flashlight, the smallest alarm clock you can find, a padlock, dental floss and a basic medical kit.

✓ Pack photocopies of essential documents like passport, visas and traveller's cheque receipts just in case you lose the originals.

✓ Photographers should take all the film that they will require for the trip, ideally in a bag that is both water and dust proof.

✗ Don't load yourself down with toiletries. They're heavy and can be bought everywhere. Items like contact lens solutions and tampons may be harder to find, so stock up in major cities.

Disabled travellers

In most of South America, facilities for the disabled are severely lacking. For those in wheelchairs, ramps and toilet access are limited to some of the more upmarket, or most recently-built hotels. Visually or hearing-impaired travellers are similarly poorly catered for, but there are experienced guides in some places who can provide individual attention. Some travel companies outside South America specialize in holidays which are tailor-made for the individual's level of disability. PromPerú has initiated a programme to provide facilities at airports, tourist sites, etc and Quito's trolley buses are supposed to have wheelchair access, but they are often too crowded to make this practical. While disabled South Americans have to rely on others to get around, foreigners will find that people are generally very helpful. For general information, consult the **Global Access - Disabled Travel Network** website, www.geocities.com/Paris/1502.

Useful organizations

Directions Unlimited, 123 Green Lane, Bedford Hills, NY 10507, T1-800-533-5343, T914-241 1700. A tour operator specializing in tours for disabled US travellers.

Disability Action Group, 2 Annadale Ave, Belfast BT7 3JH, T01232-491011. Information about access for British disabled travellers.

Disabled Persons' Assemble, PO Box 27-524, Wellington 6035, New Zealand, T04-801-9100, gen@dpa.org.nz. Has lists of tour operators and travel agencies catering for the disabled.

Drugs

While many illegal drugs are easily available, any one caught in possession will automatically be assumed to be a drug trafficker. Drug use or purchase is punishable by up to 15 years' imprisonment in Peru (up to 10 years in Ecuador and up to 16 years in Bolivia). There have been reports of drug-planting by the PNP on foreigners in Lima. If you are asked to have your bags searched, insist on having a witness present at all times. Be aware of tricks to plant drugs on you at all times. Planting of drugs on travellers by both traffickers and police is not unknown in Bolivia but never answer offers by anyone selling drugs on the street as they may be a plain-clothes officer. In Ecuador, police drug-planting is relatively rare, though they may seek to make an example of you or attempt to squeeze you for as much money as they can.

Electricity

Peru 220 volts AC, 60 cycles throughout the country except Arequipa (50 cycles). Most four- and five-star hotels have 110 volts AC. Plugs are American flat-pin.
Bolivia Varies. Generally 110 volts AC, 50 cycles in La Paz; 220 volts AC, 50 cycles elsewhere but be sure to check first. US-type plugs can be used in most hotels.
Ecuador 110 volts AC, 60 cycles. US-type flat-pin plugs.

Embassies and consulates

Peruvian

Australia, 40 Brisbane Av Suite 8, Ground Floor, Barton ACT 2600, Canberra, PO Box 106 Red Hill, T61-2-6273 8752, www.emba peru.org.au Consulate in Sydney.
Bolivia, F Guachalla 300, Sopocachi, La Paz, T02-2441250, embbol@caoba. entelnet.bo.
Canada, 130 Albert St, Suite 1901, Ottawa, Ontario K1P 5G4, T1-613-238 1777, emperuca@bellnet.ca. Consulates in Montréal, Toronto and Vancouver.
Ecuador, República de El Salvador 495 e Irlanda, edif Irlanda, T02-2468410, embpeecu@uio.satnet.net.
New Zealand, Level 8, 40 Mercer St, Cigna House, Wellington, T64-4-499 8087, embassy.peru@xtra.co.nz.
UK, 52 Sloane St, London SW1X 9SP, T020-7235 1917, www.peruembassy-uk.com.
USA, 1700 Massachusetts Av NW, Washington DC 20036, T1-202-833 9860, www.peruemb.org. Consulates in Los Angeles, Miami, New York, Chicago, Houston, Boston, Denver, San Francisco.

Bolivian

Australia and New Zealand, 74 Pitt St, Level 6, Sydney, NSW 2000, T923-51858.
Canada, 130 Albert St, Suite 416, Ottowa, ON K1P 5G4, T613-236 5730, bolcan@ iosphere.net.
Peru, Los Castaños 235, San Isidro, Lima 27, T01-4228231, postmast @emboli.org.pe.
UK, 106 Eaton Sq, London SW1 9AD, T0207-235 4248, http://bolivia. embassyhomepage.com..
USA, 3014 Massachusetts Av NW, Washington DC 20008, T202-483 4410, or 211 East 43 Road St, Suite 702 New York, NY 10017, T212-499 7401, www.bolivia-usa.org.

Ecuadorean

Australia, 11 London Circuit, 1st floor, Canberra ACT 2601, T6-6262 5282, embecu@hotkey.net.au.
Canada, 50 O'Connor St No 316, Ottawa, ON K1P 6L2, T613-563 8206, mecuacan@rogers.com.
New Zealand (consulate), Peace Tower, level 9, 2 St Martins Lane, Auckland, T09-377 4321, jmorlaconsulacuadorxtra.co.nz.
Peru, Las Palmeras 356, San Isidro (6th block of Av Javier Prado Oeste), T01-4409991, embjecau@amauta.rcp.net.pe.
UK, Flat 3B, 3 Hans Cres, Knightsbridge, London SW1x 0LS, T7584 1367, embajada@ecuador.freeserve.co.uk.
USA, 2535 15th St NW, Washington, DC 20009, T202-234 7200, embassy@ecuador.org Also 1101 Brickell Av, Suite M-102, Miami, Fl 33131, T305-539 8214, consecumia@aol.com.

Gay and lesbian

Much of Latin America is quite intolerant of homosexuality. Rural areas tend to be more conservative in these matters than cities. It is therefore wise to respect this and avoid provoking a reaction. For the gay or lesbian traveller, however, Lima and Quito have active communities and there are local and international organizations which can provide information. In Ecuador: www.quitogay.net (in Spanish and English). In Peru: gaylimape.tripod.com/about.htm (good site, in English, lots of links and information).

Health

See your GP or travel clinic at least six weeks before departure for general advice on travel risks and vaccinations. Try phoning a specialist travel clinic if your own doctor is unfamiliar with health in the region. Make sure you have sufficient medical travel insurance, get a dental check, know your own blood group and if you suffer a long-term condition such as diabetes or epilesy, obtain a Medic Alert bracelet/necklace (www.medicalalert.co.uk).

Vaccinations
The list of obligatory vaccinations is thin, only Yellow Fever is a pre-requisite for entering the region. Nonetheless, it is advisable to vaccinate against Polio, Tetanus, Typhoid, Hepatitis A and, if going to more remote areas, Rabies. Malaria is a danger throughout the lowland tropics and coastal regions. Specialist advice should be taken on the best anti-malarials to take before you leave. Among the most common are Chloroquine and Paludrine.

Health risks
The major risks posed in the region are those caused by insect disease carriers such as mosquitoes and sandflies. The key parasitic and viral diseases are malaria, South American tyrpanosomiasis (Chagas Disease) and Dengue Fever. Be aware that you are always at risk from these diseases, Dengue Fever is particularly hard to protect against as the mosquitoes can bite throughout throughout the day as well as night (unlike those that carry malaria and Chagas disease); try to wear clothes that cover arms and legs and also use effective mosquito repellent. Mosquito nets dipped in permethrin provide a good physical and chemical barrier at night. Some form of diarrhoea or intestinal upset is almost inevitable, the standard advice is to be careful with drinking water and ice. Always buy bottled water and ask from where any water that is served in a restaurant came from. Food can also pose a problem, be wary of salads if you don't know whether they have been washed or not. There is a constant threat of tuberculosis (TB) and although the BCG vaccine is available, it is still not guaranteed protection. It is best to avoid unpasteurised dairy products and try not to let people cough and splutter all over you. One of the major problems for travellers in the region is altitude sickness, it is essential to get acclimatized to the thin air of the Andes before undertaking long treks or arduous activities. The altitude of the Andes means that strong protection from the sun is always needed, regardless of how cool it may feel.

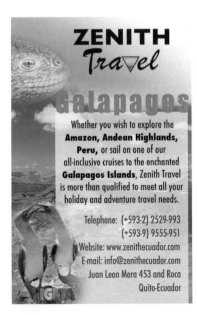

www.btha.org British Travel Health Association.

www.cdc.gov US government site that gives excellent advice on travel health and details of disease outbreaks.

www.fco.gov.uk British Foreign and Commonwealth Office travel site has useful information on each country, people, climate and a list of UK embassies/consulates.

www.fitfortravel.scot.nhs.uk A-Z of vaccine/health advice for each country.

www.travelscreening.co.uk Travel Screening Services gives vaccine and travel health advice, email/SMS text vaccine reminders and screens returned travellers for tropical diseases.

Insurance

Always take out comprehensive insurance before you travel, including full medical cover and extra cover for any activities (rafting, biking, riding etc) that you may undertake. Check exactly what's being offered, the maximum cover for each element and also the excess you will have to pay in the case of a claim. Keep details of your policy and the insurance company's telephone number with you at all times and get a police report for any lost or stolen items.

Internet

Internet cafés are becoming more and more common throughout the region, both in large and small towns. Rates and speed vary from café to café and from place to place but you should generally expect to pay between US$0.50-2 in the major cities. Outside of these places connections are slower and prices higher.

Regional websites

www.latinworld.com/sur Links to individual Latin American countries.

www.lanic.utexas.edu The Latin American Network Information Centre: loads of information on everything.

www.andes.org Quechua language lessons, music, songs, poems, stories and resources.

www.southamericadaily.com Links to newspapers, plus environment, health, business and travel sites.

Language

Without some knowledge of Spanish you will become very frustrated and feel helpless in many situations. English, or any other language, is absolutely useless off the beaten track. Not all the locals speak Spanish, of course; you will find that some Indians in the more remote highland parts of Bolivia and Peru, and lowland Indians in Amazonia, speak only their indigenous

languages (Quichua in Ecuador, Quechua in Peru and Bolivia, also Aymara in southern Peru and Bolivia), though at least one person in each village usually speaks Spanish. Some initial study or a beginners Spanish course are strongly recommended, as is a pocket phrasebook and dictionary. Quito is a particularly good place to head for cheap language courses. **AmeriSpan**, PO Box 58129, Philadelphia, PA 19103, T1-800-879 6640 (USA & Canada), T215-751 1100 (Worldwide), www.amerispan.com, programmes are offered in Sucre, Cuenca, Quito and Cusco. In Ecuador, they also offer a discount card for use in hotels, restaurants and shops. **LanguagesAbroad.com** 317 Adelaide St West, Suite 900, Toronto, Ontario, Canada, M5V 1P9, T416-925 2112, toll free 1-800-219 9924, www.languages abroad.com, offers Spanish and Portuguese programmes in all three countries. They also have language immersion courses throughout the world. **Spanish Abroad**, 5112N, 4th St, suite 103, Phoenix, A285018, USA, T1-888-722-7623 (USA), T602-778 6791 (Worldwide), www.spanishabroad.com, year round classes catering for small groups and individuals. Can arrange accomodation.

Media

Latin America has more local and community radio stations than practically anywhere else in the world. A shortwave radio will allow you to absorb local culture, as well as pick up **BBC World Service** (www.bbc.co.uk/worldservice) or the **Voice of America** (www.voa.gov).

Essentials Essentials A-Z

There are several main morning papers in Lima, *El Comercio* has good international news, *La República* has liberal-left views and *Gestión* is the major business daily. Most provinicial cities will have at least one widely read newspaper each. The *Andean Report* is a weekly economic and political magazine produced in English that has useful information and articles. Similarly, *Rumbos* is a good bi-monthly magazine in Spanish and English that focuses on tourism and culture. For good online news coverage, the following websites are the most useful: www.perualdia.com, www.yachay.com.pe, www.peru.com.

Bolivia

The main cities and towns all have their own daily, in La Paz *Presencia* and *El Diario* are the most popular while in Santa Cruz it is *El Día*. Sucre has a number of papers that are good for foreign coverage, amoung these are *El Correo*, *El Mundo* and *La Razón*. The *Bolivian Times* is an Enlish language weekly and is available in the big cities. Of particular use to travellers is the *Llama Express* which is a free monthly paper in English that covers many travel and cultural features as well as local news reports, it is available across the country. It is only possible to find some foreign national papers in La Paz.

Ecuador

The main newspapers in Quito are *El Comercio* and *Hoy* and in Cuenca *El Mercurio*. There are also many local and regional publications throughout the rest of the country. Foreign newspapers can only be found in the luxury hotels and some speciality bookshops in Quito.

Money

Withdrawing cash from ATMs with a credit or debit card is by far the easiest way to stay in funds but do not rely exclusively on credit cards or ATMs when travelling in South America. ATMs are common, but cannot always be relied on and have been known to confiscate valid cards. The affiliations of banks to the Plus and Cirrus systems change often, so ask around. Always bring some US dollar bills, traveller's cheques, or both. A good strategy is to gradually convert your traveller's cheques to cash in the larger cities. US dollar notes may only accepted if they are in excellent condition. Low-value US dollar bills are very useful for shopping: shopkeepers and *casas de cambio* give better exchange rates than hotels or banks. Banks and the better hotels will normally change traveller's cheques for their guests (often at a poor rate) although some may ask to see a record of purchase before accepting. Take plenty of local currency, in small denominations, when making trips off the beaten track. Frequently, the rates of exchange on ATM withdrawals are the best available but check if your bank or credit card company imposes handling charges. Credit card transactions are normally at an officially recognized rate of exchange but are often subject to a sales tax. **For lost or stolen cards**, call **Visa** T1-800-999-0115; **MasterCard** T1-800-999-1480; **American Express** T1-800-999-0245. Whenever possible, change money at a bank or *casa de cambio* rather than from money changers on the street. Change any local currency before you leave the country or at the border.

Cost of travelling

A realistic budget for the region is roughly US$35-50 per person per day, based on two people travelling together, sleeping in comfortable, mid-range accommodation and eating reasonably well. Those spending more time in large cities and main tourist centres and taking frequent flights between destinations could easily spend more than this, up to as much as US$100 a day. Of course, you could quite easily get by on less (US$25-30) without enduring any hardship, especially in

Ecuador and Bolivia. In all three countries budget travellers can find a basic but clean hotel room for as little as US$5-10 per person, and a simple meal for only US$1.50-2, and travelling by bus is relatively cheap. For sleeping and eating categories, see p26 and p30.

Peru

The monetary unit is the sol (s/), in Mar 2005 the conversion rate was **US$1 = s/3.3**. Some prices are quoted in dollars in more expensive establishments, to avoid changes in the value of the sol. A large number of forged US dollar notes (especially US$20 and larger bills) are in circulation. Posters in public places explain what to look for in forged soles. Visa, Maestro, MasterCard, American Express and Diners Club are all valid and widely accepted. There is often an 8-12% commission for all credit card charges. Most of the main banks accept American Express and Visa traveller's cheques but it can be very difficult in cashing them in the jungle and other remote areas. Banks are the most discreet places to change traveller's cheques into soles. Some charge commission from 1% to 3%, some don't. ATMs are widespread and usually give dollars if you don't request soles. There are no restrictions on foreign exchange, banks always give a lower exchange rate

than *cambistas* or *casas de cambio*. For changing into or out of small amounts of dollars cash, the street changers give the best rates, avoiding paperwork and queuing, but they also employ many ruses to give you a bad deal.

Bolivia

The monetary unit is the boliviano (Bs), in Mar 2005 the conversion rate was **US$1 = 8.4Bs**. Bolivianos are often referred to as pesos; expensive items, including hotel rooms, are often quoted in dollars. When changing money, try to get notes in small denominations. Bs 100 notes are very difficult to change in La Paz and impossible elsewhere. Change is often given in forms other than money: eg, cigarettes, sweets, or razor blades. It is difficult to buy dollars at points of exit when leaving or to change bolivianos in other countries. It can be impossible to change traveller's cheques outside the major cities. Changing dollars cash presents no problems anywhere but it is not worth trying to change other currencies. All the larger *casas de cambio* will give dollars cash in exchange for traveller's cheques, usually with a commission. Credit/debit cards are commonly used to obtain cash. American Express is not as useful as Visa or MasterCard. ATMs displaying the *Enlace* sign are the best, accepting both Visa, Visa Electron and MasterCard (and therefore

In much of the Andes, life has changed little since Inca times.

pretty much every foreign card). You can usually take out US dollars or bolivianos. For credit card purchases an extra charge, up to 10%, may be made.

Ecuador

The United States Dollar is the only official currency of Ecuador. Only US Dollar bills circulate, in the following denominations: US$1, US$2 (rare), US$5, US$10, US$20, US$50 and US$100. US coins are used alongside the equivalent size and value Ecuadorean coins for 1, 5, 10, 25 and 50 cents and US$1 (US-minted bronze dollar). It is best to bring US dollars cash, in small denominations, as this is universally accepted. All other currencies are hard to exchange and fetch a very poor rate. The most commonly accepted credit cards are Visa, Mastercard, Diners and, to a lesser extent, American Express. Some banks allow a cash advance but a surcharge (at least 10%) may be applied in some hotels and restaurants. Places with credit card stickers do not necessarily take them. Traveller's cheques (American Express is most widely accepted) are safe, but can only be exchanged for cash in the larger cities and up to 5% commission may be charged.

Opening hours

Peru

Banks are generally open 0930-1200 and 1500-1800 but those in Lima operate from 0945-1700. Branches in Lima and Cusco may also open 0945-1200 Sat. Businesses are most open to the same hours while shops open 0900 or 1000-1230 and 1500 or 1600-2000. Supermarkets don't usually close for lunch and some in Lima are 24 hours.

Bolivia

Business hours are 0900-1200 and 1400-1800 with a half day on Sat. Afternoon opening and closing hours in the provinces are often several hours later than in towns and cities. Banks operate 0900-1200 and 1400-1630 as well as 0900-1200 or 1300 Sat.

Ecuador

Banks are open Mon-Fri 0900-1600. Government offices Mon-Fri variable hours but most close for lunch. Other offices 0900-1230, 1430-1800. Shops 0900-1900, close at 1200 in smaller towns, open until 2100 on the coast.

Police and the law

Typically, law enforcement exists on a systematic basis and the most obvious is a round-up of criminals in the cities just before Christmas. You may well be asked for identification at any time, and if you cannot produce it, you will be jailed. In the event of a vehicle accident in which anyone is injured, all drivers involved are automatically detained until blame has been established, and this does not usually take less than two weeks. Never offer a bribe unless you are fully conversant with the customs of the country. Do not assume that an official who accepts a bribe is prepared to do anything else that is illegal. If an official suggests that a bribe must be paid before you can proceed on your way, be patient (assuming you have the time) and he may relent.

Post

All mail should be registered and it is worth checking whether your embassy will hold mail in preference to the poste restante service (*lista de correos*), although this is available at most major post offices. If mail is sent here, check under both your surname and your first name when collecting and be prepared to show your passport. In general, postal services are very slow and unreliable.

Peru

The postal service is named **Serpost** and sending mail and parcels is possible from any post office although the office the Plaza de Armas in Lima is best. Sending packages out of Peru is incredibly expensive and is not really worth it but letters are much more reasonable; rates are US$1 to anywhere in the Americas, US$1.50 to Europe and US$1.70 to Australia. It is possible to pay an extra US$0.55 (for the Americas) or US$0.90 (for the rest of the world) for an '*expresso*' service.

Bolivia

Airmail letters to and from Europe should take 5-10 days. Letter/postcard up to 20 g to Europe US$0.90, to North America US$0.75, rest of the world US$1; letter over 30 g to Europe US$2.20, to North America US$1.50, rest of the world US$2.30. Packages up to 2 kg can be posted from the ground floor of the main post office in La Paz between 1200-1430; to Europe a 2 kg parcel costs US$30, to North America US$20.30, to the rest of the world US$42. Surface mail parcels up to 2 kg cost US$16 to North America, US$19 to Europe and US$21 to the rest of the world.

Ecuador

Airmail up to 20 g are US$0.90 to the Americas, US$1.05 to the rest of the world. Registered mail costs an additional US$0.95 per item. Parcels up to 30 kg, maximum dimensions permitted are 70 by 30 by 30 cm. Air parcel rates are: to the Americas approximately US$14.55 for the first kg, US$4.45 for each additional kg; to the rest of the world approximately US$24 for the first kg, US$13 for each additional kg. There is no surface (sea) mail service from Ecuador. Postal branches in small towns may not be familiar with all rates and procedures.

Public holidays

Aside from the national holidays listed below, local holidays are also taken during the main festivals (see p63). Most businesses such as banks, airline offices

and tourist agencies close for the official holidays while supermarkets and street markets may be open. This depends a lot on where you are so try to find out before you leave home. Sometimes holidays that fall during mid-week will be moved to the following Monday to make a long weekend, or some places will take a *dia del puente* (bridging day) taking the Friday or Monday as a holiday before or after an official holiday on a Thursday or Tuesday.

Peru

1 Jan New Year's Day; **6 Jan** Bajada de Reyes; **Carnival Week** (Mon, Shrove Tue, Ash Wed); **Easter** (Maundy Thu, Good Fri and Sat); **1 May** Labour Day; **Corpus Christi** (moveable); **28-29 Jul** Independence (Fiestas Patrias); **8 Oct** Battle of Angamos; **2 Nov** All Souls' Day; **24-25 Dec** Christmas.

Bolivia

1 Jan New Year's Day; **Carnival** (Mon and Tue before Lent); **Easter** (Maundy Thu, Good Fri, Sat); **1 May** Labour Day; **Corpus Christi** (moveable); **16 Jul** La Paz Municipal Holiday; **5-7 Aug** Independence; **2 Nov** All Souls' Day; **25 Dec** Christmas Day.

Ecuador

1 Jan New Years Day; **6 Jan** Reyes Magos y Día de los Inocentes; **27 Feb** Día del Civismo; **Carnival** (Mon and Tue before Lent); **Easter** (Maundy Thu, Good Fri, Sat); **1 May** Labour Day; **24 May** Battle of Pichincha, Independence Day; **Corpus Christi** (moveable); **10 Aug** 1st attempt at Independence; **12 Oct** Columbus' arrival in America; **2 Nov** All Souls' Day; **6 Dec** Foundation of Quito; **25 Dec** Christmas Day.

Safety

The region is generally safe but you should always take sensible precautions to protect yourself and your baggage. Be especially careful in Lima, La Paz and

Quito, particularly on public transport, in and around markets and when handling money in public places. While the Police presence in the major cities in **Peru** has been improved, there have been alarming increases in violent muggings along the Gringo Trail. Check with **South American Explorers** for updates and advice. **Bolivia** remains safe and hospitable with strikes and demonstrations being the major problem. However, Police advise tourists not to stray from the main road in the main coca-growing country around Villa Tunari. In **Ecuador**, in response to urban street crime and highway robbery, mixed army and police patrols now operate in some areas so don't be shocked to see troops on duty. Some provinces along the border with Colombia have come under the influence of insurgents so enquire locally before travelling there. Visitors are strongly advised to seek up-to-date advice from hotels and other travellers. See also Drugs, p33 and Police and the law, p40.

It is better to seek advice on security before you leave from your own consulate than from travel agencies. Before you travel you can contact: **British Foreign and Commonweath Office** ① *Travel Advice Unit, T0870 606 0290.* Footprint is a partner in the Foreign and Commonwealth Office's 'Know before you go campaign', www.fco.gov.uk/travel. US State Department's **Bureau of Consular Affairs**, Overseas Citizens Services ① *T202-647 4000 (travellers' hotline T647 5225), travel.state.gov/travel_warnings.html* **Australian Department of Foreign Affairs** ① *T+61-2-6261 3305, www.dfat.gov.au/consular/advice/advices_mnu.html*

Student travellers

If you are in full-time education you will be entitled to an **International Student Identity Card** (ISIC), which is distributed by student travel offices and agencies in 70 countries. The ISIC gives you special prices on transport and access to a variety of other concessions and services, including an emergency helpline (T+44-20-8762-8110). Discounts are often extended to teachers, who are entitled to an **International Teacher Identity Card** (ITIC). Both are available from www.isic.org.

Telephone

Peru
IDD +51

All Peruvian phone numbers are made up of 6 digits except Lima which has 7, plus the area code. All area codes are given with each number in the text. If calling Peru from abroad, dial the international access code (00 from the UK), followed by the Peru country code (51) and then dial in the area code and number. Local, national and international calls can be made from public phone boxes with coins and the more common pre-paid phone cards. The most popular phone cards are issued by the main service provider, **Telefónica**. Also available are long-distance phone cards, among which are **AT&T**, **Americatel**, **Nortek** and **Perusat**. Each of these has its own code which must be dialled in first, followed by the secret code on the card and not all cards work in every phone. For collect calls (reverse charge), dial 108 to reach the international operator. You can also receive calls at many **Telefónica** offices at about US$1 for 10 mins. Growing in popularity are **net-phones**, especially in Lima. Rates may be cheaper than normal phones, particularly if calling the US.

Bolivia
IDD +591

Bolivian phone numbers consist of 7 digits and all area codes are made up of 2 digits. To make a regional call, dial 0 before the regional code and the number. If dialling from a private phone, an access number of the service provider must be

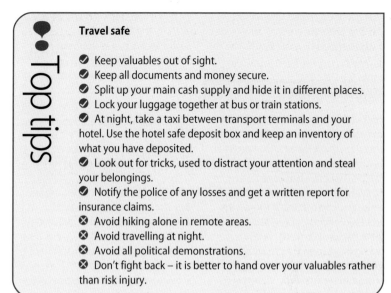

Top tips

Travel safe

- ✔ Keep valuables out of sight.
- ✔ Keep all documents and money secure.
- ✔ Split up your main cash supply and hide it in different places.
- ✔ Lock your luggage together at bus or train stations.
- ✔ At night, take a taxi between transport terminals and your hotel. Use the hotel safe deposit box and keep an inventory of what you have deposited.
- ✔ Look out for tricks, used to distract your attention and steal your belongings.
- ✔ Notify the police of any losses and get a written report for insurance claims.
- ✘ Avoid hiking alone in remote areas.
- ✘ Avoid travelling at night.
- ✘ Avoid all political demonstrations.
- ✘ Don't fight back – it is better to hand over your valuables rather than risk injury.

dialed between the 0 and area code; the providers are **Entel** (10), **AES** (11), **Telecel** (17) and **Boliviatel** (13). Coins and tokens are being phased out of use in public phones, pre-paid phone cards are currently the best option for local and long distance calls. Collect calls can be made by accessing the provider in the recieving country and asking for a collect call there. Such providers in the US are **AT&T** 0800 1111, **MCI** 0800 2222, **Sprint** 0800 3333 and **IDB (TRT)** 0800 4444; in the UK, **BT** 0800 0044.

Ecuador
IDD +593

All phone numbers are 7 digits, including cell phones (should be preceeded by area code 09). The country is divided between 3 regional state companies, **Andinatel** in the northern highlands and northern Oriente; **Pacifictel** on the coast, the southern highlands and southern Oriente; and **Etapa** in Cuenca. Many towns now have public cell phones provided by **Bell South** and **Porta**, while these services can be convenient (they are used where there are no other phones), they are expensive. Standard coin and debit-card operated

phone booths are also being installed throughout the country. Telephone company offices are the best places to go to make local, national and international calls and there will be at least one in every city or town. To make international calls you may be asked to specify the number of minutes you want to speak for and pay in advance. International rates should be under US$0.50 per min but may be more in small towns.

Time

Bolivia is 4 hrs behind GMT while Peru and Ecuador are both 5 hrs behind. The Galápagos are 6 hrs behind GMT.

Tipping

Mid-range to expensive restaurants in Peru add up to 17% service charge to the bill while those in Ecuador will include up to 10%. You should give up to 10% service for good restaurants, cheaper establishments do not expect anything, although it is welcome. Do not tip taxi drivers in Peru or Ecuador and give about US$0.50-1 to porters and cloakroom attendents. Car 'watch' boys expect US$0.20. In Bolivia, anyone that provides a service should be given Bs0.50-1 on top of the fee.

Tourist information

Contact details for tourist offices and other information resources are given in 'Ins and outs' throughout the text. The internet is an invaluable source of information, with countless websites dedicated to each country. For tourist information on the region from outside, visit the respective embassies and consulates of each country (p34). See also Ron Mader's website **www.planeta.com**, which contains masses of useful information on ecotourism, conservation, travel, news, links, language schools and articles. **South American Explorers** is a non-profit educational organization staffed by volunteers, widely recognized as the best place to go for information on South America. Highly recommended as a source for specialized information, with member-written trip reports, maps, lectures, library resources. SAE publishes a 64-page quarterly journal, helps members plan trips and expeditions, stores gear, holds post, hosts book exchanges, provides expert travel advice, etc. Annual membership fee is US$50 individual (US$80 couple) plus US$10 for overseas postage of its quarterly journal, *The South American Explorer*. The SAE membership card is good for many discounts throughout Ecuador and Peru. The Clubhouses, in **Quito** (Jorge Washington 311 y Leonidas Plaza, T02-2225228, quitoclub@saeexplorers.org), **Lima** (Piura 135, Miraflores, T01-4453306, limaclub@saeexplorers.org) and **Cusco** (Choquechaca 188, T084-245484, cuscoclub@saeexplorers.org), are helpful and friendly. SAE will sell used equipment on consignment (donations of used equipment, unused medicines, etc are welcome). The SAE Headquarters are located in the **USA** ⓘ *126 Indian Creek Rd, Ithaca, NY, 14850, T607 277 0488, F607-277 6122, ithacaclub @saexplorers.org*. For information and travel tips on-line, visit www.sa explorers.org. If signing up in UK please allow 4-6 weeks for receipt of membership card.

Peru

PromPerú, Edificio Mitinci, located at the head of Avenida Carnaval y Moreyra in Corpac, 13th and 14th floor, San Isidro, Lima, T01-224 3279, www.peru.org.pe; they also run the information and assistance service, **i perú** (24 hr calls on T01-574 8000). The main office is in Lima, Jorge Basadre 610, San Isidro, T421 1227, iperulima@promperu.gob.pe There is a 24 hr office at Jorge Chávez airport as well as offices in the major cities across the country. **Idecopi** is the government-run consumer protection and tourist complaint bureau, they are friendly and helpful, T01-224 7888 (Lima), T0800-42579 (rest of Peru), tour@indecopigob.pe.

Bolivia

Dirección Nacional De Turismo, Edificio Ballivián, piso 18, C Mercado, La Paz, T02-236 7463/4. Also involved is the **Viceministerio de Turismo**,

www.desarrollo.gov.bo/turismo/turismo.htm. Information on national parks can be found from the **Servicio Nacional de Area Protegidas**, Sernap, Av 20 de Octubre 2659, La Paz, T02-243 4420, www.sernap.gov.bo.

Ecuador

Ministerio de Turismo, Eloy Alfaro N32-300 Carlos Tobar, Quito, T02-250 7559, mtur1@ec-gov.net The **Cámara Provincial de Turismo de Pichincha** (CAPTUR) has information booths at Quito airport and in the Old and New City, their administrative offices are located at 6 de Diciembre 1424 y Carrión, T02-222 4074, www.captur.com. On the Galápagos Islands, the **Ministerio de Turismo** has an office on Avenida Charles Darwin in Puerto Ayora, T05-252 6174, cptg@pa.ga.pro.ec.

Tour operators

In the UK

4starSouth America, T0871-711 5370 (UK), T1-800-747 4540 (USA), www.4starSouthAmerica.com (tours), www.4starFlights.com (flights).

Condor Journeys & Adventures, 2 Ferry Bank, Colintraive, Argyll PA22 3AR, T01700-841318, www.condorjourneys-adventures.com

Dragoman, Camp Green, Debenham, Suffolk IP14 6LA T0870-499 4475, www.dragoman.co.uk

Exodus Travels, Grange Mills, 9 Weir Rd, London SW12 ONE, T020-8675 5550, www.exodus.co.uk

Explore, 1 Frederick St, Aldershot, Hants GU11 1LQ, T01252 760100, www.explore.co.uk

Essentials Essentials A-Z

Galapagos Classic Cruises, 6 Keyes Rd, London NW2 3XA, T020-8933 0613, www.galapagoscruises.co.uk. An experienced company with excellent service providing specialist and adventure tours for individuals and groups to meet personal requirements.

Journey Latin America, 12 and 13 Heathfield Terr, Chiswick, London W4 4JE, T020-8747 8315, and 12 St Ann's Sq (2nd Fl), Manchester M2 7HW, T0161-832 1441, www.journeylatinamerica.co.uk.

Latin American Travel Association, 46 Melbourne Rd, London SW19 3BA, UK, T020-8715 2913, www.lata.org.

Peruvian Secrets, Unit 4, Brynsiencyn Business Units, Brynsiencyn, Anglesey, LL61 6HZ, T01248-430621, www.peruviansecrets.co.uk. Tailor made tours to the Galapagos and Peru.

Specializes in trips to Northern Peru.

Select Latin America (incorporating Galapagos Adventure Tours), 79 Maltings Pl, 169 Tower Bridge Rd, London SE1 3LJ, T020-7407 1478, www.selectlatinamerica.com. Quality tailor-made holidays and small group tours.

Travelbag, 3-5 High St, Alton, Hants GU13 1TL, T0870-814 4440, www.travelbag.co.uk.

Trips Worldwide, 9 Byron Pl, Clifton, Bristol BS8 1JT, T0117-311 4400, www.tripsworldwide.co.uk.

In North America

GAP Adventures, 355 Eglinton Av East, Toronto, Ontario M4P 1M5, T1- 800-465 5600, www.gapadventures.com.

Quasar Nautica, 7855 N.W. 12th St, Suite

221, Miami, Florida 33126, www.quasar expeditions.com. Tours to sights throughout Ecuador and Peru, including the Galapagos and Machu Picchu.

Tambo Tours, 20919 Coral Bridge Lane, Suite 225-A, Spring, TX, 77388, USA, T1-888-2-GO-PERU (246-7378) T001-281 528 9448, www.2GOPERU.com. Long established adventure and tour specialist with offices in Peru and the USA. Customized trips to the Amazon and archaeological sites of Peru and Ecuador. Daily departures for groups and Individuals.

Tropical Nature Travel, PO Box 5276, Gainsville, Fl 326270 5276, USA, T1-877-827-8350/919-380-0966, www.tropicalnaturetravel.com. Eco tour company with itineraries to Ecuador, Peru and Bolivia.

Peru

No visa is necessary for citizens of Western Europe, Asia, North or South America, the Caribbean, or citizens of Australia, New Zealand or South Africa. Visitors from Fiji and India do need a visa. A Tourist Card is free on flights arriving in Peru, or at border crossings for visits up to 90 days. Insist on getting the full 90 days. It is in duplicate, the original given up on arrival and the copy on departure. A new tourist card must be obtained for each re-entry or when an extension is given. If your tourist card is stolen or lost, get a new one at **Migraciones** Av España 700 y Av Huaraz, Breña, Lima, 0900-1330, Mon-Fri. You can also get extensions here (expect to pay about US$30) as well as in Cusco, Puno, Puerto Maldonado, and Iquitos, but in the provinces it can take more time. For citizens of countries not listed above, tourist visas cost £21.60 (US$36 approximately) or equivalent, for which you require a valid passport, a departure ticket from Peru (or a letter of guarantee from a travel agency), two colour passport photos, one application form and proof of economic solvency.

All foreigners should be able to produce on demand some recognizable means of identification, preferably a passport. You must present your passport when reserving tickets for internal, as well as, international travel. Travellers arriving by air are not asked for an onward flight ticket at Lima airport. If you let your tourist visa expire you can be subject to a fine of US$20 per day.

Bolivia

A passport only, valid for one year beyond the date of visit, is needed for citizens of almost all Western European countries, Israel, Japan, North and South American countries (except Venezuela), South Africa, Australia and New Zealand. Irish citizens are advised to check with a Bolivian embassy before leaving home as there has been confusion over requirements for them in recent years. Many are granted 90 days on entry, others are entitled to only 30. Extensions can be easily arranged at immigration. Nationals of all other countries require a visa. Some nationalities must gain authorization from the Bolivian Ministry of Foreign Affairs, which can take six weeks. Other countries which require a visa do not need authorisation (visas in this case take 1-2 working days). You must check with a Bolivian consulate in advance. The cost of a visa varies from nationality to nationality. Visas (or permit to stay), which are valid for 30 days, can be renewed at any *migración* office for up to 90 days at no cost. After this time renewal is at the

discretion of the immigration officer. If refused, leave the country and return. There should be a statutory 72 hs period outside Bolivia before renewing a visa but 24 hrs is usually acceptable. On arrival ensure that visas and passports are stamped with the same, correct date of entry or this can lead to 'fines' later. If you outstay your visa the current fine is US$1.50 per day. **Immigration Office** (La Paz), Av Camacho 1480, T0800-3007, Mon-Fr 0830-1600 i.

Ecuador

Citizens of (among others) all European countries, the USA, Canada, Australia and New Zealand only need a valid passport and in principle, an onward or return ticket although this is rarely asked for. Also required but rarely asked for is an international vaccination certificate. Only citizens of some countries in the Middle East, Central America, Asia and Africa require a consular visa to visit Ecuador as tourists. Members of the Sikh religion, irrespective of nationality, also need a visa.

Tourists are entitled to visit Ecuador for up to 90 days during any 12 month period. This may be extended, at the discretion of the **Policía Nacional de Migración** (national immigration police). In practice, those travelling by land from Peru or Colombia are seldom granted more than 30 days on arrival, but this can usually be extended. When arriving at Quito airport you will be asked how long you plan to stay in the country, say 90 days if you don't know. All visitors must complete an international embarkation/disembarkation card. Keep this card in your passport, losing it can cause difficulties when leaving the country or at a spot check. Extensions up to 90 days total stay may only be requested in Quito, Cuenca, Baños, and Puerto Baquerizo Moreno.

About the region

A sprint through history

9000 BC	Earliest evidence of human presence found at three sites in Peru.
3500-1500 BC	Valdivia culture exists along the coast of Ecuador, based around the town of the same name.
2000 BC	Climatic change dries up the lomas ('fog meadows'), and drives sea shoals to deeper water. Coastal peoples turn to farming and begin to spread inland along river valleys.
2000 BC-100 BC	Formative Period when the initial signs of the high culture of Andean society appear. Sophisticated irrigation and canal systems are developed, farming productivity increases and communities have more time to devote to building and producing ceramics and textiles. The development of pottery also leads to trade and cultural links with other communities.
900 BC	A new era begins with the rise of two important centres in Peru; Chavín de Huantar in the central Andes and Sechín Alto on the north coast. Chavín is the first of several 'horizon styles' that are of greatest importance in Peru and have very widespread influence.
500 BC	There is evidence of an El Niño flood that devastates the north coast of Peru. Social order is disrupted and the Chavín cult takes hold.
300 BC	The Chavín hegemony, which is also known as the Middle Formative Period (or Early Horizon), breaks up and regional diversification of Andean cultures begins.
Up to AD 500	This is the Regional Development Period, a time of great social and cultural development. Sizable towns of 5-10,000 inhabitants grow on the south coast of Peru, populated by artisans, merchants, government administrators and religious officials. One of the most famous cultures of this period is the Nasca, famed for the Nasca Lines
AD 100-800	The militaristic Moche build an empire on the north coast of Peru. Their greatest achievement is their artistic genius, especially their pottery.
AD 600-700	The collapse of the Moche Empire is thought to have been started by a 30-year drought at the end of the sixth century, followed by one of the periodic El Niño flash floods (identified by meteorologists from ice thickness in the Andes) and finished by the encroaching forces of the Huari Empire. The decline of the Moche signals a general tipping of the balance of power in Peru from the north coast to the southern sierra.

AD 500-1200	The Tiahuanaco region of Bolivia becomes one of the most densely populated areas of the Altiplano. The influence of the culture spreads to other areas, through military conquest or trade, and absorbs the militaristic Huari of the central Peruvian highlands. From circa AD 600 the Huari-Tiahuanaco have spread their empire and influence from Cajamarca and Lambayeque in the north and across much of southern Peru, northern Bolivia and Argentina. The civilization reaches its high point around AD 1000, after which a period of decline sets in, leading to its complete collapse around AD 1100-1200.
1200-1450	After the decline of the Huari-Tiahuanaco Empire, the unity imposed on the Andes is broken. A new stage of autonomous regional or local political organizations begins. Among the cultures corresponding to this period are the Kuelap, centred in the Chachapoyas region and the Chimú, based near present-day Chiclayo and Trujillo. In Bolivia, the most powerful kingdoms are the Lupaca, based at Chuquito, southwest of Lake Titicaca, and the Colla, with their capital at Huatuncolla, near present-day Puno.
1438-1527	The expansion of the Inca Empire (see page 57) begins in earnest with the reign of Pachacútec. At its peak, the Inca Empire stretches from the Río Maule in central Chile, north to the present Ecuador-Colombia border, containing most of Ecuador, Peru, western Bolivia, northern Chile and northwest Argentina. The Aymara people of the Titicaca basin are not finally conquered until the latter part of the 15th century in the reign of Inca Túpac Yupangi (1471-1493).
1492	In the same year that Columbus makes his first landfall in South America, Quito is finally captured by the Inca armies and becomes the base from which they extend their territory even further north. A great road is built between Cusco and Quito.
1527	The Inca ruler, Huayna Capac dies and civil war breaks out in the confusion over his rightful successor. One of his legitimate sons, Huáscar, rules the southern part of the empire from Cusco. Atahualpa, Huáscar's half-brother, governs Quito, the capital of Chinchaysuyo.
1532	Soon after Atahualpa has won the civil war, Francisco Pizarro arrives in Tumbes on the north Peruvian coast with 179 *conquistadores*, many on horseback. Atahualpa's army is marching south, when he clashes with Pizarro at Cajamarca. Pizarro captures the Inca leader and puts him to death in 1533. This effectively ends Inca resistance and their empire collapses.
1534	Pizarro claims the northern kingdom of Quito, and his lieutenants Sebastián de Benalcázar and Diego de Almagro take the city.
1535	Pizarro founds Lima in 1535 as capital of the whole region, and four years later replaces Benalcázar at Quito with Gonzalo, his brother.
1535-1542	The Inca's political capital, Cusco, falls and soon afterwards the Spanish begin the conquest of Bolivia. In 1542 the entire area is annexed as the Audencia of Charcas of the Viceroyalty of Peru.

1538	La Plata, now Sucre, is founded and, in 1559 becomes capital of the Audiencia of Charcas (it is still the official capital of Bolivia). Another administrative centre, La Paz, is founded in 1548.
1541-1542	Gonzalo Pizarro sets out on an exploration of the Oriente. He moves down the Napo River and sends Francisco de Orellana ahead to prospect. Orellana does not return, but instead drifts down the river, finally to reach the mouth of the Amazon, nearly two years later, thus becoming the first white man to cross the continent in this way.
1545	Bolivia's destiny is sealed with the discovery of silver at Cerro Rico (Rich Mountain) in Potosí. Charcas becomes one of the most important centres of the Spanish colonial economy, sending a constant supply of silver to Spain. The mining town of Potosí grows rapidly and by 1610 has a population of over 160,000, making it for a long time, by far the largest city in Latin America.
1545-1572	Each succeeding representative of the Kingdom of Spain tries to subdue the Inca successor state of Vilcabamba, north of Cusco, and to unify the fierce Spanish factions. Francisco de Toledo (appointed 1568) solves both problems during his 14 years in office: Vilcabamba is crushed in 1572 and the last reigning Inca, Túpac Amaru, put to death.
From 1700	Following economic recession, the Spanish begin to take over the remaining areas of land in Indian hands and turn them into huge private estates, called haciendas, for which the indigenous population provide the labour force. This new form of serfdom survives until the land reforms of the 20th century.
1780-1814	After nearly 200 years of unbroken Spanish rule, the Peruvian Indians rise in 1780, under the leadership of an Inca noble who calls himself Túpac Amaru II. He and many of his lieutenants are captured and put to death under torture at Cusco. Another Indian leader in revolt suffers the same fate in 1814, but this last flare-up has the sympathy of many of the locally born Spanish, who resent their status, inferior to the Spaniards born in Spain, the refusal to give them any but the lowest offices, the high taxation imposed by the home government, and the severe restrictions upon trade with any country but Spain.
1808-1810	Taking advantage of the chaos produced in Spain by Napoleon's invasion and the forced abdication of the Spanish king, some members of the Quito élite form a junta and declare independence. This lasts only three months before being put down by royalist troops. Meanwhile, in Bolivia, the University of San Francisco Xavier, at Sucre, calls for the independence of all Spain's American colonies.
1820-22	José de San Martín's Argentine troops; convoyed from Chile under the protection of Lord Cochrane's squadron, land in southern Peru. San Martín proclaims Peruvian independence at Lima on 28 July 1821, though most of the country is still in the hands of the Viceroy, José de La Serna. Simón Bolívar, who has already freed Venezuela and Colombia, sends Antonio José de Sucre to Ecuador where, on 24 May 1822, he gains a victory over La Serna at Pichincha.

Essentials About the region A sprint through history

1824-1825   On 9 December General Antonio José de Sucre, wins the decisive battle of Ayacucho in Peru and invades Alto Perú (Bolivia), defeating the Spaniards finally at the battle of Tumusla on 2 April 1825. Bolivia is declared independent on 6 August in Sucre. In honour of its liberator, the country is named República de Bolívar, soon to be changed to Bolivia. La Plata becomes the capital and Sucre becomes the first president.

1820-1895   Following the collapse of Gran Colombia under the leadership of Simón Bolívar, Ecuador becomes an independent state but becomes a chronic example of the political chaos and instability which affects much of Spanish America in the 19th century. Of the 21 individuals and juntas who occupy the presidency for a total of 34 times between 1830 and 1895, only six complete their constitutional terms of office.

1829-1839   The longest lasting government of the 19th century is that of Andrés Santa Cruz, but when he tries to unite Bolivia with Peru in 1836, Chile and Argentina intervene to overthrow him. Between 1825 and 1982 there are no fewer than 188 coups d'état in Bolivia.

1879-1883   The disastrous War of the Pacific is fought between Peru and Bolivia and Chile. Peru and Bolivia are defeated by Chile and Peru loses its southern territory. Defeat discredits civilian politicians even further and leads to a period of military rule in Peru in the 1880s. In Bolivia, there is greater stability, but opposition to the political dominance of the city of Sucre culminates in a revolt in 1899 led by business groups from La Paz and the tin-mining areas, as a result of which La Paz becomes the centre of government.

1895   In Ecuador, the seizure of power by the coastal élite, led by the Radical Liberal *caudillo* Eloy Alfaro (president 1895-1901 and 1906-11), is followed by important changes as the Radical Liberals begin to implement a programme to bring Ecuador into the modern world and to reduce the power of the church. The overthrow of the Radical Liberals by a group of military officers leads to the restoration to power of the Quito élite.

1924   The formation in Peru of the Alianza Popular Revolucionario Americana (APRA) by Víctor Raúl Haya de la Torre. APRA eventually becomes the largest and best-organized political party in Peru, but the distrust of Haya de la Torre by the military and the upper class for Haya de la Torre ensures that he will never become president.

1931-1948   The onset of the Great Depression leads to severe economic problems in Ecuador. In the following years the country experiences its worst period of political instability. Between 1931 and 1948 there are 21 governments, none of which succeeds in completing its term of office.

1932-35   The long-running dispute between Bolivia and Paraguay over the Chaco erupts into war and ends in ignominious defeat for Bolivia and the loss of three quarters of the Chaco.

1936	The Bolivian army seizes power for the first time since the War of the Pacific. Defeat in the Chaco War has bred nationalist resentment among junior army officers who had served in the Chaco and among the Indians who had been used as cannon-fodder.
1936-1944	The growing national malaise among different sectors of society in Bolivia leads to a group of young intellectuals setting up a nationalist party, the Movimiento Nacional Revolucionario (MNR) headed by Víctor Paz Estenssoro, Hernán Siles Zuazo, Walter Guevara Arce and Juan Lechín Oquendo. In 1944 Víctor Paz Estenssoro succeeds in taking the MNR into the radical government of young army officers led by Major Gualberto Villaroel. However, in 1946 Villaroel is overthrown and publicly lynched and Paz Estenssoro has to flee to Argentina.
1948-1960	Political stability is restored to Ecuador when it enters a period of economic expansion based on the production of bananas on coastal plantations. Bananas account for two-thirds of exports. Between 1948 and 1960 three successive presidents manage to complete their terms of office.
1951-1953	Bolivian elections won by Víctor Paz, the MNR candidate. However, the incumbent government refuses to recognize the result and transferred power to a military junta. The organized and radicalized miners react immediately and revolution breaks out on 9 April 1952, backed by sections of the police as well as the campesinos, urban factory workers and the lower middle classes. Two days later the army surrenders to the MNR's militias. Paz Estenssoro becomes president and his MNR government nationalizes the mines, introduced universal suffrage and begins the break-up and redistribution of large estates under the Agrarian Reform programme of 1953 which ends the feudal economic conditions of rural Bolivia.
1962	In Peru, Haya de la Torre is at last permitted to run for the presidency. But although he wins the largest percentage of votes he is prevented from taking office by the armed forces who seize power and organize fresh elections for 1963 in which the military obtain the desired result. The victor, Fernando Belaúnde Terry, attempts to introduce reforms, particularly in the landholding structure of the sierra. When these reforms are weakened by landowner opposition in Congress, peasant groups begin invading landholdings in protest. At the same time, under the influence of the Cuban revolution, guerrilla groups begin operating in the sierra. Military action to deal with this leads to the deaths of an estimated 8,000 people.
1968-1975	Belaúnde's attempts to solve a long-running dispute with the International Petroleum Company (a subsidiary of Standard Oil) result in him being attacked for selling out to the unpopular oil company. The armed forces seize power.
1964-1969	The military regime of Barrientos in Bolivia. Political opponents and trade union activists are brutally persecuted and miners' rebellions are put down violently. Barrientos dies in 1969 in a mysterious air crash.

1971-1978 The military incumbent in Bolivia is overthrown by the right-wing General Hugo Banzer. During his rule, tens of thousands of Bolivians are imprisoned or exiled for political reasons. In 1978 Banzer is forced to call elections, partly as a result of the pressure which US President Jimmy Carter exerts on the military government because of its human rights abuses.

1978-1982 Another period of chronic instability, political unrest and military violence in Bolivia, with three presidential elections and five coups. Civilian rule returns on 10 October 1982, but not before the notoriously brutal military coup led by General García Meza (1980-1981). In August 1982 the military return to barracks and Siles Zuazo assumes the presidency in a leftist coalition government with support from the communists and trade unions. Inflation spirals out of control.

1980-1984 Belaúnde returns to power in Peru winning the first elections after military rule. His government is badly affected by the 1982 debt crisis and the 1981-1983 world recession, and inflation reaches over 100 per cent a year in 1983-1984. His term is marked by the growth of the Maoist guerrilla movement Sendero Luminoso (Shining Path) and the smaller Marxist Túpac Amaru (MRTA).

1985-1990 APRA, in opposition for over 50 years, finally comes to power in Peru. With Haya de la Torre dead, the APRA candidate Alan García Pérez wins the elections and is allowed to take office by the armed forces. By the time his term of office ends in 1990, Peru is bankrupt and García and APRA are discredited.

1990-1992 In Peru, Alberto Fujimori of the Cambio 90 movement defeats the novelist Mario Vargas Llosa. Fujimori fails to win a majority in either the senate or the lower house but duly dissolves congress and suspends the constitution on 5 April 1992. In elections to a new, 80-member Democratic Constituent Congress (CCD) in November 1992, Fujimori's Cambio 90/Nueva Mayoría coalition wins a majority of seats, though three major political parties boycott the elections.

1992-1995 The terrorist activities of Sendero Luminoso and Túpac Amaru are effectively ended with the capture of both their leaders, Abimael Guzmán and Víctor Polay, in 1992. Many of Sendero's members take advantage of guaranteed lighter sentences in return for surrender.

1995 Fujimori stands for re-election and wins by a resounding margin. The coalition that supports him also wins a majority in Congress.

1995-1998 Ecuador's long-running border conflict with Peru flares up. Massive display of national unity in Ecuador temporarily diverts attention away from yet another major corruption scandal. Jamil Mahuad, a former mayor of Quito, is elected president in 1998, amid renewed border tensions with Peru. He immediately diffuses this explosive situation and in less than three months he signs a definitive peace treaty, putting an end to decades – even centuries – of conflict.

17 Dec 1996	14 Túpac Amaru guerrillas infiltrate a reception at the Japanese Embassy Siege in Lima, taking 490 hostages. Among the rebels' demands are the release of their imprisoned colleagues, better treatment for prisoners and new measures to raise living standards. Most of the hostages are released and negotiations are pursued during a stalemate that lasts until 22 April 1997. The president takes sole responsibility for the successful, but risky assault which frees all the hostages (one died of heart failure) and kills all the terrorists. By not yielding to Túpac Amaru, Fujimori regains much popularity.
1997	The worst El Niño of the 20th century hits Peru, causing chaos, many deaths and devasting damage.
1997-2000	Bolivian presidential elections are won by former dictator General Hugo Banzer. Banzer pursues economic austerity and the US-backed policy of eradicating coca production. Economic hardship in rural areas, together with unemployment and anger at a plan to raise water rates to fund an expensive new reservoir project lead to violent protests and road blocks in many parts of the country. Several people are killed and Banzer calls a state of emergency. Amid the confusion, the police seize the moment to go on strike for higher pay. Within 48 hours the government capitulates.
1997	Abdalá Bucaram of the Partido Roldosista Ecuatoriano (PRE) is swept to power but his erratic government lasts barely six months and by February 1997 all manner of scandal has implicated his entire government and family. There follows a period of political chaos during which Ecuador has three simultaneous presidents. Bucaram flees to Panama. The interim government is marred by further accusations of corruption and continuing economic decline and the acting President is imprisoned for several months on corruption charges. A constituent assembly is convened during the interim government and draws up the country's 18th constitution.
1999-2002	Ecuador's social, political and economic situation is completely out of control and Mahuad decrees the adoption of the US dollar as the national currency in a desperate bid for monetary stability. Less than a month later, on 21 January 2000, he is forced out of office by Ecuador's indigenous people and disgruntled members of the armed forces in the first overt military coup in South America in more than two decades. It lasts barely three hours before a combination of local intrigue and international pressure hands power to vice-president Gustavo Noboa. The colonels involved in the coup are subsequently pardoned but dismissed from the military. Colonel Lucio Gutiérrez, the leader of the coup, goes on to found his own political party and is elected president in 2002.
28 May 2000	Fujimori stands for re-election in Peru but foreign observers say the electoral system is unprepared and flawed, proposing a postponement. The authorities refuse to delay. Fujimori's opponent, Toledo, boycotts the election and Fujimori returns unopposed.

Essentials About the region A sprint through history

14 Sep 2000	Fujimori's close aide and head of the National Intelligence Service (SIN), Vladimiro Montesinos, is caught on film allegedly handing US$15,000 to a congressman, Alberto Kouri, to persuade him to switch allegiances to Fujimori's coalition. Fujimori's demise is swift. Montesinos is declared a wanted man and he flees to Panama, where he is denied asylum. In early 2001 he is eventually captured in Venezuela and returns to Peru where he is tried on a multitude of charges. Fujimori is exiled in Japan from where, on 20 November 2000, he sends congress an email announcing his resignation. Congress rejects this, firing him instead on charges of being "morally unfit" to govern.
2001-2004	Alejandro Toledo is elected President in Peru but the first half of his presidency is marked by slow progress on both the political and economic fronts. A series of damaging strikes by farmers, teachers and government workers forces him to declare a state of emergency in May 2003 to restore order and further violent protests take place. In July 2002 Montesinos is convicted of usurping power and sentenced by the Peruvian anti-corruption court to nine years and four months in prison. In 2004, prosecutors also seek to charge exiled Fujimori with ordering the deaths of 25 people in 1991 and 1992. This follows the Truth and Reconciliation Committee's report (2003) into the civil war of the 1980s-1990s, which stated that over 69,000 Peruvians had been killed. Members of both Sendero Luminoso and MRTA are arrested in May 2004 on suspicion of infiltrating educational establishments.
2001-2004	In Bolivia, demonstrations large and small against social conditions are held throughout the country. President Banzer is forced to resign in August 2001 because of cancer. Gonzalo Sánchez de Lozada wins the election in 2002 but the following year tension between the government and *campesinos* boils over and more than 100 people are killed in various protests. Lozada is forced from office and into exile in the United States, to be succeeded by his deputy, Carlos Mesa. Mesa continues to walk the fine line between the demands of the militant left and pressure from big business and the United States.
26 Jan 2005	Up to 250,000 Ecuadoreans march in Guayaquil in protest at rising crime and corruption and to demand the reinstatement of the Supreme Court which was suspended by President Gutiérrez on 8 December 2004. Gutiérrez is under mounting pressure, following allegations of corruption. Rising costs of basic services, due to privatization and increased military ties with the US in their campaign against Colombian guerillas, also threaten his government's future.
Mar 2005	Bolivia's President, Carlos Mesa, announces his resignation in the face of continued protests over new laws governing the country's oil and gas resources. Parliament refuses to accept his resignation so Mesa carries on amidst threats by Evo Morales, who heads the Movement Towards Socialism, the second largest force in parliament, to block all the highways and take over the electricity and gas plants. Mesa promises not to use force to open highways but sends troops to oil fields to prevent disruption of supplies.

The Incas

The origins of the Inca Dynasty are shrouded in mythology. The best known story reported by the Spanish chroniclers talks about Manco Cápac and his sister rising out of Lake Titicaca, created by the Sun as divine founders of a chosen race. This was in approximately AD 1200. Over the next 300 years the small tribe grew to supremacy as leaders of the largest empire ever known in the Americas, the four territories of Tawantinsuyo, united by Cusco as the umbilicus of the Universe. The four quarters of Tawantinsuyo, all radiating out from Cusco, were: 1 Chinchaysuyo, north and north-west; 2 Cuntisuyo, south and west; 3 Collasuyo, south and east; 4 Antisuyo, east.

At its peak, just before the Spanish Conquest, the Inca Empire stretched from the Río Maule in central Chile, north to the present Ecuador-Colombia border, containing most of Ecuador, Peru, western Bolivia, northern Chile and northwest Argentina. The area was roughly equivalent to France, Belgium, Holland, Luxembourg, Italy and Switzerland combined (980,000 sq km).

The first Inca ruler, Manco Cápac, moved to the fertile Cusco region, and established Cusco as his capital. Successive generations of rulers were fully occupied with local conquests of rivals, such as the Colla and Lupaca to the south, and the Chanca to the northwest. At the end of Inca Viracocha's reign the hated Chanca were finally defeated, largely thanks to the heroism of one of his sons, Pachacútec Inca Yupanqui, who was subsequently crowned as the new ruler.

Inca society

The Incas were a small aristocracy numbering only a few thousand, centred in the highland city of Cusco, at 3,400 m. They rose gradually as a small regional dynasty, similar to others in the Andes of that period, starting around AD 1200. Then in the mid-1400s, they began to expand explosively under Pachacútec, a sort of Andean Alexander the Great, and later his son, Topa. Under a hundred years later, they fell before the rapacious warriors of Spain. The Incas were not the first dynasty in Andean history to dominate their neighbours, but they did it more thoroughly and went further than anyone before them.

Empire building

Enough remains today of their astounding highways, cities and agricultural terracing for people to marvel and wonder how they accomplished so much in so short a time. They seem to have been amazingly energetic, industrious and efficient – and the reports of their Spanish conquerors confirm this hypothesis.

They must also have had the willing cooperation of most of their subject peoples, most of the time. In fact, the Incas were master diplomats and alliance-builders first, and military conquerors only second, if the first method of expansion failed. The Inca skill at generating wealth by means of highly efficient agriculture and distribution brought them enormous prestige and enabled them to 'out-gift' neighbouring chiefs in huge royal feasts involving ritual outpourings of generosity, often in the form of vast gifts of textiles, exotic products from distant regions, and perhaps wives to add blood ties to the alliance. The 'out-gifted' chief was required by the Andean laws of reciprocity to provide something in return, and this would usually be his loyalty, as well as a levy of manpower from his own chiefdom.

Thus, with each new alliance the Incas wielded greater labour forces and their mighty public works programmes surged ahead. These were administered through an institution known as **mit'a**, a form of taxation through labour. The state provided the materials, such as wool and cotton for making textiles, and the communities provided skills and labour.

Mit'a contingents worked royal mines, royal plantations for coca leaves, royal quarries and so on. The system strove to be fair, and workers in such hardship posts as high altitude mines and lowland coca plantations were given correspondingly shorter terms of service.

Organization

Huge administrative centres were built in different parts of the empire, where people and supplies were gathered. Articles such as textiles and pottery were produced there in large workshops. Work in these places was carried out in a festive manner, with plentiful food, drink and music. Here was Andean reciprocity at work: the subject supplied his labour, and the ruler was expected to provide generously while he did so.

Aside from mit'a contributions there were also royal lands claimed by the Inca as his portion in every conquered province, and worked for his benefit by the local population. Thus, the contribution of each citizen to the state was quite large, but apparently, the imperial economy was productive enough to sustain this.

Another institution was the practice of moving populations around wholesale, inserting loyal groups into restive areas, and removing recalcitrant populations to loyal areas. These movements of **mitmakuna**, as they were called, were also used to introduce skilled farmers and engineers into areas where productivity needed to be raised.

Communications

The huge empire was held together by an extensive and highly efficient highway system. There were an estimated 30,000 km of major highway, most of it neatly paved and drained, stringing together the major Inca sites. Two parallel highways ran north to south, along the coastal desert strip and the mountains, and dozens of east-west roads crossed from the coast to the Amazon fringes. These roadways took the most direct routes, with wide stone stairways zig-zagging up the steepest mountain slopes and rope suspension bridges crossing the many narrow gorges of the Andes. The north-south roads formed a great axis which eventually came to be known as **Capaq Ñan** – "Royal, or Principal Road", in Quechua – which exceeded in grandeur not only the other roads, but also their utilitarian concept. They became the Incas' symbol of power over men and over the sacred forces of nature. So marvellous were these roads that the Spaniards who saw them at the height of their glory said that there was nothing comparable in all Christendom.

Every 12 km or so there was a **tambo**, or way station, where goods could be stored and travellers lodged. The tambos were also control points, where the Inca state's accountants tallied movements of goods and people. Even more numerous than tambos, were the huts of the **chasquis**, or relay runners, who sped royal and military messages along these highways.

The Inca state kept records and transmitted information in various ways. Accounting and statistical records were kept on skeins of knotted strings known as **quipus**. Numbers

Markets remain the primary focus of Andean commerce.

employed the decimal system, and colours indicated the categories being recorded. An entire class of people, known as quipucamayocs, existed whose job was to create and interpret these. Neither the Incas nor their Andean predecessors had a system of writing as we understand it, but there may have been a system of encoding language into quipus.

Archaeologists are studying this problem today. History and other forms of knowledge were transmitted via songs and poetry. Music and dancing, full of encoded information which could be read by the educated elite, were part of every major ceremony and public event information was also carried in textiles, which had for millennia been the most vital expression of Andean culture.

Textiles

Clothing carried insignia of status, ethnic origin, age and so on. Special garments were made and worn for various rites of passage. It has been calculated that, after agriculture, no activity was more important to Inca civilization than weaving. Vast stores of textiles were maintained to sustain the Inca system of ritual giving. Armies and mit'a workers were partly paid in textiles. The finest materials were reserved for the nobility, and the Inca emperor himself displayed his status by changing into new clothes every day and having the previous day's burned.

Most weaving was done by women, and the Incas kept large numbers of 'chosen women' in female-only houses all over the empire, partly for the purpose of supplying textiles to the elite and for the many deities to whom they were frequently given as burned offerings. These women had other duties, such as making *chicha* – the Inca corn beer which was consumed and sacrificed in vast quantities on ceremonial occasions. They also became wives and concubines to the Inca elite and loyal nobilities. And some may have served as priestesses of the moon, in parallel to the male priesthood of the sun.

Religious worship

The Incas have always been portrayed as sun-worshippers, but it now seems that they were mountain-worshippers too. Recent research has shown that Machu Picchu was at least partly dedicated to the worship of the surrounding mountains, and Inca sacrificial victims have been excavated on frozen Andean peaks at 6,700 m. In fact, until technical climbing was invented, the Incas held the world altitude record for humans.

Human sacrifice was not common, but every other kind was, and ritual attended every event in the Inca calendar. The main temple of Cusco was dedicated to the numerous deities: the Sun, the Moon, Venus, the Pleiades, the Rainbow, Thunder and Lightning, and the

Textiles continue to play a vital part in people's lives.

countless religious icons of subject peoples which had been brought to Cusco, partly in homage, partly as hostage. Here, worship was continuous and the fabulous opulence included gold cladding on the walls and a famous garden filled with life-size objects of gold and silver. Despite this pantheism, the Incas acknowledged an overall Creator God, whom they called **Viracocha**. A special temple was dedicated to him at Raqchi, about 100 km southeast of Cusco. Part of it still stands today.

Military forces

The conquering Spaniards noted with admiration the Inca storehouse system, still well-stocked when they found it, despite several years of civil war among the Incas. Besides textiles, military equipment and ritual objects, they found huge quantities of food. Like most Inca endeavours, the food stores served a multiple purpose: to supply feasts, as provisions during lean times, to feed travelling work parties and to supply armies on the march.

Inca armies were able to travel light and move fast because of this system. Every major Inca settlement incorporated great halls where large numbers of prople could be accommodated or feasts and gatherings held, and large squares or esplanades where public assemblies could take place.

Inca technology is usually deemed inferior to that of contemporary Europe. Their military technology certainly was. They had not invented iron-smelting and basically fought with clubs, palmwood spears, slings, wooden shields, cotton armour and straw-stuffed helmets. They did not even make much use of the bow and arrow, a weapon they were well aware of. Military tactics, too, were primitive. The disciplined formations of the Inca armies quickly dissolved into melees of unbridled individualism once battle was joined.

This, presumably, was because warfare constituted a theatre of manly prowess, but was not the main priority of Inca life. Its form was ritualistic. Battles were suspended by both sides for religious observance. Negotiation, combined with displays of superior Inca strength, usually achieved victory, and total annihilation of the enemy was not on the agenda.

Architecture

Other technologies, however, were superior in every way to their 16th-century counterparts: textiles; settlement planning, and agriculture, in particular, with its sophisticated irrigation and soil conservation systems, ecological sensitivity, specialized crop strains and high productivity under the harshest conditions. The Incas fell short of their Andean predecessors in the better-known arts of ancient America – ceramics, textiles and metalwork – but it could be argued that their supreme efforts were made in architecture, stoneworking, landscaping, roadbuilding and in the harmonious combination of these elements.

These are the outstanding survivals of Inca civilization, which still remain to fascinate the visitor: the huge, exotically close-fit blocks of stone, cut in graceful, almost sensual curves; the astoundingly craggy and inaccessible sites encircled by great sweeps of Andean scenery; the rhythmic layers of farm terracing that provided land and food to this still-enigmatic people. The finest examples of Inca architecture can be seen in the city of Cusco and throughout the Sacred Valley. As more evidence of Inca society is uncovered each year, our knowledge of these remarkable people can only improve: in 2002 alone two new cities in the Vilcabamba region were revealed, as well as the huge cemetery at Purucucho, near Lima, and a mummy at Machu Picchu.

Ruling elite

The ruling elite lived privileged lives in their capital at Cusco. They reserved for themselves and chosen insiders certain luxuries, such as the chewing of coca, the wearing of fine vicuña wool, and the practice of polygamy. But they were an austere people, too. Everyone

Inca stonework in Cusco.

had work to do, and the nobility were constantly being posted to state business throughout the empire. Young nobles were expected to learn martial skills, besides being able to read the quipus, speak both Quechua and the southern language of Aymara and know the epic poems.

The Inca elite belonged to royal clans known as panacas, which each had the unusual feature of being united around veneration of the mummy of their founding ancestor – a previous Inca emperor, unless they happened to belong to the panaca founded by the Inca emperor who was alive at the time. Each new emperor built his own palace in Cusco and amassed his own wealth rather than inheriting it from his forebears, which perhaps helps to account for the urge to unlimited expansion.

This urge ultimately led the Incas to overreach themselves. Techniques of diplomacy and incorporation no longer worked as they journeyed farther from the homeland and met ever-increasing resistance from people less familiar with their ways. During the reign of Wayna Cápac, the last emperor before the Spanish invasion, the Incas had to establish a northern capital at Quito in order to cope with permanent war on their northern frontier. Following Wayna Cápac's death came a devastating civil war between Cusco and Quito and, immediately thereafter, came the Spanish invasion. Tawantisuyo, the empire of the four quarters, collapsed with dizzying suddenness.

The region today

The dominant adjective that links Peru, Bolivia and Ecuador is "Andean", because of the mountain range that is such a massive physical presence and the people, whose historical associations and present-day culture contribute such striking images of the region. But Andean is an imperfect description, as Ecuador and Peru have an extensive Pacific seaboard; a great proportion of national territory is made up of Amazonian lowlands; and Bolivia also has areas of Chaco and Pantanal.

The Spaniards, after conquering the already divided Incas, plundered the riches they found, enslaved the people and deliberately fragmented their society. Neither the *conquistadores*, however, nor the leaders of the subsequent war of independence from Spain could prevent internal differences tearing their visions apart. The contemporary legacy of this fractured past is mirrored by, for example, the Peruvian-Ecuadorean border disputes which lasted into the 20th century, the rivalry between coast and sierra in Ecuador, or between highlands and eastern lowlands in Bolivia, and pockets of wealth amid areas of extreme poverty. Moreover, there is a general lack of unifying principles in public life, seen most obviously in corruption by those in power. The sense of disillusion in political institutions is not surprising when, for instance, Peruvian President Fujimori's administration was shown to be as corrupt as those he was professing to eradicate (2000), or Ecuador's President Bucaram could only manage six months in office (1996). This is not to downplay the difficulties presidents face, from unpopularity because of unfulfilled promises, to intense international pressures, most obviously in the calls for solidarity in the so-called war against drugs.

Where it would appear that a shared history is failing to hold the region together, there are many issues which cement a common bond. The marginalization of indigenous communities has forged a new drive towards human rights. Indigenous people were instrumental in the overthrow of presidents Mahuad in Ecuador (2000) and Sánchez de Lozada in Bolivia (2003). Furthermore, they are now major actors in international bodies such as the United Nations. This newfound assertiveness is but one aspect of Andean peoples' legendary cultural endurance. Although their customs and beliefs have blended with those imported from Spain and even Africa, these remain as cherished as ever. When you are urged to join a festival parade, be it Corpus Cristi in Pujilí (Ecuador) or Carnaval in Oruro (Bolivia), you can easily see why. And thanks in part to visitors, Andean music, dance and textiles have become part of the world's cultural language.

The mountains and the jungle still hold vast natural resources which perennially promise prosperity. But neither Peru's enormous Yanacocha gold mine, nor Ecuador's reserves of oil, nor Bolivia's natural gas, will contribute to improved social conditions if they only benefit foreign interests. And when, at the other end of the scale, a pittance is paid for produce sweated from precipitous hillsides or extracted from the forest several days' walk from town, it's not surprising that inequality breeds discontent. To make matters worse, the exploitation of natural resources (from minerals, to food crops, to shrimp, to coca) is at times inflicting terrible damage on the natural environment.

Like the Andes themselves, Peru, Bolivia and Ecuador are young and growing. Greater than the deceptions of the past or the challenges of the present are hopes for the future, and sustainable tourism has its part to play. From the local to the global, many travellers embrace the cause of conservation, while others struggle alongside residents to improve life for dispossessed farmers, shanty town dwellers and street kids. And all visitors contribute just by being here. Running a small hotel or tour agency can be a local family's ticket out of poverty. Recognizing this is the first step towards gringos giving something back to the Andes, not plundering like the *conquistadores* of the past.

Indigenous people are increasingly asserting their political rights.

Festivals

One of the major considerations of deciding when to travel, aside from knowing where to go and what the weather will be like, is the festival calendar. Fiestas are a fundamental part of life for most South Americans, taking place up and down the length and breadth of the continent and with such frequency that it would be hard to miss one, even during the briefest of stays. This is fortunate, because arriving in any town or village during these inevitably frenetic celebrations is one of the great travelling experiences.

Invariably, fiestas involve drinking – lots and lots of it. There's also non-stop dancing, which can sometimes verge on an organized brawl, and water throwing (or worse). What this means is that, at some point, you will fall over, through inebriation or exhaustion, or both. After several days of this, you will awake with a hangover the size of the Amazon rainforest and probably have no recollection of what you did with your backpack.

Not all festivals end up as massive unruly parties, however. Some are solemn and elaborate holy processions, often incorporating Spanish colonial themes into predominantly ancient pagan rituals. Many of the major fiestas, such as Carnival (throughout February) and Semana Santa (March/April) take place during the wet season. Here is a brief list of the most important festivals in each country:

Peru

First two weeks of Feb: La Virgen de la Candelaria, Puno and the shores of Lake Titicaca, masked dancers and bands compete in a famous festival in which local legends and characters are represented.

Mar/Apr: Semana Santa, Arequipa and Ayacucho, both cities celebrate Holy Week with fine processions, but each has its unique elements: the burning of an effigy of Judas in Arequipa and beautiful floral 'paintings' in Ayacucho, where Easter celebrations are among the world's finest.

Jun: Semana de Andinismo, Huaraz, international climbing and skiing week. In late Jun in this region also, San Juan and San Pedro are celebrated.

Jun: there are several major festivals in and around Cusco: **Corpus Christi**, on the

Carnival at Oruro.

Background →

Day of the Dead

One of the most important dates in the indigenous people's calendar is 2 November, Day of the Dead (*Día de los Difuntos* or *Finados*). This tradition has been practised since time immemorial. In the Incaic calendar, November was the eighth month and meant *Ayamarca*, or land of the dead. The celebration is another example of religious adaptation in which the ancient beliefs of ethnic cultures are mixed with the rites of the Catholic Church. According to ancient belief, the spirit visits its relatives at this time of the year and is fed in order to continue its journey before its reincarnation. The relatives of the dead prepare for the arrival of the spirit days in advance. Among the many items necessary for these meticulous preparations are little bread dolls, each one of which has a particular significance. Horse-shaped breads are prepared that will serve as a means of transport for the soul in order to avoid fatigue.

Inside the home, the relatives construct a tomb supported by boxes over which is laid a black cloth. Here they put the bread, along with various other items important in the ritual. The tomb is also adorned with the dead relative's favourite food and drink. Most households also share a glass of *colada morada*, a syrupy, purple-coloured drink made from various fruits and purple corn. Once the spirit has arrived and feasted with its living relatives, the entire ceremony is then transported to the graveside in the local cemetery, where it is carried out again, along with the many other mourning families.

This meeting of the living and their dead relatives is re-enacted the following year, though less ostentatiously, and again for the final time in the third year, the year of the farewell. It does not continue after this, which is just as well as the costs can be crippling for the family concerned. Today, such elaborate celebrations are rare and most people commemorate *Día de los Difuntos* in more prosaic fashion; by visiting the cemetery and placing flowers at the graveside of their deceased relatives.

Thu after Trinity; mid-Jun, **Q'Olloriti**, the ice festival at 4,700 m on a glacier; 24th, **Inti Raymi**, the Inca festival of the winter solstice at Sacsayhuaman (this is preceded by a beer festival and, one week later, the Ollanta-Raymi in Ollantaytambo). Also in mid-Jun is the **Wiracocha** dance festival at Raqchi. **Last week of Sep**: Festival de la **Primavera**, Trujillo, with beauty pageant, Caballos de Paso horse shows and events.

Bolivia

24 Jan to first week in Feb: Alacitas Fair, La Paz, a celebration of Ekeko, the household god of good fortune and plenty.
2 Feb: La Virgen de la **Candelaria**, Copacabana, processions, fireworks, dancing and bullfights on the shores of Lake Titicaca (also celebrated in many rural communities).

5 Best

Festivals

Oruro Carnival Dancing, music, great costumes, lots of alcohol and hundreds of water bombs all add up to a lot of fun ▸▸ *p286*

Phujllay One of Bolvia's wildest celebrations, with lots of dancing, colourful costumes, gallons of *chicha* (maize beer) and no sleep ▸▸ *p254*

Santa Cruz Carnival Not quite Rio but wild and raucous with music and dancing in the streets, fancy dress and the coronation of a carnival queen ▸▸ *p310*

Festival de la Primavera This celebration of the arrival of Spring is one of Peru's most important tourist events and features the famous *Caballos de Paso* ▸▸ *p186*

Día de Quito A week of elaborate parades, bullfights, performances and music in the streets, and a great deal of drinking, with a day to sleep it all off ▸▸ *p337*

Feb/Mar: La Diablada, Oruro, celebrations in the high Andes with tremendous masked dancers and displays. **Carnival** is also worth seeing in the lowland city of Santa Cruz de la Sierra.

Mid-Mar: Phujllay, Tarabuco (Sucre), a joint celebration of carnival and the Battle of Jumbate (12 Mar 1816), with music and dancing.

May/Jun: Festividad del Señor del Gran Poder, La Paz, thousands of dancers in procession through the centre of the city.

Jun-Aug (movable): Masked and costumed dances are the highlight of the four-day **Fiesta de la Virgen de Urkupiña** in Quillacolla, near Cochabamba.

Ecuador

Feb: Fiesta de las Frutas y las Flores, Ambato, carnival with parades, festivities and bullfights; unlike other Andean carnivals, throwing of water and other mess is banned.

Jun: Los San Juanes, the combined festivals of (21st) **Inti Raymi**; (24th) San Juan Bautista; and (29th) San Pedro y San Pablo, Otavalo and Imbabura province, mostly indigenous celebrations of the summer solstice and saints' days, music, dancing, bullfights, regattas on Laguna San Pablo.

Second week of Sep: Yamor and Colla Raimi, Otavalo, lots of festivities and events to celebrate the equinox and the festival of the moon.

6 Dec: Día de Quito, Quito, commemorating the founding of the city with parades, bullfights, shows and music. The city is busy right through Christmas up to the 31st, Años Viejos, the New Year celebrations which take place all over the country.

Christmas time: Cuenca, many parades, the highlight being the **Pase del Niño Viajero**, the finest Christmas parade in the country.

Lima and the South Coast

Pomp and ceremony in Lima's Plaza de Armas

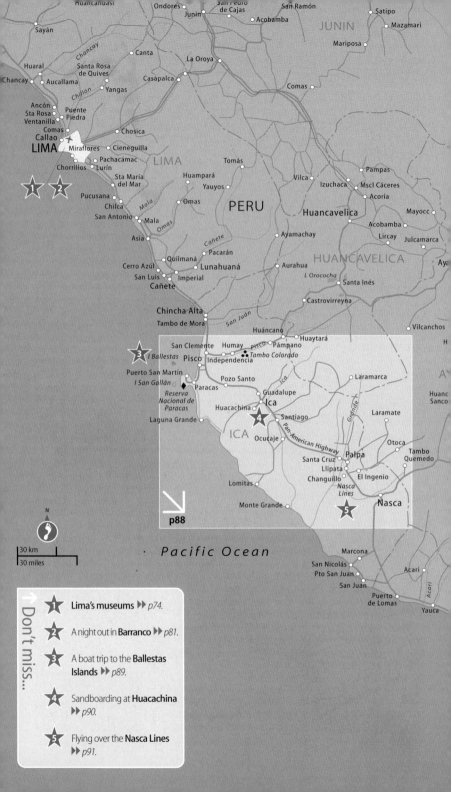

Don't miss...

1 Lima's museums ▶▶ *p74.*

2 A night out in **Barranco** ▶▶ *p81.*

3 A boat trip to the **Ballestas Islands** ▶▶ *p89.*

4 Sandboarding at **Huacachina** ▶▶ *p90.*

5 Flying over the **Nasca Lines** ▶▶ *p91.*

Peru's capital gets a bad press, but scratch beneath its coating of grime and decay and you'll find one of the most vibrant and hospitable cities anywhere. Lima boasts some of the finest historical monuments and museums in the country. The colonial centre, with its grand Plaza de Armas, fine churches and beautiful wooden balconies, is one of Peru's ten UNESCO World Heritage sites and strenuous efforts are being made to refurbish the historical districts. The city's cuisine has earned it the title 'Gastronomic Capital of the Americas' and the bars, clubs and peñas of Barranco and Miraflores ring to the sounds of everything from techno to traditional music.

Stretching south from the capital is the long desert coast, washed by seas full of marine life, punctuated by beautiful oases such as Huacachina and decorated by a series of massive lines etched in the sand. These ancient works of art, depicting various animals, plants and geometrical patterns, continue to engage the minds of intrigued scientists as well as attract visitors who come to gaze in awe at their sheer scale.

Ratings

Culture
★★★★★

Landscape
★★★

Wildlife
★★★

Activities
★★★

Chillin'
★

Costs
$$$$

Lima

Lima is a city of contradictions. Here in this sprawling metropolis of 8,000,000 inhabitants you'll encounter grinding poverty and conspicuous wealth in abundance; the rubbish-strewn districts between airport and city and the shantytowns on the outskirts constrast sharply with the shiny, upmarket suburbs of Miraflores, San Isidro or Barranco. Lima's image as a place to avoid or quickly pass through is enhanced by the thick grey blanket of cloud that descends in May and hangs around for the next seven months, but when the blanket is pulled aside in November to reveal bright blue skies, Limeños descend in droves on the city's popular coastal resorts for raucous weekends of sun, sea, salsa and ceviche.

⊘ Getting there International and domestic flights. Buses to all parts of the country.
⊖ Getting around Taxis and frequent public buses.
⊖ Time required 2 days.
⊚ Weather Sunny Nov-Apr; damp and foggy May-Nov.
⊖ Sleeping 5-star luxury to backpacker guesthouses.
⊘ Eating The gastronomic capital of South America.
▲▲ Activities and tours Sightseeing in the colonial centre.
★ Don't miss... Barranco nightlife ▸▸ p81.

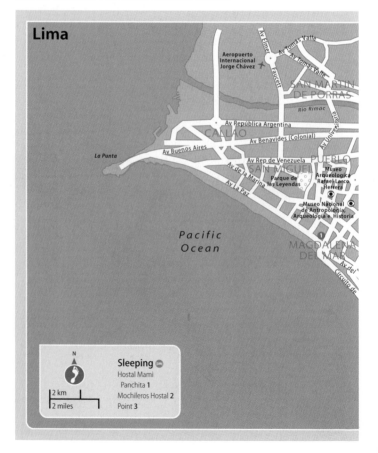

Lima

Pacific Ocean

Aeropuerto Internacional Jorge Chávez ✈
Av Elmer Faucett
Av Tomás Valle
SAN MARTÍN DE PORRAS
Río Rímac
Av República Argentina
CALLAO
Av Benavides (Colonial)
La Punta
Av Buenos Aires
Av Rep de Venezuela
PUEBLO
SAN MIGUEL
Av de la Marina
Parque de las Leyendas
Museo Arqueológico Rafael Larco Herrera
Av La Paz
Museo Nacional de Antropología, Arqueología e Historia
MAGDALENA DEL MAR

N

2 km
2 miles

Sleeping ⊖
Hostal Mami Panchita **1**
Mochileros Hostal **2**
Point **3**

Getting there

All **international flights** land at Jorge Chávez Airport, 16 km northwest of the historic centre. Transport into town is easy. Remise taxis (Mitsui or CMV) have representatives at desks outside International Arrivals and National Arrivals, charging US$11.75 to the city centre, US$14.50 to San Isidro and Miraflores, US$17.50 to Barranco. This is the safest option, but also the most expensive. There are many taxi drivers offering their services outside Arrivals. An illuminated sign outside the airport shows official taxi charges and there is usually a policeman monitoring the taxis. It helps to have exact change in soles to avoid having to break a large bill along the way. If you are feeling confident and not too jet-lagged, go to the car park exit and find a taxi outside the perimeter, by the roundabout. They charge US$3 to the city centre. The security guards may help you find a taxi. All vehicles can enter the airport for 10 minutes at no charge. After that, it's S/.3.50 (US$1) every 30 minutes. Taxis that have been waiting for more than the allotted free time will try to make the passenger pay the toll upon leaving the airport. Always establish who will pay before getting in. There is a bus service (called Urbanito) from the airport to the centre (US$3), Pueblo Libre, San Isidro and Miraflores (US$5). It's a slow journey, calling at all hotels. T01-424 3650 or T9957 3238 (mob), urbanito@terra.com.pe.

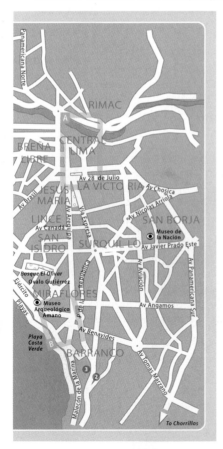

All hire companies have offices at the airport. The larger international chains, **Avis**, **Budget**, **Dollar**, **Hertz**, are usually cheaper and have better-maintained vehicles than local firms. The airport in Lima is the best, most cost-effective place to arrange car hire. 🚗 ▸▸ *p84*.

Getting around

Downtown Lima can be explored on foot in the daytime, but take all the usual precautions. The central hotels are fairly close to many of the tourist sites. At night taxis are a safer option. Miraflores is about 15 km south of the centre. Many of the better hotels and restaurants are located here and in neighbouring San Isidro.

The Lima public transportation system, at first glance very intimidating, is actually quite good. There are three different types of vehicles that will stop whenever flagged down: buses, *combis* (small vans) and *colectivos* (shared taxis). All are very cheap, charging from US$0.35. On public holidays, Sunday and from 2400 to 0500 every night, a small charge is added to the fare. Always try to have the exact fare. Routes on any public transportation vehicle are posted on windscreens with coloured stickers. Destinations written on the side of any

Lima's impressive cathedral dominates the Plaza de Armas.

vehicle should be ignored. Several blocks, with their own names, make up a long street, which is called a jirón (often abbreviated to Jr). You will be greatly helped by the corner signs which bear both names, of the jirón and the name of the block. The new and old names of streets are used interchangeably: remember that Colmena is also Nicolás de Piérola, Wilson is Inca Garcilaso de la Vega, and Carabaya is also Augusto N Wiese.

Best time to visit

Only 12° south of the equator, you would expect a tropical climate, but Lima has two distinct seasons. The winter is from May-November, when a damp *garúa* (sea mist) hangs over the city, making everything look greyer than it is already. It is damp and cold, 8° to 15°C. The sun breaks through around November and temperatures rise as high as 30°C.

Tourist information

i perú has offices at ⓘ *Jorge Chávez International Airport, T01-574 8000, open 24 hrs a day; Casa Basadre, Av Jorge Basadre 610, San Isidro, T01-421 1627, Mon-Fri 0830-1830; Larcomar shopping centre, Módulo 14, Plaza Gourmet, Miraflores, T01-445 9400, Mon-Fri 1200-2000*. **Info Perú** ⓘ *Jr de la Unión (Belén) 1066, of 102, T01-424 7963, infoperu@qnet.com.pe, Mon-Fri 0930-1800, Sat 0930-1400*, is a very helpful office with lots of good advice, English, French spoken. Ask for the helpful, free, *Peru Guide* published in English by **Lima Editora** ⓘ *T01-444 0815*, available at travel agencies or other tourist organizations.

As much an agency as tourist office, but highly recommended nonetheless, is Siduith Ferrer Herrera, CEO of **Fertur Perú** ⓘ *Schell 485, Miraflores, T01-445 1974, http://ferturperu.tripod.com, 0900-1900*. Her agency not only offers up to date, correct tourist information on a national level, but also great prices on national and international flights, discounts for those with ISIC and Youth cards and **South American Explorers** members. Other services include flight reconfirmations, hotel reservations and transfers to and from the airport or bus stations.

Central Lima

The heart of the old city is the Plaza de Armas, which has been declared a World Heritage site by UNESCO. Around the great plaza stands the **Palacio de Gobierno** ⓘ *tours in Spanish and English Mon-Fri, 0845 and 0945, Sat 0900, 1000, 1100, and last 45 mins, free, register a day in advance on T01-311 3908, or at the office of public relations, Edificio Palacio 269, oficina 201 (ask guard for directions).* Also on the plaza is the **Cathedral** ⓘ *T01-427 9647, Mon-Sat 0900-1630, all-inclusive entrance ticket is US$1.50,* built in 1755 on the site of the original, destroyed in the earthquake of 1746. The interior is immediately impressive, with its massive columns and high nave. Also of note are the splendidly carved stalls (mid-17th century), the silver-covered altars surrounded by fine woodwork and mosaic-covered walls. The assumed remains of Francisco Pizarro lie in a small chapel, on the right of the entrance, in a glass coffin, though later research indicates that they reside in the crypt. There is a **Museo de Arte Religioso** in the cathedral, with free guided tours (English available, give tip). Next to the cathedral is the **Archbishop's Palace**, rebuilt in 1924, with a superb wooden balcony.

A few blocks east of the Plaza de Armas, on the corner of Lampa and Ancash, is the baroque **San Francisco Church and monastery** ⓘ *T01-4271381, daily 0930-1730, US$1.50, US$0.50 children, guided tours only,* finished in 1674 and one of the few buildings to withstand

the 1746 earthquake. The nave and aisles are lavishly decorated in the Moorish, or Mudéjar, style. The choir, which dates from 1673, is notable for its beautifully-carved seats in Nicaraguan hardwood and its Mudéjar ceiling. There is a valuable collection of paintings by the Spanish artist, Francisco de Zuburán (1598-1664). The monastery is famous for the Sevillian tilework and panelled ceiling in the cloisters (1620). The Catacombs under the church and part of the monastery are well worth seeing. This is where an estimated 25,000 Limeños were buried before the main cemetery was opened in 1808.

Two blocks southeast from San Francsico is Plaza Bolívar, from where General José de San Martín proclaimed Peru's independence. The plaza is dominated by the equestrian statue of the Liberator. On the plaza is the **Museo del Tribunal de la Santa Inquisición** ① *C Junín 548, near the corner of Av Abancay, Mon-Sun 0900-1700, free, students offer to show you round for a tip; good explanations in English*. The Court of Inquisition was first held here in 1584 and in the basement is an accurate recreation *in situ* of the gruesome tortures. The whole tour is fascinating, if a little morbid. A description in English is available at the desk.

Lima suburbs

A visit to the **Museo de la Nación**, ① *Javier Prado Este 2465, San Borja, T01-476 9878, Tue-Sun 0900-1700, closed major public holidays, US$1.80, 50% discount with ISIC card*, is recommended before you go to see the archaeological sites themselves. There are displays of the tomb of the Señor de Sipán, artefacts from Batán Grande near Chiclayo (Sicán culture) and reconstructions of the friezes found at Huaca La Luna and Huaca El Brujo, near Trujillo, and other sites. There are good explanations in Spanish and English on Peruvian history, with ceramics, textiles and displays of many ruins in Peru. It is arranged so that you can follow the development of Peruvian precolonial history through to the time of the Incas. Also included is the **Museo Peruano de Ciencias de la Salud**, which has a collection of ceramics and mummies, plus an explanation of pre-Columbian lifestyle. Temporary exhibitions are held in the basement, where there is also an Instituto de Cultura bookshop. The museum also has a cafetería. From Avenida Garcilaso de la Vega in downtown Lima take a combi with a window sticker that says 'Javier Prado/Aviación'. Get off at the 21st block of Javier Prado at Avenida Aviación. From Miraflores take a bus down Avenida Arequipa to Avenida Javier Prado (27th block), then take a bus with a window sticker saying 'Todo Javier Prado' or 'Aviación'. A taxi from downtown Lima or from the centre of Miraflores costs US$2.

In the suburb of Pueblo Libre, southwest of the historic centre, are some of the city's finest museums. On Plaza Bolívar (not to be confused with Plaza Bolívar in the centre), is the **Museo Nacional de Antropología, Arqueología e Historia** ① *T01-463 5070, Tue-Sat 0900-1700, Sun 0900-1600, US$3, photo permit US$5, guides are available,* the original museum of archaeology and anthropology. On display are ceramics of the Chimú, Nasca, Mochica and Ichma (Pachacámac) cultures, various Inca curiosities and works of art, and interesting textiles. The museum houses the Raimondi Stela and the Tello obelisk from Chavín (see page 195), and a reconstruction of one of the galleries. It also has a model of Machu Picchu. Next door is the **Museo Nacional de Historia** ① *T01-463 2009,* housed in a mansion once occupied by San Martín (1821-1822) and Bolívar (1823-1826). The exhibits comprise colonial and early republican paintings, manuscripts, portraits, uniforms, etc. To get to both museums from the centre, take any bus on Avenida Brasil with a window sticker saying 'Todo Brasil.' Get off at the 21st block called Avenida Vivanco. Walk about five blocks down Vivanco. The museum will be on your left. From Miraflores, take bus SM 18 Carabayllo-Chorrillos, marked 'Bolívar, Arequipa, Larcomar', get out at block eight of Bolívar, by the Hospital Santa Rosa, and walk down Avenida San Martín for five blocks till you see the 'blue line'; turn left. The 'blue line' marked on the pavement, a bit faded in places, links the Museo Nacional de Antropología, Arqueología e Historia to the Museo

Arqueológico Rafael Larco Herrera (10 minutes' walk). A taxi from downtown Lima is US$2 and from Miraflores US$2. The **Museo Arqueológico Rafael Larco Herrera** ① *Av Bolívar 1515, T01-461 1312, http://museolarco.perucultural.org.pe, 0900-1800; texts in Spanish, English and French, US$6.35 (half price for students), disabled access, guides, no photography*, gives an excellent overview on the development of Peruvian cultures through their pottery. It has the

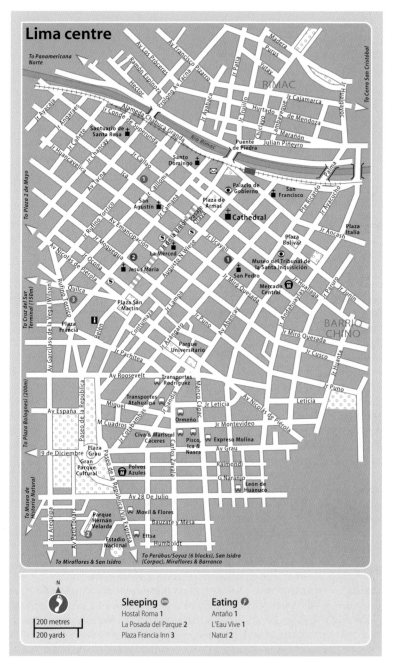

Lima centre

Sleeping 🛏
Hostal Roma 1
La Posada del Parque 2
Plaza Francia Inn 3

Eating 🍽
Antaño 1
L'Eau Vive 1
Natur 2

200 metres
200 yards

Top tips

Finding the right hotel

✅ Regular taxis do not use meters, so make sure you fix the price before getting in and insist on being taken to the hotel of your choice, not the driver's.

✅ If you arrive in Lima by bus, it is likely you'll pull into the main terminal at Jr Carlos Zavala, just south of the historical centre. Take a taxi to your hotel even if it's close, as this area is not safe day or night. Some bus companies have terminals in safer areas.

✅ Miraflores has a good mix of places to stay, as well as bars, restaurants and cinemas. From here you can commute to the centre by bus (30-45 minutes) or by taxi (20-30 minutes).

✅ Barranco is a little further out but has the best nightlife and is overall the best choice.

❌ The central colonial heart of Lima is not as safe at night as the more upmarket areas of San Isidro, Miraflores or Barranco.

world's largest collection of Moche, Sicán and Chimú pieces. There is a Gold and Silver of Ancient Peru exhibition, a magnificent textile collection and a fascinating erotica section. It is surrounded by beautiful gardens.

Miraflores is one of Lima's smartest suburbs, a world away from the grime of the old centre. It is home to fashionable shops, cafés, restaurants, bars, clubs, upmarket hotels and guesthouses. At the end of Avenida Larco and running along the promenade is **Parque Salazar** and the ultra-modern **Centro Comercial Larcomar**, which houses expensive shops, cafés and restaurants, an open-air internet café and clubs and from where there are beautiful views of the ocean and the sunset. There are a few sights worth searching out in Miraflores, one of which is the **Museo Arqueológico Amano** ⓘ *C Retiro 160 near the 11th block of Av Angamos Oeste, T01-441 2909, open by appointment Mon-Fri in the afternoons only, free, photography prohibited,* a very fine private collection of artefacts from the Chancay, Chimú and Nasca periods, owned by the late Mr Yoshitaro Amano, and boasting one of the most complete exhibits of Chancay weaving. Take a bus or *colectivo* to the corner of Avenida Arequipa y Avenida Angamos and another one to the 11th block of Avenida Angamos Oeste. Alternatively a taxi from downtown costs US$2 or from Parque Kennedy US$1. The other is the **Poli Museum** ⓘ *Almte Cochrane 466, T01-422 2437, tours cost US$10 per person irrespective of the size of the group, allow 2 hrs, call in advance to arrange tours,* one of the best private collections of colonial paintings, silver, cloth and furniture in Peru. It also has a fine collection of pre-Columbian ceramics and gold, including material from Sipán. Guided tours are given in Spanish only and delivered rapidly by Sr Poli or his son, whose views are often contrary to long-held opinions about the symbolism of Peruvian cultures.

North or Miraflores, the district of **San Isidro** combines some upscale residential areas, many of Lima's fanciest hotels and restaurants and important commercial zones with a huge golf course smack in the middle. South of Miraflores, **Barranco** is something of an intellectual haven, with artists' workshops and chic galleries, and though it's a quiet, sleepy suburb during the day, it comes alive at night when the city's young flock here to party at weekends. Squeezed together into a few streets are dozens of good bars and restaurants.

Budget busters

Luxury in Lima

LL Miraflores Park, Av Malecón de la Reserva 1035, Miraflores, T01-242 3000, www.mira-park.com, mirapark@ peruorientexpress.com.pe. At the top of the range in Lima, an Orient Express hotel with excellent service and facilities, beautiful ocean views from the luxurious rooms. Check with the hotel for monthly offers.

L Libertador, Los Eucaliptos 550, T01-421 6666, www.libertador.com.pe. A luxurious hotel overlooking the golf course in San Isidro. Full facilities for business travellers, comfortable rooms, bar, gym, sauna, jacuzzi, good restaurant, excellent service.

Sleeping

Foreign nationals do not pay the 19% state tax (IVA) but some hotels also add a service charge which is not included in the prices given here.

Central Lima *p73, map p75*

B Hostal La Posada del Parque, Parque Hernán Velarde 60, near 2nd block of Av Petit Thouars, Santa Beatriz, T01-433 2412, www.incacountry.com. Run by Sra Mónica Moreno and her husband Leo Rovayo who both speak good English, a charmingly refurbished old house in a safe area, excellent bathrooms, cable TV, breakfast US$3 extra, airport transfer 24 hrs for US$14 for up to 3 passengers. Excellent value.

C Hostal Roma, Jr Ica 326, T/F01-427 7572, www.hostalroma.8m.com. With bathroom, **D** without bath, hot water all day, safe to leave luggage, basic but clean, often full, internet extra but good, motorcycle parking (**Roma Tours**, helpful for trips, reservations, flight confirmations, Dante Reyes speaks English).

D Plaza Francia Inn, Jr Rufino Torrico 1117 (blue house, no sign, look for 'Ecología es vida' mural opposite), near 9th block of Av Garcilaso de la Vega (aka Wilson), T01-330 6080, T9945 4260 (mob), franciasquareinn@ yahoo.com.

Dormitory **E**, very clean and cosy, hot water 24 hrs, safety box in each room for each bed, kitchen and laundry facilities, airport pick up for up to 4 people US$12 (send flight details in advance), discounts for ISIC cardholders. SAE members and same owners as **Posada del Parque**.

Lima suburbs *p74, map p78*

AL Antigua Miraflores, Av Grau 350 at C Francia, Miraflores, T01-241 6116, www.peru-hotels-inns.com. A beautiful, small and elegant hotel in a quiet but central location, very friendly service, tastefully furnished and decorated, 35 rooms, gym, cable TV, good restaurant.

A Casa Andina, Av 28 de Julio 1088, Miraflores, T01-241 4050, www.casa-andina.com. Part of the recommended chain of hotels. Very neat, with many useful touches, such as smoke detectors, emergency lighting and local maps given to all guests. Friendly service, comfortable beds, 10 minutes free internet, a/c, fridge, safe, laundry service, buffet breakfast, other meals available.

A Hostal La Castellana, Grimaldo del Solar 222, Miraflores, T01-444 4662, lacastellan@terra.com.pe. Pleasant, with a nice garden, safe, good value, but the restaurant is expensive, laundry, English spoken, special price for South American Explorers (SAE) members.

A San Antonio Abad, Ramón Ribeyro 301, Miraflores, T01-447 6766, www.hotelsanantonioabad.com. Clean, secure, quiet, good service, welcoming, tasty breakfasts, one free airport transfer with reservation.

B El Carmelo, Bolognesi 749, Miraflores, T01-446 0575, carmelo@amauta.rcp. net.pe. With bath and TV, in a great location a couple of blocks from the Parque del Amor, small restaurant downstairs serving *criolla* food and

ceviche, price includes breakfast, good value and comfortable.

B Hostal El Patio, Diez Canseco 341, Miraflores, T01-444 2107, www.hostalelpatio.net. Includes continental breakfast, reductions for long stays. The patio has a fountain, lots of flowers and bird cages; there are terraces for sitting outside. Very nice suites with big bathroom and kitchen, clean, comfortable standard rooms, gay-friendly, English

Miraflores

100 metres
100 yards

and French spoken, convenient, *comedor* with wood fire.

C Hostal Mami Panchita, Av Federico Callese 198, Magdalena del Mar, T01-263 7203, San Miguel, raymi_travels @perusat.net.pe. Dutch-Peruvian owned, English, French, Dutch, Spanish and German spoken, includes breakfast and welcome drink, comfortable rooms with bath, hot water, living room and bar, patio, recently extended, email service, book exchange, have their own **Raymi Travel agency** (good service), 15 mins from airport, 15 mins from Miraflores, 20 mins from historical centre.

C Home Perú, Av Arequipa 4501 (no sign), Miraflores, T01-241 9898, www.homeperu.com. In a 1920s mansion with huge rooms, antiques in the public areas, with breakfast, rooms with and without bath, **E** per person with shared bath, group discounts. You'll be made to feel most welcome here. Use of kitchen, luggage store, English spoken, laundry service, internet, very helpful staff, safe, near Plaza Vea hypermarket. Can help with bus and plane tickets, connected to other *hostales* in the country.

C Pensión Yolanda, Domingo Elias 230, Miraflores, T01-445 7565, pensionyolanda@hotmail.com or erwinpension@yahoo.com. Price includes breakfast. English and French spoken, family house, quiet, safe, laundry, book exchange, internet and luggage store. They have travel information, can reserve flights and hotels.

C-D Imperial Inn, Bolognesi 641, Miraflores, T01-445 2504, imperialinn@viabcp.com. With shower, hot water, most expensive rooms have cable TV, orthopaedic beds, price includes coffee and a roll, close to Parque del Amor, good value, very friendly.

E per person **Albergue Turístico Juvenil Internacional**, Av Casimiro Ulloa 328, San Antonio between San Isidro and

Miraflores, T01-446 5488, www.limahostell.com.pe. Youth hostel, dormitory accommodation, **C** in a double private room, US$2.50 discount for IHA card holders. Basic cafeteria for breakfasts, travel information, lounge with cable TV, cooking (minimal) and laundry facilities, swimming pool often empty, extra charge for kitchen facilities, clean and safe, situated in a nice villa.

E per person **Flying Dog Backpackers**, Diez Canseco 117, Miraflores, T01-445 6745, www.flyingdog.esmartweb.com. Price includes breakfast in *El Parquetito* café, dormitories or private rooms, shared bath (**C** in en suite room). This is a popular place so it's best to reserve through the web. Very central, comfortable, hot water, secure, friendly, free internet and local calls, lounge with DVD and videos, book exchange, kitchen facilities. Full transport information and tickets can be arranged.

E per person **Mochileros Hostal**, Av Pedro de Osma 135, 1 block from main plaza, Barranco, T01-247 8643, fenallo@hotmail.com. Beautiful house, completely redecorated late 2004, friendly English-speaking owner, huge shared rooms with lockers, gay friendly, use of kitchen, good pub on the premises, a stone's throw from Barranco nightlife.

E-F per person **The Point**, Malecón Junín 300, Barranco, T01-247 7997. Rooms in this 80-year old house range from doubles to large dormitories, all with shared bath. Quickly becoming very popular with budget travellers (book in advance at weekends), breakfast included, internet, cable TV, laundry, kitchen facilties, welcomes gay and lesbian travellers, party atmosphere most of the time, *The Pointless Pub* open 2000 till whenever, weekly barbecues, therapeutic massage next door, can arrange bungee jumping, flight tickets and volunteering.

🍴 Eating

In restaurants, both foreigners and Peruvians have to pay 19% state tax (IVA) and the service charge.

Central Lima *p73, map p75*

On Sat and Sun, 1100-1700, traditional dishes from all over Peru are served in Plaza Italia. East of the historical centre of Lima, next to the *Mercado Central*, is Lima's Chinatown, or *barrio chino*, with lots of good Chinese restaurants.

🍴 **Antaño**, Ucayali 332, opposite the Torre Tagle Palace. Good, typical Peruvian food, nice patio.

🍴 **L'Eau Vive**, Ucayali 370, also opposite the Torre Tagle Palace, T01-427 5612. Run by nuns, open Mon-Sat, 1230-1500 and 1930-2130, fixed-price lunch menu in interior dining room, or à la carte in either of the dining rooms that open onto the patio, profits go to the poor, *Ave Maria* is sung nightly at 2100. Heavenly.

🍴 **Wa Lok**, Jr Paruro 864, Barrio Chino, T01-427 2656. Owner Liliana Com speaks fluent English and is very friendly. Highly recommended *chifa*.

🍴 **Natur**, Moquegua 132, 1 block from Jr de la Unión, T01-427 8281. Vegetarian, the owner, Humberto Valdivia, is one of the *South American Explorers'* advisers, good for food and casual conversation.

Lima suburbs *p74 map p78*

C San Ramón, more commonly known as Pizza St (across from Parque Kennedy), is a pedestrian walkway lined with outdoor restaurants, bars and clubs, all open until the wee small hours of the morning. It's a very popular place with good-natured touts trying to entice diners and drinkers with free offers.

🍴 **Antica Pizzería**, Av Dos de Mayo 728, San Isidro, T01-222 8437. Very popular, great ambience, great food, Italian owner.

🍴 **Astrid y Gaston**, Cantuarias 175, Miraflores, T01-444 1496. Excellent local and international cuisine, one of the best in Lima, also has a bar.

🍴 **Café Voltaire**, Av Dos de Mayo 220, Miraflores. International cuisine with emphasis on French dishes, beautifully-cooked food, pleasant ambience, good service, closed Sun.

🍴 **Cuarto y Mitad**, Av Espinar 798, Miraflores, T01-446 2988. This popular grill is close to the Ovalo Gutiérrez, it's one of the places to go if you're looking for meat (beef or ostrich); they also serve seafood.

🍴 **El Kapallaq**, Av Petit Thouars 4844, Miraflores, T01-444 4149. Prize-winning

Pizza Street in Miraflores is lined with numerous al fresco dining and drinking options.

Budget busters

For a romantic meal, especially for those Brits with a nostalgia for seaside holidays, you can't beat **La Rosa Náutica** (T01-445 0149, www.larosanautica.com). The restaurant is built on a pier, No 4, that juts out from the Lima Beach Circuit below the cliffs of Miraflores. It's a dining institution, delightfully opulent with its pillars, glass and lamps, and charges high prices (ⓉⓉⓉ) for the privilege of eating there. The menu concentrates on fish and seafood, but has Peruvian daily specials, meat dishes, pastas, salads and desserts. There are various dining rooms and a bar. If you wish, you can just sample the atmosphere by buying an expensive beer at sunset, but why not take in the full experience and have a meal to remember?

A contender for the best seafood in Lima, and similarly expensive, is **La Costa Verde**, on Barranquito beach in Barranco (T01-441 3086). It's open daily 1200-2400.

Peruvian restaurant specializing in seafood and fish, excellent *ceviches*. Open Mon-Fri 1200-1700 only.

Ⓣ **El Señorío de Sulco**, Malecón Cisneros 1470, T01-441 0183, Miraflores, http://senoriodesulco. com. Overlooking a clifftop park, with ocean views from upstairs. This is a 'five-fork' restaurant which some believe is the best in Lima, all Peruvian food, à la carte and buffet, piscos, wines, piano music at night.

Ⓣ **Las Brujas de Cachiche**, Av Bolognesi 460, Miraflores, T01-447 1883. An old mansion converted into bars and dining rooms, almost Alpine in appearance. It specializes in traditional food (menu in Spanish and English), best *lomo saltado* in town, live *criollo* music.

Ⓣ **Dalmacia**, San Fernando 401, Miraflores. Spanish-owned, casual gourmet restaurant serving tapas and main meals, excellent, seating on the terrace.

Ⓣ **Segundo Muelle**, Av Conquistadores 490, San Isidro, T01-421 1206, and Av Canaval y Moreyra (aka Corpac) 605. Worth a visit for its excellent *ceviche* and other very good seafood dishes, popular with the younger crowd.

Ⓣ **Naturaleza**, Av Larco 870, Miraflores. Good value vegetarian restaurant, with good fixed menu, side dishes and fabulous desserts.

Cafés

Café Café, Martín Olaya 250, near the Parque Kennedy roundabout, Miraflores. Very popular, good atmosphere, over 100 different blends of coffee, good salads and sandwiches, very popular with well-to-do Limeños.

C'est si bon, Av Cdte Espinar 663, Miraflores. Excellent cakes by the slice or whole, best in Lima.

La Tiendecita Blanca, Av Larco 111 on Parque Kennedy, Miraflores. One of Miraflores' oldest, expensive, good people-watching, very good cakes, European-style food and delicatessen under the Café Suisse brand.

San Antonio, Av Angamos Oeste 1494, Miraflores, also Vasco Núñez de Balboa 770, Rocca de Vergallo 201, Magdalena del Mar and Av Primavera 373, San Borja. A fashionable *pastelería* chain, serving good coffee, cakes and snacks, not too expensive.

ⓘ Bars and clubs

Barranco is the capital of Lima nightlife. Pasaje Sánchez Carrión, right off the main plaza, is lined with watering holes and clubs and Av Grau, just across the street from the plaza, is also lined with bars. Many of the bars in this area turn into nightclubs as the evening goes on. Often there is a cover charge ranging from US$3-10 per person.

Barcelona, Larcomar Shopping Centre, Miraflores, T01- 445 4823. One of the best pubs in the city.

Bosa Nova, Bolognesi 660, Barranco. Chilled student- style bar with good music.

Cocodrilo Verde, Francisco de Paula 226 near corner with Bellavista, Miraflores. Relaxed, stylish bar, slightly pricey but worth it for the Wed night jazz, and live music at weekends, occasionally charges cover for music at weekends.

Juanitos, Av Grau, opposite the park. Barranco's oldest bar, a perfect place to start the evening.

La Noche, Bolognesi 307, at Pasaje Sánchez Carrión, Barranco. A Lima institution with great live music, Mon is jazz night, kicks off around 2200 (also in Central Lima).

Media Naranja, C Schell 130, at the bottom of Parque Kennedy, Miraflores. Brazilian bar with typical drinks and food.

Murphys, C Schell 627, T01-242 1212, Miraflores, www.murphysperu.com. Great Irish pub, now doing food such as fish and chips, lookout for special events and happy hours.

Punto G, Av Conquistadores 512, San Isidro. Very popular, really small.

Santa Sede, Av 28 de Julio 441, San Isidro. Very popular, great music, fun crowd, gay friendly.

Sargento Pimienta, Bolognesi 755, Barranco. Live music, always a favourite with Limeños.

⊕ Entertainment

Cinemas

Most films are in English with subtitles and cost around US$4-5. Among the best of the cinemas are **Cine Roma**, C Teniente Fernández 242, 9th block of Av Arequipa, Santa Beatriz, T01-433 8618, and **Multicine Starvision El Pacífico**, on the Ovalo by Parque Kennedy, in Miraflores, T01-445 6990.

Peñas

Del Carajo, San Ambrosio 328, Barranco, T01-247 7977. All types of traditional music, Thu-Sat from 2200.

La Candelaria, Av Bolognesi 292, Barranco, T01-247 1314. This is a good Barranco peña, Fri-Sat 2130 onwards.

Las Brisas de Titicaca, Pasaje Wakuski 168, at the 1st block of Av Brasil near Plaza Bolognesi, Central Lima, T01-332 1881, www.brisasdeltiticaca.com. A Lima institution for folkloric music and dance, workshops, restaurant and bar.

Peña Poggi, Av Luna Pizarro 578, Barranco, T01-247 5790. Over 30 years old, a traditional favourite.

⊛ Festivals and events

On **18 Jan** is the anniversary of the **founding of Lima**. It is preceded, on the evening of the 17th, by the **Gran Serenata** in the Plaza de Armas with some of Peru's best musicians. **Semana Santa**, or Holy Week, is a colourful spectacle with processions. The **end of May** sees a **beer festival** which attracts many famous singers from Peru and some from abroad. **28-29 Jul** is **Independence**, with music and fireworks in the Plaza de Armas on the evening before. **Oct** is the month of **Our Lord of the Miracles** with impressive processions. On **3 Nov** is San Martín de Porres.

⊙ Shopping

Handicrafts

Since so many artesans have come from the Sierra to Lima, it is possible to find any kind of handicraft in the capital. Among the many items which can be bought here are silver and gold handicrafts, Indian hand-spun and hand-woven textiles and manufactured textiles in Indian designs. You can find llama and alpaca wool products such as ponchos, rugs, hats, blankets, slippers, coats, sweaters, etc. Although Lima is more expensive, it is often impossible to find

the same quality of goods elsewhere.
Kuntur Wasi, Ocharan 182, Miraflores,
T01-444 0557. English-speaking owner,
very knowledgeable about Peruvian
textiles, frequently has exhibitions of fine
folk art and crafts.
La Casa de la Mujer Artesana, Juan
Pablo Ferandini 1550, Av Brasil cuadra 15,
Pueblo Libre, T01-423 8840, F01-423
4031. A co-operative run by the
Movimiento Manuela Ramos, excellent
quality work mostly from the
shantytowns (*pueblos jóvenes*), open
Mon-Fri 0900-1300, 1400-1700.

Markets
Av Petit Thouars cuadras 51 a 54
(parallel to Av Arequipa, a few blocks
from Parque Kennedy). Here you'll find an
unnamed crafts market area with a large
courtyard and lots of small flags. This is
the largest crafts arcade in Miraflores.
From here to Av Ricardo Palma the street
is lined with crafts markets.

Tour operators
Lima is bursting at the seams with
tour and travel agencies. Some are
good and reliable, many are not. If
possible, use agencies in or close to
the area you wish to visit and always
shop around. Bargaining ability is a
plus. See also Fertur Peru, Ins and outs
p72. We have received complaints
about agencies, or their representatives
at bus offices or the airport, arranging
tours and collecting money for
companies that either do not exist or
which fall far short of what is paid for.
Do not conduct business anywhere
other than in the agency's office and
insist on a written contract.
Class Adventure Travel, Av Pardo 231,
Miraflores, T01-444 1652,
www.cat-travel.com. Dutch-owned
and run, one of the best.
Coltur, Av José Pardo 138, Miraflores,
T01-241 5551, www.coltur.com.pe. With
offices in Cusco and Arequipa, very
helpful, well-organized.
Cóndor Travel, Mayor Armando
Blondet 249, San Isidro, T01-442 7305,
www. condortravel.com.pe. Also has
a branch in Cusco and another in
Quito, Ecuador, for tours throughout
the Andes.
Dasatariq, Jr Francisco Bolognesi 510,
Miraflores, T01-447 7772,
www.dasatariq.com. Also in Cusco. A
well-organized company with a good
reputation and helpful staff.
Domiruth Travel Service, Jr Río de
Janeiro 216-218, Miraflores,
T01-610 6022, www.domiruth.com.pe.
Over 20 years of experience, offers a
huge range of tours ranging from
historical and archeological to
adventure and ecological. Also offices
in major towns throughout the country,
including Arequipa and Cusco.
Explorandes, C San Fernando 320,
T01-445 8683, www.explorandes.com.pe.

Award-winning company with a wide range of adventure and cultural tours throughout the country. Also offices in Cusco, see p137, and Huaraz.

InkaNatura Travel, Manuel Banón 461, San Isidro, Lima 27, T01-440 2022, www.inka natura.com. Also in Cusco, offers good tours with knowledgeable guides, special emphasis on sustainable tourism and conservation.

Lima Tours, Jr Belén 1040, Lima centre, T01-424 5110, and Av Pardo y Alliaga 698, San Isidro, T01-222 2525, www.limatours.com.pe. Recommended for tours in the capital and around the country.

Peru Expeditions, Av Arequipa 5241-504, Lima 18, T01-447 2057, www. Peru-expeditions.com. Specializing in expeditions in 4WD vehicles and Andes crossings.

⊖ Transport

Air

For all information on international flight arrivals and departures, see p19. For all information on domestic flights, see Getting around p22. Domestic flight schedules are given under the relevant destinations. To enquire about arrivals or departures, T01-595 0666, www.lap.com.pe. For all information on how to get from the airport to the city, see Ins and outs p22.

Airline offices

Domestic Aero Cóndor, C Juan de Arona 781, San Isidro, T01-614 6000. Lan, Av José Pardo 513, Miraflores, T01-213

8200, open 0900-1900, Sat 0900-1300. **LC Busre**, Los Tulipanes 218, Lince, T01-619 1313. **Star Up**, Av José Pardo 269, Miraflores, T01-447 7573. **Tans**, Jr Belén 1015, Lima centre, and Av Arequipa 5200, Miraflores, T01-213 6000.

International Air France, Av José Pardo 601, Miraflores, T01-444 9285. **American Airlines**, Av Canaval y Moreyra 390, San Isidro, and in Hotel Las Américas, Av Benavides y Av Larco, Miraflores, T01-211 7000. **British Airways**, C Andalucía 174, Miraflores, T01-411 7800. Continental, C Victor Belaúnde 147, oficina 101, San Isidro, and in the Hotel Marriott, 13th block of Av Larco, Miraflores, T01-221 4340. **Delta**, C Victor Belaúnde 147, San Isidro, T01-211 9211. **Iberia**, Av Camino Real 390, p 9, San Isidro, T01-411 7800. **KLM**, Av José Pardo 805, p6, Miraflores, T01-421 9500. **Lloyd Aéreo Boliviano**, Av José Pardo 231, Miraflores, T01-241 5510.

Bus

Local

Lima centre to Miraflores Av Arequipa runs 52 blocks between the downtown Lima area and Parque Kennedy in Miraflores. There is no shortage of public transport on this avenue; they have 'Todo Arequipa' on the windscreen. When heading towards downtown from Miraflores the window sticker should say 'Wilson/Tacna'. To get to Parque Kennedy from downtown look on the windshield for 'Larco/Schell/Miraflores', 'Chorrillos/Huaylas' or 'Barranco/Ayacucho'.

Long distance

Cruz del Sur buses leave from their terminal at Jr Quilca 531, Lima centre, T01-424 6158, www.cruzdelsur.com.pe, to many destinations in Peru. Their luxury buses, which are more expensive and direct, leave from another terminal at Av Javier Prado Este 1109, San Isidro, T01-225 6163. The website accepts Visa bookings without surcharge. **Ormeño**

buses depart from and arrive at Av Carlos Zavala 177, Lima centre, T01-427 5679; also Av Javier Prado Este 1059, Santa Catalina, T01-472 1710, www.grupo-ormeno.com. They also offer a variety of services. Javier Prado is the best place to buy tickets. They also have buses to **Quito** (38 hrs). A maximum of 20 kg is allowed per person. Depending on the destination, extra weight penalties range from US$1-3 per kg. For prices and approximate duration of trip, refer to the destination.

Car

It's recommended to test-drive car before signing contract as quality varies. **Alkila**, Av La Paz 745, Miraflores, T01-242 3939, www.alkilarenatcar.com. **Avis Rent A Car**, Av Javier Prado Este 5233, T01-434 1111, www.avis.com. **Budget Car Rental**, Canaval y Moreyra 569, San Isidro, T01-442 8703, www.budget.com. **Hertz**, Av Cantuarias 160, MIraflores, T01-445 5716, www.hertz.com.pe. **National**, Av España 543, Lima, T01-433 3750, www.nationalcar.com. **Paz Rent A Car**, Av Diez Canseco 319, oficina 15, Miraflores, T01-446 4395, T9993 9853 (mob).

Taxi colectivos

Regular private cars acting as taxis (*colectivos*) charge US$0.50. They are a faster, more comfortable option than municipal public transportation, but they are no safer. They run between Av Arequipa and Av Tacna which runs from Miraflores to the centre of Lima. Look for the coloured sticker posted on the windscreen. These cars will stop at any time to pick people up. When full (usually 5 or 6 people) they will only stop to let someone off, then the process begins again to fill the empty space.

Taxis

Conventional taxis operate without meters so agree the fare before you get in. Tips are not expected. As driving a taxi in Lima (or anywhere in Peru) simply requires a windshield sticker saying 'Taxi', they come in all colours and sizes. By law, though, all must have the vehicle's registration number painted on the side. If it does not, don't take it. Yellow taxis are usually the safest since they have a number, the driver's name and radio contact. A large number of taxis are also white. To/from the centre to Miraflores, Pueblo Libre and San Isidro expect to pay US$2-4, depending on your bargaining skills and level of Spanish. Official taxi companies are the safest option but cost much more than just picking one up in the street. These include: **Taxi América**, T01-265 1960; **Moli Taxi**, T01-479 0030; **Taxi Real**, T01-470 6263; **Taxi Seguro**, T01-241 9292; **Taxi Tata**, T01-274 5151; **TCAM**, run by Carlos Astacio, T01-983 9305, safe, reliable.

❶ Directory

Banks

All the main Peruvian banks have branches in the centre and in Miraflores, with Visa/Plus ATMs. Most will change Amex TCs. They are mostly open Mon-Fri 0900-1800, Sat 0930-1230. They include: **BCP, Banco de Comercio, BBVA Continental, Banco Financiero, Banco Santander Central Hispano (BSCH). Banco Wiese Sudameris** branches have ATMs for Mastercard, Maestro and Cirrus. **Interbank** branches have ATMs for Visa/Plus, Mastercard, Maestro, Cirrus and AmEx.

There are many *casas de cambio* on and around Jr Ocoña off the Plaza San Martín. There are also several *cambios* and

cambistas on Av José Pardo, Miraflores. A good one is **LAC Dolar**, Jr Camaná 779, 1 block from Plaza San Martín, p 2, T01-428 8127, also at Av La Paz 211, Miraflores, T01-242 4069. Mon-Sat 0930-1800, good rates, very helpful, safe, fast, reliable, 2% commission on cash and TCs (Amex, Citicorp, Thomas Cook, Visa). Changing money on the street should only be done with official street changers wearing an identity card with a photo. Around Parque Kennedy and down Av Larco in Miraflores are dozens of official *cambistas* with ID photo cards attached to their usually blue, sometimes green vest.

Embassies and consulates
Australia, Av Víctor Belaúnde 147, Vía Principal 155, ed 3, of 1301, T01-222 8281. **Bolivian Consulate**, Los Castaños 235, San Isidro, T01-422 8231, postmast@ emboli.org. pe. (0900-1330), 24 hrs for visas (except those requiring clearance from La Paz). **Canada**, Libertad 130, Miraflores, T01-444 4015, lima@dfait -maeci.gc.ca. **Ecuadorean Consulate**, Las Palmeras 356, San Isidro (6th block of Av Javier Prado Oeste), T01-461 8217, embjecua@amauta.rcp.net.pe. **New Zealand Consulate**, Av Camino Real 390, Torre Central, p 17 (Casilla 3553), San Isidro, T01-221 2833, reya@nzlatam.com. Open Mon-Fri 0830-1300, 1400-1700. **UK**, Torre Parque Mar, Av Larco 1301, p 22, T01-617 3000, www.britemb.org.pe. Open 1300-2130 (Dec-Apr to 1830 Mon and Fri, and Apr-Nov to 1830 Fri), good for security information and newspapers. **USA**, Av Encalada block 17, Surco, T01-434 3000, for emergencies after hours T434 3032, http://peru.usembassy.com. The consulate is in the same building.

Internet
Lima is full of internet cafés, so you'll have no problem finding one. An hour will cost you approximately S/3-5 (US$0.85-1.50).

Medical services
For hospitals, doctors and dentists, contact your embassy or consulate for recommendations. **Backpackers Medical Care**, Dr Jorge Bazan, T01-9735 2668, backpackersmc@yahoo.com. About US$13 per consultation, speaks English, frequently recommended. **Clínica Anglo Americano**, Av Salazar 3rd block, San Isidro, a few blocks from Ovalo Gutiérrez, T01-221 3656. Stocks Yellow Fever for US$18 and Tetanus for US$3.

Post
The central post office is on Jr Camaná 195 in the centre of Lima near the Plaza de Armas. Open Mon-Fri 0730-1900 and Sat 0730-1600. In Miraflores the main post office is on Av Petit Thouars 5201 in Miraflores (same hrs).

Useful addresses
Immigration, Av España 700 y Jr Huaraz, Breña , open 0900-1330. Visa extensions on 3rd floor given the same day, usually within 30 mins (expensive). Provides new entry stamps if passport is lost or stolen. **Tourist Police**, administrative office at Jr Moore 268, Magdalena at the 38th block of Av Brasil, T01-460 1060, open daily 24 hrs; for public enquiries etc, Jr Pachitea at the corner of Belén (Jr de la Unión), Lima, T01-424 2053. They are friendly and very helpful, English spoken.

Nasca and the southern desert

The Pan-American Highway runs all the way south from Lima to the Chilean border and the desert coast has some distinctive attractions, the most famous, and perhaps the strangest, are the enigmatic Nasca Lines, whose origin and function continues to puzzle scientists. More designs on the desert, plus tomb finds at neighbouring Palpa are casting new light on the mystery. Paracas peninsula is one of the world's great marine bird reserves and was formerly home to one of Peru's most important ancient civilizations. As you bob in a boat to the Ballestas Islands to watch the seabirds, look for the giant Candelbra, drawn on the cliffs by unknown hands.

⊘ **Getting there** Buses from Lima to Pisco, Nasca and Ica.
⊜ **Getting around** Buses between main towns; boat tours to the Ballestas Islands; flights over the Nasca Lines.
⊖ **Time required** 3 days.
⊚ **Weather** The coast is foggy May-Nov, otherwise hot, sunny and dry. Nasca sunny all year.
⊖ **Sleeping** Nasca has a reasonable selection, but elsewhere the choice is limited.
⊘ **Eating** Better known for the drinking than the eating: try the local pisco and wines.
▲ **Activities and tours** Birdwatching at the Islas Ballestas, sandboarding at Huacachina, flights over the Nasca Lines.
★ **Don't miss...** the Nasca Lines ➤ *p91.*

Pisco, Paracas Peninsula and Ballestas Islands

The workmanlike fishing port of Pisco, unofficially named after the famous local brandy, is the jumping off point for visiting the Paracas Peninsula. The whole peninsula, a large area of coast to the south and the Ballestas Islands are all part of **Paracas National Reserve** ⓘ *US$1.50 per person*, which covers a total of 335,000 ha on land and sea. It is one of the most important marine reserves in the world, with the highest concentration of sea birds. The wildlife on view also includes a wide variety of sea mammals and rare and exotic birds. Condors can even be seen in February and March from the rough road between Paracas and Laguna Grande. These

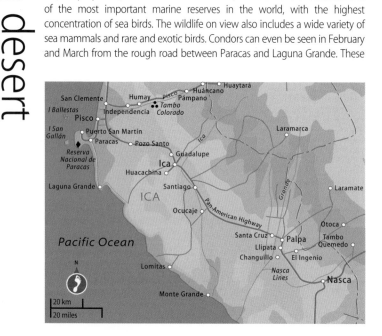

> ## The cost of nodding off
>
> ### Travellers' tales
>
> There are times when you have no choice but to ignore your own guide book's advice. I had to get from Nasca to Lima and the only option was a night bus. "If at all possible, avoid night buses or arriving in a big city in the dark", it states in the *South American Handbook*. The bus left before midnight and arrived before dawn, but what the heck, the journey had to be done and there was no flight. I settled into my reserved seat and prepared myself mentally for a few uncomfortable, sleepless hours. A man sat next to me, said good evening, and settled down too. Once we were on our way, my neighbour offered me a sweet. "Finally," the `How to keep safe' paragraph urges, "never accept food, drink, sweets or cigarettes from unknown fellow-travellers... They may be drugged and you would wake up hours later without your belongings." I can't recall how many times I have read that phrase, but I don't recall it flashing through my mind. I must have been on autopilot when I declined. Unusually for me, I did fall asleep and when I awoke as the bus pulled into Lima, my neighbour had gone – so had my wallet. Waiting for the dawn in the grubby bus terminal, I clung to my belongings as tightly as I could and turned down every destitute hawker's offer of food or drink, factory-sealed or not. *Ben Box.*

massive vultures feed on the ready supply of sea lion carcasses. Rather more delicate are the flamingos which feed in Paracas bay, a short walk from the museum (see below). From January to March the flamingos head for the sierra.

The **Julio Tello site museum** ⓘ *0900-1700, US$2*, is at the entrance to the reserve with a shop which sells guide books, film and drinks, and a visitors' centre, information in Spanish only. The exhibits are from the burial sites discovered by the Peruvian archaeologist, Julio C Tello, under the Paracas desert in 1925. The best examples of textiles and funerary bundles can be found in the Museo de la Nación in Lima (see page 74). About 14 km from the entrance to the Reserve is the pre-Columbian **Candelabro** (or Candelabra) traced in the hillside. At least 50 m long, it is best seen from the sea (see below). There are differing theories as to its exact purpose. Some believe it to be linked to the Nasca Lines (see page 91), 200 km to the south, others that it is related to the Southern Cross constellation and was used to help guide ancient sailors. Still others contend that it represents the cactus used by the ancient high priests for its hallucinogenic powers.

The **Ballestas islands**, dubbed the poor man's Galápagos by many, are nonetheless spectacular in their own right and well worth visiting. They are eroded into numerous arches and caves, hence their name – *ballesta* means bow, as in archery. These arches provide shelter for thousands of seabirds, some of which are very rare, and countless sea lions. Boat trips to the islands leave from the jetty at El Chaco, the beach and fishing port by Paracas village, usually at 0730, returning at 1100 to avoid rougher seas in the afternoon. Tours may be cancelled if the sea is too rough. Few tours include Isla San Gallán, where there are thousands of sea lions. All boats are speedboats with life jackets, but some are very crowded. Wear warm clothing, but also take protection against the sun and wear sunglasses. You will see, close up, sea lions, guano birds, pelicans, penguins and, if you're lucky, dolphins swimming in the bay. The boats pass Puerto San Martín and the Candelabra en route to the islands. See Activities and tours, page 95.

The city of Ica is Peru's main wine centre. Most travellers spend little time in Ica itself, preferring to stay at **Huacachina**, an attractive desert oasis and summer resort 5 km from the city. Set round a palm-fringed lake and amid impressive sand dunes, its green sulphur waters are said to possess curative properties and attract thousands of visitors. Paddleboats can be rented for US$3 for 30 minutes of boating around the lake. **Sandboarding** on the dunes has become a major pastime here, attracting fans from Europe and elsewhere. Board hire is US$1.50 per hour. **Dune buggies** also do white-knuckle, rollercoaster tours for US$12, or you can hire a buggy and scare yourself for US$6 per person for 3-4 hours.

Nasca and around » pp93-97

Set in a green valley surrounded by mountains, Nasca would be just like any other anonymous desert oasis were it not for the 'discovery' of a series of strange lines etched on the plains to the north. Tourists in their thousands now flock to the town to fly over the famous Nasca Lines, whose precise purpose still remains a mystery. Overlooking the town is Cerro Blanco (2,078 m), the highest sand dune in the world, which is popular for sandboarding and paragliding.

Ins and outs

Getting there and around   There is no central bus station in Nasca, but offices are at the western end of town, close to the Panamericana Sur. Do not pay attention to people selling tours or offering hotels on the street, especially near bus stations. Head straight to a hotel and find an official agency to handle your flights and tours. For more information, see Activities and tours, page 95. Most of the hotels are spread out along Jr Lima and around the Plaza de Armas and are within easy walking distance of the bus stations.

A monkey is only one of the many animal figures etched in the Nasca desert.

Sights

The **Museo Antonini** ⓘ *Av de la Cultura 600, at the eastern end of Jr Lima, ring the bell to get in, T056-523444, cahuachi@terra.com.pe, 0900-1900, US$3, including a local guide, US$1.50 extra to use a camera,* is a 10-minute walk from the plaza, or a short taxi ride, but well worth it. It houses the discoveries of Professor Orefici and his team from the huge pre-Inca city at Cahuachi (see next page), which, Orefici believes, holds the key to the Nasca Lines. Many tombs survived the *huaqueros* and there are displays of ceramics, textiles, amazing *antaras* (panpipes) and photos of the excavations and the Lines.

The **Maria Reiche Planetarium** ⓘ *Hotel Nasca Lines, T056-522293, shows are at around 1900 and 2100 nightly, US$6 (half price for students),* was opened in May 2000 in honour of Maria Reiche (see box on page 92). It is run by Edgardo Azabache, who speaks English, Italian and French, and Enrique Levano, who speaks English and Italian. Both give stimulating lectures every night about the Nasca Lines, based on Reiche's theories, which cover archaeology and astronomy. The show lasts about 45 minutes (commentary in English), after which visitors are able to look at the moon, planets and stars through sophisticated telescopes.

Nasca Lines

Cut into the stony desert are large numbers of lines, mostly parallels and geometrical figures, but also designs such as a killer whale, a monkey, birds (one with a wing span of over 100 m), a spider and a tree. The lines, which can best be appreciated from the air, were etched on the Pampa sands by the Nasca people. It's estimated that they were begun around 400 BC and continued to be made for perhaps another thousand years. The famous lines are above the Ingenio valley on the Pampa de San José, about 22 km north of Nasca, and across the Ingenio river, on the plain around Palpa. The Pan-American Highway passes close to, even through, the Lines. Note that the wind gets up every afternoon, peaking at around 1500.

In 1976 Maria Reiche (see box, page 92) had a 12-m platform called the Mirador put up at her own expense, from which three of the designs can be seen – the Hands, the Lizard and the Tree. This is included on some tours, enquire with your agency to be sure. If you get a taxi to the Mirador, make sure it will wait for you and take you back. Taxis charge US$4-6 per hour.

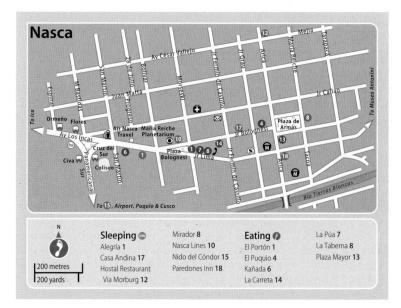

Nasca

Sleeping ⊜
Alegría 1
Casa Andina 17
Hostal Restaurant
Via Morburg 12

Mirador 8
Nasca Lines 10
Nido del Cóndor 15
Paredones Inn 18

Eating ⑦
El Portón 1
El Puquio 4
Kañada 6
La Carreta 14

La Púa 7
La Taberna 8
Plaza Mayor 13

200 metres
200 yards

(vertical text, right margin) Lima & the South Coast Nasca & the southern desert

Background

→ **Drawing conclusions from the lines**

Since the Nasca Lines were first spotted from the air 70 years ago, their meaning, function and origin have tormented scientists around the world. The greatest contribution to our awareness of the lines is that of Maria Reiche, who lived and worked on the *pampa* (plain) for over 50 years. Her meticulous measurement and study of the lines led her to the conclusion that they represented a huge astronomical calendar that not only recorded celestial events but also had a practical day-to-day function such as indicating the times for harvest, fishing and festivals. Maria Reiche died in June 1998.

There are many competing theories as to the function of the Nasca lines. One of the most far-fetched was that of Erich Von Daniken, who believed that the lines were an extraterrestrial landing strip. This idea, however, only succeeded in drawing to the site thousands of sci-fi freaks who tore across the lines on motorbikes, four-wheel drives, horses and whatever else they could get their hands on, leaving an indelible mark.

The most recent theory regarding the true purpose of the Nasca lines is results of six years' work by Peruvian archaeologist Johny Isla and Markus Reindel of the Swiss-Liechtenstein Foundation. It ties together some of the earlier ideas and discredits both the astronomical calendar and extraterrestrial theories. They have deduced that the lines on the Nasca plains are offerings dedicated to the worship of water and fertility. These two elements were vital to the coastal people in this arid environment and they expressed their adoration not only in the desert, but also on their ceramics and on the engraved stones of the Paracas culture. This new research proposes the theory that the Nasca culture succumbed not to drought, but to heavy rainfall, probably during an El Niño event.

Around Nasca

The Nasca area is dotted with over 100 cemeteries and the dry, humidity-free climate has preserved perfectly invaluable tapestries, cloth and mummies. Some 30 km south of Nasca is **Chauchilla**, a cemetery site where grave robbing *huaqueros* ransacked the tombs and left remains all over the place. Bones, skulls, mummies and pottery shards litter the desert. A tour is worthwhile and takes about two hours. It should cost about US$10 per person, plus the cost of entrance to the cemetery, with a minimum of two people.

There are other cemeteries in the vicinity, all of which can be visited on a tour from Nasca (see page 96). A good cemetery, with mummies still to be seen, is in the valley of **Jumana**, one hour west of Nasca in the river bed. Cemetery tours usually include a visit to a gold shop. Gold mining is one of the main local industries and a tour includes a visit to a small family processing shop where the techniques used are still very old-fashioned.

Cahuachi, to the west of the Nasca Lines, comprises several pyramids and a site called **El Estaquería**. The latter is thought to have been a series of astronomical sighting posts, but more recent research suggests the wooden pillars were used to dry dead bodies and therefore it may have been a place of mummification. Tours of the ruins of Cahuachi costs US$10 per person for a minimum two people. The town of **Palpa**, 43 km northwest of Nasca,

The arid desert conditions have preserved many mummified remains around Nasca.

is close to several archaeological sites, of different periods. On the desert near Palpa there are drawings similar to those found at Nasca: a sun dial (*Reloj Solar*), a whale, a pelican, the so-called *Familia Real*, a man, woman and child (30 m tall) and another 1,000 or so lines and figures. There are no travel agencies in town; ask for information and guides in Nasca.

● Sleeping

Pisco *p88*

The town is full at weekends with visitors from Lima. Mosquitoes are a problem at night in the summer.

B Hostal Villa Manuelita, San Fransisco 227, T056-535218, hostalvillamanuelita@ hotmail. com. Very charming, elegantly decorated colonial mansion converted into hotel, all rooms with private bath, cable TV, fan, cafeteria, restaurant. Helpful staff, tranquil patios and warm atmosphere.

D Posada Hispana Hotel, Bolognesi 236, T056-536363, www.posadahispana.com. Rooms each with loft and bathroom, also rooms with shared bath (**G** per person), hot water, TV, can accommodate groups, comfortable, clean, breakfast extra, information service, email, laundry facilities, luggage store, English, French, Italian and Catalan spoken.

D Hostal San Isidro, San Clemente 103, T/F056-536471, www.hostalsanisidro.com. With bath, **E** without, hot water, safe, clean and welcoming, nice pool and cafeteria, free laundry facilities, use of kitchen, but no fridge, games room, English spoken, parking. Arranges dune buggy tours.

E Hostal Los Inkas Inn, Prol Barrio Nuevo Mz M Lt 14, Urb San Isidro, T056-536634, los_inkas_inn@hotmail.com. 5 blocks from the Plaza de Armas, some may think it's too far to stay, but this hostal is comfortable and straightforward. The pool may not always be full but there is internet, cafetería, sauna, laundry services and garage. There are single and double/matrimonial rooms with bath and cable TV, and **E** dorms with shared bathrooms. Tours can be arranged.

Paracas Peninsula and Ballestas Islands *p88*

A Paracas, T056-545100, hparacas@terra. com.pe. Bungalows on the beach, good food, good buffet lunch on Sun US$25, fine grounds facing the bay, TCs can be changed at good rates. Good centre for excursions to the Peninsula and flights over Nasca, it has tennis courts and open-air swimming pool (US$2 for non-residents), also houses the Masson ceramics collection. Dune-buggy trips of 2 hrs can be arranged for US$25 per person; you decide how risky you want to be, good fun.

Hotels are fully booked during the harvest festival and prices rise greatly.

A Hotel Mossone, Huacachina, at the eastern end of the lake, T056-213660, reserva@derrama.org.pe. An elegant hacienda-like hotel to relax at, full board available, with bath, pool (US$4 including snacks, for non-residents), bicycles and sandboards for guests' use. End the day with a Perú libre in the majestic bar/restaurant with a fantastic view over the lake.

B Hostería Suiza, Malecón 264, Huacachina, T056- 238762, hostesuiza@terra.com.pe. Nice house with a huge terrace overlooking the lake, quiet, friendly, clean, includes breakfast.

E Princess, Urb Santa María D-103, Ica, T/F056-215421, www.geocities.com/hotel_princess. A mototaxi ride from the main plaza, with hot water, TV, pool, tourist information, helpful, peaceful neighbourhood, clean, very good.

Nasca *p91, map p91*

If arriving by bus, beware being told that the hotel of your choice is closed, or full. Go to the hotel and find out for sure.

AL Casa Andina, Jr Bolognesi 367, T056-523563, www.casa-andina.com. One of this new chain of hotels with standardized services in distinctive style. Bright, modern decor, clean, a/c, pool, friendly staff, TV, internet, restaurant open all day.

AL Nasca Lines, Jr Bolognesi, T056-522293, reservanasca@derramaje.org.pe. Large remodelled hotel with a/c, comfortable, rooms with private patio, hot water, peaceful, price includes American breakfast, restaurant, good but expensive meals, safe car park, pool (US$4.50 for non-guests, or free if having lunch), they can arrange package tours which include 2-3 nights at the hotel plus a flight over the lines and a desert trip: enquire about the price.

B Nido del Cóndor, opposite the airport, Panamericana Sur Km 447, T056-522424, contanas@terra.com.pe. Large rooms, hot water, good restaurant, bar, shop, videos, swimming pool, camping US$3, parking, English, Italian, German spoken, free pick-up from town, reservation advised.

C-E per person Alegría, Jr Lima 166, T056-522702, www.nazcaperu.com. Continental breakfast and tax included. Rooms with bathroom, carpet and a/c, rooms with shared bath **G** per person, hot water, cafeteria, pool, garden, English, Hebrew, Italian and German spoken, laundry facilities, safe luggage deposit, book exchange, email facilities for US$2 per hr, netphone also US$2, free video on the lines at 2100, very popular. Efraín Alegría also runs a tour agency and guests are encouraged to buy tours (see Activities and tours), flights and bus tickets arranged. Don't listen to anyone who says that Alegría is closed, or full, and no longer runs tours; if you phone or email the hotel they will pick you up at the bus station free of charge day or night (Alegría gives 1 hr free internet use to those who email in advance).

C Paredones Inn, Jr Arica 115, T056-522181, paredoneshotel@terra.com. One block from the Plaza de Armas, nice, ample rooms with cable TV, clean bathrooms, modern, great views from rooftop terrace, laundry service, bar, suites with jacuzzi, helpful staff. Good.

D Mirador, Tacna 436, T056-523121. On main plaza, rooms with shower, cheaper with shared bath, hot water, good breakfast, TV downstairs, modern, clean.

E Hostal Restaurant Via Morburg, JM Mejía 108, 3 blocks from Plaza de Armas, T/F056-522566, hotelviamorburg@hotmail. com. Rooms are a bit small, with bathroom, hot water, small swimming pool, TV room, excellent and cheap restaurant on top floor, very helpful staff, luggage store.

● Eating

Pisco *p88*

♥-♥ As de Oro, San Martín 472, T056-532010. Good food at decent prices, closed Mon. Also a disco and karaoke bar on Sat.

¶¶-¶ El Bossa Nova, Av San Martín 176, p 2, T056-807388. This new café/bar is a stylish place for an espresso or a drink. Good night and day.

¶¶-¶ La Casona Restaurant and Churrascaría, San Martín. New restaurant specializing in grilled meats, large portions, good value.

Ica and Huacachina *p90*

¶¶-¶ La Sirena, Huacachina. Best place to eat. The big corvina fish steaks are excellent, also serves good sandwiches.

Nasca *p91, map p91*

¶¶-¶ El Portón, Moresky 120, in front of Hotel Nasca Lines. A popular stopover with tours, and well worth the visit. Specializes in Peruvian food, has a great indoor/outdoor setting with wood decor.

¶¶-¶ El Puquio, Bolognesi 50 m from plaza. Good food, especially pastas, pleasant atmosphere, good for drinks, popular.

¶¶-¶ La Carreta, Bolognesi. Good for *Nuevo Andino* dishes using traditional Andean ingredients, rustic, lively atmosphere.

¶¶-¶ La Taberna, Jr Lima 321, T056-521411. Good food, live music, popular with gringos, worth a look for the graffiti on the walls.

¶¶-¶ Plaza Mayor, on the Plaza. New restaurant, specializes in barbecue of all types, roasted chicken, steaks, anticuchos, great salads. Large portions, friendly staff.

¶ Kañada, Lima 160, nazcanada@yahoo. com. Cheap menú, excellent *pisco sours*, nice wines, popular, display of local artists' work, email service, English spoken, owner Juan Carlos Fraola is very helpful.

¶ La Púa, Jr Lima, next to La Taberna. Great espresso, also serves pizzas, pastas and sandwiches, good, also offers courtesy *pisco sour*.

⊛ Festivals and events

Ica and Huacachina *p90*

The wine harvest festival (**Festival Internacional de la Vendimia**) is held in early **Mar**. In **May**, the third Sun, is **Día**

Internacional del Pisco. In the first 2 weeks of **Oct** the image of **El Señor de Luren**, in a fine church in Parque Luren, draws pilgrims from all Peru, when there are all-night processions.

▲ Activities and tours

Paracas Peninsula and Ballestas Islands *p88*

Tours to the islands cost US$9-10 per person, and to the peninsula US$20 per person, but are a lot cheaper out of season. Operators usually go to Ballestas in the morning and the Paracas Reserve in the afternoon.

Amigos Adventure Travel Agency, Jr Progreso 167, p 2,T056-311984, amigos_adventures@hotmail.com. Island tours, Reserve tours, sandboarding, English, Italian, French, Dutch and Hebrew spoken.

Blue Sea Tours, C Chosica 320, San Andrés, Pisco; also at El Chaco. Guides Jorge Espejo and Hubert Van Lomoen (speaks Dutch) are frequently recommended, no time limit on tours.

The Zarcillo Connection, San Francisco 111, T056-536543, www.zarcillotravel.com. For Paracas National Reserve, Tambo Colorado, trekking and tours to Ica, Chincha and the Nasca Lines and surrounding sites.

Ica and Huacachina *p90*

Many *hostales* in Huacachina help their guests arrange tours.

Desert Adventures, T01-981 69352, desertadventures@hotmail.com, are frequently recommended for sandboarding and trips into the desert, French and English spoken.

Ica Desert Trip, icadeserttrip@yahoo.es, Robert Penny Cabrera (speaks Spanish and English) and Marc Romain (speaks, Spanish, French and English) offer 1-, 2- and 3-day trips off-road into the desert, archaeology, geology, etc. US$50 per person per day (maximum 4 people), contact by email in advance.

All guides must be approved by the Ministry of Tourism and should have an official identity card. Only conduct business with agencies at their office, or phone or email the company you want to deal with in advance. Some hotels are not above pressurising guests to buy tours at inflated prices. Taxi drivers usually act as guides, but most speak only Spanish. Taxis will charge from US$4-6 per hr to wait for you at the sites and bring you back to the city.

Aerial tours

Small planes take 3-5 passengers. Flights last 30-35 mins and are controlled by air traffic personnel at the airport. A taxi to the airport costs US$1.35; bus, US$0.10. Reservations should be made at the airport for flights with companies listed below. These companies are well-established and recommended. There are others. The price for a flight is US$40 per person (special deals are sometimes available, eg *hostal* included; touts charge US$50; shorter flights on sale for US$25). You also have to pay US$2 airport tax. It is best to organize a flight direct with the airlines at the airport. Flights are bumpy with many tight turns – many people are airsick. Best times to fly are 0800-1000 and 1500-1630 when there is less turbulence and better light (assuming there is no fog, in which case chaos may ensue).

Aerocóndor, Panamericana Sur Km 447, T056-522404, www.aero condor.com.pe. The outfit offers flights over the lines from Lima in a 1-day tour (lunch in Nasca) for US$260 per person; or flights from Ica for US$130 per person.

Aero Ica, in Jr Lima and at the airport, Lima T01-446 3026, aeroica@terra.com.pe. Also offers flights from Lima and a night in Maison Suisse plus flight for US$65, but book 48 hrs in advance.

Alas Peruanas, T056-522444, www.alasperuanas.com. Their flights can also be booked at Hotel Alegría (experienced pilots fluent in English).

They also offer 1-hr flights over the Palpa and Llipata areas (US$60 per person, minimum 3). They can also organize flights from Pisco (US$130) and Ica (US$120). All flights include a BBC film.

Tour operators

Air Nasca Travel, Jr Lima 185, T056-521027, guide Susi recommended. Very helpful and friendly staff, very competitive prices. Can do all types of tours around Nasca, Ica, Paracas and Pisco.

Alegría Tours, Lima 168, T056-522444, (24 hrs), www.nazcaperu.com. Run by Efraín Alegría, offer inclusive tours (see Sleeping) which have been repeatedly recommended. They have guides who speak English, German, French and Italian, with tours to Palpa, Puerto Inca, Sacaco and the San Fernando Reserve to see the marine wildlife, to Chauchilla, Cantalloc, etc. Tours go as far as Ica, Paracas and the Ballestas Islands. Also sandboarding on Cerro Blanco. Alegría run a bus from Nasca to Pisco every day at 1000 (returns at 1000 from Pisco's Plaza de Armas), via Ica, Huacachina and bodegas. Efraín Alegría can arrange a taxi to one of the sites outside Nasca.

Nasca Trails, Bolognesi 550, T056-522858, nascatrails@terra.com.pe. Juan Tohalino Vera speaks English, French, German and Italian.

Félix Quispe Sarmiento, El Nativo de Nazca, Fedeyogin5@hotmail.com. He has his own museum, Hantun Nazca, Panamericana Sur 447, and works with the Instituto Nacional de Cultura, tours off the beaten track, can arrange flights, knowledgeable, ask for him at Kañada restaurant.

◉ Transport

Pisco *p88*

All the bus terminals are in the centre near the Plaza de Armas. However, if arriving by bus, make sure it is going into town and will not leave you at the Repartición right on the Panamericana, which is 5 km from the centre, a 10-min taxi (US$1) or mototaxi ride (US$0.50), and not a particularly safe area after dark. Transport from the Repartición stops at Hostal Comercio by Plaza Belén.

Bus To **Lima**, 242 km, 3-4 hrs, US$4 with **Ormeño** (San Francisco, 1 block from the plaza) and **San Martín** (San Martín 199). For buses from Lima, see p85. There is regular transport to **Ica**, US$0.90 by bus, 45 mins, 70 km; with **Ormeño** and **Saky** (Pedemonte y Arequipa). To **Nasca**, 210 km, US$5, 3 hrs by bus, via Ica, at 0830 with **Oropesa** and 3 daily with Ormeño. To **Arequipa**, US$12, 10-12 hrs, 2 daily.

Paracas Peninsula and Ballestas Islands *p88*
A taxi from Pisco to Paracas costs about US$2.50-3. Combis to/from El Chaco beach (marked 'Chaco-Paracas-Museo') leave when full, US$0.50, 25 mins. The last one returns at around 2200. There is no public transport on the peninsula.

Ica and Huacachina *p90*
To **Pisco** (70 km), 45 mins, US$0.90, every half hour. To **Lima** (302 km), 4 hrs, US$5-10, several daily. To **Nasca** (140 km), 2 hrs, minimum US$1.50; **Cueva** (José Elias y Huánuco), hourly on the hour 0600-2200. To **Arequipa** the route goes via Nasca, US$15-25, see also under Nasca; most reliable buses with **Ormeño**, **Cruz del Sur** and **Flores**.

Nasca *p91, map p91*
Bus To **Lima** (446 km), 6 hrs, several buses and *colectivos* daily.
Ormeño,T056-522058, Royal Class at 0530 and 1330, US$20, from Hotel Nasca Lines, Jr Bolognesi, arrive in Santa Catalina, a much safer area of Lima, see p85. **Cruz del Sur**, Av Guardia Civil 290, T056-523713, 4 buses daily, US$6. To **Ica**, 2 hrs, US$1.50, 4 a day, and to **Pisco** (210 km), 3 hrs, US$5, also 3 a day. Note that buses to Pisco don't go into the centre (see previous page). To

Arequipa, 565 km, 9 hrs. **Ormeño** Royal Class at 2100, US$15, 8 hrs. **Cruz del Sur** has 4 buses daily between 1900 and 2400, with prices ranging between US$10 and US$27. Delays are possible out of Nasca because of drifting sand across the road or mudslides in the rainy season. Travel in daylight. To **Cusco**, 659 km, 14 hrs. **Expreso Wari** have 6 services a day, normal US$17, and Imperial at US$20 (bus may run if not enough passengers). Their offices are at the exit from Nasca on the road to Puquío. Also **Cruz del Sur**, at 2000, 2015, US$22.

⊕ Directory

Pisco *p88*
Banks ATMs at banks on Plaza de Armas, mostly Visa. **Interbank**, for Mastercard. **Internet** At various places in town. **Telephone** On the Plaza de Armas between Av San Martín y Callao.

Ica and Huacachina *p90*
Banks Avoid changing TCs if possible as commission is high. If you need to, though, **BCP** is reasonable. **Post** At Callao y Moquegua, Ica. **Telephone** At Av San Martín y Huánuco, Ica.

Nasca *p91, map p91*
Banks **BCP**, Lima y Grau. Changes cash and Visa TCs at decent rates, also cash advance on Visa, Visa ATM. Some street changers will change TCs, but at 8% commission. **Internet** Many places on Jr Bolognesi. **Lucy@com**, Bolognesi 298. US$0.75 per hr. **Migsu Net**, Arica 295, p 2. Daily 0800-2400, good, US$1 per hr. Facilities at Hotel Alegría and Casa Andina. **Post** Fermín de Castillo 379, T056-522016. Also at Hotel Alegría. **Police** Av Los Incas, T056-522105. **Telephone** Telefónica for international calls with coins on Plaza Bolognesi. Also on Plaza de Armas and at Lima 359.

Lima & the South Coast Nasca & the southern desert Listings

Cusco & Southern Peru

The Inca Trail to Machu Picchu.

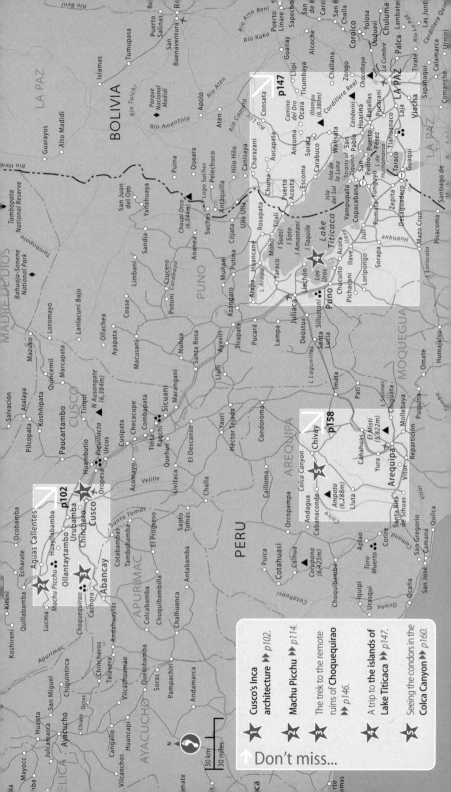

The main focus of Peru's tourist activity is the southern highlands, centred on an axis of three cities: Cusco, Arequipa and Puno. Here lie many of the country's premier attractions, including the big three of Lake Titicaca, the Colca Canyon and Machu Picchu. From the ancient Inca capital, Cusco, the Urubamba Valley – or Sacred Valley of the Incas – snakes its way down to the eastern edges of the Andes, passing on its way a string of Inca sites, each more fantastic than the last, until it genuflects at the feet of that great tourist icon, Machu Picchu, Peru's answer to the Taj Mahal.

South from Cusco a new paved road runs to the shores of Lake Titicaca, from whose deep waters the first Inca emerged to found an empire. West across the Andes is Arequipa, a colonial beauty with alabaster-like skin. From here, visitors can take a tour to enjoy the grandeur of the Colca Canyon. Twice as deep as the Grand Canyon and, until quite recently, believed to be the deepest canyon in the world, this is a magical place of ancient peoples, smoking volcanoes and some very, very large birds.

Ratings

Culture
★★★★★

Landscape
★★★★★

Wildlife
★★★

Activities
★★★★★

Chillin'
★★★★

Costs
$$$

Cusco and the Sacred Valley

Cusco stands at the head of the Sacred Valley of the Incas and is the jumping-off point for the Inca Trail and famous Inca city of Machu Picchu. Not surprising, then, that this is the prime destination for the vast majority of Peru's visitors. In fact, the ancient Inca capital is now the 'gringo' capital of the entire continent. And it's easy to see why. The city's beauty cannot be overstated. It is a fascinating mixture of Inca and colonial Spanish architecture: colonial churches, monasteries and convents and numerous pre-Columbian ruins are interspersed with hotels, bars and restaurants that have sprung up to cater for the hundreds of thousands of tourists. Almost every central street has remains of Inca walls, arches and doorways. Many streets are lined with Inca stonework, now serving as the foundations for more modern dwellings.

⊘ Getting there Flights from Lima and Arequipa, bus from Nasca, Arequipa and Puno.

⊜ Getting around Lots of buses and tours from Cusco to the Sacred Valley.

⊖ Time required 5-6 days; if trekking to Machu Picchu allow an extra 4 days.

⊚ Weather May-Sep is dry season; Nov-Apr wet season but cheaper and still pleasant enough.

⊜ Sleeping Cusco has hotels for any budget. The Sacred Valley has a range of good-value options.

⊘ Eating Every kind of cuisine in Cusco, from Novo Andino to Asian.

▲ Activities and tours Rafting, trekking, mountain biking, Inca ruins.

★ Don't miss... the Inca Trail. ▸▸ p117.

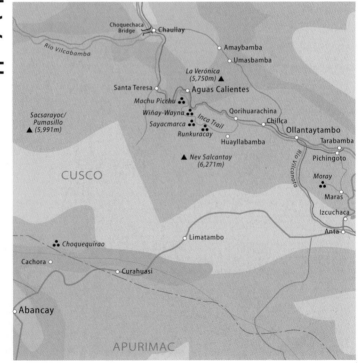

Ins and outs 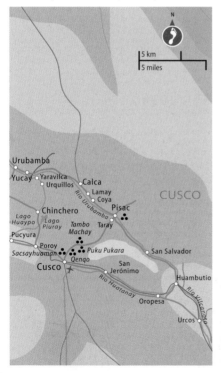 → *pp119-146*

Getting there

Most travellers arriving from Lima will do so by **air**. There are regular daily flights and none arrive at night. The airport is at Quispiquilla, near the bus terminal, 1½ km southeast of the centre. A taxi to and from the airport costs US$1-2 (US$3.50 by radio taxi). Colectivos to the centre cost US$0.20 from outside the airport car park to the centre.

All long-distance **buses** arrive and leave from the bus terminal near the Pachacútec statue in Ttio district. Transport to your hotel is not a problem as bus company representatives are often on hand.

There are two **train** stations in Cusco. To **Juliaca and Puno**, trains leave from the Estación Wanchac on Calle Pachacútec (T084-221992). The office here offers direct information and ticket sales for all **PerúRail** services. Look out for special promotional offers. When arriving in Cusco, a tourist bus meets the train to take visitors to hotels whose touts offer rooms on the train. **Machu Picchu trains** leave from Estación San Pedro, opposite the Santa Ana market (T084-221313). ⊙ → *p84; for trains to Juliaca and Puno, p141; to Machu Picchu, p114.*

Getting around

The centre of Cusco is small and is easily explored on foot. Bear in mind, however, that at this altitude walking up some of the city's steep cobbled streets may leave you out of breath, so you'll need to take your time. Combis (minivans) are the main form of public transportation in the city: well-organized, cheap and safe. Taxis in Cusco are also cheap and recommended when arriving by air, train or bus. When you fly into Cusco, consider staying in the Sacred Valley for the first couple of days; it's at a lower altitude and it'll help you get acclimatized for the height of Cusco itself.

Tourist information

Tourist offices Official tourist information ① *Portal Mantas 117-A, next to La Merced church, T084-263176, Mon-Fri 0800-1900, Sat 0800-1400.* There is also an **i perú tourist information desk** ① *T084-237364, daily 0600-1300, at the airport, and another at Portal de Carrizos 250, Plaza de Armas, T084-252974, daily 0830-1930.* **Dirección Regional de Turismo** ① *Av de la Cultura 734, 3rd floor, T084-223701, Mon-Fri 0800-1300.* See box on page 104 for OFEC offices and INC office for Machu Picchu.

Tourist Police ① *C Saphi 511, T084-249654.* If you need a *denuncia* (a report for insurance purposes), which is available from the **Banco de la Nación**, they will type it out. Always go to the police when robbed, even though it will take a bit of time. The **Tourist Protection Bureau (Indecopi)** ① *at the tourist office at Portal Carrizos, Plaza de Armas (see above), toll free T0800-42579 (24-hr hotline, not available from payphones).*

Cusco & Southern Peru Cusco & the Sacred Valley

Top tips

Just the ticket

A combined entry ticket to most of the sites of main historical and cultural interest in and around Cusco, called the **Boleto Turístico Unificado (BTU)**, costs US$10 (S/.35) and is valid for five to 10 days. It permits entrance to: Santa Catalina Convent and Art Museum, Museo de Sitio Qorikancha, Museo Histórico Regional (Casa Inca Garcilazo de la Vega), Museo Palacio Municipal de Arte Contemporáneo, Museo de Arte Popular, Centro Qosqo de Arte Nativo, Monumento Pachacútec, Sacsayhuaman, Qenqo, Puka Pukara, Tambo Machay, Pisac, Ollantaytambo, Chinchero, Tipón and Piquillacta. There is also a US$6 ticket for only Sacsayhuaman, Qenqo, Puka Pukara and Tambo Machay. The BTUs can be bought at the **OFEC** office (Casa Garcilazo) ① *Plaza Regocijo, esquina C Garcilazo, T084- 226919, Mon-Sat 0800-1600, Sun 0800-1200, or Av Sol 103, T227037, Mon-Fri 0800-1800, Sat 0830-1230*, or at any of the sites included in the ticket. There is a 50% discount for students with a green ISIC card, which is only available at the OFEC office (Casa Garcilazo) upon presentation of the student card. Take your ISIC card when visiting the sites, as some may ask to see it. There is no student reduction for the one-day card. Entrance tickets for the Cathedral, Museo de Arte Religioso del Arzobispado, Museo Inka (El Palacio del Almirante), Santo Domingo/ Qorikancha and La Merced are sold separately. Machu Picchu ruins and Inca trail entrance tickets are sold at the **Instituto Nacional de Cultura (INC)** ① *San Bernardo s/n between Mantas y Almagro, T084-236061, Mon-Fri 0900-1300, 1600-1800, Sat 0900-1100.*

Head office: Av de la Cultura 732-A, p 1, T084-252987, mmarroquin@indecopi.gob.pe. Also at the airport, T084-237364. This organization protects the consumer rights of all tourists and helps with any problems or complaints and can be helpful in dealing with tour agencies, hotels or restaurants.

Sights

Since there are so many sights to see in Cusco city, not even the most ardent tourist would be able to visit them all. For those with limited time, or for those who want a whistle-stop tour, a list of must-sees would comprise: the combination of Inca and colonial architecture at Qoricancha; the huge Inca ceremonial centre of Sacsayhuaman; the paintings of the Last Supper and the 1650 earthquake in the cathedral; the churches of La Compañía de Jesús and La Merced; and the view from San Cristóbal. If you have the energy catch a taxi up to the White Christ and watch the sunset as you look out upon one of the most fascinating cities in the world. If you visit one museum make it the Museo Inka; it has the most comprehensive collection.

Plaza de Armas and around

The heart of the city is the Plaza de Armas. This was the great civic square of the Incas, flanked by their palaces, and was a place of solemn parades and great assemblies. On the northeast side of the square, the early 17th-century baroque **Cathedral** ⓘ *Mon, Tue, Wed, Fri and Sat 1000-1130, daily 1400-1730, daily until 1000 for worshippers, Quechua Mass at 0500-0600, US$3,* forms part of a three-church complex: the cathedral itself, **Iglesia Jesús y María** (1733) on the left as you look at it and **El Triunfo** (1533) on the right. There are two entrances; the cathedral doors are used during Mass but the tourist entrance is on the left-hand side through Iglesia Jesús y María. The cathedral itself was built on the site of the Palace of Inca Wiracocha (*Kiswarcancha*) using stones from Sacsayhuaman.

The view from Cusco's Plaza de Armas looking towards La Merced church.

The gleaming, newly renovated gilded main altar of the **Iglesia Jesús y María** draws the eyes to the end of the church. However, take the time to look up at the colourful murals which have been partially restored. Walking through into the cathedral's transept, the oldest surviving painting in Cusco can be seen. It depicts the 1650 earthquake (much of modern-day Cusco was built after this event). At the far right-hand end of the cathedral is an interesting local painting of the Last Supper. But this is the Last Supper with a difference, for Jesus is about to tuck into a plate of *cuy*, washed down with a glass of *chicha*! Entering **El**

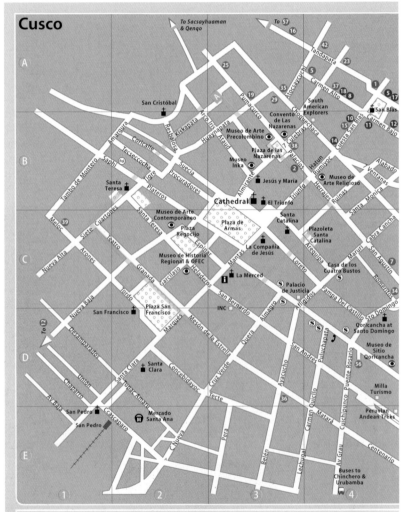

Cusco

To Sacsayhuaman & Qenqo

To 57

16

San Cristóbal

Convento de Las Nazarenas

South American Explorers

San Blas

Museo de Arte Precolombino

Plaza de las Nazarenas

Museo Inka

Santa Teresa

Jesús y María

Museo de Arte Religioso

Cathedral

El Triunfo

Museo de Arte Contemporáneo

Plaza Regocijo

Plaza de Armas

Santa Catalina

Plazoleta Santa Catalina

La Compañía de Jesús

Museo de Historia Regional & OFEC

La Merced

Casa de los Cuatro Bustos

Palacio de Justicia

Plaza San Francisco

San Francisco

INC

Qoricancha at Santo Domingo

Museo de Sitio Qoricancha

Santa Clara

Milla Turismo

San Pedro

Mercado Santa Ana

Peruvian Andean Treks

San Pedro

Centenario

Buses to Chinchero & Urubamba

100 metres
100 yards

Triunfo there is a stark contrast between the dark, heavy atmosphere of the cathedral and the light, simple structure of this serene church, the first in Cusco.

On the southeast side of the plaza is the beautiful 17th century church of **La Compañía de Jesús**, built on the site of the Palace of the Serpents (*Amarucancha*, residence of the Inca Huayna Cápac). The original church was destroyed in the earthquake of 1650. One of the main features is the magnificent baroque altarpiece, resplendent in gold leaf. Further west, on Calle Márquez, is the church of **La Merced** ⓘ *monastery and museum 1430-1700, church Mon-Sat 0830-1200, 1530-1730, except Sun, US$0.85.* Originally built in 1534, it was razed in the 1650 earthquake and rebuilt by indigenous stonemasons in the late 17th century. Inside the church are buried Gonzalo Pizarro, half-brother of Francisco, and the two Almagros, father and son. Attached is a very fine monastery. The first cloister is the most beautiful with its two floors, archways and pillars.

Just north of the Plaza de Armas is the interesting **Museo Inka** ⓘ *C Ataud, T084-237380, Mon-Fri 0800-1700, Sat 0900-1600, US$3,* housed in the **Palacio del Almirante**, one of Cusco's most impressive colonial buildings. The museum exhibits the development of culture in the region from pre-Inca, through Inca times to the present day. They have an excellent collection of miniature turquoise figures and other objects made as offerings to the gods. The display of trepanned skulls is fascinating, as is the full-size tomb complete with mummies stuck in urns. During the high season local Quechuan weavers can be seen working, and selling, in the courtyard. Their weavings are expensive but of very good quality.

In the Casa Cabrera, on the northwest side of the plaza, is the beautiful **Museo de Arte Precolombino** ⓘ *Plaza de las Nazarenas 231, T084-233210, daily 0900-2200, US$4.60, US$2.30 with student card.* Set around a spacious courtyard, it is dedicated to the work of the great artists of pre-Colombian Peru. Within the expertly lit and well-organized galleries are many superb examples of pottery, metalwork (largely in gold and silver) and wood carvings.

The magnificent church, convent and museum of **Santa Catalina** ⓘ *Arequipa at Santa Catalina Angosta, Sat-Thu 0900-1730, Fri 0900-1500, entrance with BTU visitors' ticket, guided tours by English-speaking*

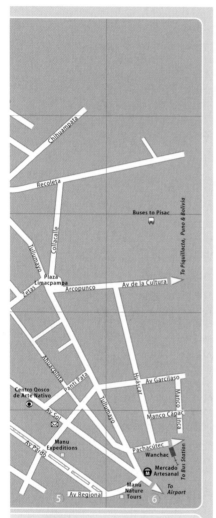

Eating 🍴
Greens **5** *A4*
Jack's Café **14** *B4*
La Bodega **8** *A4*
Macondo **10** *B4*
Muse **17** *A4*
Pacha-Papa **11** *B4*
Planet Cusco **18** *A4*

Witches Garden **12** *B4*

Bars & clubs 🍸
Km 0 (Arte y Tapas) **1** *A4*
Mandela's Bar **2** *B3*

Background

→ **Navel gazing**

The ancient Inca capital is said to have been founded around AD 1100. According to the central Inca creation myth, the Sun sent his son, Manco Cápac and the Moon sent her daughter, Mama Ocllo, to spread culture and enlightenment throughout the dark, barbaric lands. They emerged from the icy depths of Lake Titicaca and began their journey in search of the place where they would found their kingdom. They were ordered to head north from the lake until a golden staff they carried could be plunged into the ground for its entire length. The soil of the altiplano was so thin that they had to travel as far as the valley of Cusco where, on the mountain of Huanacauri, the staff fully disappeared and the soil was found to be suitably fertile. This was the sign they were looking for and they duly named the place Cusco, meaning 'navel of the earth'.

students (tip is expected), church daily 0700-0800, is built upon the foundations of the *Acllahuasi* (House of the Chosen Women), whose nobility, virtue and beauty permitted them to be prepared for ceremonial and domestic duties – some were chosen to bear the Inca king's children. Today the convent is a closed order where the nuns have no contact with the outside world. The church has an ornate, gilded altarpiece and a beautifully carved pulpit. The museum has a wonderful collection of Cuzqueño school paintings spanning the decades of Spanish rule – a good guide can point out how the style changes from the heavy European influence to the more indigenous style.

Much original Inca stonework can be seen in the streets and most particularly in the **Callejón Loreto**, running southeast past La Compañía de Jesús from the main plaza. The walls of the *Acllahuasi* are on one side, and of the *Amarucancha* on the other. There are also Inca remains in Calle San Agustín, to the east of the plaza. The famous **Stone of 12 Angles** is in **Calle Hatun Rumiyoc** half-way along its second block, on the right-hand side going away from the plaza. The finest stonework is in the celebrated curved wall beneath the west end of Santo Domingo. This was rebuilt after the 1950 earthquake and excavations have revealed Inca baths below here, and more Inca retaining walls. Another superb stretch of late-Inca stonework is in **Calle Ahuacpinta**, outside Qoricancha, to the east or left as you enter. True Inca stonework is wider at the base than at the top and features ever-smaller stones as the walls rise. Doorways and niches are trapezoidal. The Incas clearly learnt that the combination of these four techniques helped their structures to withstand earthquakes. This explains why, in two huge earthquakes (1650 and 1950), Inca walls stayed standing while colonial buildings tumbled down.

One of the most fascinating sights in Cusco is the **Qoricancha at Santo Domingo** ⓘ *Mon-Sat 0800-1700, Sun 1400-1600 (except holidays), US$1.80 (not on the BTU Visitor Ticket), guides outside charge around US$2-3*. Behind the walls of the Catholic church are remains of what was once the centre of the vast Inca society. The Golden Palace and Temple of the Sun was a complex filled with such fabulous treasures of gold and silver it took the Spanish three months to melt it all down. The Solar Garden contained life-sized gold sculptures of men, women, children, animals, insects and flowers which were placed in homage to the Sun God. On the walls were more than 700 gold sheets weighing about 2 kg each. The *conquistadores* sent these back intact to prove to the King of Spain how rich their discovery was. There would also have been a large solar disc in the shape of a round face with rays and flames. This disc has never been found. The first Inca, Manco Cápac, is said to have built the temple when he left Lake Titicaca and founded Cusco with Mama Ocllo. However, it was the ninth Inca, Pachacútec, who transformed it. When the Spaniards arrived, the complex was awarded to Juan Pizarro, the younger brother of Francisco. He in turn willed it to the Dominicans who ripped much of it down to build their church.

On entering the courtyard you will see behind you Santo Domingo. This was where the **Temple of the Sun** stood, a massive structure 80 m wide, 20 m deep and 7 m in height. Only the curved wall of the western end still exists and will be seen (complete with a large crack from the 1950 earthquake), when you later walk left through to the lookout over the Solar Garden. Also in the baroque cloister are the remains of the **Temple of the Moon**, identifiable by a series of niches. Beyond this is the so-called **Temple of Venus and the Stars**. Stars were special deities used to predict weather, wealth and crops. On the other side of the courtyard is the **Temple of Lightning**.

Sacsayhuaman and other sites near Cusco

On a hill in the northern outskirts of Cusco are the magnificent Inca walls of the ruined ceremonial centre of **Sacsayhuaman** ⓘ *daily 0700-1730, entry with BTU Visitors' Ticket (and to other sites below)*. For centuries this was thought to be a fortress, but the layout and architecture suggest a great sanctuary and temple to the Sun, rising opposite the place previously believed to be the Inca's throne – which was probably an altar, carved out of the solid rock. Broad steps lead to the altar from either side. Zigzags in the boulders round the 'throne' are apparently '*chicha* grooves', channels down which maize beer flowed during festivals. Up the hill is an ancient quarry, the *Rodadero*, now used mainly as a rock slide. Near it are many seats cut perfectly into the smooth rock.

The site survived the first years of the conquest. Pizarro's troops had entered Cusco unopposed in 1533 and lived safely at Sacsayhuaman, until the rebellion of Manco Inca, in 1536, caught them off guard. The bitter struggle which ensued became the decisive military action of the conquest, for Manco's failure to hold Sacsayhuaman cost him the war, and the empire. The destruction of the hilltop site began after the defeat of Manco's rebellion. The 360 m-long outer walls still stand and you can see the massive rocks, weighing up to 130 tons, fitted together with absolute perfection, but the complex of towers and buildings was razed to the ground. From then, until the 1930s, Sacsayhuaman served as a kind of unofficial quarry of pre-cut stone for the inhabitants of Cusco. The site is about a 30-minute walk from the town centre. Walk up Pumacurco from Plaza de las Nazarenas. A taxi costs US$1.50.

Along the road from Sacsayhuaman to Pisac, past a radio station, at 3,600 m, is the temple and amphitheatre of **Qenqo**. These aren't exactly ruins, but are one of the finest

Calle Hatun Rumiyoc shows some of the best examples of Inca walls in Cusco.

Top tips

Visiting Sacsayhuaman and other sites near Cusco

✔ Taking a guide to Sacsayhuaman and sites near Cusco is a good idea and you should visit in the morning for the best photographs and before the tour groups arrive.

✔ Carry your multi-site ticket as there are roving ticket inspectors.

✔ You can visit the sites on foot. It's a pleasant walk through the countryside requiring half a day or more, though remember to take water and sun protection, and watch out for dogs.

✔ An alternative to walking both ways is to take the Pisac bus up to Tambo Machay (which costs US$0.35) and walk back. Another way to see the ruins is on horseback, arranged at travel agencies.

✔ An organized tour (with guide) will go to all the sites for US$6 per person, not including entrance fees. A taxi will charge US$15-20 for three to four people.

✔ Some of these ruins are included in the many City Tours available. For details, see page 135.

examples of Inca stone carving *in situ*, especially inside the large hollowed-out stone that houses an altar. The rock is criss-crossed by zigzag channels that give the place its name and which served to course *chicha*, or perhaps sacrificial blood, for purposes of divination. The open space that many refer to as the 'plaza' or 'amphitheatre' was used for ceremonies. The 19 trapezoidal niches, which are partially destroyed, held idols and mummies.

Known as an Inca fortress, **Puka Pukara**, whose name translates as 'Red Fort', was more likely to have been a *tambo*, a kind of post-house where travellers were lodged and goods and animals housed temporarily. It is worth seeing for the views alone.

A few hundred metres up the road is the spring shrine of **Tambo Machay**, still in excellent condition. There are many opinions as to what this place was used for. Some say it was a resting place for the Incas and others that it was used by Inca Yupanqui as a hunting place. There are three ceremonial water fountains built on different levels. It is possible that the site was a centre of a water cult. Water still flows by a hidden channel out of the masonry wall, straight into a little rock pool traditionally known as the Inca's bath.

The Sacred Valley ⊜❶✿⊜❶ ›› *pp119-146*

The Río Urubamba cuts its way through fields and rocky gorges beneath the high peaks of the Cordillera. This beautiful valley, which stretches from Sicuani (on the railway to Puno) to the gorge of Torontoi, to the northwest of Cusco, has come to be known as The Sacred Valley due to its great significance. The Incas built a number of strategic sites here; Pisac, Ollantaytambo and Machu Picchu among them.

Ins and outs

Getting there and around Paved roads, plentiful transport and a good selection of hotels and eating places make this a straightforward place to explore. You can choose either a quick visit from the city or, better still, linger for a few days. Don't hurry; most organized tours are too fast. Explore it on foot, by bike or on horseback. Using public transport and staying overnight in Urubamba, Ollantaytambo or Pisac allows much more time to see the ruins and markets. See under each destination for transport details. For Cusco tour operators, see page 135.

The great Inca ceremonial site of Sacsayhuaman was largely destroyed but the huge outer walls remain.

Pisac

Only 30 km north of Cusco is the little village of Pisac, which is well worth a visit for its superb **Inca ruins** ① *0700-1730, entry by BTU multi-site ticket*, perched precariously on the mountain above the town. This is one of the largest Inca ruins around Cusco and it clearly had defensive, religious and agricultural functions, as well as being an Inca country estate. To appreciate the site fully, allow five or six hours if going on foot. If possible arrive very early, around 0700, before the tourists. Avoid Sunday afternoons, when tour groups from Pisac descend in their hundreds. Guides charge US$5, but the wardens on site are very helpful and don't charge anything to give out information.

Walking up to the ruins, although tiring, is recommended for the views. It's at least one hour uphill all the way. The walk begins from the plaza, passing the Centro de Salud and a control post. The path goes through working terraces, giving the ruins a context. The first group of buildings is **Pisaqa**, with a fine curving wall. Climb up to the central part of the ruins, the **Intihuatana**, a group of temples showing magnificent Inca masonry. From here a path leads around the hillside through a tunnel to **Q'Allaqasa** (military area). Across the valley at this point, a large area of Inca tombs in holes in the hillside can be seen. The end of the site is **Kanchiracay**, where the agricultural workers were housed. At dusk you will hear, if not see, the *pisaca* (partridges), after which the place is named. Road transport approaches from the Kanchiracay end. If you don't fancy walking, horses are available for US$3 per person. Combis charge US$0.60 per person and taxis US$3 one way up to the ruins from near the bridge. Then you can walk back down (if you want the taxi to take you back down negotiate a fare). Strangely, most visitors don't come to Pisac for the ruins. Instead, they come in droves for its Sunday morning **market**, which comes to life after the arrival of tourist buses around 1000, and is usually over by 1500. Pisac has other, somewhat less crowded, less expensive markets on Tuesday and Thursday morning; it's best to get there before 0900. Pisac is usually visited as part of a tour from Cusco but this often allows only 1½ hours in the town, which is not enough time to take in the ruins and splendid scenery.

Urubamba

Like many places along the valley, Urubamba has a fine setting, with views of the Chicón snow-capped peaks and glaciers, and enjoys a mild climate. **Seminario-Behar Ceramic Studio** ① *C Berriózabal 111, a right turning off the main road to Ollantaytambo, T084-201002, kupa@terra.com.pe, open every day, just ring the bell,* founded in 1980, is located in the beautiful grounds of the former **Hostal Urpihuasi**. Pablo Seminario has investigated the techniques and designs of pre-Columbian Peruvian cultures and has created a style with strong links to the past. Each piece is handmade and painted, using ancient glazes and minerals, and is then fired in reproduction pre-Columbian kilns. The resulting pieces are very attractive. Reservations to visit the studio and a personal appointment with the artists (Pablo and Marilú) are welcomed.

Chinchero
ⓘ *Daily, 0700-1730. Can be visited on the BTU combined entrance ticket (see box on page 104).*
Chinchero is northwest from Cusco, just off a direct road to Urubamba. The streets of the village wind up from the lower sections, where transport stops, to the plaza which is reached through an archway. The great square appears to be stepped, with a magnificent Inca wall separating the two levels. Let into the wall is a row of trapezoidal niches, each much taller than a man. From the lower section, which is paved, another arch leads to an upper terrace, upon which the Spaniards built an attractive church which is open on Sunday for mass and at festivals. Opposite the church is a small local museum. Excavations have revealed many Inca walls and terraces. The local produce **market** on Sunday morning is fascinating and very colourful, and best before the tour groups arrive. It's on your left as you come into town. There's also a small Sunday handicraft market by the church. Chinchero attracts few tourists, except on Sunday.

Moray and Maras
Some 46 km from Cusco is the little town of **Maras**, famous for a series of spectacular terraced Inca *salineras* (salt pans), which are still in production today. These are now a fixture on the tourist circuit and can become congested with buses. The walk to the salt pans takes about 30 minutes. Take water as it can be very hot and dry here. There is public transport from Chinchero to Maras and regular pick-up trucks which carry people and produce in and out. Transport stops running between 1700 and 1800; it costs between US$0.60-1. If you cannot get transport to Maras, take any combi going between Urubamba and Chinchero, get out at the junction for Maras and walk 4 km from there.

Some 9 km west of Maras is **Moray** (US$1.45). This remote but beautiful site is well worth a visit. There are three huge terraced amphitheatres, descending to a depth of 150 m, and each with its own micro-climate. These 'hanging gardens' were used by the Incas, according to some theories, as a sort of open-air crop nursery. It is a very atmospheric place, which, some claim, has mystical power. The scenery around here is absolutely stunning, especially in the late afternoon

The little town of Pisac is renowned for its weekly market.

> ## Downhill from here
>
> We set off from a mountain village and then went off road. Soon I was out ahead and shot through a valley where farm dogs gave chase. We had lunch and then checked out a well-preserved Inca site in the valley below: an amazing irrigation system with a massive image of the sun at its epicentre. The next section was difficult, mostly downhill but along steep gorges, requiring mountain bike technique, distributing weight to avoid going over the handlebars. A young German girl joined the party there. The guide suggested that wheeling the bike would be safer, which is what I did. The German girl was ahead of me and she went over the handlebars. Had she fallen sideways she would have gone down 300 feet. I got to her quickly. She had a few cuts and bruises but I had everything she needed in my medical kit. *Glenn Simpson.*

Travellers' tales

light. There is little indication of the scale of the terraced amphitheatres until you reach the rim. It's about a 1½-hour walk to Moray from Maras but the most interesting way to get there is from Urubamba via the Pichingoto Bridge over the Río Urubamba. The climb up from the bridge is fairly steep but easy, with great views of Nevado Chicón. The **Hotel Incaland** in Urubamba can arrange horses and guide and a pick-up truck for the return, all for US$30-40 per person (see page 126). Another option is to hire a taxi with driver to take you to Moray.

Ollantaytambo

The ancient Inca town of Ollantaytambo stands at the foot of a spectacular Inca fortress ⓘ *0700-1730, admission is by combined entrance ticket (see page 104), which can be bought at the site, otherwise it's US$6.50, guides at the entrance charge US$2*, scene of one of the greatest acts of resistance by the Incas against the *conquistadores*, in 1536. Behind the great high-walled trapezoidal esplanade known as *Mañariki* rise a series of 16 massive, stepped terraces of the very finest stonework. Beyond these imposing terraces lies the so-called Temple of Ten Niches, a funeral chamber once dedicated to the worship of Pachacútec's royal household. Immediately above this are six monolithic upright blocks of rose-coloured rhyolite, the remains of what is popularly called The Temple of the Sun. You can either descend by the route you came up, or follow the terracing round to the left (as you face the town) and work your way down to the Valley of the Patacancha. Here are more Inca ruins in the small area between the town and the temple fortress, behind the church. Most impressive is the **Baño de la Ñusta** (Bath of the Princess), a grey granite rock, about waist high, beneath which is the bath itself.

The town itself is built directly on top of the original Inca town, or Llacta. The Inca canchas (blocks of houses) are almost entirely intact, and shouldn't be missed. Also worth seeing is **El Museo Catcco** (Centro Andino de Tecnología Tradicional y Cultural de las Comunidades de Ollantaytambo) ⓘ *Casa Horno, Patacalle, 1 block from the plaza, T084-204024, www.cbc.org.pe/rao, daily 0900-1800, US$1.45 (donations welcome)*, which houses a fine ethnographical collection and its Information Center gives tips on day-hikes, things to see and places to stay. Local guides are available for tours of the town and surrounding areas. Ceramics and textiles are sold in the museum shop and there's internet access. From Ollantaytambo you can continue to Machu Picchu by train but you won't be allowed on the station unless you have previously bought a ticket for the train.

The Inca fortress at Ollantaytambo, scene of defiant resistance against the Spanish invaders.

Machu Picchu and the Inca Trails 🖥️🚌 ▶ *pp119-146*

It's a cliché to say it, but Machu Picchu is not be missed. No amount of hype can detract from the sheer magnificence of this awesome sight. The ancient citadel, 42 km from Ollantaytambo by rail, straddles the saddle of a high mountain with steep terraced slopes falling away to the fast-flowing Río Urubamba snaking its hairpin course far below. Towering overhead is Huayna Picchu, and green jungle peaks provide the backdrop for the whole majestic scene.

If you take the Inca Trail to Machu Picchu, following in the footsteps of its creators, you are making a true pilgrimage and all the sweat and toil is worth it when you finally set eyes on this mystical site from the Inca sun gate. Afterwards you recover in Aguas Calientes and soothe those aching limbs in the hot springs. The introduction of new regulations for walking the Inca Trail opened up additional options for trekking to Machu Picchu, some shorter, some longer than the old route. So if you fancy widening the perspective of how the Incas walked to their sacred city, ask your chosen tour operator to show you the alternatives.

Ins and outs

Getting there There are two ways to get to Machu Picchu. The easy way is by train from Cusco, Ollantaytambo or Urubamba, with a bus ride for the final climb from the rail terminus at Aguas Calientes to the ruins. The most rewarding way is to hike one of the Inca Trails (see page 117). 🖥️ ▶ *p142*.

Machu Picchu ruins

ⓘ *The site is open from 0700 to 1730. Entrance fee is US$20. It is possible to pay in dollars, but only clean, undamaged notes will be accepted. You cannot take backpacks into Machu Picchu; leave them at the entrance for US$0.50. Guides are available at the site, they are often very knowledgeable and worthwhile, and charge US$15 for 2½ hrs. See Top tips box on page 115.*

For centuries Machu Picchu was buried in jungle, until Hiram Bingham stumbled upon it in July 1911. It was then explored by an archaeological expedition sent by Yale University. Machu Picchu was a stunning find. The only major Inca site to escape 400 years of looting and destruction, it was remarkably well preserved. And it was no ordinary Inca settlement. It sat in an inaccessible location above the Urubamba Gorge, and contained so many fine buildings that people have puzzled over its meaning ever since.

Top tips

Seeing Machu Picchu

✅ Permission to enter the ruins before 0630 to watch the sunrise over the Andes, which is a spectacular experience, can be obtained from the Instituto Nacional de Cultura(INC) in Cusco, but it is often possible if you talk to the guards at the gate.

✅ The ruins are also quieter after 1530, but don't forget that the last bus down from the ruins leaves at 1730. Walking down to Aguas Calientes, if staying the night there, takes between 30 minutes and one hour.

✅ Many hotels in Aguas Calientes seem to have increased their prices sharply in recent years, perhaps in response to the rising costs of train services and excursions on the Inca Trail. You should bargain hard for good value.

❌ The climb up to Huayna Picchu is not for those with vertigo.

Once you have passed through the ticket gate you follow a path to a small complex of buildings which now acts as the main entrance to the ruins. It is set at the eastern end of the extensive terracing which must have supplied the crops for the city. Above this point, turning back on yourself, is the final stretch of the Inca Trail leading down from **Intipunku** (Sun Gate), see page 119. From a promontory here, on which stands the building called the **Watchman's Hut**, you get *the* perfect view of the city (the one you've seen on all the postcards), laid out before you with Huayna Picchu rising above the furthest extremity. The main path into the ruins comes to a dry moat that cuts right across the site. At the moat you can either climb the long staircase which goes to the upper reaches of the site, or you can enter by the baths and Temple of the Sun.

The more strenuous way into the site is by the former route, which takes you past quarries, on your left as you look down to the Urubamba on the west flank of the mountain. To your right are roofless buildings where you can see in close up the general construction methods used. Proceeding along this level, above the main plazas, you reach the **Temple of the Three Windows** and the **Principal Temple**, which has a smaller building called the **Sacristy**. The two main buildings are three-sided and were clearly of great importance, given the fine stonework involved. The wall with the three windows is built onto a single rock, one of the many instances where the architects did not merely put their construction on a convenient piece of land. They used and fashioned its features to suit their concept of how this sacred site should be tied to the mountain, its forces and the alignment of its stones to the surrounding peaks. In the Principal Temple, a diamond- shaped stone in the floor is said to depict the constellation of the Southern Cross.

Continue on the path behind the Sacristy to reach the **Intihuatana**, the 'hitching-post of the sun'. The name comes from the theory that such carved rocks (*gnomons*), found at all major Inca sites, were the point to which the sun was symbolically 'tied' at the winter solstice, before being freed to rise again on its annual ascent towards the summer solstice. The steps, angles and planes of this sculpted block appear to indicate a purpose beyond simple decoration and researchers have sought to define the trajectory of each alignment. Whatever the motivation behind this magnificent carving, it is undoubtedly one of the highlights of Machu Picchu.

Climb down from the Intihuatana's mound to the **Main Plaza**. Beyond its northern end is a small plaza with open-sided buildings on two sides and on the third, the **Sacred Rock**. The outline of this gigantic, flat stone echoes that of the mountains behind it. From here you can proceed to the entrance to the trail to Huayna Picchu (see below). Returning to the Main Plaza and heading southeast you pass, on your left, several groups of closely packed buildings which have been taken to be **Living Quarters and Workshops**, **Mortar Buildings** (look for the house with two discs let into the floor) and the **Prison Group**, one of whose constructions is known as the **Condor Temple**. Also in this area is a cave called **Intimachay**.

A short distance from the Condor Temple is the lower end of a series of **Ceremonial Baths** or fountains. They were probably used for ritual bathing and the water still flows down them today. The uppermost, **Principal Bath**, is the most elaborate. Next to it it is the **Temple of the Sun**, or Torreón. This singular building has one straight wall from which another wall curves around and back to meet the straight one, but for the doorway. From above it looks like an incomplete letter P. It is another example of the architecture being at one with its environment as the interior is taken up by the partly worked summit of the outcrop onto which the building is placed. All indications are that this temple was used for astronomical purposes. Underneath the Torreón a cave-like opening has been formed by an oblique gash in the rock. Fine masonry has been added to the opposing wall, making a second side of a triangle, which contrasts with the rough edge of the split rock. But the blocks of masonry appear to have been slotted behind another sculpted piece of natural stone, which has been cut into a four-stepped buttress. Immediately behind this is a two-stepped buttress. This strange combination of the natural and the man-made has been called the **Tomb or Palace of the Princess**. Across the stairway from the complex which includes the Torreón is the group of buildings known as the **Royal Sector**.

Synonymous with the ruins themselves is **Huayna Picchu** ⓘ *access 0700-1300, with the latest return time being 1500*, the verdant mountain overlooking the site. There are also ruins on the mountain itself, and steps to the top for a superlative view of the whole magnificent scene. The climb takes up to 90 minutes but the steps are dangerous after bad weather and you shouldn't leave the path. You must register at a hut at the beginning of the trail. The other trail to Huayna Picchu, down near the Urubamba, is via the Temple of the Moon, in two caves, one above the other, with superb Inca niches inside, sadly blemished by graffiti. To reach the **Temple of the Moon** from the path to Huayna Picchu, take the marked trail to the left; it is in good shape, but descends further than you think it should. After the Temple you may proceed to Huayna Picchu, but this path is overgrown, slippery when wet and has a

Machu Picchu - a sight to relieve tired legs at the end of the four-day Inca Trail.

Advice and information for the Inca trail

🕭 The new rules for trekking the Inca Trail are getting ever more complex and obstructive. If your heart is set on the classic trail, book as early as possible, even up to a year in advance, then confirm nearer the time.

🕭 Only a restricted number of agencies are licensed to operate Inca Trail trips. INRENA, Av José Gabriel Cosio 308, Urb Magisterial, 1 etapa, T084-229297, www.inrena.gob.pe, will verify operating permits. The INC website publishes the regulations and lists of licensed tour operators and guides: www.inc-cusco.gob.pe.

🕭 Other agencies will sell Inca Trail trips, but pass clients on to the operating agency. This can cause confusion and booking problems at busy times.

🕭 Up to date comments of the various tour operators can be found in the trip reports in the South America Explorers' clubhouse at Choquechaca 188 (for members only).

🕭 If you have any doubts about carrying your own pack, porters/guides are available through Cusco agencies.

🕭 Although security has improved in recent years, it's still best to leave all your valuables in Cusco and keep everything inside your tent, even your shoes.

🕭 Remove all your rubbish, including toilet paper, or use the pits provided. The Trail is closed each February for cleaning and repair.

🕭 In the dry season sandflies can be a problem, so take insect repellent and cover up.

🕭 Carry a day-pack, water and snacks in case you walk faster or slower than the porters and you have to wait for them to catch you up or you have to catch them up.

🕭 Take around US$30 extra per person for tips and a drink at the end of the trail.

✖ You are not allowed to walk back along the Inca Trail though you can pay US$4.50 at Intipunku to be allowed to walk back as far as Wiñay-Wayna.

✖ Avoid the July-August high season and the rainy season from November to April. In the wet it is cloudy and the paths are very muddy and difficult.

crooked ladder on an exposed part about 10 minutes before the top (not for the faint-hearted). It is safer to return to the main trail to Huayna Picchu, but this adds about 30 minutes to the climb. The round trip takes about four hours.

The Inca Trails

The wonder of Machu Picchu has been well documented over the years. Equally impressive is the centuries-old Inca Trail that winds its way from the Sacred Valley near Ollantaytambo, taking three to four days. What makes this hike so special is the stunning combination of Inca ruins, unforgettable views, magnificent mountains, exotic vegetation and extraordinary ecological variety. The government acknowledged all this in 1981 by including the trail in a

Porters are available for those not up to carrying their own backpack on the Inca Trail .

325 sq-km national park, the Machu Picchu Historical Sanctuary. Machu Picchu itself cannot be fully understood without the Inca Trail. Its principal sites are ceremonial in character, apparently in ascending hierarchical order. The trail is essentially a work of spiritual art, like a Gothic cathedral, and walking it was formerly an act of devotion.

Entrance tickets and tours An entrance ticket for the trail or its variations must be bought at the **Instituto Nacional de Cultura (INC)** office in Cusco; no tickets are sold at the entrance gates. Furthermore, tickets are only sold on presentation of a letter from a licensed tour operator on behalf of the visitor. There is a 50% discount for students, but note that officials are very strict, only an ISIC card will be accepted as proof of status. Tickets are checked at Km 82, Huayllabamba and Wiñay-Wayna. From Km 82 or Km 88 to Machu Picchu it costs US$50, students and children under 15 US$25. The **Camino Real de los Inkas**, from Km 104 to Machu Picchu, costs US$25, US$15 for students and children (or US$20 and US$10 respectively if you don't camp at Wiñay-Wayna).

Travel Agencies in Cusco arrange transport to the start, equipment, food, etc, for an all-in price. Prices vary from about US$200 to US$300 per person for a four day, three night trek. If the price is under US$180, you should be concerned as the company will be cutting corners and may not be paying the environment the respect the new rules were designed to instil. All the necessary equipment can be rented in Cusco. For a list of recommended agencies in Cusco, see page 135.

The route From Km 82, **Piscacucho**, or Km 88, **Qorihuayrachina**, at 2,600 m, it's a gentle start. The route from Km 88 goes via the village of **Huayllabamba**, a popular camping spot for tour groups though some continue up a steep climb for about an hour up to the next site. For most people the second day is by far the toughest. It's a steep climb to a flat meadow, followed by an exhausting 2½-hour haul up to the first pass – aptly named **Warmiwañusqa** (Dead Woman) – at 4,200 m. After a well-earned break it's a sharp descent on a treacherous path down to the Pacamayo Valley. Halfway up the second pass comes the ruin of **Runkuracay**, which was probably an Inca *tambo* (post-house). A steep climb up an Inca staircase leads to the next pass, at 3,850 m, with spectacular views of Pumasillo (6,246 m) and the Vilcabamba Range. The trail then descends to **Sayacmarca** (Inaccessible town), a spectacular site over the Aobamba Valley.

A blissfully gentle two-hour climb on a stone highway, leads through an Inca tunnel and along the enchanted fringes of the cloudforest, to the third pass. This is the most rewarding part of the trail, with spectacular views of the entire Vilcabamba Range. Then it's down to the extensive ruins of **Phuyupatamarca** (Cloud-level town), at 3,650 m, where Inca observation platforms offer awesome views of nearby Salkantay (6,270 m) and surrounding peaks. From here an Inca stairway of white granite plunges more than 1,000 m to the spectacularly sited and impressive ruins of **Wiñay-Wayna** (Forever Young), where, appropriately, there is a youth hostel. The last day starts from Wiñay-Wayna with a gentle hour's walk to a steep Inca staircase which leads up to **Intipunku** (Sun gate), where you look down, at last, upon Machu Picchu, basking in all her reflective glory. Your aching muscles will be quickly forgotten and even the presence of the functional hotel building cannot detract from one of the most magical sights in all the Americas.

A short Inca Trail, the **Camino Real de los Inkas**, is used by those who don't want to endure the full hike. It starts at Km 104, where a footbridge gives access to the ruins of Chachabamba and the trail ascends to the main trail at Wiñay-Wayna. Half way up is a good view of the ruins of Choquesuysuy. The first part is a steady, continuous three-hour ascent (take water) and the trail is narrow and exposed in parts. About 15 minutes before Wiñay-Wayna is a waterfall where fresh water can be obtained (best to purify it before drinking).

Aguas Calientes

Only 1½ km back along the railway from Puente Ruinas, this is a popular resting place for those recovering from the rigours of the Inca Trail. It is called Aguas Calientes (or just Aguas) after the hot springs above the town. It is also called the town of Machu Picchu. Most activity is centred around the old railway station, on the plaza, or on Avenida Pachacútec, which leads from the plaza to the thermal **baths** ⓘ *0500-2030. US$1.50*, which consist of a rather smelly communal pool, 10 minutes' walk from the town. You can rent towels and bathing costumes for US$0.65 at several places on the road to the baths. There are basic toilets and changing facilities and showers. Take soap and shampoo and keep an eye on your valuables.

⬤ Sleeping

Cusco *p102, maps p106 and p122*
AL **Casa Andina Plaza**, Portal Espinar 142, T084-231733, www.casa-andina.com. 1½ blocks from the plaza, this brand new hotel has 40 rooms with cable TV, bath, safe deposit box, heating, duvets on the beds and all the facilities common to this chain. Equally recommendable are the **Casa Andina Koricancha**, San Agustín 371, T084-252633, and the **Casa Andina Catedral**, Santa Catalina Angosta 149, T084-233661, both of which are in the same vein and price range.

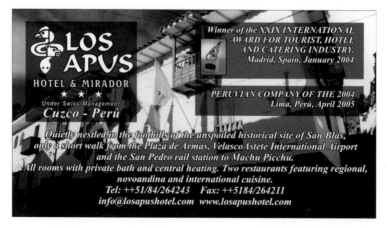

Top tips

Sleeping soundly

⊘ You should book more expensive hotels well in advance through a good travel agency, particularly for the week or so around Inti Raymi, when prices are much higher.

⊘ Also, prices in the mid to upper categories are often lower when booked through tour agencies.

⊘ Taxis and tourist minibuses meet arriving trains and take you to the hotel of your choice for US$0.50, but be insistent.

⊘ Nights are cold in Cusco and many hotels do not have heating. It is worth asking for an *estufa*, a heater, which some places will provide for an extra charge.

⊘ When staying in the big, popular hotels, allow yourself plenty of time to check out if you have a plane or train to catch: front desks can be very busy.

⊘ All the Cusco hotels listed here offer free luggage storage unless otherwise stated.

⊘ Assume hotels have 24-hr hot water in pre-heated tanks unless otherwise stated.

⊘ Cusco's low-power electric showers often do a poor job of heating the very cold water and their safety is sometimes questionable.

⊗ Be wary of unlicensed hotel agents for mid-priced hotels, they are often misleading about details; their local nickname is *jalagringos* (gringo pullers), or *piratas* (pirates).

AL Los Apus Hotel y Mirador, Atocsaycuchi 515 y Choquechaca, T084-264243, www.losapushotel.com. Price includes buffet breakfast and airport pick-up; laundry US$1 per kg. Swiss-owned, very clean and smart with beamed bedrooms fitted with cable TV and real radiators.

B Hostal Casa de Campo, Tandapata 296-B (at the end of the street), T084-244404, info@hotelcasadecampo.com. Price (10% discount for Footprint owners) includes continental breakfast and free airport/rail/bus transfer with reservations. Bedrooms have fabulous views but it's quite a climb to get to them! Safe deposit box, laundry service, meals on request and a sun terrace. Dutch and English spoken; take a taxi there after dark.

B Hostal El Arqueólogo, Pumacurco 408, T084-232569, reservation@ hotelarqueologo. com. Price includes buffet breakfast. Services include oxygen, a library and hot drinks. A colonial building on Inca foundations, this has rustic but stylish decor. Lovely sunny garden with comfy chairs and a small restaurant that serves interesting Peruvian food and fondue. French and English spoken. Also has tour agency.

B Hostal Rumi Punku, Choquechaca 339, T084-221102, www.rumipunku.com. A genuine Inca doorway leads to a sunny, tranquil courtyard. 20 large, clean, comfortable rooms, helpful staff and safe.

B Los Portales, Matará 322, T084-223500, reservas@portalescusco.com. Price includes continental breakfast and airport pick-up; ask for a heater at no extra charge. Safe deposit box, laundry (US $3 per kg), oxygen and a money exchange. Modern, friendly and helpful, children welcome.

B Pensión Loreto, Pasaje Loreto 115, Plaza de Armas (it shares the same entrance as Norton's Rat pub), T084-226352, hloreto@terra.com.pe. Price includes continental breakfast and a heater for the spacious rooms with original Inca walls. Great location; they will serve you breakfast in bed. Laundry service, will help organize travel services including guides and taxis, free airport pick-up.

C Hostal Amaru, Cuesta San Blas 541, T084-225933, www.cusco.net/amaru. (**D** without bathroom), price includes

breakfast and airport/train/bus pick-up. Services include oxygen, kitchen for use in the evenings only, laundry and free book exchange. Rooms around a pretty colonial courtyard, good beds, pleasant, relaxing, some Inca walls. Rooms in the first courtyard are best.

C Hostal María Esther, Pumacurco 516, T084-224382. Price includes continental breakfast; heating extra. This very friendly, helpful place has a lovely garden, lounge and a variety of rooms, car park.

C Marani, Carmen Alto 194, T084-249462, www.hostalmarani.com. Breakfasts

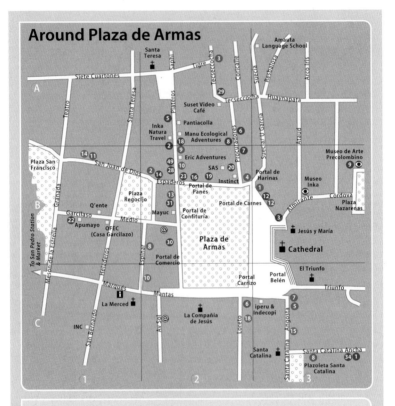

Around Plaza de Armas

| 50 metres |
| 50 yards |

Sleeping ⊜
Casa Andina Catedral **15** *C3*
Casa Andina Plaza **10** *C2*
Hostal Royal
  Frankenstein **14** *B1*
Pensión Loreto **18** *C2*
Sonesta Posada
  del Inca **8** *B2*

Eating ❼
Al Grano **1** *C3*
Ama Lur **2** *B2*

Auliya **22** *B1*
Ayllu **3** *B3*
Babieca **29** *A2*
Café Halliy **5** *A2*
Chez Maggy Clave de Do **6** *A2*
Chez Maggy El Corsario **7** *B2*
Chez Maggy La Antigua **8** *A2*
Deli **12** *B3*
El Encuentro **34** *C3*
Fallen Angel **9** *B3*
Inka Grill **16** *B2*
Kusikuy **18** *A2*
La Retama **19** *B2*
La Tertulia **20** *B2*
Café Amaru **49** *B2*
Pachacútec Grill & Bar **23** *B2*
Pucará **28** *B2*
Trotamundos **30** *B2*

Tunupa **31** *B2*
Varayoc **14** *B2*

Bars & clubs ❶
Blueberry Lounge **12** *B3*
Cross Keys Pub **13** *B2*
Excess **1** *B3*
Kamikaze **2** *B2*
Los Perros **3** *A2*
Mama Africa **4** *B2*
Mama América **5** *C3*
Norton Rat's Tavern **6** *C2*
Paddy Flaherty's **7** *C3*
Rosie O'Grady's &
  Sky Travel **8** *C3*
Spoon **5** *B2*
Tangible Myth **11** *B1*
Ukuku's **10** *B2*

MIRAFLORES PARK
HOTEL

ORIENT-EXPRESS HOTELS
TRAINS & CRUISES

Av. Malecón de la Reserva 1035, Miraflores
Lima 18 - Perú ☎ (51-1) 242-3000 / 610-4000
Fax: (51-1) 242-3393
E-mail: res-mirapark@peruorientexpress.com.pe
www.mira-park.com   www.orient-express.com

El Parador del Colca

Reservas / Oficinas Lima
T 242 3425 **F** 242 3365
E res-mirapark@peruorientexpress.com.pe

MACHU PICCHU
SANCTUARY LODGE

ORIENT-EXPRESS HOTELS
TRAINS & CRUISES

Carretera Hiram Bingham s/n
Ciudadela Machu Picchu Urubamba - Cusco
☎ (084) 211167 / 211039 / 211038 / 211052
Fax (084) 211053
E-mail: res-mapi@peruorientexpress.com.pe
www.monasterio.orient-express.com

HOTEL MONASTERIO

ORIENT-EXPRESS HOTELS
TRAINS & CRUISES

Calle Palacio 136, Plazoleta Nazarenas
Cusco - Perú ☎ (51 84) 241777
Fax: (51 84) 246983
E-mail: reservas@peruorientexpress.com.pe
www.monasterio.orient-express.com
The Leading Small Hotels of the World

ORIENT-EXPRESS HOTELS
TRAINS & CRUISES

www.orient-express.com

Budget busters

LL **El Monasterio**, Palacio 136, T084-241777, www.monasterio.orient-express.com. This 5-star, beautifully restored Seminary of San Antonio Abad is central and quite simply the best hotel in town for historical interest; it is worth a visit even if you cannot afford the price tag. Soft Gregorian chants follow you as you wander through the baroque chapel, tranquil courtyards and charming cloisters, admiring the excellent collection of religious paintings. Rooms have all facilities, including cable TV, some even offer an oxygen-enriched atmosphere to help clients acclimatize, for an additional fee of US$25. Staff, who all speak English, are very helpful and attentive. The price includes a great buffet breakfast (US$17 to non-residents) which will fill you up for the rest of the day. The restaurant serves lunch and dinner à la carte.

LL **Libertador**, in the Casa de los Cuatro Bustos at Plazoleta Santo Domingo 259, T084-231961, www.libertador.com.pe. Buffet breakfast is US$15 extra. This splendid 5-star, award-winning hotel is built on Inca ruins (the walls can be seen in the restaurant and bar) and is set around courtyards. It has 254 well-appointed rooms; the attention to detail is so great there are even Nazca Lines drawn in the sand of the ashtrays! Enjoy Andean music and dance over dinner in the excellent Inti Raymi restaurant.

available. Book exchange and information on Andean life and culture. Large rooms with heaps of character, set around a courtyard. The Hope Foundation (www.stichtinghope.org) operates here: Walter Meekes and his wife, Tineke, have built 20 schools in poor mountain villages and *barrios*, established a programme to teach teachers and set up a 30-bed burns unit in Cusco general hospital. Good value and a great cause.

C **Niños Hotel**, C Meloc 442, T084-231424, www.ninoshotel.com. Price does not include the excellent breakfast, which costs US$1.70-2.50. Services include the cafeteria and laundry service (US$1.15 per kg), Dutch, English, German and French spoken. Spotless, beautiful rooms in a 17th-century colonial house funding a fantastic charity established by Dutch couple, Titus and Jolande Bovenberg. Recently opened is the new Niños 2, on C Fierro, a little further from the centre, 20 nicely decorated, clean and airy rooms, surrounding the central courtyard.

C **Posada del Sol**, Atocsaycuchi 296, T084-246394. Includes American breakfast, heater and airport pick-up. Cheerfully decorated, sun terrace with great views, fantastic showers. Use of kitchen, laundry service, food is available. Cannot be reached by taxi.

D **El Arcano**, Carmen Alto 288, T084-232703. Breakfast and laundry available, cheaper rooms with shared bath. Lovely little communal area with comfortable seating and a small breakfast area with cable TV and a book exchange. Friendly owners will help arrange trips and own 2 lodges; one in the jungle and another in cloudforest.

D **Hostal Kuntur Wasi**, Tandapata 352-A, T084-227570. E without bath, services include a safe, use of the kitchen (for US$0.60 a day) and laundry. Great views from the terrace where you can breakfast. Very welcoming, helpful owners, a very pleasant place to stay.

D-E **Hostal Royal Frankenstein**, San Juan de Dios 260, 2 blocks from the Plaza de Armas, T084-236999, ludwig_roth@hotmail.com. This unforgettable place, with its ghoulish theme, has good services: fully equipped kitchen (just US$0.30 a day), cable TV in the living room, safe, laundry facilities, excellent mattresses but few rooms have outside windows. German owner.

E Hostal Familiar Mirador del Inka, Tandapata 160, off Plaza San Blas, T084-261384, miradordelinka @latinmail.com. This *hostal* looks very stylish with its Inca foundations and white colonial walls; completely redeveloped in 2003. Bedrooms with bath are spacious and some have great views. The owner's son Edwin runs trekking trips and has an agency on site.

E-F Maison de la Jeunesse, (affiliated to Hostelling International), Av Sol, Cuadra 5, Pasaje Grace, Edificio San Jorge (down a small side street opposite Qoricancha), T084-235617, elia25@msn.com. Price includes breakfast. Very friendly French/Peruvian-run hostel with a selection of dormitories and private rooms. TV and video room, cooking facilities and very hot water.

AL Royal Inca Pisac, Carretera Ruinas Km 1.5, T084-203064, royalin@terra.com.pe. It is a short distance out of town, on the road that goes up to the ruins, a taxi ride after dark. Price includes taxes and breakfast. Camping is available for US$5 per person. A guide for the ruins can be provided. The rooms are comfortable, in a number of blocks in the grounds of a converted hacienda; they are pleasantly furnished, with all conveniences. There is a pool, sauna and jacuzzi (US$7), tennis court, horse riding and bicycle rental. The restaurant is good and there is a bar. Staff are very helpful and accommodating.

E per person Ulrika's Hostal and Café, at the corner of Pardo, on the plaza in front of the church and marketplace, Casilla Postal 1179, Cusco, T084-203062, hotelpisaq@ terra.com.pe. There are 2 double rooms with bath in our **D** range. All others share bathrooms, which are spotless. Breakfast is US$2.50 extra (a bit more if you have eggs). Excellent brownies are on sale and pizza is served on Sun. There is hot water 24 hrs, pleasant decor, and a sauna. Friendly and knowledgeable staff who speak English, German and French.

Cusco & Southern Peru Cusco & the Sacred Valley Listings

Urubamba *p111*

AL Incaland Hotel and Conference Center, Av Ferrocarril s/n, 5 mins' walk from the centre, T084-201126, www.incalandperu.com. Special rates are also available. 65 comfortable, spacious bungalows set in extensive gardens, English-owned, good restaurant serving buffet meals, bar, disco, 2 pools, also horse riding (eg to Moray), mountain biking, kayaking and rafting. The staff are helpful and service is good.

B Perol Chico, Km 77 on the road to Ollantaytambo, office Grau 203, Casilla postal 59, Correo Central, Urubamba, T084-201694, stables T084-624475, www.perolchico.com. Dutch/Peruvian-owned, private bungalows with fireplace and kitchen on a ranch. Specializes in horse riding, 1- to 12-day trips out of Urubamba, 1-day trip to Moray and the salt pans costs US$60 (6 hrs).

D per person **Las Chullpas**, 3 km west of town in the Pumahuanca Valley, T084-976 1193, www.laschullpas.com. Very peaceful, includes excellent breakfast, vegetarian meals, English and German spoken, Spanish classes, natural medicine, treks, horse riding, mountain biking, camping US$3 with hot shower. Mototaxi from town US$0.85, taxi (ask for Querocancha) US$2.

D Macha Wasi, Jr Nicolás Barre, T084-201612, www.unsaac.edu.pe/machawasi. Canadian-owned guesthouse with comfortable rooms and a dormitory, delicious breakfast extra, safe, lovely garden, laundry. Spanish courses and treks can be arranged.

Ollantaytambo *p113*

AL Ñustayoc Mountain Lodge and Resort, about 5 km west of Ollantaytambo, just before Chillca and the start of the Inca Trail, T084-204098 or Lima T01-275 0706, www.nustayoclodge.com Large and somewhat rambling lodge in a wonderful location with great views of the snowy Verónica massif and other peaks. Lovely flower-filled garden and grounds. Nicely decorated, spacious rooms, all with private bath. Price includes continental breakfast served in the large restaurant area.

AL Pakaritampu, C Ferrocarril s/n, T084-204020, www.pakaritampu.com. The price includes breakfast and taxes. This modern, 3-star hotel has 20 rooms with bath and views. There is a TV room, restaurant and bar, internet service for guests, laundry, safe and room service. Adventure sports such as rafting, climbing, trekking, mountain biking and horse riding can be arranged. Meals are extra: buffet US$13, dinner US$12-15. Excellent quality and service.

C-D Albergue Kapuly, at the end of the station road, T084-204017. Prices are lower in the off season. A quiet place with spacious rooms, some with and some without bath. The garden is nice and the price includes a good continental breakfast.

D El Albergue Ollantaytambo, within the railway station gates, T084-204014, www.rumbosperu.com/elalbergue/. Owned by North American Wendy Weeks, the *albergue* has 8 rooms with shared bathrooms. Price (per person) includes breakfast; box lunch costs US$4, full dinner US$7 on request. The rooms are full of character and are set in buildings around a courtyard and lovely gardens. Great showers (24 hrs a day) and a eucalyptus steam sauna (US$5). The whole place is charming, very relaxing and homely. It's very convenient for the Machu Picchu train and good place for information. Private transport can be arranged to the salt mines, Moray, Abra Málaga for birdwatching and taxi transfers to Cusco airport.

E Hostal Chaskawasi, Chaupicalle (also C Taypi) north of the plaza, T084-208085, anna_machupicchu@hotmail.com. New *hostal* hidden in the small alleys behind the plaza. Owner Anna is very friendly.

Budget busters

LL Machu Picchu Sanctuary Lodge, under the same management as the Hotel Monasterio in Cusco, T084-2111167, www.monasterio.orient-express.com. This hotel, at the entrance to the ruins, was completely refurbished in 2001 and has included some environmentally friendly features. They will accept American Express TCs at the official rate. The rooms are comfortable, the service is good and the staff helpful. Electricity and water are available 24 hrs a day. Food in the restaurant is well cooked and presented; the restaurant is for residents only in the evening, but the buffet lunch is open to all. The hotel is usually fully booked well in advance; if struggling for a booking try Sun night as other tourists find Pisac Market a greater attraction.

LL Machu Picchu Pueblo Hotel, Km 110. Reservations: Jr Andalucia 174, San Isidro, Lima, T01-6100404; in Cusco at Plaza las Nazarenas 211, T084-245314, www.inkaterra.com. Beautiful colonial-style bungalows have been built in a village compound surrounded by cloudforest 5 mins' walk along the railway from the town. The hotel has lovely gardens in which there are many species of birds, butterflies and orchids. There is a pool, an expensive restaurant, but also a campsite with hot showers at good rates. It offers tours to Machu Picchu, several guided walks on the property and to local beauty spots. The buffet breakfasts for US$12 are great. It also has the Café Amazónico by the railway line. The hotel is involved in a project to rehabilitate spectacled bears, and re-release them back into the wild. Recommended, but there are a lot of steps between the public areas and rooms.

E Hostal La Ñusta, C Ocobamba, T084-204035. Ask about accommodation in the shop/restaurant of the same name on the plaza or in the **Pizzería Gran Tunupa**. This is a decent although uninspiring budget option. Proprietor Rubén Ponce loves to share his knowledge of the ruins with guests. You get a good view of the ruins from the balcony. Also has restaurant.

F Hostal Chuza, just below the main plaza in town, T084-204113. Very clean and friendly with safe motorcycle parking. They have a TV in the front room for guests and one of the rooms features a wonderful view of the ruins with the Nevado de Verónica framed perfectly behind – a wonderful sight to wake up to in the morning.

Aguas Calientes *p119*

B Gringo Bill's (Hostal Q'oñi Unu), Colla Raymi 104, T084-211046, gringobills @yahoo. com. Price includes bathroom and continental breakfast. An Aguas Calientes institution, it's friendly, relaxed, with a lot of coming-and-going, hot water, good beds, luggage store, laundry and money exchange. Good but expensive meals are served in **Villa Margarita** restaurant; breakfast starts at 0530; US$4 packed lunch to take up to the ruins.

B La Cabaña, Av Pachacútec M20-3, T084-211048. Price includes bathroom and continental breakfast. Rooms have hot water. There is a café, laundry service and a DVD player and TV (with a good selection of movies) for clients in the lounge. The staff are helpful and can provide information on interesting local walks. The hotel is popular with groups.

C Hostal Machu Picchu, at the old station, T084-211212. Price includes breakfast and taxes. A clean, functional establishment, quiet and friendly (especially Wilber, the owner's son). There is hot water, a nice balcony over the Urubamba, a grocery store and travel information is available.

C Rupa Wasi, C Huanacaure 180, T084-211101, www.rupawasi.org. Rustic and charming 'eco-lodge', located up a small alley off Collasuyo. The lodge and its owners have a very laid-back, comfortable style, and there are great views from the balconies of the first floor rooms. Great breakfasts for US$3.

C-D Jardín Real, C Wiracocha 7, T084-211234, jardinrealhotel @hotmail.com. A clean, modern hotel with good hot water. At the unofficial price this hotel represents great value, so bargain hard. Same owner as **Pizzería Los Jardines** on Pachacútec.

D Hostal Pachakúteq, up the hill beyond Hotel La Cabaña, T084-211061. Rooms with bathroom and 24-hr hot water. Good breakfast is included, quiet, family-run.

D Hospedaje Quilla, Av Pachacútec, T084-211009, between Wiracocha and Túpac Inka Yupanki. Price includes breakfast, bath and hot water. They rent bathing gear for the hot springs if you arrive without your costume and towel.

D Hostal Wiracocha Inn, C Wiracocha, T084-211088. Rooms with bath and hot water. Breakfast included. There is a small garden at this very friendly and helpful *hostal*. It's popular, particularly with European groups.

🍴 Eating

Cusco *p102, maps p106 and p122*
Procuradores (Gringo Alley) and Plateros lead off the northwest side of the Plaza de Armas. Procuradores, or Gringo Alley as the locals call it, is good for a value feed and takes the hungry backpacker from Mexico to Italy, to Spain and Turkey with its menus. None is dreadful, many

are very good indeed, especially for the price; do not be too worried if a tout drags you into one (demand your free *pisco sour*) before you've reached the restaurant you have chosen from the list here. Parallel with Gringo Alley but further southwest, Plateros also has good-value places to eat. It is also lined with a great many tour operators, so you can wander up and down checking what deals are on offer. Many of the more upmarket restaurants are serving *Novo Andino* cuisine, which uses native ingredients and 'rescued' recipes.

Fallen Angel, Plazoleta Nazarenas 221, T084-258184, fallenangelincusco@hotmail. com. Under the same ownership as **Macondo** (see below), this is an art gallery like nowhere else that just happens to serve great food, in an original *conquistador* residence. The menu features steaks of a quality to equal any in Peru, and there are some innovative pasta dishes. Cocktails are excellent. Regular parties/fashion shows are always events to remember.

Inka Grill, Portal de Panes 115, T084-262992, 1000-2400 (Sun 1200-2400). According to many the best food in town is served here, specializing in *Novo Andino* cuisine and innovative dishes, also home-made pastas, wide vegetarian selection, live music, excellent coffee and home-made pastries 'to go'. A good place to spoil yourself.

La Retama, Portal de Panes 123, 2nd floor. Excellent *Novo Andino* food and service. Try the mouth-watering trout sashimi as a starter followed by steak. Also a balcony, an enthusiastic music and dance group and art exhibitions.

Pachacútec Grill and Bar, Portal de Panes 105. International cuisine including seafood and Italian specialities, also features folk music shows nightly. Excellent value quality *menú* for just US$2.50.

Tunupa, Portal Confiturías 233, 2nd floor (same entrance as Cross Keys). One of the finest restaurants on the plaza (often used by tour groups). Also has the longest (glassed-in) balcony but this is narrow and best for couples only. Food is international, traditional and *Novo Andino*; wine list, as everywhere in Cusco, is limited. Also an excellent buffet for US$15 including a *pisco sour* and a hot drink. In the evenings there is an excellent group playing 16th and 17th-century-style *Cusqueñan* music of their own composition accompanied by dancers.

Al Grano, Santa Catalina Ancha 398, T084-228032, 1000-2100, closed on Sun. Lunchtime menu US$2.15 is a good option if you are fed up with other menus. In the evening they serve 5 authentic Asian dishes for US$5.50, menu changes daily. Without doubt some of the best coffee in town, vegetarian choices and breakfasts, including a 'Full English'.

Greens, Tandapata 700, behind the church on Plazoleta San Blas, T084-243820, greens_cusco@hotmail.com. Open 0700-2300. Modern international food in warm and relaxed setting with sofas to kick back in while sipping wine and reading English magazines. Famous for huge roasts (Sun, US$10, booking essential) as well as English breakfasts (0700-1500) and curries. Vegetarian options. Desserts and toasted sandwiches available 1500-1830. Games, book exchange and library.

Jack's Café, on the corner of Choquechaca and San Blas. T084-806960. Opens at 0630. Excellent varied menu with generous portions, all in a light and relaxed atmosphere. Great American-style pancakes and freshly ground local coffee. Lunchtime can be very busy.

Kusikuy, Plateros 348B, T084-262870. 0800-2300 Mon-Sat. Some say this place serves the best *cuy* (guinea pig) in town and the owners say if you give them an hour's warning they will produce their absolute best. Many other typical Cusco dishes on the menu. Set lunch is unbeatable value at only US$2. Good service, live music.

La Bodega, Carmen Alto 146. Snug Dutch- and Peruvian-owned café/restaurant serving hot chocolate by candlelight in the afternoons, evening meals - dishes come with side trip to salad bar, American breakfast and a US$1.50 lunch menu.

Macondo, Cuesta San Blas 571, T084-229415, macondo@ telser.com.pe. Bit pricier than others in this range but fantastic. A casual, cosy, arty and comfortable restaurant with sofas of iron bedsteads covered in dozens of cushions mixed with chairs, tables and candles. Walls are decorated with local art. Popular, gay-friendly and a steep 3-block walk from the central plaza. Dishes of local ingredients with an artistic twist.

Pachapapa, Plazoleta San Blas 120, opposite church of San Blas, T084-241318. Open 1000-2200. A beautiful patio restaurant in a wonderful old colonial house, under same ownership as Inka Grill. Very good Cusqueña dishes, including *pachamanca* (previous reservation required for 6 people). At night diners can sit in their own, private colonial dining room.

Pucará, Plateros 309. 1230-2200, closed Sun. Peruvian and international food. Japanese owner does very good US$2 set lunch, pleasant atmosphere.

Varayoc, Espaderos 142, T084-232404. Open daily 0800-2400. Swiss-owned restaurant including Peruvian ingredients (the only place in Cusco that serves cheese fondue). Also has a variety of pastas, good desserts, 'tea time' beverage and pastry for US$2.80 accompanied by Andean harp music. Pleasant, literary atmosphere.

Witches Garden, Carmen Bajo 169, just off Plazoleta San Blas, T084-9623866, witchesgardenrestaurant @hotmail.com. Good *Novo Andino* and international cuisine served in this warmly decorated little restaurant. There is a TV and video, with a selection of movies, available for patrons.

Ama Lur, Plateros 325. This is the restaurant below **Amalu** where you go for breakfast. Clean, cheap, very good set

Cusco & Southern Peru Cusco & the Sacred Valley Listings

menu for US$2 as well as tasty evening meals.

¶ **Auliya**, C Garcilaso 265, 2nd floor. Beautifully renovated colonial house, excellent vegetarian food, also stocks a wide range of dried food for trekking.

¶ **Babieca**, Tecseccocha 418, T084-221122. Walk to the top of Procuradores, turn left and this place is on the corner opposite the **Sunset Video Bar**. Serves excellent pizzas with light, crispy bases and a varied selection of menus ranging from US$2-6. Cosy decor and efficient service.

¶ **Chez Maggy**, has 3 branches: La Antigua (the original) at Procuradores 365 and, on the same street, **El Corsario** No 344 and **Clave de Do** No 374 (opens at 0700 for buffet breakfast). Hotel delivery T084-234861. All have good atmosphere, serving pizzas freshly baked in a wood-burning oven, pastas, Mexican food and soups. All are popular.

¶ **El Encuentro**, Santa Catalina Ancha 384. One of the best-value eateries in Cusco, 3 courses of good healthy food and a drink will set you back US$1.

Cafés and delis

Ayllu, Portal de Carnes 208, to the left of the cathedral. Probably one of the oldest cafés in Cusco and a great place to go. Fantastic breakfasts (have the special fruit salad, US$2.30), sandwiches, coffee and classical music as well as wonderful apple pastries. Very much a local venue with superb service.

Café Amaru, Plateros 325, 2nd floor. Limitless coffee, tea, great bread and juices served, even on non-buffet breakfasts (US$1.15 for simple). Colonial balcony.

Café Halliy, Plateros 363. Popular meeting place, especially for breakfast, good for comments on guides, has good snacks and *copa Halliy* (fruit, muesli, yoghurt, honey) and chocolate cake, also good vegetarian menu and set lunch.

La Tertulia, Procuradores 50, 2nd floor. Breakfast, served 0630-1400, includes

muesli, bread, yoghurt, eggs, juice and coffee, eat as much as you like for US$3, superb value, book exchange, newspapers, classical music.

Planet Cusco, Carmen Alto 162, T084-223010. Great buffet breakfast in a warm, stylish atmosphere for only US$1.40, plus 10 mins free internet.

The Deli, Portal de Carnes 236, next to the Blueberry Lounge. This is closest you'll get in Peru to a European delicatessen, and very nice it is too! Great salad bar, good takeaway including sandwiches, pricey, but worth it.

The Muse, Tandapata 682, Plazoleta San Blas. Funky little café with a cosy feel and great views over the plaza. Fresh coffee, good food, including vegetarian lasagne, chicken curry and carrot cake. There's often live music in the afternoons and evenings with no cover charge. English owner Clair is very helpful. **The Muse** will refill water bottles for a small charge in an attempt to minimize plastic waste in Cusco.

Trotamundos, Portal Comercio 177, 2nd floor. Open Mon-Sat 0800-2400. One of the most pleasant cafés in the plaza if a bit pricey. Has a balcony overlooking the plaza and a warm atmosphere especially at night with its open fire. Good coffees and cakes, safe salads, *brochetas*, sandwiches and pancakes as well as 4 computers with internet access.

Pisac *p111*

¶ **Doña Clorinda**, on the plaza opposite the church, doesn't look very inviting but cooks tasty food, including vegetarian options. A very friendly place.

Urubamba *p111*

¶¶¶ **Tunupa**, on left side of the road on the riverbank, in a new, colonial-style hacienda (same ownership as Tunupa in Cusco), zappa@ terra.com.pe. Excellent food served indoors or outdoors, bar, lounge, library, chapel, gardens, stables and an alpaca-jewellery shop. Outstanding exhibition of pre-Columbian objects and colonial paintings, and **Seminario's** ceramics feature in the decor. Lunch and dinner (1800-2030) is available daily.

La Casa de la Abuela, Bolívar 272, 2 blocks up from the Plaza de Armas, T084-622975. Excellent restaurant with rooms grouped around a small courtyard. The trout is fantastic and food is served with baskets of roasted potatoes and salad.

El Maizal, on the road before the bridge, T084-201454. Country-style restaurant with a good reputation, buffet service with a variety of typical *Novo Andino* dishes, plus international choices, beautiful gardens with native flowers and fruit trees.

Pintacha, Bolognesi 523. Pub/café serving sandwiches, burgers, coffees, teas and drinks. Has games and book exchange, cosy, open till late.

Pizzonay, Av Mcal Castilla, 2nd block. Pizzas, excellent spinach ravioli (not so good lasagne). Mulled wine served in a small restaurant with nice decor. Clean, good value.

Ollantaytambo *p113*

Il Cappuccino, just before the bridge on the right-hand side. Offers the best cappuccino in town, great coffee generally, also café latte and expresso. Good continental and American breakfasts. Slightly more sophisticated ambience and service in comparison with many other establishments in town.

Mayupata, Jr Convención s/n, across the bridge on the way to the ruins, on the left, T084-204083 (Cusco). Serving international choices and a selection of Peruvian dishes, desserts, sandwiches and coffee. It opens at 0600 for breakfast, and serves lunch and dinner. The bar has a fireplace; river view, relaxing atmosphere.

Alcázar Café, C del Medio s/n, 50 m from the plaza, T084-204034, alcazar@ollantaytambo.org. Vegetarian restaurant, also offering fish and meat dishes, pasta specialities. Offers excursions to traditional Andean communities.

Bahía, on the east side of the plaza. Very friendly, vegetarian dishes served on request.

Aguas Calientes *p119*

Pizza seems to be the most common dish in town, but many of the pizzerías serve other types of food as well. The old station and Av Pachútec are lined with eating places. At the station (where staff will try to entice you into their restaurant), are, among others: **Aiko**, which is recommended; **La Chosa Pizzería**, with pleasant atmosphere, good value; **Las Quenas**, which is a café and a baggage store (US$0.30 per locker); and 2 branches of **Pizzería Samana Wasi**. See also under Sleeping, above.

Café Inkaterra, on the railway, just below the Machu Picchu Pueblo Hotel. US$15 for a great lunch buffet with scenic views of the river.

Indio Feliz, C Lloque Yupanqui, T084-211090. Great French cuisine, excellent value and service, set 3-course meal for US$10, good *pisco sours*.

Inka's Pizza Pub, on the plaza. Good pizzas, changes money and accepts TCs.

Toto's House, Av Imperio de los Incas, on the railway line. Same owners as **Pueblo Viejo**. Good value and quality *menú*.

Govinda, Av Pachacútec y Túpac Inka Yupanki. Vegetarian restaurant with a cheap set lunch.

Inka Machu Picchu, Av Pachacútec 122. Another good place on the avenue. The menu includes vegetarian options.

Inti Killa, Av Imperio de los Incas 47. Good-value *menú* with excellent food and plenty of it. Credit cards accepted.

☻ Bars and clubs

Cusco *p102, maps p106 and p122*
Bars

Blueberry Lounge, Portal de Carnes 235, T084-742472. Dark, moody and sophisticated, this is a slice of London's Soho on the Plaza de Armas. There's a good menu, featuring many Asian dishes.

Cross Keys Pub, Portal Confiturías 233 (upstairs). 1100-0130. Run by Barry Walker of **Manu Expeditions**, a Mancunian and

Top tips

On the house

● Before your evening meal, collect the flyers being handed out around the Plaza de Armas. Then, over dinner, you should work out your free drink circuit – for each coupon not only gives you free entry, it is worth a *cuba libre*.

● During your subsidized tour of the clubs you can check out which is the 'in' place to be that week – they are constantly changing.

● If you fancy learning a few Latin dance steps before hitting the dancefloor, many of the clubs offer free lessons. Ask at the door for details or look out for flyers.

ornithologist, darts, cable sports, pool, bar meals, happy hours 1830-1930 and 2130-2230, plus daily half price specials Sun-Wed, great *pisco sours*, very popular, loud and raucous, great atmosphere.

Km 0 (Arte y Tapas), Tandapata 100, San Blas. Lovely Mediterranean-themed bar tucked in behind San Blas. Good snacks and tapas (of course), affordable, and with live music every night (around 2200 – lots of acoustic guitar, etc).

Los Perros Bar, Tecseccocha 436, above Gringo Alley (Procuradores). A great place to chill out on comfy couches listening to excellent music. There's a book exchange, English and other magazines and board games. Opens 1100 for coffee and pastries; kitchen opens at 1300. Occasionally hosts live music and special events.

Mandela's Bar, Palacios 121, 3rd floor, T084-222424, www.mandelasbar.com. Contemporary bar/restaurant with an African theme. Good atmosphere and lots of space to spread out and relax. Serves breakfast, lunch and drinks in the evening, also barbecues on Sun and special events through the year. Great 360° panorama from the rooftop.

Norton Rat's Tavern, Loreto 115, 2nd floor, on the plaza but has a side entrance off a road to the left of La Compañía (same entrance as Hostal Loreto), T084-246204, nortonrats@yahoo.com. Pleasant pub with a pool table, dart board, cable TV and lots of pictures of motorbikes. There's a balcony which

offers great views of the Plaza de Armas. Also has a juice bar serving Amazonian specials. Happy hour 1900-2100 every night with other daily specials.

Paddy Flaherty's, C Triunfo 124 on the corner of the plaza, 1300-0100. An Irish theme pub, deservedly popular, with great food (jacket potatoes, shepherd's pie, etc).

Rosie O'Grady's, at Santa Catalina Ancha 360, T084-247935. Open 1100 till late (food served till 2400, happy hours 1300-1400, 1800-1900, 2300-2330). Has good music, tasty food.

Clubs

Excess, on Suecia, next door to Magtas Bar (see below). An old Cusco staple. Movies are shown in the late afternoon and early evening, but after midnight this place really gets going with an extremely eclectic range of music, from 60s and 70s rock and pop to techno and trance. This place seems to give out more free drinks than most, so it's a good option for kicking off a big night on the town!

Kamikaze, Plaza Regocijo 274, T084-233865. Peña at 2200, good old traditional rock music, candle-lit cavern atmosphere, entry US$2.50 but usually you don't have to pay.

Mama, Portal Belén 115, 2nd floor. The mother of all clubs in Cusco, **Mama Africa**, has become 2 separate entities: **Mama América** is decorated in a jungle theme, with a dancefloor and a large video screen, although people dance anywhere they can. The music is middle of the road, from local music through 70s classics to the latest releases. **Mama Africa** now resides in the Portal de Harinas, 2nd floor. It claims to have cooler music and be more of a serious clubber's spot. It also serves good food from a varied menu, happy hour till 2300, good value and friendly.

Spoon, Plateros 334, 2nd floor, spoonclub@ peru.com. 2000-0500. This joint tends to play more hard-core dance, trance and techno tunes than other nightspots, but it still verges into hip-hop and funk on occasion. Happy hour 2300-2400.

Tangible Myth, San Juan de Dios 260 (on the 2nd floor, next to Hostal Frankenstein), T084-260519. Live jazz, sometimes edging into funk and Latin rhythms, Mon to Sat, usually warming up at around 2100. This is a great place to enjoy a relaxed night out.

Ukuku's, Plateros 316. US$1.35 entry or free with a pass. This is somewhat different to the other clubs as every night there is a live band that might play anything from rock to salsa. The DJ then plays a mixture of Peruvian and international music but the emphasis is on local. It has a good mix of Cusqueños and tourists. Happy hour 0730-0930.

⊙ Entertainment

Cusco *p102, maps p106 and p122*
Centro Qosqo de Arte Nativo, Av Sol 604, T084-227901. There's a regular nightly folklore show here 1900-2030, entrance on the BTU visitors' ticket.

Sunset Video Café, inside Hostal Royal Qosqo, turn left at the top of Gringo Alley. Shows 3 films a day: 1600, 1900, 2130. It has good sound and you can order popcorn and other snacks while you watch. US$0.70.

Teatro Inti Raymi, Saphi 605. Music nightly at 1845, US$4.50 entry and well worth it.

⊙ Festivals and events

Cusco *p102*
Carnival in Cusco is a messy affair with flour, water, cacti, bad fruit and animal manure thrown about in the streets. Be prepared. **Easter Mon** sees the procession of **El Señor de los Temblores** (Lord of the Earthquakes), starting at 1600 outside the cathedral. A large crucifix is paraded through the streets, returning to the Plaza de Armas around 2000 to bless the tens of thousands of people who have assembled there. On **2-3 May** the **Vigil of the Cross**, which takes place at all mountaintops with crosses on them, is a boisterous affair.

In **Jun** is **Corpus Christi**, on the Thu after Trinity Sunday, when all the statues of the Virgin and of Saints from Cusco's churches are paraded through the streets to the cathedral. This is a colourful event. The Plaza de Armas is surrounded by tables with women selling *cuy* (guinea pig) and a mixed grill called *chiriuchu* (*cuy*, chicken, tortillas, fish eggs, water-weeds, maize, cheese and sausage) and lots of Cusqueña beer. In **early Jun**, 2 weeks before Inti Raymi (see box on next page) is the highly recommended **Cusqueño Beer Festival**, held near the rail station, which boasts a great variety of Latin American music. The whole event is well-organized and great fun.

Also in **Jun** is Qoyllur Rit'i (Snow Star Festival), held at a 4,700-m glacier north of Ocongate (Ausangate), 150 km southeast of Cusco. It has its final day 58 days after Easter Sun. To get there involves a two hour walk up from the nearest road at Mawayani, beyond Ocongate, then it's a further exhausting climb up to the glacier. It's a good idea to take a tent, food and plenty of warm clothing. Many trucks leave Cusco, from Limacpampa, in the days prior to the full moon in mid-Jun; prices from US$2 upwards. This is a very rough and dusty overnight journey lasting 14 hrs, requiring warm clothing and coca leaves to fend off cold and exhaustion. Several agencies offer tours (see p135).

On the **last Sun in Aug** is the **Huarachicoy Festival** at Sacsayhuaman, a spectacular re-enactment of the Inca manhood rite, performed in dazzling costumes by boys of a local school. On **8 Sep**, the **Day of the Virgin**, there is a colourful procession of masked dancers from the church of Almudena, at the southwest edge of Cusco, near Belén, to the Plaza de San Francisco. There is also a fair at Almudena, and a bull fight on the following day.

Urubamba *p111*

May and **Jun** are the harvest months, with many processions following mysterious ancient schedules. Urubamba's main festival, **El Señor de Torrechayoc**, takes place during the first week of Jun.

Ollantaytambo *p113*

On **6 Jan** there is the **Bajada de Reyes Magos** (the Magi), with traditional dancing, a bull fight, local food and a fair. **End May-early Jun**: Pentecostes, 50 days after Easter, is the **Fiesta del Señor de Choquekillca**, patron saint of Ollantaytambo. There are several days of dancing, weddings, processions, masses, feasting and drinking (the last opportunity to see traditional Cusqueño dancing). On **29 Jun**, following Inti Raymi in Cusco, there is a colourful festival, the **Ollanta-Raymi**, at which the Quechua drama, *Ollantay*, is re-enacted. **29 Oct** is the **Aniversario de Ollantaytambo**, a festival with dancing in traditional costume and many local delicacies for sale.

⚪ Shopping

Cusco *p102, maps p106 and p122*
Camping equipment
There are several places on Plateros which rent out equipment but check it carefully as it is common for parts to be missing.

An example of prices per day: tent US$3-5, sleeping bag US$2 (down), US$1.50 (synthetic), stove US$1. A deposit of US$100 is asked, plus credit card, passport or plane ticket. You can also rent equipment through travel agencies. **Soqllaq'asa Camping Service**, Plateros 365 No 2F, T084-252560. Owned by English-speaking Sra Luzmila Bellota Miranda, is recommended for equipment hire, from down sleeping bags (US$2 per day) to gas stoves (US$1 per day) and **ThermaRest** mats (US$1 per day); pots, pans, plates, cups and cutlery are all provided free by the friendly staff. They also buy and sell camping gear and make alpaca jackets, open Mon-Sat 0900-1300, 1600-2030, Sun 1800-2030.

Handicrafts
Cusco has some of the best craft shopping in all Peru. In the Plaza San Blas and the surrounding area, authentic Cusco crafts still survive and woodworkers can be seen in almost any street. A market is held on Sat. In its drive to 'clean up' Cusco, the authorites have moved the colourful artisans' stalls from the pavements of Plaza Regocijo to the main market at the bottom of **Av Sol**. There are, however, small markets dotted around the city which offer goods made from alpaca as well as modern materials. Cusco is also the weaving centre of Peru and excellent textiles can be found at good value; but watch out for sharp practices when buying gold and silver objects and jewellery.
Agua y Tierra, Plazoleta Nazarenas 167, and also at Cuesta San Blas 595, T084-226951. Excellent quality crafts from lowland rainforest communities, largely the Shipibo and Ashaninka tribes from the Selva Central whose work is considered to be among the finest in the Amazon Basin.
Center for Traditional Textiles of Cusco, Av Sol 603-A, T084-228117, www.incas.org. A non-profit organization that promotes the weaving traditions of

Background

Inti Raymi

On **24 June** is one of Peru's biggest celebrations, Inti Raymi, the Inca festival of the winter solstice, which takes place at the fortress of Sacsayhuaman. The spectacle starts at 1000 at the Qoricancha, then proceeds to the Plaza de Armas. From there performers and spectators go to Sacsayhuaman for the main event, which starts at 1300. It lasts 2½ hours and is in Quechua. Locals make a great day of it, watching the ritual from the hillsides and cooking potatoes in pits in the ground. Tickets for the stands can be bought in advance from the Emufec office, Santa Catalina Ancha 325 (opposite the Complejo Policial), and cost US$35. Standing places on the ruins are free but get there at about 1030 as even reserved seats fill up quickly, and defend your space. Travel agents can arrange the whole day for you, with meeting points, transport, reserved seats and packed lunch. Don't believe anyone who tries to persuade you to buy a ticket for the right to film or take photos. On the night before Inti Raymi, the Plaza de Armas is crowded with processions and food stalls. Try to arrive in Cusco before Inti Raymi. The atmosphere in the town during the build up is fantastic and something is always going on (festivals, parades, etc).

the area. Tours of workshops in Chinchero and beyond can be arranged, also weaving classes. In the Cusco outlet you can watch weavers at work. Excellent quality textiles at prices reflecting the fact that over 50% goes direct to the weaver.

Josefina Olivera, Portal Comercio 173, Plaza de Armas. She sells old ponchos and antique *mantas* (shawls), without the usual haggling. Her prices are high, but it is worth it to save pieces being cut up to make other items, open daily 1100-2100.

Markets

San Jerónimo, just out of town, is the new location of the wholesale Sat morning fruit and vegetable market, but food just as good and not much more expensive (and washed) can be bought at the markets in town: **Huanchac**, Av Garcilaso (not to be confused with C Garcilaso), or **Santa Ana**, opposite Estación San Pedro, which sells a variety of goods. The best

value is at closing time or in the rain. Take care after dark. Sacks to cover rucksacks are available in the market for US$0.75. Both Huanchac and Santa Ana open every day from 0700.

▲ Activities and tours

Cusco *p102, maps p106 and p122*
There are a million and one tour operators in Cusco, most of them around the Plaza de Armas. The sheer number and variety of tours on offer is bewildering and prices for the same tour can vary dramatically. You should only deal directly with the agencies and seek advice from visitors returning from trips for the latest information. For Manu and Tambopata, see p213.

Amazonas Explorer, Av Collasuyo 910, Miravalle, PO Box 722, Cusco, T084-252846, 084-976 5448 (mob), www.amazonas-explorer.com. T01437-891743 in UK. Experts in rafting, hiking, biking and multi-activity tours. English owner Paul Cripps has great experience, but takes most bookings from

Budget buster

Extravagance amongst the ruins

If you are looking for something really special and, let's face it, expensive with a capital E, take the *Hiram Bingham* train service from Cusco to Machu Picchu. Named after the American explorer who uncovered the Incas' `lost' citadel, it is the height of luxury and costs US$476 return (in 2005). While the train climbs out of Cusco and heads for the Sacred Valley, you take breakfast. Once at Aguas Calientes you are whisked up by bus to the Machu Picchu Sanctuary Lodge for lunch. The afternoon is taken up with a private guided tour of Machu Picchu before an early evening return to town. On the 3½-hour journey back to Cusco, you are served cocktails and dinner, with live entertainment.

overseas. However, he may be able to arrange a trip for travellers in Cusco.
Apumayo, C Garcilaso 265 interior 3, T084-246018 (Lima: T01-444 2320), www.apumayo.com. Mon-Sat 0900-1300, 1600-2000. Rafting on the Urubamba and the Apurímac. Also mountain biking and treks. This company also offers tours for disabled people, including rafting.
Ch'aska, Plateros 325, p 2, T084-240424, www.chaskatours.com. A Dutch-Peruvian owned company offering cultural, adventure, nature and esoteric tours. Specialize in the Inca Trail, but also llama treks to Lares, and other major treks (their Choquequirao trip is recommended). They can tailor tours throughout Peru.

Ecotrek Peru, Totorapaccha 769, San Blas, T084-247286, T976 2162 (mob), www.ecotrekperu.com. (The office is above San Blas, to the left of the plaza, on a Royal Inca trail.) Scot and long-time Cusco resident Fiona Cameron runs this environmentally friendly tour agency; she is often involved in river clean-ups in the area. Tour specialities currently focus on adventurous mountain biking trips in remote highland areas and jungle expeditions (see box p217).
Eric Adventures, Plateros 324, T084-228475, www.ericadventures.com. Specialize in adventure activities, rafting, mountain biking, also rent motorcross bikes. They clearly explain what equipment is included in their prices and what you will need to bring. Prices are

higher if you book by email, you can get huge discounts if you book in the office. A popular company.

Explorandes, Av Garcilaso 316-A (not to be confused with C Garcilaso in the centre), T084-245700, www.explorandes.com. Experienced high-end adventure company. Their main office is in Lima, but trips can also be arranged from Cusco. Award-winning environmental practices.

Instinct, Procuradores 50, T084-233451, www.instinct-travel.com. Tailor-made trips, working a lot through the internet, plenty of involvement with community projects and opening up new routes. Mountain biking in the Sacred Valley; they also hire mountain bikes; also some rafting. Juan and Benjamín Muñiz speak good English.

Manu Expeditions, Av Pardo 895, PO Box 606, T084-226671, www.ManuExpeditions.com. As well as Manu trips (see p214), also runs tailor-made bird trips in cloud and rainforest around Cusco and Peru, and has horse riding and a 9-day/8-night trip to Machu Picchu along a different route from the Inca Trail, rejoining at Sun Gate. Barry runs horse-supported treks to Choquequirao, starting from Huancacalle.

Mayuc Expediciones, Portal Confiturías 211, Plaza de Armas, T084-232666, www.mayuc.com. Rafting on the Urubamba and Apurímac rivers. **Mayuc** have a permanent lodge, **Casa Cusi**, on the upper Urubamba, which forms the basis of 2-day, Class III-IV trips in the area. Also trekking and combinations of horse-trekking and walking can be organized.

Cusco & Southern Peru Cusco & the Sacred Valley Listings

Milla Tourism, Av Pardo 689 y Portal Comercio 195 on the plaza, T084-231710, www.millaturismo.com. Mon-Fri 0800-1300, 1500-1900, Sat 0800-1300. Mystical tours to Cusco's Inca ceremonial sites such as Pumamarca and the Temple of the Moon. Also private tours arranged to Moray agricultural terracing and Maras salt mines in Sacred Valley. Guide speaks only basic English. They also arrange cultural and environmental lectures and courses.

Peru Treks & Adventure, Garcilaso 265 oficina 11 (2nd floor), T084-805863, www.perutreks.com. Trekking agency set up by Englishman Mike Weston and his partner Koqui González. They pride themselves on good treatment of porters and support staff (and tourists!). Treks offered include Salkantay, the Lares Valley and Vilcabamba Vieja (not Inca Trail). Mike also runs the **Andean Travel Web**, www.andeantravelweb.com/peru, with a focus on sustainable tourism.

Peruvian Andean Treks, Av Pardo 705, T084-225701, www.andeantreks.com. Open Mon-Fri 0900-1300, 1500-1800, Sat 0900-1300. Manager Tom Hendrickson has 5-day/4-night Inca Trail using high-quality equipment and satellite phones. His 7-day/6-night Vilcanota Llama Trek to Ausangate (the mountain visible from Cusco) includes a collapsible pressure chamber for altitude sickness.

Q'ente, Garcilaso 210, int 210b, T084-222535, www.qente.com. Their Inca Trail service is recommended. They will organize private treks to Salkantay, Ausangate, Choquequirao, Vilcabamba and Q'eros. Also horse riding to local ruins. Very good, especially with children.

SAS Travel, Portal de Panes 143, T084-237292 (staff in a 2nd office at Medio 137, mainly deal with jungle

information and only speak Spanish), www.sastravel.com. Inca Trail price includes the bus down from Machu Picchu to Aguas Calientes and lunch on the last day. SAS have their own hostel in Aguas Calientes – if clients wish to stay in Aguas after the trail and return the next morning this can be arranged at no extra cost. Group sizes are between 8 and 16 people. To go in a smaller group, costs rise considerably. Also Manu, mountain bike, horse riding and rafting trips can be organized. All guides speak English (some better than others). Responsible, good equipment and food.

Tambo Tours, 20919 Coral Bridge Lane, Suite 225-A, Spring, TX, 77388, USA, T1-888-2GO-PERU (246-7378), T001-281 528 9448, www.2GOPERU.com. Long-established adventure and tour specialist with offices in Peru and USA. Customized trips to the Amazon and archaeological sites of Peru, including Machu Picchu. Daily departures for groups and individuals.

Wayki Trek, Procuradores 351, T084-224092, www.waykitrek.net. Budget travel agency, recommended for their Inca Trail service. Owner Leo grew up in the countryside near Ollantaytambo and knows the area very well. They run treks to several almost unknown Inca sites and many interesting variations on the 'classic' Inca Trail. They also run treks to Ausangate, Salkantay and Choquequirao.

Sacred Valley tours

To organize your own Sacred Valley transport, try one of these taxi drivers, recommended by **South America Explorers: Movilidad Inmediata**, T962 3821 (mob), runs local tours with an English-speaking guide. **Angel Salazar**, Marcavalle I-4 Huanchac, T084-224679 (to leave *messages)*, is English-speaking and arranges good tours, very knowledgeable and enthusiastic. **Milton Velásquez**, T084- 222638, T968 0730 (mob), is an anthropologist and tour guide and speaks English.

⊖ Transport

Cusco *p102, maps p106 and p122*
Air
Airport information T084-222611/601. There is a post office, phone booths, restaurant and cafeteria at the airport. There is also a Tourist Protection Bureau desk, which can be very helpful if your flight has not been reconfirmed (not an uncommon problem). Do not forget to pay the airport tax at the appropriate desk before departure. For details of getting to and from the airport, see p103. For contact details for finding out flight times, see the Essentials chapter, p22.

Bus
Local Combis run (0500-2200 or 2300, US$0.15) to all parts of the city, including the bus and train stations and the airport, but are not allowed within 2 blocks of the Plaza de Armas. Stops are signed and the driver's assistant calls out the names of stops. After 2200 combis may not run their full route; demand to be taken to your stop, or better still, use a taxi late at night.
El Tranvía de Cusco is a motor coach which runs on the route of the original Cusco tramway system. The route starts in the Plaza de Armas (except on Sun morning) and ends at Sacsayhuaman. There is a 10-min stop at the mirador by the Cristo Blanco before descending to the Plaza de Armas. Departures 1000, 1150 and 1500, 1 hr 20 mins, with explanations of

the city's history, architecture, customs, etc; US$2, US$1.40 for students with ID. For group reservations, T084-740640.
Long distance The bus terminal, Terminal Terrestre, is on Av Vallejo Santoni, block 2 (Prolongación Pachacútec). Colectivo from centre US$0.15, taxi US$0.60. Platform tax US$0.30. Buses to **Lima** (20-24 hrs) go via **Abancay** and **Nasca**, on the Panamerican Highway. This route is paved, but floods in the wet season can damage sections of the highway. At night take a blanket or sleeping bag to ward off the cold. All buses leave daily from the Terminal Terrestre. **Cruz del Sur**'s comfortable *Imperial* service departs at 1500 and 1600. To **Abancay** US$3.40, **Nasca** US$17-20, **Lima** US$20 up to US$32 (**Cruz del Sur**, *Imperial* class).
    To **Puno**, there is a good service with Ormeñoat 0900, US$10, 6 hrs. This service continues to **La Paz**, Bolivia. **Tour Perú** offers a direct service to **La Paz**, US$15.
    To **Arequipa**, 521 km, **Cruz del Sur** have standard services leaving daily (10½ hrs, US$7), and an *Imperial* service at 1930, 10 hrs, US$10.

Car
Avis, Av El Sol 808 and at the airport, T084-248800, avis-cusco@terra.com.pe. **Touring y Automóvil Club del Perú**, Av Sol 349, T084-224561, cusco@touringperu.com.pe. A good source of information on motoring, car hire and mechanics (membership is US$45 per year).

Taxi
Local Taxis have fixed prices: in the centre US$0.60 (a little more after dark); and to the suburbs US$0.85-1.55 (touts at the airport and train station will always ask much higher fares). In town it is safest to take taxis which are registered; these have a sign with the company's name on the roof, not just a sticker in the window. Taxis on call are reliable but more expensive, in the centre US$1.25 (**Ocarina**

T084-247080, **Aló Cusco** T084-222222).

Long distance Taxi trips to **Sacsayhuaman** cost US$10; to the ruins of **Tambo Machay** US$15-20 (3-4 people); a whole-day trip costs US$40-70. For US$50 a taxi can be hired for a whole day (ideally Sun) to take you to **Chinchero**, **Maras**, **Urubamba**, **Ollantaytambo**, **Calca**, **Lamay**, **Coya**, **Pisac**, **Tambo Machay**, **Qenqo** and **Sacsayhuaman**.

Train

The train to **Juliaca** and **Puno** leaves at 0800, on Mon, Wed and Sat, arriving in Puno at 1800 (sit on the left for the best views). Trains return from Puno on Mon, Wed and Sat at 0800, arriving in Cusco at 1645. Fares: tourist/backpacker class, US$16.66, 1st class US$119.

Tickets can be bought up to 5 days in advance. The ticket office at Wanchac station is open Mon-Fri 0800-1700, Sat 0900-1200. Tickets sell out quickly and there are queues from 0400 before holidays in the dry season. In the low season tickets to Puno can be bought on the day of departure. You can buy tickets through a travel agent, but check the date and seat number. Meals are served on the train. Always check whether the train is running, especially inthe rainy season, when services might be cancelled. All details of the train services out of Cusco can be found on www.perurail.com.

Pisac *p111*
Bus
From C Puputi on the outskirts of Cusco, near the Clorindo Matto de Turner school and Av de la Cultura. 32 km, 1 hr, US$0.85. Colectivos, minibuses and buses leave when full, between 0600 and 1600. Also from Av Tullumayo 800 block, Wanchac, US$1. Buses returning from Pisac are often full. The last one back leaves around 2000. Taxis charge about US$20 for the round trip.

Bus
Buses from Cusco leave from Av Tullumayo 800 block, Wanchac, US$1.The bus and combi terminal in Urubamba is just west of town on the main road. To **Calca**, **Pisac** (US$0.80, 1 hr) and **Cusco** (2 hrs, US$1), from 0530 onwards. Also buses to Cusco via **Chinchero**, same fare.

Colectivos to **Cusco** can be caught outside the terminal and on the main road, US$1.15. Combis run to **Ollantaytambo**, 45 mins, US$0.30. Hotels such as the **Incaland** (see page 126) run a twice-daily shuttle between Cusco airport and Urubamba for US$10. There are also buses from here to Quillabamba.
Train See p142 for the Sacred Valley Railway from Urubamba to **Aguas Calientes**.

Chinchero *p112*
Combis and colectivos for Chinchero leave from 300 block of Av Grau, **Cusco**, 1 block before crossing the bridge, 23 km, 45 mins, US$0.45; and for **Urubamba** a further 25 km, 45 mins, US$0.45 (or US$1 Cusco-Urubamba direct, US$1.15 for a seat in a colectivo). To **Ollantaytambo**, 0745 and 1945 direct, or catch a bus to Urubamba from Av Grau.

Ollantaytambo *p113*
Ollantaytambo can be reached by bus from Cusco, Urubamba and Chinchera. There is a direct bus service from Ollantaytambo to **Cusco** at 0715 and 1945; the fare is US$2.85. The station is 10-15 mins walk from the plaza (turn left at the sign that says 'Centro de Salud' between the Plaza de Armas and the ruins). There are colectivos at the plaza for the station when trains are due. Also, a bus leaves the station at 0900 for **Urubamba** (US$0.30) and **Chinchero** (US$1).
Train For details of the train service to and from Machu Picchu, see below.

Machu Picchu ruins *p114*

Bus

From **Aguas Calientes** for Machu Picchu every 30 mins, 0630-1300, US$9 return, valid for 48 hrs. Buses run down from the ruins 1200-1730. It is also possible to take a bus down between 0700 and 0900. The ticket office is opposite the bus stop. Tickets can also be bought in advance at **Consetur**, Santa Catalina Ancha, Cusco, which saves queuing when you arrive in Aguas Calientes.

Train

PerúRail (www.perurail.com) trains to Machu Picchu run from San Pedro station in **Cusco**, passing through Ollantaytambo on the way to Aguas Calientes (the official name of this station is Machu Picchu). The station for the tourist trains at Aguas Calientes is on the outskirts of town, 200 m from the **Pueblo Hotel** and 50 m from where buses leave for Machu Picchu ruins. The ticket office is open 0630-1730; there is a guard on the gate. A paved road in poor condition runs from Aguas Calientes to the start of the road up to the ruins.

There are 2 classes of tourist train: **Vistadome** and **Backpacker**. From **Cusco** the **Vistadome** costs US$101.15 return and the **Backpacker** costs US$65.45 return (a 1-way ticket is available for US$29.75, but only 48 hrs before departure). The **Vistadome** leaves Cusco daily at 0600, stopping at Ollantaytambo at 0805 and Machu Picchu at 0940. It returns from Machu Picchu at 1530, passing Ollantaytambo at 1700, reaching Cusco at 1920. The **Backpacker** leaves Cusco at 0615, passing Ollantaytambo at 0835 and Machu Picchu at 1010. It returns at 1555, passing Ollantaytambo at 1740, getting to Cusco at 2020.

The **Sacred Valley Railway Vistadome** service runs from **Urubamba** to Machu Picchu and costs US$69 return. It leaves Urubamba at 0600, reaching Machu Picchu at 0820, returning at 1645, reaching Urubamba at 1910. Price includes breakfast on the way out and a soft drink on the way back.

There are further **Vistadomes** and Backpackers from **Ollantaytambo** to Machu Picchu, at US$69 and US$51.17 return, respectively. The Ollantaytambo **Vistadome** leaves at 1030 and 1455, journey time 1 hr 20 mins, returning from Machu Picchu at 1320 and 1645. The Ollantaytambo **Backpacker** leaves at 0925, arriving at 1100, returning from Machu Picchu at 1700, reaching Ollantaytambo at 1840. Seats can be reserved even if you're not returning the same day. The **Vistadome** tickets include food in the price. These trains have toilets, video, snacks and drinks for sale. Tickets should be bought at Wanchac station in Cusco, Av Pachacútec. The **Sacred Valley Railway** office, Av El Sol 803, Cusco, T084-249076, or Casa Estación, Av Ferrocarril s/n, Urubamba, T084-201126/27, www.sacredvalleyrailway.com.

There is a cheaper way to travel by train to Machu Picchu, but you have to check on this train's existence at the time of travel. Backpacker coaches are added to the local train which leaves Ollantaytambo at 1945, arriving Aguas Calientes 2120. It returns from Aguas at 0545, arriving Ollantaytambo at 0740. Tickets cost US$12.50 and can only be bought 1-2 days before departure (they sell out fast). Tourists are not allowed to travel in the carriages for local people. If you use this service you have to stay 2 nights in Aguas Calientes if you want to see Machu Picchu. Timetables are not published for this train and the inclusion of Backpacker coaches is not guaranteed.

ⓘ Directory

Cusco *p102, maps p106 and p122*
Banks

All the banks along Av Sol have ATMs (most of which have 24-hr police protection) from which you can withdraw dollars or soles at any hour. Whether you use the counter or an ATM, choose your time carefully as there can be long

PERURAIL

Discovering the Andes

PeruRail - the service comprising some of the world's most scenic railways, and linking the tourist highlights of the Andes. It operates from historic Cusco to the famous Citadel of Machu Picchu and Puno's Lake Titicaca, connecting the most spectacular attractions of Peru. The trains are comfortable, the service is splendid and the views are unmatched. It is an unparalleled way to travel within Peru.

www.perurail.com
reservas@perurail.com

queues at both. Most banks are closed between 1300 and 1600. As well as those on Av Sol, there are ATMs on the Plaza de Armas at the entrance to Inka Grill, Portal de Panes, Supermercado Gato's, Portal Belén, and the entrance to Cross Keys and Tunupa, Portal de Confiturías. There are other ATMs on Av la Cultura, beside Supermercado Dimart and beside Supermercado La Canasta. Many travel agencies and **casas de cambio** change dollars. Some of them change TCs as well, but charge 4-5% commission. There are many *cambios* on the west side of the Plaza de Armas (eg Portal Comercio Nos 107 and 148) and on the west side of Av Sol, most change TCs (best rates in the *cambios* at the top of Av Sol). **LAC Dólar**, Av Sol 150, T084-257969, Mon-Sat 0900-2000, with delivery service to central hotels, cash and TCs, is recommended. The **street changers** hang around Av Sol, blocks 2-3, every day and are a pleasure to do business with. Some of them will also change TCs. In banks and on the street check the notes.

Embassies and consulates
Ireland, Charlie Donovan, Santa Catalina Ancha 360 (Rosie O'Grady's), T084-243514. **UK**, Barry Walker, Av Pardo 895, T084-239974, bwalker@amauta.rcp.net.pe. **US Agent**, Dra Olga Villagarcía, Apdo 949, Cusco, T084-222183, F084-233541, or at

the Binational Center (ICPNA), Av Tullumayo 125, Wanchac.

Internet
You can't walk for 2 mins in Cusco without running into an internet café, and new places are opening all the time. Most have similar rates, around US$0.60 per hr, although if you look hard enough you can find cheaper places. The main difference between cafés is the speed of internet connection and the facilities on offer. The better places have scanners, webcams and CD burners, among other gadgets, and staff in these establishments can be very knowledgeable.

Language classes
Academia Latinoamericana de Español, Av Sol 580, T084-243364, latinocusco@goalsnet. com.pe. Professionally run with experienced staff. Many activities per week, including dance lessons and excursions to sites of historical and cultural interest. Private classes US$170 for 20 hrs, groups, with a maximum of 4 students US$125, again for 20 hrs. **Amauta**, Suecia 480, 2nd floor, T084-241422, PO Box 1164, www.amautaspanishschool.org. Spanish classes, individual or in small groups, also Quechua classes and workshops in Peruvian cuisine, dance and music, US$9.50 per hr individual, but cheaper

and possibly better value for group tuition (2-6 people), US$88 for 20 hrs. Free internet café for students. They also have a school in Urubamba and can arrange courses in the Manu rainforest, in conjunction with Pantiacolla Tours.
Amigos Spanish School, Zaguán del Cielo B-23, T084-242292, www.spanishcusco.com. Profits from this school support a foundation for disadvantaged children. Private lessons for US$8 per hr, US$100 for 20 hrs of classes in a group. Homestays available.
Excel, Cruz Verde 336, T084-232272 , www.Excel-spanishlanguageprograms-pe ru.org. Very professional, US$7 per hr for private one-to-one lessons. US$200 for 20 hrs with 2 people, or US$80 per person in groups of 3 or more. The school can arrange accommodation with local families. **The Spanish Centre**, T084-993 0177, www.studyspanishincusco.com. Discounts for SAE and ISIC card holders, special offers, homestays, can arrange cultural activities and trekking and provides travel advice.

Laundry
There are several cheap laundries on Procuradores, and also on Suecia and Tecseccocha.

Medical services
Clínica Pardo, Av de la Cultura 710, T084-240387, T993 0063 (mob), www.clinicapardocusco.com. 24-hr emergency and medical attention, international department, trained bilingual personnel, handles complete medical assistance coverage with international insurance companies, free ambulance service, visit to hotel, discount in pharmacy, dental service, X-rays, laboratory, full medical specialization. The most highly recommeded clinic in Cusco.

Post offices
Central office, Av Sol at the bottom end of block 5, T084-225232. Mon-Sat 0730-2000, 0800-1400 Sun and holidays.

Poste restante is free and helpful. Sending packages from Cusco is not cheap. **DHL**, Av Sol 627, T084-244167. For sending packages or money overseas.

Telephone
Telefónica, Av del Sol 386, T084-241111. For telephone and fax, Mon-Sat 0700-2300, 0700-1200 Sun and holidays. International calls can be made by payphone or go through the operator – a long wait is possible and a deposit is required.

Useful addresses
Immigration Av Sol, block 6, close to post office, T084-222740. Mon-Fri 0800-1300. Reported as not very helpful.
Perú Verde Ricaldo Palma J-1, Santa Mónica, T084-243408, acss@telser.com.pe. For information and free video shows about Manu National Park and Tambopata National Reserve. They are friendly and have information on programmes and research in the area of Madre de Dios.

Pisac *p111*
Internet and telephone On the same side of the plaza as the museum are the municipal building with a computer centre (internet for US$0.75 per hr, closed Sun morning) and a public phone booth.

Urubamba *p111*
Banks ATM on the main road not far from the bridge. **Internet** Connections, corner of Av M Castilla and Av La Convención. **Post** Serpost, post office, Plaza de Armas.

Ollantaytambo *p113*
Internet Internet Ollanta, just before the Plaza Ruinas on the left-hand side, opposite the Santiago Apóstol church. 3 machines, US$2 per hr, US$0.90 for 15 mins.

Aguas Calientes *p119*
Banks and money exchange There are no banks in Aguas Calientes. Those

Going further

Choquequirao – the next lost city of the Incas

The ruins of Choquequirao lie off the road from Cusco to Abancay. To get to the ruins is a tough but rewarding trip, requiring an expedition of four days or more. Choquequirao is built on a ridge spur almost 1,600 m above the Apurímac. Although only 30 per cent has been uncovered, it is believed to be a larger site than Machu Picchu, but with fewer buildings. A number of high-profile explorers and archaeologists, including Hiram Bingham, researched the site, but its importance has only recently been recognized. Now tourists are venturing there. With new regulations being applied to cut congestion on the Inca Trail, Choquequirao is destined to replace the traditional hike as the serious trekker's alternative.

Sleeping Accommodation, guides (Celestino Peña is the official guide) and mules are available in Cachora. Cheap accommodation is available at La Casona de Ocampo, San Martín 122, Cachora, T084-237514, lacasonadeocampo@yahoo.es, with hot showers and free camping. Owner Carlos Robles is very friendly and knowledgeable, rents camping equipment and organizes treks to Choquequirao and beyond.

Transport There are three ways to reach Choquequirao. None is a gentle stroll. The shortest way is from Cachora, a village in a magnificent location on the south side of the Apurímac, reached by a side road from the Cusco-Abancay highway, near Saywite. It is four hours by bus from Cusco to the turn-off, then a two-hour descent from the road to Cachora (from 3,695 m to 2,875 m). Buses run from Abancay to Cachora. From Cachora to Abancay there are buses at 0630 and 1100 (2 hours, US$1.50) and colectivo taxis.

businesses that change money will not do so at rates as favourable as you will find in Cusco. **Qosqo Service**, corner of Av Pachacútec and Mayta Cápac, has *cambio*, postal service and guiding service.
Internet Yanantin Masintin, Av Imperio de los Incas 119, US$3 per hr, is part of the Rikuni group, as is **Tea House**, which is opposite. Both serve coffees,

teas, snacks, etc. The town has electricity 24 hrs. **Post Serpost** (post office), just off the plaza, between the Centro Cultural Machu Picchu and Galería de Arte Tunupa, and on the railway line.
Telephone Oficina on C Collasuyo, and there are plenty of phone booths around town. There are lots of places to choose from for exchange, shop around.

Lake Titicaca

Straddling Peru's southern border with landlocked Bolivia are the deep, sapphire-blue waters of mystical Lake Titicaca, everyone's favourite school geography statistic. This gigantic inland sea covers up to 8,500 square km and is the highest navigable lake in the world, at 3,856 m above sea level. Its shores and islands are home to the Aymara and Quechua, who are among Peru's oldest peoples, predating the Incas by a thousand years. Here you can wander through old traditional villages where Spanish is still a second language and where ancient myths and beliefs hold true. The main town on the lake is Puno, where chilled travellers gather to stock up on warm woollies to keep the cold at bay. The high-altitude town is the departure point for the islands of Taquile and Amanataní, as well as the floating reed islands of Los Uros.

⊘ Getting there Flights to Juliaca, then bus or taxi to Puno; bus or train from Cusco to Puno, and bus from Arequipa.

⊜ Getting around Buses run around the lake; boats sail across it.

⊕ Time required 2-4 days.

⊚ Weather May-Sep are generally dry months, but cold at night, especially Jun-Aug. Nov-Apr are wetter months.

⊜ Sleeping Puno has decent options in the mid-range and cheap brackets. Elsewhere, options are mostly basic.

⊘ Eating Mostly tourist fare in Puno. Otherwise restaurants are basic.

▲▲ Activities and tours Visits to islands on and communities around the lake.

★ Don't miss... Llachón ▸▸ *p149.*

Cusco & Southern Peru Lake Titicaca

Puno and the islands ⊜⊘⊕⊗⊜⊚▲⊜⊜ ▸▸ *pp152-157*

On the northwest shore of Lake Titicaca, at 3,855 m, Puno is a major folklore centre and a great place to buy handicrafts, particularly those amazingly tactile alpaca jumpers, hats and gloves. It also boasts a rich tradition of music and dance and is a good place to enjoy a number of Andean festivals, some wild,

some solemn. Puno isn't the most attractive of cities, especially at night when temperatures plummet, but it has a certain vitality, helped by the fact there is a large student population.

Ins and outs

Getting there and around The railway station for trains from Cusco is within walking distance of the centre, but if you've got heavy bags, it's a good idea to hire a 3-wheel cycle cart, trici-taxi, which costs about US$0.35 per km per person. The new bus station and the depots for local buses are further away, southeast of the centre, but trici-taxis and conventional taxis serve this area. The centre of town is easy to walk around, but as said above, a trici-taxi can make life a lot easier. Colectivos (buses) in town charge US$0.20. ● ▸▸ *p155*

Best time to visit Puno gets bitterly cold at night, especially in June-August, when the temperature at night can plummet to -25°C. Days are bright and the midday sun is hot. The first two weeks in February, when the Fiesta de la Candelaria takes place, and 4-5 November, the pageant of the emergence of the founding Incas, are good, but crowded, times to visit.

Tourist information i perú, ⓘ *Lima y Deústua, T051-365088, near Plaza de Armas, open Mon-Sun 0830-1930*, are friendly and helpful with general information and they provide all maps and information free. www.punored.com is a portal for the Puno area. Visit also www.titicacaalmundo.com, which has good information on Puno, sponsored by several local businesses (they also distribute a free CD-Rom).

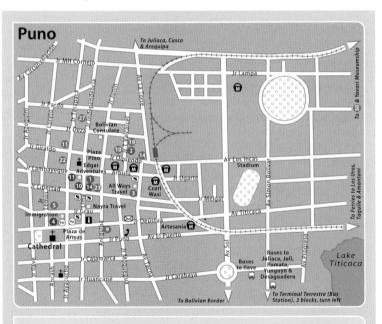

Puno

Sleeping ●
Casa Andina Plaza **5**
Casa Andina Tikarani **27**
Colón Inn **3**
Hostal Hacienda **9**
Hostal Italia **10**
Hostal Los Pinos **11**
Hostal Q'oñiwasi **14**

Libertador Isla Esteves **30**
Los Uros **19**
Posada Don Giorgio **22**
Pukara **23**

Eating ●
Casa del Corregidor **4**
IncAbar **10**

Keros **11**
Pizzería El Buho **14**

Bars & clubs ●
Pub Ekeko's **1**
The Rocks **2**

200 metres
200 yards

Top tips

Visiting the islands

✅ If staying the night on Taquile or Amantaní, take warm clothes and a sleeping bag.

✅ Tourism to both islands is community-based: the less you pay, the smaller the amount that goes to the islanders. Bear this in mind when you shop around for a good value tour (there is not much variation at the lower end of the price range).

✅ The influx of tourists on Taquile and Amantaní unfortunately prompts persistent requests by children for sweets or to have their photo taken. Buy their handicrafts instead of handing out sweets indiscriminately. Gifts of fruit, sugar, salt, spices, torches/flashlights (there is no electricity), moisturizer or sun block are appreciated.

✅ Watch out for the many unofficial street tour sellers – or jalagringos – in Puno. They are everywhere: train station, bus offices, airport and hotels. Ask to see their guide's ID card. Only use agencies with named premises and compare prices.

❌ When not taking a tour to the islands, do not buy your boat ticket from anyone other than the boat operator at the harbour, do not believe anyone who says you can only visit the islands on a tour and do not be pressurized by touts.

Sights

Puno sits on a bay at the northwest end of the lake. The port and lakeside quarters are several blocks from the centre, whose focus is the Plaza de Armas. The **Yavari** ⓘ *www.yavari.org, open 0800-1700, then illuminated till 2230 for 'Happy Hour' managed by hotel staff, entry free in daytime, but donations welcome,* is the oldest ship on Lake Titicaca. It was restored in the port of Puno and turned into a museum, before being moved to its present location, near the entrance to the Sonesta Posada del Inca Hotel (see page 153). The ship is being restored by an Anglo-Peruvian Association. Visitors are very welcome on board and will be shown over the ship and its exhibition of archival documentation and memorabilia on the Lake Fleet by the captain or a volunteer. To get there you can go by taxi, bus, or trici-taxi, but the most charming way is by boat from the port, about US$2 return, including wait.

A highly recommended trip is to the *chullpas* (pre-Columbian funeral towers) of **Sillustani** ⓘ *US$2.25,* in a beautiful setting on a peninsula in **Lago Umayo** (3,890 m), 32 km from Puno on an excellent road. These burial towers of the Aymara-speaking Colla tribe mostly date from the period of Inca occupation in the 15th century. There is a museum and handicraft sellers in traditional costume wait at the exit. Guides are also available here. Take an organized tour, which lasts about 3 to 4 hours and leaves at 1430, US$6.30. Tours usually stop at a Colla house on the way, to see local products, alpacas and guinea pigs. Alternatively, take a Juliaca bus to the Sillustani turn-off (US$0.35); from here a 15-km paved road runs across the altiplano to the ruins. Take warm clothing, water and sun protection. Go early to avoid tour groups at the site. A taxi from Puno should cost about US$12, including the driver waiting for you.

The pretty farming village of **Llachón**, sitting at the eastern end of the Península de Capachica, has recently become a focus of community-based tourism. The sandy beaches, pre-Inca terracing and trees and flowers dotted around, make it a charming place to visit. You'll be welcomed with a necklace of cantuta flowers and then invited to share in local

The inhabitants of the Uros islands are always eager to sell their handicrafts to visiting tourists.

activities; 70 per cent of all produce served is from the residents' farms. The peninsula is also good for hiking and mountain-biking and sailing boats can be hired. After all that activity, take in the sunset from the Auki Carus hill. Twelve families offer accommodation on a rotational basis, see page 152. Llachón is great place to start a visit to Lake Titicaca, especially if you are flying in. It is closer to come here directly from Juliaca and you can go from Llachón to the islands or to Puno by boat.

The islands

Puno's tourist raison d'être is as the jumping off point for a visit to the islands on Lake Titicaca. Dozens of agencies in Puno run tours of varying quality but for those with a little more time and imagination, travelling independently is more rewarding, allows more flexibility and is fairly easy. Those is search of a few days of quiet contemplation in which to experience life at a slow pace should head for Amantaní.

Several tour operators in Puno offer two- to three- day excursions to Amantaní, Taquile and a visit to the floating islands. These cost from US$12 per person upwards, including meals, depending on the season and size of group. This gives you one night on Amantaní and three or four hours on Taquile. There is little difference in price visiting the islands independently or on a tour, but going independently means that the islanders get all the proceeds, with no commission paid to Puno tour companies, you can stay as many nights as you wish and you will be able to explore the islands at your own pace.

The best known islands on the Peruvian side of the lake are **Los Uros**, an estimated 32 floating islands made entirely of totora reeds and on which the Uros people have lived for centuries. Only 15 of these islands are regularly visited by tour boats and these are little more than floating souvenir stalls where the residents, though friendly, are also very poor and sometimes subject visitors to a hard-sell approach for handicrafts. But the Uros cannot live from tourism alone, and the extra income they glean from tourists merely supplements their more traditional activities of fishing, hunting birds and living off the lake plants, most important of which are the totora reeds they use for their boats, houses and the very foundations of their islands. On the more far-flung islands, reached via narrow channels through the reed beds, the Uros do not like to be photographed and continue to lead relatively traditional lives outside the monetary economy.

Children on Taquile enjoying an impromptu game of football.

The quiet and hospitable island of **Taquile**, 45 km from Puno, is also a favourite with tour boats. However, you need to spend a night on Taquile fully to appreciate its beauty and, therefore, it may be better to travel independently and go at your own pace. The island is only about 1 km wide and 6-7 km long but has numerous pre-Inca and Inca ruins, and Inca terracing. At the highest point is a ruin from which to view the sunset (the path is signed). On the main plaza is the (unmarked and free) **museum of traditional costumes** and a co-operative shop selling exceptional woollen goods (they are cheaper in the market at Puno). Visitors pay US$1 to land. Shops on the plaza sell film, postcards, water, chocolate bars and dry goods.

Another island well worth visiting is **Amantaní**. It is very beautiful and peaceful, and many say is less spoiled, more genuine and friendlier than Taquile. There are six villages and ruins on both of the island's peaks, Pacha Tata and Pacha Mama, from which there are excellent views. Small shops sell water and snacks, but these are more expensive than Puno. The residents make beautiful textiles and sell them at the *Artesanía Cooperativa*, at the east end of El Pueblo. They also make basketwork and stoneware. The people are Quechua speakers, but understand Spanish.

Border with Bolivia

The most popular and straightforward route across the Peru-Bolivia border is the direct route from Puno to La Paz, or vice versa if travelling the other way. The route goes via Yunguyo and Copacabana. Peruvian immigration is just 100m from its Bolivian counterpart and is open 24 hrs. Bolivian immigration is only open 0830-1930.

Three bus companies in Puno sell bus tickets for this route (see Puno Transport, page 156 for details). They stop at the borders and one hour for lunch in Copacabana, arriving in La Paz at about 1700. Passengers change buses at Copacabana and it seems that the Bolivian bus may not be of the company indicated and may not be of the same standard as the Peruvian bus. You only need to change money into bolivianos for lunch on this route. You can also get off at Copacabana (US$4.40-5.80 from Puno) and continue from there to La Paz independently. It is also possible to cross the border by hydrofoil or catamaran as part of a tour (see box, page 156).

🔵 Sleeping

Puno *p143, map p148*

Puno sometimes suffers from power and water shortages. Check if breakfast is included in the price. Note also that some hotels are full of dubious street tour sellers. Others are linked to tour operators which may or may not belong to them, so are not above pressurized tour selling (see Tour operators, p155).

AL Casa Andina Plaza, Jr Grau 270, T051-367520, www.casa-andina.com. Price includes breakfast and 10% service. One of this chain's modern hotels, a block from the plaza, rooms with bath, TV and heating, non-smoking rooms, clean, safe and central. Business centre with internet for guests, parking. Also **Casa Andina Tikarani**, Independencia 143, T051-365803, www.casa-andina.com. Same price and similar in most respects.

A Colón Inn, Tacna 290, T051-351432, www.titicaca-peru.com. Price includes tax and buffet breakfast. Colonial style, good rooms with hot shower, good service, safe, internet for guests, restaurant Sol Naciente and pizzería Europa, the Belgian manager Christian Nonis is well known, especially for his work on behalf of the people on Taquile island.

A Hostal Hacienda, Jr Deústua 297, T/F051-356109, haciendahostal@hotmail.com. Price includes breakfast. Refurbished colonial house, comfortable rooms with bath and hot water, TV, café. Rooms facing the front have private balconies.

B Hostal Italia, Teodoro Valcarcel 122, T051-352521, www.hotelitaliaperu.com. 2 blocks from the station. With continental breakfast, cheaper in low season. Good, safe, hot water, good food, small rooms, helpful staff.

B Hostal Pukara, Jr Libertad 328, T/F051-368448, pukara@terra.com.pe. Includes good American breakfast.

Popular, with bath, hot water and heating. English spoken, central, quiet, free coca tea in evening.

C Posada Don Giorgio, Tarapacá 238, T051-363648, dongiorgio @titicacalake.com. Breakfast included. Large, comfortable, pleasantly decorated rooms with bath, hot water, TV, parking US$1.50 extra.

D Los Uros, Teodoro Valcarcel 135, T051-352141, huros@speedy.com.pe. Cheaper without bath. Hot water, plenty of blankets, breakfast is available (at extra cost), quiet at the back, good value. They make a small charge to leave luggage, laundry, often full, changes TCs at reasonable rate.

D-E Hostal Los Pinos, Tarapacá 182, T/F051-367398, hostalpinos @hotmail.com. Cheaper without bath. Family run, electric showers, good breakfast, clean, safe, luggage store, laundry facilities, helpful, cheap tours organized.

D-E Hostal Q'oñiwasi, Av La Torre 119, opposite the rail station, T051-365784, qoniwasi@mundomail.net. **E** without bath and in low season. Heating is extra, but hot water available all day, laundry facilities and service, luggage store, breakfast extra from 0600-0900, lunch on request, safe, very helpful.

Around Puno *p143*

E Valentín Quispe is the organizer of tourism in **Llachón**. He offers lodging and meals (breakfast US$1.20, other meals US$2). To contact Don Valentín, T051-360226/7, T051-9821392 (mob), llachon@yahoo.com or visit www.titicaca-peru.com/capachicae.htm. Another family is that of Tomás Cahui Coila, Centro Turístico Santa María Llachón, T051-992 3595 (mob); Tomás can arrange boat transport to Amantaní. There is a campsite towards the end of the peninsula. See Transport, below.

Budget busters

Luxury around Lake Titicaca

L **Libertador Isla Esteves**, on an island linked by a causeway 5 km northeast of Puno (taxi US$3, or red *colectivo* No 16, or white Nos 24 and 33), T051-367780, www.libert ador.com.pe. Built on a Tiahuanaco-period site, the hotel is spacious with good views. Bar, good restaurant, disco, good service, electricity and hot water all day, parking.

L **Sonesta Posada del Inka**, Av Sesquicentenario 610, Huaje, 5 km from Puno on the lakeshore (take same transport as for Isla Esteves), T051-364111, www.sonesta.com/peru_puno/. 62 large rooms with heating, in similar vein to other hotels in this group but with local touches, such as the textile decorations and the Andean menu in the Inkafé restaurant. Has facilities for the disabled, fine views, attractive, good service, folklore shows.

To get away from it all you cannot find a more remote piece of luxury than the hotel on the Isla de Suasi. It's a tiny island just off the north shore of Lake Titicaca, with its own microclimate. This allows for beautiful terraced gardens and solar-powered facilities. The island is small enough to roam around, even row around (there are kayaks) and the sunsets from the highest point are out of this world. The hotel is in the **Casa Andina Private Collection** (www-casa-andina.com, T051-962 2709) and is in our AL range. Rooms are spacious and comfortable and the food is excellent.

The islands *p150*

Taquile

Plentiful accommodation can be found in private houses and, on arrival, you are greeted by a *jefe de alojamiento*, who oversees where you are going to stay. You can either say where you are going, if you (or your guide) know where you want to stay, or the jefe can find you a room. The average rate for a bed is F, plus US$1.50 for breakfast. Other meals cost extra. Several families now have sizeable alojamientos (eg **Pedro Huille**, on the track up from the north entry, with showers, proper loos, no sign). Instead of staying in the busy part around the main square, the Huayllano community is hosting visitors. This is on the south side of the island. Contact **Alipio Huata Cruz**, T051-952 4650 (mob, you can leave a voicemail that he will retrieve from Puno as there is no reception on the island) or

you can arrange a visit with **Allways Travel** (see p155).

Amantaní

Ask your boat owner where you can stay; families living close to the port tend to receive tour company business and more tourists. Accommodation is in our F range. This includes three meals of remarkable similarity. It's very good value for visitors, but the prices have been forced down to unrealistically low levels, from which the islanders benefit hardly at all. Some contacts for accommodation are: **Hospedaje Jorge Wasi**, basic, but nice family, great view of lake from room, or **j.mamani.cari@eudoramail.com**, or **Familia Victoriano Calsin Quispe**, Casilla 312, Isla Amantaní, T051-360220 (Irma) or 363320 (Puno contact).

Eating

Puno *p143, map p148*

¶¶ **IncAbar**, Lima 356-A. Open for breakfast, lunch and dinner, interesting dishes in creative sauces, fish, pastas, curries, café and couch bar, nice décor.

¶¶-¶ **Keros**, Lambayeque 131. Bar/restaurant with very good food, mostly Peruvian, good service, pleasant surroundings, good drinks.

¶¶-¶ **Pizzería El Buho**, Lima 349 and at Jr Libertad 386. Excellent pizza, lively atmosphere, open 1800 onwards, pizzas US$2.50-3.

¶ **Casa del Corregidor**, Deústua 576, aptdo 2, T051-355694. In restored 17th century building, sandwiches, good snacks, coffee, good music, great atmosphere, nice surroundings with patio.

The islands *p150*

On **Taquile** there are many small restaurants around the plaza and on the track to the Puerto Principal (eg Gerardo Hualta's **La Flor de Cantuta**, on the steps; **El Inca** on the main plaza). Meals are generally fish (the island has a trout farm), rice and chips, tortilla and fiambre – a local stew. Meat is rarely available and drinks often run out. Breakfast consists of pancakes and bread.

Bars and clubs

Puno *p143, map p148*

Peña Hostería, Lima 501. Good music, also restaurant with good value set menu.
Pub Ekeko's, Jr Lima 355, p 2. Live music every night, happy hour 2000-2200.
The Rocks, Valcarcel 181, T051-337441. New in 2004, live music starts at 2000 on Fri and Sat.

Festivals and events

Puno *p143*

The very colourful **Fiesta de la Virgen de la Candelaria** takes place during the first 2 weeks in **Feb**. Bands and dancers from all the local towns compete in this Diablada, or Devil Dance, with the climax coming on Sun. The festival is famous for its elaborate and grotesque masks. The festivities are better at night on the streets than the official functions in the stadium. Check in advance on the actual date. Other festivals include a candlelight procession through darkened streets, which takes place on **Good Friday**, with bands, dignatories and statues of Jesus. On **3 May** is Invención de la Cruz, an exhibition of local art. On **29 Jun** is the colourful festival of **San Pedro**. Another takes place on **20 Jul**. In fact, it is difficult to find a month in Puno without some sort of celebration. On **5 Nov**, there's an impressive pageant dedicated to the founding of Puno and the emergence of Manco Cápac and Mama Ocllo from the waters of Lake Titicaca.

The islands *p150*

Numerous festivals take place on Taquile. These include: **Semana Santa**, a festival from **2 to 7 Jun**, the Fiesta de Santiago, held over **2 weeks in mid-Jul**, and on **1 and 2 Aug**. Weddings take place each **May and Aug**. The priest comes from Puno and there is a week-long party. On Amantaní, on **15 Jan** (or thereabouts) there's a very colourful, musical and hard-drinking fiesta. There is also a festival on the **1st Sun in Mar** with brass bands and colourful dancers.

Shopping

Puno *p143, map p148*

The markets between Av Los Incas and Arbulu (Ccori Wasi) and on the railway between Av Libertad and Av El Puerto are two of the best places in the entire region for **llama and alpaca wool** articles, but bargain for a good price when buying in quantity (and you will!), especially in the afternoon. In the covered part of the market (bounded by Arbulu, Arequipa, Oquendo and Tacna) mostly **foodstuffs** are sold (good cheeses), but there are also model **reed boats**, attractive **carved stone amulets** and Ekekos (**household gods**). This central market covers a large area and on Sat it expands down to the stadium (mostly fruit and vegetables) and along Av Bolívar (potatoes and grains). **Cooperación Artesanal Ichuña**, Jr Libertad 113, www.ichunia.org, is the outlet for a cooperative of about 100 women from Ichuña, 90km southwest of Puno, selling hand-woven textiles made of alpaca wool.

▲ Activities and tours

Puno *p143, map p148*
Agencies organize trips to the Uros floating islands and the islands of Taquile and Amantaní, as well as to Sillustani, and other places. Make sure that you settle all details before embarking on the tour. Alternatively, you can easily go down to the lake and make your own arrangements with the boatmen.

Tour operators
Most agencies will go and buy train tickets for you, at varying rates of commission, similarly for bus tickets. The following have been recommended as reliable and helpful and offer good value. **Allways Travel**, Tacna 234, T/F051-355552, www.titicacaperu.com. Very helpful, kind and attentive to visitors' needs. Reliable, staff speak German, French, English and Italian. They offer a unique cultural tour to the islands of Anapia and Yuspique in Lake Wiñaymarka, beyond the straits of Tiquina, 'The Treasure of Wiñaymarka', departures Thu and Sun. You can contribute to owner Víctor Lazo's educational project by donating children's books for schools. They also have a speedboat for 40 passengers. Also doing an alternative visit to Taquile where you go to the south of the island to visit the Huayllano community, this is a lot less touristy then the regular Taquile visit.

Edgar Adventures, Jr Lima 328, T/F051-353444 (office)/354811 (home), www.titicacalake.com. Run by Edgar Apaza F and Norka Flórez L who speak English, German and French, very helpful. **Kontiki Tours**, Jr Melgar 188. T051-353473, www.kontikiperu.com. Local tour agency specializing in special interest excursions. **Nayra Travel**, Jr Lima 419, of 105. T051-364774, www.nayratravel.com. Small but very helpful staff, offering local tours. **Turpuno**, Lima 208, stand 8-II, upstairs in Gallery, T051-352001, www.turpuno.com. Open 0700-1230, 1430-1800. Very good service for local tours, transfers and ticketing, DHL and Western Union agent.

⊖ Transport

Puno *p143, map p148*
Air
The nearest airport is at Juliaca. The airport is small but well-organized. There are daily flights to/from Lima (2¼ hrs) with **Tans**, and **Lan**, all via **Arequipa** (30 mins). Lan also flies to Cusco. Minibuses 1-B, 6 and 14 to airport from 2 de Mayo at either Núñez or San Román, US$0.15; from airport to town they take you to your hotel. Taxi from Plaza Bolognesi, US$1.75. **Tourist buses** run direct from Puno to the airport and vice versa; US$3.50 pp, 1 hr. You can book ahead with **Rossy Tours** T051-366709, 968 9852 (mob). Rosa has minibuses and will drop you off/pick you up at your hotel for US$3.50. Also taxis, US$11.75. If taking a public colectivo from Puno to Juliaca for a flight, allow plenty of time as they drive around Puno looking for passengers to fill the vehicle first.
   Airline offices: **Lan**, Tacna y Libertad, T051-367227.

Bus
All long-distance buses, except some Cusco services and buses to La Paz (see below), leave from the new Terminal Terrestre, which is between Av Simón Bolívar and the lake, southeast of the

Budget buster

Border crossing with a difference

Those who wish to cross the border in style and comfort can do so on board Crillon Tours' hydrofoil or Transturin's catamaran (prices range from US$90-US$250, depending on the service). **Crillon Tours'** services can be booked at **Arcobaleno**, Jr Lambayeque 175, T/F051-351052, www.titicacalake.com, or at their head office in La Paz (see p237). The Puno office will take care of all documentation for crossing the border into Bolivia. The main itinerary is: Puno-Copacabana by bus or hydrofoil; Copacabana-Isla del Sol-Huatajata (Bolivia) by hydrofoil; Huatajata-La Paz by bus. Similar services, by more leisurely catamaran, are run by **Transturin**. Bookings can be made through Transturin's offices in La Paz (see p237) or at Av Libertad 176, Puno, T051-352771. The main route is Puno-Copacabana by bus; Copacabana-Isla del Sol (including a land tour); Isla del Sol-Chúa by catamaran; Chúa-La Paz by bus. The trip can be done in one day, or with a night on board the catamaran, moored at the Isla del Sol. Transturin also run buses between Puno and La Paz, with no change of bus at the border.

centre. It has a tourist office, snack bars and toilets. Platform tax US$0.30. Bus prices to Cusco and La Paz have seasonal variations. Daily buses to **Arequipa**, 5-6 hrs via **Juliaca**, US$8.60. **Cruz del Sur** (at Lima 442), among others, have a morning and evening bus – better quality buses go at night. To **Lima**, 22 hrs, US$18-43, all buses go through **Arequipa**, sometimes with a change of bus. To **Cusco**, 5 hrs, US$8-9, several daily from Terminal. **First Class**, Jr Tacna 280, T051-365192, firstclass@terra.com.pe, and **Inka Express**, Jr Tacna 314-B, T051-365654, both at 0830 arriving 1800, US$25, daily. This service, while higher in price than the turismo train or other buses, leaves a little later and is comfortable, with a good lunch stop and visits to Pukará, La Raya, Raqchi and Andahuaylillas en route. This option is recommended and has become very popular so book in advance, especially in high season. Do not take night buses to Cusco: many robberies were wreported in 2004.

To Bolivia In Puno 3 companies sell bus tickets for the route to La Paz, via Copacabana, which takes 6-8 hrs (the fare does not include the Tiquina ferry crossing, US$0.25). These are: **Colectur**, Tacna 221, T051-352302, 0730, US$6.50, combines with Galería in Bolivia; **Panamericano**, Tacna 245, T051-354001, 0730, US$7.35, combines with Diana Tours; **Tour Perú** (at terminal and Tacna 282, T051-352991), 0800, US$8.75, combines with Combi Tour (fares rise at holiday times). For details of border procedures, see p151 .

Trains

To **Cusco** on Mon, Wed, Thu and Sat at 0800, arriving in Juliaca at 0910 and in Cusco at about 1800 (try to sit on the right hand side for the views). The train stops at **La Raya**. In the high season (Jun especially), tickets sell well in advance. In the wet season services may be cancelled for short periods. Always check, www.perurail.com. **Fares** Puno-Cusco, turismo/backpacker, US$15; first class, US$90 including meal. The ticket office is open 0630-1030, 1600-1900 Mon-Sat, and on Sun in the afternoons only. Tickets can be bought in advance, or 1 hr before departure if there are any left. The station is well-guarded by police and sealed off to those without tickets.

Around Puno *p143*
Public boats leave Puno for Llachón at 0830, usually daily, 3 hrs. Private boat services take 1½ hrs: contact tour agencies in Puno for details. There is no direct road transport on the unpaved road to the peninsula that branches east from the main road half way between Puno and Juliaca. Take a colectivo from Bellavista market in Puno to the village of Capachica, then another colectivo to Llachón. Tour operators in Puno arrange visits, about US$25 per person staying overnight, in groups of 10-15.

The islands *p150*
Motorboats charge US$3 per person to take tourists to the **Uros** islands for a 2-hr excursion. Boats leave from the harbour in Puno about every 30 mins from about 0630 till 1000, or whenever there are 10 or more people to fill the boat. The earlier you go the better, to beat the crowds of tourists. Almost any agency going to the other islands in the lake will stop first at Los Uros. Just to Los Uros, agencies charge US$6.

Boats leave Puno harbour for **Taquile** daily at 0700-0800. The journey takes 3 hrs. Boats return at 1430, arriving in Puno at 1730. It costs US$7 one way. This doesn't leave enough time to appreciate the island fully in one day. Organized tours can be arranged for about US$10-16 per person, but only give you about 2 hrs on the island. Make sure you and the boatman know exactly what you are paying for.

Boats for **Amantaní** from the harbour in Puno leave at 0700-0800 daily, and return at 0800, arriving in Puno around 1200. The trip costs US$5.80 one way. The journey takes 4-5 hrs. A one-day trip is not possible as the boats do not always return on the same day. If you wish to visit both Taquile and Amantaní, it is better to go to Amantaní first. From there

boats go to Taquile at around 0800, costing US$2.50 per person. There is no regular service – boats leave if there are enough passengers. You would then take the 1430 boat from Taquile to Puno.

ℹ️ Directory

Puno *p143*
Banks BCP, **Interbank** and **Banco Continental**, all on Lima, have Visa ATMs, **Banco Wiese Sudameris**, at Lima with Deústua, has a Mastercard ATM. For cash go to the cambios, the travel agencies or the better hotels. Best rates with money changers on Jr Lima, many on 400 block, and on Tacna near the market, eg Arbulu y Tacna. Check your Peruvian soles carefully. Exchange rates from soles to bolivianos and vice versa are sometimes better in Puno than in Yunguyo; check with other travellers. **Consulates Bolivia**, Jr Arequipa 136, T051-351251. Issues a visa on the spot, US$10, open 0830-1400 Mon-Fri. **Internet** There are offices everywhere in the centre. Average price is US$0.60/hr. Good ones include **Chasquinet**, Jr Libertad 239, 0730-2230. **Chozanet**, Jr Lima 339, 0800-2300. **Kupidos**, Jr Libertad 233, 0730-2230. **Laundry Don Marcelo**, head office at Ayacucho 651, T352444, has agencies in several places in the centre, including on Lima 427, and will collect and deliver laundry. US$1.50 per kg, good service. **Post office** Jr Moquegua 267. **Telephone Telefónica** at Puno y Moquegua for local and international calls. Another phone office is at Lima 489. **Useful addresses Immigration**, Ayacucho 240, T051-352801. For renewing entry stamps, etc. The process is very slow and you must fill in 2 application forms at a bank, but there's nothing else to pay. **Indecopi**, Lima y Fermín Arbulú, p 2, T/F051-366138 odipun@indecopi .gob.pe. The office of the tourist protection bureau.

Arequipa and the Colca Canyon

Arequipa stands in a beautiful valley at the foot of El Misti volcano, a snow-capped, perfect cone, 5,822 m high. The distinctive volcanic sillar used in the building of Arequipa has given it its nickname of the 'White City'. Spanish churches, mansions and the 19th-century Plaza de Armas all shine with this stonework. In contrast, the city's most famous colonial legacy, the Santa Catalina convent, is painted in bright colours, a gorgeous little city within a city. But this is only one attraction in a region of volcanoes, deep canyons and terraced valleys, and ancient peoples. The famous Colca Canyon offers excellent trekking and riding on its vast terraces, but above all, Colca is the best place in the world to get a close up view of the majestic condor as it rises from the bottom of the canyon the morning thermals.

Getting there Flights to Arequipa from Lima; buses from Lima and Cusco.

Getting around Local buses and tours to the Colca Canyon.

Time required 1-2 days in Arequipa, 2 days minimum in Colca.

Weather Arequipa has 360 days of warm sunshine. May-Dec is the dry, cold season in Colca, Jan-Apr is wet.

Sleeping Good range of hotels in Arequipa; more expensive options are opening in Colca to complement the more basic places.

Eating Guinea pig and spicy foods are popular in Arequipa.

Activities and tours Climbing, trekking, rafting and tours to Colca.

★ **Don't miss...** Cruz del Cóndor ▶▶ p162.

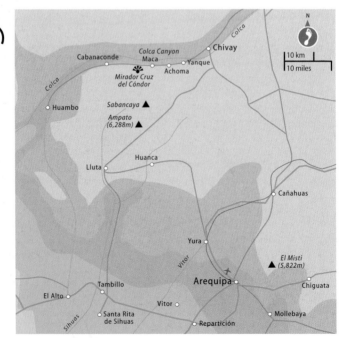

Arequipa ⬤🚆👤✳️🚌⚠️⬤🌙 ›› *pp163-171*

Founded in 1540, Arequipa has grown into a magnificent city, one that exudes an air of intellectual rigour and political passion. It is now the main commercial centre for the south and its fiercely proud people resent the general tendency to believe that everything is run from Lima.

Ins and outs

Getting there Rodríguez Ballón airport is 7 km from town. For transport to and from the airport, see page 170. The bus terminal is a 10-15 minute drive south of the centre. The train station is a 15-minute walk from the centre (see map on page 164). Theft is a serious problem in the bus station area. Take a taxi to and from the bus station and do not wander around with your belongings. No one is allowed to enter the terminal 2100-0500, so new arrivals cannot be met by hoteliers between those hours; best not to arrive at night. ⬤ ›› *p170*

Getting around Arequipa is a compact city with the main places of interest and hotels within a few blocks of the Plaza de Armas. Take a bus or taxi if you want to the visit the suburbs. Taxis (can be shared) charge US$4-5 from the airport to the city. Fares around town are US$0.70-0.85, including to bus terminal.

One of the many delightful little, flower-filled plazas in Arequipa's amazing Santa Catalina Convent.

Cusco & Southern Peru Arequipa & the Colca Canyon

Tourist information i perú ⓘ *In the Municipalidad on the south side of the Plaza de Armas, T054-221228, iperuarequipa@ptomperu.gob.pe, 0830-1930 daily. Airport, 2nd floor, T054-444564, 0630-1730 daily.* **Indecopi** (tourist protection bureau) ⓘ *Moral 316, T054-212054, mcornejo@indecopi.gob.pe and Quezada 104, Yanahuara, T054-270181, rneyra@indecopi. gob.pe or T0800-42579, 24 hrs, toll-free.* **Tourist Police** ⓘ *Jerusalén 315, T054-251270/239888*, are helpful with complaints or giving directions. Useful websites are www.arequipa-tourism.com, in Spanish and English; www.aqplink.com/arequipa/ in Spanish and www.perupass.com, who also publish the *Arequipa Tourist Magazine*.

Climate Arequipa enjoys a wonderful climate, with a mean temperature before sundown of 23°C, and after sundown of 14°C. The sun shines on 360 days of the year. Annual rainfall is less than 150 mm.

Sights

The **Santa Catalina Convent** ⓘ *Santa Catalina 301, T054-229798, www.santacatalina.org.pe, 0900-1600, US$7.25*, opened in 1970 after four centuries of mysterious isolation, is the most remarkable sight in Arequipa and a complete contrast to what you would expect from nuns who had taken vows of poverty. The convent has been beautifully refurbished, with period furniture, pictures of the Arequipa and Cusco schools and fully equipped kitchens. It is a complete miniature walled colonial town of over 2 ha in the middle of the city. About 450 nuns lived here in total seclusion, except for their women servants.

The few remaining nuns have retreated to one section of the convent, allowing visitors to see a maze of cobbled streets and plazas bright with geraniums and other flowers, cloisters and buttressed houses. These have been finely restored and painted in traditional white, orange, deep red and blue. The tour offered at the entrance is worthwhile and lasts 1½ hours; there's no set price and many of the guides speak English or German (a tip of US$2-3 is expected). There is a good café, which sells cakes made by the nuns and a special blend of tea.

The elegant **Plaza de Armas**, beautifully laid-out with palm trees, gardens and fountain, is faced on three sides by arcaded colonial buildings (rebuilt after an earthquake in 1863) with many restaurants, and on the fourth by the massive **cathedral**, founded in 1612 and largely rebuilt in the 19th century. Despite the care taken in building techniques, the June 2001 earthquake caused one of the cathedral's twin towers famously to collapse. Repairs were completed in 2003. The entrance to the Cathedral is on the plaza.

Firmly established as one of the major sites in Arequipa is the **Museo Santuarios Andinos** ⓘ *La Merced 110, T054-200345, www.ucsm.edu.pe/santury, Mon-Sat 0900-1800, Sun 0900-1700; the US$5 entry fee includes a 20 min video of the discovery in English followed by an hour-long guided tour in English, French, German, Italian or Spanish (tip the guide), discount with student card*. It contains the frozen mummies recently found on Ampato volcano. The mummy known as 'Juanita' is particularly fascinating (see p162). From January to April, Juanita is often jetting round the world, and is replaced by other child sacrifices unearthed in the mountains.

Colca Canyon ▣❶◐▣ ▸▸ *pp163-171*

Twice as deep as the Grand Canyon and once thought to be the deepest canyon in the world (until the nearby Cotahuasi Canyon was found to be all of 163 m deeper), the Colca Canyon is an area of astounding beauty. Giant amphitheatres of pre-Inca terracing become narrow, precipitous gorges, and in the background looms the grey, smoking mass of Sabancaya, one of the most active volcanoes in the Americas, and its more docile neighbour, Ampato (6,288 m). Unspoiled Andean villages lie on both sides of the canyon, inhabited by the Cabana and Collagua peoples. The Río Colca snakes its way through the length of this massive gorge, 3,500 m above sea level at Chivay (the canyon's main town) falling to 2,200 m at Cabanaconde, at the far end of the canyon. Now, the Colca Canyon is best known for its associations with some rather large birds. Would-be David Attenboroughs flock here for a close encounter with the giant Andean condor at the aptly-named Cruz del Cóndor.

Ins and outs

Getting there and around Buses to Colca all leave from the main terminal in Arequipa but you can get your ticket the previous day at the bus company offices in Calle San Juan de Dios. It is a rough route and cold in the morning, reaching 4,825 m at the Pata Pampa pass, but the views are worth it. In the rainy season it is better to travel by day as the road can get icy and slippery at night. Combis and colectivos run from Chivay to the villages in the canyon. ⊖ ➤➤ *p170*

Best time to visit May to December is the dry, cold season when there is more chance of seeing condors. January to April is the rainy season, but this makes the area green, with lots of flowers, though this is not the best time to see the birds.

The 3,500 m-deep Colca Canyon offers one of Peru's great wildlife experiences.

Background

Appeasing the gods

In September 1995, anthropologist, Johan Reinhard, of Chicago's Field Museum of Natural History, accompanied by Peruvian climber, Miguel Zárate, were climbing Ampato in the Colca Canyon when they made a startling discovery, at about 6,000 m. They found the perfectly preserved mummified body of an Inca girl. Wrapped tightly in textiles, this girl in her early teens must have been ritually sacrificed and buried on the summit.

Mummies of Inca human sacrifices have been found before on Andean summits, but the girl from Ampato, nicknamed Juanita, was the first frozen Inca female to be unearthed and her body may be the best preserved of any found in the Americas from pre-Columbian times.

Ampato was one of the principal deities in the Colca Canyon region. The Incas appeased the mountain gods, who were said to supply water to their villages and fields, with children as sacrifices. The Cabana and Collagua people even bound their children's heads to make them look like the mountains from which they believed they were descended.

A subsequent ascent of Ampato revealed a further two mummies at the summit. One is a young girl and the other, though badly charred by lightning, is believed to be a boy. If so, it may mean that these children were ritually sacrificed together in a symbolic marriage.

Nowadays, villages in the Colca continue to make offerings to the mountain gods for water and good harvests, but thankfully the gods have modified their tastes, now preferring chicha to children.

Chivay to Cabanaconde

Chivay is the gateway to the canyon and the overnight stopping point for two-day tours run by agencies in Arequipa. The hot springs of **La Calera** ⓘ *entry US$3*, are 4 km away. To get there take one of the regular *colectivos* (US$0.25) from beside the market or it's a pleasant hour-long walk. There are several large hot pools and showers but only one pool is open to tourists. The hot springs are highly recommended after a hard day's trekking. There is a very helpful **tourist office** in the Municipalidad on the west side of the plaza which gives away a useful map of the valley. The tourist police, also on the plaza, can give advice about locally trained guides.

From Chivay the road winds its way on to the Mirador, or **Cruz del Cóndor** ⓘ *entrance fee of US$4 is charged (may rise to US$10), not included in agency prices*, at the deepest point of the canyon. The view from here is wonderful but people don't come for the view. This is where the immense Andean vulture, the condor, can be seen rising on the morning thermals to swoop by in startling close up, so close, in fact, that you feel you could reach out and touch them. It is a breathtaking and very humbling experience. The condors, more punctual than most Peruvians, usually arrive around 0900 as they fly off to look for carrion on the higher slopes of the surrounding peaks. Get there by 0800 for a good spot, any earlier and you may be faced with a long, chilly wait (this may be unavoidable by public transport – buses from Chivay stop here very briefly). The condors can also be seen returning from a hard day's food

searching at around 1600-1800. Just below the Mirador is a rocky outcrop, which allows a more peaceful viewing but take great care on the loose scree (or you'll end up on the menu). Binoculars are recommended. Snacks and drinks are available.

To get to the Mirador from Cabanaconde, take one of the return buses which set off at around 0730, and ask to be dropped off at the Mirador, just in time for the morning performance. Or you can walk along the road, which takes about three hours. Horses can be hired to save you the walk; arrange the night before in Cabanaconde. To walk from the Mirador to Cabanaconde, follow the road until Cabanaconde is in sight, then turn off the road 50 m after a small reservoir down a walled track. After about 1 km turn left on to an old Inca road and continue down to rejoin the road into Cabanaconde.

From the Mirador it is a 20-minute bus ride to the tumbledown village of **Cabanaconde** at 3,287 m, the last in the Colca Canyon. The views into the canyon are excellent from here and condors can be seen from the hill just west of the village, a 15-minute walk from the plaza, which also gives views of the amazing terraces, arguably the most attractive in the valley, to the south of the village. There's a tourist information office, T054-280212, attended by friendly locals willing to give plenty of advice, if not maps. It's a good place to find trekking guides and muleteers and there are many hiking possibilities in the area. Make sure to take enough water as it gets very hot and there is not a lot of water available. Moreover, sun protection is a must. Some treks are impossible if it rains heavily in the wet season, but this is rare. Ask locals for directions as there are hundreds of confusing paths going into the canyon. Buy food for longer hikes in Arequipa. Topographical maps are available at the **Instituto Geográfico Militar** in Lima, from **Colca Trek** or **Pablo Tour** in Arequipa, and good information can be obtained from **South American Explorers**.

◉ Sleeping

Arequipa *p158, map p164*
LL-L Libertador, Plaza Simón Bolívar, Selva Alegre, T054-215110, www.libertador.com.pe. Safe, large comfortable rooms, good service, swimming pool (cold), gardens, good meals, pub-style bar, cocktail lounge, squash court.
AL-A Casa Andina, C Jerusalén 603, T054-202070, www.casa-andina.com. Part of the attractive Casa Andina chain,

with breakfast, comfortable and colourful, central, modern, good restaurant, safe, cable TV, phones, friendly staff, car parking.
B Casa de Mi Abuela, Jerusalén 606, T054-241206, www.lacasdemia buela.com. Very clean, friendly, safe, hot water, laundry, cable TV, swimming pool, rooms at the back are quieter and overlook the garden (but the room at the very back beyond the garden is dark and has no hot water), **D** without bathroom, self-catering if desired, English spoken,

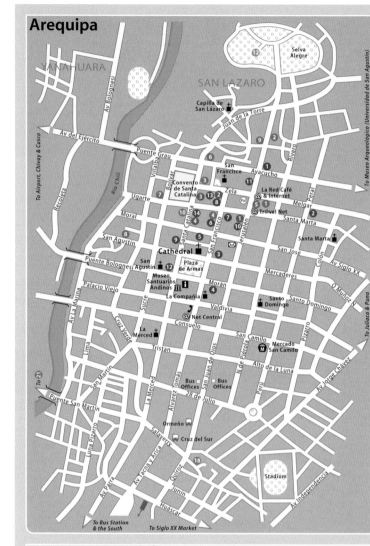

Arequipa

Sleeping
Casa Andina **9**
Casa de Melgar **1**
Casa de Mi Abuela **2**
Hostal la Reyna **3**
Hostal Regis **4**
Hostal Tumi de Oro **8**
La Casa de Margott **5**
La Estación **21**
La Posada del Cacique **6**
Las Torres de Ugarte **7**
Posada de Sancho **10**
Libertador **12**
Tambo Viejo **18**

Eating
Ary Quepay **1**
Café Manolo **3**
Café Valenzuela **4**
Casa Vegetariana **5**
Colibri Café **6**
El Turko **7**
El Turko II **8**
Ganesh **9**
Mandala **10**

Nómadas **2**
Pizzería Los Leños **11**
Sonccollay **12**
Zig Zag **13**
Zig Zag Crêperie **14**

Bars & clubs
Ad Libitum **1**
Dejá Vu **2**
Las Quenas **3**
Siwara **4**

internet access US$3 per hr, tours and transport organized in own agency (Giardino, T054-221345, www.giardinotours.com), which has good information (expensive), small library of European books, breakfast or evening snacks on patio or in beautiful garden, parking, **A-B** for apartment for 4, lots of tour groups.

C Casa de Melgar, Melgar 108, T/F054-222459, www.lared.net.pe/lacasademelgar/. Excellent rooms, all different, delightful 18th century building, with bathroom, hot water all day (solar panel), safe, clean, friendly, nice courtyard, good breakfast in café open in the morning and 1730-2100, book exchange, luggage store. Can arrange good taxi tours with driver, Angel.

C La Casa de Margott, Jerusalén 304, T229517, lacasademargotthostal@hotmail.com. Bright with a massive palm tree in patio, spotless, small bar/café, new, cable TV, phone, security box.

C La Casa de Tintin, Urbanización San Isidro F1, Vallecito, T054-284700, www.lacasadetintin.com. New B&B place 15 mins' walk, 5 mins by taxi from the Plaza de Armas, Belgian/Peruvian owned, with bath, hot water 24 hrs, cable TV, garden, terrace, sauna, laundry service, restaurant, café and bar and internet, mountain bike rental, very pleasant, clean. Breakfast included in the price.

C-F Tambo Viejo, Av Malecón Socabaya 107, IV Centenario, 5 blocks south of the plaza near the rail station, T054-288195, www.tamboviejo.com. Family home, quiet, very friendly, English and Dutch spoken, walled garden, hot water, expensive laundry service, cable TV, safe deposit, coffee shop, bar book exchange (2 for 1), money changed, tourist information for guests, use of kitchen, internet, phone for international calls, bike rental, popular with young travellers, luggage store extra, tours arranged. For a small fee, you can use the facilities if passing through. When arriving by bus or train, do not believe taxi drivers who say

the hotel is closed or full; ring the door bell and check for yourself. Better still, telephone the hostel and they will pick you up free of charge 0500-2100. In high season rooms with garden view are **C**, **D-E** with shared bath, **F** pp in dormitory.

D per person **Hostal Regis**, Ugarte 202, T054-226111. Colonial house, French-style interior, clean, hot water all day, **E** without bath, cooking and laundry facilities (good laundry service), sun terrace with good views, safe deposit, luggage store, video rental, book exchange, very helpful, tours arranged.

D Hostal Tumi de Oro, San Agustín 311A, 2 blocks from the Plaza de Armas, T/F054-281319. With bathroom, French and English spoken, hot water, roof terrace, book exchange, tea/coffee facilities, safe.

D La Estación, Loreto 419, Umacollo, T273852, www.backpackerperu.com. Unusual dormitory accommodation in two train carriages, includes breakfast, hot water, restaurant next door, friendly, clean and fresh. 10 mins' walk from Plaza, ask directions for 'el Ovalo del Vallecito', English spoken.

D La Posada del Cacique, Puente Grau 219, T202170, posadadelcacique @yahoo.es. Old house with tall ceilings, tiny patio, sun terrace, friendly, good hot water, English spoken, family atmosphere, **E** without bath, also dorm accommodation, safe storage facilities, breakfast available, laundry service, will pick up from terminal.

D Las Torres de Ugarte, Ugarte 401-A, T/F054-283532, hostaltorresdeugarte @star.com.pe. Next to Santa Catalina convent, hot water all day, cable TV, roof terrace, laundry service, parking, safe, luggage store, helpful staff, discount for longer stays, price includes breakfast served in a sunny room.

D Posada de Sancho, Santa Catalina 213 A and 223 A, near the convent, T/F054-287797, posadasancho @terra.com.pe. Hot showers, cheaper without bath, clean, safe, nice patio and terrace with a view of El Misti, good breakfast extra, very friendly owners, English, French and German spoken, information on travel and Spanish classes, offer cheap tours.

E Hostal La Reyna, Zela 209, T054-286578. With or without bath, two more expensive rooms at the top of the house (very good), hot water 24 hrs, clean, can be noisy because of location, the daughter speaks English, laundry, breakfast for US$1.15, pizza available at any hour, rooftop seating, can arrange Spanish classes, will store luggage and arrange trips to the Colca Canyon and volcanoes (a bit chaotic, but recommendable nonetheless). Can also arrange cars, vans and 4WDs with drivers.

Colca Canyon p160

Ask if your hotel can provide heating. Many of the better hotels are regularly used by tour groups. There are several other hotels and family homes where you can stay; ask around.

AL Colca Lodge, between Coporaque and Ichupampa (in Arequipa Jerusalén 212, T054-202587, www.colca-lodge.com). Very pleasant and relaxing, safe, heating, restaurant with good buffet, widescreen TV with pirated DVDs. Beautiful hot springs beside the river, trekking, cycling, riding, rafting, spend at least a day there to make the most of what's on offer.

AL Parador del Colca, T054-288440, res-mirapàrk@peruorientexpress.com.pe. 3½ km from Yanque, 10 km from Chivay, owned by Orient Express. Built of local materials, with solar power, on an old estate, the hotel offers lots of activities; comfortable cabin-like suites, typical food and home-grown vegetables, meals extra, due for expansion in 2005.

A Casa Andina, Huayna Cápac s/n, Chivay, T054-531020, www.casa-andina.com. Attractive cabins with hot showers and a cosy bar/dining area, another member of this recommended hotel chain, heating, internet, parking.

B Kuntur Wassi, on the hill above the plaza, Cabanaconde, T054-252989, kunturwassi@terra.com.pe. Attractive and original, restaurant/bar, great views, helpful.

B Colca Inn, Salaverry 307, Chivay, T054-531111, www.hotelcolcainn.com. A good mid-range option, modern, very clean, with a decent restaurant.

C Posada del Conde, C San Pedro, Cabanaconde, T054-440197, 993 6809 (mob), pdelconde@yahoo.com. Cheaper in low season, with hot shower, excellent value but can be a bit noisy, very good restaurant. Booking advisable.

C Tradición Colca, on main road, Yanque. Contact Carelia and Emmanuel Derouet, Jerusalén 300C, T205336, www.tradicioncolca.com Price is per unit, D in low season and includes breakfast, with gardens, restaurant, bar, games room, also have backpackers' rooms; they also have a travel agency.

D El Posada del Inca, Salaverry 330, T054-521032. Modern, with hot showers, carpeted rooms, safe, hot water bottles, clean and friendly.

F Hostal Valle del Fuego, 1 and 2 blocks from the plaza, Cabanaconde, T054-280367 (Arequipa 054-203737), www.pablotour.com. Good but basic, has two places (E in newer annex), both with restaurants serving good meals for around US$3, breakfast overpriced. The owner and his son, both Pablo Junco, are a wealth of information. They usually meet the incoming buses but otherwise turn left facing the church on the plaza and the first place is 1 block along on the right.

🍴 Eating

Arequipa p158, map p164

🍴🍴🍴 **Tradición Arequipeña**, Av Dolores 111, Paucarpata, T054-246467. Restaurant serving excellent food, popular with tourists and locals alike, also dancehall.

🍴🍴 **Ary Quepay**, Jerusalén 502. Excellent local meat and vegetarian dishes, open 1000-2400.

¶¶ **El Turko II**, San Francisco 315. Turkish, local and international.

¶¶ **Nómadas**, Melgar 306. Swiss and South American owned, breakfasts, wide menu including vegetarian, sandwiches.

¶¶ **Pizzería Los Leños**, Jerusalén 407. Excellent, good atmosphere, evenings only, popular, especially with tourists.

¶¶ **Sonccollay**, Portal de San Agustin 149. Serving 'Inca and Pre-Inca' dishes, this restaurant gives a new twist to 'traditional' food. Stone-cooked alpaca steaks and meats are a speciality. Hosted by an entertaining owner, plenty of home-made chicha.

¶¶ **Zig Zag**, Zela 210. In a colonial house, European (including Swiss) and local dishes, excellent meats include ostrich and alpaca, top class. They also have a creperie in the Alianza Francesa.

¶¶ **Zig Zag Crêperie**, Santa Catalina 208. Excellent crêpes, good value set lunch, also snacks, cocktails, coffee.

¶¶ ¶ **Ganesh**, Santa Catalina 111, upstairs. Asian food and a limited number of vegetarian options, good service, relaxed atmosphere, bar.

¶ **Casa Vegetariana**, Moral 205. Vegetarian and Asian, typical local food and western dishes.

¶ **El Turko**, San Francisco 216. Kebabs, coffee, good breakfasts and sandwiches, open 0700-2200.

¶ **Mandala**, Jerusalén 207, mandala26 @correoweb.com. Good value vegetarian, breakfast, 3 set menus for lunch, buffet, dinner, friendly staff.

Cafés

Café Manolo, Mercaderes 107 and 113. Great cakes and coffee, also cheap lunches, pastas, sandwiches and juices.

Café Valenzuela, Moran 114. Fantastic coffee, locals' favourite.

Colibri Café, San Francisco 225. Excellent value set lunches and dinners, open plan, attractive, good coffee.

Colca Canyon *p160*

There are several good, attractively decorated restaurants in Chivay, which are both cosy and friendly. They serve good-value set meals for around US$3 which offer a choice of dishes. Not all restaurants are open at night.

¶¶-¶ **Casa Blanca**, on the main plaza, good, main dishes US$2.50-7.50, reasonable food, also has *peña* show with set meal.

¶¶-¶ **Fonda del Cazador**, on the north side of the plaza, serves delicious alpaca steaks.

¶¶-¶ **Lobos Pizzería**, on the plaza. Has good pizzas and fast food, internet access, pool, and a happy hour bar.

¶¶-¶ **Los Sismos**, by the petrol station. Also serves great alpaca steaks, often has live folklore shows.

¶ **Farren's**, bar run by a Peruvian and an Irishman, handmade Guinness sign outside, warm, friendly, good selection of drinks, sandwiches and music, also bikes for hire.

There are several basic restaurants around the plaza in Cabanaconde (all ¶), including **Rancho del Colca**, which is mainly vegetarian, and **Don Piero**, signposted just off main plaza, excellent choice and good information.

● Bars and clubs

Arequipa *p158, map p164*

Ad Libitum, Jerusalén y Ugarte. Friendly, unpretentious local bar, open late.

Las Quenas, Santa Catalina 302. For *peña* music, Mon-Fri 2100.

Le Café Art Montreal, Santa Catalina 300B-1. Atmospheric Canadian-run jazz/blues restaurant/bar with live music Wed and Sat.

Siwara, Santa Catalina 210. Trendy hangout, lively in the evenings, good food, and some live music.

✸ Festivals and events

This is a region of wild and frequent festivals. On **2-3 Feb** Virgen de la Candelaria is celebrated in the towns of

Chivay and Cabanaconde, with dancing in the plaza, and over 5 days in Maca and Tapay and in the churches of Cayma, Characato, Chiguata and Chapi with masses, processions of the Virgin through the streets, and fireworks.

The **Semana Santa** celebrations in Arequipa are carried out Sevillano style, with the townsfolk turned out in traditional mourning dress. There are huge processions every night, culminating in the burning of an effigy of Judas on **Easter Sun** in the main plazas of Cayma and Yanahuara, and the reading of his 'will', containing criticisms of the city authorities.

On **1 May** the Fiesta de la Virgen de Chapi is a great pilgrimage to the sanctuary of Chapi and one of the most important religious ceremonies in the region. **May** is known as the 'Month of the Crosses', with ceremonies on hilltops throughout the city. On **15 May** the popular fiesta of San Isidro Labrador takes place in Sachaca, Chuquibamba and other towns and villages in the valley, and lasts for 7 days.

On **29 Jun**, in Yanahuara, the **Fiesta de San Juan**, the local patron saint, is held with mass and fireworks.

On **14-17 Jul** the Fiesta de la Virgen del Carmen is held in Cabanaconde and Pampacolca, when folk dancing takes place in the streets. Of particular interest is the dance of Los Turcos, which represents the indigenous peoples' struggle against the conquistadors. This fiesta is also held in the churches of Yura, Carmen Alto, Congata, Tingo Grande and the Convent of Santa Teresa in Arequipa city.

On **6-31 Aug** is the Fiesta Artesanal del Fundo del Fierro, a sale and exhibition of artesanía from all parts of Peru, taking place near Plaza San Francisco. At the same time, **6-17 Aug** is the celebration of the city's anniversary; various events are held, including music, dancing and exhibitions. On the eve of the actual day, the 15th, there is a splendid firework display in the Plaza de Armas and a decorated float parade. There is also a mass ascent of El Misti from the Plaza de Armas. It is virtually impossible to find a hotel room during the celebrations. On **15 Aug** in Chivay is the fiesta of the **Virgen de la Asunta**, the town's patron saint, which lasts 8 days. On **8 Dec**, **Inmaculada Concepción** is held in Chivay and Yanque, when groups of musicians and dancers present the traditional dance, the Witite, lasting 5 days. On **25 Dec** once again in Yanque, just in case you haven't had enough, the **Witite** is held over 6 days.

○ Shopping

Arequipa *p158, map p164*
Arequipa is noted for its leather work. The main street of saddlers and leather workers is Puente Bolognesi. The handicraft shop in the old prison opposite San Francisco is particularly good for bags. There are markets which are good for general handicrafts. The covered market opposite the Teatro Municipal on Mercaderes is recommended for knitted goods, bags, etc. Also worth a try is the market around Valdivia and Nicolas de Piérola. The large **Fundo del Fierro** handicraft market behind the old prison on Plaza San Francisco is also worth a visit. Shop 14 sells alpaca-wool handicrafts from Callalli in the Colca Canyon.

Arequipa is an excellent place to buy top quality alpaca knitwear.
Alpaca 21, Jerusalén 115, of 125, T054-213425, is recommended.
Colca Trading Company, Santa Catalina 300B, T054-242088 (Lima 01-254 1885), colcatradingperu@yahoo.com, sells a wide variety of naturally-coloured cotton and alpaca clothing for adults and children.
Lanificio, La Pampilla sin número, T054-225305, is a factory selling high-quality alpaca cloth at better prices than Lima outlets.
Patio del Ekeko, Mercaderes 141, T054-215861, www.patiodelekeko.com,

Top tips

Colca Canyon tours

✅ Many agencies on Jerusalén, Santa Catalina and around Plaza de Armas in Arequipa sell air, train and bus tickets and offer tours of Colca, Cotahuasi and city. Prices vary greatly so shop around.

✅ Find out exactly what you are paying for. Travel agents frequently work together in a 'pooling' system to fill buses. This can mean that a busload of tourists will come from different agencies, all paying different prices, but all expecting the same level of service. On occasion the company providing the transport may not have the same high standards as the operator through whom the tour was booked.

❌ Many people, especially those with altitude problems, will find a one-day tour too much to cope with (the only advantage is that you don't have to sleep at high altitude). It's also more dangerous since drivers get tired on the way back.

is a shopping and entertainment and cultural centre. Shops include **Alpaca 111** for alpaca and vicuña (recommended for high-quality alpaca and wool products), **Ilaria** for fine jewellery and silverware, **La Ibérica** for chocolates and **Artesanías del Ekeko**. There is also the **Café del Ekeko**, which has internet (a bit more expensive than elsewhere, but a good place), as well as sandwiches, desserts, coffee and a bar.

▲ Activities and tours

Arequipa *p158, map p164*
Travel agencies in Arequipa arrange a 'one-day' tour to the **Cruz del Cóndor** for US$18-20. They leave Arequipa at 0400, arriving at the Cruz del Cóndor at 0800-0900, followed by an expensive lunch stop at Chivay and back to Arequipa by 2100. Two day tours start at US$20-30 per person with an overnight stop in Chivay; more expensive tours range from US$45 to US$90 with accommodation at the top of the range.

Tour operators
Colca Trek, Jerusalén 401 B, T054-206217, www.trekinperu.com. Run by the knowledgeable and English-speaking Vlado Soto. The

company is recommended for climbing, trekking and mountain biking in the Colca Canyon. Vlado is one of the best guides for the Cotahuasi Canyon. He also rents equipment and has topographical maps.
Holley's Unusual Excursions, T/F054-258459 (home) any day 1700-0700, or all day Sat and Sun, or Mon-Fri 0800-1600 T054-222525 and leave a message, angocho@terra.com.pe. Expat Anthony Holley runs trips in his Land Rover to El Misti, Toro Muerto, the desert and coast.
Naturaleza Activa, Santa Catalina 211, T054-204182, naturactiva@yahoo.com. Experienced guides, knowledgeable, climbing and trekking.
Pablo Tour, Jerusalén 400-A, www.pablotour.com. Father-and-son agency that owns several hostals in Cabaconde; they know the area well.
Santa Catalina Tours, Santa Catalina 219-223, T054-216994. Offer unique tours of Collagua communities in the Colca Canyon. Daily 0800-1900.
Servicios Aéreos AQP, Santa Catalina 210, T054-281800, www.saaqp.com.pe. For private hire and tourist flights to the Colca Canyon and around the country.
Transcontinential Arequipa, Puente Bolognesi 132, oficina 5, T054-213843,

transcontinental-aqp@terra.com.pe
Cultural and wildlife tours in the
Colca Canyon.
Volcanyon Travel, C Villalba 414,
T054-205078, mario-ortiz@terra.com.pe.
Trekking and some mountain bike tours
in the Colca Canyon, also volcano
climbing.

⊖ Transport

Arequipa *p158, map p164*

Air

Airport information T054-443464. At the
airport are two desks offering hotel
reservations (not always accurate) and free
transport to town, a travel agency
(**Domiruth**) and **Avis** car rental. To and
from **Lima**, several flights daily with **Lan**
and **Tans**. These airlines also serve **Juliaca**.
Also daily flights to Cusco with **Lan**.

A reliable means of transport to and
from the airport to the hotel of your
choice is with **King Tours**, T054-243357,
US$1.30 per person. You need to give 24
hrs notice for the return pick-up from
your hotel. The journey takes 30-40 mins
depending on the traffic. Transport to the
airport may be arranged when buying a
ticket at a travel agency, for US$1 per
person, but it's not always reliable. **Local
buses and combis** go to about 500 m
from the airport, look for ones marked
'Río Seco', 'Cono-Norte' or 'Zamacola'.

Airline offices Lan, Santa Catalina
118-C, T054-201100.

Bus

All buses leave from either of the two
terminals at Av Andrés A Cáceres s/n,
Parque Industrial, opposite Inca Tops
factory, south of the centre; 15 mins by
colectivo US$0.20, or taxi US$1.75. The
older terminal is called **Terminal
Terrestre**, which contains a tourist office,
shops and places to eat. The newer
terminal is **Terrapuerto**, the other side of
the carpark, also with a tourist office
(which makes hotel reservations with free
transfer to affiliated hotels and its own

hostal, T054-421375). A terminal tax of
US$0.30 must be paid on entry to the
platform. Check which terminal your bus
will leave from as it may not depart from
the terminal where you bought your
ticket. All the bus companies have their
offices in the Terminal Terrestre and
several also have offices in Terrapuerto.
Some companies also have offices around
C San Juan de Dios (5-6 blocks from the
Plaza de Armas), where tickets can be
bought in advance, saving a trip to the
terminal. Be especially careful in this area,
however (addresses are given below).
Some tour operators also make bus
reservations for a small fee.

To **Lima**, 16-18 hrs, 'normal' service
US$8.70, 'imperial' US$17.40 (video, toilet,
meals, comfortable seats, blankets),
'crucero' US$23-29 several daily. Ormeño
(T054-424187, or booth in Carsa shop at
San Juan de Dios 657, only open Mon-Fri
for about 2 hrs a day) and **Cruz del Sur**
(T054-217728, or Av Salaverry 121,
T054-213905) are recommended (prices
quoted are for Cruz del Sur). The road is
paved but drifting sand and breakdowns
may prolong the trip. Buses will stop at
the major cities en route, but not always
Pisco. To **Nasca**, 566 km, 9 hrs,
US$7.25-10 (US$30 on Ormeño Royal
service), several buses daily, mostly at
night and most buses continue to Lima.
Beware, some bus companies to Nasca
charge the Lima fare. To **Cusco**, all buses
now go via Juliaca or Puno, US$12-15,
10 hrs. Most companies use
double-decker buses (bath, TV, hostess,
etc), including **Cruz del Sur** and **Ormeño**,
running one in the morning and, in some
instances, one in the afternoon. To **Puno**,
6 hrs, US$6.

Cars and taxis

Car hire Avis, Palacio Viejo 214,
T054-282519, or at the airport
T054-443576. **Transjesa**, Urb Guardia Civil
III Etapa E-6, Paucarpata, T054-460403,
www.planet.com/transjesa. Also at the
airport. Good value and new vehicles.

Genesis, Jerusalén y Puente Grau,
T054-202033. Rents 4WDs in good
condition, can also arrange drivers.
Radio taxis Nova Taxi, T054-252511;
Telemóvil, T054-221515; Taxitur,
T054-422323.

Colca Canyon *p160*

Cristo Rey, **La Reyna** (recommended)
and **Andalucia** have 7 departures daily
from Arequipa to **Chivay**, continuing to
Cabanaconde; a further 75 km, 2 hrs,
US$1. La Reyna has the quickest service,
about 6 hrs, US$3.85, others US$3. Buy a
ticket in advance to ensure a seat (many
agencies can buy them for you for a fee).
Buses return to Arequipa from the
market. For **Cabanaconde** and **Cruz del
Cóndor** catch the 0500 bus from Chivay
which stops briefly at the Mirador at
0700 (if this doesn't seem likely, ask),
US$0.75. Combis run infrequently in
each direction, fewer on Sun. You could
also try hitching a lift with a tour bus.
Combis and colectivos leave from the
new terminal, 3 blocks from the main
plaza in Chivay to any village in the area.
Ask the drivers for details.

Buses leave Cabanaconde for **Arequipa**
between 0730 and 1500.

ℹ Directory

Arequipa *p158, map p164*
Banks Interbank, Mercaderes 217.
Mastercard representative and ATM, US$5
commission on TCs. BCP, San Juan de
Dios 125, also at Santo Domingo y
Jerusalén. Accepts Visa Card (has ATM)
and gives good rates, no commission.
Recommended. BBV Continental, San
Francisco 108. Visa ATM, US$12
commission on TCs. BSCH, C Jerusalén,
close to the Post Office. Changes Visa and
Citicorp TCs, low rates, accepts
Mastercard, has Visa ATM. Banco Wiese,
Mercaderes 410. Change money at
cambios on Jerusalén and San Juan de
Dios, and several travel agencies. Sergio A

del Carpio D, Jerusalén 126, T054-242987,
good rates for dollars. **Via Tours**, Santo
Domingo 114, good rates. **Casa de
Cambio**, San Juan de Dios 109,
T054-282528, good rates. It is almost
impossible to change TCs on Sat
afternoon or Sun; try to find a
sympathetic street changer. Better rates
for cash dollars in banks and casas de
cambio. **Internet** C@tedr@l, Pasaje
Catedral 101, T054-220622,
internetcatedral@hotmail.com
0800-2400, fast machines, international
calls. **Chips Internet**, San Francisco 202-A,
chips@chips.com.pe **La Red Café
Internet**, Jerusalén 306, café
@LaRed.net.pe 0830-2200, US$0.45 per
hr. : Tr@vel Net, Jerusalén 218, US$0.75
per hr and international phone calls. **Net
Central**, Alvarez Thomas 219, netcentral
@netcentral. lared.net.pe 0900-2300, fast
machines. **Cybercafé.com**, Santa Catalina
115-B, at Easy Market. US$0.75 per hr.
Another at Puente Bolognesi 108.
0700-2300. See also Patio del Ekeko in
Shopping, above.
Laundry Magic Laundry, Jerusalén
404B and La Merced 125. Coin-operated,
open daily. Don Marcelo, T054-421411
(morning), T054-229245 (afternoon).
Delivery service. **Medical
services** Clínica Arequipa SA, esquina
Puente Grau y Av Bolognesi,
T054-253424/416. Fast and efficient with
English-speaking doctors and all hospital
facilities. **Pharmacy** Farmacia Libertad,
Piérola 108. Owner speaks English. **Post
office** Central office is at Moral 118,
opposite Hotel Crismar. Letters can only
be posted at the post office during
opening hrs. Mon-Sat, 0800-2000, Sun
0800-1400.

Colca Canyon *p160*
Banks TCs, dollars and credit cards
are seldom accepted in Chivay or
Cabanaconde so take plenty of cash
in soles.

Northern Peru

Cordillera Blanca

p176

p193

50 km
50 miles

The northern half of the country does not hold the tourist cachet of the southern highlands, its charm and appeal are of an altogether more esoteric nature. The Cordillera Blanca, for instance, specifically attracts visitors who come to climb its numerous challenging peaks and hike or bike its tough trails. Less active souls need not flinch, however, as the sumptuous scenery is reward enough for braving the chilly bus journey. Down on the coast the landscape changes dramatically, a uniform adobe-brown swathe of desert that is home to some of the world's largest and most important ancient sites. There seems to be no end to the number of spectacular finds along Peru's northern coast, each one seemingly more earth-shattering than the next. Chan Chán, Huaca de la luna, Sipán, Sicán and Túcumé are only a few of the great pyramid complexes and cities uncovered by archaeologists and now accessible to the curious visitor. Incredible as it may seem, these coastal sites are dwarfed by Kuelap, a monumental pre-Inca site buried deep in the eastern highlands, and once inhabited by the mysterious 'Cloud People'.

Introduction

Northern Peru

Ratings
Culture
★★★★
Landscape
★★★★
Wildlife
★
Activities
★★★
Chillin'
★★★
Costs
$$$

Peru's north coast could well be described as the Egypt of South America. This is a region of numerous monumental ruins, built by the many highly skilled pre-Inca cultures that once thrived here. Not far from the elegant city of Trujillo, one of the finest examples of colonial architecture in the country, is Chan Chán, former capital of the Chimú Kingdom and largest adobe city in the world. Nearby, the Huaca de la Luna of the Moche empire is revealing fabulous, multicoloured friezes of gods from the first millennium AD. Further north, near Chiclayo, the adobe brick pyramids of Túcume, Sipán and Sicán rise massively from the coastal plains. The wealth from some of their tombs is now displayed in new, state-of-the-art museums. There are also charming towns such as Huanchaco, a surfers' mecca, with bizarre-looking reed fishing rafts, superb seafood and hospitality.

⊘ Getting there Regular flights and buses to Trujillo and Chiclayo from Lima; buses from Huaraz to Trujillo and southern Ecuador to Piura.

⊖ Getting around Buses run between the cities; take buses, taxis or tours to local sites.

⊖ Time required Trujillo 2 days; Chiclayo 2 days.

⊚ Weather The coast can be misty May-Nov, otherwise hot and dry.

⊖ Sleeping Good selection of mid-range and cheaper establishments in Trujillo, Huanchaco and Chiclayo.

⊘ Eating Seafood is good, especially in Huanchaco, goat is a local speciality.

▲ Activities and tours Tours to archaeological sites; surfing.

★ Don't miss... Huaca de La Luna and Sipán ▸▸ *p178 and p181.*

Trujillo and around ⊜🎵🏠✳️📷▲🔷🍷 ›› *pp183-192*

Trujillo, capital of the Department of La Libertad, disputes the title of second city of Peru with Arequipa. There is enough here to hold the attention for several days. The area abounds in pre-Columbian sites, there are beaches and good surfing within easy reach and the city itself still has many old churches and graceful colonial homes, built during the reigns of the viceroys. Perhaps Trujillo's greatest attractions are the impressive pre-Inca ruins which surround it: the Moche pyramids of Huaca del Sol and de la Luna, Chan Chán and the more distant El Brujo. All can be reached by public transport or as part of a tour, though many tours don't allow enough time for a full explanation of Chan Chán and Huaca La Luna. If you are all ruined-out, just a few minutes up the coast from Trujillo is the seaside town of Huanchaco, long a favourite of travellers for surfing, watching the fishermen on their reed boats and just hanging out.

Ins and outs

Getting there The airport is to the west of town. There is no central bus terminal and none of the bus stations is in the centre. They are spread out on three sides of the city, beyond the inner ring road, Avenida España. Plenty of taxis and *colectivos* can be found at the terminals to get you to your hotel (insist on being taken to the hotel of your choice). ⊖ ›› *p188.*

Getting around With its compact colonial centre and mild, spring-like climate, Trujillo is best explored on foot. However, should you need a taxi, there are plenty of them. Always use official taxis, which are mainly yellow. The major sites outside the city, Chan Chán, the Moche pyramids and Huanchaco beach are easily reached by public transport or taxi/*colectivo*, but care is needed when walking around. A taxi can be hired from in front of the Hotel Libertador for US$7 an hour (about the same rate as a tour with an independent guide or travel agent for one to two people). A number of recommended guides run expert tours to these and other places.

Tourist information i perú ⓘ *Municipalidad, Pizarro 402, p 2, Plaza Mayor, T044- 294561, iperutrujillo@prompertu.gob.pe, Mon-Sat 0800-1900, Sun 0800- 1400.*

Chan Chán, the giant adobe city of the Chimú kings, still stands, despite invasion and El Niño floods.

Northern Peru North Coast

The focal point is the pleasant and spacious **Plaza Mayor** (a rare departure from the ubiquitous Plaza de Armas), on which stands the 17th-century **cathedral**, with its museum of religious paintings and sculptures next door. The buildings that surround the Plaza, and many others in the vicinity, are painted in bright pastel colours, and the ornate street lamps add to the charm of the centre. Of all the city's fine colonial mansions, the **Casa Ganoza Chopitea**, Independencia 630 opposite San Francisco church, is considered the most outstanding. The **Museo de Arqueología** ⓘ *Casa Risco, Junín 682 y Ayacucho, T044-249322, Tue-Fri 0900-1300, 1500-1900, Sat and Sun 0930-1600, US$1.40, guided tours in Spanish available*, houses a large collection of thematic exhibits from pre-Hispanic cultures of the area.

A popular alternative to staying in Trujillo is the fishing and surfing town of **Huanchaco**, which is full of hotels, guesthouses and restaurants (see page 183). The town is famous for its narrow pointed fishing rafts, known as *caballitos* (little horses), made of totora reeds. These are still a familiar sight in places along the northern Peruvian coast. Unlike those used on Lake Titicaca, they are flat, not hollow, and ride the breakers rather like surfboards. Fishermen offer trips on their *caballitos* for US$1.50. You can see them returning to shore in their reed rafts about 0800 and 1600 when they stack the boats upright to dry in the hot sun.

Archaeological sites around Trujillo

A few kilometres south of Trujillo are the huge Moche pyramids, **Huaca del Sol and Huaca de la Luna** ⓘ *0830-1600, US$3, with a professional or student guide, some of whom speak European languages (students half price, children US$0.30). A booklet in English or Spanish is sold for US$2.85.* The Huaca del Sol was once, before the Spanish diverted the nearby river and washed a third of it away in a search for treasure, the largest man-made structure in the western hemisphere, reaching a height of 45 m. Today, about two-thirds of the pyramid have been lost. The Huaca de la Luna, 500 m away, is the more important of the two. Here, many fascinating brightly coloured moulded decorations have been found. The yellow, white, red and black paint has faded a little over the centuries but many metres of the intricate geometric patterns and fearsome feline deities depicted are virtually complete. The visitors' centre has a café showing videos and a souvenir shop selling attractive ceramics, T-shirts, woven bags, wooden boxes, etc. In an outside patio craftsmen reproduce ceramics in designs from northern Peru. A taxi to the site costs US$3 (there are plenty at the site for the return). *Colectivos* (blue and yellow) every 15 minutes from Suárez y Los Incas, US$0.30, run to the visitors' centre.

Chan Chán ⓘ *site entrance is a 20-min walk from the main road, daily 0900-1630, US$2.85, half price for students with an official ISIC card*, the crumbling imperial city of the Chimú, is the largest adobe city in the world and lies about 5 km from Trujillo. The ruins consist of nine great compounds built by Chimú kings. The 9-m high perimeter walls surrounded sacred enclosures with usually only one narrow entrance. Inside, rows of storerooms contained the agricultural wealth of the kingdom, which stretched 1,000 km along the coast from near Guayaquil, in

Totora reed fishing boats drying out in Huanchaco.

Ecuador, to beyond Paramonga. The dilapidated city walls enclose an area of 28 sq km containing the remains of palaces, temples, workshops, streets, houses, gardens and a canal. The city has, over the centuries, been ravaged by floods, earthquakes and *huaqueros* (grave robbers) but what is left of the adobe walls bears well-preserved moulded decorations showing small figures of fish, birds and various geometric motifs. One of the great compounds, the **Ciudadela of Tschudi** has been restored. The **site museum** on the main road, 100 m before the turn-off, has a son-et-lumière display of the growth of Chan Chán as well as objects found in the area. A guide for the site costs US$5.80 per hour. A map and leaflet in English is on sale for US$0.75. Buses and combis leave from Zela, on the corner of Los Incas, near the market (No 114A) inTrujillo, but it's safer to catch a bus at the north corner of Huayna Cápac y Avenida Los Incas or from the corner of España and Manuel Vera (114B); US$0.35, 20 minutes; US$0.25 to Chan Chán entrance. A taxi is US$3 from Trujillo, US$0.85 from museum to ruins, US$2.85 to Huanchaco from the ruins. It is relatively safe to walk on the dirt track from turn-off to the site but preferably go in a group. If alone, contact the Tourist Police in Trujillo to arrange for a policeman to accompany you (should be no charge).

Sixty kilometres north of Trujillo, **El Brujo** is considered one of the most important archaeological sites on the entire north coast. The complex, covering 2 sq km, consists of Huacas Prieta, Cortada and Cao Viejo and was a ceremonial centre for perhaps 10 cultures, including the Moche. **Huaca Cortada** (or El Brujo) has a wall decorated with high-relief, stylized figures. **Huaca Prieta** is, in effect, a giant rubbish tip dating back 5,000 years, which once housed the very first settlers to this area. **Huaca Cao Viejo** ① *US$1.40*, has extensive friezes, polychrome reliefs up to 90 m long, 4 m high and on five different levels, representing warriors, prisoners, sacrificer gods, combat and more complex scenes, with a total of seven colours in reliefs. The excavations at the site will last many years, but some parts are already open to the public. On view, but extensively sheltered by awnings to prevent further fading of the colours, is the sacrificer god, warriors and prisoners and what may be a line of priests (photography is allowed). There are exhibitions in the Chan Chán site museum, Banco Wiese in Trujillo and Museo de la Nación in Lima. The complex can be reached by taking one of the regular buses from Trujillo to Chocope, US$0.55, and then a colectivo (every 30 minutes) to Magdalena de Cao, US$0.45, then a taxi to the site, including wait, US$4.50, or a 5-km walk to the site. Alternatively, take a tour from Trujillo. ▲▲ ▸▸ *p187.*

One of the fearsome Moche feline deities uncovered at Huaca de la Luna, near Trujillo.

Chiclayo and around  ➧ *pp183-192*

Chiclayo, founded in the 1560s as a rural Indian village by Spanish priests, has long since outgrown other towns of the Lambayeque Department. Sandwiched between the Pacific Ocean and the Andes, Lambayeque is one of Peru's principal agricultural regions, and Chiclayo is the major commercial hub. The city, though, is not without its charms. Dubbed 'The Capital of Friendship', there is an earthiness and vivacity about its citizens that definitely sets it apart.

Ins and outs

Getting there José Abelardo Quiñones González airport is 1 km from the town centre; taxi from centre costs US$2. There is no terminal terrestre; most buses stop outside their offices, many on or around Bolognesi, which is south of the centre. ➧ *p188*.

Getting around Calle Balta is the main street but the markets and most of the hotels and restaurants are spread out over about five blocks from the Plaza de Armas. Mototaxis are cheap.

Chiclayo

Sleeping	Santa Rosa 9	Tradiciones 19	Cruz del Sur 9
América 1			Emtrafesa 10
El Sol 3	**Eating**	**Transport**	Línea 12
Europa 4	Govinda 6	Brüning Express to	Tepsa 14
Gran Chiclayo 5	Hebrón 7	Lambayeque 1	Transportes
Inca 10	La Fiesta 17	Civa 3	Chiclayo 15
Las Musas 23	Mi Tía 13	Colectivos to	
Paraíso 15	Romana 16	Lambayeque 4	

N

100 metres
100 yards

They cost US$0.50 anywhere in city, but are not allowed in the very centre. The surrounding area is well-served by buses/combis, most of which leave from north of the market.

Tourist information Centro de Información Turística CIT ⓘ *Sáenz Peña 838, T074-238112.* There are tourist kiosks on the Plaza and outside **El Rancho restaurant.**

Sights

Chiclayo boasts an unparalleled number of important archaeological sites which are scattered around the surrounding countryside. In the city itself the only real sight of note is the famed **Mercado de Brujos** (witchdoctors' market), considered by many to be one of the most comprehensive in South America. It is filled with herbal medicines, folk charms, curing potions and exotic objects used by *curanderos* and *brujos* to cure all manner of real and imagined illnesses. The stallholders are generally very friendly and will explain the uses of such items as monkey claws, dried foetuses and dragon's blood. **Casa La Cabalonga,** stand 43, near the corner of Arica and Héroes Cíviles, has been recommended as particularly helpful and informative.

Twelve kilometres northwest from Chiclayo is the quiet town of **Lambayeque**, home to two excellent museums. The **Brüning Archaeological Museum** ⓘ *0900-1700, US$2, a guided tour costs an extra US$2.85,* specializes in Mochica, Lambayeque/Sicán and Chimú cultures, and has a fine collection of Lambayeque gold. Most exhibits are labelled in English. Three blocks east and shaped like a pyramid is the **Museo de las Tumbas Reales de Sipán** ⓘ *Tue-Sat 0900-1700, US$3, a guide is advisable as no explanations are in English, http:// sipan.perucultural.org.pe.* The magnificent treasure from the tomb of 'The Old Lord of Sipán', found in 1987, and a replica of the Lord of Sipán's tomb are displayed here (see below).

Archaeological sites around Chiclayo

Sipán ⓘ *site open 0800-1600, museum 0800-1700, tombs and museum US$2, students half price,* is an imposing twin pyramid complex, 35 km southeast of Chiclayo. Excavations since 1987 have brought to light a cache of funerary objects considered to rank among the finest examples of pre-Columbian art: no fewer than 12 royal tombs filled with 1,800-year-old offerings worked in precious metals, stone, pottery and textiles of the Moche culture (circa AD 1-750). Among the tombs are the extraordinary **El Señor de Sipán** and '**The Old Lord of Sipán'.** Three tombs are on display, containing replicas of the original finds. Replicas of

the Old Lord and the El Señor are awaited. You can wander around the previously excavated areas of the Huajada Rajada to get an idea of the construction of the burial mound and adjacent pyramids. For a good view, climb the large pyramid across from the excavated Huaca Rajada. A guide at the site costs US$2.85 (may not speak English). Small boys offer to guide you (other kids hang around the handicraft stalls and pester for a tip for doing nothing). Allow about 3-4 hours. The site museum features photos and maps of excavations, technical displays and replicas of some finds.

About 35 km north of Chiclayo, beside the old Panamericana to Piura, lie the ruins of

One of many precious objects uncovered at Sipán. **Túcume** ⓘ *0800-1700, museum 0800-1600,*

US$2, guides charge US$2.85, a vast city built over a thousand years ago. A short climb to the two miradores on **Cerro La Raya**, or **El Purgatorio**, as it is also known, offers an unparalleled panoramic view of 26 major pyramids, platform mounds, walled citadels and residential compounds flanking a ceremonial centre and ancient cemeteries. The entire complex covers well over 200 ha and measures 1.7 km from east to west and 2 km from north to south. One of the pyramids, Huaca Larga, is the longest adobe structure in the world, measuring 700 m long, 280 m wide and over 30 m high.

The **site museum** has architectural reconstructions, photographs and drawings, highlighting the finds, which include weaving paraphernalia, a ceremonial oar and a fabulous bas relief and mural depicting maritime scenes suggesting former sea trade and interregional contact. Traditional dishes and drinks are available at the site. The town of Túcume is a 15-minute walk from the site, or a US$0.85 mototaxi ride.

The colonial town of **Ferreñafe**, 18 km northeast of Chiclayo, is worth a visit, especially for the **Museo Nacional Sicán** ① *T074-286469, Tue-Sat 0900-1700, US$2 plus US$4 per guide (Spanish only)*. This excellent new museum is designed to house objects from Sicán (see below). There is a helpful Mincetur tourist office on the Plaza de Armas ① *T074-282843, citesipan@mincetur.gob.pe*.

The ruins of **Sicán** ① *0700-1600, T074-963 2390, bosquepomac@ecoportal.zzn.com*, 16 km beyond Ferreñafe along the road to Batán Grande, have revealed several sumptuous tombs dating to the middle Sicán period, AD 900-1100. The ruins comprise some 34 adobe pyramids (*huacas*), arranged around a huge plaza, measuring 500 m by 250 m. They range in size with the largest reaching 40 m in height and approximately 100 sq m. The site as a whole covers 45 sq km. The very arid conditions, lack of marked trails and distances involved mean that walking around the site is only for the intrepid and well prepared (it is 10 km to the nearest pyramid). But don't despair, at the visitors' centre, a guide (Spanish only) can be hired with transport (US$3 with motorbike and US$7 with mototaxi), which includes the entrance fee. This covers a two-hour tour of the area which includes a mirador (viewpoint) over the forest, some of the most ancient algarrob trees and at least two *huacas*. Food and drinks are available at the centre and camping is permitted. The most valuable objects have been removed to private collections and museums, but many are in the excellent **Museo Nacional Sicán** (see above).

Piura and north to Ecuador ◌◌◐ » *pp183-192*

A proud and historic city, 264 km from Chiclayo, Piura was founded as San Miguel at Tangarará in 1532, three years before Lima, by the *conquistadores* left behind by Pizarro. There isn't a huge amount to see and do in the city but a worthwhile trip is to the little village of **Chulucanas**, 50 km northeast of Piura and 10 km off the old Pan-American Highway,

---

Peru to Ecuador

If crossing from Peru to Ecuador, don't take the Panamericana from Piura to Tumbes for the Aguas Verdes/Huaquillas border. Instead, take the Coop Loja bus from **Piura** straight through to **Loja** (for details see p192). The border crossing is problem-free, open 24 hours and officials are helpful. Go to Peruvian immigration at the end of the bridge, get a stamp, walk across and then go to Ecuadorean immigration. There are no customs searches (vehicles, including *colectivos*, are subject to full searches, though). There are banks at each side for changing cash only, open during the week; rates are a little better in Macará. There is also a connecting *colectivo* to Vilcabamba from Loja (see p386). For full details on facilities at the border, see p376.

where an ancient pottery technique has been discovered and revived since the 1960s. The most highly prized pieces are signed and sold in galleries and shops in Lima and abroad. Excellent ceramics can also be bought in the town, at a shop on the plaza and three others are within one block. Piura's **tourist office** is on the Plaza de Armas ⓘ *next to Municipio, Mon-Fri 0900-1300, 1600-2000, Sat 0900-1300.*

● Sleeping

Trujillo and around *p177,*
maps p184 and p186

L **Libertador**, Independencia 485 on Plaza de Armas, T044-232741, trujillo@libertador.com.pe. Price includes tax, pool (can be used by non-guests if they buy a drink), cafeteria and restaurant, continental breakfast US$5, excellent buffet lunch on Sun.

AL **El Gran Marqués**, Díaz de Cienfuegos 145-147, Urb La Merced, T/F044-249366, www.elgranmarques.com. Includes tax and breakfast, modern, free internet connection, pool, sauna, jacuzzi, restaurant.

C-D **Colonial**, Independencia 618, T044-258261, hostcolonialtruji@hotmail. com. Price includes basic breakfast. Clean, attractive, friendly, rooms are a bit small, hot showers, good restaurant, especially for the set lunch.

D **San Martín**, San Martín 749, T/F044-252311, www.publinet.com.pe/hotelsan martin. Good value, with bath and TV, small restaurant, good for breakfast, clean but noisy neighbouring establishments.

Huanchaco

B **Las Palmeras**, Av Larco 1150, sector Los Tumbos, T044-461199, www.lasplameras dehuanchaco.com. One of the best hotels in town, rooms with terrace, bath, TV, hot water, small dining room, pool and gardens.

C **Hostal Bracamonte**, Los Olivos 503, T044-461162, www.hostalbraca monte.com. Comfortable, good, chalets with private bathroom **B** , you can camp on the grass (US$4.25), pool, secure, good restaurant, English spoken.

D **Hostal Sol y Mar**, Los Pinos 570, T044-461120. With pool, restaurant, friendly owner, garden.

F **Hostal Solange**, Los Ficus 484, 1 block from the beach, T044-461410, hsolange@yahoo.es. With bathroom, hot water, good food, laundry facilities, limited use of kitchen.

G per person **La Casa Suiza**, Los Pinos 451, T044-461285, www.huanchaco.net/casa suiza. 3 blocks from the beach, run by Heidi and Oscar Stacher, speak German and English, cheaper with shared bathroom, 4 rooms with bath, others share bathroom, hot water, nice roof balcony, excellent breakfast for US$1.50, friendly, family home, surf boards to rent, book exchange, internet access.

Chiclayo and around *p180, map p180*

AL **Gran Hotel Chiclayo**, Villareal 115, T074-234911, granhotel1@terra.com.pe. Refurbished to a high standard, price includes taxes and breakfast, pool, jacuzzi, entertainments, restaurant, safe car park, changes dollars, casino.

A **Las Musas**, Los Faiques 101, by Parque Las Musas, T074-239885, reservaslasmusas@hotmail.com. Quiet area, large rooms, bath-tubs, TV, minibar, affable service, internet available, tours arranged.

B **Inca**, Av L González 622, T074-235931, www.incahotel.com. Recently refurbished, with TV and a/c, **A** with jacuzzi, restaurant, garage, comfortable and helpful.

C **América**, Av L González 943, T074-229305, americahotel@ latinmail.com. Comfortable, friendly, breakfast included, restaurant, good value (except for the expensive laundry).

C-D **El Sol**, Elías Aguirre 119, T074-232120, hotelvicus@hotmail.com. Price includes taxes, with bathroom, hot water, restaurant, pool, TV lounge, clean, parking, good value.

D **Europa**, Elías Aguirre 466, T074-237919, hoteleuropachiclayo@terra.com.pe. With bath (**F** without, single rooms can be small), hot water, restaurant, good value.

D **Santa Rosa**, L González 927, T074-224411. With bathroom, clean, laundry service, international phone service, breakfast downstairs in snack bar. Good value.

Piura and north to Ecuador *p182*

C **Esmeralda**, Loreto 235, Piura, T/F073-327109, www.hotelesmeralda. com.pe. With bathroom, hot water, fan (**B** with a/c), clean, comfortable, good, restaurant.

D **El Sol**, Sánchez Cerro 411, Piura, T073-324461. With bathroom, hot water, small pool, snack bar, parking, accepts dollars cash or TCs but won't change them.

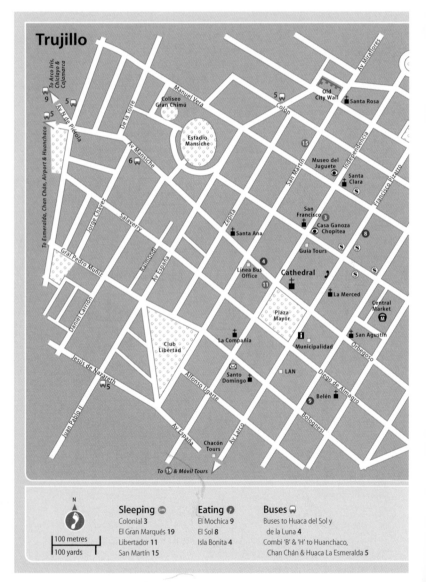

Trujillo

Sleeping
Colonial **3**
El Gran Marqués **19**
Libertador **11**
San Martín **15**

Eating
El Mochica **9**
El Sol **8**
Isla Bonita **4**

Buses
Buses to Huaca del Sol y
 de la Luna **4**
Combi 'B' & 'H' to Huanchaco,
 Chan Chán & Huaca La Esmeralda **5**

100 metres
100 yards

E Hostal Moon Night, Junín 899, Piura, T073-336174. Comfortable, modern, with bath, **F** without, clean, good value.

⦿ Eating

Trujillo and around *p177,*
maps p184 and p186

¶¶¶ Big Ben, Víctor Larco 836, near A Sánchez, Huanchaco, T461869. Seafood

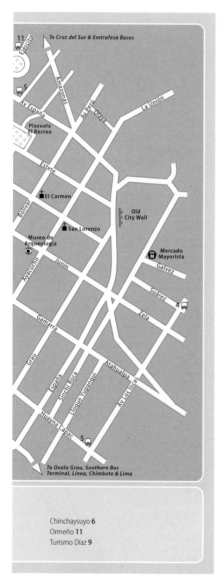

and international menu, most expensive but very good.

¶¶ El Mochica, Bolívar 462. Typical restaurant with a good reputation, the food is good and, on special occasions, has live music. There is another branch on the road to Las Delicias beach and another in Huanchaco.

¶¶-¶ Isla Bonita, Orbegoso 341, T044-204272. Mon-Sat 0800-2300. Run by a Peruvian-Swiss couple, offering a wide variety of dishes, including Swiss and other European fare. They also do breakfast, lunch menú and have a bar, German, Italian and French spoken.

¶ El Sol, Pizarro 660. The original and best vegetarian, cheap set meals, also serves other dishes.

Huanchaco
¶¶¶ El Mococho, Bolognesi 535. Said to be one of the best seafood restaurants, caters for groups.

¶¶ La Barca, Unión 320 (and Raimondi 111). Very good seafood, well-run, popular, but loud music or TV usually playing.

¶¶ Mamma Mia, on the seafront. Good value Italian food and delicious home-made ice cream, English spoken by owner Fernando, good lodging (F per person, shared showers) available next door, rents surfboards.

¶¶-¶ Otra Cosa, Av Larco 921, www.otracosa.info. Vegetarian restaurant, European run, also has a volunteering agency, massage, tourist information and surfing services.

¶ Casa Tere, Víctor Larco 280, Plaza de Armas. For best pizzas in town, also pastas, burgers and breakfasts.

¶ Piccolo, Los Abetos 142, 5 blocks from the plaza. Cheap, friendly, live folk music weekend evenings, excellent, surf and art shop.

Chiclayo and around *p180, map p180*
¶¶¶ La Fiesta, Av Salaverry 1820 in 3 de Octubre suburb, T074-201970. Local specialities, first class.

Hebrón, Balta 605. For more upmarket than average chicken, but also local food and parrilla. Also does an excellent breakfast and a good buffet at weekends.

Romana, Balta 512, T074-223598. First-class food, usually good breakfast, popular with locals.

Tradiciones, 7 de Enero Sur 105, T074-221192. Open 0900-1700 daily. Good variety of local dishes, including ceviche, and drinks, nice atmosphere and garden, good service.

Govinda, Balta 1029. Good vegetarian, open daily 0800-2000.

Mi Tía, Aguirre 650, just off the plaza. Huge portions, great value menú, very popular at lunchtime.

Piura and north to Ecuador *p182*
Carburmer, Libertad 1014, Piura. Very good lunches and dinners, also pizza.
Romano, Ayacucho 580, Piura. Popular with locals, extensive menu, excellent set meal for US$1.55.

⋒ Bars and clubs

Huanchaco *p178, map p186*
Sabes?, V Larco 920, T044-461555, ysabes@yahoo.com. Pub with food, internet café, popular, American run.
El Tribu, Pasaje M Seoane 140, Plaza de Armas. Atmospheric bar in an old house, live music on Fri, opens 1900.

⊛ Festivals and events

Trujillo and around *p177*
One of the most important festivals is the **National Marinera Contest** held at the end of **Jan** for 2 weeks. It consists of hundreds of couples competing in six categories, from children to seniors. In Huanchaco in the **first week of May** is the **Festival del Mar**, a celebration of the disembarkation of Taycanamo, the leader of the Chimú period. A procession is made in Totora boats. **30 Jun**, in Huanchaco, is **San Pedro**, patron saint of fishermen: his statue is taken out to sea

on a huge totora-reed boat. **Festival de la Primavera** is held in the last week in **Sep**. It is a celebration of the arrival of Spring

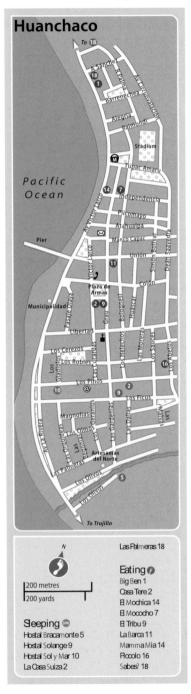

Huanchaco

Pacific Ocean

To Trujillo

200 metres
200 yards

Sleeping ⊖
Hostal Bracamonte 5
Hostal Solange 9
Hostal Sol y Mar 10
La Casa Suiza 2
Las Palmeras 18

Eating ⊘
Big Ben 1
Casa Tere 2
El Mochica 14
El Mococho 7
El Tribu 9
La Barca 11
Mamma Mía 14
Piccolo 16
Sabes? 18

and has grown over the years to become one of Peru's most important tourist events. It features Trujillo's famous **Caballos de Paso**, a fine breed of horses with a tripping gait that has made them renowned worldwide. (see www.rcp.net.pe/rcp/caballos).

Chiclayo and around *p180*
On **4 Feb** are the Túcume devil dances. During **Holy Week** are traditional Easter celebrations and processions in many villages. Túcume celebrates the **Fiesta de la Purísima Concepción**, the town's Patron Saint, 8 days prior to Carnival in **Feb**, and also in **Sep**. This is the most important festival, with music, dancing, fireworks, cockfights, sports events and, of course, much eating and drinking. During the Dance of the Devils (which is common in northern Peru), the participants wear horned masks, forked tails and long capes and are said to represent the diabolical drunken Spanish priests from colonial times.

○ Shopping

Trujillo and around *p177,*
maps p184 and p186
APIAT, Av España near Zela, open daily 0900-2300, Sun 0900-1400. The largest crafts market in Trujillo, selling ceramics, woodcarvings, totora boats, etc, and kiosks selling shoes and leather goods at competitive prices.
Artesanías del Norte, Los Olivos 504, T044-461220, marycortijo@usa.net. Sells mostly items of her own design, using prehispanic methods and motifs, primarily ceramics, but also cotton and alpaca goods and hand-painted products in wood.
    A small market selling a wide range of artesanía is on the seafront beside the pier in Huanchaco.

Chiclayo and around *p180, map p180*
Mercado Modelo, five blocks north of the main plaza on Balta, is one of northern Peru's liveliest and largest daily markets.

Don't miss the colourful fruits, handicrafts stalls and the **Mercado de Brujos** (witch doctors' market), see p181.

▲ Activities and tours

Trujillo and around *p177,*
maps p184 and p186
Surfing
La Marea, Pilcomayo 173, near the market, in Huanchaco, for rental and instruction; **Picolo**, Los Abetos 142. Instruction, rent wet suits and boards, owner is a local champion; **The Wave**, Av Larco 525, next to Mamma Mia. Staff speak English; **Un Lugar**, Pilcomayo 176, T044-992 1371. Ask for English-speaking Juan Carlos.

Tour guides
Many hotels work on a commission basis with taxi drivers and travel agencies. If you decide on a guide, make your own direct approach. The tourist police (see Directory, p192) has a list of official guides; average cost is US$7 per hr.
Clara Bravo, Cahuide 495, T044-243347, www.xanga.com/TrujilloPeru. An experienced tourist guide with her own transport, who speaks Spanish, German and understands Italian. She takes tourists on extended circuits of the region and is good for information (archaeological tour US$16 for 6 hrs, city tour US$7 per person, US$53 per car to El Brujo, with extension to Sipán, Brüning Museum and Túcume possible). Clara works with English chartered accountant **Michael White** who speaks German, French and Italian and provides transport.
Zaby Miranda Acosta, Camelias 315, Huanchaco, T044-461246, Zaby_miranda@hotmail.com. Works at the tourist office, speaks German, Italian, US$10 per day.
José Ocas Cuenca, Túpac Amaru 596, Villa del Mar, T044-583556, jocas_cuenca@hot mail.com. Speaks English, German and French, very knowledgeable.

Prices vary and competition is fierce so shop around for the best deal. Average tour costs are: to Chan Chán, El Dragón and Huanchaco, 3 hrs for US$8.50 per person, not including entrances. To Huacas del Sol and de la Luna, 2 hrs for US$7 per person. To El Brujo, US$17 per person. City tours cost US$5.65 per person (minimum of 2 people; discounts for 4 or more). Few run tours on Sun and often only at fixed times on other days. Check exactly which sites are included in the tour, if transport, entry and guide are included and whether guides speak anything other than Spanish.
Chacón Tours, Av España 106-112, T044-255212. Open Sat afternoon and Sun morning.
Guía Tours, Independencia 580, T044-234856, guiatour@amauta.rcp.net.pe. Jannet Rojas Sánchez (T044-401184, jannarojas@hotmail.com) speaks English and can also be hired independently.
Tesores del Perú, Pizarro 575, of 03, T044-582381, oscarcampos10 @hotmail.com. Oscar Campos Santa María organizes custom-made tours at affordable prices to archaeological sites, as far as Lambayeque.

Chiclayo and around *p180, map p180*
Expect to pay US$18-25 per person for a 3-hr tour to Sipán, and US$25-35 per person for Túcume and the Brüning Museum (5 hrs). Brüning Museum, Sipán and Túcume, however, can easily be done by public transport. Sicán, which has less frequent public transport, is US$45-55 per person for a full-day tour including Ferreñafe and Pómac.
Indiana Tours, Colón 556, T074-222991, indianatours@terra.com.pe. Daily tours to Sipán (US$15), archaeological excavations in Túcume, Brüning Museum in Lambayeque, Sicán and a variety of other daily and extended excursions with 4WD vehicles, as well as reservations for national flights and hotels. English and Italian spoken and Footprint users welcome.
InkaNatura Tours, Gran Hotel Chiclayo

lobby (see Sleeping above), T074-209948, www.inkanatura.com. Tours to sites around Chiclayo and Trujillo and to Kuelap.

Transport

Trujillo and around *p177,*
maps p184 and p186
Air
There are daily flights to and from **Lima** with **Aero Cóndor** and **Lan**. To **Cajamarca** daily with **Aero Cóndor**. Taxi to airport costs US$4; or take a bus or *colectivo* to Huanchaco, get out at airport turn-off then walk 2 km (US$0.25). **Airline offices** Aero Cóndor, T044- 255212. Lan, Pizarro 340-42, T044-221469.

Bus
Local Buses and combis, on all routes, cost US$0.15-0.30; *colectivos* (cars carrying 6 passengers), US$0.25, tend to run on main avenues starting from Av España. Combis between Trujillo and

Huanchaco are routes A, B and C run 0500-2100 every 5-10 mins. A and B do an anti-clockwise circuit of Huanchaco and enter Trujillo by the roundabout on Av Mansiche, 3 blocks northwest of Av España in front of the Cassinelli museum, then A goes round the west side of Trujillo onto Av 28 de Julio, while B goes round the east side on Av Manuel Vera, España as far as Bolívar. At night they go only to España y Grau. Fare is US$0.30 for the 20-min journey. Slower 'micros', B and H, follow similar routes to América; leaving Trujillo B goes north of the centre on España, H goes south (convenient stops are shown on the Trujillo map), in daylight only. There are also colectivos and taxis, minimum fare US$3, more likely US$4-5.

Long distance Concentrations of companies are around Avs Ejército/Amazonas/Túpac Amaru; on Av Nicolás de Piérola, blocks 10-13 for northbound buses; and on Av La Marina, between Ovalos Grau and La Marina, for southbound buses. The better bus companies maintain their own terminals. To and from **Lima**, 8 hrs in the better class buses, average fare US$14.30-18.50 in luxury classes, 10 hrs in the cheaper buses, US$7.15-11.50. There are many bus companies doing this route, among those recommended are **Ormeño**, Av Ejército 233, T044-259782, 3 levels of service, 5 daily; **Cruz del Sur**, Amazonas 437 near Av Ejército, T044-261801; and **Línea**, Av América Sur 2855, T044-297000, ticket office at San Martín y Orbegoso, T245181. To **Huaraz**, with **Móvil**, **Línea** (see above), 8 hrs, US$8.60 special, and **Chinchaysuyo**, Av Mansiche 391, at 2030; US$7.15, 10 hrs. To **Chiclayo**, with **Línea**, as above, and **Emtrafesa**, almost hourly from 0530-2015, US$3.35. To **Piura**, hourly with **Línea** and **Emtrafesa**.

Taxi
Taxis charge US$0.55 within Av España and US$0.70 within the Av América ring road (drivers may ask for more at night).

To **Chan Chán** US$3 per car, to the airport is US$4; to **Huanchaco**, US$3-5.

Chiclayo and around p180, map p180
Air
Daily flights to and from **Lima** and **Piura** with **Lan**.

Bus
Local For **Lambayeque**, colectivos from Chiclayo; US$0.45, 25 mins. They leave from Pedro Ruíz at the junction with Av Ugarte. Also **Brüning Express** combis from Vicente de la Vega between Angamos and Av L Ortiz, every 15 mins, US$0.20. Buses to **Sipán** leave from Terminal Este Sur-Nor Este on C Nicolás de Piérola, east of the city (take a taxi there, US$1), US$0.45, 1 hr. Colectivos leave from 5-6 blocks east of Mercado Modelo. For **Túcume** combis go from Chiclayo, Angamos y Manuel Pardo, US$0.70, 45 mins. A combi from Túcume to **Come** passes the ruins hourly. Colectivos from Chiclayo to **Ferreñafe** leave every few minutes from 8 de Octubre y Sáenz Peña, 15 mins, U$0.30, but only run to Ferreñafe town centre so take a mototaxi on to the museum, 5 mins, US$0.50. Combis for **Batán Grande** depart from the Terminal Nor-Este, in Av N de Piérola in Chiclayo, and pass the museum every 15-20 mins, 20 mins, US$0.50.
Long distance To **Lima**, 770 km, US$12 and US$22 for bus cama, with **Cruz del Sur**, **Ormeño** and **Línea** (see map for office locations). Most leave leave from 1900 onwards. To **Trujillo**, with **Línea**, as above, and **Emtrafesa**, almost hourly from 0530-2015, US$3.35. To **Piura**, US$3.65, **Línea** and **Trans Chiclayo** leave hourly throughout the day; also **Emtrafesa**. **Ormeño** goes direct to Quito (Tue at 0100). To **Chachapoyas**, 230 km, US$6-10.60: with **Civa** at 1730 daily, 10-11 hrs, and **Móvil** at 1900.

Piura and north to Ecuador p182
A taxi to the airport costs US$1.85 by day, more by night. There are daily flights to and from **Lima** and **Chiclayo** with Lan.

▶▶ **Visiting the cloud people**

Stretching from the western foothills of the Andes right across the mountains and down to the fringes of the Amazon jungle is the vast Chachapoyas Region, which contains Peru's most spectacular pre-Columbian ruins, some of them built on a massive scale unequalled anywhere in the Americas. Great pre-Inca cities, immense fortresses and ancient effigies which gaze over a dramatic landscape reward the visitor to a region which is due to become a major tourist destination as soon as a regular air service begins. The town of Chachapoyas is the best base for visiting this region. As there are no scheduled flights, it has to be reached overland from Chiclayo. **Civa** and **Móvil Tours** offer reasonably comfortable bus services from Lima, travelling Chiclayo-Chachapoyas by day. Bus schedules starting from Chiclayo all involve an overnight journey (see page 189). The dry season is best (normally May-September). During the rains, roads may become impassable due to landslides and access to the more remote areas may be impossible, or involve weeks of delay.

The undisputed highlight among the archaeological riches around Chachapoyas is **Kuélap** ⓘ *0800-1700, US$3, 50% discount for students with identification*, a spectacular pre-Inca walled city. Even the most exaggerated descriptions fail to do justice to the sheer scale of this great fortress. Kuélap was built over a period of 200 years, AD 900-1100 and contained three times more stone than the Great Pyramid at Giza in Egypt. The site lies sprawled along the summit of a mountain crest, more than 1km in length. It is divided into three parts: at the northwest end is a small outpost; at the southeast end of the ridge is a spread out village in total ruin; and the cigar-shaped fortress lies between the two, 585 m long by 110 m at its widest. The walls are as formidable as those of any pre-Columbian city. They vary in height between 8 m and 17 m and were constructed in 40 courses of stone block, each one weighing between 100 and 200 kg. It has been estimated that 100,000 such blocks went into the completion of this massive structure.

You would need at least a week to even begin to appreciate the remarkable legacy of the Chachapoyans, who are also known as 'The Cloud People'. We have only given details here of one site, but there are opportunities to venture off into the wilds to explore others, such as the spectacular Laguna de los Cóndores, which involves a three-day trek by horse. Ask the tour operators or hotels for details.

Most hotels will organize tours to Kuélap and other archaeological sites when there are sufficient people. Expect to pay around US$12-18 per person for a full-day trip, including guide and lunch. When booking a tour, request a guide who speaks English, if you so wish. Tours leave at 0800 and, after a spectacular 3-hour drive, you arrive at Kuélap. The tours usually allow a sufficient 3-4 hours for exploration before returning to Chachapoyas, with a possible stop along the way for a late lunch. Recommended agencies include: **Chachapoyas Tours SAC**, Grau

534, Plaza Armas, p 2 (Hotel El Tejado), T041-778078 www.kuelapperu.com, or in the USA T(1-800)743-0945/(407)851-2289. Reliable, English-speaking guide; **Vilaya Tours**, c/o Gran Hotel Vilaya, Jr Grau 624, T041-777506, www.vilayatours.com, or internationally T(1-416) 535-1163; Robert Dover is British, contact him through the **Café de Guías**. Also Luis, who speaks good English.

Sleeping

There is plentiful accommodation in Chachapoyas. Best is the comfortable C **Gran Vilaya**, Ayacucho 755, T041-777664, vilaya@wayna.rcp.net.pe. English is spoken and Gumercindo 'Gumer' Zegarra, the owner, is knowledgeable about happenings in the area. Their Café de Guías serves snacks, meals and local organic coffee and has lots of local information. A cheaper alternative is D **Revash**, Grau 517, Plaza de Armas, T041-777391, www.chachapoyasperu.com.pe. It has private bathrooms with plenty of hot water, patio, laundry and restaurant. Staff are friendly and helpful. The owner, Carlos Burga, can organize tours.

Eating

There are several decent restaurants. Among the best are **El Tejado**, on the Plaza de Armas, and **Matalache**, corner of Amazonas and Grau.

Transport

Civa buses return to Chiclayo at 1600 daily, 10 hrs (may be longer in the rainy season), US$9-10.60. Civa and Móvil Tours have buses to Lima at 0800, 20-22 hrs, US$21-24.

Directory

A bank on the Plaza de Armas in Chachapoyas has an ATM (Visa/Plus) and **Hostal Revash** changes cash. Tourist information at **iperú** ⓘ *Jr Ortiz 588, Plaza de Armas, Chachapoyas, T041-777292, iperuchachapoyas@promperu.gob.pe, Mon-Sat 0800-1300. Also check out www.regionamazonas.gob pe and www.chachapoyas.com.pe.*

Taxis in town charge US$1, mototaxis US$0.50. Transport to nearby towns is easy to find, likewise buses going on to Ecuador. Most bus companies are on Av Sánchez Cerro, blocks 11, 12 and 13. To **Lima**, 1,038 km, 14-16 hrs, from US$7, on the Panamericana Norte. Most buses stop at the major cities en route. To **Chiclayo**, 190 km, 3 hrs, US$3.65, several buses daily. To **Trujillo**, 7 hrs, 487 km, US$7, several daily. For **Chulucanas** combis from Piura charge US$1.50. **Coop Loja**, Av Prol Sánchez Cerro 2-28 y Av Vice, T073-309407, office opens 0700 (mototaxi US$0.70 from centre, taxi US$2), have direct buses to **Loja** in Ecuador, 4 a day, 8 hrs, US$8, via the La Tina-Macará border crossing.

❶ Directory

Trujillo and around *p177, maps p184 and p186*

Banks There are banks with ATMs in the centre, these include BCP, at Gamarra 562, Interbank, Pizarro y Gamarra, and Banco Wiese Sudameris, Pizarro 314. **Internet** There are offices all over the centre, mostly on Pizarro, blocks 1 and 6, and Av España, blocks 1 and 8. **Medical services** Clínica Peruano Americana, Av Mansiche 702, T044-231261. English spoken, good. Dr César Aníbal Calderón Alfaro, T044-255591, 948 2466 (mob). Understands English. **Post** Independencia 286 y Bolognesi. 0800-2000, Sun 0930-1300, stamps only on special request. **Telephone** Telefónica, headquarters at Bolívar 658. Private call centre at Pizarro 561, Ayacucho 625, Gamarra 450, others on 5th block of Orbegoso and Av España 1530. **Tourist police** Independencia 630, Casa Ganoza Chopitea, T044-291705,

policia_turismo_tru @hotmail.com. Open Mon-Sat 0800-2000. They provide useful information.

Chiclayo and around *p180, map p180*

Banks BCP, Balta 630, has ATM for Visa. Opposite, at Balta 625, is **Banco Wiese Sudameris**, with ATM for Visa/Plus. **Interbank**, on the Plaza de Armas, has Mastercard and Visa ATM. You may have to wait for a while in the banks. **Internet** Lots of places, particularly on San José and Elías Aguirre, average price US$0.60 per hr. **Post office** On the first block of Aguirre, 6 blocks from the plaza. **Telephone** Telefónica, headquarters at Aguirre 919; bank of phone booths on 7th block of 7 de Enero behind Cathedral for international and collect calls. Phone card sellers hang around here. **Useful addresses** Indecopi, Av Balta 506, T074-209021, ctejada@indecopi. gob.pe, Mon-Fri 0800- 1300, 1630-1930, for complaints and tourist protection. **Tourist police**, Av Sáenz Peña 830, T074- 236700, ext 311, 24 hrs a day, are very help- ful and may store luggage and take you to the sites themselves.

Piura and north to Ecuador *p182*

Banks BCP, Grau y Tacna, Visa ATM. Interbank, Grau 170, ATM for Visa, Mastercard and AmEx. Casas de cambio are at Arequipa 722, and Ica 429 and 460. Street changers can be found on Grau outside BCP. **Consulates** Honorary British Consul, c/o American Airlines, Huancavelica 223, T073-305990. Honorary German Consul, Jutta Moritz de Irazola, Las Amapolas K6, Urb Miraflores, Casilla 76, T073-332920. **Internet** Arequipa 728 and others in the centre. 10 machines in the Biblioteca Municipal, Urb Grau, US$0.60 per hr.

The Cordillera Blanca

The Cordillera Blanca is a region of jewelled lakes and sparkling white mountain peaks, which attracts mountaineers, hikers, cyclists and rafters in their thousands. Here stand the highest mountains in South America, with some 20 snow-crested peaks of over 6,000 m, including Huascarán, the highest mountain in Peru at 6,768 m. To the east of the Cordillera Blanca lies another set of valleys, the Callejón de Conchucos, containing the archaeological treasures of Chavín de Huantar, which can be visited by bus from Huaraz, while farther afield are the Cordilleras Huayhash and Raura for those in search of the ultimate trekking challenge.

✅ **Getting there** By bus from Lima or Trujillo.
◉ **Getting around** Buses and minibuses.
◉ **Time required** If trekking or climbing, 1 week minimum, otherwise 2-3 days.
◉ **Weather** Dry May-Sept.
◉ **Sleeping** Plenty of hotels in Huaraz. Caraz also has a good, but smaller selection.
◉ **Eating** Mostly international food aimed at travellers.
⛰ **Activities and tours** Adventure sports and tours to Chavín, mountain lakes and scenery.
★ **Don't miss...** Llanganuco lakes
▶▶ *p194*.

Northern Peru The Cordillera Blanca

Huaraz and around 🌐🚌🍴🎿⛰🏨🍸 ▶▶ *pp196-203*

The main town in the valley is Huaraz, a major tourist and commercial centre, especially on market days (Monday and Thursday). The city was half destroyed in the earthquake of May 1970 so don't expect red-tiled roofs or overhanging eaves. However, the Plaza de Armas has been rebuilt, with a towering, white statue of

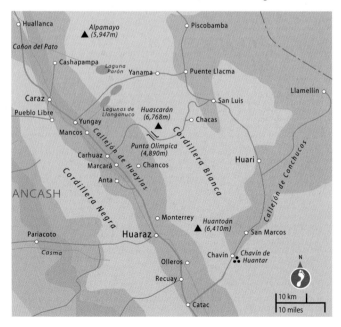

Christ and a new cathedral is still being built. What the reconstructed city lacks in colonial charm, it makes up by its spectacular setting between the mountains of the Cordilleras Blanca and Negra. The peaks of Huamashraju, Churup, Rima Rima and Vallunaraju loom so close as to seem almost a part of the architecture while, in the distance, the giants Huascarán and Huandoy can be seen.

Ins and outs

Getting there and around There are two main routes to reach Huaraz, one is from Lima and the other from Trujillo. The bus offices are in the centre of town and are conveniently close to many of the hotels and hostels. Huaraz is small enough to get around by foot. ❍ ›› *p196*.

Best time to visit The dry season (May-September) is the best time to visit the region, and the only time for climbing most summits. Trekking is also possible at other times of the year, but conditions are less amenable and the views are less rewarding. School groups flock to the city from mid-September to mid-December and book up all accommodation.

Tourist information iPerú ① *Luzuriaga on Plaza de Armas, T043-728812, iperuhuaraz @promperu.gob.pe, Mon-Fri 0800-1300, 1700-2000, Sat-Sun 0800-1300.*

Sights

The main thoroughfare, Avenida Luzuriaga, is bursting at the seams with travel agencies, climbing equipment hire shops, restaurants, cafés and bars. There's very little in the way of sights as such in the town but north of Huaraz, 6 km along the road to Caraz, are the thermal baths at **Monterrey**. It's a good place for a day trip to soak in the **thermal baths** and an alternative place to stay for those seeking peace and quiet. The baths are run by the Hotel Baños Termales Monterrey and, owing to the high iron content, the water is dark brown but not dirty. There are two pools: the lower pool is US$0.85; the upper pool, which is nicer is US$1.35. There are also individual and family tubs which cost US$1.35 per person for 20 minutes. The upper pool is closed on Monday for cleaning. It gets crowded at weekends and holidays. City buses along Avenida Luzuriaga go as far as Monterrey (US$0.22) until 1900. A taxi costs US$2-3.

North from Huaraz

The road north out of Huaraz goes through the beautiful Callejón de Huaylas, giving access to some wonderful treks which go up into, or over the mountains of the Cordillera Blanca.

Yungay is 55 km north of Huaraz. The original town was completely buried during the 1970 earthquake by a massive mudslide caused when a piece of Huascarán's glacier was pried loose by the quake and came hurtling towards the town. It was a hideous tragedy in which 20,000 people lost their lives. The earthquake and its aftermath are remembered by many residents of the Callejón de Huaylas and the scars remain part of the local psyche.

Northeast from Yungay, a road runs up to the **Lagunas de Llanganuco**, two very beautiful lakes nestling 1,000 m below the snowline beneath Huascarán and Huandoy. The first you come to is Laguna Chinancocha (3,850 m), the second Laguna Orconcocha (3,863 m). A nature trail, Sendero María Josefa (sign on the road), takes 1½ hours to walk to the western end of Chinancocha where there is a control post, descriptive trail and boat trips on the lake (a popular area for day-trippers). Walk along the road beside the lake to its far end for peace and quiet among the quenoal trees.

The pleasant town of **Caraz** is a good centre for walking and the access point for many excellent treks and climbs. It is increasingly popular with visitors as a quieter alternative to Huaraz. In July and August the town has splendid views of Huandoy and Huascarán from its lovely plaza, filled with rose bushes, palms and jacarandas. In other months, the mountains

Lagunas de Llanganuco

are often shrouded in cloud. Caraz has a milder climate than Huaraz and is more suited to day trips. The **tourist office** ⓘ *on Plaza de Armas, in the municipality, T043-791029, Mon-Fri 0745-1300, 1430-1700,* has limited information.

From Caraz a narrow, rough road goes east 32 km to **Laguna Parón**, in a cirque surrounded by several, massive snow-capped peaks, including Huandoy, Pirámide Garcilazo and Caraz. It is a long day's trek from Caraz for acclimatized hikers (25 km) up to the lake at 4,150 m, or a 4-5 hour walk from the village of Parón, which can be reached by combi. Where possible follow the walking trail which is much shorter than the road. By climbing up the slippery moraine to the south of the lake towards Huandoy, you get a fine view of Artesonraju. Camping is possible next to the Duke Energy refuge. You will need a map if you are going past Laguna Parón. A taxi from Caraz costs US$25 for four, with two hours' wait.

Chavín de Huantar

ⓘ *Daily 0800-1700. US$3, students US$1.50, US$5 for a group with Spanish-speaking guide.*
A trip to Chavín de Huantar is a must if you are in the area, as it is one of the most important archaeological sites in the country. The famous ruins lie just to the south of the town of Chavín. The fortress temple, built about 800 BC, is the only large structure remaining of the Chavín culture which, in its heyday, is thought to have held influence in a region between Cajamarca and Chiclayo in the north to Ayacucho and Ica in the south. In 1985, UNESCO designated Chavín a World Heritage Trust site.

The site is in good condition despite the effects of time and nature. The main attractions are the marvellous carved stone heads and designs in relief of symbolic figures and the many tunnels and culverts which form an extensive labyrinth throughout the interior of the structures. The carvings are in excellent condition, though many of the best sculptures are in Lima. The famous Lanzón dagger-shaped stone monolith of 800 BC is found inside one of the temple tunnels. In order to protect the site some areas are closed to visitors. All galleries open to the public have electric lights. The guard is also a guide and gives excellent explanations of the ruins. There is a small museum at the entrance, with carvings and some Chavín pottery.

Chavín can be visited on a day trip from Huaraz but it's a long day. Once the road from Huaraz is fully paved, the trip will take about two hours. In high season, the site is busy with tourists all day through. You will receive an information leaflet in Spanish at the entrance.

The nearby town of Chavín has several good, simple hotels and restaurants, but there is nowhere to change money. There are hot sulphur baths, **Baños Termales de Chavín**, about

2 km south of Chavín (US$0.30), at Km 68 in the village of **Quercos**. They consist of one small pool and four individual baths in a pleasant setting by the Río Mosna. Tip the boy who cleans the bath for you (he doesn't get paid). Camping is possible here.

◉ Sleeping

Huaraz *p193, map p197*

Hotels are plentiful (there are many more than those listed below) but fill up rapidly during the high season (May-Sep), especially during public holidays and special events (such as the Semana de Andinismo in Jun) when prices rise. Lodging in private homes is common at these times. Avoid touts at bus stations offering accommodation and tours.

AL Andino Club, Pedro Cochachín 357, some way southeast from the centre (take a taxi after dark), T043-721949, www.hotelandino.com   The best in town, expensive Swiss restaurant, free internet for guests, safe parking, Swiss run, friendly, 2nd floor rooms with balconies and views of Huascarán are more expensive.

B San Sebastián, Jr Italia 1124, T043-726960, www.hotelhuaraz.com. 2-star (price rises to **A** in high season), very helpful, breakfast included, good views.

C Edward's Inn, Bolognesi 121, T/F043-722692. Cheaper without bathroom, clean, not always hot water, laundry, friendly, breakfast extra and other meals available, insist on proper rates in low season, popular, Edward speaks English and knows a lot about trekking and rents gear (not all guides share Edward's experience).

D Albergue Churup, Jr Figueroa 1257, T043-722584, www.churup.com. Price includes breakfast and bath, **F** in dormitory without breakfast, hot water, nice garden and fire in sitting room, internet access, cafeteria, use of kitchen, lots of information and travel agency, luggage store, laundry, book exchange, English spoken, Spanish classes, extremely helpful, motorcycle parking.

D Alojamiento Soledad, Jr Amadeo Figueroa 1267, T043-721196, ajsoled@terra.com.pe. Prive includes breakfast and bath, **E** without, some hard beds, hot water, kitchen, use of internet, family-run and very friendly, secure, trekking information.

D La Casa de Zarela, J Arguedas 1263, T043-721694, www.lacasadezarela.com. With bath, hot water, breakfast available, use of kitchen, laundry facilities, popular with climbers and trekkers, owner Zarela, who speaks English, organizes groups and is very knowledgeable, stores luggage, has a nice terrace.

The Way Inn, Jr Buenaventura Mendoza 821, near Parque Fap, T043-728714, thewayinn@hotmail.com.   No fixed fee for staying, people are asked to pay what they think it`s worth. Run by Alex and Bruni, all mattresses are orthopaedic, fully-functioning kitchen (including oven and fridge), huge video library, laundry facilities, camping equipment for hire, free information on treks, places to eat, hanging out/etc, a health food bar, sauna and steam facilities as well as exercise equipment to help with the acclimatization.

E Alojamiento Marilia, Sucre 1123, T043-728160, alojamaril@latinmail.com. Good views, modern, clean rooms with bath, **F** without bath, also dormitory accommodation, hot water, breakfast available, kitchen facilities, luggage store, knowledgeable, friendly owners.

E Hostal Copa, Jr Bolívar 615, T043-722071, F722619. Cheaper without bathroom, hot water, laundry facilities, clean, owner's son Walter Melgarejo is a well-known guide, popular with trekkers, restaurant, travel agency with local tours.

E Hostal Quintana, Mcal Cáceres 411, T043-726060. Cheaper without bathroom, hot shower, laundry, clean, basic, stores luggage, breakfast extra, friendly, popular with trekkers, climbing gear for rent.

E Jo's Place, Jr Daniel Villayzan 276, T043-725505. Safe, hot water, kitchen facilities, nice mountain views, garden, terrace, warm atmosphere, English owner.

E La Cabaña, Jr Sucre 1224, T723428, www.huaraz.com/lacabana or www.huaraz.org/lacabana Shared and double rooms, hot showers, laundry, kitchen, computer, DVD, friendly, popular (especially with Israelis), safe parking, bikes and luggage, English and French spoken.

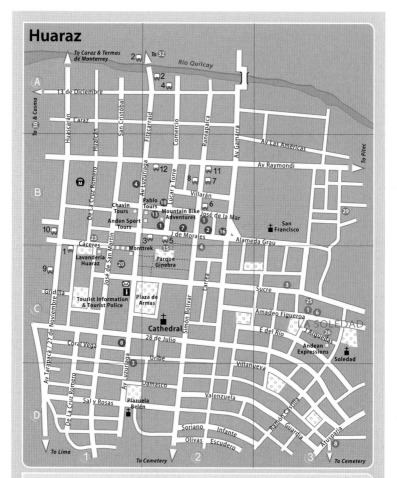

Huaraz

E **Lodging Caroline** , Urb Avitentel Mz D – Lt 1, T043-722588. Price includes breakfast, free pick-up from bus station (phone in advance), hot water, kitchen facilities, tourist information and guides, laundry, very helpful.

F per person **Alojamiento Alpes Andes**, at Casa de Guías, Plaza Ginebra 28-g, T043-721811, casa_de_guias@ hotmail.com Member of the Peruvian Youth Hostel Association, 1 dormitory with 14 beds and another with 6 beds, hot water, with very good restaurant (open 0700-1100, 1700-2300), laundry, free luggage store, the owner Sr López speaks English, French and German and is very helpful, he is the mountain guides administrator.

North from Huaraz   *p194*

C **Chamanna**, Av Nuev Victoria 185, 25 mins walk from centre, Caraz, T043-978 1094 (mob), www.chamanna.com. Clean cabañas in beautiful garden, hot water, secure, excellent French and international cuisine in pricey restaurant, German run.

C-E **Los Pinos**, Parque San Martín 103, Caraz, 5 blocks from plaza, T043-791130, lospinos@apuaventura.com. Rooms with and without private bath, hot water, comfortable and airy, garden open to all travellers, camping US$2.50, use of internet US$0.50 per hr, use of kitchen US$3, laundry service, clean, safe, book exchange, information and travel agency Apu-Aventura (see below). Breakfast and dinner are available, bar with movies every night.

D **Caraz Dulzura**, Sáenz Peña 212, about 10 blocks from the town centre, Caraz, T043-791523, hostalcarazdulzura@ hotmail.com. Modern building in an old street, 6 double rooms, hot water, with bathroom and TV, very comfortable, great service, very helpful owner (Carlos), clean and airy rooms, breakfast included, very good food available.

E **Hostal Gledel**, Av Arias Grazziani, north past the plaza, Yungay, T043-793048. Owned by Sra Gamboa, who is hospitable and a good cook, very clean but tiny

rooms, shared bathroom, hot water, no towels or soap, meals prepared on request, nice courtyard.

E **Hostal Sol de Oro**, Santo Domingo 07, Yungay, T043-793116. Private bath, hot water, comfortable, good value. The best in town.

Chavín   *p195*

D **La Casona**, Wiracocha 130, Plaza de Armas, T043-754048, lacasonachavin @peru.com. In an old house with attractive courtyard, private bathroom, cheaper with shared bath, insufficient hot water, friendly, one room with a double bed, motorcycle parking.

E **Hostal Chavín**, Jr San Martín 141-151, half a block from the plaza, T/F043-754055. Set around a pleasant courtyard, F without bath, hot water, provides breakfast for groups, best of the more basic hotels, friendly and helpful.

● Eating

Huaraz *p193, map p197*

♦♦♦ **Bistro de los Andes**, J de Morales 823, T/F043-726249. Great food, owner speaks English, French and German.

♦♦♦ **Pizza Bruno**, Luzuriaga 834. 1600-2300. Excellent pizzas, crêpes and pastries, good service. French owner Bruno Reviron also has a 4WD with driver for hire.

♦♦♦ **Monte Rosa**, J de la Mar 661. 1000-2300. Pizzería, also fondue and other Swiss specialities. Swiss owner is *Victorinox* representative, offering knives for sale and repair service, also *Suunto* (altimeters, GPS), sells mountaineering gear and excellent postcards, rents skiis and snowboards and has climbing and trekking books to read.

♦♦♦ **Crêperie Patrick**, Luzuriaga 422. Excellent crêpes, fish, quiche, spaghetti and good wine.

♦♦♦-♦♦ **Siam de Los Andes**, Gamarra corner J de Morales. Authentic Thai cuisine, has an excellent buffet dinner with 2 starters and a main course. There is a nice fireplace, too.

♦♦ **Pachamama**, San Martín 687. Bar, café and restaurant, concerts, art gallery, garden, nice place to relax, good toilets, pool table and table-tennis, information on treks, Swiss-owned.

♯ **Pizza B&B**, La Mar beside laundry of same name. Pizza is excellent, as is their dessert specialty *tarte flambée*, wood oven, pleasant décor and atmosphere, attentive service.

♯ **El Querubín**, J de Morales 767. Clean, friendly, good breakfast and set meals (high season only), also vegetarian, snacks and à la carte, very good, decorated with nice regional paintings.

Cafés
Café Andino, Lúcar y Torre 538, T721203, cafeandino@hotmail.com   American run café and book exchange, extensive lending library in many languages, a nice place to relax and write postcards, great atmosphere, good meeting place, occasional movies, new Huayhuash maps for sale, owner guides treks in Cordillera Huayhuash, lots of advice offered.

North from Huaraz *p194*

♯-♯ **La Punta Grande**, D Villar 595, 10 mins' walk from centre, Caraz. Best place for local dishes, good, open for lunch only till 1700.

♯ **Alpamayo**, Av Arias Grazziani s/n, at the northern entrance to town, Yungay. Best in town, excellent value local dishes such as trout, cuy, tamales and pachamanca at weekends. Open lunch only.

♯ **Esmeralda**, Av Alfonso Ugarte 404, Caraz. Good set meal, breakfast, friendly.

♯ **Café de Rat**, Sucre 1266, above Pony's Expeditions, Caraz. Serves breakfast, vegetarian dishes, pizzas, drinks and snacks, darts, travel books, nice atmosphere.

Chavín *p195*

♯ **R'ickay**, see Sleeping, above. Pasta and pizza dishes in the evenings.

♯-♯ **La Portada**, 17 de Enero. In an old house with tables set around a garden.

♯ **La Ramada**, 17 de Enero. Regional dishes, also trout and set lunch.

● Bars and clubs

Huaraz *p193, map p197*
Extreme, Jr Gabino Uribe near Luzuriaga. Popular with gringos. 1900-0200.
Makondo's, José de la Mar opposite Cruz del Sur bus station. Bar and nightclub, safe, popular.

Huaraz and around *p194*
Taberna Disco Huandy, Mcal Cáceres 119, Caraz. Reasonable prices, good atmosphere, young crowd, Latin music. Fri-Sat.

● Festivals and events

Huaraz *p193*
Semana Santa, or Holy Week, is widely celebrated and always colourful and lively. The town's Patron saints' day is **El Señor de la Soledad**, during the week starting **3 May**, with parades, dancing, music, fireworks and much drinking. Semana del Andinismo is an international climbing and skiing week, held in **Jun**. San Juan and **San Pedro** are celebrated throughout the region during the last week of **Jun**. On the eve of San Juan fires are lit throughout the valley to burn the chaff from the harvest. The following day the entire valley is thick with smoke.

North from Huaraz *p194*
Yungay   Oct 28 is the anniversary of the founding of the town, celebrated with parades, fireworks and dances.
Caraz   Holy Week features processions and streets carpeted with flower petals. Semana Turística takes place during the last week in **Jul**, with sports festivals, canoeing, parasailing and folkloric events.

○ Shopping

Huaraz *p193, map p197*
Food and drink
The central market offers a wide variety of canned and dry goods, including nuts and

Mountain biking in the Cordillera Blanca.

dried fruit, as well as fresh fruit and vegetables. Check expiry dates. **Militos**, Sucre 775. A well-stocked supermarket. **Ortiz**, Luzuriaga 401 corner Raymondi. Another well-stocked supermarket with a good selection of items, but expensive.

Handicrafts

Local sweaters, hats, gloves, ceramics, and wall hangings can be bought from stalls on Pasaje Mcal Cáceres just off Luzuriaga, in the stalls off Luzuriaga between Morales and Sucre, also on Bolívar cuadra 6 and elsewhere. **Andean Expressions**, Jr J Arguedas 1246, near La Soledad church, T043-722951, olaza@qnet.com.pe 0800-2200, run by Lucho, Mauro and Beto Olaza, and recommended for hand-printed T-shirts and sweatshirts with unusual motifs.

▲▲ Activities and tours

Huaraz *p193, map p197*
Climbing and trekking
Trekking tours cost US$40-70 per person per day. Pricing is extremely variable. **Andean Kingdom**, Luzuriaga 522. Free information, maps, climbing wall, rock and ice climbing, treks, equipment rental, very helpful, English and some Hebrew spoken, can be very busy.

Anden Sport Tours, Luzuriaga 571, T043-721612. Have a basic practice wall. They also organize mountain bike tours, ski instruction and river rafting. **Hirishanka Sport**, Sucre 802, T043-722562. Climbing, trekking, horse riding, 4WD hire, they also rent rooms, E per person, with bath, hot water, breakfast. **Kallpa**, José de la Mar y Luzuriaga, T043-727868, www.peruviantrek.com. Organizes treks, rents gear, arranges arrieros and mules, very helpful. **Monttrek**, Luzuriaga 646, upstairs, T043-721124. Good trekking and climbing information, advice and maps, run ice and rock climbing courses (at Monterrey), tours to Laguna Churup and the 'spectacular' Luna Llena tour; also hire out mountain bikes, run ski instruction and trips, and river rafting. Next door is a climbing wall, good maps, videos and slide shows.

Horseriding
Posada de Yungar, at Yungar (about 20 km on the Carhuaz road), T043-721267, 967 9836 (mob). Swiss run. Ask for José Flores or Gustavo Soto. US$4.50 per hr on nice horses; good 4-hr trip in the Cordillera Negra with fabulous views.

Mountain biking
The Callejón de Huaylas offers superb variety for mountain bikers. Local agencies

Top tips

Trekking in the Cordillera Blanca

The Cordillera Blanca offers the most popular – and some of the best – trekking in Peru, with a network of trails used by the local people and some less well-defined mountaineers' routes. There are many possibilities for day-hikes, trekking and climbing. One of the best and most heavily used walks in the Cordillera Blanca is from Santa Cruz to Llanganuco, taking four to five days, but there are many other, less popular, options. Most circuits can be hiked in five days.

The **Dirección de Turismo** issues qualified guides and *arrieros* (muleteers) with a photo ID. Always check for this when making arrangements; note down the name and card number in case you should have any complaints. Prices for specific services are set so enquire before hiring someone. You should also state your priorities to the muleteer in advance of the trek (pace, choice of route, campsites, etc).

Casa de Guías, Plaza Ginebra 28-g in Huaraz, T043-721811, agmp@terra. com.pe or casa_de_guias@hotmail.com, Mon-Sat 0900-1300, 1600-1800, Sun 0900-1300. This is the climbers' and hikers' meeting place. It has information, books, maps, arrangements for guides, arrieros, mules, etc. They have a full list of all members of the **Asociación de Guías de Montaña del Perú** (AGMP) throughout the country. A great site for trekking is www.huaylas.com.

can supply bikes, guides and full back-up. **Mountain Bike Adventures**, Lúcar y Torre 530, T043-724259, julio.olaza@erra.com.pe, or www.chakinaniperu.com. Contact Julio Olaza. US$20 for 5 hrs, various routes. Julio speaks excellent English and also runs a book exchange, sells maps and climbing books.

River rafting and canoeing
Rafting on the Río Santa is also available (US$15 for half a day), year round, Grade II-III, not special, but in pretty

surroundings. **Ario Ferri**, T043-961 3058 (mob, between 1800-2000), www.yurakyaku.com, or contact through Café Andino. Multilingual rafting guide and certified kayak instructor.

Tour operators

Huaraz is overflowing with agencies and quality varies. Try to get advice from someone who has recently returned from a tour, climb or trek. All agencies run conventional tours to Llanganuco, Pastoruri (both US$8.50 per person) and Chavín (8-10 hrs, US$6-10 per person), entry tickets not included. Most agencies provide transport, food, mules and guides. Prices are generally 20% lower during the low season, which is from Oct-Apr.

Two reputable agencies for local tours are **Chavín Tours**, Luzuriaga 502, T043-721578, and **Pablo Tours**, Luzuriaga 501, T043-721142.

North from Huaraz *p194*

Cycle World, Arias Graziani 3ra cuadra, near bridge at south end of Yungay, T043-303109. Bike rentals at US$10/day including helmet and gloves. For US$3 a combi will take you and your rented bike to Llanganuco. The ride down is beautiful and exhilarating, but cold.

La Almeda bakery, at 4 km south of Caraz, 5 mins by combi towards Yungay, T043-791935. Offers a variety of horse riding routes, across the Río Santa and up in to the Cordillera Negra, US$5 per hr, with guide. Horses for both experienced and novice riders available.

Pony's Expeditions, Sucre 1266, near the Plaza de Armas, Caraz, T/F043-791642, www.ponyexpeditions.com. Open Mon-Sat 0800-2200, English, French and Quechua spoken, reliable information about the area. Owners Alberto and Aidé Cafferata are very knowledgeable about treks and climbs. They arrange local and trekking tours and transport for day excursions, maps and books for sale, also equipment for hire, mountain bike rental (US$15 for a full day).

⊖ Transport

Huaraz *p193, map p197*

Bus

Many bus companies have offices selling tickets in the centre, but buses leave from the edge of the centre. To/from **Lima**: 7-8 hrs, US$6-14. There is a large selection of buses to Lima, both ordinary and luxury coaches, with departures all day. Many companies have their offices along Av Raymondi and on Jr Lúcar y Torre. Some recommended companies are:

Cruz del Sur, Bolívar y José de la Mar, T043-723969, with terminal at Prolongación Raymondi 242; **Transportes Rodríguez**, Tarapacá 622, T043-721353; **Civa**, Morales opposite Lúcar y Torre; **Móvil Tours**, Bolívar 452, T043-722555; **Empresa 14**, Fitzcarrald 216, T043-721282, terminal at Bolívar 407. To **Trujillo**, all buses go at night, 8-9 hrs, US$10: **Chinchaysuyo** (J de Morales 650, T043-726417), **Línea** (Simón Bolívar 450, T043-726666), **Empresa 14** and, **Móvil Tours**.

Several buses and frequent minivans run daily, 0500-2000, between Huaraz and **Caraz**, 1 hr, US$1. They stop at all the places in between and depart from the parking area under the bridge on Fitzcarrald and from the open space beside the bridge on the other side of the river (beware of thieves here). To **Chavín**, 110 km, 4 hrs (sit on left side for best views), US$3: **Chavín Express**, Mcal Cáceres 338, T043-724652, daily at 0730, 0830, 1100 and 1400, Sun 1500; and **Trans Sandóval**, 27 de Noviembre 582, T043-726930, 0800 and 1300.

Taxis

The standard fare for a taxi in town is about US$0.60, US$0.70 at night. The fare to Monterrey is US$1.45. Radio taxis T043-721482 or 043-722512.

North from Huaraz *p194*

Yungay Most transport leaves from Jr 28 de Julio. Buses, colectivos run all day to **Caraz** (12 km, US$0.30), and **Huaraz** (54 km, 1½ hrs, US$1). To lakes **Llanganuco**, combis leave when full, especially 0700-0900, from Av 28 de Julio 1 block from the plaza, 1 hr, US$1.50, US$9 to hire a vehicle to drop you off, US$12 with 2 hrs wait.

Caraz To **Lima**, 470 km; several buses (5 companies, on D Villar and Jr Córdova) leave daily, US$7. To **Trujillo**, via Huaraz and Pativilca, with **Chinchaysuyo** (Córdova 830, T791930), at 1845 daily, US$9.10, 11-12 hrs. To **Huaraz**, frequent combis leave daily, 0400-2000, 1¼ hrs, US$1.10, the road is in good condition. They are supposed to leave from a terminal on the way out of town, but if there is no police control they pick up passengers by the market and along Jr José Gálvez. By combi to **Yungay**, 12 km, 15 mins, US$0.30. To the village of **Parón** (for trekking in Laguna Parón area) combis leave from the corner Santa Cruz and Grau by the market, from Mon to Sat 0400 and 1300, and Sun 0300 and 1300, 1 hr, US$1.20. They return from Parón at 0600 and 1400.

Chavín *p195*

It is much easier to get to Chavín than to leave the place by bus. All buses to **Huaraz** originate in Huari or beyond. They pass through Chavín at irregular hours and may not have seats available. Buying a ticket at an agency in Chavín does not guarantee you will get a seat or even a bus. The journey to Huaraz takes 2½ hrs, US$3. For buses from **Huaraz**, see under Huaraz. **Chavín Express** passes through around 1200, 1600 and 1700 daily. All schedules are subject to change during road construction, expected to continue to late 2005.

❶ Directory

Huaraz *p193, map p197*
Banks BCP and Interbank, on Plaza de Armas, both have ATMs. Banco Wiese, Sucre 766, changes cash and cheques. Casa de Cambio Oh Na Nay, across the street from Interbank. Gives good rates for cash dollars, but poor rates for other currencies. **Internet** There are internet places everywhere, US$0.30 per hour on average. Sayuri, Jr Bolívar 683. As well as internet, has digital photo services (including scanning, burning to CD, printing) and international phone calls. **Post office** Serpost is on Luzuriaga opposite the Plaza de Armas. 0800-2000 daily. **Telephone** Telefónica, Sucre y Bolívar, corner of Plaza de Armas. National and international phone and fax. 0700-2300 daily. There are many other private calling centres along Luzuriaga, plus coin phones everywhere. **Useful addresses** Policía de Turismo, on second floor of same building, T043-721341, ext 315, Mon-Fri 0900-1300, 1600-1900, Sat 0900-1300, is the place to report all crimes and mistreatment by tour operators, hotels, etc.

Caraz *p194*
Banks BCP, D Villar 217. Cash and TCs at good rates, no commission. Mon-Fri 0915-1315, 1630-1830, Sat 0930-1230. Pony's Expeditions (see above) cash only, good rates. Importaciones América, Sucre 721, T043-791479 (Esteban). Good rates and service, open weekends and evenings. **Internet** Many places around the plaza and throughout town, US$0.30. **Post office** At San Martín 909.

Peruvian Amazon

One of the Amazon's famous clay licks.

↑ Don't miss...

1 A night under canvas in the heart of **Manu Reserve** ▶▶ p208.

2 The spectacular but rough **road from Cusco to Manu** ▶▶ p210.

3 A trip to the beautiful **Lago Sandoval** ▶▶ p210.

4 Staying in a jungle lodge on the **Rio Tambopata** ▶▶ p212.

5 Breakfast time at a **macaw clay lick** ▶▶ p212.

Introduction

Peru's immense Amazon Basin covers a staggering 4,000,000 square kilometres, an area roughly equivalent to three quarters the size of the United States. But despite the fact that 60% of Peru is covered by this green carpet of jungle, less than 6% of its population lives here, meaning that much of Peru's rainforest is still intact. The Peruvian jungles are home to a diversity of life unequalled anywhere on Earth. It is this great diversity which makes the Amazon Basin a paradise for nature lovers. The area is home to 10,000,000 living species, including 2,000 species of fish and 300 mammals. It also has over 10% of the world's 8,600 bird species and, together with the adjacent Andean foothills, 4,000 butterfly species. The two major tourist areas in the Peruvian Amazon Basin are the northern and southern jungles. We focus only on the southern parts of the Amazon Bason – namely Manu Biosphere Reserve and Tambopata National Park – as they offer the best wildlife-viewing possibilities and the distinct advantage of being accessible from Cusco.

Peruvian Amazon

Ratings
Culture
★★
Landscape
★★★★
Wildlife
★★★★★
Activities
★★★
Chillin'
★★★
Costs
$$$$$

Southern Jungle

Both the Manu Biosphere Reserve and Tambopata National Park offer amazing wildlife spotting, large parts being remote and pristine, with such highlights as macaw clay licks and birdwatching on undisturbed lakes. One of the most striking features of the Southern Sierra is the former river channels that have become isolated as ox-bow lakes (*cochas*). These are home to black caiman and giant otters and a host of other living organisms. Other rare species living in the forest are jaguar, puma, ocelot and tapir. There are also capybara, 13 species of primate and many hundreds of bird species. If you include the cloud forests and highlands of the Manu Biosphere reserve, the bird count almost totals 1,000.

Getting there Charter flights to Manu, scheduled flights to Puerto Maldonado, long bus journey from Cusco.

Getting around By river boat.

Time required 4-5 days, unless going overland from Cusco (add a day).

Weather Apr-Oct is the dry season. In the wet, temperatures can get up to 40°C but the rain isn't usually heavy enough to prevent you going.

Sleeping Jungle lodges, except in Puerto Maldonado where there are some reasonable hotels.

Eating Lodges provide good food.

Activities and tours Wildlife tours in or near the protected areas around the rivers Madre de Dios and Tambopata.

★ Don't miss... Parrot clay lick ➤➤ *p212*.

Ins and outs

Getting there and around To visit Manu you must go as part of a tour leaving from Cusco, either by road or by air. The frontier town of Puerto Maldonado is the starting point for expeditions to the Tambopata National Reserve and is only a 30-minute flight from Cusco. ➤➤ *p213 and p216*.

Best time to visit The climate is warm and humid, with a rainy season from November to March and a dry season from April to October. Cold fronts from the South Atlantic, called *friajes*, are characteristic of the dry season, when temperatures drop to 15-16°C during the day, and 13°C at night. Always bring a sweater at this time. The best time to visit is during the dry season when there are fewer mosquitoes and the rivers are low, exposing the beaches. This is also a good time to see birds nesting and to view the animals at close range, as they stay close to the rivers.

Information Perú Verde ① *Ricaldo Palma J-1, Santa Mónica, Cusco, T084-243408, www.peruverde.org*, is a local NGO that can help with information and has free video shows about Manu National Park and Tambopata Reserve. The staff are friendly and helpful and also have information on programmes and research in the jungle area of Madre de Dios.

Manu Biosphere Reserve ➤➤ *pp211-216*

No other rainforest can compare with Manu for the diversity of its life forms. This is, quite simply, one of the world's great wilderness experiences. The reserve is

Manu wildlife (clockwise): scarlet macaw; giant otter; jaguar; capybara.

one of the best bird-watching spots in the world as well as offering the best chance of seeing giant otters, jaguars, ocelots and several of the 13 species of primates which abound in this pristine tropical wilderness. The more remote areas of the reserve are home to uncontacted indigenous tribes and many other indigenous groups with very little knowledge of the outside world. Covering an area of 1,881,000 ha, Manu Biosphere Reserve is also one of the largest conservation units on Earth, encompassing the complete drainage of the Manu river, with an altitudinal range from 200 m to 4,100 m above sea-level.

The park areas
The Biosphere Reserve formally comprises the **Manu National Park** (1,692,137 ha), where only government sponsored biologists and anthropologists may visit with permits from the Ministry of Agriculture in Lima, the **Manu Reserved Zone** (257,000 ha), set aside for applied scientific research and ecotourism, and the **Cultural Zone** (92,000 ha), containing acculturated native groups and colonists, where the locals still employ their traditional way of life. In 2003 the former Manu Reserved Zone was absorbed into the Manu National Park, increasing its protected status. Ecotourism activities have been allowed to continue in specially designated tourism and recreational zones along the course of the Lower Manu River. These tourism and recreational areas are accessible by permit only. Entry is strictly controlled and visitors must enter the area under the auspices of an authorized operator with an authorized guide. Permits are limited and reservations should be made well in advance, though it is possible to book a place on a trip at the last minute in Cusco. In the former Reserved Zone there are two lodges, the rustic **Casa Machiguenga** run by the Machiguenga communities of Tayakome and Yomibato

Jungle tours

✅ Package tours booked in Lima or abroad are much more expensive than those booked in Cusco or Puerto Maldonado and personal approaches to lodge operators will often yield better prices than booking through an agency or the internet.

✅ Take a long-sleeved shirt, waterproof coat and shoes or light boots on jungle trips and a good torch, as well as *espirales* to ward off the mosquitoes at night – they can be bought from pharmacies in Cusco. Premier is the most effective local insect repellent.

✅ A pair of binoculars is essential for wildlife viewing and insect repellent is a must.

with the help of a German NGO, and the upmarket **Manu Lodge** (see page 214). In the Cocha Salvador area, several companies have tented safari camp infrastructures, some with shower and dining facilities, but all visitors sleep in tents. Some companies have installed walk-in tents with cots and bedding. The Cultural and Multiple Use Zones are accessible to anyone and several lodges exist in the area. It is possible to visit these lodges under your own steam, but it's best to go with an organized tour (see page 213 for a list of operators). ▲ ▸▸ *p213.*

Among the ethnic groups in the Multiple Use Zone (a system of buffer areas surrounding the core Manu area) are the Harakmbut, Machiguenga and Yine in the Amarakaeri Reserved Zone, on the east bank of the Alto Madre de Dios. They have set up their own ecotourism activities, which are entirely managed by indigenous people. Associated with Manu are other areas protected by conservation groups, or local people (for example the Blanquillo reserved zone and a new conservation concession in the adjacent Los Amigos river system) and some cloud forest parcels along the road. The **Nuhua-Kugapakori Reserved Zone** (443,887 ha), set aside for these two nomadic native groups, is the area between the headwaters of the Río Manu and headwaters of the Río Urubamba, to the north of the Alto Madre de Dios.

Puerto Maldonado and Tambopata ◐◖🛈▲▣◑ ▸▸ *pp211-216*

Puerto Maldonado is an important starting point for visiting the rainforest, though most visitors won't see much of the place because they are whisked through town on their way to a lodge on the Río Madre de Dios or the Río Tambopata. The road from Cusco to Puerto Maldonado can only be described as a challenge. The journey is very rough, but the changing scenery is magnificent. This road is rarely passable in the wet season.

Sights

Overlooking the confluence of the rivers Tambopata and Madre de Dios, Puerto Maldonado is a major logging and brazil-nut processing centre. From the park at the end of Jr Arequipa, across from the Capitanía, you get a good view of the two rivers, the ferries across the Madre de Dios and the stacks of lumber at the dockside.

The beautiful **Lago Sandoval** ⓘ *costs US$5, you must go with a guide (see page 215); this can be arranged by the boat driver,* is a one-hour boat ride along the Río Madre de Dios from Puerto Maldonado, and then a 5-km walk into the jungle. There is an interpretation centre at the start of the trail and a 35-m high observation tower overlooking the lake. It is possible to see giant river otters early in the morning and several species of monkeys, macaws and

hoatzin. There are two jungle lodges at the lake, see pagexxx. At weekends, especially on
Sundays, the lake gets quite busy. Upstream from Lago Sandoval, towards Puerto
Maldonado, is the wreck of the **Fitzcarrald**. The steamer (a replica of Fitzcarrald's boat) lies a
few metres from the Madre de Dios in the bed of a small stream. The German director,
Werner Herzog, was inspired to make his famous film of the same name by the story of
Fitzcarrald's attempt to haul a boat from the Ucuyali to the Madre de Dios drainage basins
(this happened in what is now the Manu National Park).

Tambopata National Reserve (TNR)

From Puerto Maldonado you can visit the Tambopata National Reserve by travelling up the
Tambopata river or down the Madre de Dios river. The area was first declared a reserve in
1990 and is a very reasonable alternative for those who do not have the time or money to
visit Manu. It is a close rival in terms of seeing wildlife and boasts some superb oxbow lakes.
There are a number of lodges here which are excellent for lowland rainforest birding. In an
effort to ensure that more tourism income stays in the area, a few local families have
established their own small-scale 'Casas de Hospedaje', which offer more basic facilities
and make use of the nearby forest.

● Sleeping

Manu Biosphere Reserve *p208*
For details of all-inclusive tours to the
Biosphere Reserve, including jungle
lodges or camps, see p213.

Puerto Maldonado *p210, map p211*
A **Wasai**, Billinghurst opposite the
Capitanía, T082-572290,
www.wasai.com. Price includes
breakfast, a/c, TV, shower. In a beautiful
location overlooking the Madre de Dios,
with forest surrounding cabin-style
rooms which are built on a slope down
to the river, small pool with waterfall,
good restaurant if slightly expensive,
very good though service can be
stretched if hotel is full. They run local
tours and the **Wasai Lodge**, see below.
C **Cabañaquinta**, Cusco 535,
T082-571045, cabanaquinta
@webcusco.zzn.com. With bathroom, fan,
good restaurant, friendly, lovely garden,
very comfortable but could be cleaner,
airport transfer.
C **Casa de Hospedaje Mejía**, to book
T082-571428, visit **Mejía Tours**, L Velarde
333, or just turn up. An attractive rustic
lodge on Lago Sandoval, with 10 double
rooms, full board can be arranged, canoes
are available.

Peruvian Amazon Southern Jungle Listings

E **Amarumayo**, Libertad 433, 10 mins from centre, T082-573860, residenciamarumayo @hotmail.com. Price includes breakfast. Comfortable, with pool and garden, good restaurant.

E **Hospedaje La Bahía**, 2 de Mayo 710, T082-572127. Cheaper without bath or TV, large rooms, clean. Best of cheaper options.

Tambopata National Reserve (TNR) *p211*

Lodges close to Puerto Maldonado are less likely to have as great a variety of wildlife as those further away.

L **Las Piedras Biodiversity Station** is, in effect, a casa de hospedaje, T/F082-573922, info@tambopataexpeditions.com. A small lodge located 90 km up the Río Las Piedras, visitors camp en route to the lodge. With only 20 beds the lodge looks to offer a more personalized experience of the rainforest. Central dining-room, shared bath, no electricity, library, guiding in English/ Spanish. Owing to the remoteness of the lodge the minimum package is for 5 days/4 nights, US$410 pp based on a group of 4 people. Special rates offered for those wanting to stay longer than 2 weeks.

L **Libertador Tambopata Lodge**, on the Río Tambopata, make reservations at Suecia 343, Cusco, T084-245695, tplcus@terra.com.pe. Associated with the Libertador hotel chain, the lodge has rooms with solar-heated water, accommodates 60. Good guides, excellent food. Trips go to Lake Condenado, some to Lake Sachavacayoc, and to the Collpa de Chuncho, guiding mainly in English and Spanish, package US$210 per person for 3 days/2 nights, naturalists programme provided.

L **Reserva Amazónica Lodge**, 45 minutes by boat down the Río Madre de Dios. Lodge with 6 suites and 38 rustic bungalows with private bathrooms, solar power and good food. Caters mainly for large groups. Jungle tours available with multi-lingual guides, the lodge is surrounded by its own 10,000 ha but

most tours are to Lago Sandoval. A naturalists programme is also provided, negotiable out of season. The lodge has a Monkey Island (Isla Rolín). It is run by **Inkaterra**, Andalucía 174, Lima 18, T01-610 0400, Cusco T084- 245314, Puerto Maldonado.

L **Sandoval Lake Lodge**, 1 km beyond Mejía on Lago Sandoval, usually accessed by canoe across the lake after a 3-km walk or rickshaw ride along the trail. Can accommodate 50 people in 25 rooms, bar and dining area, electricity, hot water. Short system of trails nearby, guides are available in several languages. Also have a small lodge on the Río Heath. It is run by **InkaNatura**, Manuel Bañon 461, San Isidro, Lima, T01-440 2022, www.inkanatura.com. Also have an office in Cusco, see facing page.

AL **Explorer's Inn**, jungle lodge 58 km from Puerto Maldonado. It's a 2½-hr ride up the Río Tambopata (1½ hrs return, in the early morning, so take warm clothes and rain gear), one of the best places in Peru for seeing jungle birds, butterflies and even giant river otters, but you will need more than a 2-day tour to benefit fully from the location. The guides are biologists and naturalists from around the world who undertake research in the reserve in return for acting as guides. They provide interesting wildlife-treks, including to the macaw lick (collpa). Run by **Peruvian Safaris**, Alcanfores 459, Miraflores, Lima, T01-447 8888, or Plateros 365, T084-235342 Cusco, www.peruviansafaris.com. The office in Puerto Maldonado is at Fitzcarrald 136, T/F082-572078.

AL **Posada Amazonas Lodge** is 2 hours upriver from Puerto Maldonado. A unique collaboration between a tour agency the local native community of Infierno. There are 24 large attractive rooms with bathroom and with good birdwatching opportunities including the Tambopata Collpa. Tourist income has helped the centre become self-funding. Service and guiding is very good. Prices start at

US$190 for a 3 day/2 night package, or US$690 for 5 days/4 nights including the Tambopata Research Centre, the company's older, more intimate, but comfortable lodge, which is next to the famous Tambopata macaw clay lick.

Rainforest Expeditions, Aramburú 166, of 4B, Miraflores, Lima 18, T01-421 8347, or Portal de Carnes 236, Cusco, T084-246243, www.perunature.com.

AL Wasai Lodge, on the Río Tambopata, 120 km (3½ hrs) upriver from Puerto Maldonado. Small lodge with 7 bungalows for 40 people, 20 km of trails around the lodge, guides in English and Spanish. The Collpa de Chuncho, one of the biggest macaw licks in the world, is only 1 hr upriver; 3 day/2 night trips US$275, 4 day/3 nights US$375, both including a visit to Lake Sandoval plus two nights in Puerto Maldonado. Just to spend a night in the jungle without guided tours costs US$50.

🍴 Eating

Puerto Maldonado *p210, map p211*
The best restaurant in town is at the **Hotel Wasai**, the best lunchtime menu is at the **Cabañaquinta**.
🍴-🍴 **El Califa**, Piura 266. Often has bushmeat, mashed banana and palm hearts on the menu.
🍴-🍴 **El Hornito/Chez Maggy**, on the plaza. Cosy atmosphere, good pizzas, but pasta dishes are not such good value.
🍴 **El Buen Paladar**, González Prada 365. Good value lunch menu.

🍸 Bars and clubs

Puerto Maldonado *p210, map p211*
El Witite, Av León Velarde 153. A popular, good disco, latin music, open Fri and Sat.

⛰ Activities and tours

Manu Biosphere Reserve *p208*
The tour operators listed below are all based in Cusco.
Expediciones Vilca, Plateros 363, T084-251872, www.cbc.org.pe/manuvilca/ Manu jungle tours: 8-day/7-night, other lengths of stay are available. Will supply sleeping bags at no extra cost. Minimum 5 people, maximum 10 per guide. This is the only economical tour which camps at the **Otorongo** camp, which is supposedly quieter than Salvador where many agencies camp. There are discounts for students. In the low season they will organize other tours. Very efficient, good service.
InkaNatura Travel, C Ricardo Palma number J1, Urb Santa Monica, T084-255255 (in Lima: Manuel Bañón 461, San Isidro, T01-440 2022), www.inkanatura.com. A non-profit organization with proceeds directed back into projects on sustainable tourism and conservation. Arranges trips to the Manu Reserved Zone, Manu Wildlife Centre, The

❝ A new best friend

We were greeted by Loretta, a green parrot who had been confiscated by a park warden from a local farmer who had illegally clipped her wings. She had been given to Laurel, at the Research Centre, to regrow her feathers and return to the wild. The feathers were now regrown but Loretta was no fool and showed no signs of answering any call of the wild. She gave love bites to those she favoured and simply bit the rest... As I lay in my hammock (after a jungle walk), Loretta perched at the end trying to undo the supporting knot and slipping nearer to my tempting toes. I persuaded her onto the balcony where she sat muttering and continued to eye my toes... I decided it was time to clarify my relationship with Loretta: were we friends or foes? I had a technique of scratching behind the ears that had never failed me with cats or dogs. I wondered if it would work with parrots? It did and I became one of the favoured few who received love bites for the rest of our stay. My toes felt safer in the hammock after that... A local hawk once attacked Loretta and, had she been an ordinary parrot, that would have been the end of her. However, as she fluttered, dazed, having been knocked off her branch, instead of squawking, she let out a loud and offended "Oi!" The hawk was so disconcerted that it misjudged its killer run completely. *Mike McKinley*

Biotrip, 6-day/5-night, which takes you through the Andes to lowland jungle, the **Sandoval Lake Lodge**, in Tambopata (see below), and also a tour into Machiguenga Indian territory, including the Pongo de Mainique. They have also opened the remote **Heath River Wildlife Center**, 1 hr up the Río Heath (4-5 hrs from Puerto Maldonado) on the Peru/Bolivia border, a cooperative project with traditional Ese'eja community of Sonene. See also box, p217).

Manu Ecological Adventures, Plateros 356, T084-261640, www.manuadventures.com. Manu jungle tours, either economical tour in and out overland, or in by land and out by plane, giving you longer in the jungle, both leave on Sun. Other lengths of stay are available leaving on Mon and Tue. Options include a mountain biking descent through the cloudforest and 3 hrs of white-water rafting on the way to **Erika Lodge** on the

upper Río Madre de Dios. They operate with a minimum of 4 people and a maximum of 10 people per guide.
Manu Expeditions, Av Pardo 895, PO Box 606, T084-226671, www.ManuExpeditions. com. English spoken, Mon-Fri 0900-1300, 1500-1900; Sat 0900-1300. Run by ornithologist and British Consul Barry Walker of the **Cross Keys Pub**. 3 trips available to the reserve and Manu Wildlife Centre. Two of the trips visit a lodge run by Machiguenga people on the first Sun of every month and cost an extra US$150.
Manu Nature Tours, Av Pardo 1046, T084- 252721, www.manuperu.com. Owned by Boris Gómez Luna. English spoken. This company aims more for the luxury end of the market and owns 2 comfortable lodges in the cloudforest and reserved zone. Tours are very much based around these sites, thus entailing less travel between different areas. **Manu Lodge** has an extensive trail system and

also offers canopy climbing for an additional US$45 per person. In the cloudforest zone a novel 'Llama Taxi' service is offered, in conjunction with local community of Jajahuana.

Pantiacolla Tours, Plateros 360, T084-238323, www.pantiacolla.com. Manu jungle tours: 5- and 7-day trips include return flights, the 9-day trip is an overland return. Prices do not include park entrance fee. Guaranteed departure dates regardless of number, maximum 10 people with 1 guide. The trips involve a combination of camping, platform camping and lodges. Dutch owner, Marianne van Vlaardingen, a biologist, is extremely friendly and helpful. Marianne and her Peruvian husband Gustavo have recently opened an ecotourism lodge in conjunction with the Yine native community of Diamante.

Tambopata National Reserve (TNR) *p211*

The usual price for trips to Lago Sandoval is US$25 per person per day (minimum of 2 people), and US$35 per person per day for longer trips lasting 2-4 days (minimum of 4-6 people). All guides should have a carnet issued by the Ministry of Tourism (DIRCETUR), which also verifies them as suitable guides for trips to other places and confirms their identity. Check that the carnet has not expired. Reputable guides are **Hernán Llave Cortez**, **Romel Nacimiento** and the **Mejía** brothers, all of whom can be contacted on arrival at Puerto Maldonado airport, if available. **Perú Tours**, Av 2 de Mayo 400, Puerto Maldonado, T082-803064, perutoursytravel@hotmail.com, organize local trips.

⊖ Transport

ⓘ Directory

Puerto Maldonado *p210, map p211*
Air
To **Lima**, daily with **Tans** and **Lan**. Both fly via Cusco, but **Tans** also has a direct flight from Lima on Fri and Sun. Combis to the airport run along Av 2 de Mayo, 10-15 mins, US$0.60. A moto-taxi from town to the airport is US$2. If on the last flight of the day into Puerto Maldonado, usually Lan, don't hang around as most vehicles return to town quickly.

Motorcycles/taxis
Scooters and mopeds can de hired from San Francisco, and others, on the corner of Puno and G Prada for US$1.15 per hour or US$10 per day. No deposit is required but your passport and driving licence need to be shown. Mototaxis around town charge US$0.50; riding pillion on a bike is US$0.20.

Puerto Maldonado *p210, map p211*
Banks BCP, cash advances with Visa, no commission on TCs (Amex only). **Banco de la Nación**, cash on Mastercard, quite good rates for TCs. Both are on the south side of the Plaza. The best rates for cash are at the casas de cambio/gold shops on Puno 6th block, eg Cárdenas Hnos, Puno 605. **Internet** All over town, along Av León Velarde and most main streets. **Post** Serpost: at Av León Velarde 6th block. **Telephone** Telefónica, on west side of the Plaza, adjoining the Municipalidad. A phone office on the Plaza, next to **El Hornito**, sells all phone cards for national and international calls.

→ **Pongo de Mainique**

Going further

Before the Río Urubamba enters the vast plain of the Amazon Basin it carves its way through one last wall of foothills and the result is spectacular. The Pongo de Mainique, frequently described as one of the most beautiful places on earth, is a sheer rainforest canyon, hundreds of metres deep with the Urubamba surging through its centre and many small waterfalls tumbling in on either side. The Machiguenga people who live in the area believe this to be a portal to the afterlife. They are, however, very private people and do not take kindly to uninvited strangers. **Ecotrek Peru** run tours in the region, but those with enough time can go it alone. Take a bus from Cusco to Quillabamba. It's an incredibly bumpy, but beautiful ride taking approximately 8 hours, although expect 14 hours or more in the rainy season, because of landslides. Buy tickets in advance, US$3-4. From Quillabamba, take a bus to Ivochote. The road can be in terrible condition in places. The journey takes 10 hours and costs around US$4. (Buses back to Cusco depart in the morning around 0700 and in the evening; there are extra services at weekends.)

Ivochote is the end of the road. From here, lanchas (boats) head downstream early in the morning on most days during the dry season. In the wet season (roughly December to April) the river may be too dangerous to navigate, especially the rapids in the Pongo itself. Depending on your bargaining ability, passage downriver to the Pongo or to the Casa de los Ugarte (see below) will set you back between US$6 and US$8.50, providing the captain has trading business downstream. Hiring a boat independently will cost a lot more. To return upstream prices are roughly one third higher, owing to the increased amount of gasoline required to motor against the current.

Just beyond the Pongo, on the left bank of the river (if heading downstream), is the **Hostal La Casa de los Ugarte** (G), the small hacienda of Ida and Abel Ugarte. They are very helpful and will let you camp on their land for a small fee. They have a modest general store and basic supplies, fruit and very fresh eggs are available. The forest behind the hacienda is rich in wildlife and the family may be able to arrange expeditions in the jungle, given time to make the arrangements. Two to three hours downstream from the Casa de los Ugarte, on the right-hand bank of the river, you pass the Machiguenga community of Timpia, home of a high-level ecotourism project and comfortable lodge, run in co-operation with InkaNatura Travel (see Manu Tour operators, page 213).

La Paz and around

Chacaltaya, near La Paz

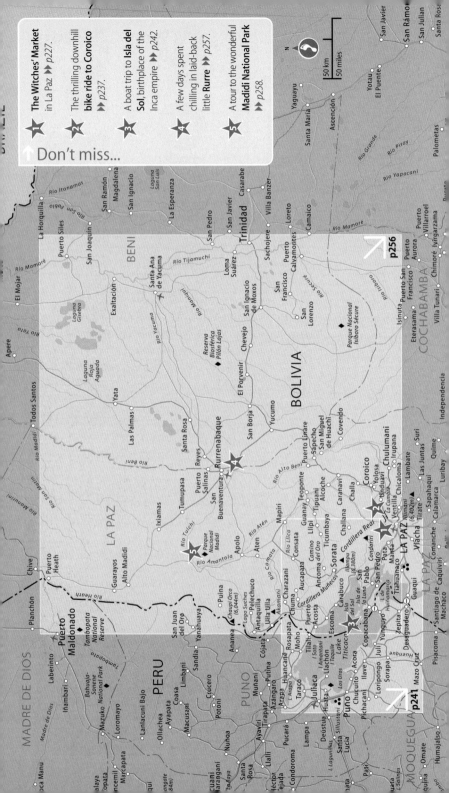

↑ Don't miss...

★ 1 The Witches' Market in La Paz ▶▶ *p227*.

★ 2 The thrilling downhill bike ride to Coroico ▶▶ *p237*.

★ 3 A boat trip to Isla del Sol, birthplace of the Inca empire ▶▶ *p242*.

★ 4 A few days spent chilling in laid-back little Rurre ▶▶ *p257*.

★ 5 A tour to the wonderful Madidi National Park ▶▶ *p258*.

50 km
50 miles

N

p256

p241

Few cities can boast such an impressive setting as La Paz. Lying huddled at the bottom of a huge canyon, the first view of the city is one that leaves most visitors breathless – literally – for La Paz stands at over 3,500 m, making it the highest capital city in the world. Airborne visitors touch down at the highest commercial airport in the world, and can then play golf at the highest golf course in the world, or ski (just about) on the highest ski slope in the world. No visit to Bolivia would be complete without witnessing the sapphire-blue expanse of mystical Lake Titicaca, the highest navigable lake in the world, at 3,856 m above sea level. In the mountains of the Cordillera Real, to the east of the Lake, Sorata is a neglected old colonial town enjoying one of the most beautiful settings in the whole country. To the southeast the valleys drop steeply towards the Amazon Basin through the Yungas, where Coroico is a good place for chilling, especially if you've just cycled down the 'world's most dangerous road'. Farther east still, the little town of Rurrenabaque, in the northern Beni lowlands, is a peaceful and attractive base from which to explore the wonders of the Bolivian Amazon, home to world's greatest collection of plants and animals.

Ratings

Culture
★★★

Landscape
★★★★

Wildlife
★★★★★

Activities
★★★★

Chillin'
★★★★

Costs
$$$

La Paz

Architecturally, La Paz is no beauty. There are few surviving examples of colonial architecture and little in the way of classic tourist attractions – no great museums or art galleries. Yet La Paz is arguably the most fascinating 'capital city' in all of South America. What sets it apart are not only the sights, sounds and smells of the streets but the phenomenal views of the triple-peaked Illimani and the encircling mountains. The other striking feature about La Paz is that it appears to be one gigantic street market. Every square inch of street space is taken up by Aymara women in traditional bowler hats and voluminous skirts, squatting on their haunches yelling at passers-by to buy their handicrafts, fake designer labels, bags of coca leaves – everything under the sun, in fact.

Getting there International and domestic flights; buses from Peru.

Getting around *Micros* (buses), *combis* (minivans) and *trufis* (shared taxis)

Time required 2-3 days.

Weather Nov-Apr wet season; cold nights Jun-Aug.

Sleeping Wide choice in all price ranges.

Eating Everything from llama steaks to sushi.

Activities and tours Tiahuanaco, downhill biking at Chacaltaya.

★ **Don't miss**… Museo de Coca
▸▸ *p227*.

Ins and outs ▸▸ *pp230-240*

Getting there

Air The **airport** (T02-2810122), is at El Alto, high above the city and the highest commercial airport in the world, at 4,058 m. It is connected to the city by motorway. A taxi between the centre and airport takes about 20 minutes and costs Bs45 (US$5.70), or Bs15 (US$1.90) each for a shared taxi. Current prices, including luggage, should be on display at the airport exit. Enquire at the tourist office in town, or at the airport. **Cotranstur** minibuses, white with 'Cotranstur' and 'Aeropuerto' written on the side and back, go from Plaza Isabel La Católica or anywhere on the Prado to the airport between 0800-0830 to 1900-2000; Bs3.50 (US$0.44) per person, allow about one hour (it's best to have little luggage). They leave from the airport every five minutes or so. *Colectivos* from Plaza Isabel La Católica charge US$3 per person, carrying four passengers. Flight details are given on pages 22 and 237.

There is an **Enlace** ATM that accepts Cirrus, Plus, VISA and Mastercard credit/debit cards in the international departures hall for taking out local cash when you arrive as well as a bank which changes cash at reasonable rates. To change money when the bank is closed, ask at the departure tax window. The international departures hall is the main concourse, with all the check-in desks, and is also the hall for all domestic arrivals and departures. There's a small **tourist office** at the airport with some maps available, where English is spoken, and is helpful (when staffed). There's an expensive bar/restaurant and a cheaper café/comedor upstairs, as well as a duty-free shop. Flights with **TAM** leave from the military airport next door to the main commercial one.

Bus Buses to Oruro, Potosí, Sucre, Cochabamba, Santa Cruz and all points south of La Paz leave from the raucous main terminal at Plaza Antofagasta, as do international buses (these desks are further back in the building). For information, T02-2280551. Touts find passengers the most convenient bus and are paid commission by the bus company. *Micros* 2, M, CH or 130 go there from the centre of town. The terminal (open 0700-2300) has a post office, Entel, restaurant, luggage stores (0530-2200), internet and even hot showers. There is also a **tourist information** booth outside. When arriving at the terminal, pay no more than Bs8 (US$0.90) for a taxi to hotels in the centre. Buses to Peru with agencies such as **Turisbus** (see page 237), **Diana** and **Vicuña** (see page 254) can also be caught from here and may be cheaper than buying tickets from their respective offices. Buses for Sorata, Copacabana and Tiahuanaco leave from the cemetery district. Those for the Yungas and Rurrenabaque leave from Villa Fátima. ● ›› *p237.*

Getting around

Most of the centre of La Paz can be walked around, though this is often a slow process, especially as you get used to the altitude. For trips further down the valley, possibly to Sopocachi and definitely to Zona Sur, you'll want to take a bus or taxi. Taxis are cheap and plentiful – those marked 'Radio Taxi' charge per journey rather than per passenger and so are cheaper for more than one person, around US$1 for a journey, slightly more to Zona Sur. Taxis can be flagged down in the street or your hotel will order you one. *Micros* (shared minibuses, around US$0.15-0.25 per person depending on the journey) are worth experiencing, but not with anything more than the bare minimum of luggage. La Paz's buses are colourfully painted antiques which chug around the streets for about US$0.20 a journey.

Tourist information

The **tourist information office** ⓘ *at the bottom end of Av 16 de Julio (Prado) on Plaza del Estudiante on the corner with C México, Mon-Fri 0830-1200, 1430-1900*, has staff who speak English but very little in the way of information to disseminate. There are a few free leaflets and a map of La Paz (US$2.25). There are smaller offices at: Calle Linares 932, which has a good selection of guidebooks for reference, purchase or exchange, and outside the main bus terminal. **Secretaria Nacional de Turismo (Senatur)** ⓘ *Edificio Ballivián, 18th floor, C Mercado, T02-2367463/64, F02-2374630, Casilla 1 868.*

The Prado, La Paz's main traffic artery and the street by which all visitors find their bearings.

La Paz

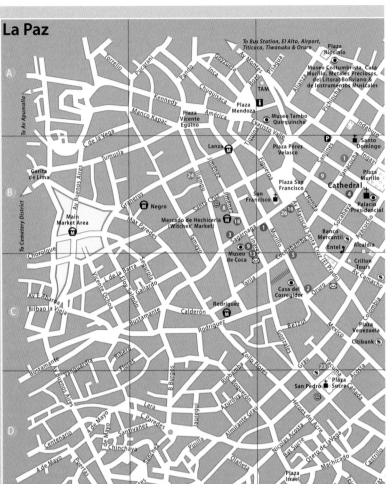

To Bus Station, El Alto, Airport, Titicaca, Tiwanaku & Oruro

Plaza Riosinio

Museo Costumbrista, Casa Murillo, Metales Preciosos, del Litoral Boliviano & de Instrumentos Musicales

TAM

Plaza Mendoza

Museo Tambo Quirquincho

Plaza Pérez Velasco

Lanza

Plaza San Francisco

San Francisco

Cathedral

Santo Domingo

Plaza Murillo

Palacio Presidencial

Negro

Mercado de Hechicería (Witches' Market)

Banco Mercantil

Entel

Alcaldía

Museo de Coca

Crillon Tours

Av Camacho

Casa del Corregidor

Plaza Venezuela

Citibank

Rodríguez

Calderón

Rodríguez

Plaza Sucre

San Pedro

Plaza Israel

Plaza Confederacion

Medinacelli

N

200 metres
200 yards

Sleeping
Austria **1** B3
España **7** E4
Gloria **9** B3
Hostal Cactus del
  Milenio **8** B2
Hostal Naira **26** B3
Hostal República
  13 B4

Residencial Sucre
  23 C3
Rosario **24** B2

Eating
Andrómeda **2** E5
Angelo Colonial
  13 C2
Banais **16** B3
Bodeguita
  Cubana **6** C4
Café Alexander **4** B3
Chifa Emy **5** F5
Jalapeños **17** F6
La Comedie **12** E5
La Terraza **8** D4
Laksmi **1** B3

Mongo's **19** E5
Osteria Pettirosso **11** E5
Pepe's **18** B2
Pot Pourri des
  Gourmets **9** B2
Pronto **20** E5
Vienna **7** D4
Wagamama **10** E6
Yussef's **3** B2

Bars & clubs
Café Montmartre **6** E5
Diesel Nacional **1** E5
La Luna **2** C3
La Salsa del Loro **3** E5
Sol y Luna **5** C3
Thelonius Jazz **4** E4

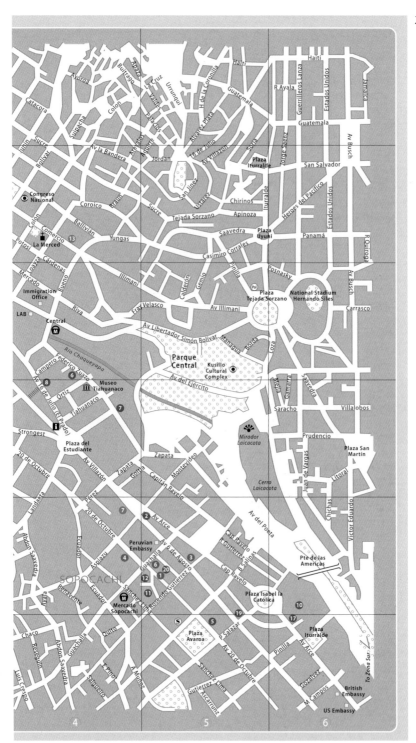

Plenty to cheer about

One of the most intriguing items for sale in Andean markets is *Ekeko*, the god of good fortune and plenty and one of the most enduring and endearing of the Aymara gods and folk legends.

He is a cheery, avuncular little chap, with a happy face to make children laugh, a pot belly due to his predilection for food and short legs so he can't run away. His image, usually in plaster of Paris, is laden with various household items, as well as sweets, confetti and streamers, food, and with a cigarette dangling from his lower lip. Believers say that these statues only bring luck if they are received as gifts.

Ekeko figure adorned with miniature objects at Alacitas, see page 235.

Orientation

Orientation around the centre is relatively simple. Running along the bottom of the canyon is the broad main street called El Prado (though it has four official names, starting in the north: Avenida Montes, Avenida Mariscal Santa Cruz, Avenida 16 de Julio and Avenida Villazón). El Prado runs southeast from Plaza San Francisco down to the Plaza del Estudiante. To its northeast is the grander area of the city, with government buildings and much of La Paz's remaining colonial architecture. To the southwest of the Prado the streets rise into the city's indigenous heart, teeming with markets and budget hostels. At the southern end of the Prado, Plaza del Estudiante is, as the name suggests, the epicentre of student life, while a short distance on down the valley, the smart area of Sopocachi has many of the city's best restaurants, bars and nightclubs. Five kilometres further south, Zona Sur is another world: the modern flipside of the city centre, full of shiny office blocks, businessmen and supermarkets.

Sights

Plaza Murillo, three blocks northeast of the Prado, is the traditional centre of the city. Here stand the the huge, modern, **cathedral**, the Italian renaissance-style **Palacio Presidencial** which has twice been gutted by fire in its stormy 130-year history, and the **Congreso Nacional**. In front of the Palacio Quemado is a statue of former President Gualberto Villarroel who was dragged into the plaza by an angry mob and hanged in 1946.

Northwest of Plaza Murillo is Calle Jaén, home to the city's finest examples of colonial architecture, as well as craft shops and four museums: **Museo Costumbrista** ⓘ *on Plaza Riosinio, at the top of C Jaén, T02-2378478, single ticket for all 4 museums US$0.50*, has miniature displays depicting the history of La Paz and well-known Paceños; **Museo Casa Murillo** ⓘ *C Jaén 790, T02-2375273, Tue-Fri 0930-1230, 1500-1900, Sat and Sun 1000-1230*, has a good collection of paintings, furniture and national costumes of the period; **Museo de Metales Preciosos** ⓘ *C Jaén 777, T02-2371470, Tue-Fri 0930-1230, 1500-1900, Sat and Sun 1000-1230*, pretty much does what it says on the label; and **Museo del Litoral Boliviano** ⓘ *C Jaén 789, T02-2378478, Tue-Fri 0930-1230, 1500-1900, Sat and Sun 1000-1230*, houses artefacts of the War of the Pacific.

Also on Jaén, but not included on the combined ticket, is the **Museo de Instrumentos Musicales de Bolivia** ⓘ *C Jaén 711, T02-2331075, Tue-Fri 0930-1230, 1500-1900, Sat and Sun 1000-1230, US$0.75, students US$0.15,* run by Ernesto Cavour and based on 30 years of research. Further west, on the other side of Avenida Montes, at Calle Evaristo Valle, near Plaza Mendoza, is the excellent **Museo Tambo Quirquincho** ⓘ *Tue-Fri 0930-1230, 1500-1900, Sat and Sun, 1000-1230, US$0.15, (Sat and students free).* It is housed in a restored colonial building, displaying modern painting and sculpture, carnival masks, silver, early-20th-century photography and city plans.

At the southern end of the Prado is the aptly named **Plaza del Estudiante**, only a stone's throw from the Universidad Mayor San Andrés. A few blocks north of the plaza, back from the Prado on the right by the Hotel Plaza and María Auxili church, a flight of stairs leads down to the **Museo Nacional de Arqueología** ⓘ *Mon-Fri 0900-1230, 1500-1900, Sat 1000-1200, 1500-1830, Sun 1000-1300, US$0.75, includes a good video show, students US$0.10.* This modern building, built in mock-Tiahuanaco style, contains good collections of the arts and crafts of ancient Tiahuanaco and items from the eastern jungles. It also has a two-room exhibition of gold statuettes and objects found in Lake Titicaca.

At the upper end of Avenida Mariscal Santa Cruz is the Plaza San Francisco, with the church and monastery of **San Francisco** ⓘ *local indigenous weddings can be seen on Sat 1000-1200, otherwise the church opens for Mass at 0700, 0900, 1100 and 1900, Mon-Sat and also at 0800, 1000 and 1200 on Sun*, dating from 1549. This is one of the finest examples of colonial religious architecture in South America and is well worth seeing. The plaza outside the church is always a hive of activity and often the focal point for frequent political protests.

Behind the San Francisco church a network of narrow cobbled streets rises steeply up the side of the canyon. Much of this area is a permanent street market. The lower part of **Calle Sagárnaga**, from Plaza San Francisco to Calle Illampu, is lined with shops and stalls selling handicrafts, clothes, guitar covers, silver and leatherware. Further up, on Calle Linares between Calle Sagárnaga and Santa Cruz, is the **Mercado de Hechicería** (Witches' Market), where you can find everything you need to put a spell on that annoying hotel guest or crooked tour operator. Here also is where you'll find the infamous dried llama foetuses which are used to protect a dwelling from evil spirits.

Don't miss out on the provocative **Museo de Coca** ⓘ *daily 1000-1800, US$1.05*, also on Linares, at number 906. It presents a historic and scientific explanation of the production and effects of this controversial plant, chewed for thousands of years by indigenous Bolivians.

The Witches' Market.

Mount Illimani dominates the La Paz skyline.

Further up Sagárnaga turn right onto Max Paredes and, between Santa Cruz and Graneros, is the **Mercado Negro** (Black Market), a bewildering labyrinth of stalls where you can pick up a cheap pair of Levi jeans, or almost anything else. Continuing west towards the cemetery district, Max Paredes meets **Avenida Buenos Aires**, one of the liveliest streets in the indigenous quarter and the main market area, where streets are crammed with stalls selling every imaginable item. Do not expect to go anywhere in a hurry in this part of the city. Heading back southwards along Max Paredes, where it meets Calle Rodríguez and becomes Calle Zoilo Flores, is the **Mercado Rodríguez**, a riot of colour, fruit, vegetables and unidentifiable parts of animals. The main market days are Saturday and Sunday mornings but stalls are here every day.

Running south from Plaza del Estudiante is Avenida Villazón which then becomes Avenida Arce and heads southwards towards the suburbs of Zona Sur. Branching off to the right at the bridge is Avenida 6 de Agosto which takes you into the district of **Sopocachi**, more upmarket than street market and packed with good bars and restaurants. At Cerro Laicacota Hill, on Avenida del Ejército to the east of Avenida Arce , is the **Kusillo Cultural Complex** ① *T02-2226371, www.quipusbolivia.org, Tue-Sun 1030-1830, Tue-Fri US$0.75, Sat and Sun US$1.50, children US$0.75,* featuring interactive exhibits on Bolivian culture and textiles, craft shops, a Museum of Science and Play and the world's highest funicular railway. From the top you get great views of the city, especially at dusk, when all the lights begin to twinkle on the surrounding hillsides.

The **Zona Sur** district is in the valley 15 minutes south of the city (US$0.40 by *trufi* or minibus – take any minibus marked Calacoto, San Miguel, Achumani or Chasquipampa from the centre). Home to the resident foreign community, it has developed into an important area in its own right. It has international shopping centres, supermarkets stocked with imported items and some of the smartest restaurants and bars in La Paz. The area begins after the bridge at La Florida where there is an attractive park, Plaza Humboldt, which has exhibitions of local art work on Sundays and a collection of kiosks selling cheap snacks. The main road, Avenida Ballivián, begins here at Calle 8 and continues up the hill to the shopping district of San Miguel on Calle 21 (about a 20-minute walk). The place comes alive in the evenings, when La Paz's affluent youth cram the streets in their parents' flashy cars and the city's ex-pats visit national-themed cafés and bars to talk about home.

You can buy just about anything in La Paz's street markets, including a hundred varieties of potato.

Tiahuanaco

ⓘ *Daily 0900-1700, US$3.50, including entry to the museum. Allow 4 hrs to see the ruins and village. Hiring a good guide at the site costs US$10. See page 237 for transport details.*

The most popular excursion from La Paz is the remarkable site of **Tiahuanaco**, 72 km west of the city. Rising out of the vast flatness of the altiplano are the remains of pyramids and temples of a civilization which predated the Incas and was one of the world's greatest and longest-running empires.

The Tiahuanaco Empire comprised nearly half of present-day Bolivia, southern parts of Peru, the northwest section of Argentina and nearly half of Chile. Its armies reigned supreme over many different cultures and its engineers built a vast system of paved highways over mountains and through jungles and deserts, which enabled it to maintain a constant flow of goods throughout the empire. All these roads led to one place – next to the little market town of today, and once the site of a mighty imperial capital of 50,000 inhabitants. By 100 BC Tiahuanaco was emerging as the most important urban centre on Lake Titicaca and by AD 100 it ruled all of its neighbouring kingdoms at the southern end of the lake. By AD 400 it had defeated its main rivals, the Pukara people of Peru, and ruled the entire lake basin. Tiahuanaco was the longest-running empire of all the Andean civilizations, but it collapsed between AD 1150 and AD 1200 and no one really knows why. There are several theories but perhaps the most credible is that the empire was ended by a prolonged drought.

Tiahuanaco today bears little relation to its former magnificence but the site is still impressive. The main structure is the **Kalasasaya Temple**, which was the holiest part of the site and the burial place of the ruling elite. The name means 'standing stones', referring to the statues found in that part. Two of them, the Ponce monolith (in the centre of the inner patio) and the Fraile monolith (in the southwest corner), have been re-erected. In the northwest corner of the Kalasasaya is the **Puerta del Sol**, or Gateway of the Sun, which was originally at Pumapunku. This massive carved portal was hewn from a single block of stone 3 m high, nearly 4 m wide and weighing 10 tonnes. The central motif is a figure common throughout the empire. It displays many of the typical Tiahuanaco features: puma faces looking downwards, condor faces, two left hands and the snake with a human face. This is thought to represent the principal deity of Tiahuanaco. The complex markings are thought to be part of an elaborate calendar.

The Kalasasaya Temple (and Ponce monolith in the background) seen from the Templo Semisubterránneo.

In front of the Kalasasaya is a large sunken courtyard, the **Templo Semisubterráneo**. Around 1,500 years ago this was filled with the sacred monolithic icons of the kingdoms conquered by Tiahuanaco. They were positioned there for all to see that Tiahuanaco's gods were more powerful than any others. According to some theories, though, the faces on the walls depicted states of health, the temple being a house of healing. The **Akapana**, next to the Kalasasaya, originally a pyramid, was the largest structure, but is now no more than a hill. A little way from the main site, on the other side of the railway, is **Pumapunku**, a mysterious collection of massive fallen stones, some of which weigh up to 100 tonnes. The widespread confusion of fallen stones has led some to suggest a natural disaster putting a sudden end to the construction before it was finished. This part of the site is often not included on tours.

There is a good **museum** near the entrance. It has well illustrated explanations of the raised field system of agriculture as well as ceramics, textiles and distended skulls – apparently the result of a belief that long heads were a sign of high class. Many other artefacts are in the **Museo Nacional de Arqueología** (see page 227) in La Paz, including the **Bennett** megalith.

Sleeping

Much of the upmarket accommodation can be found in Zona Sur and on the Prado, more especially south of Plaza del Estudiante, around Av Villazón and Av Arce. Most of the budget accommodation is concentrated in 2 areas: in the streets which lead steeply up from behind San Francisco, especially Sagárnaga, Illampu and Santa Cruz; and around Plaza Murillo, in the triangle formed by the Prado, C Ingavi and C Loayza.

B Hostal Naira, C Sagárnaga 161, T02-2355645, F02-2311214, hostalnaira @entelnet.bo. Big, carpeted, fairly modern rooms are arranged around an internal courtyard with potted plants. Rooms at the front have balconies overlooking Sagárnaga; others lack much natural light. Staff are friendly but speak little English. Price includes a decent buffet breakfast downstairs at *Café Banais*. Try bargaining.

B Rosario, Illampu 704, above Plaza San Francisco, T02-2451658, www.hotel rosario.com. Almost on the doorstep of the Witches' Market, this very popular, attractive and modern 42-room, colonial-style hotel has a Turisbus travel agency downstairs (see page 237) as well as a fair trade shop. A 'Cultural

Interpretation Centre' explains everything for sale in the nearby markets, from textiles to llama foetuses. All rooms have cable TV, safes and excellent showers – two have bathtubs. Price includes a huge buffet breakfast. There is also a family suite for up to 6, an excellent restaurant (see Eating, next page) and a café with free internet. Stores luggage, friendly and helpful experienced staff.

B Gloria, Potosí 909, T02-2407070, F02-2406622, www.boliviantravel.com. All rooms at this modern and central hotel have bathtubs and cable TV. The attached French-style *Café Pierrot* is good. There is also a canteen restaurant serving good *almuerzo* for US$3, also buffet breakfast, and dinner (US$2.20) after 1900, Sun 0700-1000, and a tour agency, *Gloria Tours*.

C Hostal República, Comercio 1455, T02-2202742, F02-2202782. With bathroom (**D** without). In the beautiful old colonial-era house of a former president, friendly República has attractive courtyards and a helpful travel information desk. The café, opposite reception, has free internet for hotel guests and serves good breakfasts. Book ahead.

D España, Av 6 de Agosto 2074, T02-2442643, F02-2441329, www.hotel-espana.com. Set back from the Prado near Plaza del Estudiante, Hotel España is an unexpectedly peaceful gem. Rooms have shared bathroom, hot water and cable TV and those at the back are set around a beautiful garden. There is a restaurant as well as free internet and a travel agency just outside.

D-E Residencial Sucre, Colombia 340, on Plaza San Pedro, T02-2492038, F02-2486723. A friendly and helpful place with big rooms set around a courtyard with a beautiful garden. There's a quiet area, warm water, it's clean and luggage is stored. Cheaper without bathroom.

F Austria, Yanacocha 531, T02-2408540. There are no private bathrooms and it can be gloomy (make sure you get a room with a window) but rooms are clean and staff are generally friendly. The 3 showers (for the 22 rooms) have hot water and there is also a safe deposit, laundry and TV lounge.

G per person. **Hostal Cactus del Milenio**, C Jiménez 818. In what used to be just 'Milenio', the downstairs rooms are dark; those upstairs are better though still very simple. Kitchen, limited hot water, very peaceful, excellent position.

● Eating

Most of the top-class restaurants are found in Sopocachi. Av 20 de Octubre has become *the* trendy place to eat and be seen eating, with new arty, funky cafés and restaurants springing up all the time. There are several great *chifas* along Av 6 de Agosto offering tasty and cheap food. Pick any one of them for a delicious lunch menu.

Budget buster

LL **Presidente**, Potosí 920 and Sanjines, near Plaza San Francisco, T02-2406666, F02-2407240. 'The highest 5-star in the world' has great views from top floor and pool, gym and sauna all open to non-residents. Some of the Las Vegas styling (mirrored ceilings and indoor waterfalls) feels out of place but it's comfortable and service is excellent.

LL **Radisson Plaza**, Av Arce 2177, T02-2441111, F02-2440593, www.radisson. com/lapazbo. Formerly Hotel La Paz (and still referred to as the Sheraton), this 5-star hotel has 239 rooms, all modern facilities, good views and an excellent buffet in its restaurant (🍴) Mon and Wed, 2000-2300, US$5.50.

🍴🍴🍴 **Chalet Suisse**, C23, Zona Sur, T02-2793160. On the main avenue, up the hill between C 24 and 25, Chalet Suisse is expensive but highly recommended, with excellent fondue and steaks. Booking is essential on Fri evenings.

🍴🍴 **Chifa Emy**, Av 20 de Octobre 927, Plaza Avaroa, T02-2440551. Mon-Fri 1130-1430, Sat 1130-1500, Sun 1130-1530, Mon-Wed 1800-2300, Thu 1800-0000, Fri-Sat 1800-0100, Sun 1800-2200. One of the best Chinese restaurants in town, with good service, over 170 dishes and a big screen TV. Accepts credit cards. Shows and concerts Wed-Fri at 2130.

🍴🍴 **Jalapeños**, Av Arce 2549, T02-2435288. Excellent Mexican food, main course up to US$6.50.

🍴🍴 **Tambo Colonial**, in Hotel Rosario (see page 230), Illampu 704. Huge buffet breakfast with fruit, yoghurt, pancakes and excellent wholemeal bread (there are even toasters) from 0700 for US$2.84. In the evenings it becomes one of La Paz's best restaurants, with excellent local and international cuisine, including good llama steaks.

🍴🍴 **La Comedie**, Pasaje Medinacelli 2234, T02-2423561. Branding itself as an 'art-café restaurant', La Comedie is a cool, terracotta-coloured, contemporary place with good salads, a predominently French menu, round windows and plenty of candles. Also good for cocktails.

🍴🍴 **La Quebecoise**, Av 20 de Octubre 2387, T02-2121682. With an interior rather like a 19th-century French living room, this French-Canadian restaurant has an open fire and top-notch service.

🍴🍴 **Osteria Pettirosso**, Pasaje Medinacelli 2282, T02-2423700. Tue-Fri 1200-1430, Sun 1200-1530, Mon-Sat 1900-2300. A welcoming Italian restaurant, Pettirosso has live music Fri and Sat, cool jazz at other times, fig trees, terracotta walls, an open fire, proper wood-burning pizza ovens, Italian wine and even an Italian chef. Takeaway pizzas are also available and are slightly cheaper.

🍴🍴 **Pronto**, Jauregui 2248, T02-2441369, Mon-Sat 1830-2230. In a basement and not easy to find. It's well worth the effort though for its upmarket Italian cuisine. There are 3 different types of pasta – regular, integral and *de quinoa*. Popular, good service.

🍴🍴 **Vienna**, Federico Zuazo 1905, T02-2441660. Mon-Fri 1200-1400, 1830-2200, Sun 1200-1430. www.restaurantvienna.com. A smart, European-style restaurant with excellent German, Austrian and local food, excellent service, antique prints, a great atmosphere and huge, juicy steaks at moderate prices.

🍴🍴 **Wagamama**, Pasaje Pinilla 2557, T02-2434911. Tue-Sat 1200-1430, 1900-2000, Sun and Mon closed. Huge plates of amazing sushi. Complimentary tea and excellent service. Popular with ex-pats – hardly a Bolivian in sight.

♈ **Andromeda**, Av Arce 2116, T02-2440726. European-style and vegetarian food, with an excellent 5-course set lunch. Closed evenings.

♈ **Angelo Colonial**, Linares 922. Fantastic, affordable food at candelit tables in a ramshackle upstairs room overflowing with antiques. Good and plentiful vegetarian options and delicious steaks. Jazzy music with regular smatterings of The Beatles. One of the best central restaurants.

♈ **Bodeguita Cubana**, Federico Zuazo 1653. Cuban favourites such as *ropa vieja* and excellent mojito cocktails in an atmospheric Cuban setting. Strictly meat and fish so vegetarians will have to concentrate on the drinks.

♈ **Laksmi**, Piso 1, Galeria Chuquiago, Sagárnaga. A genuinely vegetarian Indian at back of one of the courtyards off Sagárnaga. Indian hippie influenced, but with an unexpected lack of curry. *Almuerzos* are thali-like, with everything served together on a metal dish and the vegetarian burgers are excellent. There are some sunny tables outside overlooking the courtyard. Set lunch US$1.25, dinner US$1.

♈ **Marbella**, Av 16 de Julio 1655, T02-2317075. Daily 0800-0000, lunch until 1430. The friendly Marbella is enshrouded in plastic foliage and flowers, and has a peculiar mock-Arabian mural. The music is heartfelt Bolivian and the place fills up with businessmen. A big menu has Bolivian, Mexican and international food and some good breakfast options, including fruit, yoghurt and cereal.

♈ **Mongo's**, Hermanos Manchego 2444, near Plaza Isabela la Católica, T02-2440714. Mon-Thu 100-0130, Fri-Sun 1800-0300. There are plans to take Mongo's upmarket but until that happens it remains the most popular gringo spot in town. There's an open fire, cable TV for

sports, US$2.90 set lunches which change every day and excellent food including fish and chips, great burgers, and Mexican dishes. Service can be slow for food but there's always the fastest and coldest beer in town to keep you going.

♈ **RamJam**, C Presbitero Medina 2421, T02-242-2295. Above Plaza Avaroa, RamJam, set up in 2004 by some of the team that created Mongo's, offers everything a homesick gringo could want, from coffee to curry, Sunday roasts to cable TV. Expect some late nights and wobbly walks home.

♈ **Pot Pourri des Gourmets**, Linares 906. In an attractive barrel-vaulted, wood and brick room, Pot Pourri offers an excellent value set lunch (US$2.20) with choice of soup, main course and dessert. Bolivian/French owners have produced a good mixture of local drinks and food combined with many international options. Exceptional value, great atmosphere and very friendly.

♈ **Yussef's**, Sagárnaga 380. Poorly signposted and well hidden on the right of Sagárnaga as you go up the hill, but well worth the effort for wonderful Lebanese food. Excellent vegetarian options as well as meaty choices. The mixed plate of mezes for US$4.50 is a real feast, or you can mix and match individual portions for US$0.75. Friendly service, relaxed atmosphere.

Cafés

Banais, Sagárnaga 161. Below Hostal Naira, one of central La Paz's grooviest cafés has wooden floors, laid-back music and especially good lemon meringue pie, salads and sandwiches. Downstairs there's a room of computers with internet access for US$0.50 per hr. The buffet breakfast (US$1.50) is simple but good, with delicious crusty bread and fruit salad.

Café Alexander, Av 16 de Julio 1832, T02-2312790, also on C Potosí 1091, T02-2406482. Mon-Fri 0800-2230, Sat and Sun 0900-2230. A modern, international-style café serving excellent coffee, smoothies and muffins. The cakes, salads and sandwiches are also good. Usually referred to as 'Café Alex', there's also a branch in Zona Sur.

La Terraza, Av 6 de Agosto 2296, Av 16 de Julio (next to Burger King) and at Gutiérrez in Zona Sur. A mini chain with wooden floors and chairs and a modern US feel. Pancakes and 80s pop. You can make your own salad from a selection of ingredients on menu. Bs10-18 for breakfast options, also excellent sandwiches and coffee.

Pepe's, Pasaje Jimenez 894 (off Linares between Sagárnaga and Santa Cruz), T02-2450788, pepcoff@hotmail.com. Service can be a little slow but is invariably friendly in this chilled and welcoming little café. Great all-day breakfasts range from US$1-3 and sandwiches and omelettes are also good. You can relax at an outside table in the sun after scouring the textiles and handicraft shops nearby, play with the provided dominoes and cards, or leaf through the guidebooks and magazines. The local pottery found in many cafés in the city is also for sale here.

🍷 Bars and clubs

For up-to-the-minute information, check out *The Llama Express* or *Quéhacer*, a free magazine with Sat's *La Razón* newspaper, or visit www.la-razon.com. Some cafés and restaurants stay open late and some have regular music. **Mongo's**, **RamJam** and **La Comedie** are good places for a drink. Check flyposters for details of gigs. Many of the good bars and clubs are in Sopocachi. C Belisario Salinas is full of bars, starting just below Plaza Abaroa and continuing all the way up to Av Ecuador, beyond Plaza España.

Café Montmartre, Fernando Guachalla 399, off Av 6 de Agosto; also in Zona Sur on Av Mariscal de Montenegro, T02-2442801. Mon-Sat 1200-1500, 1700-0200. Fashionable bar with live jazz some weekends, also good French menu, set lunch US$4. Sandwiches, salads and crêpes too.

Diesel Nacional, Av 20 de Octubre between Gutiérrez and Guachalla. A hip, modern club with an industrial theme.

La Luna, C Oruro 197 and Murillo, 1900-late, publalunabolivia@ hotmail.com. Good value cocktails and other drinks in a friendly environment, though it can get very crowded. Cable TV and board games. Happy hour 2000-2100.

La Salsa del Loro, Rosendo Gutiérrez, corner of Av 6 de Agosto. Thu-Sat. A salsa club where once you hit the dancefloor there will be no respite until you're carted off on a stretcher suffering from exhaustion. It's probably a good idea to take a few lessons first: try *Gym Cec*, Illampu 868, 1st floor, T02-2310158, US$4 per hr.

Sol y Luna, Murillo and Cochabamba, 1800-late. The best bar in the centre of town, and possibly in La Paz, Sol y Luna is warm, comfy and cosy. A Dutch-run place, it has stone walls and wooden floors, a good range of bottled beers, a travel book library, candles, and laid-back sounds. There are also different teas and coffees on offer, bar snacks and toasted sandwiches and a wide choice of cocktails including 'Mojito Boliviano' (with coca leaves) and 'Bolivia Libre' (with Singani instead of rum).

Thelonius Jazz Bar, Av 20 de Octubre, 2172, T02-2337806. Tue-Sat from 1700. Good jazz bar.

🎭 Entertainment

Cinemas

The good films are mainly in English. Some of the best cinemas are: **Cine 16 de Julio**, on the Prado by Plaza del Estudiante, T02-2441099, films at 1530, 1900 and 2130; **Monje Campero**, on the Prado, Av 16 de Julio 1495, T02- 2330192, next to *Eli's Pizzeria*, films at 1000, 1530, 1900 and 2130; and **6 de Agosto**, 6 de Agosto,

T02-2442629, films at 1545, 1930 and 2130. Expect to pay around US$2.50. For film buffs there is the excellent **Cinemateca Boliviana**, Capitán Ravelo and Rosendo Gutiérrez, 2 blocks from Puente de las Américas. This is La Paz's art film centre with festivals, courses, etc; entry is US$1.20, students US$0.60.

Peñas

The best traditional entertainment for visitors are the folk shows, or *peñas*. Various restaurants also have shows worth seeing. At these, visitors will be able to listen to the wide variety of local musical instruments. Enquire at the *Rumillajta* shop (in the galería close to San Francisco church) about future performances by the eponymous folk group.

There's a good peña at **Casa del Corregidor**, dinner show Mon-Thu, no cover charge, Fri and Sat *peña* both start at 2100, US$4, colonial atmosphere, traditional music and dance. Another peña is **Marko Tambo** on C Jaén 710. US$7 all inclusive (also sells woven goods). **El Parnaso**, Sagárnaga 189, corner with Murillo, T02-2316827. This is a *peña* purely for tourists but a good way to see local costumes and dancing.

⊛ Festivals and events

Jan-Feb Alacitas is an extravaganza of miniature objects where you can buy anything from tiny bags of flour to trucks and houses. Held from the last week of Jan to the first week of Feb, in Parque Central up from Av del Ejército, and Plaza Sucre/San Pedro.

May-Jun At the end of May/early Jun is the **Festividad de Nuestro Señor Jesús del Gran Poder** (generally known simply as the 'Gran Poder'), the most important festival of the year, with a huge procession of costumed dancers.

Jun Other festivals include **Corpus Christi**, at the beginning of Jun; and **San Juan**, on 21 Jun, which is based on the Aymara New Year. People used to mark the passing of the old year by burning all their rubbish in the streets, especially old tyres; now it is mainly an excuse to let off fireworks.

Jul Fiestas de Julio, is a month of concerts and performances at the Teatro Municipal and offers a wide variety of music, including the **University Folkloric Festival**.

31 Dec On **New Year's Eve** fireworks are let off and make a spectacular sight – and din – best viewed from a high vantage point.

◎ Shopping

You need never go into a shop in La Paz. Everything is available on the street – from computers and cellular phones to tummy trimmers, and a few useful things like food.

Bookshops

Los Amigos del Libro, Mercado 1315, T02-2204321, also branches at Edificio Alameda, Av 16 de Julio (1 block from Plaza Hotel), El Alto airport and Montenegro in the Zona Sur. Large stock of English, French and German books, and US magazines here; they also sell a few tourist maps of the region from Puno to the Yungas, and walking-tour guides; and will ship books.

Handicrafts

On C Sagárnaga, by the side of San Francisco church (behind which are many handicraft stalls in the Mercado Artesanal), are booths and small stores with interesting local items of all sorts, especially textiles, leather and silverware. It's best to go on Sun morning when prices are reduced. At Sagárnaga 177 is an entire gallery of handicraft shops. There are also many shops on Linares, between Sagárnaga and Santa Cruz. **Artesanía Sorata**, Linares 862 and Sagárnaga 311. Mon-Sat 0930-1900, and Sun 1000-1800 in high season. Specializes in dolls, sweaters and weavings made using natural dyes by a women's co-operative, and handmade textiles.

Millma, Sagárnaga 225, and in *Hotel Radisson*, for alpaca sweaters (made in their own factory) and antique and rare textiles.

Rumillajta, one of the Galería shops adjacent to the San Francisco church entrance. For musical instruments.

Mother Earth, Linares 870. High-quality alpaca sweaters with natural dyes. Good-quality alpaca goods also at **LAM** shops on Sagárnaga.

Markets

The markets are a good place for ponchos and local handicrafts. Many local objects are sold near Av Buenos Aires, and musical instruments can be found much cheaper than in the shops on C Granier, near the main cemetery. Mercado Rodríguez street market is good for fresh food. Sat and Sun mornings are the main days but the market is open every day. The street of Eloy Salmón is packed with shops selling cheap electronic goods, cameras and computer components.

▲▲ Activities and tours

Skiing

Ninety minutes by car from La Paz (36 km) is Chacaltaya, the highest ski run in the world at 5,345 m and incorporating the first ski lift in South America, opened in 1940. Unfortunately there has been little development in the last 50 years and the lift is no longer working. Furthermore, ski equipment is very limited and of poor quality (equipment-hire costs US$10). The only time you can really ski is immediately following a fresh snowfall. However, it's still fun to visit and take plastic bags for a spot of poly-bag tobogganing.

The **Club Andino Boliviano**, organizes the cheapest regular transport to Chacaltaya; US$10 per person for the 2½-hour bus journey, leaving La Paz at 0800 on Sat and Sun, and returning about 1530. A taxi or minibus costs US$30 (whole car) for a half-day trip. Hiring a

jeep and driver for the trip costs US$70. The trip can be hair-raising as buses carry no chains. Often the buses and tours only go half way. Many agencies do day trips for US$12.50, often combined with Valle de la Luna. The Club Andino Boliviano are converting the old clubhouse into a plush *refugio*, complete with all mod cons. This will appeal to serious hikers and also mountain bikers, as the ride down from the top is wonderful.

Tour operators

America Tours, Av 16 de Julio 1490 (opposite the Monje Campero Cinema), inside Edif Avenida, office 9, T02-2374204, F02-2310023, www.america-ecotours.com. Highly recommended for tours to all parts of the country, especially to Chalalán where they have special rates. Also now running trips to Noel Kempff Mercado and Amboró National Parks. This genuine ecotourist agent helps local communities benefit from responsible tourism.

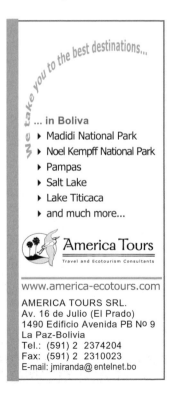

Bolivian Mountains, C Murillo 947 (entre Sagárnaga y Cochabamba), Galeria Siglo XIX, T02-2313197, www.bolivianmountains.com. A high-quality mountaineering outfit using very experienced guides and top quality equipment, though their climbs don't come cheap. They also have an office in the UK.

Crillon Tours, Av Camacho 1223, (PO Box 4785), T02-2337533, www.titicaca.com. For trips on Lake Titicaca, see page 252.

Deep Rainforest, C Illampu 626 (in Hotel Continental), T02-2150385. Professionally run biking, trekking climbing and jungle tours with small groups. Branch in Rurrenabaque, from where they run a jungle survival tour.

Detour, Av Mariscal Santa Cruz, Edif Camara Nacional de Comercio (next door to Varig), T02-236 1626. Mon-Fri 0900-1200, 1400-1900, Sat 0930-1230. Excellent for flight tickets. Very professional, English spoken.

Gravity Assisted Mountain Biking, Av 16 de Julio 1490, T02-2374204, www.gravitybolivia.com. Office Mon-Fri 0900-0700, Sat 1000-1300. No rides on Mon. Top tours with excellent bikes and guides to Coroico ('world's most dangerous road') for US$50. Also trips to Sorata, Zongo and other locations, depending on demand. More expensive

than others but definitely the most highly recommended, especially for the risky but exhilarating Coroico trip. Book early as trips genuinely fill up fast. The office is well hidden on the Prado.

Toñito Tours, Office 9, Comercio Doryan, Sagárnaga 189, T/F02-2336250, www.bolivianexpeditions.com. Organizes trips to Uyuni salt flats. Run by American Chris and Bolivian wife Suzy. Friendly and helpful, will take reservations by internet. Also rent sleeping bags for US$5 the whole trip.

Transturin , C Ascarrunz 2518 (off our main map), PO Box 5311, T02-2422222, www.travelbolivia.com. Full travel services, with tours ranging from La Paz to the whole country (for full details of their Lake Titicaca services see page 252).

Turisbus, Illampu 704, T02-2451341, www.turisbus.com. Agent for Peruvian railways (ENAFER), tickets to Puno and Cusco, also local and Bolivian tours.

⊖ Transport

Air

LAB and **Aero Sur** fly to the main cities and towns and **TAM** (Transportes Aéreo Militar) and **Amaszonas** fly to destinations in the eastern and northern lowlands. Fares are comparatively low for internal flights. For details, see under destinations.

La Paz & around La Paz Listings

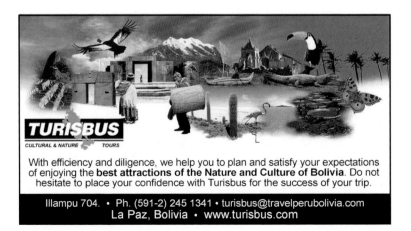

Airline offices

Aero Sur, Av 16 de Julio 616,
T02-2430430, F02-2313957,
www.aerosur.com.
Lloyd Aéreo Boliviano (LAB),
Camacho 1460, T02-0800- 3001,
www.labairlines.com.
Transportes Aéreo Militar (TAM), Av
Montes 738, on the corner with Serrano,
T02-2379286. Mon-Fri 0830-1200 and
1430-1830.

Bus

Local

Don't expect to get anywhere fast in
the centre as *micros* (Bluebird-type
buses which charge US$0.18 in the
centre, US$0.24 from outside the centre)
and *combis* (minivans which are quicker,
US$0.20/0.34) often have to stop every
few metres to let passengers on and
off. Note: if you can't keep your
backpack on your lap, you may be
charged extra in *combis*.
To Tiahuanaco Transportes Ingavi,
José María Azin and Eyzaguirre (take any
micro marked 'Cementerio') all go to
Tiahuanaco; US$0.90, 1½ hrs. They leave
almost hourly from the Cemetery district,
from 0700. The frequency may change
according to demand, so the earlier you
go the better. They are usually full but
tickets can be bought in advance. Return
buses leave from the plaza in the village.
The last one back is at around 1730-1800.
A taxi for 2 costs about US$20 for the
return trip with unlimited time at the site.
Most tours from La Paz cost US$15 return;
they usually stop at Laja and the highest
point on the road before Tiahuanaco, and
sometimes also at the Valle de la Luna.

Long distance

Buses to **Sorata** and **Copacabana** and
destinations north of La Paz leave from
various streets around the Cemetery
district. To get to the **Cemetery district**,
take any bus or *combi* marked
'Cementerio' going up C Santa Cruz
(US$0.17). Look out for the cemetery arch

on your left. Buses to **Coroico** and the
Yungas leave from Villa Fátima, which is
25 mins by *micros* B, V, X, K, 131, 135, or
136, or *trufis* 2 or 9, which pass Pérez
Velasco on the way down from Plaza
Mendoza – get off at the service station.
Details of bus times and fares are given
under each relevant destination.

Buses to **Oruro**, **Potosí**, **Sucre** and
Santa Cruz, and all points south of La
Paz, leave from the main terminal at Plaza
Antofagasta. To **Oruro**, 3 hrs, US$1.80. To
Santa Cruz, 17 hrs, US$10.50, from 1630.
To **Sucre**, 19 hrs, US$9, from 1830. To
Potosí, 10 hrs, US$9, from 1830.
To Peru via Copacabana   Colectivos
and agency buses leave daily to **Puno**
with different companies and are most
easily booked through travel agencies,
US$12-15.50, 10 hrs. Of the various La
Paz-**Puno** services, only **Transturin** does
not make you change to a Peruvian bus
once over the border. For further details
of bus services to Puno via Copacabana,
see page 254.

**To Peru via Guaqui and
Desaguadero**   Minibuses depart from
Transportes Ingavi office in the
Cementerio district in La Paz every half
hour, US$1.55, 2½ hrs. They are usually full
but tickets can be bought in advance. If
entering Bolivia here, the last bus from
Desaguadero to La Paz departs at 1700
though buses may leave later if there are
enough passengers, but will charge a lot
more. The bus terminal is 3 blocks up from
Migraciones, then 3 blocks on the right; ask
for *Entel* which is nearby. There are
frequent buses from the Peruvian side to
Puno until 1930, US$1.50, 2¼ hrs.
Exprinter/Cruz del Sur, T02-2362708, leave
from La Paz to Puno via Desaguadero on
Tue, Thu and Sat 0800, US$7.20.

There are buses to **Cusco**, direct with
Trans Litoral on Wed, Fri and Sun at 0800,
12 hrs, US$17.

Car hire

Imbex, Av Montes 522, T02-2455432,
F02-2455433, www.imbex.com.

Crossing the altiplano.

Well-maintained Suzuki jeeps from US$60 per day, including 200 km free for 4-person 4WD. **Kolla Motors**, Rosendo Gutiérrez 502, T02-2419141. Well-maintained 6-seater 4WD Toyota jeeps, insurance and fuel extra.
Petita Rent-a-car, C Valentín Abecia 2031, T02-2420329, www.rentacar petita.com. Swiss owners Ernesto Hug and Aldo Rezzonico are recommended for well-maintained VW beetles and 4WD jeeps, etc, they also offer recommended adventure tours, ('Jeeping Bolivia'), German, French and English spoken. Ernesto also has a garage for VW and other makes at Av Jaimes Freyre 2326, T02-2342279.

Taxis

Normal taxis charge US$0.75 (5Bs) for short trips within city limits. *Trufis* are fixed-route collective taxis with a little flag on the front which charge US$0.28-0.40 per person within city limits. Taxi drivers are not tipped. Radio taxis (eg **Alfa** T02-2322427, **La Rápida** T02-2392323) charge US$1.45 in the centre and US$2.80 to the suburbs. They are also good value for tours for 3 or more people, but negotiate the price.

❶ Directory

Banks

ATMs for Visa and Mastercard can be found at several sites in the city as well as at the airport. Among the major banks are **Banco Mercantil**, **Banco Popular**, **Banco Nacional**, **Banco Boliviano Americano** and **Banco Santa Cruz de la Sierra** (branch in Shopping Norte is open Sat afternoon). It is difficult to change TCs at the weekend, especially on Sun. Take care accepting large bills – not only are they almost impossible to change, there have been forgeries circulating. Visa has an office on Av Camacho 1448, 11th and 12th floors, T02-2318585 (24hrs), F02-2816525, for cancelling lost or stolen credit cards.
Exchange houses (*casas de cambio*) are generally faster for money changing than the banks. **Sudamer**, Colón 256, has good rates, also for currencies other than US dollars, no commission on TCs into bolivianos, 2% commission into dollars, frequently recommended. There are several others around Mercado and Colón. Money changers can be found on street corners around Plaza del Estudiante, Camacho, Colón and Prado. Always count your money immediately, in front of the money changer.

Embassies and consulates

Canada, Edif Barcelona, 2nd floor, C Victor Sanjinez 2678, Plaza España, T02-2414453. Mon-Fri, 0900-1200. **Peru**, Edif Alianza office 110, Av 6 de Agosto 2190 and C F Guachalla, T02-2440631, F02-2444199. Mon-Fri 0900-1300, 1500-1700, visa costs US$10 in US dollar bills, issued same day if you go early. **UK**, Av Arce 2732, T02-2433424, F02-2431073, Casilla 694. Mon-Fri 0900-1200, Mon, Tue, Thu also 1330-1630, visa section open 0900-1200 has a list of travel hints for Bolivia, doctors, etc. **USA**, Av Arce 2780 and Cordero, T02-2433520, F02-2433854, Casilla 425. Mon-Fri 0800-1700.

Internet

There are many internet cafés in La Paz and the number is increasing almost daily. Most charge US$0.75-1.00 per hr and are open Mon-Sat 0900-2100/2300. Connections are normally faster in the mornings and at weekends.

Laundry

Wash and dry, 6-hr service, at **Lavaya Lava-Sec**, 20 de Octubre 2019, suite 9, helpful service, US$1.40 for 1 kg. **Limpieza Rosario**, Av Manco Kapac, near Hotel Andes, US$1 per kg, quick and highly recommended. **Lavandería Select**, Av Arce 2341, 3-hr service.

Medical services

Contact your embassy or the Tourist Office for a recommended doctor who speaks your language. The following clinics are recommended: **Clínica Alemana**, 6 de Agosto 2821, San Jorge, T02-243676, has English-speaking doctors; **Clínica Santa María**, Av 6 de Agosto 2487, English-speaking doctors, consultation costs US$16, simple analysis US$24, course of antibiotics US$8.

Pharmacies

There are lots of pharmacies and prescriptions are unnecessary. Every day the newspapers print a list of those that will be open that night. For contact lenses, **Optaluis**, Comercio 1089, has a stock of 5,000 lenses, including 'semiduros'.

Post Office

Correo Central is at Av Mariscal Santa Cruz and Oruro. Open Mon-Fri 0800-2000, Sat 0830-1800 and Sun 0900-1200. Stamps are sold only at post offices and by some hotels as a service to their guests.

Telephone

Entel (T02-2367474) office for telephone calls and fax is at Ayacucho 267 (the only one open on Sun), and in Edificio Libertad, C Potosí. For international and national calls, rather than wait for a booth, buy a phonecard (5, 10, 20 or 100 Bs) and use it in the phones to the left in the main Entel office and in the Entel offices or phone boxes throughout the city. Buy a *ficha* (token) for US$0.10 from the person selling them next to the booth. Or use a phone in any shop or stall with 'teléfono' sign (US$0.20), or pay one of the many people renting out mobiles.

Useful addresses

To renew a visa go to **Migración Bolivia**, Av Camacho 1433 (opposite Banco de Santa Cruz), T02-2379385/2370475. Open Mon-Fri 0900-1200, 1600-1800, fast and efficient service. **Tourist Police**, Plaza del Estadio, Miraflores, next to *Love City* disco, T02-2225016, for insurance claims after theft, English spoken, helpful.

Lake Titicaca and Sorata

The startlingly limpid waters of Lake Titicaca straddle Bolivia and Peru only a few hours from La Paz. This is an area of almost preternatural beauty and serenity, where the white-topped peaks of the Cordillera Real appear much closer than they are due to the thin altiplano air. Lake Titicaca is officially two lakes joined by the Straits of Tiquina. The larger, northern lake – Lago Mayor, or Chucuito – contains Isla del Sol, site of the Inca creation legend. You can spend a few days here relaxing and witnessing a way of life unchanged in centuries, or simply marvelling at the beauty of the lake's waters, reflecting the distant cordillera, mirroring the sky in the rarified air and changing colour when it is cloudy or raining.

⊘ **Getting there** Buses from La Paz or from Puno.
⊜ **Getting around** Boat trips from Copacabana to Isla del Sol; buses from La Paz to Sorata.
⊕ **Time required** 3-5 days.
⊛ **Weather** May-Sep are dry months, but cold nights, especially Jun-Aug.
⊜ **Sleeping** Decent options in Copacabana and Sorata. Basic lodgings only on Isla del Sol.
⊘ **Eating** Good trout in Copacabana; a few decent options in Sorata. Limited elsewhere.
▲▲ **Activities and tours** Boat trips to islands; trekking around Sorata.
★ **Don't miss…** Spending a night on Isla del Sol ⇒ *p248*.

Copacabana ⊜⊘⊛⊜⊙ ⇒ *pp247-255*

This attractive town with red-tiled roofs is nestled between two hills on the shores on Lake Titicaca. It is a popular stopping-off point on the way to or from Peru and definitely worth a brief visit. Its main plaza is dominated by the impressive and heavily restored Moorish-style cathedral. Every Sunday in front of the cathedral a line of cars, trucks, buses and minibuses, all decorated with garlands of flowers, waits to be blessed, as a spiritual form of accident insurance, see box, page 244.

Copacabana Cathedral's gleaming white basilica.

Ins and outs

A paved road runs northwest from La Paz across the Altiplano for 114 km to the village of San Pablo on the eastern shore of the **Straits of Tiquina**. It then continues from San Pedro, on the opposite side of the straits, for a further 44 km to Copacabana. By car from La Paz takes about four hours. There are several agency buses that go from La Paz to Puno in Peru and vice-versa, all stopping at Copacabana for lunch, as well as public transport (see page 254). New arrivals may be pressurized into paying for 'entry' to the town; the fee is in fact for the sanctuary (see below). The **Tourist Information kiosk** ① *Plaza 2 de Febrero,* is helpful when open.

Sights

Dominating the main plaza is the huge **cathedral** ① *Mon-Fri, 1100-1200, 1400-1800, Sat and Sun, 0800-1200, 1400-1800, only groups of 8 or more can visit, US$0.60,* with its gleaming white basilica, built between 1610 and 1620 to accommodate the huge numbers of pilgrims who flocked to the town when miracles began happening in the Sanctuary of Copacabana after the presentation of a black wooden statue of the Virgin Mary, carved in the late 1570s by Francisco Yupanqui, grandson of the Inca Túpac Yupanqui. The Virgin is known both as the Dark Virgin of the Lake, or the *Virgen de la Candelaria*, the patron saint of Bolivia. Sunday vehicle blessings (which are supposed to bring good luck, and prevent accidents) outside the cathedral involve large quantities of fresh flowers and petals, garlands, firecrackers, beer scattered around and on the tyres and money tucked behind the steering wheel.

Don't miss the walk to the top of **Cerro Calvario**, up a long series of steps, especially at sunset, though you're unlikely to be alone. It's a steep climb up some rough steps but there are great views of the town and the lake from the top and on Sundays you can buy miniature items (cars, suitcases and money, plus a myriad of other things) and have them blessed. Head north and uphill from the centre of town.

Isla del Sol and around ⬤⬤ ›› *pp247-255*

Though only a short distance by boat from Copacabana, Isla del Sol has an altogether different feel to it. It has a quiet, almost serene beauty and makes the perfect place to relax

for a few days. It is worthwhile staying overnight on the island for the many beautiful walks
through villages and Inca terraces, some of which are still in use. A sacred rock at its
northwestern end is worshipped as the birthplace of the first Incas, Manco Kapac and
Mama Ocllo, son and daughter of Viracocha and the first Incas.

Ins and outs

Isla del Sol is, by Bolivian standards, intensively inhabited (an estimated 5,000 people live
there) and cultivated, and so is covered in trails. The wilder west side has the highest point
on the island. The most impressive ruins are at the far north at Chincana and the Labyrinth.
It is possible to arrange a motor launch to take you there and then walk back across the
island to be picked up at the Inca Steps at the other end, where there are a second set of
ruins (much more visited) at Pilcocaina and the Inca Spring. Walking from one end of the
island to the other takes five hours, so it's not really possible to see all the sites on the island
and return to Copacabana in one day.

Around the island

Starting at the north end of the island is the village of **Challapampa,** not far from the
sacred rock of **Titicaca** (after which the lake is named), the ruins of **Chincana**, and the
temple del Inca, which have been restored by the National Institute of Culture. There is a
good little **museum** ⓘ *0800-1230, 1400-1800, US$1.45*, in Challapampa, containing
artefacts from archaeological excavations at the nearby island of Koa, plus maps and
pictures with excellent explanations in English. You will see hollow stones in which
offerings were placed and dropped into the lake. These were retrieved by two American
and Bolivian archaeologists working together.

Isla del Sol

Background

An answer to your prayers

In Copacabana all your dreams will come true. At least that's what the local people believe. And when you see them fervently blessing all manner of material goods on the Cerro Calvario perhaps you will start to believe it, too.

On Sunday, a procession of the faithful makes its way up the steps to the summit of the Calvario to perform this ritual – a strange mix of the spiritual and the material. The many believers, old and young alike, climb the steep stairs past the 14 stations of the cross, pausing at each station to bless themselves and to enjoy a brief respite from the lung-bursting ascent. Once at the top, they find an array of stalls offering a veritable multitude of miniature items to pray for: cars, trucks, minibuses, houses (for the more optimistic), bricks and sacks of cement, cookers, wheelbarrows, tiny bags of pasta, suitcases stuffed with dollar bills, even mini certificates to ensure a successful graduation from university.

The devout take their pick before descending to a series of little altars where, for a small fee, they get a bag of incense to burn during the blessing of their desired object. Cars and money seem to be the favourite choices. These are carefully arranged before a miniature version of Copacabana's famous Virgen de la Candelaria.

The ceremony then begins, in either Latin or Aymara. Those choosing the latter get chanting, dancing, histrionics and even flames emitting from a large cup. The alternative ceremony is a more sedate affair: only smoke instead of flames, a few lines of Latin, a song and some sprinkled flower petals. At a signal from the priest, a cholita then dutifully rushes over with a few bottles of beer which are shaken up and sprayed over the altar.

The ceremony over, the priest and his small congregation drink a toast to good fortune before the weekend pilgrims depart, happy in the belief that their heavenly benefactor will deliver the goods before the year is out.

About 1½ hours from Challapampa, in the middle of the island, is the friendly village of **Challa**, which is worth a stay. To get there from Challapampa walk past the northern beach (about an hour), then up a hill (20 minutes) to the open area where you'll see the village church. From here head down into the valley of southern Challa (another 20 minutes) and you'll reach the excellent little museum dedicated to the Aymara culture, the **Museo Comunitario de Etnografía** (although over the door it also bears the name Museo Templo del Sol) ① *daily 0900-1200, 1300-1800, if it looks closed just wait for a few minutes and someone will show you around, entry by voluntary contribution.* The interior is nothing to shout about, with bare concrete floors, but there are some fascinating displays of traditional Aymara costumes worn for dances and in daily life, as well as artefacts from around the island. There are also excellent explanations in flawless English. The museum is run by members of the community to commemorate and preserve their traditions.

Totora reed boats are still used on Lake Titicaca, but seem only to appear with the arrival of tour buses.

From Challa it's about two hours southeast to **Yumani**, where there are a number of places to stay. Below Yumani is the jetty for **Crillon Tours**' hydrofoils and other boats (see page 237). A series of steep **Inca steps** leads up from the jetty to the **Fuente del Inca**, three natural springs said to aid in matters of love, health and eternal youth. A 2-km walk from the spring takes you to the main ruins of **Pilcocaina** ① *US$1.20*, a two-storey building with false domes and superb views. The Sun Gate from the ruins is now kept in the main plaza in Copacabana. There is accommodation by the ruins.

Isla de la Luna
Southeast of the Isla del Sol is the Isla de la Luna (or Coati), which can also be visited as part of a day tour, though this doesn't leave you enough time on Isla del Sol. The best ruins on Isla de la Luna are an Inca temple and nunnery, both sadly neglected.

Sorata and around ◉◉◉▲◉◉ ▸▸ *pp247-255*

Northeast of Lake Titicaca and four hours from La Paz is the gorgeous little mountain town of Sorata, the starting point for some of Bolivia's most spectacularly arduous treks. It is also a pleasant place to visit for lesser mortals, with some good walks in the surrounding countryside.

Ins and outs
Buses from La Paz leave daily from the Cemetery district (see page 237). Buses to La Paz leave from the main plaza in Sorata every hour or so through the day. ◉ ▸▸ *p255*.

The town itself has little of real interest but is a fine example of Bolivian small-town life. From the main plaza, on a clear day, you can see Illampu (on the left) and Ancohuma (on the right), though the view of the mountains is better from the smaller Plaza Obispo Bosque. One of the most popular walks near Sorata is to the **San Pedro Caves** ⓘ *daily 0800-1700, US$1, beyond* the village of San Pedro. The caves, despite the warm (21°C) lake and nectar-sipping bats, are not much in themselves but the walk there and back (2½ hours each way) is worth it. Where the road splits after San Pedro take the lower road (signed to the caves) and look for the white building above. It is also possible to walk to the cave along the Río Cristóbal, but either way get clear directions and take at least one litre of water per person before setting out. For your entry fee the guardian will fire up a generator to light your eerie path into the depths; but take a torch in case the power fails. Continue past the cave for 30 minutes to reach a point on the ridge which gives great views over the surrounding valleys. You can camp here, too. Plans have been approved to spend enormous amounts of money on sprucing up the caves.

To Peru via Copacabana

There are two main routes into Peru from La Paz. The more common route leaves from Copacabana. An unpaved road leads to the Bolivian frontier at Kasani, 20 minutes away, then on to Yunguyo and from there to Puno. Note that Peruvian time is 1 hr behind Bolivian time.

Peruvian immigration is open 24 hours, but the Bolivian side, and therefore the border, is only open 0830-1930 (Bolivian time). Buses/*colectivos* stop at **Kasani** and on the Peruvian side; or you can walk (400 m), between the two posts. There should be a statutory 72-hour period spent outside Bolivia before renewing a visa but 24 hours is usually acceptable. Ask for a 90-day visa on return: 30 days is often given on entering Bolivia, but there are no problems extending it in La Paz; 90 days is normally given on entering Peru.

Money can be changed in Yunguyo, in Peru, at better rates than at the border. Coming into Bolivia, the best rates are given at the border, on the Bolivian side. Peruvian soles can be changed in Copacabana (see page 255).

Transport Agency buses will take you from La Paz or Copacabana to Puno and stop for border formalities and to change money in Yunguyo. For details of these buses see under Copacabana Transport (see page 254), La Paz International buses (page 237) or La Paz Tour operators (page 236).

To Peru via the west side of Lake Titicaca

The less-used route takes the road to Tiahuanaco and goes along the west side of the lake to Guaqui, then onto Desaguadero on the border. The road heads west from La Paz 91 km to **Guaqui**, then crosses the border at **Desaguadero**, a dusty and dreary (and freezing cold at night) place 22 km further west, and runs along the shore of the lake to Puno. The road is paved all the way to Peru. For details of bus services, see page 238.

Bolivian immigration ⓘ *0830-1230 and 1400-2030*, is just before the bridge in Desaguadero. A 30-day visa is normally given on entering Bolivia, so ask for more if you need it. Get your exit stamp, walk 100 m across the bridge, then get an entrance stamp on the other side. Both offices may also close for dinner around 1830-1900. Get a visa in La Paz if you need one.

Peruvian immigration opens same hours (Peruvian time) and has been known to give 90-day visas. Money changers just over the bridge on the Peruvian side give reasonable rates for bolivianos or dollars.

Inca ruins on the Isla del Sol.

A good one-day walk is to **Cerro Istipata**. Either take a La Paz-bound bus to below the cross on Cerro Ulluni Tijja (US$0.40), and follow the ridge up and over Cerro Lorockasini and on to Cerro Istipata, or walk the whole way from Sorata. Follow the La Paz road until just before the YPFB garage opposite the Gran Hotel. Drop down right, cross the Río San Cristóbal and head up through the spread-out village of Atahuallani and then up to join the ridge between Cerro Lorockasini (on the right) and Cerro Istipata.

● Sleeping

Copacabana *p241, map p251*
A Hotel Rosario del Lago, Rigoberto Paredes, between Av Costanera and Av 16 de Julio, T02-8622141, www.hotelrosario. com/lago. Same ownership as **Rosario** in La Paz (see page 230) and a similar modern colonial-style building. Excellent shared spaces with internet (US$0.60 per hr), views and free tea. Rooms all have good lake views but are small and lack much character. Bathrooms are good though, with powerful, hot showers. The restaurant – *Kota Kauhaña* – has good fish specialities and the price includes a generous buffet breakfast. **Also has Turisbus** office (see page 237).
C Hotel Chasqui de Oro, Av Costanera 55, T02-8622343. 3-star, includes buffet breakfast and parking. Lakeside hotel, 50 rooms all with comfy beds, bathrooms and even some bathtubs. Café/breakfast room has great views. Also has video room.

C-D La Cúpula, C Michel Pérez 1-3, T02-8622029, www.hotelcupula.com. A short and steep walk from the centre of town, La Cúpula is one of Bolivia's best hotels. There are fantastic views, the design (incorporating the eponymous white domes) is imaginative and innovative, and the attention to the needs of travellers is exceptional. The price depends on the room: of 17 bright and comfortable rooms 7 have private bathrooms and 1 has a kitchen. The honeymoon suite is so spectacular it might just make you propose. There's also a sitting room with DVD showings, a library, a garden with hammocks, a book exchange and a great restaurant (see Eating, below). Run by German Martin Strätker.
E Hotel Utama, Michel Peréz and San Antonio (50 m from La Cúpula), T02-8622013. Spotless rooms are arranged around an orange coloured covered courtyard. Free oranges and

maté on arrival. Good evening set meal. Book exchange. Price includes a good breakfast.

E-F Ambassador, C Jauregiu s/n, on Plaza Sucre, T02-8622216. This pink colonial building has big sunny shared spaces, rooms with balcony, a rooftop restaurant, great beds and a shrine. US$2 discount with an ISIC or YHA card. Heaters available, US$2 per day.

G Hostal La Sonia, Calle Murillo s/n, T7196-8441 (mob). Most rooms have private bathrooms and big, light windows overlooking the town, though a couple of smaller rooms are a bit dark. There's a great roof terrace, a sink for laundry, a kitchen, and breakfast can be served in bed on request. Exceptionally friendly and helpful, and, at less than US$2 for a double room, the best value around.

Isla del Sol *p242, map p243*

Apart from places to stay in Challapampa, Challa and Yumani (see below) there are plenty of places to camp, especially on the western side of the island where it is possible to camp in a secluded bay. If camping take all food and water (or water sterilisers).

Yumani

Most of the accommodation is at Yumani. There are hostels opening all the time and plenty of options. With no real streets or signs on this rambling hillside community, the best thing to do is to agree a tip with one of the children at the jetty and ask them to take you to the hostel of your choice. It is worth hiking to the top of the hill where there are superb views for no extra money.

D Puerta del Sol, at the peak of the hill. Rooms with bath (**G** without).

F El Imperio del Solis, a peach-coloured building with no running water but very comfortable and friendly, breakfast US$0.60, other meals US$1.50-2.

G Inti Huayra, up the hill from La Posada del Inca, basic but clean, no electricity or hot water, meals provided for US$1-2.

G Mirador del Inca, further up the hill, slightly cheaper and more comfortable, clean, friendly, no shower, breakfast US$0.75, meals US$1.50-2.

G Posada de las Ñustas, at the top of the hill with great views all around, has 9 rooms, solar-heated shower, breakfast US$1, also snacks and meals for US$1.50-2.

G Templo del Sol, near to Puerta del Sol (see above) and owned by the same family. Clean rooms, electric showers and a restaurant.

Challapampa

There are several *alojamientos* around the plaza straight up from the landing jetty, near the church. Ask for Lucio Arias or his father, Francisco, who have opened 2 basic hostels: **G Posada Manco Kapac** has rooms for 35 people and a garden for camping, hot showers and views of Illampu; the second hostel has the same name but is further up the

beach. Friendly Lucio is planning to build a reed boat for guests to use and can provide guides, all of whom speak Spanish and very basic English.

Sorata *p245, map p249*

E **Residencial Sorata**, on the corner of the main plaza and Villavicencio, T/F02-8135218, resorata@ceibo. entelnet.bo. A huge, fascinating and ramblingly antique old place with original fixtures, fittings and drawing room, and massive 18-20 ft long snake skins on the walls. The more expensive rooms overlook the beautiful internal garden. These have sepia prints and antique furniture but the beds are either saggy or lumpy and hard. Those in the modern section are not much better. Unless you're after flies in your coffee, dirty crockery, soggy pancakes and surly service, breakfast is best avoided. Run by French-Canadian Louis Demers, who is helpful and has lots of good trekking information.

F **Altai Oasis**, T02-71519856, resaltai@ hotmail.com. At the bottom of the valley, Altai's beautiful setting has a camping area by the river and cabins and rooms higher up. It's very quiet except for the sounds of the river, and the pet parrot shouting 'ola'. The cabins are thoughtfully designed and constructed, with fireplaces, kitchens and lots of wood and tiles. There are also outside areas for barbecues and fires. A bridge crosses straight over the river to the bottom of town but the path is steep and not recommended with heavy rucksacks or after a drink or two. The long way around, via one of the bridges further upstream, is easier. The restaurant does good breakfasts including porridge, pancakes and fruit salad, great goulash and T-bone steaks, soy burgers and good coffee. Fresh vegetables are home-grown and

Sorata

Old Spanish Trail to Lakathiya

Sleeping 🛏
Hostal Las Piedras 12
Hostal Panchita 5
Residencial Sorata 10

Eating 🍴
Altai Oasis 2
Café Illampu 3
Pete's Place 1

200 metres
200 yards

The sacred lake

Lake Titicaca has played a dominant role in Andean beliefs for over two millennia. This, the highest navigable body of water in the world, is the most sacred lake in the Andes. The people who depend on the lake's resources still make offerings to her, to ensure sufficient totora reeds for their houses and boats, for successful fishing, for safe passage across its waters and for a mild climate. If someone falls into the lake, it is traditional not to rescue them, but to let them drown as an offering to the Earth Goddess Pachamama. Storms do blow up on the lake, so Pachamama is given offerings every year, but don't let that put you off taking a trip!

honey comes from beehives in the garden. Transport is available to town, US$3 for 5 people. Camping US$1.25 per person, with showers and a basic kitchen. Double rooms with private bathrooms are US$5pp, with shared bathrooms US$2.50pp. Cabins cost US$37.50 for 5 people, US$19 for a couple.

F Hostal Las Piedras, just off Ascarrunz, T02-71916341. There's a very good mellow feel to this new hotel, just off to the left on the way down to the cave. It's well designed, European run, very friendly, and gets its breakfast bread from Café Illampu (see Eating below) across the river.

G Hostal Panchita, on the corner of the Plaza with Guachalla, T02-8135038. All the rooms are large and have shared bathrooms. Clean and modern, there's a sunny courtyard with flowers and a sitting room. Hot water, good restaurant, has Entel office in the entrance. Very friendly, very good value.

Eating

Copacabana *p241, map p251*
Fantastic fresh fish is served from lots of beach shacks. In some you can choose your own fish before it's cooked and in all the food is cheap. It's hard to choose between them – pick by popularity or smell.

♥♥ **La Cúpola**, C Michel Pérez 1-3, T02-8622029, 0730-1500, 1800-2130, closed Tue am. Attached to the hotel of the same name (see above), La Cúpola serves up fantastic food, including a range of fondues, a mouth-wateringly good moussaka and a memorable 'aubergine baked in the oven'. Portions are generous, you can also select the music from a 'music menu' (there's also live music) and even the Bolivian wine is excellent.

♥♥ **La Orilla**, Av 6 de Agosto, close to lake, T8622267, miguelzamorano @hotmail.com. Daily, generally 1000-2200 but depends on demand. One of the warmest, tastiest, most atmospheric places in town. Owners Lucas and Miguel are excellent hosts and have created a menu with great local and international combinations. The peppered steak is to die for and the stuffed trout superb. There's a terrace, an open fire, Cuban jazz, masks and dreamcatchers. Arachnaphobics should avoid looking up at the stuffed creatures in the ceiling. Main dishes cost around US$3.

♥ **Kalá U'ta**, Av 6 de Agosto, T02-01573852. Run by same people as Sujma Wasi, warm atmosphere and good vegetarian food, organic coffee and chocolate and good music and fabrics.

♥ **Sujma Wasi**, C Jauregui 127, T02-8622091. Open 0730-2300 every day from breakfast to dinner. Excellent food and atmosphere (lovely and warm) in the café/restaurant plus a very good collection of books on Bolivia in their *sala cultural*. Breakfasts are themed on a health/mountaineer/worldwide basis. A vegetarian lunch changes daily and there's a cobbled square courtyard with stone benches, plants and flowers.

Sorata *p245, map p249*
♦ **Café Illampu**, a 20-min walk from town via the short-cut, on the way to Gruta San Pedro. Run by Swiss masterbaker Stefan, it's the best in Sorata for views of Illampu.

Breakfasts include home-baked raspberry and strawberry cakes and yoghurts. Also sandwiches, hammocks and camping. There are basic mountain bikes for hire (US$4.50 per half day) which eases a trip to the caves. Open 0930-1830 daily except Tue when Stefan walks his pet llamas around town. Closed Feb and Mar.
♦ **Pete's Place**, Plaza General Peñaranda, T02-2895005, 0830-2200. On the corner of the plaza, Pete's is the epicentre of gringo life in Sorata. Fantastic veggie and non-veggie food, great value breakfasts, set lunches and dinners. Very friendly and

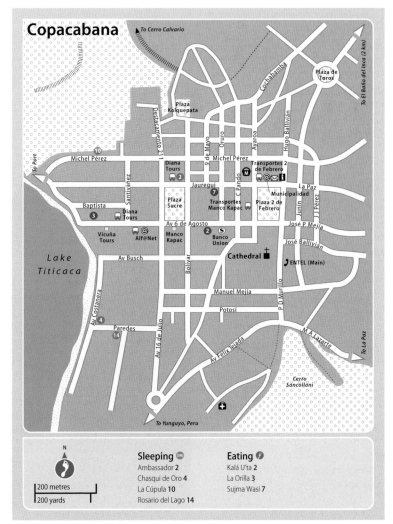

Copacabana

Lake Titicaca

Sleeping ●
Ambassador 2
Chasqui de Oro 4
La Cúpula 10
Rosario del Lago 14

Eating ●
Kalá U'ta 2
La Orilla 3
Sujma Wasi 7

200 metres
200 yards

gets copies of the *Guardian Weekly* delivered. Will change TCs for 3% commission if there is enough cash in the till. East Londoner Pete Good himself is a great source of local info (especially on trekking) and there's a good selection of books on Bolivia and maps to browse through. You may find it hard to leave.

⊛ Festivals

Copacabana *p241, map p251*
Festivals in Copacabana are frequent and frantic and to be heartily recommended, especially to those who like drinking, dancing, eating and more drinking.
1-3 Feb, Virgen de la Candelaria a massive procession of the Dark Virgin takes place, this is a real highlight with much music, dancing, fireworks and bullfights.
End Feb/beginning Mar, Carnival.
Easter, during **Semana Santa**, there is a huge pilgrimage to the town.
2-5 May, Fiesta del Señor de la Cruz, this is very colourful with dances in typical costumes.
23 Jun, San Juan, this is also celebrated throughout the region and on Isla del Sol.
24-25 Jul, Fiesta del Señor Santiago, dancing in typical costumes.
4-6 Aug, La Virgen de Copacabana, the town fills with people, the plaza becomes a huge market and there is dancing and fireworks. Petty crime rises massively at this time so take extra precautions.

⊘ Shopping

Sorata *p245, map p249*
Artesanía Sorata, Mon-Sat 0900-2000, Sun 0900-1600, on the main plaza near the Transportes Unificado office, sells postcards, handicrafts, jumpers, gloves and wall hangings. It also cashes traveller's cheques and accepts them as payment.

▲ Activities and tours

Lake Titicaca *p147*
Crillon Tours (address in La Paz Tour operators, page 237), run a hydrofoil service on Lake Titicaca with excellent bilingual guides. **Crillon's** tours stop at the Andean Roots cultural complex at their **Inca Utama Hotel**. The hydrofoil trips visit the Andean Roots complex, Copacabana, Isla del Sol and Isla de la Luna, the Straits of Tiquina and totora-reed fishing boats. You can also stay on Isla del Sol at the very comfortable **La Posada del Inca** . Trips can be arranged to/from Cusco and Machu Picchu: hydrofoil and train one-way and flight the other.
Transturin (address on page 237) run catamarans on Lake Titicaca, either for sightseeing or on the La Paz-Puno route. From their dock at Chúa, 3-hr trips go to Copacabana, with a bar, video, sun deck and music on board. One-night tours to Copacabana are also available. The catamarans are slower than the hydrofoils of **Crillon** so there is more room and time

Fiesta at Achacachi, on the road to Sorata

for on-board entertainment. **Transturin** also runs services to Puno without a change of bus, and without many of the usual formalities at the border.

Sorata *p245, map p249*
Tour operators
Sorata Guides and Porters, C Sucre 302, T02-22136698, guiasorata@hotmail.com. Opposite **Residencial Sorata**, this outfit can arrange all kinds of trips, though most of their guides speak only Spanish and have no glacier-climbing experience. They charge US$12 per day for groups of 1-3, US$16-17 per day for 4-6 and US$22-23 per day for up to 10; food not included. They also rent out mules, porters and equipment and can organize transport to/from the beginning and end of treks.
Hoodoo Bike Tours, Plaza General Peñeranda, T02-71276685, www.hoodoo biketours.com. Lots of good mountain bike routes, with the emphasis on fairly extreme rides. One multi-day trip passes through mountains, desert, Inca ruins, down into jungle and then has a three-day boat trip to Rurrenabaque at the end of it. You can also contact Travis in La Paz, C Sagarnaga and Illampu, T02-2411102.

⊖ Transport

Copacabana *p241, map p251*
Bus
Regular bus travel to/from **La Paz** costs US$2 plus US$0.20 for the Tiquina crossing. There are several departures daily between 0700-1800 with **Manco Kapac**, T02-8622234 (or T02-2453035 in La Paz) and **2 de Febrero**, T02-8622233 (or T02-2377181, La Paz). Both have offices on Copacabana's main plaza and Plaza Sucre, and in La Paz at Plaza Reyes Ortíz, opposite the entrance to the cemetery (see La Paz buses, page 237). Book ahead for Fri travel. 1-day trips from La Paz are not recommended as they allow only 1½-2 hrs in Copacabana.
To Peru Several agency buses go from **La Paz** to **Puno** in Peru and vice-versa, stopping at Copacabana for lunch. They

charge US$12-15 and leave La Paz at 0800. They leave Copacabana after lunch around 1300-1400. The journey from La Paz to Copacabana takes 4 hrs. These agencies continue to the Peruvian border at Yunguyo and on to Puno, stopping for immigration formalities and to change money in Yunguyo. It takes around 3½ hrs from Copacabana to Puno and costs US$2.50-US$4, depending on the season. Agencies include: **Diana Tours**, at Hotel Ambassador, Plaza Sucre, and on Av 6 de Agosto near the lake; **Vicuña Tours**, 6 de Agosto, just down from Plaza Sucre, T02-8622155, open 0900-1400, 1630-1900; and **Turisbus**, in Hotel Rosario, see Sleeping above). Alternatively, *colectivos* leave from Plaza Sucre in Copacabana to **Kasani** (border) for US$0.50 per person, and from Kasani to **Yunguyo**, 600 m across the border, for US$0.60 per person.

It is also possible to catch a tour bus to **Cusco** (see pages 236 and237). You change bus in Puno; the tour company arranges the connection.

Rental
Motorcycles and bicycles can be hired on the beach, but bargain. You can also hire a kayak or rowing boat on the beachfront for US$2.50 per hr. Pedalos, complete with sunshades and life jackets, are US$2/hr. You can even rent a donkey.

Isla del Sol *p242, map p243*
Inca Tours and **Titicaca Tours** run motor boats to **Isla del Sol** and **Isla de la Luna**; both have offices on 6 de Agosto in Copacabana. **Andes Amazonia** run smaller boats – for maximum 10 people – which are more pleasant, but less good with waves. A full-day tour (US$4-5) leaves Copacabana at 0815 and returns from the island at 1600, arriving back at 1730. A half-day tour returns at 1030, arriving back at 1200. With the same ticket you can stay on the island and return another day. Half-day tours, or full-day tours which include the north and south of

Isla del Sol and Isla de La Luna, are not recommended as too much time is spent on the water and not enough on dry land.

Tickets can be bought at the agency offices, or through your hotel. Note that boats stop only briefly at the jetty by the Fuente del Inca, leaving punctually at 1600. Make sure the boat is equipped with life-jackets; some are not. Conditions on the lake can change very quickly and you don't want to end up as the next offering to the gods.

You can also take a boat to the island from **Yampupata**, a 17 km (4-hr walk) north of Copcabana at the end of the peninsula. Motor launches from Yampupata to Fuente del Inca on the southern end of the Isla del Sol cost US$8. A rowing boat costs US$3 (or US$1 per person) and takes 40 mins. Arrange the time and day of your return beforehand.

Sorata *p245, map p249*
Bus
From La Paz Buses to **Sorata** leave daily from C Manuel Bustillos, on the corner with Av Kollasuyo, 2 blocks up from the Cementerio, in La Paz (see La Paz buses, page 237) US$1.65, 4½ hrs. Booking recommended on Fri. **To La Paz** These leave from the main plaza in Sorata at least every hr, from 0400 to 1400; 1700 on Fri and Sun. There's a military checkpoint at Achacachi, so keep your passport handy.

Directory

Copacabana *p241, map p251*
Banks Banco Unión, 6 de Agosto, 0830-1230, 1430-1800 closed on Mon. Reasonable rates, changes traveller's cheques for US$2 commission, cash advance on Visa and Mastercard at 3% commission. Several *artesanías* on 6 de Agosto buy and sell US dollar bills and Peruvian soles. **Internet** Alf@Net, Av 6 de Agosto, next to Hostal Colonial, 0830-2200, US$2 but sliding scale, very fast connection. **Medical services Hospital**, see map on page 251 for location. Offers medical and dental treatment and a 24-hr pharmacy, but if you're seriously ill you should go to La Paz. **Pharmacy**: opposite Entel (open Tue-Sun 0900-1200, 1400-1800).
Police On Plaza 2 de Febrero, next to the post office. **Telephone** Entel open 0800-1230, 1330-2000 every day, for national and international phone and fax. They also accept dollars at a good rate.

Sorata *p245, map p249*
Banks There are no banks or official money-changing outlets. Try Artesanía Sorata or Residencial Sorata. **Internet** Buho's internet café. US$2.50/hr. A cosy little café on the plaza but painfully slow and expensive dial-up connection.

La Paz & around Lake Titicaca & Sorata Listings

The Yungas and northern Amazon

Only a few hours from La Paz are the subtropical valleys known as the Yungas. These steep, forested slopes are squeezed in between the high Cordillera and the vast green carpet of jungle that stretches east, providing a welcome escape from the breathless chill of the capital as well as a convenient stopping point for those hardy souls travelling overland to the jungle. The town of Coroico, in the Nor Yungas, is a firm favourite and the road which winds its tortuous way down from the high mountains has achieved near legendary status in South American travelling lore as the most dangerous in the world. Many tourists now opt for the relative safety of two wheels rather than four for the terrifying and spectacular 70-km downhill ride.

⊘ **Getting there** Buses or bike tour from La Paz to Coroico; flight or bus to Rurrenabaque.
⊘ **Getting around** Limited bus services; river boats from Rurre into jungle.
⊖ **Time required** 7-8 days if taking a jungle tour.
⊚ **Weather** Rainy season Nov-Apr; best time May-Sep.
⊜ **Sleeping** Plenty of choice in Coroico; luxury jungle lodges near Rurre.
⊘ **Eating** Standard gringo fare in Coroico and Rurre.
⊿ **Activities and tours** Jungle and pampas tours; biking down the 'world's most dangerous road'.
★ **Don't miss…** Chalalán Eco-lodge ▸▸ *p264*.

The Bolivian Amazon accounts for over two-thirds of the country. This vast region, covered by steamy jungles and flat savannah lands, is bursting with all manner of wildlife. Parque Nacional Madidi, Bolivia's newest preservation area, boasts the greatest biodiversity of any protected area on earth, and is also home to one of Bolivia's newest, and most authentic, ecotourism ventures, Chalalán Eco-lodge, which is owned and run by the indigenous population.

50 km
50 miles

Coroico ⬤🏵️👤❀⛰️🚌☕ ▸▸ pp260-267

The little town of Coroico has long been a favourite with visitors to Bolivia and residents of La Paz. It clings to the flanks of a steep, forested mountain amid orange and banana groves and coffee plantations, with stupendous views, particularly to the southwest, where you can see the distant snowy peaks of the Cordillera Real. Coroico isn't a place for the hyperactive. There's not a huge amount to do here, except lay by the hotel pool soaking up the sun and sipping ice-cold beer as you enjoy the views, swap travelling tales with your equally chilled-out fellow travellers and recover from the bus trip or thrilling bike ride, see page 237.

Ins and outs

Buses leave La Paz several times daily, all from the Villa Fátima district for the three hour trip to Coroico. There are also daily buses from Coroico to La Paz. Buses, trucks and pick-ups run from Yolosa to Caranavi, Guanay and Rurrenabaque.. **Tourist information** ⓘ *Cámera Hotelera on the plaza.* ⊖ ▸▸ *p266.*

Sights

There are a number of good walks around Coroico. One is up to the waterfalls, starting from **El Calvario**. Follow the Stations of the Cross by the cemetery, off Calle Julio Zuazo Cuenca, which leads steeply uphill from the plaza. Facing the chapel at El Calvario, with your back to the town, look for a path on the left, which soon becomes well-defined. It leads in one hour to the **Cascada y Toma de Agua de Coroico**, the source of the town's water supply. Walk beyond this to a couple of waterfalls further on which are better for swimming. We have received reports of several incidents of assault on the trail. Women should definitely not go alone.

Rurrenabaque and around ⬤🏵️👤⛰️🚌☕ ▸▸ pp260-267

Rurrenabaque, or 'Rurre' as the locals call it, is the jumping-off point for the many Amazon jungle and pampas tours now available in this once-remote area of northwest Bolivia, approximately 200 km northeast of La Paz. Situated on the banks of the Río Beni, with San Buenaventura on the opposite bank, Rurrenabaque is an important trading centre and transportation link for Beni Department. A rapidly growing town, its status as a gateway to the Amazon has brought it some degree of prosperity, and many of its citizens are now involved in one way or another with the burgeoning ecotourist trade.

The sleepy Yungas town of Coroico is an established favourite on Bolivia's 'Gringo Trail'.

Getting there There are flights to and from La Paz. Check flight times in advance as they change frequently, and expect delays and cancellations in the dry season and severe delays in the rainy season. On average, 8 % of flights in and out of Rurre's airport are cancelled. Buses from La Paz leave from Villa Fátima, on Calle Santa Cruz. ● ›› *p266*.

Getting around Unlike most Bolivian towns, the businesses, restaurants and offices in Rurre are not centred around the plaza (2 de Febrero), but instead are clustered together a few blocks north along Calle Vaca Diez and Santa Cruz. Just north of Calle Santa Cruz a small branch of the river effectively divides the town in half. The vast majority of businesses, including the many tour operators, are south of the estuary. Both of the town's markets are above it: the main market, on Calle Avaroa, between Anecito Arce and the old tributary; and the farmer's market, two blocks north and three blocks east.

Information Rurrenabaque's **tourist information office** ① *Av Santa Cruz, between Bolivar and Avaroa, T03-03-71289664, 0800-2000, and often later*, is probably the most helpful in the whole of Bolivia. The ranking system they run for tour companies in town has been a resounding success, meticulously quantifying customers' thoughts on nearly every conceivable aspect of tours and charting the results with glee in massive wall displays.

Sights

Rurre is an astonishingly beautiful place whatever your interests. Whether it is the lush Amazon jungle, the savannah-like pampas, the sub-tropical lowlands, or the wonderful eco-lodges upriver in the national parks, this is the logical starting point. In spite of the usually humid climate, the town has a charming quality, and even if your itinerary doesn't include one of the many tours around the area, just walking about the town itself is an unusual experience. It is with good reason that the settlement is considered the most picturesque in the Beni. The hotels almost all have hammocks, there are plenty of good bars and restaurants, an interesting **market**, and even a **spa**, complete with sauna (see page 266). The local **swimming pool** is excellent and, although most come and go on tours fairly rapidly, it's also very easy to spend a few days here doing very little. The only real drawback is the occasional flooding of the Río Beni. It rarely overflows its banks, but when it does the place becomes a real mess.

Parque Nacional Madidi

Bolivia's Madidi National Park is one of the world's most important conservation areas, and is quite possibly the most biodiverse of all protected areas on the planet's surface. Quite simply, there are more plant and animal species here than any other place on Earth. Parque Nacional Madidi in the La Paz Department, is now roughly four times the size of Amboró, at 1,895,740 ha (almost half the size of Holland). A primary Amazonian watershed, like Amboró, it also contains a pristine ecosystem, one that is home to nearly one-half of all the mammal species known in the Western Hemisphere. It also provides shelter for more than one-third of the known amphibian and bird species in the New World. At last count, almost 1,200 different species of bird had been identified, representing more than 90 % of all known types in Bolivia. It also has what may well be the largest number of plants anywhere in the world, with almost 6,000 classified. By comparison the continental United States and Canada account for some 700 species. Birdlife ranges from minute hummingbirds to the Andean Condor, with a wingspan of 3 m, and the magnificent harpy eagle, the most powerful member of the raptor family. Mammals include: 10 species of primates, including the large spider and red howler monkeys; five species of cat, with healthy populations of jaguar and puma; giant anteaters

Top tips

Jungle trips from Rurrenabaque

Many tour agencies (see page 266) offer jungle tours from Rurrenabaque. Anyone wanting to join a tour should investigate carefully what the various companies are offering. The tourist information centre is a great place to start and, if you can, speak to people returning from tours. Tour prices have been set by the government. Jungle tours cost US$25 per person per day, pampas tours US$30. Acute competition means that some companies cut their prices to be even lower than this, but quality suffers. The usual minimum group size is three (four in the low season).

Pampas tours are usually four days, three nights and involve a bumpy, dusty, four-hour jeep ride at either end. They also involve boat travel in long canoes, though this is a lot smoother and more enjoyable. The pampas is wetland savannah to the northeast of Rurre and there's little or no dry land at all – accommodation usually consists of wooden huts on stilts and most moving around is done in boats. It is an eerily beautiful and peaceful place, with watery wildlife sounds all around, fireflies at night. Expect to see caiman, monkeys, all sorts of birds and probably pink river dolphins. Anaconda are harder to see, and though you may be promised piranha-fishing, this will probably be a stop-off at a pond on the way home. Generally wildlife is easier to see here than in the denser vegetation of the jungle. However, there are also more mosquitoes and sandflies.

Jungle trips offer the advantage of being able to leave Rurrenabaque in a boat and travel up the beautiful river Beni. Accommodation is either in special purpose-built, and relatively luxurious camps (such as Mapajo, page 262, or Chalalán, page 264) or tents. Note also that not all trips offer English-speaking guides and that accommodation is usually spartan (bring insect repellent, mosquito netting, toilet paper and a torch).

- ⬤ Insist that your tour be conducted in an environmentally sound manner.
- ⬤ Set the price in advance and make sure it includes all expenses.
- ⬤ Most groups are of between five and ten people – either find a group before choosing a tour agency or turn up and put yourself on the list. If you arrive early in the morning you probably won't have too much problem getting on a tour straight away, if you so wish.
- ⬤ The best season is July-October. Avoid trips during the rainy season; the humidity and insects will conspire to annoy even the most enthusiastic adventurer, and there are far fewer opportunities to see animals.
- ⬤ Take insect repellent to ward off sandflies and mosquitoes.
- ✖ One-day trips are a waste of time as it takes three hours to reach the jungle.

Capuchin monkey near Rurrenabaque

and a myriad of lesser-known species. Reptiles are represented most spectacularly by the anaconda and the black caiman, which can reach lengths of 9 and 6 m respectively. There are also several types of venomous snake, the most feared being the bushmaster and the fer de lance. Chances of encountering such snakes are very low, but caution is required.

There are lots of guides and tour agencies in Rurrenabaque offering **tours to Madidi** with widely varied and fluctuating standards. Most of these offer trips for small groups at US$25 per person per day. Beyond the usual three- to five-day jungle tour it's possible to arrange a customized itinerary for the same daily rate. It's hard to recommend agencies, other than the operation at Chalalán, as the standards vary between tours and between guides. Ask around when in Rurrenabaque; especially question travellers recently returned from trips for recommendations. ▶ *p266*.

🛏 Sleeping

Coroico *p257*

For such a small town, Coroico has a large variety of accommodation. Due to its popularity, however, the best hotels are booked up during holiday weekends when prices rise.

B El Viejo Molino, a 20-min walk out of town on the road to Caranavi, T02-8136004, valmar@waranet.com, or book through Valmar Tours, T02-2361076, F02-2352279 (La Paz). Expensive option with a sauna, jacuzzi and pool.

D Bella Vista, C Heroes Chaco (2 blocks from the main square), T02-71569237 (mob). **E** without bath but much smaller. Modern, smart and clean rooms with beautiful views. 2 racquetball courts (15Bs per hr) but no pool. Terrace, bikes for rent.

D Esmeralda, 10-15 mins steep walk uphill from the plaza, T/F010-22136017,

www.hotelesmeralda.com. This large hotel is worth the walk up the hill. There's a great pool, a fantastic sauna and a lovely garden and around 200 videos which can be played on demand from your room. Rooms at the front have great views and good hot showers; those at the back are cheaper. The owner Fernando speaks English, German and Spanish and is a good source of local information. There's a free pick-up service (ring from **Totai Tours**) from the plaza and Visa and Mastercard are taken with no commission. The excellent restaurant has a buffet, there's a terrace, a laundry service, free internet access for 2hrs each night, the possibility of burning Cds of digital images and satellite TV. The only downside might be that sweaty bikers arrive en masse every day from 2 'world's most dangerous road' groups and hog the showers.

D-F Sol y Luna, a 15-min walk beyond Hotel Esmeralda, T02-2362099 (La Paz), www.solyluna-bolivia.com. A dreamily rustic set-up among verdant woods and flowery gardens, Sol y Luna is a sprawling fairy tale place with winding paths connecting well designed wooden 'cottages', a swimming pool and hammocks with stunning views across the valley to the distant mountains. Meals are also available, try their superb Indonesian banquet. 7 rooms, US$3.50-6 per person; 5 cottages USUS$14-20; camping US$2.50 by prior booking. For US$12 you can even have a 50-min shiatsu massage.

E Hostal Kory, at the top of the steps leading down from the plaza, T02-2431311. F without bathroom. Bang in the middle of town, Kory offers discounts for stays any longer than a couple of days. There's a big pool, a lovely terrace with good views, a video room and comfy beds in the smallish rooms.

F El Cafetal, Miranda, T02-719-33979 (mob). Hammocks, great views, clean rooms, friendly, though a fair walk from the centre of town. Also a fantastic restaurant. See under Eating, below, for directions.

Rurrenabaque *p258, map p263*

Most hotels in Rurrenabaque are safe, good and relatively inexpensive. Most offer laundry and breakfast (usually not included in the price), although only a few take credit cards. The better ones have ceiling fans, almost none have air conditioning.

B Jataumba Lodge, T03-71255763. www.jataubalodge.com. Just upriver (2.5 km away) on the other side, you need to take a boat to Jataumba. Two pools. Honeymoon packages for $299, trips over the Pampas in a light aircraft $US200.

B Safari, C Comercio, T03-8922410. At the far north end of town, a 10-min walk along C Comercio from the centre, this relatively expensive but lovely hotel has a clean swimming pool sunk into immaculate and extensive green lawns. Palm trees create shade and all rooms have wooden floors and firm comfortable beds. Especially attractive family rooms have front doors which open onto the lawn, and double beds upstairs. The restaurant is good and the hotel accepts Visa. Prices include breakfast. Perfect for a small dose of luxury after a long hard tour.

D Hostal Beni, Comercio (near ferry), T03-03-8922408. A big hotel on the other side of the stream, the colonial style Beni has lots of stairs and landings, a/c and good big wooden beds. Accepts credit cards.

E Bella Vista, Plaza 2 de Febrero. On the plaza, this low pink building has a garden behind leading down to the river. Quiet rooms overlook either the square or garden. No double beds.

E Oriental, Plaza 2 de Febrero, T03-8922401. On the plaza, Oriental has a long courtyard leading into a garden strung with comfortable hammocks. Showers in private bathrooms are electric. A simple breakfast is included, but prices are higher than in other comparable hotels in town. However, it's very cheap (**G** per person) without bathroom or breakfast.

F El Porteño, C Comercio, esq. Vaca Díez, T03-8922558. This central hotel has an attractive courtyard with hammocks and a starfruit tree, from which, if you're lucky, you'll get a welcoming glass of carambola juice on arrival. Some rooms are especially big, with TV, private bathrooms, hot water, firm comfortable beds, ceiling fans and even wardrobes. The owner speaks no English though and you may have to put up with the late night sounds of soft rock from Moskkito Bar.

F Hostal El Eden, at the southern end of C Bolivar, T03-8922452. All on the ground floor at the far southern end of town, El Eden is good value and has a good sandy area out the back with a few hammocks and tables. Rooms have fans, wardrobes and, mostly, private bathrooms (**G** without). Price includes breakfast.

Jungle lodges near Rurrenabaque
A Mapajo Ecotourism Indigena, candlelit walkways link beautifully built cabañas in a prime model of sustainable ecotourism. Constructed and run by the local people, Mapajo combines expertly guided trips into the jungle to see wildlife with visits to the local community. The camp itself, fully owned and operated by the indigenous people of the Quiquibey River, is about 2 hrs upstream (less on the way back down) from Rurrenabaque. It's a rare chance to stay in the pristine jungle of the Reserva Biosférica Pilón Lajas and learn about local music, crafts and local medicine. A trip to Mapajo includes a visit to the nearby village of Asunción and a chance to meet some of its 123 inhabitants, fire their arrows, try your hand at grinding and weaving, visit the school funded by the camp and even the

opportunity to play the locals at football. Towels and mosquito nets are provided and some cabañas have private bathrooms and shower. The food is good and there is a maximum of 16 visitors at any time. As with Chalalán (see page 264), the buildings have been built utilizing environmentally sound methods, with forest materials and traditional construction. Staff are courteous and friendly, though they speak no English, so some Spanish is definitely an advantage. It's well worth the outlay, especially as all profits go back into the local community. Office at C Commercio, Rurrenabaque. T/F03-8922317, www.mapajo.com.

● Eating

Coroico *p257,*

♦♦ **Bamboo**, Iturralde. Good Mexican food in an atmospheric little restaurant. Live music some nights with a small cover charge; otherwise usually recorded reggae. Happy hour 1800-1900.

♦♦ **El Cafetal**, Miranda, T02-719-33979 (mob). A 10-min walk from town, some of which is poorly lit, some of which is not lit at all. Soon after the road starts going downhill there is a turning off on the right, down steps. French-run, with excellent French cuisine. Laid-back jazz, roof, stone tables, good caipirinhas, menu includes pastas, savoury souffles, steak, llama and trout. Try the *Copa cafetal* – ice cream of the house, with fruit, chocolate, cream and nuts. Good value.

♦ **Back-Stube**, next to Hostal Kory, T02-71935594 (mob). Closed Tue. Excellent cakes and German breads, delicious vegetarian lasagne, lots of breakfast options and a friendly atmosphere. They also have a fully equipped house for rent, for up to 5 people for 3 or more days.

♦ **Café de la Senda Verde**, Plazuela Julio Zuzo Cuenca, T02-71532703. Mon-Sun 0630-1900. The home-roasted Yungas coffee is the highlight in this friendly café on the corner of Hostal Kory. Healthy breakfasts, oven-toasted sandwiches and cinnamon rolls are also available.

Rurrenabaque *p258, map p263*

For a town of its size, Rurre has a large number of places to eat. Though none are 5-star, and only the pizza restaurant next door to the **Mosskito Bar** accepts credit cards, many are excellent and almost all are good value.

♦♦ **Juliano**, C Comercio. Offering excellent 'French-Italian' cuisine. Blue-painted tables, a bar outside and a friendly atmosphere create a vaguely Southern Pacific feel. Some good pasta dishes, excellent fish and delicious crème brulée, but avoid the soggy gnocchi ('ñoqui').

♦♦ **La Perla de Rurre**, corner of Bolivar and Vaca Díez. With a big, walled courtyard under a large shady tree decked in

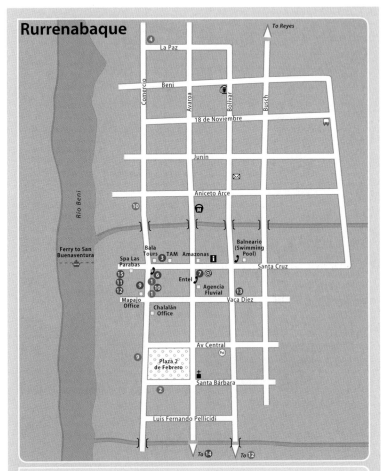

Rurrenabaque

To Reyes

La Paz

Comercio
Beni
Ayaroa
Bolivar
Busch

18 de Noviembre

Junín

Aniceto Arce

Río Beni

Ferry to San Buenaventura

Bala Tours
TAM
Amazonas
Balneario (Swimming Pool)
Santa Cruz

Spa Las Parabas

Entel
@
Agencia Fluvial
Vaca Díez

Mapajo Office
Chalalán Office

Av Central

Plaza 2 de Febrero
Santa Bárbara

Luís Fernando Pellicidi

To 14
To 12

N

200 metres
200 yards

Sleeping	Eating	La Perla de Rurre 13
Bella Vista 9	Café Bar Madidi 9	Pachamama 14
El Porteño 1	Café Motacú 3	Pizzeria Italia 6
Hostal Beni 10	Camila's 7	Playa Azul 15
Hostal El Eden 12	Juliano 10	
Oriental 2	La Cabaña 11	**Bars & clubs**
Safari 4	La Chocita 12	Moskkito 1

Chalalán Eco-lodge ⓘ *T/F03-02-2434058, www.ecotour.org/destinations/chalalan.htm. Also information at www.snids.gov.bo/forestal/apbmp/Madidi.htm.*
Around six hours upriver from Rurre is the excellent Chalalán Eco-lodge, built by the Bolivian government in conjunction with Conservation International. The lodge is surrounded by primary rainforest with an amazing variety of birds and mammals. The nearby lake is home to caiman, turtles, monkeys, hoatzin, macaws and other wildlife. Chalalán is, in many people's eyes, the finest example of community/indigenous ecotourism in Latin America. It has been built utilizing environmentally sound methods, with forest materials, traditional construction and solar power for lighting. The lodge is operated exclusively by the Quechua/Tacana community of San José de Uchupiamonas, a village further upstream. Guides, food and lodging all come highly recommended. The lodge is also an invaluable source of information on the park and is worth the trip to Madidi alone. Tours to Chalalán cost around US$100 per person per night, but vary depending on the size of group and length of tour. Prices include one night in a hotel in Rurre, airport transfers, local guides, meals and transport in Chalalán but not flights to/from Rurre, which cost an extra US$110 return. The cabins have capacity for 14, with great showers, drinking water, library, 25 km of trails, viewing stations, canoe trips and night hikes. There's a booking office ⓘ *Rurrenabaque on C Comercio, near the plaza, T03-8922519*, but tours are best booked in advance for no extra commission through **América Tours** in La Paz (address under La Paz Tour operators, page 236).

Chalalán Lake at Chalalán Eco-lodge.

coloured lights at night, La Perla is Rurre's smartest restaurant. Meaty and fishy menu.

☝ **Camila's Restaurant**, Santa Cruz. Good restaurant, next to Camilla's internet café. Lots of outside tables, plants, jungle murals and 1980s music. A big menu is good for fish dishes. Service can be slow. There's a separate *heladeria* just down the road towards the river.

☝ **La Chocita**, just south of the ferry stop by the river, next to La Cabaña. A riverside fish restaurant with a few red-clothed tables outside under awning. Simple but popular, esecially for the *almuerzo*. The special dish of *Pescado Taquara* is reportedly great here, but needs ordering a day in advance.

☝ **Pizzeria Italia**, Comercio, T03-8922611. Next to *Moskkito*, the restaurant is open to the bar next door, so you can watch games of pool as you eat. 25 types of pizza, though many seem to have the same ingredients in a different order. 3 sizes, medium is about enough for one. A young atmosphere and a creatively translated menu.

☝ **Café Motacú** Santa Cruz, next door to TAM. Mon, Wed, Thu, Fri and Sat 0830-1200 and 1730-2000. Very good and cheap veggie food: 3 types of veggie burgers, burritos, lentil dahl and quiche. Excellent breakfasts too (US0.60-1.50), good cakes and cookies, including delicious hot chocolate brownies. Run by a Scot, a Peruvian, an Argentine and a Bolivian, Motacú also has a book exchange, handicrafts and you can buy some locally produced organic products – coffee, sun-dried tea, honey, peanut butter and dried fruit.

☝ **Pachamama**, C Avaroa, T03-03-8922620. 1200-2230. At the southern end of town, a friendly café-bar run by an English/Bolivian couple with snacks, a balcony with a view over the river, a film room, playstation, internet,

table football and a book exchange.

🍷 Bars and clubs

Coroico *p257*
Barpension Los Jasmies, Iturralde, up from *Bamboo*. Bar, disco, popular with locals.
Wiskería Taurus, C Julio Zuazo Cuenca. Good for a beer.

Rurrenabaque *p258, map p263*
The town's fun swings chiefly around *Moskkito Bar* and karaoke bars. Follow the music on Fri and Sat nights to find them. There are also 2 dodgy discos. The one opposite *Hotel Tuichi* is best for gringos.
Moskkito Bar, C Comercio. With rock music and pool tables (and now an attached t-shirt shop), the Moskkito bar is a good place to drink away an evening in the company of new-found friends. Lots of beer and tales of large anacondas. You can also order in pizzas from the restaurant next door. Happy hour with half-price cocktails 1900-2100.

✹ Festivals

Coroico *p257*
19-22 Oct Colourful 4-day **festival**, accommodation is hard to find. It is great fun, but it might be an idea to wait a day or two before returning to La Paz, in order to give your driver time to recover.
2 Nov All Souls' Day. The local cemetery is festooned with black ribbons.

⛰ Activities and tours

Coroico *p257*
Horse riding Ask Dany at *El Cafetal* for information. Also T02-8136015; US$6 per 2 hrs, group rates and organized trips.

Tour operators
Eco Adventuras and Inca Land Tours, both on the main plaza.

Rurrenabaque *p258, map p263*
Spas
Spa las Parabas, at the end of Av Santa Cruz, near the ferry port, T71120883. A beautifully designed dry and wet sauna with a cold plunge pool, massage, treatments, and a snack bar with great views. Even if you don't fancy the sauna itself, it's a great place to come and chill out. Use of the spa, US$5.

Tour operators
Agencia Fluvial, at Hotel Tuichi, T03-8922372, is run by Tico Tudela. They offer jungle tours on the Río Tuichi, normally 4 days, but shorter by arrangement, including food, transport and mosquito nets. Three nights are spent in the jungle, learning about plants, survival and the foods of the region. Fluvial also run 3-day 'pampas tours' on a boat to Río Yacuma, US$30 per person per day.
Bala Tours, next door to TAM on C Santa Cruz, T03-8922527, www.balatours.com. Runs jungle tours and has a private camp for the pampas tour well away from other groups.
Turismo Ecologico Social (TES), next door to the tourist information office, T03-03-71289664, turismoecologicosocial @hotmail.com. Mon-Sat 0730-1740. They offer excellent day-long tours to 4 local communities. In groups of a maximum of 10 people, minimum 3, you travel around 40 km from Rurrenabaque by road to the buffer zone of Pilón Lajas Biosphere Reserve and see the ways communities in the area live and the sustainable ways in which the rainforest can be used. Tours touch on forest management, handicrafts, agroforestry and fruit. U$25 per person includes lunch, water and well-informed guides.

⊖ Transport

Coroico *p257*
From La Paz all bus companies serving **Coroico** (3 hrs, US$2) are in Villa Fátima.

Turbus Totai, Yanacachi y América, have big buses which leave several times daily from 0730-1630 as does **Trans Totai** further up Yanacachi. **Flota Yungueña**, C Yanacachi y Alcoche (T02-2213513), have *micros* from 0730-1630.

To La Paz buses leave daily from Coroico, 0730-1630, although **Turbus Totai** claims to start at 0300. Extra services run on Sun. It's worth booking in advance, and note that it can be difficult to book journeys to La Paz on holidays and on Sun evenings/Mon mornings.

Rurrenabaque *p258, map p263*
Air
TAM fly to/from **La Paz**; US$58 one-way; you'll be charged Bs3 for every kilo over 15 kg. They have an office on C Santa Cruz, T03-8922398. Check flight times in advance as they change frequently, and expect delays and cancellations in the rainy season. **TAM** flies 4 days a week.

Amazonas fly twice daily and are usually cheaper (US$50 return). Their office is opposite Camila's on Santa Cruz (T03-8922472) or contact travel agents (eg **America Tours** in La Paz, T02-2374204).

Taxis and motorcycle taxis meet flights. A motorcycle taxi to or from town costs US$1, a normal taxi US$3. **Amazonas** and **TAM** also run their own minibuses to and from the airport from their offices in the centre of town, US$0.60. There is a small tourist tax and flight tax at the airport.

Road
To/from **La Paz** (you have to go to Villa Fátima to leave the capital) via Caranavi daily at 1100 with **Flota Yungueña** and **Totai**; 18-20 hrs, US$8.20. Returns at 1100. **Flota Unificada** leaves La Paz (also from Villa Fátima) on Tue, Thu, Fri and Sat at 1030, same price but, as it continues on to far-off Riberalta and Guayamerin, its return departure time depends on how well the driver copes with the road on the way back; ask in Rurre.

Travellers' tales

Jungle ennui

The rain, which all night has drowned out the sounds of soft rock and loud travellers' tales of anacondas from the pizza place next door, is still cascading down out of a grey sky when we wake up. This is the jungle, and airports are narrow strips of rough grass cut through the endless trees. Rain and jungle air travel don't mix.

My shoes are still soaked from walking thigh-deep through a pampas bog the day before, so in sandals I wade across what was once a road, wondering where yesterday's kerb begins. At the airline office they seem unfeasibly optimistic. We leave our bags and head off to a café for breakfast. Several breakfasts and brunches later we're still sitting watching the rain and the sky and waiting for news, always half an hour away. Locals come by, smiling, telling us how the last time it rained nobody left for a week. We meet a couple of Irish girls and talk to a pair we'd met before in La Paz. In a homemade kit car, an American man drives around selling banana cake and giving out conspiracy theory literature about the FBI. Hours pass. There are no spectacled bears, no active volcanoes, no enormous expanses of white, or blue, not even any weird potatoes, just a few bedraggled dogs, some muddy motorbikes and some stranded travellers. Eventually the call goes up from somewhere that we're off to another airport, where they have a solid runway and far too many muddy people pile into a tiny minibus and we are driven bumpily away into the mist.

There is nothing especially unusual about today, but, alongside all of spectacular Bolivia, along with dinosaur footprints and candlelit cabins I'll remember this too, fondly. *Julius Honnor*

⊙ Directory

Coroico *p257*
Banks Banco Mercantil on central plaza. Mon-Fri 0830-1230, 1430-1830, Sat 0900-1230, cash advances (no commission) on Mastercard, VISA and Maestro. You can change TCs at *Turbus Totai*, but the rates are poor. Better rates at *Hostal Kory* or *Hotel Esmeralda*.
Internet Carlos has a small internet café on C Caja de Agua, T/F02-8136041. He will also exchange Spanish for English lessons.

Rurrenabaque *p258, map p263*
Banks Getting money in Rurre is very difficult; bring plenty of it with you. There are no banks or casas de cambio. **Beni**, **Moskkito** and **Red Oriental** (next to Indigena Tours) all change cash for 5-10% commission. TCs in dollars can be used to pay for tours but are difficult to cash; try **Agencia Fluvial**, who charge 5% commission. Most if not all tour companies will accept credit cards for tours. **Internet** Camila's, next to the restaurant of the same name on Santa Cruz charges US$3 per hr, minimum US$0.75 for 15 mins. **Laundry** Speed Queen, Vaca Díez between Bolívar and Avaroa. US$1/kg, ready in 3½ hrs. **Telephone** Entel, C Comercio, 2 blocks north of the plaza, T03-8922205, and C Santa Cruz and C Bolivar.

South & Central Highlands

The Salar de Uyuni's mirror-like surface

Don't miss...

1 Riding around on the cheesy **Dino Truck** ▶▶ *p275*.

2 Exploring the **weaving villages around Sucre** ▶▶ *p276*.

3 Descending into the **'Mouth of Hell'** at **Potosí** ▶▶ *p278*.

4 The wild celebrations of Phujllay at **Tarabuco**, near Sucre ▶▶ *p284*.

5 Driving across the blinding white expanse of the **Salar de Uyuni** ▶▶ *p291*.

p272

p290

50 km
50 miles

Bolivia's extremities add a whole new dimension to the concept of remote. In the far southwest, you can travel for hours without seeing another soul, save for the occasional 4WD packed with tourists heading to or from the Salar de Uyuni, the largest salt lake in the world and biggest attraction in these parts. People also go out of their way to travel here for the dream-like landscapes, peppered with smoking volcanoes, kaleidoscopic lakes full of flamingos and belching geysers. Equally surreal, but in a more sinister way, is the experience of burrowing down into the bowels of the aptly-named Cerro Rico (Rich Mountain), a pink-hued colossus that has, during its 400-plus years of silver mining, devoured many hundreds of thousands of indigenous slaves as well as turning Potosí into a booming, 17th century version of Las Vegas, before the lodes wore thin and the city went bust. A few hours away is the distinctly soigné Sucre, famed for its whiter than white beauty and near which is the greatest concentration of dinosaur footprints in the world, hundreds of them, all within the perimeter fence of the local cement factory.

Ratings

Culture
★★★★

Landscape
★★★★★

Wildlife
★★★

Activities
★★★★

Chillin'
★★

Costs
$$

Central Highlands

Sucre and Potosí are the finest examples of Bolivia's colonial heritage and two of its main tourist attractions. Sucre exudes the assured confidence and charm befitting the country's official capital, legal centre and major university city. Its near neighbour, Potosí, is not only the highest city in the world, at over 4,000 m, but was once the largest and wealthiest city in the Americas. All around are reminders of its silver-mining heyday, from the many crumbling colonial buildings, to the massive mint, where the silver was smelted into coins for the Spanish Crown. Towering over the city is Cerro Rico – Rich Mountain – from which the silver was extracted, at an unimaginable human cost. Visitors can burrow into its bowels through a series of tunnels and shafts, meet the devil face to face, and experience what life was like many centuries ago for those who were forced to enter the 'Mouth of Hell'.

Getting there Flights/buses to Sucre and Potosí from La Paz and to Sucre from Santa Cruz; buses to Potosí from La Paz, Sucre and Uyuni.

Getting around Frequent buses between Sucre and Potosí; buses and *micros* to outlying towns and villages.

Time required 3-4 days, more if attending one of the festivals.

Weather Sucre is mild year-round; nights in Potosí are freezing cold, especially May-Oct.

Sleeping Wide choice in Sucre, fewer upmarket options in Potosí.

Eating Regional specialities and international cuisine in Sucre, a few decent options in Potosí.

Activities and tours Dinosaur hunting and weaving villages in and around Sucre, mine tours in Potosí.

★ **Don't miss...** Mine tour in Potosí ▶ *p278*.

Sucre ⊖🚹🌸⊛⊙▲⊖🌓 ↦ *pp280-289*

Sucre, Bolivia's official capital, is proud of its colonial legacy. Also known as 'La Ciudad Blanca' (the White City), owing to the fact that, by tradition, all the buildings in its centre are whitewashed every year, Sucre is not just a series of pretty façades but also a thriving university city and thousands of young students fill every street, plaza, bar and café. Surrounding this sparkling white colonial masterpiece is a hinterland of traditional weaving villages which burst into life during their frequent market days and festivals. Dinosaur-hunters are also making tracks for Sucre, with the discovery of many prehistoric footprints. Sucre enjoys a mild climate with an average daytime temperature of 24°C in July-August and 7°C at night .

Ins and outs

Getting there Juana Azurduy de Padilla **airport** is 5 km northwest of town (T04-6454445). The airport minibus goes from the entrance and will drop you off on Hernando Siles y Junín, in the centre. It returns from here, usually 1½ hours before flights leave; US$0.70, 20-30 minutes. A taxi from the centre is US$2-3. *Trufis* 1 and F go from the entrance to Hernando Siles y Loa, one block from the main plaza, US$0.55, 25 minutes. The **bus terminal** is on the northern outskirts of town, 3 km from centre on Ostria Gutiérrez, T04-6452029. A taxi to and from the centre is US$0.75 (5Bs) per person inside the terminal compound or US$0.45 (3Bs) outside. Alternatively take *micro* A or *trufi* 8 (going to the bus station, from Av H Siles, between Arce and Junín). ⊖ ↦ *p288.*

Getting around Sucre is a small, compact city and easy to explore on foot. Its busy narrow streets generally run uphill from the plaza eastwards and downhill west towards the train station. Taxis around town are always US$0.45 (Bs3) per person; pay no more.

Information **Tourist information** is available downstairs in the **bus terminal** ⓘ *Mon-Fri 1000-1230 and 1500-1730, Sat 0800-1200 (but often shut)*; and the **airport**, to coincide with incoming flights; also and upstairs at the **Casa de la Cultura** ⓘ *Argentina 65, T04-6427102, Mon-Fri 0800-1200, 1400-1600.*

South & Central Highlands Central Highlands

Sucre, Bolivia's 'White City'.

Sights

The city's heart is the spacious, elegant **Plaza 25 de Mayo**, on which stands the **Casa de la Libertad** ⓘ *25 de Mayo 11, T04-6454200, Mon-Fri 0900-1115, 1430-1745, Sat 0930-1115; US$1.50, photo permit US$1.50 more, videos US$3, includes guided tours in English or Spanish*, where the country's Declaration of Independence was signed on 6 August 1825. The actual document is on display. Also among its treasures is a famous portrait of Simón Bolívar, said to be the most accurate.

Also on the plaza is the beautiful 17th-century **cathedral** ⓘ *Mon-Fri 1000-1200, 1500-1700, Sat 1000-1200, US$1.50, if the door is locked wait for the guide*, which houses the famous jewel-encrusted *Virgen de Guadalupe*

(1601), as well as works by the Italian Bernardo Bitti, the first great painter of the New World. Entrance to the cathedral is through the museum, halfway down Calle Nicolás Ortiz, opposite La Vieja Bodega. If you're outside opening hours, the main door will obviously be unlocked during mass. Times either change frequently, or are not observed at all.

The church of **Santa Mónica**, at the corner of Arenales y Junín, is perhaps one of the finest gems of Spanish architecture in the Americas, but has been closed to visitors since 1995. Another one of Sucre's fine churches is the church of **San Miguel** ⓘ *1130-1200, no shorts, short skirts or short sleeves*. Completed in 1628, it has been restored and is very beautiful with Moorish-style carved and painted ceilings, pure-white walls and a gold and silver altar. In the Sacristy some early sculpture can be seen. It was from San Miguel that Jesuit missionaries went south to convert Argentina, Uruguay and Paraguay.

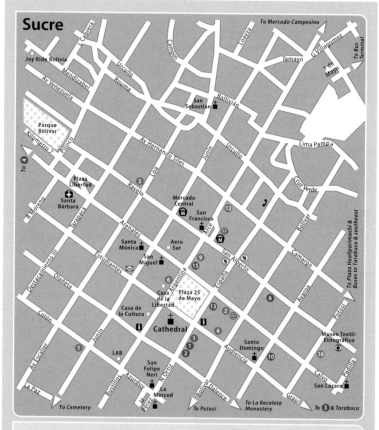

Sucre

To Mercado Campesino
To Bus Terminal
Joy Ride Bolivia
Tamayo
G Villagomez
1 de Mayo
Av Venezuela
Mendizabel
Cabrera
Campos
Rouma
Urcullo
Loayza
San Sebastián
Ballivián
Parque Bolívar
Kilometro 7
Bolívar
Av Hernando Siles
Junín
Urcullo
Lima Pampa
Plaza Libertad
Santa Bárbara
Ravelo
Loa
Cruz Verde
R Moreno
Tarapacá
Arenales
Mercado Central
San Francisco
Bolívar
Santa Mónica
Aero Sur
Arce
San Alberto
Camargo
Estudiantes
San Miguel
España
Destacamento III
Olañeta
Argentina
Colón
Casa de la Libertad
Plaza 25 de Mayo
Avaroa
Potosí
Casa de la Cultura
Cathedral
Santo Domingo
Museo Textil-Etnográfico
Av Escalier
Junín
LAB
San Felipe Neri
Audiencia
Kultur-Café Berlin 10
Grau
Bustillos
Azurduy
N Ortiz
La Merced
Bolívar Dalence
Calvo
San Lázaro
Padilla
La Paz
Pérez
To Cemetery
To Potosí
To La Recoleta Monastery
To Tarabuco
To Plaza Huallparimachi & Buses to Tarabuco & southeast

Sleeping ⊜
Colonial 6
Grand 9
Hostal Colón 1
Hostal Independencia 2
Hostal Recoleta 3
Hostal San Francisco 12
La Posada 4

Real Audiencia 16

Eating ⓐ
Arco Iris 1
Bibliocafé Sureña 2
Café Hacheh 4
Café Mirador 3
El Germen 6

Kultur-Café Berlin 10
La Plaza 13
La Taverne 15

Bars & clubs ⓝ
Joy Ride Café 1

N

100 metres
100 yards

> **Birth on a bus**

> We were on a bus heading south from Potosí, admiring the stunning scenery outside as we bounced past on the less than smooth road. Gradually, we became aware of a commotion a few seats ahead of us and what sounded like a woman in pain. As I got up to see what was going on and, more importantly, if I could help, someone tapped me on the shoulder. I turned round and a pair of rather rusty looking scissors were thrust in my face, accompanied by a gesture to pass them forward. As I duly passed them on a sudden scream emanated from the seat in front. There was no mistaking it – a baby's scream. And sure enough, when we squeezed through to take a peep, there was a newborn baby wrapped in a shawl and feeding at its mother's breast. The scissors, having been used to cut the umbilical cord and now wiped clean of blood, were already being returned to their owner at the rear of the bus. What happened next, though, was truly amazing. Within a few hours of giving birth on the bus, the mother shouted at the bus driver to stop, then got off the bus with her new baby, retrieved her luggage from the hold and then set off down a track towards her home. And the driver hadn't even charged for the extra fare! *A. Thomson, Toronto.*

Travellers' tales

Highly recommended for explanations of local indigenous groups and their distinctive textiles is the **Museo Textil-Etnográfico** ⓘ *San Alberto 413 y Potosí, T04-6453841, www.bolivianet.com/asur, Jul-Sep Mon-Sat 0830-1200, 1430-1800, Oct-Jun Mon-Fri 0830-1200, 1430-1800, Sat 0930-1200,* housed in the Caserón de la Capellanía. Their Jalq'a exhibit is perhaps the finest display of Bolivian ethnography now available. It includes superb examples of contemporary daily dress, as well as ritual costumes, a film of dances, live weaving demonstrations, photographs of earlier weavings and clear and fulsome explanations of their history and descriptions of the iconography of the textiles. The knowledgeable and helpful staff can also arrange visits to the villages where the textile traditions have been revived. There's also a handicrafts shop downstairs which supports the project. There's a lot to see but tickets can be used again the following day.

Southeast of the city, on Plaza Pedro de Anzúres at the top of Calle Dalence, is the Franciscan monastery of **La Recoleta** with good views over the city. The monastery, which was founded in 1601 by the Franciscans, is notable for the beauty of its cloisters and gardens. Inside the monastery is the **Museo de la Recoleta** ⓘ *Mon-Fri 0900-1130, 1430-1630, Sat only with guides from tourist agency and minimum of 10 people, US$1.20 for entrance to all collections, guided tours only – you may have to wait; US$0.30 for use of camera.* In the grounds is the *Cedro Milenario*, a 1,000-year-old cedar tree.

Around Sucre

The best known and most accessible of the region's many dinosaur tracks are at **Cal Orcko**, at the Fanseca cement factory, 3 km out of town. There are around 5,000 footprints, making it possibly the world's largest paleontological site. The footprints are on the steep side of a rockface but it's not hard to imagine that once this was a flat muddy plain. One single set of footprints continues for 350 m. The tracks were discovered by the workers in 1994, but it took

The ubiquitous coca leaves on sale at Tarabuco market, near Sucre.

some time for them to be fully identified as those of a Sauropdos, or Titanosauros, Anguilosaurios and Teropodos. Access is through the factory, and you should be accompanied by a company employee. Take the fantastically cheesy **DinoTruck**, which leaves every day at 0930, 1200 and 1430, costing US$3.75. You'll ride in the back of a red and yellow lorry with a painted stegosaurus on its side. Excellent explanations in good English. The tourist office can recommend taxi drivers who have trained as guides, US$10. Untrained drivers charge US$6 per person.

One of the most interesting trips from Sucre is to the village of **Tarabuco**, 64 km southeast on a good road. It is famous for its very colourful **market** on Sunday. The local people still wear their traditional dress of *conquistador*-style helmets, multi-coloured ponchos, *chuspas* (bags for carrying coca leaves) and the elaborate *axsu*, an overskirt worn by women. The market starts around 0930-1000 and could be described as a bit of a tourist trap, but many still find it an enjoyable experience. Those in search of a bargain should have an idea about the quality on offer before buying. Many of the sellers also come to Sucre through the week.

The weavers' village nearby include **Candelaria** (two hours by truck from Tarabuco), **Macha** (eight hours from Sucre), **Pocata** (one hour from Macha), or **Ravelo** (59 km northwest of Sucre). ➡ ▸▸ p288.

Potosí ⬛🚻🅿❄✳🛏🔺🔲ℹ ▸▸ pp280-289

Potosí is not only the highest city in the world, but also one of the most beautiful, saddest and fascinating places you'll ever experience. Towering over the city like a giant pink headstone is the 4,824-m **Cerro Rico** (Rich Mountain). Silver from this mountain made Potosí the biggest city in the Americas and one of the richest in the world, rivalled only by Paris, London and Seville. But Cerro Rico also claimed the lives of countless thousands of Indian slaves. This painful history still haunts the city and is as much a part of its colonial legacy as the many magnificent old buildings which led it to be declared Patrimony of Mankind by UNESCO in 1987. The Spanish still have a saying 'vale un Potosí' ('it's worth a Potosí') for anything incredibly valuable, but though Potosí's wealth is now only a distant memory, it remains one of Bolivia's greatest attractions and is certainly well worth a visit.

Getting there and around The airport is 5 km out of the city on the road to Sucre. There are flights to and from La Paz. The bus terminal, T02-6243361, is on Avenida Universitaria, beyond the old train station. It's a 30-minute lung-busting walk uphill to the town – or a short taxi or *micro* ride. You have to pay US$0.10 terminal tax. When you buy your ticket you check your luggage into the operator's office and it is then loaded directly onto your bus. *Micros* within the city cost US$0.12. Taxis cost US$1. ● ▸▸ *p289*.

Climate Bring warm clothes – average temperature is 9°C and there are 130 sub-zero nights a year. Also, take it easy on arrival. Remember Potosí is higher than La Paz.

Information **Tourist office** ⓘ *Plaza 6 de Agosto, ½ block above the main Plaza 10 de Noviembre, T02-6227405, gobmupoi@cedro.pts.entelnet.bo.* It is supposed to be open Monday to Friday 0800-1200 and 1400-1800 but is often closed during these hours.

Sights

Just wandering around the centre of Potosí is fascinating in itself and will take you past many colonial buildings. While Viceroy Toledo tried to bring order to the city's layout in 1574, the silver boom had led to fast and unplanned development which has left Potosí with a less-than-gridiron plan full of small streets with unexpected twists and turns which adds to the city's charm. There are lots of beautiful and ornate religious buildings well worth seeing but restoration work means buildings can be closed to visitors for months. Check with the tourist office if there is anywhere you particularly want to visit.

Below the main plaza, on Calle Ayacucho and Quijarro, is the huge and impressive **Casa Nacional de Moneda** ⓘ *T02-6222777, Tue-Fri 0900-1200, 1400-1830, Sat and Sun 0900-1300, entry US$3, by 2-hr guided tour only (in English at 0900, usually only for groups of 10 or more).* All silver mined in Potosí had to be brought to the *Casa* (or Mint) to be turned into ingots so the Spanish Crown could tax it. Founded in 1572, rebuilt 1759-73, it is one of the chief monuments of civil building in Hispanic America. It has 160 rooms and the walls are fortress-thick. You cannot fail to notice the huge, grinning Bacchus (mask) over an archway

Entrance to Casa Nacional de Moneda.

The red-tiled roofs of colonial Potosí.

between two principal courtyards. This was put up in 1865 – according to some, the smile is said to be ironic and aimed at the departing Spanish. The 50-odd room museum has a good collection of paintings including works by the best of the Bolivian colonial painters.

Those who are into colonial architecture could do worse than begin in **Calle Quijarro**, one of Potosí's best-preserved streets. In colonial times it was known as Calle Ollería (potmakers) and Calle de los Sombreros (hats). At the bottom of Calle Ayacucho, on the corner with Chichas, is the convent, church and **Museo de Santa Teresa** ⓘ *T02-6223847, admission only with 2-hr tour (in English and Spanish), daily 0900-1100 and 1500-1700, US$3.15, plus US$1.50 to take photos, US$25 to video*. The building was started in 1685 and has an impressive amount of giltwork inside. There is an eye-opening collection of flagellation tools (a must for sado-masochists), colonial paintings, religious architecture and furniture.

Potosí's first church, built in 1547, is the **Museo y Convento de San Francisco**, ⓘ *C Tarija esquina Nogales, T02-6222539, Mon-Fri 0900-1200 and 1430-1700, Sat 0900-1200, US$1.50, US$1.50 to take photos, to video US$3*. The current building, begun in 1707 has the oldest surviving cloisters in Bolivia. It contains a museum of ecclesiastical art, with more than 200 paintings including one of Melchor Pérez de Holguín's best works, *The Erection of the Cross*. Don't miss going up on the roof, which provides one of the best viewpoints over the city.

Mine tours

Most people come to Potosí for the incredible experience of visiting one of the myriad mine workings of the infamous **Cerro Rico**. ▲▲ ▶▶ *p286*.

Cerro Rico was described by one Spanish chronicler in the mid-16th century as 'the mouth of hell', and visitors should be aware that descending into its bowels is both physically and emotionally draining. The tour, as *Koala Tours* proclaim, is 'not for wimps or woosies'. The mine entrances are above 4,000 m and you will be walking, or rather crouching, around breathing in noxious gases and seeing people working in appalling conditions in temperatures up to 40°C. You should be acclimatized, fit and not have any heart or breathing problems, such as asthma.

The standard price of a tour is US$10 per person – less in the low season. Make sure you are getting a helmet, lamp and protective clothing (but wear old clothes anyway). Tours follow a set itinerary. A full tour lasts four to five hours and does not give you time to join a tour of the Casa Nacional de Moneda afterwards. A trip to the thermal baths to clean up is a better option. The size of tour groups varies – some are as large as 20 people, which is excessive. Tours last from around 0800 to mid-afternoon, with around four hours inside the mines.

The tour begins with a visit to **Mercado Calvario** where you are expected to buy gifts for the miners such as dynamite, coca leaves, meths, ammonium nitrate and cigarettes. Then it's up to the mine where you get kitted up and enter one of the tunnels. A tour will usually go down all the way to the fourth level, meeting and talking to working miners on the way. You will see how dynamite is used and also meet *El Tío*, the god of the underworld (Friday afternoon is the main day for making offerings to *El Tío*). A good guide will be able to explain mining practices, customs and traditions little changed since the Spanish left and enable you to communicate with the miners. Many tours also include some sort of dynamite pyrotechnics. A contribution to the miners' cooperative is appreciated as are medicines for the new health centre (*Posta Sanitaria*) on Cerro Rico. New projects such as a radio and drinking water have been, or will shortly be, realized.

Around Potosí

The thermal baths at **Tarapaya**, 25 km outside the city on the road to Oruro, are worth visiting to freshen up after crawling around in mine tunnels. There are public baths (US$0.30) and private (US$0.60); the private baths, higher up, may be cleaner. On the other side of the

Background

→ **Fight for the right to party**

A tradition peculiar to the Potosí Department is the *tinku* ritual fight. Basically, what happens is that two neighbouring communities meet up and beat the living daylights out of one another – literally. For death, though much less common these days, is always a possibility.

The *tinku* may look like a drunken Saturday night pub brawl, but it is loaded with symbolism and carries a deep spiritual significance. It is a meeting of equals and is not about winning, but of recognizing your rivals, respecting them and defining your territory. It symbolizes the need to co-exist with other people. It is also a celebration of forgiveness of family or personal enemies. In the *tinku* any problem is solved and all debts are paid.

Before the fight, the combatants meet and drink *chicha* and stronger alcohol. The alcohol is to give them courage for the impending battle. For protection, the pugilists wear a leather helmet, treated so that it is hard as steel, and a leather groin protector. Fighting is hand-to-hand and reaches a fever pitch of noisy violence. The losers begin to retreat and then stones rain down on both groups.

The winner of each fight then enjoys one year of dominance over his defeated opponent. The injured are respected for standing their ground and fighting bravely and the corpses, when death was a more commonplace occurrence, were buried as an offering to Pachamama, to ensure a good harvest.

There is no sexual discrimination here. Women also fight in the *tinku* and it is said that they fight more cruelly and with more honour. During the *tinku*, bands play continuously and those who are too scared, ill, old, or sensible to fight dance around in a circle.

Tourists are a relatively new phenomenom, so be discreet. Things can get ugly after few days' hard drinking and fighting, so it's wise to get out before the end. Some agencies, for example Koala, organize trips to the Macha *tinku* on 3 May and the Uncía *tinku* on 2 August, among others.

river from Tarapaya is a small 50-m wide volcanic crater lake, with a temperature of 30°C. It's a pleasant enough spot but on no account swim in the lake. A tourist drowned here, and though agencies in Potosí still run trips, it is not safe. Nearby is **Balneario Miraflores** which also has swimming pools. Camping by the lake is possible and there's accommodation at *Balneario Tarapaya*. North of Balneario Miraflores is **Hacienda Mondragon**, set in a beautiful canyon, which is visited by most of the tour operators. Buses to Tarapaya and Miraflores leave from outside the Chuquimia market on Avenida Universitaria, up from the bus terminal, every 30 minutes or so (0700-1700, US$0.50, 30 minutes). A taxi costs US$7.50 for a group. The last bus back from Miraflores leaves at 1800.

The city of Potosí lies at the foot of Cerro Rico, whose rich silver lodes sealed its fate.

Sleeping

Sucre *p273, map p274*

AL Refugio Andino Bramadero, near Chataquila, and Gato Diabólico, 23 km from Sucre, bramader@yahoo.com, or Restaurant Salamandra, Avaroa 510, T6913433. Or book through **Joy Ride Café** (see page 286). These fairy-tale cabins are in the middle of some beautiful countryside, with great walks from the front door. Good food, candlelight, hot water. All food and transport is included in the US$35 per person price. Family cottages or doubles and a big house too.

A Real Audiencia, Potosí 142, T04-6460823, F04-6460823. 4-star, excellent restaurant, swimming pool, sauna, massages, views from lounge, all rooms have cable TV, room service, modern.

B La Posada, C Audencia 92, T6460101, www.laposadahostal.com. A smart, central, colonial-style hotel with comfortable rooms with big beds and wooden beams. There's also a good courtyard restaurant (see Eating). Worth asking for a discount.

B Hostal Independencia, Calvo 31, T04-6442256, F04-6461369, jacosta@ mara.scr.entelnet.bo. Has a spectacular salón worth seeing even if you don't stay here, with gilding, chandeliers, spiral stairs and lots of velvet. The verdant courtyard is draped in greenery and towering palms and enormous rooms have oversized TVs and baths to match.

C Colonial, Plaza 25 de Mayo 3, T04-6440309, F04-6440311, hoscol@mara. scr.entelnet.bo. The Colonial is grander than its plain corridors and courtyard might suggest. Some rooms are noisy, the best room of all has a bathtub, an enormous bed and a great view overlooking the Plaza. Good continental breakfast included.

C Hostal Recoleta, Ravelo 205, T04-6454789. Bright and friendly place, clean and kitted out in a lovely colonial style. Rooms have cable TV and phone. Price includes buffet breakfast.

D Grand, Arce 61, T04-6451704, F04-6452461. Comfortable rooms with private bathrooms, hot showers and cable TV. There are lots of courtyards and plants and the price includes continental breakfast in room. Excellent central location, good value lunch in Arcos restaurant, laundry, safe, helpful.

E Hostal San Francisco, Av Arce 191 y Camargo, T04-6452117, F04-6462693, hostalsf@cotes.net.bo. A pristine white hotel where rooms have private bathrooms, TV and phone. It's quiet and comfortable and rooms are centred around a large courtyard with a fountain. Breakfast is US$0.60 extra. Excellent value for money.

F Hostal Colón, Colón 220, T04-6455823, colon220@bolivia.com. Family-run colonial house, quiet, basic but clean, laundry US$1 per kg, helpful owner speaks excellent English and German. Rooms overlook a courtyard with a flowering tree and a new coffee room opens out onto the street. Breakfast included. Small book exchange.

Potosí *p276, map p283*

Hotels have no heating, unless stated otherwise.

B Hostal Colonial, Hoyos 8, near the main plaza, T02-6224809, F02-6227146. Popular and attractive colonial house, with heating. Rooms are suprisingly plain for the price but are nevertheless comfortable.

B Hostal Libertador, Millares 58 y Nogales, T02-6227877, F02-6224629, hostalib@ cedro.pts.entelnet.bo. Colonial building, central heating in comfortable, modern rooms, quiet, helpful, parking.

C per person Hacienda Cayara, 25 km west of the city. Those wishing to avoid the freezing cold nights of Potosí can stay here. This is the best-preserved *hacienda* in the area, it has space for up to 10, price includes breakfast, other meals can be prepared on request or cook your own, lunch is US$7 and dinner US$5. For reservations, T02-6226380, cayara@cedro.pts.entelnet.bo, or go to the door to the right of the shop of the same name beside the main *Entel* office at Cochabamba 532.

C Hostal Cerro Rico, Ramos 123 (between La Paz and Millares, off map), T/F02-6223539, www.hostal cerrorico.8k.com. **D** without private bathroom. Very good rooms upstairs, cable TV, friendly and helpful, parking.

C Jerusalem, Oruro 143, T/F02-6222600, hoteljer@cedro.pts.entelnet.bo. **F** without bath. Includes buffet breakfast, TV, friendly, helpful, clean and comfortable, very good in the new section, comedor, garage parking a block away, US$1/day, laundry, good value, internet for US$2 per hr. Travel agency **Sumaj Tours**, T02-6224633, is part of the hotel.

F Casa de María Victoria, Chuquisaca 148, T02-6222132. With bathroom. Built in the 17th century as accommodation for friars from Santo Domingo, all rooms open on to a stone courtyard, clean, stores luggage, popular budget choice, travel agency offers cheap mine tours, breakfast in courtyard, owner speaks English.

F Tarija, Av Serrudo 252, T02-6222711. cheaper without bath. Clean and helpful, Tarija has no obvious sign but a big cobbled courtyard with free parking. The more expensive rooms are much nicer, with wooden beds and floors and good, newly tiled private bathrooms.

F Koala Den, Junin 56. Recently expanded and refurbished, the Koala Den is heated, with TV, video, magazines and a coffee room. Rooms for 2, 3, 5 or 10. Private bathrooms and a kitchen. Look out for a Koala pub in the future.

Eating

Sucre *p273, map p274*

Arco Iris, Bolivar 567, T46423985. Swiss restaurant, good service, expensive but good, *peña* on Sat, excellent roesti, live music some nights.

El Huerto, Ladislao Cabrera 86, T04-6451538. Take a taxi at night, set in a beautiful garden. Good *almuerzo*, international food with salad bar.

Posada, C Audencia 92, T04-6460101, www.laposadahostal.com. Mon-Sat 0700-2230, Sun 0700-1500. An upmarket restaurant in a courtyard with a palm tree. Quiet and laid-back, it is popular with local suits, generals and pilots. Great homemade lemonade.

¶ **El Germen**, San Alberto 231. Open Mon-Sat 0800-2200. Very good vegetarian with good set lunches for US1.80 and excellent healthy breakfasts, US$1-1.50. Also chocolate cake, a good book exchange and German magazines.

¶ **La Plaza**, on the Plaza at No 33, T04-6455843. Mon-Sun 1200-0000. With a wooden balcony, good food and pisco sours, lots of fish dishes, very popular with locals, set lunch US$2.10.

¶ **La Taverne**, Alliance Française, Aniceto Arce 35, ½ a block from the plaza. Mon-Sat 0800-2200. *Peñas* Fri and Sat. Good value French food in a setting with wooden beams and checked tablecloths, also regular films and cultural events. Good meeting place.

Cafés

Bibliocafé Sureña, Nicolás Ortiz 50, near the plaza. Mon-Sat 1100-0200, Sun 1800-0200. Good pasta and light meals, crêpes, music. *Almuerzos* 1100-1600 for US$3. Atmospheric but service can be slow. And despite the name, there's a distinct shortage of books.

Café Hacheh, Pastor Sainz 233. Open 1000-0100. An unlikely but exceptionally good café and cultural centre, well worth the walk from the centre. The walls are adorned with lots of sexy designer nakedness, Chomsky and chess are laid out on tables and Pink Floyd plays on the stereo. Comfy chairs, crêpes, good value juices, tasty sandwiches, real fireplace. The '70s café of your dreams. Ring the bell to be let in.

Café Mirador, Plaza de la Recoleta, esq El Mirador, opposite Recoleta Monastery. T04-6440299. Tue-Sun 1000-1800. Has the best views of Sucre from its grassy terrace below the plaza. Fantastic iced cappuccino and equally good juices. Also omelettes, crêpes, pasta, cocktails. There's a book exchange too. The café is attached to the Tanga Tanga Museum.

Kultur-Café Berlin, Avaroa 326. Mon-Sat 0800-2400. A little slice of Germany. Part of a cultural centre (the Instituto Cultural Boliviano Alemán – ICBA) which includes a library and film room. Wooden tables, candles, arches, bar stools, wooden floor, black and white photos and letters, *Sureña* on tap, MTV on the TV. *Peña* every other Fri.

Potosí *p276, map p283*

¶¶ **El Fogón**, Oruro y Frías, T02-6224969. Upmarket pub-restaurant, good food and atmosphere, open 1200-1500, 1800-2400.

¶¶ **Museo del Ingenio San Marcos,** Attached to the museum (see map facing for location). Diners sit among the old machinery, creating a great atmosphere. Speciality is llama meat. Open 0800-2300.

¶ **Belén**, 6 de Agosto, just off the plaza, 0800-2300. Has an impressive colonial façade, Bolivian music, good pizza and wine, and ladders leading up to a mirador.

¶ **Kaypichu**, Millares 24. Tue-Sun 0700-1300 and 1600-2100. Good vegetarian food and an enormous selection of breakfasts. Quality of service mixed. Cultural events.

¶ **Potocchi**, Millares 13, T02-6222759. Great restaurant for typical Potosí food and drink, traditional breakfast of *api* 0800-1200 as well as good muesli, excellent llama meat and natural soups also popular *peñas* at 2100 on Tue, Fri, Sat and Sun with dancing and traditional costumes, cover charge US$1.50.

¶ **Sumaj Orcko**, Quijarro 46. Excellent and enormous portions and a cheap set lunch. The reasonably priced food is very popular with travellers, despite the blaring TV. Lots of meaty options on a big menu. Usually open and usually warm. Next door there's a **Sumaj Pub**, which has good heating, a TV with sport events and live music on a Fri night.

Cafés

Café Internet Calendaria, C Ayacucho 5. Daily from 0700. A part of the **Koala** mini empire, the slightly decrepit Calendaria is popular with travellers for its Bolivian food, balcony, book exchange, apple pie and travel guide library. Internet for US$0.40.

Café La Plata, Plaza 10 de Noviembre, corner with Linares, T02-6226085. Mon-Sat 1500-2200, also for breakfast. A great place to relax over a coffee, wine or beer. The home-baked cookies are delicious and there are games to play. Chic, warm and friendly, the owners speak English and French.

La Casona, Frías 34, T02-6222954. Mon-Sat 1000-1230, 1800-2400. Good food (try the meat fondue, the trout or one of the good salads) and beer. There are games, a laid-back atmosphere and good service. It's warm already but the hot wine also helps heat you up.

♠ Bars and clubs

Sucre *p273, map p274*
Joy Ride Café, Nicolás Ortiz 14, T04-6425544 www.joyridebol.com. Mon-Sat 0730 until late (usually around 0200), weekends from 0900. Dutch-run. Good vibes and a popular night time haunt with great food and drink. Four types of Belgian beer are among the drinks from the bar and if you're lucky you might even find some Guinness. Try the nachos, pique a lo macho, chilli con carne, or the 'hangover eggs' (eggs fried with cheese, ham, onion, tomato and a splash of chilli), which are talked about by

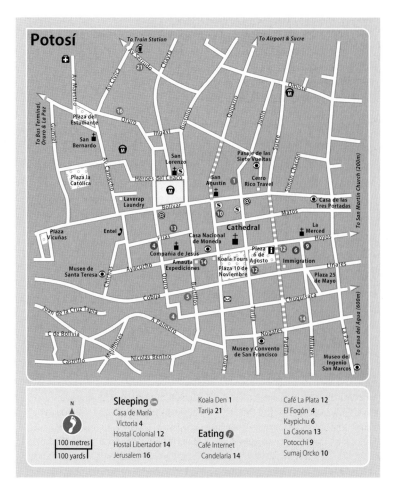

Potosí

travellers all over Bolivia. Good salads and a patio out the back with heating. A new, elegant and comfortable upstairs lounge with sofas has film showings Sun-Thu evenings. See also Tour operators, below, for details of their excellent biking and hiking trips.

Mitsubanía, Av del Maestro corner with Av Venzuela. Currently the most happening place, popular with a local, young, fashionable crowd, mixture of music with lots of cumbia, US$3 for men, women get in free.

⊕ Entertainment

Potosí *p276, map p283*
Peñas
Potocchi, Millares 13, T02-6222759. At 2100 on Tue, Fri, Sat and Sun, with dancing and traditional costumes, cover charge US$1.50 (see also Eating above).

⊛ Festivals and events

Sucre *p273, map p274*
Mar Phujllay in Tarabuco. One of the best traditional festivals in the country. It is held in celebration of the Battle of Jumbate when the local people defeated the Spaniards on 12 March 1816. It is a very colourful and lively affair with great music, local food and the obligatory *chicha*. No one sleeps during this fiesta so there are no accommodation problems.
16 Jul Fiesta de la Virgen del Carmen is similar to Alacitas in La Paz (see page 235).
8 Sep Virgen de Guadalupe is a 2-day fiesta, followed by folkloric fiesta with dances and costumes from across Bolivia.

Potosí *p276, map p283*
Feb or Mar Carnival Minero is celebrated 2 weeks before the Oruro Carnival, on a Sat and is known locally as *Tata Ckascho*. The miners parade and dance down Cerro Rico from the church near the top, to Plaza El Minero, carrying their god, El Tío. This is his one and only annual appearance outside the mine.

During Carnival itself, Shrove Tuesday is celebrated as **Martes de Cha'lla**, when offerings to Pachamama are made at the doors of people's houses and drinks are offered to passers-by. Ash Wednesday throughout the region is **Carnival Campesina** which lasts for 5 days, ending with **Domingo de Tentación** (Temptation Sunday) in many small villages. **8-10 Mar** is **San Juan de Dios**, with music, dancing and parades.

Aug On the 1st day, **Chutillo**, people walk to the village of La Puerta, 5 km from the centre on the Oruro road, to the church of San Bartolomé to pray and then climb the nearby hill. On day 2, **Majtillo**, indigenous people in costume from all over the department make their entrance into the city. Day 3 is **Thapuquillo**, when people from the city and invited groups from other parts of the country and abroad parade through the streets.

1st and 2nd Sun in Oct is Virgen de La Merced and Virgen del Rosario, with processions through decorated streets and people throwing flower petals on passing religious images.

⊙ Shopping

Sucre *p273, map p274*
Artesanías Calcha, Arce 103, opposite San Francisco Church. Recommended for handicrafts. The owner is very knowledgeable.
ASUR, Antropológicos del Sur Andino, in the **Museo Textil Etnográfico**, San Alberto 413, T04-6423841 (see also page 275). Sells weavings from around Tarabuco and from the Jalq'a; their weavings are more expensive, but of higher quality than elsewhere.
Chocolates Para Ti, San Alberto, just off the Plaza, T04-6454260, www.chocolates-para-ti.com. Chocaholics should note that Sucre is the chocolate capital of Bolivia, and this is one of its best chocolate shops.

→ **The legend of Chutillo**

Background

Legends abound surrounding the origins of the festival of Chutillo, one of Potosí's greatest annual celebrations, which runs from 24 to 26 August. Chutillo is the traditional name for a miner on muleback which is now given to the main participants in the festival – the jockeys who wear white capes. On the first day of the festival, the Chutillos ride on mules or donkeys to the chapel of San Bartolomé, also known as Cueva del Diablo (the Devil's Cave), near the village of La Puerta.

According to legend, an evil spirit called Umphurruna was banished from the House of Light and sent to earth. On the way, he saw Sapallay, the sun, and instantly fell in love with her. He carried her off to La Puerta, to hide her away from the prying eyes of men. With his mysterious power, he cut into two the huge cliffs, opening up a narrow winding passage through the middle. He took her into a dark cave. This became known as the Devil's cave and Unphurruna was given the name Chutillo, or genie who harms and then escapes. If anyone threatened to discover Devil's cave, the Chutillo would cause the cliffs to close together , thereby crushing them both to death.

This finally ended when the Jesuits of the Compañía de Jesús church in the newly-founded Villa Imperial de Carlos V took an image of the Apostle San Bartolomé and put it in a smaller cave near the Devil's residence. This caused the evil spirit to rush out screaming and smash into the cliff walls, leaving a greenish black mark which is still visible today.

Ever since then the people of Potosí have celebrated San Bartolomé by visiting the site of the cave each year.

Service can be a little unfriendly but there's a huge selection of handmade chocolates.
Mercado Central is clean and colourful, with a wide variety of goods and many stalls selling *artesanía*. There are also lots of *artesanía* shops on the pedestrianized part of Junín between Ravelo and Hernando Siles. A bus from the central market will take you to the Mercado Campesino market on the outskirts of town, which is a vast, sprawling affair, selling local produce, second-hand clothing and some *artesanía*.

Potosí *p276, map p283*
For musical instruments try Arnaud Gerard's workshop at the back of

Mercado Artesanal, which produces beautifully-made and tuned pieces, designed to be played, will make to order, open Mon-Fri 1700-1930.

Markets
Mercado Central, between Oruro, Bustillos, Héroes del Chaco and Bolívar, sells mainly food and produce, but silver is sold near the C Oruro entrance.
Mercado Artesanal, at Sucre y Omiste, sells jumpers, rugs, wall-hangings, bags, good musical instruments, some Fri the merchants organize music, food and drink (*ponche*), not to be missed.

Going further

Oruro Carnival

The normally cold, austere city of Oruro undergoes a complete transformation during its carnival. Over the week or so of celebrations the townsfolk go wild, so you can get hopelessly drunk with the locals, dance until you drop and in the process get soaked to the skin from a million water bombs. This is a rare opportunity to get involved in some serious partying with the indigenous people and not stand out like a sore thumb. You would be well advised not to miss it. For culture vultures this is also a fascinating insight into Aymara folk legends and a chance to enjoy some of the finest Bolivian music and dance. Carnival is a movable feast, usually held around the middle of February.

The main event is *Entrada* on Saturday. The parade ends at 0400 on Sunday when it reaches the Sanctuary of the Virgen del Socavón, where the dancers invoke her blessing and ask for pardon, accompanied by a cacophony of a dozen brass bands playing different tunes at the same time - a truly unforgettable experience. The *Entrada* is followed the next day (Sunday) by the *Gran Corso del Carnaval*, a very spectacular display. On Monday is *El Día del Diablo y del Moreno* in which the *Diablos* (Devils) and *Morenos* (black slaves), with their bands, compete against each other in demonstrations of dancing. Every group seems to join in the wonderfully chaotic spectacle. The action usually parades out of the amphitheatre, ending up at the Plaza de Armas. In the afternoon is the *Despedida de la Virgen* (Farewell to the Virgin). At dusk dancers and musicians go their separate ways, serenading until the early hours.

Many agencies in La Paz organize day trips from La Paz for the Saturday parade. They leave at 0430, most will pick you up from your hotel. They return at round 1600-1700, so you'll miss out on a lot of the fun. Trips cost US$30-45, and include breakfast and a snack. Alternatively, travel independently. There are numerous buses from La Paz from before sunrise till late at night, though

▲ Activities and tours

Sucre *p273, map p274*
Tour operators
Joy Ride Bolivia, C Mendizabal 229, T04-6425544, www.joyridebol.com. Speak to Gert or Hans at *Joy Ride Café* (see Eating). Recommended for top-quality bike trips and guided walks among the hills of Sucre's attractive surroundings. Includes full safety gear, insurance and experienced guides. Longer trips from 2-9 days can take in Uyuni, Tupiza and Santa Cruz; contact in advance. Prices are dependent on numbers but start at around US$18 per person per day. Paragliding is also possible though they no longer run motorbike or quad trips. Put your name on the blackboard in the café if you're interested in making up a group.

Potosí *p276, map p283*
Tour operators
All guides must have an ID card issued by the Prefectura and must work through an agency. If you go with a guide who is not working through an agency and

they charge up to three times as much as the normal fare. If you leave early enough, you should be able to find a seat. Otherwise, you'll have to join the masses standing along the route. Be sure to take a rain jacket or poncho as you're bound to get very wet from the thousands of flying water bombs. Better still, arm yourself to the teeth with your own water bombs.

Accommodation costs two to three times more than normal during Carnival and must be booked well in advance. Hotels charge for Friday, Saturday and Sunday nights. You can stay for only one night, but you'll be charged for three. A better idea, though, if you have the stamina, is to party all night on Saturday and return to La Paz by bus on Sunday - or even on Monday for serious party animals. Buses leave daily to La Paz at least every hour from 0400. Alternatively, take a train from Oruro to Uyuni, see page 297 for train times.

something goes wrong there is no insurance cover. If you want to book a Salar tour with a Potosí agency, check that they operate the service themselves – many of them subcontract and just put you on a bus to Uyuni. If you pay in Potosí and then have problems in Uyuni refunds can be difficult. It is difficult to differentiate between the agencies: they all offer (unless noted below) similar services including daily mine visits, city tours, trips to the thermal baths near Potosí, trekking to Kari-Kari or to Laguna Talacocha and trips to the Salar de Uyuni and Lagunas.

Amauta Expediciones, Ayacucho 17, T02-6225515, for trips to Uyuni, the lagoons and the mines. Claims to hand 15% of its income to the miners. Geronimo Fuertes, the owner, leads groups, of no more than 8 in size, and speaks good English and some French and Hebrew.
Andes Salt Expeditions, Plaza Alonso de Ibáñez 3 (eastern side of the plaza), T/F02-6225175, www.bolivia-travel.com.bo. English spoken, daily city tours. Also sell bus and flight tickets and run their own Uyuni tours. They have another office in Uyuni.

Cerro Rico Travel, Bolívar 853, T02-6227044, T02-71835083, jacky_gc@yahoo.com. Jaqueline knows the mines well and speaks good English. Also English and French guides for trips to village *artesanía* markets north of the city and to colonial *haciendas*, horse and mountain bike hire, treks in Kari Kari and Talacocha, trips to Toro Toro including cave visits, as well as visits to Sucre.

Koala Tours, C Ayacucho 5, T02-6224708, www.koalatoursbolivia.com. Excellent mine tours, guides are former miners and speak English, optional traditional breakfast or lunch including high protein, low fat llama meat, also *tinku* trips. Eduardo Garnica Fajardo, the owner, speaks English, French and some Hebrew. He rarely guides now but employs Juan Mamaní Choque who is also excellent. Also offer breakfast at 0600, a *plato típico* with llama meat. They also donate 15% of their US$10 fee to support on-site health-care facilities (donations can be sent to Eduardo Garnica). Also sell bus tickets, and run the **Koala Den** (see Sleeping).

⊖ Transport

Sucre *p273, map p274*
Air
Aero Sur and LAB fly to **La Paz** and **Santa Cruz**, LAB also flies to **Cochabamba**, **Tarija** and, like **Aero Sur**, to other parts of the country. Some are daily.
Airline offices Aero Sur, Arenales 31, T04-6462141, 204A, T04-6454895 (Toll free 0800 3030). **LAB**, Bustillos 127, T04-6454994, F04-6452666 (Toll free 0800 3001), Mon-Fri 0830-1230, 1430-1830, Sat 0900-1200.

Bus
All buses from Sucre bus terminal leave in the evening, except those to Potosí. There is an Enlace ATM outside and a post office inside (Mon-Sat 0800-1930, Sun 0900-1200).

Buses leave daily to/from **La Paz** at 1430 (**10 de Noviembre**, 16 hrs via Potosí, US$6), 1730 (**Flota Copacabana**,

buscama, 15 hrs, US$7.50), 1730 (**Trans Copacabana**, *buscama*, 15 hrs, US$10.45). To **Potosí**: frequently between 0630 and 1800, 3 hrs on a good paved road, US$2.25. **Silito Lindo** taxis take 4 people to Potosí with door-to-door service for US$5; T04-6441014.

To **Uyuni** at 0700 and 0800, 10 hrs, US$5.20. Alternatively you can catch a bus to Potosí and change. To **Santa Cruz** many companies go between 1600 and 1730, 15 hrs, from US$4.50.

Car hire
Imbex, Serrano 165, T04-6461222, F04-6912687. Well-maintained jeeps.

Around Sucre *p275*
Tarabuco
Buses (US$1.25) and trucks leave from 0630 or when full from Plaza Huallparimachi, Av Manco Kapac and across the railway tracks (take *micro* B or C from opposite the Mercado); 2½-hr journey. A taxi costs US$45. On Sun at least 1 bus will wait on Ravelo by the Mercado Central for travellers, leaves at 0700, US$3 return to Tarabuco. Shared taxis can be arranged by hotels, with a pick-up service, starting at 0700, US$3.25 return. The first bus back is at 1300. **AndesBus** run a tourist service which departs at 0800, and returns at 1530, US$6. Transport is more difficult on weekdays; take an early bus and return by truck. A good guide to Tarabuco is Alberto from the Sucre tourist office, US$45 for a full day in a car for 4 people.

The weavers' villages
There's regular transport to **Ravelo** from Parque Mariscal Sucre, or by the 1st bridge on the road to the airport. Most leave around 0700 with a few more until 1000; 3 hrs. Trucks back to Sucre are usually full. Daily buses to **Potolo**. A bus to **Llallagua**, passing through Ravelo, Macha, Ocuri and Uncia leaves on Thu at 1700, though the road isn't always passable in the wet season.

Potosí *p276, map p283*

Air

Aero Sur, C Hoyos 10 (T02-6222088), flies to **La Paz** 0800 Mon-Sat, 1 hr (La Paz to Potosí 0630 Mon-Sat). **TAM** fly on Mon from La Paz at 0830, returning at 1030.

Bus

To **La Paz** at 1830 and 1930, US$4.50, 11 hrs. *Bus-cama* from **Flota Copacabana** costs US$7.50. To **Sucre** at 0700, 1200, 1700 and 1800, US$3, 3 hrs. To **Santa Cruz** (must change in Sucre or Cochabamba) at 1900, US$12, 18 hrs. To **Uyuni** buses leave from either side of the railway line several blocks above the bus terminal (uphill the road is called Av Antofagasta or 9 de Abril, downhill it is Av Universitaria), daily at 1100 and 1830, US$4.75, 6-7 hrs, get there early or book in advance. **Emperador** runs to Uyuni from the terminal at 1200 (US$4.50).

ⓘ Directory

Sucre *p273, map p274*

Banks Most banks have ATMs for cash withdrawal and there are many Enlace ATMs around town. Travel agencies' rates are good and at **El Arca**, España 134, T04-6460189, good rates for TCs 3% commission into US$, commission-free for changing into Bolivianos. **Casa de Cambio Ambar**, San Alberto 7, T04-6451339. Good rates for TCs. The stalls at the corner of Camargo and Arce buy and sell dollars cash at good rates. **Cultural centres** Casa de la Cultura, Argentina 65, housed in a beautiful colonial building, presents art exhibitions, concerts, folk dancing etc, good breakfast in café, open Mon-Fri 0830-1230, 1400-2200, Sat and Sun 0830-1230. **Internet** There are many around town (especially on Colón) charging as little as US$0.25/hr but often with slow connections. **Café Internet Maya**, Arenales,

is not the cheapest, at US$0.50/hr, but it's well-equipped, well-situated just off the Plaza, and also has drinks. **Laundry** Laverap, Bolívar 617, quick, US$2.50 per full load. **Medical services Doctor**: Dr Gaston Delgadillo Lora, Colón 33, T04-6451692, speaks English, French, German, highly recommended. **Hospital**: Hospital Gastroenterológico Boliviano-Japonés, for stomach problems. **Post office** Ayacucho 100 y Junín, open Mon-Fri. **Police** T110 if in doubt about police or security matters.

Potosí *p276, map p283*

Banks You can find Enlace ATMs outside **Banco Mercantil**, Sucre, 9. Almost opposite is **Casa Fernández**, which changes US$ cash. **Banco Nacional**, Junín 4-6, between Bolívar and Matos changes dollar TCs and cash. **Banco de Crédito**, C Bolívar y Sucre. Cash withdrawals on Visa. **Internet** Tuko's Café, Junín 9, 3rd floor, 'the highest net café in the world' (4,100 m), T02-6225489, tuco25 @hotmail.com, daily 0800-2300, US$0.75/hr, good lunchtime food (burgers, llama meat and vegetarian), free city maps, tourist information, helpful English-speaking owners know pretty much everything about Potosí. **Laundry** Laverap, Camacho (next to Residencial San Andres), also at Quijarro, corner of Matos, Edificio Cademin, US$1.20 per kg, Mon-Sat 0800-1200, 1400-2000. **Medical services Clinics**: Clínica Británica, on Oruro near Alojamiento La Paz, clinics mornings and afternoons, English spoken. **Post office** Lanza 3, corner with Chuquisaca. Mon-Fri 0800-2000, Sat 0800-1930, Sun 0900-1200. **Telephone** Entel: on Plaza Arce at the end of Camacho between Frías and Bolívar, T02-6243496; also at Av Universitaria near the bus terminal. **Police** Pl 10 de Noviembre.

Southwest Bolivia

The remote southwestern corner of Bolivia stretches from the mining centre of Oruro, south to the borders of Chile and Argentina. There would appear to be little to attract the tourist to this barren plateau sitting on the roof of the world. It's a bleak, windswept terrain of parched scrub, with the occasional tiny adobe settlement blending into the uniform brown landscape. But tourists do come to this starkly beautiful corner of Bolivia, to enjoy some of the greatest visual delights that this country has to offer. In the far south is the Salar de Uyuni, an inconceivably vast expanse of blinding-white nothingness.

Further south, near the Chilean border, is a Salvador Dalí landscape of bizarre rock formations, white-capped volcanoes, sparkling soda lakes of jade and scarlet, filled with pink flamingos and steaming geysers.

⊘ **Getting there** Buses and trains to Uyuni from Oruro and Potosí.

⊜ **Getting around** 4WD tours of the salar and lagunas from Uyuni.

⊖ **Time required** 5-6 days including salar tour.

◈ **Weather** Skies are clear Jun-Jul, but any time of year is fine.

⊜ **Sleeping** Mostly budget hotels in Uyuni, basic accommodation on tours of salar.

⊘ **Eating** Mainly pizza but main concern is keeping warm at night.

▲▲ **Activities and tours** Salar de Uyuni and Lagunas.

★ **Don't miss...** A dip in a hot thermal spring with views of flamingos and volcanoes ►► p293.

Uyuni ⬤⬤⬤⬤▲⬤⬤ ⮞ *pp294-297*

Hot in the sun, cold in the shade and bitterly cold in the wind and at night, Uyuni is a railway junction founded in 1889 and the starting point for trips to the remote southwestern corner. Though once described as "a diamond encrusted in the shores of the Great Salar", Uyuni is no beauty. Once important, as the Bolivian railways have declined so has Uyuni. Despite the benefits of tourism, its functional architecture, wide, dust-blown streets and freezing winds lend it a strange, post-apocalyptic feel.

Ins and outs

Getting there and around Incoming (and outgoing) buses stop in Avenida Ferroviaria, between Arce and Bolívar. It is quite possible to spend your entire time in Uyuni within 150 m of this point. The majority of tour operators, hotels and restaurants and all the bus companies are in this area, with the station just to the south.

Tourist office There is an under-funded **tourist office** in the public clocktower on Avenida Potosí with Plaza Arce ⓘ *Mon-Fri 0900-1230, 1500-1930*. The **head office** ⓘ *Av Potosí 13, open Mon-Fri 0830-1200 and 1400-1830, Sat-Sun 0830-1200*, is where to go if you need to complain about a tour. ▲▲⮞ *p296 and box, p295*.

Sights

Once you've sorted out your **tour** there's not much to do in Uyuni, but if you have some time check out the **Cementerio de Trenes** (train cemetery) just over 1 km from the centre following Avenida Ferroviaria and then the railway line. Rusting steam engines and carriages decay slowly into the barren landscape. Some agencies throw in a swift visit at the end of a tour, thereby saving you the walk. **Pulcayo** is a small mining village northeast of Uyuni on the road to Potosí. The train cemetery here contains the first locomotive to enter Bolivia and a train robbed by Butch Cassidy and the Sundance Kid. There is a small mining museum which allows you to go underground. For times, call Señor Ciprian Nina at Uyuni tourist head office, T02-6932060.

Salar de Uyuni

The Salar de Uyuni is the highest and largest salt lake in the world at an altitude of 3,650 m and covering roughly 12,000 sq km, making it twice as big as the Great Salt Lake in the United States. Driving across it is one of the strangest, most fantastic experiences you will have, especially during June and July when the bright blue skies contrast with the blinding-white salt crust. After particularly wet rainy seasons the lake is covered in water which adds to the surreal experience. A trip to this corner of Bolivia would not be complete without continuing to see two of Bolivia's most isolated marvels, the bright red Laguna Colorada and jade green Laguna Verde. These spectacular soda lakes lie 350 km southwest of Uyuni, across a surreal desert landscape, and over unmarked, rugged truck tracks. Hundreds of pink flamingos standing in the midst of a shimmering salt lake is definitely a sight worth seeing. Tours run from Uyuni.

Ins and outs

A four-day tour across the Salar and down to Laguna Colorada and Laguna Verde in Reserva Eduardo Avaroa on the Chilean border is not to be missed, but note that this is a region of harsh extremes of climate. Temperatures can reach 30°C at midday and minus 25°C the following night. You'll need warm clothing and a good sleeping bag, and sunglasses are essential to avoid snowblindness. Many agencies will not send jeeps out when the Salar has reverted to a wet lake because the salt water destroys the engines; but shop around, someone will want your money.

South & Central Highlands Southwest Bolivia

Crossing the Salar

Some 20 km north of Uyuni is the tiny settlement of **Colchani**. A couple of minutes out of the village and you are on the salt. Workers from the village dig out piles of the stuff, which are then loaded onto trucks and taken back to the village to be ground and iodised before being sold. Next is **Hotel Playa Blanca**, 34 km from Uyuni, which apart from the roof is completely made of salt. It was closed down at the end of 2001 as a result of protests at the pollution the effluent was said to be causing. You will be allowed to take photos if you buy a drink or snack there. Suffering a similar fate is the adjacent and more upmarket **Palacio de Sal**.

It takes one to two hours from **Hotel Playa Blanca** (depending on the state of the Salar and your vehicle) to go the 80 km to **Isla de Pescadores**, which is in danger of being spoiled by development. There is even a branch of Mongo's (see La Paz page 234) bar-restaurant there and around the middle of the day the place crawls with visitors. That said, Isla de Pescadores is the most impressive of the 60-odd islands in the Salar. From among the giant cacti (some are more than 10 m high and many hundreds of years old) there are stunning views across the huge white expanse of salt to the mountains shimmering on the horizon.

In the dry season, most tours then head south across the Salar to the Colcha K military post (also known as Villa Martín) and on to **San Juan** to spend the night in a basic but clean *alojamiento* with hot showers (electricity 1900-2100). Ask your driver to take you out on to the Salar for an unforgettable sunset. **Toñito Tours** and **Colque Tours** both have their own hotels on the edge of the salt. If the Salar is under water, tours normally head back to Uyuni and then continue south on not so much terra firma but certainly terra drier.

South of the Salar

Tours continue south from San Juan, via Chiguana (a rail station and military post) and its small **Salar de Chiguana** to Laguna Hedionda. Or from Uyuni they head south, crossing the 50-cm-deep Río Grande to Villa Alota, a military checkpoint five hours away, with a number of very cheap *alojamientos*. Then on through striking collections of eroded rocks surrounded by snowcapped mountains to Laguna Hedionda in another two hours. One of these mountains – **Volcán Ollagüe** – is actually an active volcano and wisps of smoke can usually be seen coming from just below its summit. It's possible to organise a five-day tour which includes a visit to the volcano.

One of hundreds of old trains rusting away at the Cementerio de trenes.

The Arbol de Piedra.

Laguna Hedionda (literally, Stinking Lake, due to the sulphur) is popular with flamingos which are mainly white as the algae which create the pink colour are not so numerous in this lake. Continuing south, the route climbs up through a red-brown rock and sand landscape to reach the **Siloli Desert** at 4,600 m before dropping down to the bizarre **Arbol de Piedra** (rock tree), an improbably balanced piece of wind-eroded rock. It continues downwards and south to reach **Laguna Colorada** in around three hours from Laguna Hedionda.

Laguna Colorada and Laguna Verde

At 4,278 m high and 60 sq km, Laguna Colorada gets its name from the effect of wind and sun on the micro-organisms that live in it. The shores of the lake are encrusted with borax, used for soap and acid, which provides an arctic-white counterpoint to the blood-red waters. Up to midday, though, the lake is pretty normal coloured. The pink algae provide food for the rare James flamingos (the population here is the world's biggest), along with the more common Chilean and Andean flamingos, and also gives them their pink colour. Of the places to stay at Laguna Colorada, the REA (park authorities) run the best, a modern, clean, comfortable, warmish 34-bed refuge with kitchen and friendly guardian. Insist that your agency books you in there, though they will probably charge an extra Bs 10. There is also a dirty, waterless shack for US$3 per person, which remains popular with Uyuni agencies for some reason. Be careful with water – there's not much of it about.

An unpleasantly cold and early start on day three gets you to the **Sol de Mañana**, a 50-m-high steam geyser, for dawn. You then continue to the 30°C thermal waters at the edge of **Laguna Chalviri**, 30 minutes from the geysers. It's a pleasant spot and the first (and last) chance for a wash. You continue for an hour through the barren, landscape of the **Pampa de Chalviri** at 4,800 m, via a pass at 5,000 m, to the wind-lashed jade waters of **Laguna Verde** (Green Lake) at 4,400 m, the southernmost point of the tour. The stated causes of the lake's impressive colour range from magnesium, calcium carbonate, lead and arsenic. It covers 17 sq km and is at the foot of **Volcán Licancábur** (5,868 m) which is on the border between Bolivia and Chile.

From Laguna Verde, tours start the 400-km-plus journey back to Uyuni. There are a number of options for routes back; check out what your agency is offering. It is possible to go through the village of **Quetena**, Laguna Celeste (not possible during the wet season) and the *bofedales* (wet grassy areas popular with wildlife), but most take the route through

Salt piles dot the edges of the Salar de Uyuni.

the bizarre and impressive Valle de las Rocas near **Villa Alota**. All the eastern routes give views of huge glaciated mountains including **Uturuncu**, at 6,020 m, the highest in the area and the only one to exceed 6,000 m.

An attractive option is to stop at **San Cristóbal**, which is being touted as an alternative base to Uyuni with the help of some sustainable tourism funding. The town is actually brand new, having been moved from its original location in order to build Bolivia's biggest mine. The 17th-century church and churchyard, however, are original, having been moved wholesale. With the emphasis on 'adventure travel', San Cristóbal offers a **Mongo's Mad Max** bar and restaurant built from an enormous water tank, a hotel (D) and **Llama-Mama** mountain biking, www.llama-mama.com, an offshoot of La Paz's successful **Gravity Assisted Mountain Biking** (see page 237). There are condors in the area and lots of paths and bike tracks across the boulder fields with views across to the Salar. If you feel like getting off and not getting back in the jeep, you can buy tickets for onward travel from Uyuni here, and get the shuttle bus (US$2) to take you to the bus or train.

◉ Sleeping

Uyuni *p291, map p296*
It can be difficult to find a bed in the better hotels if you're arriving around 0500-0600 in the high season.
C **Kory Wasy**, Av Potosí 350, T03-6932670, kory_wasy@ hotmail.com. D in low season. Pretty basic for the price but good fun, with doors made from cactus wood and decorated with carved Indian heads; the sun streams through to the lobby and owner Lucy Laime de Pérez is very friendly. Also has its own tour agency and a restaurant on-site. Private bathrooms, heating is promised soon and

the price includes breakfast. Some rooms are dark.
C **La Casita Toñito**, 60 Av Ferroviaria, T02- 6933186, www.bolivianexpeditions. com/hotel.htm. A modern hotel with cable TV, internet, laundry, restaurant, heating in rooms, parking and big beds. Owned by **Toñito Tours** (see page 296), who will try to persuade you to go on one of their tours.
D **Mágia de Uyuni**, Av Colón between Sucre and Camacho, T02-6932541, magia_uyuni @latinmail.com. All rooms with private bathroom, price includes breakfast.

Top tips

Tours worth their salt

✅ Of the two dozen or so agencies in Uyuni, very few can be recommended without reservation and even those are by no means perfect. Companies pass in and out of favour. Speak to travellers who have just returned from a tour and try the agencies listed on page 296.

✅ Most agencies are open until at least 2000 so you can arrive, organize a tour and leave the next day. It is also not difficult to arrive during the night and get on a tour in the morning. Most don't leave until 1000. All accept traveller's cheques, and some take credit cards.

✅ The standard four-day trip (Salar de Uyuni, Lagunas Colorada and Verde) costs from US$65 up to US$220 per person depending on the agency and season and where it leaves from.

✅ Trip prices are based on a six-person group. Normally the agencies will form groups, otherwise you may have to find others to make up the numbers. This is easy in the high season (April-September). Outside this period, it is worth getting a group together before arriving. If there are fewer than six you each pay more. There is no discount for having seven people and it is uncomfortable.

✅ Take a good sleeping bag, sunglasses, sun hat, sun protection, lots of warm clothing, six litres of bottled water or water purification tablets or iodine tincture, lots of film or memory cards and your own Cds (or ipod). Snacks are a good idea too.

✅ A good tip for freezing nights on the Salar or at Laguna Colorada is to fill a water bottle with hot water last thing at night, wrap it in a sock and use it as a sleeping bag warmer. If you're lucky it might still be lukewarm for washing with the next day.

✅ It's possible to do the tour in a far more adventurous way. **Llama Mama** (www.llama-mam.com) does it on mountain bikes when the Salar is not flooded.

❌ Agencies in Potosí also organize tours, but this mainly involves putting you on a bus to Uyuni where you meet up with one of the Uyuni agencies and get the same quality tour for a higher price.

🍴 Eating

Uyuni *p291, map p296*
Avoid eating in the market. Uyuni wouldn't be a good place to get ill, worse still if you fell sick on a tour.

🍴 **Arco Iris**, Plaza Arce. The best pizza and huge pasta portions but, if it's busy, service takes an early exit.

🍴 **Cafeteria Confiteria**, Plaza Arce. Decent café and breakfast place in the middle of the square. A good place from which to watch the world go by.

🍴 **La Loco**, Av Potosí. Gringo grub plus open fires and music and drinks until late make this 'restaurant-bar-pub' a popular evening hang-out.

🍴 **San Gaetano**, Plaza Arce. A trendy restaurant with loud music, bare stone, seats outside, a warm fire in middle of the room and good breakfasts on sunny side of plaza.

🎵 Entertainment

Uyuni *p291, map p296*
One way of forgetting the night-time sensation of being locked in a deep-freeze is to pay **Universal 'Cinema'** a visit at Bolívar 60. For just US$0.90, squeeze into a 6-seat 'auditorium' to watch one of 1,000 English-language videos of your choice. The fee includes a hot drink. Open 1400-2200 every day.

🛍 Shopping

Uyuni *p291, map p296*
The **market** at Av Arce esquina Colón sells the basics. There is also a smaller **indoor market** on C Bolívar above Av Ferroviaria and another at Avaroa. Fleece jackets, scarves, long wool socks and other warm clothes are available from a shop on C Bolívar below Potosí.

⛰ Activities and tours

Uyuni *p291, map p296*
Tour operators
The tour companies listed below have been recommended, though even recommended companies have their off days. See also box, p295.
Colque Tours, Av Potosí 54, T02-6932199, www.colquetours.com. Can pay by Visa, Mastercard for a US$2 fee. The most popular agency, but not necessarily the best. There have been bad reports about the way they deal with complaints. Colque specialize in tours ending up in San Pedro de Atacama, in Chile, where they have an office offering the trip in reverse. Even if you're heading back north to La Paz, the route through Chile may not be a bad idea – it's easy to find transport via Arica and the roads are substantially smoother. However, don't let Colque bully you into this – remember that it's in their interests to have empty jeeps for their return tours.

South & Central Highlands Southwest Bolivia Listings

Uyuni

To Colchani & El Salar

Av Arce

Av Colón

Sucre

Bolívar

Avaroa

Colque Tours

Av Potosí

Immigration

Plaza Arce

Universal Cinema

To Train Cemetery (1 km)

Toñito Tours Main Office

Esmeralda Tours

Transandino Tours

Toñito Tours

Lavarap Laundry

Av Ferroviaria

Railworker's Monument

To Tupiza

N

50 metres
50 yards

Sleeping ●
Kory Wasy **3**
La Casita Toñito **5**
Mágia de Uyuni **6**

Eating ●
Arco Iris **2**
Cafetería Confitería **6**
La Loco **1**
San Gaetano **7**

Esmeralda, Av Ferroviaria esquina Arce, T02-6932130. Good tours at the cheaper end of price bracket.

Toñito, Av Ferroviaria 152, T02-6932819, www.bolivianexpeditions.com. Toñito own a hotel by the Salar and also have an office in La Paz (see page 236) which will book transport to and from Uyuni.

Transandino, Plaza Arce 2, T02-6932132. **Uyuni Andes Travel Office**, Ayacucho 222, T02-6932227. Good reports, run by Belgians Isabelle and Iver.

Licancabur, Sucre s/n, T02-6932667. Incorporates the usual trip with a journey to Tupiza, passing several beautiful and seldom-visited lagoons on the way.

⊖ Transport

Uyuni *p291, map p296*
Bus

All the bus offices are on Av Arce, on the same block as the post office. Departures are daily unless otherwise stated.
To **La Paz** (change at Oruro) 2000 (also 1930 every day with **Belgrano** except Thu when they leave at 2100), US$7.45, 11-13 hrs. **Panasur** go direct Wed and Sun at 1800. From La Paz, **Panasur** leave the bus terminal (office 39) every day at 1730 and arrive at 0730 (change at Oruro, direct Tue and Fri). To **Oruro** at 2000, (also 1930 every day with **Belgrano** except Thu when they leave at 2100), US$3, 8 hrs (take a sleeping bag, or blanket). To **Potosí** 1000 and 1900, US$3, 5-7 hrs (spectacular journey). To **Sucre** 1000, 1900, US$3.75, 9-10 hrs.

Jeep

Trans Expreso Rapido, T02-6932839, office in same place as bus companies, goes to **Potosí** and **Oruro** by special charter US$150 for up to 10 people, 5 hrs. **Colque Tours** also runs jeep trips to **Potosí**, US$200 for 6-7 people.

Train

There are 2 companies running services from **Oruro** to **Uyuni**. Nuevo Expreso del Sur leaves on Mon and Fri at 1530, arriving in Uyuni at 2156 (*Premiere Class* US$7.75, *Salon* US$5.40); **Wara Wara del Sur** leaves on Sun and Wed at 1900, arriving in Uyuni at 0200 (Salon US$4.20). From **Uyuni to Oruro**: Nuevo Expreso del Sur leaves on Tue and Sat at 2352, arriving 0625 (*Premiere* US$7.75; *Salon* US$5.40). The **Wara Wara del Sur** service leaves on Mon and Thu at 0122, arriving 0825 (*Salón* US$4.20). Check train services on arrival, T02-6932153. The ticket office opens at 0830 and 1430 each day and 1 hr before the trains leave. It closes once tickets are sold – get there early or buy through a tour agent.

⊕ Directory

Uyuni *p291, map p296*
Banks Banco de Crédito, Av Potosí, between Bolivar and Arce, does not change money, though they may give cash advances from credit cards. The exchange shop to its left changes US dollars or Chilean pesos as well as TCs as does a cambio almost opposite M@c Internet Café on Av Potosí (see below). Hotel Avenida changes dollars cash. Some shops will change cash dollars for Bolivianos. All agencies and some shops accept payment in TCs.
Internet US$1.50 per hr: M@cNet, Av Potosí near Arce, open every day 0900-2300 or later if you ask, fast satellite connection. Servinet Uyuni, Potosí y Bolívar, open every day 0800-1300, 1400-2200.
Laundry Lavarap laundry, Av Ferroviaria 253. Also at hotels. **Post office** Av Arce corner with Cabrera, Mon-Thu 0830-1200, 1400-1900, Fri 0830-1900, Sat and Sun 0900-1200.
Telephone Entel at Av Arce above Av Potosí, 0830-2200. **Useful addresses** Immigration at Av Potosí corner with Sucre, open 0800-2000 every day, for visa extensions; don't leave it to the last minute as often the officer is at the new border exit offices.

Eastern Bolivia

Noel Kempff Mercado National Park

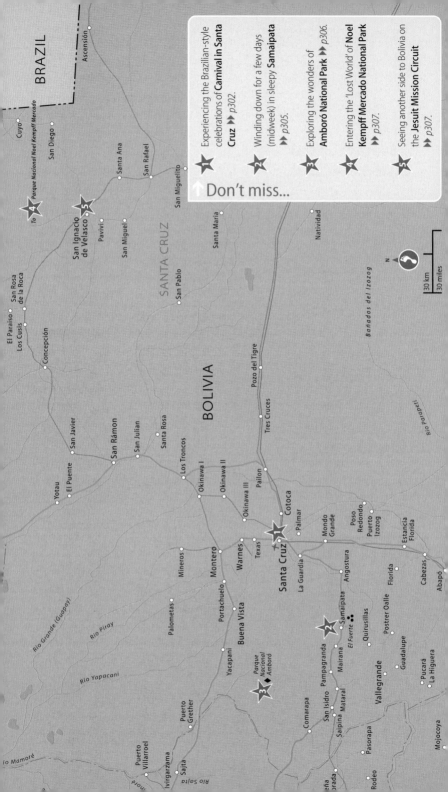

BRAZIL

Parque Nacional Noel Kempff Mercado

Ascensión
Cuyo
San Diego
Santa Ana
San Rafael
San Miguelito

To **4**

5 San Ignacio de Velasco
Pavivi
San Miguel
Santa María
Natividad

SANTA CRUZ

San Pablo

El Paraíso
Los Cusis
San Rosa de la Roca
Concepción

Pozo del Tigre

BOLIVIA

Tres Cruces

Bañados del Izozog

San Javier
San Rámon
Santa Rosa

RÍO PARAPETÍ

Yotau
El Puente
San Julian
Los Troncos

Palometas
Mineros
Okinawa I
Okinawa II
Okinawa III
Pailón
Cotoca
Palmar
Mondo Grande
Poso Redondo
Puerto Izozog
Estancia Florida

Montero
Warnes
Texas

1 Santa Cruz

Portachuelo
La Guardia
Angostura
Florida
Cabezas
Abapó

Río Grande (Guapay)
Río Piray
Buena Vista
Yacapaní

Puerto Grether
Río Yapacani

Parque Nacional Amboró **3**

San Isidro
Pampagranda
Comarapa
Saipina
Mairana
Mataral

2 Samaipata
El Fuerte
Quirusillas
Postrer Oalle
Guadalupe
Pucará
La Higuera

Vallegrande

Puerto Villarroel
Ivirgarzama
Salta
Río Solto
Rodeo
Pasorapa
Mojocoya

lo Mamoré

N
30 km
30 miles

↑ Don't miss...

1 Experiencing the Brazilian-style celebrations of **Carnival in Santa Cruz** ▶▶ *p302.*

2 Winding down for a few days (midweek) in sleepy **Samaipata** ▶▶ *p305.*

3 Exploring the wonders of **Amboró National Park** ▶▶ *p306.*

4 Entering the 'Lost World' of **Noel Kempff Mercado National Park** ▶▶ *p307.*

5 Seeing another side to Bolivia on the **Jesuit Mission Circuit** ▶▶ *p307.*

The vast eastern lowlands of Bolivia are the area of the country richest in natural resources. Bordered by Brazil to the east and Paraguay to the south, this region comprises most of the enormous Santa Cruz Department, which makes up almost 34% of Bolivia's territory and at 370,621 sq km (144,542 sq miles) is larger than Germany. The capital of the region, Santa Cruz is a booming modern city, more in tune with neighbouring Brazil and a world away from most people's image of Bolivia. It marks the jumping-off point for travels to one of the least-explored and most fascinating parts of Bolivia. To the northeast are the Jesuit Missions, a string of seven dusty cattle towns, each boasting a Jesuit church more beautiful than the next. Only three hours away are Amboró National Park, one of the country's truly great natural experiences and Samaipata, weekend retreat for Cruceños and an increasingly major player on the gringo circuit. One of the very few places to surpass Amboró in its bio-diversity is the remote and stunningly beautiful Noel Kempff Mercado National Park, in the far northeast of Santa Cruz Department, said to have been the inspiration for Sir Arthur Conan Doyle's famous Lost World.

Introduction

Eastern Bolivia

Ratings

Culture
★★★

Landscape
★★★★

Wildlife
★★★★★

Activities
★★★★

Chillin'
★★★★

Costs
$$$$-$$$

Santa Cruz has taken over from La Paz as Bolivia's largest city, with a population of roughly 1.3 million. This vast, swelteringly hot place, grown rich on oil, agriculture and and narco dollars, has largely returned to its less opulent roots, although "agribusiness" is still an important economic concern. The economic downturn has brought about a downsizing of its once many wealthy barrios, but the colonial centre remains its heartbeat. Its narrow, congested streets are lined with low, red-tiled roofs with overhanging eaves, giving much-needed relief from the fierce sun. The people of Santa Cruz – cambas – are generally more open and laid-back than their Andean counterparts. Their relaxed, fun-loving attitude is especially clear during Carnival, when proceedings can reach near-Brazilian levels of hedonism and excess.

✈ **Getting there** Regular flights and buses from La Paz and Sucre.
⊖ **Getting around** Regular transport to Samaipata, buses to Jesuit Missions, tours to Amboró and Noel Kempff Mercado.
⊖ **Time rquired** 2-3 days for Samaipata, more for Amboró; 6-7 days for Jesuit Missions.
☼ **Weather** Dry season May-Sep; rainy season Dec-Feb.
⊖ **Sleeping** Plenty of mid-range to expensive in Santa Cruz; good mid-range options in Samaipata.
✪ **Eating** International and regional in Santa Cruz; superb German cuisine in Samaipata.
▲▲ **Activities and tours** Tours to Amboró and Noel Kempff Mercado from Samaipata or Santa Cruz; to Jesuit Missions from Santa Cruz.
★ **Don't miss...** A trip to Noel Kempff Mercado ⟫ *p307*.

Santa Cruz ⊖✪⊖⊖⊛⊖⊡▲⊟⊙ ⟫ *pp308-315*

Ins and outs

Getting there Air The international airport is at Viru Viru, about 13 km from town (T181 for information). The airport bus runs every 20 minutes to and from the terminal to the city centre (25 minutes, US$0.70, operates 0530-2030). Taxis to town cost US$8.50. The airport has an emigration/immigration office, **Entel** office, luggage lockers, three duty-free shops and coffee shops. The bank, open 0830-1830, changes cash and traveller's cheques and cash can be withdrawn using Visa and Mastercard. When the bank is closed try the **AASANA** desk, where you pay airport tax (US$25 for international departures). There's a **Tourist Information kiosk** in the check-in hall, where English is spoken (free maps available).

Bus The huge new bus terminal, the **Terminal Bimodal**, for long-distance arrivals, is in the same place as the train station, on Avenida Montes between Avenida Brasil and Tres Pasos al Frente, between the second and third *anillo* (ring), T03-348 8382. There's also a bank, infirmary, luggage store and restaurants. Take a number 12 bus to/from the centre, or a taxi (US$1.50 – catch it from outside the terminal, it's cheaper). Local buses also use the new terminal.

Train The train station for east-bound trains to Puerto Suárez/Quijarro, for crossing into Brazil (see page 314), is in the same place as the long-distance bus terminal (see above), T03-346 3900, extension 307/303. They depart every day except Sunday. ⊖ ⟫ *p314*.

Information **Tourist office** ⓘ *in the Prefectura del Departamento, on the north side of the* *main plaza, T03-332770, extension 144, 0800-1600 daily.* Along with some cultural and historical videos and exhibits, they have a free and very useful city map, as do many hotels and tour agents; the map in this chapter shows the roads only in the heart of the city. There's also an information kiosk at the airport.

Orientation The city has 10 ring roads, referred to as *anillos* 1, 2, 3, 4, and so on. Equipetrol suburb, where many of the better hotels and bars are situated, is northwest of the heart of the city, between *anillos* 2 and 3; Avenida San Martin is one of its principal streets.

Climate It is usually hot and windswept from May to August. But when the cold *surazo* wind blows from the Argentine *pampas* during these months the temperature drops sharply. The rainy season is December-February.

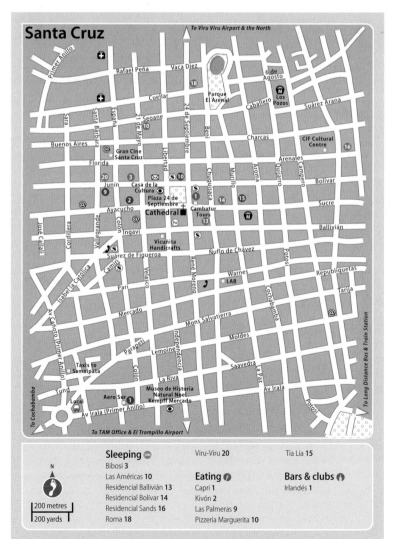

Sleeping 🛏
Bibosi **3**
Las Américas **10**
Residencial Ballivián **13**
Residencial Bolívar **14**
Residencial Sands **16**
Roma **18**

Viru-Viru **20**

Eating 🍴
Capri **1**
Kivón **2**
Las Palmeras **9**
Pizzeria Marguerita **10**

Tia Lia **15**

Bars & clubs 🍸
Irlandés **1**

N
200 metres
200 yards

Plaza 24 de Septiembre is a good place to watch Cruceño inaction.

Sights

The **Plaza 24 de Septiembre** is the city's main square, where people are so unhurried they would make the sloths who used to live in the trees here look uptight. The last sloth was removed from here in 2001 because of pollution and tree disease and there are no plans to introduce any new ones. Facing onto the plaza is the imposing brick-fronted **St Lawrence Cathedral** ⓘ *Tue, Thu, Sun 1000-1200, 1600-1800, US$0.60,* (now technically a minor basilica after Pope John Paul II's visit in 1988), with its wonderfully cool interior and a museum containing what is considered the smallest book in the world, at only 7 sq mm. The city's **Casa de la Cultura "Raúl Otero Reiche"** is also on the plaza. It hosts occasional exhibitions, an archaeological display, plays, recitals, concerts and folk dancing. It also has a wonderful free gallery devoted to the works of Bolivia's beloved painter, Armando Jordan, on the second floor. Also part of the complex is the **Museo Historical y Archivo Regional de Santa Cruz de la Sierra** ⓘ *T03-336 5533, Mon-Fri 0830-1200, 1500-1800, occasionally Sat as well,* which has several displays ranging from ceramics to explorers' routes to native handicrafts. Perhaps its finest attribute, however, is a small shop run by the non-profit group **La Mancomunidad**, where handcrafted and signed carvings, hammocks, fabrics, and jewellery can be purchased. These are made by indigenous peoples, from non-threatened woods, and all proceeds are returned to the craftsmen. The **Museo de Historia Natural Noel Kempff Mercado** ⓘ *Av Irala 565, between Velasco y Independencia, T/F03-337 1216, www.museonoelkempff.org, Mon-Fri 0800-1200, also 1500-1830 Mon and Tue, US$0.12,* has a video library. Contact them for trips and information to Noel Kempff Mercado National Park (see page 307).

An interesting area is the **Mercado Los Pozos**, which encompasses almost all of calles Quijarro, Campero, Suárez Arana, and 6 de Agosto. Here you'll see large numbers of Mennonites in their traditional clothing – the men in their high-crowned cowboy hats, check shirts and denim dungarees, the women in dark, full-length dresses, shawls and full-brimmed hats.

Samaipata and Amboró ⊜⊘⊙⛰⊜❻ ⊮ pp308-315

West from Santa Cruz on a paved and spectacular road, Samaipata is set to be one of the next big destinations but is still far enough off the beaten track to attract the more adventurous traveller. This is no sleepy, laid-back little town, however. At the weekend it bursts into life when crowds of visitors from Santa Cruz come to escape the oppressive heat and party with a vengeance. Close by is El Fuerte, one of the country's major pre-Columbian sites. Samaipata is also a major gateway into **Amboró National Park** (see next page). There's no tourist office but all the tour operators offer free information. **Roadrunners** are particularly helpful. They will arrange the purchase of tickets for buses heading to Sucre so you don't have to return to Santa Cruz; give them 24 hours notice. They'll also take bookings for *colectivos* to Santa Cruz. ⊜ ⊮ *p315.*

Sights

The **Centro de Investigaciones Arqueológicos y Antropológicas Samaipata** ⓘ *2 blocks east and 1 block north of the plaza, daily 0930-1230, 1430-1830, US$0.75, US$3 for museum and El Fuerte,* provides a valuable introduction to the nearby pre-Inca ceremonial site known as **El Fuerte**. The carved rock can no longer be walked upon at the ancient site so it is vital to see the museum's model. There is also a collection of pre-Inca lowland ceramics with anthropomorphic designs dating from around AD 300 and a good mock-up of the cave near Mataral. English-speaking Olaf Liebhart of **Roadrunners** gives an enthusiastic tour of the museum included in his El Fuerte trip which really brings it to life.

Nine kilometres east of Samaipata, and often besieged by ferocious winds, **El Fuerte** ⓘ *daily 0900-1700 US$3, ticket also valid for the museum in town,* is Bolivia's second-most visited pre-Columbian site after Tiahuanaco. There is convincing evidence this was the easternmost fortress of the Incas' Bolivian Empire. The site is 3 km along the highway, then 6 km up a signposted road. It's a 2-hour walk one-way but you really need at least 1 ½ hrs to explore the sight so it's better to take a *colectivo* taxi there (US$4.50 one-way for 1-4 people) and walk back. A round trip to the ruins by taxi from Santa Cruz will cost around US$40. Don't cut it fine – visitors must be out of the restricted zone by 1700 and this is 2 km from the ruins.

El Fuerte's chief attraction is its vast carved rock, a sacred structure which consists of a complex system of channels, basins and high-relief sculpture. The rock is 240 m by 40 m and

The huge pre-Colombian ceremonial site of El Fuerte.

Eastern Bolivia Santa Cruz & eastern lowlands

66 99 Clear as crystal, motionless as a sheet of glass, green as the edge of an iceberg, it stretched in front of us under its leafy archway, every stroke of our paddles sending a thousand ripples across its shining surface. It was a fitting avenue to a land of wonders.

Sir Arthur Conan Doyle, The Lost World

10-m high, the biggest in South America. In front is a circular relief of a puma and alongside two others, badly eroded. The wall further back forms the remains of the temple of the jaguar. Also further back are the beautiful, 24 m-long patterned channels. These are thought to symbolize rattlesnakes and sacrificial blood and, during Inca rituals, *chicha* (corn beer) released from the central temple would wriggle its way down the criss-cross rhombus carvings like a moving snake. The rest of the site, sadly, is poorly restored and overgrown. Finish by climbing to the viewpoint from where the rock can be best appreciated.

Parque Nacional Amboró

Bolivia's best-known protected area is Parque Nacional Amboró, a 637,600-ha territory only three hours west of Santa Cruz. This is one of the last untouched wildernesses on earth and a place of special beauty. The park encompasses three distinct major ecosystems – those of the Amazon River basin, the foothills of the Andes mountains, and the Chaco plain – and 11 life zones. The park is home to thousands of animal, bird, plant, and insect species, and is reputed to contain more butterflies than anywhere else on earth. In total, 712 species of bird have been discovered. Most mammals native to Amazonia are also here. They include capybaras, peccaries, tapirs, several species of monkey such as howlers and capuchins, jungle cats like the jaguar, ocelot and margay, and the increasingly rare spectacled bear, the only one found in South America. There are numerous tributaries of the Yapacani and Surutú rivers to explore, as well as numerous waterfalls and cool green swimming pools, moss-ridden caves and the fragile yet awe-inspiring virgin rainforest.

Penetration into the park's more remote areas should always be undertaken with an experienced guide or as part of an organized tour. Much of the park is wet all year round and many of the routes are riverine or along poorly (if at all) marked trails. A good supply of food and water, insect repellent, a machete, good boots and long-sleeved shirts and long trousers are a must. The best time of year to visit the park is during the May-October dry season. Tours can be organized from Samaipata (see page 311) or little Buena Vista (see page 314), a sleepy, friendly old place, reached via the lowland route from Santa Cruz to Cochabamba. Some of the hotels in Buena Vista also organize trips around the park. There is a **park information office**, just over a block away from the plaza in Buena Vista. They have information and advice on the park and some maps. They can also help with guides and suggestions and will issue a permit. There is no park fee as yet. As well as a slew of websites, sources of extensive inside knowledge are Pieter and Margarita de Radd, who operate the wonderful **Cabañas La Víspera** and tour agency **Boliviajes** in Samaipata (see page 311). The park is managed by **Fundacíon Amigos de la Naturaleza (FAN)** ⓘ *Santa Cruz office at the intersection of C Sucre and Murillo, T03-944 6017, www.fan-bo.org.rs.*

▶▶ **Parque Nacional Noel Kempff Mercado**

In the remote northeast corner of Santa Cruz Department is Parque Nacional Noel Kempff Mercado, one of the world's most stunningly diverse natural habitats. The park is astonishing in every way, especially for its Amazonian forests, spectacular waterfalls (the Catarata el Encanto, Arco Irís, and Federico Ahlfeld especially), and eerie-looking mountain ranges (serranías). There are seven distinct ecosystems within the park, the highest number in any single protected area anywhere on earth. The wildlife count in the park is staggering – so far over 620 bird species have been identified, which is approximately one-quarter of all the birds in the neotropics. Among the many large mammals frequently sighted are the tapir, grey and red brocket deer, silvery marmoset, and spider and black howler monkeys. Giant otter and capybara are relatively common along the Iténez and Paucerna rivers, as are jabiru and the maguari stork. Giant anteaters, marsh deer and the rare maned wolf inhabit the western grasslands and the endangered pampas deer roam the dry twisted forest of the Huanchaca Plateau. There's also a chance of seeing jaguars where the narrow Río Paucerna winds its way through dense towering rainforest on its way to join the Río Iténez.

Access to Noel Kempff Mercado, given its size, remains limited. Its remoteness has not only helped to preserve this great bio-diversity, but has also placed the park out of the reach of most travellers. The best known of the various routes into the park is by air, through Flor de Oro, a small border town along the Río Guapore with a tourist lodge run by **Fundacion Amigos de la Naturaleza** (FAN). It can be reached by a five-hour plane ride from Santa Cruz. Alternatively, you can fly directly from Santa Cruz to Los Fierros (two hours). Flights are sporadic, and all are arranged by Fundación Amigos de la Naturaleza (FAN), who manage the park ⓘ *Km. 7 1/2, Carretera Antigua a Cochabamba, Santa Cruz; T03-354 7383; F03-355 6800; www.fan-bo.org*. Another good source is the Proyecto de Acción Climática's website (in English or Spanish), www.noelkempff.com.

Sleeping and tours

Because of its enormous environmental importance, accommodation within Noel Kempff Mercado is deliberately kept to a minimum, and should be arranged in advance through FAN. There is a lodging in the park, at Los Fierros Camp, where cabins cost US$20 and up per person and include 3 meals for another US$20, and a campsite, US$10 per person plus US$5 to cook. There are also campsites at Ahlfeld and Flor de Oro, which also boasts an ecolodge. For details on organized trips into the park contact **International Expeditions Incorporated**, One Environs Park, Helena, AL 35080, USA, F205-428 1714, intlexp@aol.com. **Amboró Tours** in Samaipata (see page 311) runs trips for US$500 for 6 days all-inclusive travelling by jeep and staying in tents.

● Sleeping

Santa Cruz *p302, map p303*

Accommodation is relatively expensive here and good value mid-and-lower-range hotels are hard to find, but several of the 4- and 5-star hotels offer excellent package deals. Most of the budget hotels are to be found near the old bus terminal.

A Las Américas, 21 de Mayo esquina Seoane, T03-336 8778, F333 6083. A/c , discount for longer stay, parking, arranges tours and car rental, restaurant, bar, 4-star hotel, 5-star service. Excellent value in this price bracket.

B Viru-Viru, Junín 338, T03-333 5298, F336 7500. Includes breakfast, a/c, cheaper rooms with fan, pool, pleasant and central. Tour agency next door.

C Roma, 24 de Septiembre 530, T03-332 3299, F333 8388. Pleasant, a/c, cable TV, good value, helpful.

C-D Bibosi, Junín 218, T03-334 8548, F334 8887. Cheaper with shared bathroom. Cable TV, electric showers, although the bedrooms need a revamp, internet, continental buffet breakfast included.

E Residencial Sands, Arenales 749, 7 blocks east of the main square, T03-337 7776. Unbelievable value, better than some in higher price brackets – stylish 3-star standard rooms have cable TV, ceiling fans, telephone and very comfortable beds. There's even a pool.

E-F Residencial Bolívar, Sucre 131, T03-334 2500. Cheaper with shared bathroom. Hot showers, courtyard with hammocks and toucan, breakfast for US$2.10.

F Residencial Ballivián, Ballivián 71, T03-332 1960. Basic, shared hot showers, patio.

Samaipata *p305, map p308*

Accommodation in and around the town may be difficult to find at weekends in the high season but midweek the better hotels and resorts are willing to negotiate and there are some good discounts available. Most of the *cabañas,* or cabins, listed below are fully equipped with kitchens,

bathrooms and barbecues and if you turn up unannounced and there's space they'll let you sleep in a hammock outside (E).

C Landhaus, T03-944 6033. Most central of all the *cabañas*. Beautiful place with a small pool, sun loungers, garden, hammocks, parking, internet and sauna (US$20 for up to 8 people). A group of 7 can rent a house here for US$70, also has rooms only with shared bathroom (F).

C La Víspera, 1.2 km south of town, T03-944 6082, vispera@entelnet.bo. Dutch-owned organic farm with accommodation in 4 cosy cabins, 2 of which sleep up to 2, another up to 7 and another up to 12. Can provide delicious local produce for breakfast, US$3 per person. It's a very peaceful place to stay. Margarita and Pieter know plenty about the local area and can arrange all excursions. They also sell medicinal and seasoning herbs and spices.

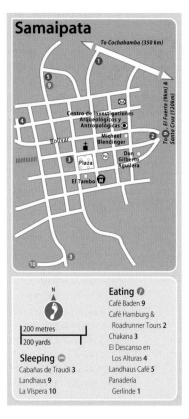

Samaipata

Eating ●
Café Baden 9
Café Hamburg & Roadrunner Tours 2
Chakana 3
El Descanso en Los Alturas 4
Landhaus Café 5
Panadería Gerlinde 1

Sleeping ●
Cabañas de Traudi 3
Landhaus 9
La Víspera 10

200 metres
200 yards

C-F **Cabañas de Traudi**, T03-944 6094, traudiar@cotas.com.bo. Has individually designed and decorated large cabins for 2-8, also (**E**) lovely rooms (**F** with shared bathroom), heated pool US$1.50 for non residents, sitting area with open fire, TV and music system, ceramics shop and lessons, a great place.

Parque Nacional Amboró
The best option for accommodation is in Buena Vista. All accommodation within the park is basic and should be secured before entry. This is done by registering in person at the **Amboró National Park Headquarters** in Buena Vista. Expect to pay about US$2 per person.
B Pozazul, out on the bypass, Buena Vista, T03-932 2091. A/c, clean, kitchen, pool, restaurant, friendly and helpful owners, also **A** *cabañas* and camping for US$14 per person night with use of showers and pool.
D Cabañas Quimori, Buena Vista. Prices negotiable in low season, includes buffet breakfast, shared kitchen and hammocks, building a pool, offer guide service with 4WD transport into the park and horse riding to its boundary (US$10 per day).

Eating

Santa Cruz *p302, map p303*
▮▮▮ **La Sierra**, a bit out of town at Km 23 on the old road to Cochabamba, T03-384 0009. In an idyllic setting on the banks of the Río Paraí. Open only at weekends and during holidays. This is genuine Bolivian cooking at its best, both regional and national. The emphasis is on meat (roast duck, pork, steaks). Considered by the locals to be the best Bolivian restaurant around.
▮▮ **Capri**, Av Irala 634, next to *AeroSur*. Said to serve the best pizzas in town.
▮▮ **Churrasquería Los Lomitos**, Av Uruguay 758, T03-332 8696. A culinary highlight. Outstanding Argentine cuisine, real *parrillada* and *churrasco*; open round the clock. Also has branch on Av Mons Rivero 201, T03-334 3229.

▮▮ **Pizzeria Marguerita**, on the plaza at corner of C Libertad and Junín, T03-337 0285. Mon-Fri 0900-2400, Sat/Sun 1600-2400. Serves pizzas and burgers and a superb filet mignon. It's a big hit with gringos and the staff are very friendly and helpful. Bar, a/c. Also recommended for breakfast and liqueurs (not necessarily at the same time!), credit cards accepted, no commission.
▮ **Las Palmeras**, Junín 381 and (bigger place) nearby at Ayacucho 590 and José Callau. Mon-Sat 0700-2200, Sun 0700-1600. Popular, good vegetarian meals.
▮ **Tia Lia**, Murillo 40, T03-336 8183. Mon-Fri 1100-1500, Sat-Sun 1100-1600. One of the best places to eat in town. For just US$1.50 (US$2.25 weekends) you can eat all the beef, chorizos, pork and chicken you want from a *parillada* as well as choose from a huge selection of salads, pasta and bean dishes. Also has *feijoada* (the famous Brazilian stew) on Sat with *caipirosca* (Brazil's lethal sugar cane spirit-based drink).

Cafés
There are lots of very pleasant air-conditioned cafés and ice cream parlours, where you can get coffee, ice cream, drinks, snacks and reasonably-priced meals.
Fridolin has 2 central locations: one at Av Cañoto esq. Florida, T3340274; the other at Pari 254, T3323768. Excellent coffee and pastry spot.
Kivón, Ayacucho 267, which is highly recommended for ice cream (also at Quijarro 409 in Mercado Los Pozos).

Samaipata *p305, map p308*
▮▮▮ **El Descanso en Los Alturas**, wide choice including excellent steaks and pizzas.
▮▮▮ **Landhaus Restaurant**, German-run, good for steaks and salad buffet, open only Thu-Sat 0800-2200.
▮▮ **Andoriña Galeria de Fotografias**, Calle Campero. Run by a Dutch-Bolivian couple, this laid-back place offers photo

exhibitions, local info and internet alongside healthy breakfasts and lunches.
¶¶ **Café Hamburg**, on Bolívar, is a great place to hang out. The atmosphere is laid back, there's a bar, food (curry, chorizo, spaghetti and vegetarian), well-stocked book exchange as well as internet US$2.25 per hr (only after 1900). They are also recommended for their *Roadrunners* tour agency (see next page), they have very good tourist advice; private rooms are available too.
¶¶ **Chakana**, Dutch-owned bar/restaurant/ café open every day 0900-late, a relaxing place with *almuerzos* for US$2.25, good snacks and salads, seats outside, book exchange, and ice cream.

Cafés

Café Baden, 1 km towards Santa Cruz. Good for ice cream and torts as well as steak and schweizer *würstsalat* (by now you'll be wondering if you've gone to sleep and woken up in Bavaria).
Landhaus Café, Mon-Thu 1400-1900, Sat and Sun 0800-1900. Pure German cuisine with lovely decor and delicious apple and banana pie.
Panadería Gerlinde, open daily 0700-2200. For superb value and tasting biscuits, bread, homemade pastas, herbs, cheese, yoghurts and cold meats, try this Swiss-run café which also has a weekend stall in the market.

Bars and clubs

Santa Cruz *p302, map p303*
See also listings in the local press for nightclubs and bars. Most of the most happening clubs are in the Equipetrol suburb (to the north of the map on p303).
Bar Irlandes, on the east side of the main plaza and on 3rd Anillo, near the Cristo Redentor statue, T03-343 0671, open late. Irish theme pub. Probably the city's best-known watering hole for gringos, it boasts an owner from the Emerald Isle. Clean and fairly low

volume, so some may find it a bit tame. Reasonable priced drinks, snacks and light meals. Most of the staff speak English and it even has a dartboard. A pleasant and central place to drink and have a late bite of food.
MAD, Av San Martín 155, T03-336 0333. One of the best known and most popular clubs.
Moosehead Bar Restaurant, next door to Bar Irlandes, T03-343 4757. Canadian-run bar/restaurant.
New Palladium, C Boqueron 83, T03-334 0034. One of the best-known clubs.

Entertainment

Santa Cruz *p302, map p303*
Cinemas
Gran Cine Santa Cruz, 21 de Mayo 247, T03-332 4503, showings at 1530, 1730, 1930 and 2130. **Palace**, Pl 24 de Septiembre, T03-332 2617, showings at 1700, 1930 and 2200. **René Moreno**, C René Moreno 448, T03-334 7448, showings at 1630, 1930 and 2100.

Festivals and events

Santa Cruz *p302, map p303*
Cruceños are famous as fun-lovers and their music, the *carnavalitos*, can be heard all over South America.
15 days before Lent Carnival Of the various festivals, this is the best. It's a wild and raucous time with music and dancing in the streets, fancy dress and the coronation of a carnival queen. As with all Bolivian festivals at this time, you're almost certainly going to get very wet, and we're not going to gloss over the fact that people also throw paint at passers by. Well-dressed foreigners are not shown any mercy. The *mascaritas* balls also take place during the pre-Lent season, when girls wear satin masks covering their heads completely, thus ensuring anonymity.

○ Shopping

Santa Cruz *p302, map p303*
Handicrafts and jewellery
Vicuñita Handicrafts, corner of C
Independencia and Ingavi, 1 block west
of the main plaza, T03-334 059,
www.santacruz virtual.com. The best
artesanía in town. The owners are fair
and honest and can ship goods to
anywhere in the world. There are 4
shops in a row (plus another at C René
Moreno 150) selling everything from
sweaters to jewellery and pottery, and
much more. It's an excellent place for
advice on what to buy and what to pay
for it. Some English and French spoken
(ask for Zulema).

Markets
Mercado Los Pozos takes up the whole
block between 6 de Agosto, Suárez Arana,
Quijarro and Campero. It is clean and
good for midday meals – the food aisles
serve local and Chinese food, and is worth
visiting in the summer for its exotic fruits.
The market is open daily.
Bazar Siete Calles sells mainly clothing,
but food and fruit is sold outside. The
main entrance is in 100 block of Isabel La
Católica and there's another entrance on
Camiri and Vallegrande, past Ingavi.

Samaipata *p305, map p308*
There is an amazing array of homemade
food and drink in Samaipata which will
satisfy many a traveller. Particularly good
is Argentinian **Don Alex** who sells
hand-made wines and liqueurs from a
stall on the plaza Sat 1500-2000, Sun
0900-2000, and holidays 1000-2200.
His wine is expensive (US$15) but he
offers free tasting and sells truffles,
brownies, homemade jam, cakes and
biscuits which are all excellent in taste
and value. Also in the market at
weekends, is the delicious German cold
meat kiosk which sells mustards and
bread to go with the cold cuts.

Cabañas Traudi. For locally-made
ceramics; you can arrange to have
ceramics lessons too.
El Tambo, on the Plaza, 1000-2100,
closed Mon. Sells a range of local crafts
and has a good selection of books.
Landhaus Café not only sells homemade
biscuits and cakes but crafts and ceramics
made in their own workshops.

▲ Activities and tours

Santa Cruz *p302, map p303*
Tour operators
Bracha, at the train station, T03-346 7795.
Open Mon, Wed and Fri 0800-1800,
otherwise 0830-1230, 1430-1830, Sun
closed. For rail tickets to Quijarro.
Fremen, Beni 79, T03-333 8535, F336
0265. Run city and local tours to Amboró,
Samaipata etc, also tours of the Jesuit
Missions, jungle river cruises on the Flotel
Reina del Enin, all-inclusive packages
covering the Che Guevara Trail and they
run the Hotel El Puente in Villa Tunari.
Kayara Tours, Casilla 3132, home address
Tapiosí 113 (near the zoo), T03-342 0340.
Mario Berndt is highly recommended for
tours in the high Andes and the lowlands,
he is a photographer, is knowledgeable
about culture, flora and fauna, and speaks
English, German and Spanish.

Samaipata *p305, map p308*
Tour operators
Samaipata is blessed with good tour
operators. All those listed below come
highly recommended and offer trips to El
Fuerte and other attractions around
Samaipata . Their offices are marked on
the map. Expect to pay around
US$15-US$20 per person in a group of 4.
Amboró Tours, T03-9446293,
erickamboro@cotas.com.bo. Run by local
Erick Prado who only speaks Spanish but
can organize trips to Noel Kempff Mercado
(see page 307).
Don Gilberto Aguilera, T03-944 6050, is
considered by many in Samaipata to be
the most knowledgable guide around

Jesuit Mission Circuit

Northeast of Santa Cruz is la Gran Chiquitanía, a vast, sprawling, sparsely populated area, mainly given over to cattle ranching and seemingly of little interest to the traveller. But this is a part of Bolivia with a fascinating history and a precious heritage. Here lie the seven surviving Jesuit Mission churches of San Javier, Concepción, San Ignacio de Velasco, Santa Ana, San Rafael, San Miguel and San José de Chiquitos, all of which became UNESCO World Heritage sites in 1990. These are perhaps the finest examples of colonial religious art and craftsmanship in the country and will impress even those travellers who would not normally set foot inside a church.

You should spend at least five days on the Jesuit Mission circuit. The most interesting time to visit is Holy Week or at the end of July when many of the settlements celebrate their patron saint festivals. As rich as the region is in cultural heritage, it is still very much a frontier. This is one of the best regions outside of the Altiplano to sample true Bolivian culture. Tours can be organized from Santa Cruz (see p311).

Amongst the highlights of the circuit is **Concepción**, one of the loveliest and friendliest of the mission settlements. Its beautiful church (open 0700-2000, free but donation invited, guided tours at 1000 and 1500), completed in 1756, was totally restored between 1975 and 1982. On the plaza, Museo Misional (Monday-Saturday 0830-1200, 1400-1730, Sunday 1000-1200, US$0.50), has photographs of the appalling condition into which the church fell.

From **San Ignacio de Velasco**, a hot and dusty commercial centre lying on the main transport route going east to Brazil, it is possible to visit the most beautiful of the mission churches at **Santa Ana**, **San Rafael** and **San Miguel**. At the southern end of the circuit is **San José de Chiquitos**, capital of Chiquitos province, which retains the feel of a dusty, frontier town. The town centre is dominated by the architecturally unique mission church and compound (daily 0600-1200, 1430-2100, free), which occupies the whole of one side of the plaza. There is a bank on the plaza in San José, (Monday-Friday only, 0800-1200, 1430-1800) which changes US dollars cash only but dollars are accepted everywhere. It's a good idea to change money in Santa Cruz.

Sleeping

There are a few decent options in Concepción and San Ignacio de Velsaco, otherwise only the most basic of accommodation is available. A **Gran Hotel Concepción**, on the plaza in Concepción, T03-964 3031, granhotelconcepcion@ hotmail.com. Very comfortable, beautiful courtyard garden, excellent service, includes buffet breakfast, pool, bar. Owner Sra. Martha Saucedo speaks some English and German.

E **Casa Suiza**, at the end of Calle Sucre, 5 blocks west of the plaza in San Ignacio (taxi US$0.60). Small guesthouse run by Horst and Cristina Schultz and a real home from home, includes breakfast, full board available (excellent food), they can arrange fishing trips, hire horses (US$3 per hr) and provide a packed lunch, Cristina is a former nurse and can help with medical problems.

E-F **Raquelita**, on the plaza San José de Chiquitos, T03-972 2037. The best of a bad bunch, comfortable beds, a/c, good value, laundry service, snack bar serves breakfast; owners know all latest bus and train times.

Getting there

There Jesuit mission circuit can be completed in two ways: clockwise by road from Santa Cruz to San José de Chiquitos, via Concepción and San Ignacio de Velasco, then catch the Quijarro-Santa Cruz train back to Santa Cruz (see p314); or do the tour in reverse by taking the Santa Cruz-Quijarro train to San José and from there travel north by road to visit the other mission towns. To do the circuit clockwise, take a *Flota Chiquitana* bus for San Ignacio de Velasco (US$6.70, 10 hours) from the new terminal in Santa Cruz at 1900. From San Ignacio you can then visit the mission settlements of San Rafael, Santa Ana and San Miguel (*micros* leave from the market area in San Ignacio, there are no tickets on sale, just turn up about 30 minutes before departure and hope to get a seat). A day trip by taxi from San Ignacio to San Miguel, Santa Ana and San Rafael costs US$35-40, but bargain hard. There are buses from San Ignacio to San José de Chiquitos via San Miguel and San Rafael (8 hours, US$4.50), with *Trans Carreton* (Tuesday, Thursday, Sunday at 0800). From San José de Chiquitos you can then return to Santa Cruz by train (see p314).

314 simply because he was brought up here. He speaks only Spanish, is very affordable and seems to get everywhere in his car.

Michael Blendinger, T03-944 6186, mblendinger@cotas.com.bo. For avid birdwatchers and nature lovers. Michael is a biologist and very knowledgeable but the most expensive. A German raised in Argentina, he speaks excellent English. His free horse- riding promotion is monthly only, on Thu mornings, limited to 4 beasts.

Roadrunners, T03-944 6193. Olaf and Frank here also speak excellent English. Olaf is an enthusiastic authority on many sights but especially El Fuerte which he brings alive with informed description. Frank has a great sense of humour and is fun as well as knowledgeable for trips to Amboró and other sights. They are a good port of call for free tourist information.

La Víspera, T03-944 6082, www.la vispera.org. Margarita and Pieter (who run **Boliviajes**) are Dutch and helped forge the tourist service of Samaipata and can arrange any trip. Their knowledge of the area is perhaps the best of all operators, which is saying quite a bit. They also run 'eco' horse and cart trips and a tour along the beautiful old trade route to Sucre, arriving in Tarabuco in time for the market.

Parque Nacional Amboró

Amboró Tours, on the corner of the plaza, Buena Vista, T03-9322093, (mob) 71633990, amborotours@yahoo.com. Open 0730-2000 daily. Marcos Velasco is highly recommended. His English is excellent and he can book Laura Gutiérrez, an English- speaking biologist, for trips to all the destinations, US$27 per person in a group of 4 for 1 day, US$33 per person for 2 days, including transport, guide and tent but not food (US$10 extra). Also has keys to a birding tower 1 km from the town centre, US$6 per person for early morning trip, 20 species promised in 2 hrs.

⊖ Transport

Santa Cruz *p302, map p303*
Air
LAB (Lloyd Aéreo Boliviano), T03-337 1459, flies at least twice daily to **La Paz** and **Sucre.**
Aero Sur, T03-336 7400, flies to **La Paz** several times daily.

Airline offices
Aero Sur, Irala 616, T03-336 7400. Mon-Fri 0800-1230, 1430-1830, Sat 0830-1230.
LAB, Warnes y Chuquisaca, T03-334 4159.

Buses
Local/regional *Micros* that serve the first few *anillos* and don't venture out beyond the 4th ring use the new bus terminal but also pick up passengers anywhere along their appointed routes instead. Look out for the destination posted in the windscreen and flag the bus down if it's going in the right direction, but always double-check with the driver that it's going where it says it is.

Buses and *micros* to **Viru-Viru International Airport** can be hailed from anywhere along their route or can be boarded at the new terminal. A *colectivo* taxi service runs to **Samaipata** from C Tundy 70, near the old bus terminal.

Long distance There are daily direct buses to **La Paz**, via Oruro, between 1700 and 1930 (851 km, 16 hrs, US$10.45), some of which are *bus-cama*. There are direct buses to **Sucre** daily between 1700 and 1800 (14 hrs, US$6-7.50). To **San Ignacio de Velasco**, see box on p312.

Car hire
A. Barron's, Av Alemena 50 esq. Tajibos, T03-342 0160, F342 3439, www.rentacar bolivia.com. Best in town, honest and reasonable rates, English spoken. Several models, US$60 per day for Suzuki 4WD with insurance, tax extra.

Taxis

Expect to pay 8 Bs (about US$1.15) inside the 1st ring (US$1.50 at night) and US$1.30 up to the 3rd ring. Fix the fare before getting in.

Trains

Trains to **Quijarro** on the border with **Brazil** go via **San José de Chiquitos**. **Expreso del Oriente Pullman** trains leave Santa Cruz Mon-Sat at 1530, arriving in **Quijarro** at 1000. Coming back, they leave Quijarro Mon-Sat at 1500, arriving 0900-1000; 1st class is US$16, 2nd class is US$6.30. The faster (by 6½ hrs) and plusher *Ferrobus* leaves on Tue, Thu and Sun 1900, returning on Mon, Wed and Fri at 1900. It has a/c , meals and videos, US$35.40 for *cama*, US$30.60 for *semi-cama*.

Tickets can be bought the day prior to travel. The ticket counter opens at 0800, but go early because queues form hours before and tickets sell fast. Take your passport. Some tickets can be bought in advance at travel agencies (who can also advise on transporting vehicles by rail).

Samaipata *p305, map p308*

Buses All buses leave Santa Cruz from the new bus terminal, Mon-Sat 1600. A *colectivo* taxi service runs to Samaipata from **Santa Cruz**, from C Tundy 70, near the old bus terminal (2 hrs, US$15 per taxi for up to 4 people). They leave when full, or when everyone agrees to pay the full fare. Earlier departures are more frequent as fewer people travel later in the day. You can return to Santa Cruz by *colectivo* , which will pick you up from your hotel. Otherwise, a taxi will cost about US$15 from outside the petrol station. Also buses to Santa Cruz at 0430, 0445 and 0545 Mon-Sat from the plaza outside **El Tambo**, US$2.25 (ask at **Roadrunners**), returning at 1600, and sometimes an afternoon bus. Sun is easier as buses leave from 1100-1530.

You can get to Samaipata by bus from **Sucre**; these leave at night and arrive soon after dawn, stopping in Mairana or Mataral for breakfast, about ½ hr before Samaipata.

ⓘ Directory

Santa Cruz *p302, map p303*

Banks are open Mon-Sat 0830-1130, 1430-1730. Note that they won't change TCs on Sat afternoon. **Banco de La Paz**, **Banco Mercantil**, **Banco de Santa Cruz** and **Banco Boliviano-Americano**, all have *Enlace* cash dispensers for Visa and/or Mastercard. **Medicambio**, on Plaza 24 de Septiembre, will change TCs into dollars at 3% commission. **Menno Credit Unión**, 10 de Agosto 15, T03-332 8800, change TCs quickly with no fuss and 1% commission, Mon-Fri 0900-1700. Street money changers are to be found on the northwest corner of Plaza 24 de Septiembre. **Internet** There are plenty of places in town. **Santa Cruz BBS**, Moldes 543, T03-336 5475, and **KF@in@.com**, Velasco 75. Standard charge is US$0.60-0.90 per hr. **Medical services** There are 2 hospitals northwest of the city centre, **Hospital San Juan de Dios** and **Hospital Petrolero CNSS**. Nearby, around España and Cuellar, doctors of every speciality practise. The place is also packed with pharmacies. **Dr Pepe Arzabe Quiroga**, Clinica San José, Ingavi 720, T03-333 2970, is a specialist in tropical diseases. **Post office** C Junín 146, open 0800-2000 every day. **Telephone** Entel at Warnes 83 (between Moreno y Chuquisaca), T03-332 5526. Local and international calls and fax, open Mon-Sat 0730-2330, Sun and holidays 0730-2200.

Samaipata *p305, map p308*

Banks There are no banks in town, but you can change US dollars cash at **Alamacen Alba** on the plaza, or the **Cooperativo** 1 block east of the plaza. **Internet** Café Hamburg, Bolívar, from 1900; **El Tambo** (see Shopping p311), both US$2.25 per hr. **Laundry** Michael Blendinger Nature Tours, opposite the museum, charges US$3.75 for up to 5 kg.

Quito and the Highlands

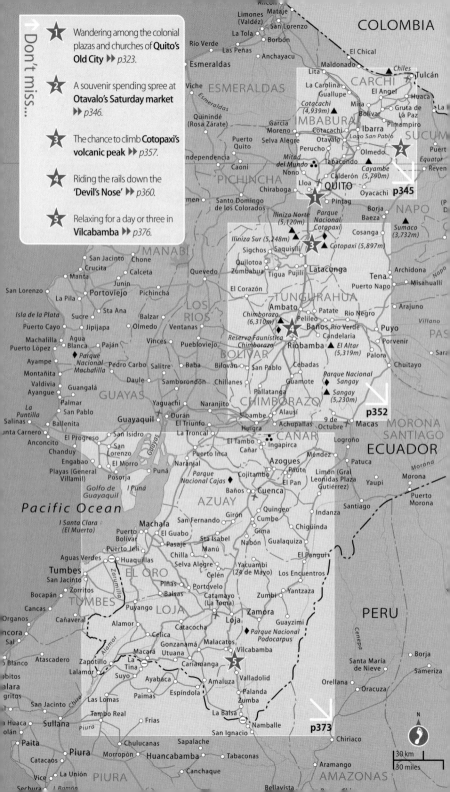

↑ Don't miss...

★1 Wandering among the colonial plazas and churches of **Quito's Old City** ►► *p323*.

★2 A souvenir spending spree at **Otavalo's Saturday market** ►► *p346*.

★3 The chance to climb **Cotopaxi's volcanic peak** ►► *p357*.

★4 Riding the rails down the 'Devil's Nose' ►► *p360*.

★5 Relaxing for a day or three in **Vilcabamba** ►► *p376*.

Introduction

Ecuador divides neatly into three parts: sierra, selva and costa. The sierra - or highlands - takes up the greater part of the country and largely defines its culture and national psyche. Here lies the capital Quito, its pastel-hued colonial Old Town presenting a counterpoint to the brash, modern shopping malls, bars and clubs of the New Town. Quito acts as a base from which to explore the surrounding mountains, volcanoes, lakes, rivers and cloud forests, and the towns and villages that nestle amongst them. To the north lies Otavalo, souvenir-central because of its peerless handicrafts market run by the country's shrewdest ethnic group. On the western Andean slopes, only a few hours from the capital, are beautiful nature reserves protecting rare bird species, while to the south, through the 'Avenue of the Volcanoes', lie timeless villages only just opening up to tourism. On the eastern slopes is Banos, jungle gateway town, spa resort and all-round favourite hang-out. In the south, Cuenca is second only to Quito for its colonial architecture, while Vilcabamba may not quite guarantee eternal life but certainly makes people want to stay.

Ratings

Culture
★★★★★

Landscape
★★★★★

Wildlife
★★★

Activities
★★★★★

Chillin'
★★★★

Costs
$$$-$$

Quito

Janus-faced Quito is a city of two halves. The Old City, a UNESCO World Heritage Trust site, is the colonial centre, where pastel-coloured houses and ornate churches line a warren of steep and narrow streets. North of the Old City is modern Quito – or New City – an altogether different place. Its broad avenues are lined with fine private residences, parks, embassies and villas. Here you'll find Quito's main tourist and business area: banks, tour agencies, airlines, language schools, smart shops and restaurants, bars and cafés, and many hotels, in the district known as La Mariscal, and further north as far as Avenida Naciones Unidas.

⊘ **Getting there** International and domestic flights. Frequent buses to all parts of the country.
◉ **Getting around** Taxis, buses and *Trole* (trolley).
⊖ **Time required** 2-3 days for the city, more for excursions.
⊚ **Weather** Springlike daytime temperatures all year, nights can be cold. Rainy season Oct-May.
◉ **Sleeping** Huge selection catering to all tastes and budgets.
⊘ **Eating** Hugely varied range of restaurants.
▲▲ **Activities and tours** Walking through the colonial Old City, nightlife in La Mariscal, trips to the Equator, Mindo or Papallacta.
★ **Don't miss...** the view from Panecillo ▶▶ *p324.*

Ins and outs

Getting there

Air Quito's airport, Mariscal Sucre, lies only about 5 km to the north of La Mariscal, the main hotel district, within the city limits. The safest and easiest way to travel between town and the airport is to take a taxi. You can catch one from the rank right outside arrivals. The fare from the airport to the New City is about US$5; to the Old City or to a first-class hotel US$6 (more at night, but beware of overcharging). Alternatively, you can use the **Trans-Rabbit** van service, they have a booth at international arrivals, T02-2276736, US$2-3 per person to the New City in a van with room for up to 15 passengers, but they don't leave until full. There is a telephone office plus a few debit card-operated public phones; buy the debit cards at one of the airport shops. There is a post office outside, between international departures and national arrivals. Upstairs at international departures is a bar-restaurant which serves meals and snacks, as well as a couple of fast food places; all are pricey. All the main car rental companies are located just outside international arrivals. For details of their offices in Quito, see page 343.

Bus The main bus station for inter-city travel is the Terminal Terrestre at Maldonado and Cumandá, south of Plaza Santo Domingo, in the Old City. Most long distance buses start and end here, and this is really the only place to get information on bus schedules. It is safest to go by taxi when arriving or leaving from the terminal, although the Cumandá Trole stop is nearby. Several companies with long-distance luxury coach services have offices and terminals in the New City. ◉ ▶▶ *p341.*

Getting around

Both the Old City and La Mariscal in the New City can be explored foot, but the distance between them and from these areas to other neighbourhoods is best

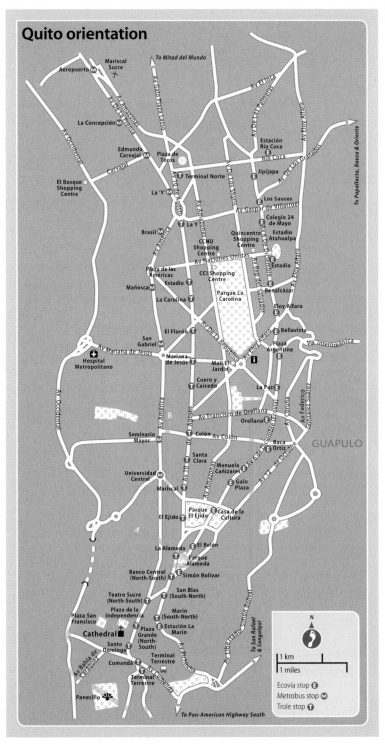

Top tips

Airport essentials

✅ Quito airport is open from 0400 to 0130. Most flights from North America arrive between 1900 and 2400, so make sure at least your first night's accommodation is booked and take a taxi from the airport.

✅ The hotels near the airport are poor, so you are better off going into the city. The hotel booking service at International Arrivals can help you enquire if they have room and the current price.

✅ Try to team up with at least one other traveller and get a taxi voucher in the arrivals area. Ask to be taken to your hotel of first choice.

✅ If you are in a group of six or more the van services from the airport can be a good deal.

✅ There are no buses from the airport after 2000.

✅ There are often long queues for international departures and airlines recommend you arrive three hours before your flight.

❌ Avoid buses and trolley if carrying a backpack, they are too crowded and the chances of having something stolen en route are very high.

❌ Beware of self-styled porters who will try to grab your luggage as you leave the terminal and offer to find you a cab in the hope of receiving a tip or stealing your bags. Legitimate porters wear ID tags and there is no shortage of taxis right at hand.

covered by some form of public transport which is plentiful. Using taxis is the best option, convenient and cheap (starting at US$1). There are city buses and three parallel transit lines running north to south on exclusive lanes: the Trole, Ecovía and Metrobus. The areas of most interest to visitors are the colonial city, with its many churches, historical monuments and museums (best accessed by Trole); La Mariscal or Mariscal Sucre district, which extends east from Av 10 de Agosto to Av 12 de Octubre, and north from Av Patria to Av Orellana, where you find most hotels, restaurants, bars, clubs, travel agencies and some banks; north of La Mariscal as far as Av Naciones Unidas and from Av 10 de Agosto east to and Av Eloy Alfaro, where the newer hotels, restaurants, main banking district, airline offices and a number of shopping malls are located. ⊖ ►► *p341.*

Climate
Quito is within 25 km of the equator, but it stands high enough to make its climate much like that of spring in England; the days pleasantly warm and the nights cool. Because of the height, visitors may initially feel some discomfort and should slow their pace for the first day or so. The rainy season is October-May, with a lull in December, and the heaviest rainfall in April.

Tourist information
The **Corporación Metropolitana de Turismo** has an excellent internet site: www.quito.com.ec, (toll free) T1-800-767767. It has information offices with English speaking personnel at International arrivals at the airport ⓘ *T02-330 0163, daily 0600-2400*; in the Old City ⓘ *Edificio El Cadisán, García Moreno N12-01 y Mejía, T02-257 2566, Mon-Sat 0900-1800, Sun 1000-1600,* it houses the tourist information office, municipal parking, gift shop and smart

Mon-Fri 0900-1700; and at the Museo del Banco Central; ⓘ *Av Patria y 6 de Diciembre, T02-222 1116, Mon-Fri 0900-1700, Sat-Sun 1000-1600.*

The **Empresa de Desarrollo del Centro Histórico**, ⓘ *Pasaje Arzobispal at Plaza de la Independencia, ground floor, T02-258 6591, daily 0900-0000,* runs walking tours (see page 338) and has an information office and an information kiosk where maps are sold, some English and French spoken. **Policía de Turismo** ⓘ *Reina Victoria y Roca, T02-254 3983, Mon-Sat 1100-2100,* have information booths in several locations in La Mariscal and one at El Panecillo. Members of the **Policía Metropolitana**, who patrol the Old City on foot, speak some English and are very helpful.

Old City ⊜🎵🎵🎴✳🅾🔺🅰️🕐🅲 ⟩⟩ *pp330-344*

The heart of the colonial city is **Plaza de la Independencia** or Plaza Grande, dominated by the **Cathedral**, built 1550-62. Facing the Cathedral is the **Palacio Arzobispal**, the Archbishop's palace. Part of the building, the Pasaje Arzobispal, now houses shops and restaurants around stone courtyards. The fine Jesuit church of **La Compañía** ⓘ *Mon-Fri 1000-1700, Sat 1000-1600, Sun 1200-1600. US$2*, on Calle García Moreno, one block south of Plaza de la Independencia, has a beautifully ornate and richly sculptured façade and interior. Several of its most precious treasures, including a painting of the Virgen Dolorosa

Church of San Francisco, standing proudly on the eponymous plaza.

framed in emeralds and gold, are kept in the vaults of the Banco Central and appear only at special festivals. Replicas of the impressive paintings of hell and the final judgement by Miguel de Santiago can be seen at the entrance.

Plaza de San Francisco (or Bolívar) is west of Plaza de la Independencia. On the northwest side of this plaza the great **church and monastery** ⓘ *Mon-Fri 0800-1200, 1500-1800, Sat-Sun 0900-1200*, built in 1553, is Quito's first and largest colonial church. It is here that the famous Quito School of Art was founded. Worth seeing are the fine wood carvings in the choir, a magnificent high altar of gold and an exquisite carved ceiling. The church is rich in art treasures, the best known of which is *La Virgen de Quito* by Legarda, which depicts the Virgin Mary with silver wings. The statue atop Panecillo is based on this painting. Adjoining San Francisco is the **Cantuña Chapel** which has impressive sculptures.

Plaza de Santo Domingo (or Sucre), to the southeast of Plaza de San Francisco, is another of Quito's busy plazas. Running off it, to the south, is **Calle Morales**, one of the oldest streets in the city and worth seeing for its narrow cobbled way and wrought-iron balconies. It is better known as Calle La Ronda and is now part of a red light district (beware of pickpockets and do not visit at night). Many of the heroes of Ecuador's struggle for independence are buried in the monastery of **San Agustín** ⓘ *Flores y Chile, Mon-Sat 0700-1200, 1300-1800*. The church has beautiful cloisters on three sides where the first act of independence from Spain was signed on 10 August 1809. It is now a national shrine.

Quito's setting, in a valley surrounded by mountains affords many views of the city itself and the encircling cones of volcanos. **El Panecillo** (the little breadloaf) ⓘ *daily 0900-1800, entry to the interior of the monument is US$2*, lies to the south of the Plaza de San Francisco. Gazing benignly over the Old City from the top of Panecillo is the impressive statue of the **Virgen de Quito**, a replica of the painting by Legarda found in the San Francisco Church. There are excellent views from the observation platform up the statue. There are craft sales at the base and **Pim's Restaurant** is along the road, before you reach the monument. Visiting Panecillo has long been considered dangerous, but neighbourhood brigades are patrolling the area and a have improved safety; they charge visitors US$0.25 per person or US$1 per vehicle. However, taking a taxi up is a lot safer than walking.

Guards outside the Presidencial Palace.

New City ⊖⚡⚙⚙⚙⚙⚙⚙ ⤳ *pp330-344*

Opposite Parque El Ejido, at the junction of 6 de Diciembre and Avenida Patria, there is a large complex housing the **Casa de la Cultura** and the excellent museum of the **Banco Central del Ecuador** ① *entrance on Patria, T02-222 3259, Tue-Fri 0900-1700, Sat-Sun and holidays 1000-1600, US$1.50, US$0.50 for students with ISIC card, children US$0.25*. Of the many fine museums in Quito, this is perhaps the most comprehensive. It has three floors, with five different sections. The **Sala de Arqueología** is particularly impressive. It consists of a series of halls with exhibits and illustrated panels with explanations in English as well as Spanish. It covers successive cultures from 12000 BC to AD 1534 with excellent diagrams and extensive collections of beautiful pre-Columbian ceramics. The **Sala de Oro** has a good collection of pre-hispanic gold objects. The remaining three sections house art collections. The **Sala de Arte Colonial** is rich in paintings and sculptures especially of religious themes. The **Sala de Arte Republicano** houses works of the early years of the Republic. The **Sala de Arte Contemporáneo** presents contemporary art. There are also temporary exhibits, videos on Ecuadorean culture, a bookshop and a cafeteria which serves good coffee. For guided tours in English, French or German call ahead and make an appointment. The **Casa de la Cultura Ecuatoriana** hosts many temporary exhibits and cultural events. In addition, the following permanent collections are presented in museums belonging to the Casa de la Cultura: **Museo de Arte Moderno**, paintings and sculpture since 1830; **Museo de Traje Indígena**, a collection of traditional dress and adornments of indigenous groups; and the **Museo de Instrumentos Musicales** ① *T02-222 3392 (ext 320), Mon-Fri 0900-1700, Sat 1000-1400, US$3*, an impressive collection of musical instruments, said to be the second in importance in the world.

Suburbs

The beautiful district of **Guápulo**, a colonial town, is perched on the edge of a ravine on the eastern fringe of Quito, overlooking the Río Machángara. It is popular with Quito's bohemian community and a worthwhile place to visit, especially if you include its beautiful 17th-century church, the **Santuario de Guápulo** (daily 0900-1800), built by Indian slaves and dedicated to Nuestra Señora de Guápulo. It is well worth seeing for its many paintings,

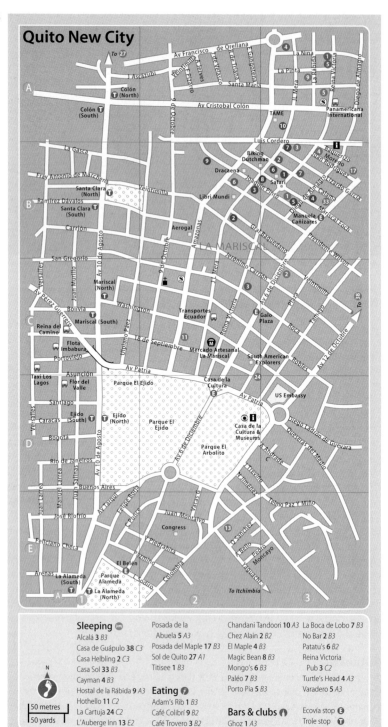

Quito New City

Sleeping

Alcalá **3** B3
Casa de Guápulo **38** C3
Casa Helbling **2** C3
Casa Sol **33** B3
Cayman **4** B3
Hostal de la Rábida **9** A3
Hothello **11** C2
La Cartuja **24** C2
L'Auberge Inn **13** E2
Posada de la
Abuela **5** A3
Posada del Maple **17** B3
Sol de Quito **27** A1
Titisee **1** B3

Eating

Adam's Rib **1** B3
Café Colibrí **9** B2
Café Trovero **3** B2
Chandani Tandoori **10** A3
Chez Alain **2** B2
El Maple **4** B3
Magic Bean **8** B3
Mongo's **6** B3
Paléo **7** B3
Porto Pia **5** B3

Bars & clubs

Ghoz **1** A3
La Boca de Lobo **7** B3
No Bar **2** B3
Patatu's **6** B2
Reina Victoria
Pub **3** C2
Turtle's Head **4** A3
Varadero **5** A3

Ecovía stop **E**
Trole stop **T**

N
50 metres
50 yards

The Casa de la Cultura and museum of the Banco Central del Ecuador are housed in the same complex.

gilded altars, stone carvings and, above all, the marvellously carved pulpit by Juan Bautista Menacho, one of the loveliest in the whole continent. To get there, take bus Hospital del Sur-Guápulo from Calle Venezuela by Plaza de la Independencia, Guápulo-Dos Puentes eastbound along Avenida Patria, or walk down the steep stairway which leads off Avenida González Suárez, near the Hotel Quito.

Around Quito 🖵 ➡ *p341*

Despite Quito's bustling big city atmosphere, it is surrounded by pretty and surprisingly peaceful countryside. Here are many opportunities for day excursions as well as longer trips. The monument on the equator, the country's best known tourist site, is just a few minutes away. There are also nature reserves, excellent thermal swimming pools, walking and climbing routes and a train ride. A combination of city and interparroquial buses and pick-up taxis will get you to most destinations around Quito. These excursions are also offered by tour operators in Quito.

Mitad del Mundo
ⓘ *T02-239 4806. Mon-Thu 0900-1800, Fri-Sun 0900-1900 (very crowded on Sun). Entry US$1.50, children US$0.75 includes entry to the pavilions; Museo Etnográfico US$3 (includes guided tour of museum in Spanish or English, guides are found near the entrance to the complex or at the information booth); parking US$1.*
Some 23 km north of Quito is the Mitad del Mundo Equatorial Line Monument. The location of the equatorial line here was determined by Charles-Marie de la Condamine and his French expedition in 1736, and agrees to within 150 m with modern GPS measurements. The monument forms the focal point of the Ciudad Mitad del Mundo, a park and leisure area built as a typical colonial town, with restaurants, gift shops etc. It is all rather touristy but the monument itself has an interesting museum with exhibits of different indigenous cultures every few steps. Worth visiting is the interesting **scale model of colonial Quito** (daily 0900-1700, US$1), about 10 sq m, with artificial day and night, which took seven years to build. .

Mitad del Mundo Equatorial Line monument.

Termas de Papallacta

ⓘ *0700-2100, US$5, children under 12 US$2.50*

Some 64 km east of Quito, on the road to the Oriente, is the village of Papallacta, whose thermal springs (*termas*) are the most attractively developed in Ecuador. The hot water is channelled into three pools large enough for swimming, three smaller shallow pools and two tiny family-size pools. There is also a steam room, hot showers and two cold plunge pools as well as access to the river. The baths are crowded at weekends but usually quiet through the week. The view, on a clear day, of Antisana from the Papallacta road or while enjoying the thermal waters is superb. In addition to the pools there is a spa centre with a therapeutic pool, jacuzzi and massage which is very clean and relaxing. The Termas de Papallacta complex includes an extension of land following the Río Papallacta upstream from the baths to forested areas. There are well maintained trails, entry US$1. Access to the complex is along a secondary road branching off the Vía Interoceánica, 1 km west of Papallacta. It is 1 km uphill from the turn-off to the complex.

Train ride to Cotopaxi

South of Quito lies the lush agricultural area of Machachi, with lovely views of the surrounding peaks. Beyond is **Parque Nacional Cotopaxi**, a very popular destination which contains one of Ecuador's best known volcanoes (see page 357). Tours are arranged by Quito agencies (see page 339). A tourist train runs from Quito to the Cotopaxi station in Area Nacional de Recreación El Boliche, abutting on Parque Nacional Cotopaxi, Saturday and Sunday at 0800, returning at 1430. The ride takes three hours, so it gives you time to walk around and enjoy the views. Dress warmly and take lunch. The ride costs US$4.60 return, children under 12 US$2.30. Plus the El Boliche park entrance fee (US$10). Tickets must be purchased in advance at Bolívar 443 y García Moreno, T02-258 2927 (Monday 1300-1630, Tuesday-Friday 0800-1600). You'll need a passport number for all the tickets you purchase and the person's age. The Quito railway station is 2 km south of the Old City, along the continuation of Calle Maldonado, reached by trolley, Chimbacalle stop if northbound, Machángara if southbound, and walk uphill along Maldonado.

Going further ▶▶

Twitching and tubing near Mindo

The Bosque Protector Mindo-Nambillo is a nature reserve covering 19,200 ha, ranging in altitude from 1,400 to 4,780 m. The reserve features spectacular flora and fauna, beautiful cloud forest and many waterfalls. Access to the reserve proper is restricted to scientists, but there is a buffer zone of private reserves which offers many opportunities for exploring. The main access town is Mindo, surrounded by dairy farms, rivers and lush cloud forest. It is an excellent base for many outdoor activities including walking, horse-riding, bathing in waterfalls, tubing (floating down the river in inner tubes), bird and butterfly watching (this is one of the best places in the country to see Cock-of-the-rock, Golden-headed Quetzal and Toucan-Barbet). A very popular activity in the Mindo area is *regattas*, the local name for inner-tubing, floating down a river on a raft made of several inner tubes tied together. Several local agencies and hotels offer this activity for US$4-6. There are several environmental groups working in the Mindo area, these operate private reserves, most of which abut on the main reserve. Some of the lodges such as Séptimo Paraiso also own private reserves and run tours on their properties.

Sleeping

AL Séptimo Paraiso, 2 km from Calacalí-La Independencia road along Mindo access road, then 500 m right on a small side road, well signed, T09-993 4133, www.septimoparaiso.com. Includes breakfast, expensive restaurant, pool, ample parking, all wood lodge, comfortable rooms, lovely grounds in a 300 ha reserve with walking trails. On its own, isolated from Mindo town.

A Hacienda San Vicente, 'Yellow House', 500 m south of the plaza, T09-276 5464. Includes excellent breakfast and dinner, family-run, friendly, nice rooms, good walking trails nearby, good value.

C per person **Centro de Educación Ambiental (CEA)**, 4 km from town, within a 17-ha buffer zone at the edge of the reserve. Run by Amigos de la Naturaleza de Mindo. Price is for full board, basic accommodation and well maintained trails, guide included when there are minimum 3 passengers, camping costs US$2 per person. Can also arrange volunteer programmes.

Getting there from Quito

Cooperativa Flor del Valle (T02-252 7495), leave from M Larrea N10-44 y Asunción (not from the Terminal Terrestre), Monday-Friday at 0800 and 1545, Saturday-Sunday at 0700, 0800, 0900, 1545; US$2.50, 2½ hours. Buses return to Quito Monday-Friday 0600, 1200, Saturday-Sunday 1400, 1500, 1600, 1700. The weekend buses fill quickly so buy tickets in advance.

Quito & the Highlands Quito

● Sleeping

Old City *p323, map p332*

C Real Audiencia, Bolívar Oe3-18 y Guayaquil at Plaza Santo Domingo, T02-295 0590, F02-258 0213. Includes breakfast, restaurant/bar, spacious, well furnished rooms, great views.

D Guest House, Julio Castro 579 y Valparaíso, T02-252 5834, marcoatm@hoy.net. Nicely restored old house, laundry and cooking facilities, good rooms and views, friendly and helpful, part of Tours Unlimited.

D Secret Garden, Antepara E4-60 y Los Ríos, T02-295 6704, www.secret gardenquito.com. Restored old house, lovely roof-top terrace restaurant serves inexpensive breakfast and dinner (vegetarian available), one room with private bath, cheaper in dorm, nice atmosphere, a popular meeting place for travellers, Ecuadorean-Australian run.

E Margarita, Los Ríos 1995 y Espinoza, T02-295 0441. Private bath, hot water, parking, good beds, sheets changed daily, great value.

D Casona de Mario, Andalucía 213 y Galicia, T/F02-223 0129, lacasona@punto.net.ec. Popular friendly hostel, shared bath, laundry facilities, well equiped kitchen, very clean rooms, sitting room, nice big garden, book exchange, helpful owner.

New City *p325, map p326*

AL-A Sol de Quito, Alemania N30-170 y Vancouver, T02-254 1773, www.sol dequito.com. Lovely converted home with large sitting room and library decorated with antiques, includes breakfast, restaurant, internet, parking, comfortable rooms, suites have beautiful carved doors.

A Hostal de la Rábida, La Rábida 227 y Santa María, T/F02-222 1720, www.hotelrabida.com. Nice home in La Mariscal, good restaurant, parking, Italian run, bright and comfortable.

A La Cartuja, Plaza 170 y 18 de Septiembre, T02-252 3577, www.hotela cartuja.com. In the former British Embassy, includes breakfast, good restaurant although menu is limited, beautifully decorated, spacious comfortable rooms, lovely garden, very helpful and hospitable.

A La Casa Sol, Calama 127 y 6 de Diciembre, T02-223 0798, www.lacasasol.com. A small quaint inn with courtyard , includes breakfast, 24-hour cafeteria, very helpful, English and French spoken.

A Santa Bárbara, 12 de Octubre N26-15 y Coruña, T02-222 5121, www.hotel-santabarbara.com. Beautiful refurbished colonial-style house and gardens, sitting room with fireplace, includes breakfast, restaurant, internet, parking, English, French and Italian spoken.

A-B Mi Casa, Andalucía N24-151 y Francisco Galavis, T/F02-222 5383, www.ecuanex.apc.org/mi_casa/ In La

Top tips

Finding a bed in Quito

✔ There are not many good places to stay near the bus station and, at present, none whatsoever by the airport. This is more than compensated for, however, by the abundance of cheap taxis.

✔ It's advisable to phone or email for advance reservations, especially in July and August.

✔ By far the greatest number of hotels are concentrated in the district of La Mariscal, between Avenida Patria to the south and Avenida Orellana to the north, Avenida 10 de Agosto to the west and Avenida 12 de Octubre to the east. Here you will be surrounded by restaurants, bars, nightlife, tour agencies, craft shops and cyber-cafés.

Floresta, includes large breakfast, sauna, comfortable rooms and suites, gardens, small, quiet, family run, multilingual owner.

A-B Posada de la Abuela, Santa María 235 y La Rábida, T02-225 334, www.posabuela.com. Cosy little inn, includes breakfast, parking, some rooms with fireplace, safety deposit box. Lovely refurbished 1920s home with pleasant sitting room in a covered patio.

B Cayman, Rodríguez E7-29 y Reina Victoria, T02-256 7616, www.hotelcaymanquito.com. Pleasant hotel, includes breakfast, cafeteria, parking, rooms a bit small, sitting room with fireplace, lovely bright breakfast room, garden, very clean and good.

B Hothello, Amazonas N20-20 y 18 de Septiembre, T/F02-256 5835. Small modern hotel, includes nice breakfast, café, rooms are bright and tastefully decorated, heating, helpful multilingual staff.

C Alcalá, Luis Cordero E5-48 y Reina Victoria, T02-222 7396, www.alcalahostal.com. Nice bright hostal, includes breakfast, sitting area, same owners and facilities as Posada del Maple.

C Posada del Maple, Rodríguez E8-49 y Almagro, T02-254 4507, www.posadadelmaple.com. Popular hostel, includes breakfast, restaurant, cheaper with shared bath and in dorm, laundry and cooking facilities, warm

atmosphere, free tea and coffee.

C-D Casa Helbling, Veintimilla E8-166 y 6 de Diciembre, T02-222 6013, www.casahelbling.de. Cheaper with shared bath, laundry and cooking facilities, parking, helpful, German spoken, family atmosphere, good information, tours arranged.

D Hostal de La Reina, Reina Victoria 836 y Wilson, T02-255 1844, queen@uio.telconet.net. Nice small hotel, popular among travellers and Ecuadoreans, includes breakfast, cafeteria, laundry and cooking facilities, sitting room with fireplace.

D L'Auberge Inn, Colombia 1138 y Yaguachi, T02-255 2912, www.ioda.net/auberge-inn. Spacious clean rooms, restaurant, cheaper with shared bath, excellent hot water, cooking facilities, parking, duvets on beds, lovely garden terrace and communal area, pool table, includes use of spa, helpful, good atmosphere, discounts for SAE members.

D Titisee, Foch E7-60 y Reina Victoria, T02-252 9063. Nice place and owner, cheaper with shared bath, cooking facilities, large rooms, lounge.

Quito suburbs p325

AL La Carriona, Km 2½ vía Sangolquí-Amaguaña, T02-233 1974, www.lacarriona.com. In a beautiful colonial hacienda, includes breakfast, pool and spa, some rooms in the old hacienda house, others in more modern section but in same style, includes horse riding.

B **San Jorge**, Km 4 Vía Antigua Cotocollao-Nono, T02-249 4002, www.hostsanjorge.com.ec. A traditional hacienda on the slopes of Pichincha, includes breakfast, restaurant, pool, sauna and turkish bath, parking, quiet, peaceful, nature reserve, horse riding and bird-watching, all within easy reach of Quito.

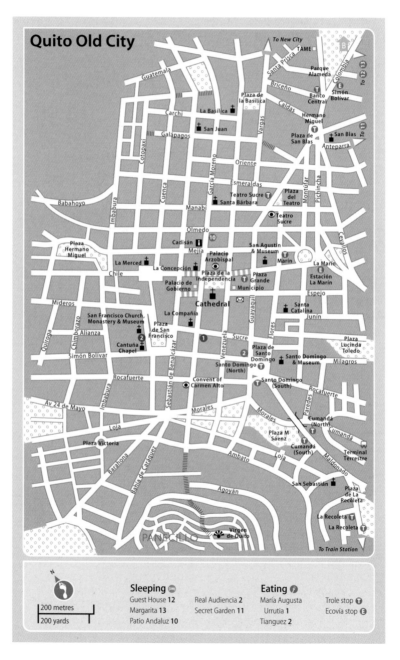

Quito Old City

To New City
TAME

Guatemala

Santa Prisca

Briceño

Caldas

Carchi

La Basílica

Plaza de la Basílica

Parque Alameda

Banco Central

Simón Bolívar

Galápagos

San Juan

Cotopaxi

Imbabura

Cuenca

Vargas

García Moreno

Oriente

Hermano Miguel

Plaza de San Blas

San Blas

Anteparra

Babahoyo

Esmeraldas

Teatro Sucre

Santa Bárbara

Plaza del Teatro

Montúfar

Pichincha

Manabí

Olmedo

Teatro Sucre

Cadisán

Plaza Hermano Miguel

Mejía

Palacio Arzobispal

San Agustín & Museum

La Merced

La Concepción

Chile

Plaza de la Independencia

Palacio de Gobierno

Municipio

Marín

La Marín

Estación La Marín

Cevallos

Espejo

Mideros

Cathedral

La Compañía

Guayaquil

Santa Catalina

Junín

San Francisco Church, Monastery & Museum

Quiroga

Chimborazo

Alianza

Plaza de San Francisco

Venezuela

Sucre

Flores

Plaza Lucinda Toledo

Cantuña Chapel

Simón Bolívar

Plaza de Santo Domingo

Santo Domingo & Museum

Milagros

Rocafuerte

Santo Domingo (North)

Sebastián de Benalcázar

Convent of Carmen Alto

Santo Domingo (South)

Rocafuerte

Av 24 de Mayo

Morales

Morales

Paredes

Cumandá (North)

Cumandá

Imbabura

Loja

Plaza Victoria

Plaza M Sáenz

Cumandá (South)

Terminal Terrestre

Barahona

Bahía de Caráquez

Ambato

Loja

Maldonado

Agoyán

San Sebastián

Plaza de La Recoleta

PANECILLO

Virgen de Quito

La Recoleta

La Recoleta

To Train Station

Colombia

To E...

To E...

Sleeping
Guest House **12**
Margarita **13**
Patio Andaluz **10**
Real Audiencia **2**
Secret Garden **11**

Eating
María Augusta **1**
Urrutia **1**
Tianguez **2**

Trole stop
Ecovía stop

200 metres
200 yards

N

Budget busters

LL Swissôtel, 12 de Octubre 1820 y Cordero, T02-256 6497, http://quito.swissotel.com Superb 5-star accommodation, includes buffet breakfast, Japanese, French and Italian restaurants, also bar, deli and café, state-of-the-art fitness centre, business centre, 3 non-smoking floors and handicapped facilities.

L Patio Andaluz, García Moreno N6-52 y Olmedo, T02-228 0830, www.hotelpatioandaluz.com. Self-styled 'boutique hotel' in the heart of the colonial city, includes breakfast, exclusive restaurant with Ecuadorean and Spanish cuisine, spa, 5-star comfort and service in a 16th century house with large arches, balconies and patios.

L Cuevas de Alvaro, 10 km east of Pifo on the way to Papallacta , T02-254 7403, birdecua@hoy.net. All rooms are in caves, built right into the rock. This is a good spot to see condors at certain times of the year. Includes 3 meals, excursions, and use of horses. Advance reservations required.

D Casa de Guápulo, C Leonidas Plaza, Guápulo, T/F02-222 0473. Includes breakfast, restaurant and bar, parking, peaceful area, multilingual staff, free transfer to airport.

Around Quito *p327*
Papallacta
AL La Posada Papallacta, opposite the Termas, T06-232 0322, www.papallacta.com.ec. Part of the Termas complex, good expensive restaurant, thermal pools both indoors and set in a lovely garden, nice lounge with fireplace, comfortable rooms heated with thermal water, some rooms have a private jacuzzi.

⊙ Eating

Old City *p323, map p332*
♥♥♥ **María Augusta Urrutia**, García Moreno 760 at the museum, T02-258 4173. Thu-Sat 1200-2300, Sun 1200-1700. Ecuadorean and international food based on Sra Urrutia's recipies, served in the elegant surroundings of this aristocratic home.
♥♥♥ **Mea Culpa**, Palacio Arzobispal, Chile y Venezuela, T02-295 1190. Mon-Sat 1230-1530, 1900-2300. International and Mediterranean gourmet cuisine,

specialties include such delicacies as and ostrich in mango sauce, housed in the 17th century Palacio Arzobispal overlooking Plaza de la Independencia, it combines the elegance of colonial decor with opulent gourmet dining. Reservations recommended, formal attire, dress code strictly enforced.
♥♥ **Hasta la Vuelta Señor**, Pasaje Arzobispal, 3rd floor. Mon-Sat 1200-2300, Sun 1200-1600. Ecuadorean comida típica and snacks, try their empanadas (pasties) or a seco de chivo (goat stew).

Cafés
Tianguez, Plaza de San Francisco under the portico of the church. Daily 0930-1830. Good coffee, snacks, sandwiches, Ecuadorean specialties. Popular with visitors, also craft shop, postcards, run by Fundación Sinchi Sacha.

New City *p325, map p326*
♥♥♥ **El Galpón**, Colón E10-53, in the back of Folklor Olga Fisch, T02-254 0209. Tue-Sun 1230-1500, 1830-2100. Very good Ecuadorean cooking featuring traditional dishes with innovative twists like lamb in naranjilla sauce. Decorated with antiques, a pleasant place for relaxed dining.
♥♥♥ **Il Risotto**, Eloy Alfaro N34-447 y Portugal, T02-224 6850. Mon-Sat 1200-

Budget busters

Cloud forest eco-lodges

There are several high quality eco-lodges to the northwest of Quito, on the western slopes of Pichincha volcano.

L **Bellavista**, T02-211 6047/6232 or in Quito T02-290 3165/6, www.bellavistacloudforest.com, is a dramatic dome-shaped lodge perched in beautiful cloud forest at Km 68 at the top of the Tandayapa Valley on the old Nono-Mindo road. The price includes accommodation with private bath, hot shower, and all meals (good vegetarian food). Camping also possible, US$5 per person. Package tours can be arranged including transport from Quito. The reserve is part of a mosaic of private protected areas dedicated to conservation of one of the richest accessible areas of west slope cloud forest. Bellavista at 2,200 m is the highest of these, and the easiest place to see the incredible plate-billed mountain-toucan. Over 300 species of birds have been seen in the Tandayapa Valley, including large numbers of hummingbirds drawn to the many feeders at the lodge. The area is also rich in orchids and other cloud forest plants.

Another recommended luxury lodge is at L **Maquipucuna Reserve**, including 3 meals, options with shared bath and/or without meals are cheaper. Contact Fundacion Maquipucuna, T02-250 7200 in Quito, www.maqui.org. The reserve has 4,500 ha, surrounded by an additional 14,000 ha of protected forest. You can arrange transport with Maquipucuna in Quito, return service from your hotel in Quito, US$100 for 4, they can also pick you up in Nanegalito, US$20. It can also be reached in two hours from Quito with a private vehicle. The cloud forest at 1,200-2,800 m contains diverse of flora and fauna, including over 325 species of birds. Especially noteworthy are the colourful tanager flocks, mountain-toucans, parrots and quetzals. The reserve has trails ranging in length from 15 minutes to all day. There is also a research station and an experimental organic garden.

1500, 1900-2200, Sun 1200-1530. Very popular and very good Italian cooking.

††† **La Jaiba**, Coruña y San Ignacio, T02-254 3887. Mon 1100-1530, Tue-Sat 1100-1600, 1900-2100, Sun 1100-1630. Varied seafood menu, an old favourite at new premises after 36 years, good service.

††† **La Paella Valenciana**, República y Almagro. Tue-Sat 1200-1500, 1900-2300, Sun 1200-1600. Huge portions, superb fish, seafood and paella, an institution.

††† **Porta Pia**, Pinto E7-85 y Almagro, T02-252 1471. Mon-Fri 1230-1500, 1800-2200, Sun 1230-1530. Tasty authentic Italian cuisine, elegant décor and very attentive service.

††† **Rincón de Francia**, Roca 779 y 9 de Octubre, T02-255 4668, www.rincondefrancia.com. Mon-Fri 1200-1600, 2000-2300, Sat 1200-1530, 2000-2200. Excellent food, reservations essential, slow service.

††† **Sake**, Paul Rivet N30-166 y Whymper, T02-252 4818. Mon-Sat 1200-1530, 1900-2300, Sun 1230-1600. Sushi bar and other Japanese dishes, very trendy, great food, nicely decorated.

†† **Adam's Rib**, Calama E6-16 y Reina Victoria. Mon-Fri 1200-2230, Sat closed,

Sun 1030-2100. Happy hour 1730-2100. Ribs, steaks, good BBQ, great pecan pie, Sun brunch 1030-1300. A popular meeting place for US expats.

Capuletto, Eloy Alfaro N32-544 y Los Shyris. Mon-Sat 0900-0000, Sun 0900-2200. Italian deli, excellent fresh pasta and desserts, lovely patio with fountain.

La Guarida del Coyote, Foch y JL Mera, Eloy Alfaro E25-94 y Catalina Aldaz, and Japón 542 y Naciones Unidas. Tue-Sun 1200-2300. Excellent Mexican food.

Mongo's, Calama E5-10 y JL Mera. Daily 1200-2200. Mongolian BBQ, select your ingredients and have them cooked on the grill. Price depends on whether you take one plate or all you can eat.

Paléo, Cordero E5-48 y Reina Victoria. Mon-Sat 1230-1530 1830-2100. Authentic Swiss cooking with specialties such as rösti and raclette. Also serve a good economical set lunch, pleasant ambience.

Pekín, Whimper 300 y Orellana. Mon-Sat 1200-1500, 1900-2230, Sun 1200-2030. Excellent chinese food, very nice atmosphere.

Puerto Camarón, 6 de Diciembre y Granaderos, Centro Comercial Olímpico. Tue-Sat 1000-1500, 1800-2100, Sun 1000-1600. A selection of fish and seafood, good quality.

The Magic Bean, Foch 681 y JL Mera. Mon-Sat 1200-1530, 1900-2200, Sun 1200-1530. Specializes in fine coffees and natural foods, more than 20 varieties of pancakes, good salads, large portions, outdoor seating.

Café Colibrí, Pinto 619 y Cordero. Daily 0800-1830. Large choice of breakfasts and German specialties, pleasant garden setting.

Chandani Tandoori, JL Mera N24-277 y Cordero. Mon-Sat 1100-2200. Simple place with good authentic Indian cuisine, cheap set meals, good variety and value, popular.

Chez Alain, Baquedano 409 y JL Mera. Mon-Fri 1200-1600, 1830-2200. Choice of good 4-course set meals at lunch, à la carte in the evening, pleasant relaxed atmosphere.

El Maple, Foch E8-15 y Almagro. Daily 0730-2330. Strictly vegetarian, varied menu, good meals and fruit juices, covered patio.

Tomato, JL Mera E5-10 y Calama. Daily 0800-0100. Good value buffet breakfast, set lunches, very good pizza and pasta.

Yu Su Café, Edificio Torres de Almagro, Almagrro y Colón. Very good sushi bar, clean and pleasant, Korean run, take-out service.

Cafés

Café del Suizo, Foch 714 y JL Mera. Nice coffee, snacks like quiche, great chocolate cake, pleasant atmosphere.

Café Trovero, JL Mera y Pinto. Mon-Fri 1230-2200, Sat 1330-2200. Espresso and sandwich bar, pastries, pleasant atmosphere, nicely decorated with plants.

Quito & the Highlands Quito Listings

🌓 Bars and clubs

Quito's nightlife is largely concentrated in La Mariscal. Clubs open Wed or Thu-Sat 2000-0300. Note that you can be arrested for not having your passport. A photocopy of the passport and entry stamp may suffice, but it depends on the particular police officer; see p42 .

Bars

La Boca del Lobo, Calama 284 y Reina Victoria, T02-223 4083. Mon-Sat 1700-0000. Café-bar, snacks and meals at mid-range prices, very laid-back, good meeting place, nice atmosphere, young crowd.

Ghoz Bar, La Niña 425 y Reina Victoria, T02-223 9826. From 1800. Swiss owned, excellent Swiss food, pool, darts, videos, games, music, German book exchange.

Kilkenny Irish Pub, Lizardo García y Reina Victoria. Typical pub scene, 80s music, microbrewery.

Kings Cross Bar, Reina Victoria 1781 y La Niña, T02-252 3597. Classic rock, good BBQ, hamburgers, wings. Popular with old hippies.

Matrioshka, Pinto 376 y JL Mera, T02-255 2668. Wed-Sat from 1900, only gets started around 2200. Gay and lesbian bar.

No Bar, Calama y JL Mera. Open till 0200, closed on Sun. Good mix of Latin and Euro dance music on weekdays, always packed on weekends, entry US$4 at weekends, happy hour 1800-2000.

Patatu's, Wilson y JL Mera. 2030-0200, closed Sun. Good drinks, pool table, happy hour all night Mon, a good place for those who want to show off their dancing skills, owner speaks English and German.

El Pobre Diablo, Isabel La Católica y Galavis, 1 block north of Madrid, T02-222 4982. Mon-Sat 1600-0000. Good atmosphere, relaxed and friendly, jazz music, sandwiches, Ecuadorean snacks and some meals, a good and popular place to hang out and chill.

Reina Victoria Pub, Reina Victoria 530 y Roca, T02-222 6369. Mon-Sat from 1700. English style pub, good selection of microbrews and of Scottish and Irish single malts, moderately priced bar meals, darts, happy hour 1800-2000, relaxed atmosphere, fireplace, popular meeting point for British and US expats.

The Turtle´s Head, La Niña 626 y JL Mera, T02-256 5544. Mon-Sat 1700-0200, Sun 1200-0200. Amazing microbrews, great fish and chips, chicken curry, also serves Sun lunch, pool table, darts.

Varadero, Reina Victoria 1721 y La Pinta, T02-254 2575. Mon-Fri 1200-0000, Sat 1800-0300. Bar-restaurant, live Cuban music Wed-Sat, meals and snacks, good cocktails, older crowd and couples.

Clubs

Mayo 68, Lizardo García N10-662 y JL Mera, T02-290 8169. Authentic salsoteca, small, mixed age crowd.

Oz, Maldonado y Pujilí, in the south near El Recreo Trole stop. Fine mix of music and people, huge place with 5 dance halls.

Le Pierrot, Carrión N22-54 y Amazonas. Good variety of live music, very smoky, popular with locals especially on Fri.

Seseribó, Veintimilla y 12 de Octubre, T02-256 3598. Thu-Sat 2100-0100. Caribbean music and salsa, a must for salseros, popular especially Thu and Fri.

🎭 Entertainment

There are always many cultural events taking place in Quito, usually free of charge. See the listings section of *El Comercio* and other papers for details, especially on Fri. Aug is a particularly active month, see festivals below.

Cinema

Films are listed daily in Section C or D of *El Comercio*, www.elcomercio.com

Cinemark, at Plaza de las Américas, Av América y República, T02-226 0301, www.cinemark.com.ec Multiplex, many salons, restaurants in the same complex, Thu-Sun US$4, Mon-Tue US$3, Wed US$2.

Multicines, CCI, Amazonas y Naciones Unidas (in the basement), T1-800-352463,

Budget buster

Dining in style

For a memorable night out in Quito, dine in style at ♛♛♛ **Theatrum** (second floor of Teatro Sucre, Plaza del Teatro, T02-228 9669, Monday-Friday 1230-1600, 1930-2330, Sat 1930-2330, Sun 1230-1600). Housed in the city's most important theatre, the plush red decor is complemented by impeccable white-glove service. No formal dress code but do dress up to make the most of the special occasion. The creative international menu features starters like zebra shrimp (prawn) with sweet tomato and eggplant. Among the main courses, the pork in lavender honey is especially recommended. There are also vegetarian options, an extensive wine list and a selection of wonderful desserts.

www.multicines.com.ec Excellent selection of movies, 8 salons, similar prices to Cinemark.
Ocho y medio, Valladolid y Guipuzcoa, La Floresta. Cinema and café, good for art films, monthly program available from Libri Mundi and other shops, US$3-4.

Dance

Teatro Demetrio Aguilera Malta, at Casa de la Cultura, 6 de Diciembre y Patria, Casa de la Cultura stop on the Ecovía, T02-295 2025. Wed at 1930. The Ecuadorean folk ballet 'Jacchigua' performs here. Entertaining, colourful and touristy, reserve ahead, US$25.

Peñas

La Casa de la Peña, García Moreno 1713 y Galápagos, by the Basílica, T02-228 4179, lacasadelapenia@hotmail.com, Thu-Sun from 2130. Show of Quito legends, Sat at 2200. Popular with locals on Fri and Sat.

✹ Festivals and events

Jan Año Nuevo On New Year's Eve *años viejos* are on display throughout the city. A good spot to see them is on Amazonas, between Patria and Colón.
Feb-Mar Carnaval Water throwing is common at Carnival and several weeks before. **Mar-Apr Semana Santa** The solemn Good Friday procession in the Old

City is most impressive, with thousands of devout citizens taking part.
24 May Independencia Independence, commemorating the Battle of Pichincha in 1822 with early morning cannonfire and parades; everything closes.
Aug Agosto Arte y Cultura Throughout the month of Aug the municipality organizes cultural events, dancing and music in different places throughout the city. **1-6 Dec Día de Quito** The city's main festival is celebrated throughout the week ending 6 Dec. It commemorates the founding of the city with elaborate parades, bullfights, performances and music in the streets. It is very lively and there is a great deal of drinking. The main events culminate on the evening of Dec 5, and the 6th is the day to sleep it all off; everything (except a few restaurants) closes.

○ Shopping

Trading hours are generally 0900-1900 on weekdays, although some shops close at 1200, as they do in smaller towns. Sat afternoon and Sun most shops are closed.

Books

Libri Mundi, JL Mera N23-83 y Veintimilla, T02-223 4791, Mon-Sat 0800-1800 and at Quicentro Shopping, open daily. Excellent selection of Spanish,

English, French and also some Italian books. Sells a wide selection of guidebooks including several Footprint titles including **Ecuador & Galápagos** and the **South American Handbook**. Knowledgeable and helpful staff, noticeboard of what's on in Quito.

Camping gear

Altamontaña, Jorge Washington 425 y 6 de Diciembre, T02-252 4422. Imported climbing equipment for sale, equipment rental, good advice, experienced climbing and trekking guides.

Supermarkets

Comisariato supermarket and department store at Quicentro Shopping and García Moreno y Mejía in the Old City. **Supermaxi** the largest chain in the city, very well stocked supermarket and department stores with a wide range of local and imported goods, not cheap, Mon-Sat 1000-2000, Sun 1000-1300. Branches at Mall El Jardín, CCI, El Bosque, Centro Comercial Plaza Aeropuerto (Av de la Prensa y Homero Salas), Multicentro shopping complex (6 de Diciembre y La Niña, about 2 blocks north of Colón), Megamaxi (6 de Diciembre y Julio Moreno), and El Recreo.

Handicrafts

Typical Ecuadorean *artesanías* include wood carvings, wooden plates, silver, textiles, ceramics, buttons, toys and other objects fashioned from tagua nuts, hand-painted tiles, naïve paintings on leather, Panama hats, hand-woven rugs and a variety of antiques dating back to colonial times. Many craft shops in La Mariscal and around the plazas in the Old City. At Parque El Ejido (Av Patria side), artists sell their crafts and paintings at weekends.
Mercado Artesanal La Mariscal, Jorge Washington, between Reina Victoria and JL Mera, daily 1000-1800. This interesting and worthwhile market, which occupies most of a city block, has a big selection of crafts.

El Indio, Roca E4-35 y Amazonas, T02-255 5227, daily 0900-1900. A craft market with stalls selling a variety of products, also has a coffee shop.
Museo de Artesanía, 12 de Octubre 1738 y Madrid, Mon-Fri 0900-1900, Sat 0900-1700. Another craft market with many vendors and products. There are also souvenir shops on García Moreno under the portico of the Palacio Presidencial in the colonial city.
Folklore, Colón E10-53 y Caamaño, near *Hotel Quito*, T02-254 1315, the store of the late Olga Fisch. It stocks a most attractive array of handicrafts and rugs, and is distinctly expensive, as accords with the designer's international reputation. Branch stores at *Hotel Hilton Colón* and *Hotel Patio Andaluz*.
Fundación Sinchi Sacha, Café Tianguez at Plaza de San Francisco, co-operative selling select ceramics and other arts and crafts from the Oriente.
Hilana, 6 de Diciembre 1921 y Baquerizo Moreno. Beautiful and unique 100% wool blankets in Ecuadorean motifs, excellent quality, purchase by metre possible.
Homero Ortega, Isabel La Católica N24-100, T02-252 67715. Outlet for one of the hat manufacturers in Cuenca.

Markets

For fruits and vegetables and to get the overall market experience, the main markets are: **Mercado Central**, Av Pichincha y Olmedo, in the Old City, refurbished in 2004, Teatro Sucre Trole stop southbound or San Blas northbound, Estación La Marín on the Ecovía. **Mercado Santa Clara**, Versalles y Ramírez Dávalos, Santa Clara Trole stop. **Mercado Iñaquito**, Iñaquito y Villalengua, west of Amazonas, La Y Trole stop.

▲▲ Activities and tours

City tours

The **Empresa de Desarrollo del Centro Histórico**, Plaza de la Independencia, Chile y García Moreno, ground floor of the

Palacio Arzobispal, T02-258 6591, offers *Paseos Culturales*, guided walking tours along two circuits in the colonial city. These include visits with English-speaking guides, who are part of the Metropolitan Police, to museums, plazas, churches, convents and historical buildings. They also have two night tours, one walking through different plazas and a bus tour to El Panecillo and La Cima de la Libertad lookouts. Tue-Sun 0900-1100 and 1400-1430. 2½-3 hours. US$10, Children and seniors US$5, includes museum entrance fees. Night tours require a minimum of 8, 1900-2000, walking tour US$5, bus tours US$12 per person, advance booking required.

For those who would rather ride in style, **Coches de la Colonia**, Plaza de la Independencia, C Chile outside the Palacio Arzobispal, T02-295 0392, will take you on a 20 minute tour of the colonial heart on a horse drawn carriage with an English speaking guide. Reservations recommended on weekends. Sun-Thu 1600-2200, Fri-Sun 1600-0000. US$4, children and seniors US$2, carriage for 4 US$12, carriage for 9 US$24.

Climbing and trekking
Alta Montaña, JL Mera 12-27 y Calama, T02-252 8769, donoso@andinanet.ne. For climbing and trekking.
Campo Base, Jacinto de Evia N60-121 (north of the airport), T02-259 9737, www.campobaseturismo.com. Climbing, trekking and cycling tours, also have a mountain lodge.

Compañía de Guías de Montaña, Jorge Washington 425 y 6 de Dicembre, T/F02-250 4773, www.compania deguias.com. Climbing and trekking specialists, but also sell other tours.

Cycling
The Biking Dutchman, Foch 714 y JL Mera, T02-254 2806, after hours T09-9730267 (mob), www.bikingdutchman.com. The pioneers of mountain biking in Ecuador, one and

several day tours, great fun, good food, very well organized, English, German and Dutch (of course) spoken.

Rafting and kayaking
All agencies in Quito offer one and two day trips on the Toachi and Blanco rivers. Some of them offer additional trips which are mentioned below.
ROW Expediciones, Pablo Arturo Suarez 191 y Eloy Alfaro, T02-2239224, F02-254 4794, www.row expediciones.com. 6-day trips on the Upano Nov-Feb, guides from Idaho, USA.
Sierra Nevada, Pinto 637 y Cordero, T02-255 3658, snevada@accessinter.net. Specialized adventure tours (climbing, trekking, whitewater rafting) and jungle expeditions.
Yacu Amu Rafting, Foch 746 y J L Mera, T02-2904054, F02-290 4055, www.yacuamu.com. 1-3 day trips on the Quijos combined with a stay at Papallacta Hot Springs Resort. Also 5-6 day trips on the Upano Oct-Feb, customized itineraries, kayaking information, equipment rental, 4-day kayak school with qualified instructors, guiding service and all-inclusive packages for those who want to leave the organizing to someone else. Highly recommended as professional and with highest quality equipment.

Tour operators
The following companies have all been recommended. Many are clustered in the Mariscal district, where you are encouraged to have a stroll and shop around. Most Quito agencies sell a variety of tours in all regions of Ecuador; they may run some of those tours themselves, while they act as sales agents for others. Jungle lodges are listed in the Oriente chapter.
Anaconda Travel, Foch 635 y Reina Victoria, 1st floor, T/F02-222 4913, anacondaec@andinanet.net. Run Anaconda lodge in the upper Napo, jungle trips, sell trips to Galápagos and tours to all other destinations.
Andando Tours, Coruña N26-311 y

Orellana, T02-256 6010, www.andandotours.com. Run first class Galápagos boats.

Canodros, Portugal 448 y Catalina Aldaz, T02-22502-6759, www.canodros.com. Luxury Galápagos cruises and jungle tours in the Kapawi Ecological Reserve (see p400).

EcoTours, www.ecotoursecuador.com. Dedicated to conservation and run 4- and 5- day tours to the Napo Wildlife Centre. Tours can only be arranged with EcoTours through other agencies.

Ecoventura, Almagro N31-80 y Whymper, T/F02-223 1034, www.ecoventura.com. Miami office: Galapagos Network, USA and Canada toll-free T1-800-633-7972, info@galapagosnetwork.com. Operate first class Galápagos cruises and sell tours throughout Ecuador.

Emerald Forest Expeditions, Pinto E4-244 y Amazonas, T02-254 1278, F02-254 1543, www.emeraldexpeditions.com. Jungle tours to Pañacocha Lodge, 4-7 day jungle trips, also have office in Coca.

The Galápagos Boat Company, Foch E5-39, T02-222 0426, www.safari.com.ec. Broker for about 60 boats in the islands, can find you the best deals around.

Galasam, Amazonas 1354 y Cordero, T02-290 3909, www.galasam.com. Has a large fleet of boats in different categories for Galápagos cruises. Full range of tours in highlands, jungle trips to their own lodge on the Río Aguarico.

Green Planet, JL Mera N23-84 y Wilson, T02-252 0570, greenpla@ interactive.net.ec. Ecologically sensitive jungle tours in Cuyabeno and the Tena area, friendly staff and guides, good food.

Kempery Tours, Ramírez Dávalos 117 y Amazonas, Edificio Turismundial, p 1, T02-250 5600, www.kempery.com. Good value tours, 4-14 day jungle trips to Bataburo Lodge in Huaorani territory and operate Galápagos cruises; also sell horse riding and other tours, multilingual service.

Klein Tours, Eloy Alfaro N34-151 y Catalina Aldaz, also Shyris N34-280 y Holanda, T02-226 7000, www.kleintours.com. Galápagos and mainland tours, tailor-made, English, French and German spoken.

Neotropic Turis, Amazonas N24-03 y Wilson, T02-252 1212, www.neotropicturis.com. Operates the Cuyabeno Lodge (see Cuyabeno Wildlife reserve, p395) jungle trips and organizes trips in all regions.

Quasar Náutica, Brasil 293 y Granda Centeno, Edificio IACA p 2, T02-244 6996, www.quasarnautica.com. Galápagos 7-10 day naturalist and diving cruises on 8-16 berth luxury sail and power yachts with multilingual guides, also tours historic sites, haciendas, national parks and jungle lodges. For UK and US contact details, see p46.

Safari, Foch E5-39 y JL Mera, T02-255 2505, USA/Canada toll free T1-800-4348182, www.safari.com.ec. Run by Jean Brown and Pattie Serrano, both

THE FINEST LODGE PROVIDING YOU ECUADOR´S BEST AMAZON WILDERNESS !

Napo Wildlife Center
Amazonian Ecuador

www.napowildlifecenter.com
www.ecotoursecuador.com

knowledgeable and informative. Excellent adventure travel, personalized itineraries, mountain climbing, cycling, rafting, trekking and cultural tours. They also book Galápagos tours, sell jungle trips and run a high-altitude glacier school. An excellent source of travel information. Open 7 days a week 0900-1900.

Tropic Ecological Adventure, República E7-320 y Almagro, Edificio Taurus 1-A, T02-222 5907, www.tropiceco.com. Run by Andy Drumm and Sofía Darquea, naturalist guides with many years experience in Galápagos, who work closely with conservation groups, winners of awards for responsible tourism. Their ecologically responsible and educational tours are recommended for anyone seriously interested in the environment, part of each fee is given to indigenous communities and ecological projects. Also sell Galápagos and highland trips.

Zenith Travel, JL Mera 452 y Roca, Chiriboga Building, 2nd floor, T02-252 9993, F02-290 5595, Mob T09-955 5951, www.zenithecuador.com. Caters to gay travellers, tours to Oriente, Highlands and Galápagos.

⊖ Transport

Air
Mariscal Sucre Airport, T02-294 4900. For airport facilities and transportation to/from the airport, see p320. For information on national flights see Getting around by air, see p22.

Bus
Local Quito has three parallel transport lines running from north to south on exclusive lanes, covering almost the length of the city. The fare is US$0.25. There are plans to integrate these lines into one transport system in late 2005. Trole is an integrated system of trolley buses and feeder bus lines (alimentadores, painted turquoise). It runs along Av 10 de Agosto in the north of the city, C Guayaquil (southbound) and C

Flores (northbound) in the Old City, and mainly along Av Pedro Vicente Maldonado in the south (see map on p321). Some trolleys run the full length of the line, while others run only a section, the destination is marked in front of the vehicle. There is a special entrance for wheelchairs. It runs Mon-Fri 0500-2345, weekends and holidays 0600-2145. There are also 3 types of city buses, selectivos are red, take mostly sitting passengers and a limited number standing, and charge US$0.25. Bus Tipo are royal blue, take sitting and standing passengers, also US$0.25. There are few populares left, these are light blue, cost US$0.18, can get very crowded. Many bus lines go through La Marín at the north end of the Old City.

Long distance The main Terminal Terrestre for all national services is in the Old City, at Maldonado y Cumandá. There is a 24-hr luggage store which is safe, US$1.75 per day. There are company booking offices in the terminal but staff shout destinations of buses leaving and you can hop on board and pay later; but confirm the fare in advance and check if another company is not leaving sooner. For the less frequent routes, or at busy times of the year (long weekends or holidays), consider purchasing your ticket a day in advance. See under the relevant destination for prices and travelling times.

When arriving in Quito by bus, you and your luggage will be unloaded next to a large taxi rank. Cab drivers wait for the buses; choose one, either agree to use the meter or agree on a price, and get going. A ride during the day to the New City should cost about US$4, less to the Old City.

Several companies have private stations, generally in the New City, buses departing from these stations will also make a stop at the Terminal Terrestre before leaving the city. These include: **Flota Imbabura**, Manuel Larrea 1211 y Portoviejo, T02-223 6940, for Cuenca; and **Panamericana Internacional**, Colón 852 y Reina Victoria, T02-250 1585, for Cuenca and Loja, also run an international service:

daily to Lima, changing buses in Aguas Verdes and Túmbes, US$70, 38 hrs. **Ormeño Internacional**, from Perú, has an office at Los Shyris N34-432 y Portugal, opposite Parque la Carolina, T02-246 0027. They go twice per week to **Lima**, US$70, 36 hrs, and **La Paz**, US$150, but it is cheaper to take a bus to the border and change there.

Taxis

Taxis are a safe, cheap and efficient way to get around the city. Rides cost from US$1 during the day, there is no increase for extra passengers. You can expect to pay about US$1-2 more at night. All taxis must have working meters (*taxímetros*) by law, so make sure the meter is running (drivers sometimes say their meters are out of order). If the meter is not running, politely fix the fare before getting in. All legally registered taxis have large numbers prominently displayed on the side of the vehicle and on a decal on the windshield. They are safer and cheaper than unauthorized taxis. At night it is safer to use a radio taxi, there are several companies including: **Taxi Amigo**, T02-222 2222, **City Taxi**, T02-263 3333 and **Central de Radio Taxis**, T02-250 0600. Some of these radio taxi companies may use unmarked vehicles, when calling ask the dispatcher exactly what car will pick you up. To hire a taxi by the hour costs from US$7 in the city, US$8 if going out of town.

Mitad del Mundo *p327*

Take a 'Mitad del Mundo' interparroquial bus from the Av del Maestro stop on the Miraflores-Carcelén line. By taxi from the New City US$12. An excursion to Mitad del Mundo by taxi, with a one hour wait is about US$20.

Termas de Papallacta *p328*

Many buses a day pass Papallacta on their way to and from Lago Agrio, Coca or Tena (drivers sometimes charge full fare). From Quito, 2 hrs, US$2. If going to the Termas, ask to be let off at the turn-off to the

springs before town; it is then a 30-min walk up the hill to the complex. At the turn-off is **Restaurante La Esquina**, they offer transport to the Termas, US$0.50-1 per person depending on the number of people. Travelling back to Quito at night is not recommended.

Directory

Airline offices

Domestic Aerogal, Amazonas 7797 opposite the airport, T02-225 7202, 1-800-2376425, aerogal@andinanet.net. **Atesa**, Guipúzcoa 122 y Gerona, T2303242, seconaca@pi.pro.ec. **Icaro**, Palora 124 y Amazonas, near airport, T2450928, T1-800-883567, www.icaro.com.ec. **TAME**, Amazonas 13-54 y Colón, Colón y La Rábida and 6 de Diciembre N26-112, T02-290 9900 to 909, www.tame.com.ec

International Lan Peru, Pasaje Río Guayas E3-131 y Amazonas, Edificio Rumiñahui, opposite Parque La Carolina, T02-299 2300, 1-800-526328, www.lan.com.

Banks

Banks are generally open Mon-Fri 0830-1800 and some also on Sat 0900-1300. Service for cash advances and TC exchange is usually only Mon-Fri until about 1500 (the earlier the better). Expect queues at all banks. The **American Express** representative is Ecuadorean Tours, Amazonas 329 y Jorge Washington, T02-256 0488, replaces lost Amex TCs and sells TCs to Amex card holders, but does not exchange TCs or sell them for cash. Mon-Fri 0830-1700. **Banco de Guayaquil**, Colón y Reina Victoria, 3rd Floor. Cirrus, Maestro or Plus ATM with maximum withdrawal of US$100. **Mastercard** headquarters, Naciones Unidas 825, next door to Banco del Pacifico. Cash advances, efficient service. Mon-Fri 0830-1700. **Banco del Pacífico**, main branch at Naciones Unidas between Los Shyris and Amazonas, also Amazonas y Roca, Mall El Jardín and Centro Comercial El Bosque. Cirrus and Maestro ATMs. **Banco del Pichincha**, Amazonas 13-54 y Colón, Venezuela y Espejo, half block from Plaza de la Independencia and many other branches. Cirrus ATM. **Casa de cambio** Vazcorp, Amazonas N21-147 y Roca, T02-252 9212. Charges 1.8% commission for US$ TCs, 2% for TCs in other currencies. Also changes other currencies and sells TCs. Mon-Fri 0845-1745, Sat 0900-1300.

Car hire
The main car hire companies have counters at the airport and city offices. The phone numbers shown without an address are at the airport. **Budget**, T02-245 9052; Amazonas 1408 y Colón T02-222 1814, www.budget-ec.com. **Ecuacars**, T02-224 7298; Colón 1280 y Amazonas, T02-252 9781. **Hertz**, T02-225 4257, www.hertz.com. **Localiza**, 6 de Diciembre E8-124 y Veintimilla, T02-227 0222, T1-800-562254, www.localiza.com.ec

Embassies and consulates
All open Mon-Fri unless otherwise noted. **Canada**, 6 de Diciembre 2816 y Paul Rivet, Edificio Josueth González p4, T02-223 2114, 0900-1200. **Ireland**, Ulloa 2651 y Rumipamba, T02-245 1577, 0900-1300. **Peru**, República de El Salvador 495 e Irlanda, Edificio Irlanda, T02-246 8410, embpeecu@uio.satnet.net, 0900-1300, 1500-1800. **United Kingdom**, Naciones Unidas y República de El Salvador, Edificio Citiplaza p14, T02-297

0800, britemq@impsat.net.ec, Mon-Thu 0730-1230, 1300-1600, Fri 0830-1230. **USA**, 12 de Octubre y Patria, T02-256 2890, 0800-1230, 1330-1700.

Internet

Quito has very many cyber cafés, particularly in the Mariscal tourist district. Rates start at about US$0.60 per hr, but US$1 per hr is more typical. Internet access is cheapest and fastest in Quito and Cuenca, more expensive and slower in small towns and more remote areas. Watch your belongings while in the internet cafés, there have been some reports of theft.

Language schools

Quito is one of the most important centres for Spanish language study in all of Latin America, with about 80 schools operating in the city. If you are short on time then it can be a good idea to make your arrangements from home, either directly with one of the schools or through an agency such as **AmeriSpan**, USA and Canada toll-free T1-800-879-6640, www.amerispan.com, who can offer you a wide variety of options. If you have more time and less money, then it may be cheaper to organize your own studies after you arrive. You can try one or two places without committing yourself for an extended period. **Internacional de Español** (IE), Selva Alegre Oe6-66 y Ruiz de Castilla, T02-310 3338, www.diplomaie.com is an organization which trains Spanish as a second language teachers, publishes textbooks and maintains a list of schools throughout Ecuador. They provide general information, help students select a school and sell course materials. **South American Explorers** also provides its members with a list of recommended schools and these may give club members discounts.

Laundry

There are many laundromats around La Mariscal, wash and dry costs about US$0.80 per kg, some deliver pre-paid laundry. Several are clustered around the corner of Foch and Reina Victoria, along Pinto and along Wilson.

Medical services

Clínica Pasteur, Eloy Alfaro 552 y 9 de Octubre, T2234004. **Clínica Pichincha**, Veintimilla E3-30 y Páez, T02-256 2296, ambulance T02-250 1565. Most embassies have the telephone numbers of doctors who speak non-Spanish languages.

Pharmacies

Fybeca is a reliable chain of 35 pharmacies throughout the city. Their 24-hr branches are at Amazonas y Tomás de Berlanga near the Plaza de Toros, and at Centro Comercial El Recreo in the south.

Post

There are 23 postal branches throughout Quito, opening times vary but are generally Mon-Fri 0800-1800, Sat 0800-1200. In principle all branches provide all services, but your best chances are at Colón y Almagro in the Mariscal district, and at the main sorting centre on Japón near Naciones Unidas, behind the CCI shopping centre.

Useful addresses

Emergencies T911 for all types of emergency in Quito. **Immigration offices** See Getting in, Extensions, page . **Police** T101. **Policía de Turismo**, Reina Victoria y Roca, T2543983. Report robberies at **Dirección de Seguridad Pública**, Cuenca y Mideros, T02-295 4604, in the Old City or **Policía Judicial**, Roca 582 y JL Mera, in La Mariscal, T02-255 0243.

North of Quito

North from Quito to the border with Colombia is an area of great natural beauty and cultural interest. The landscape is mountainous, with views of the peaks of Cotacachi, Imbabura, Chiles and glacier-covered Cayambe, interspersed with lakes. This is also a region renowned for its *artesanía*. Countless villages specialize in their own particular craft, be it textiles, hats, woodcarvings, bread figures or leather goods. And, of course, there is Otavalo, with its outstanding market, a must on everyone's itinerary. It's worth spending a few extra days here either side of the Saturday market to visit some of the local artisan villages, explore the surrounding countryside by bike or horse, stay in a converted 17th century haciends or perhaps even climb a volcano or two.

⊘ Getting there Buses and shared taxis from Quito to Otavalo.

⊖ Getting around Frequent buses run between most towns.

⊖ Time required 2-3 days.

⊚ Weather Rainy season Oct-May.

⊜ Sleeping Excellent *haciendas*, also opportunities for staying in native communities. Otavalo has wide selection in all categories.

⊘ Eating Various *hosterías* offer good *comida típica*; also standard gringo fare in Otavalo.

▲▲ Activities and tours Shopping at Otavalo market; trips to artisan villages; climbing, trekking and horseriding

★ Don't miss... Saturday in Otavalo ⟫ *p346*.

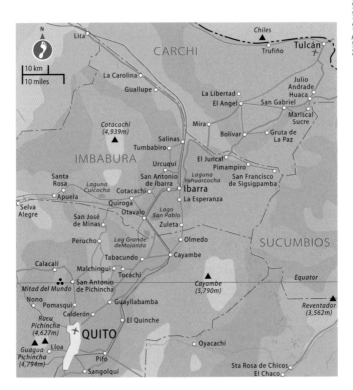

Otavalo and around ⊜🕖🕉⊛⊙▲⊜⦿ ›› pp348-351

Otavalo is set in beautiful countryside which is well worth exploring. The town itself is nothing to write home about, consisting as it does of rather functional modern buildings, but visitors still don't come here for the architecture. Otavalo is one of South America's most important centres of ethno-tourism and its enormous Saturday market, featuring a dazzling array of textiles and crafts, is second to none and not to be missed. For those interested in learning more about how local crafts are made, a visit to surrounding villages can be interesting.

Ins and outs

Getting there The bus station is at Atahualpa and Ordoñez in the northeast of the city and just off the Panamericana. Through buses going further north drop you at the highway which is not recommended, **Transportes Otavalo** and **Los Lagos** are the only long distance companies going into town. There are few hotels around the bus terminal, but most are in the centre which is within walking distance (about 6 blocks), taxis and city buses are also available. It's best to travel on Friday, in order to avoid overcrowded buses on Saturday and to enjoy the nightlife. ⊜ ›› p351.

Getting around The centre is quite small. You can walk between the craft market at Plaza de Ponchos and the produce market at Plaza 24 de Mayo. The livestock market is more of a hike. City buses go to nearby villages such as Peguche and those around Lago San Pablo.

Information Oficina Municipal de Turismo, Bolívar 8-38 y Calderón, T06-292 1313, sdt@andinanet.net Monday-Saturday 0800-1230, 1400-1730, local and regional information.

Sights

Saturday is the main event, when Otavalo's famous market can be experienced in all its glory. The Saturday market actually comprises four different markets in various parts of the town and the central streets are filled with vendors. The **artesanía** (crafts) market (0700-1800) is based around the Plaza de Ponchos (officially called Plaza Centenario). The livestock sections begin at 0500 and last until 1000. Large animals are traded outside town in the Viejo Colegio Agrícola, west of the Panamericana. To get there, go west on Calle Colón from the town centre. The small animal market is held on Atahualpa by the bus terminal. The produce market (0700-1400) is in Plaza 24 de Mayo. The artesanía market has more selection on Saturday but prices are a little higher than other days when the atmosphere is more relaxed.

Otavalo market is one of the best places in all of South America to buy handicrafts.

The Otavaleños sell goods they weave and sew themselves, as well as *artesanía* from throughout Ecuador, Peru and Bolivia. Mestizo and indigenous vendors from Otavalo, and from elsewhere in Ecuador and South America, sell paintings, jewellery, shigras, baskets, leather goods, hats, woodcarvings from San Antonio de Ibarra and the Oriente, ceramics, antiques and almost anything else you care to mention.

Around Otavalo

The Otavalo weavers come from dozens of communities, but it is easiest to visit the nearby towns of Peguche, Ilumán, Carabuela and Agato which are only 15-30 minutes away and all have a good bus service. There are also tours to these villages. In **Peguche** (a few kilometres northeast of Otavalo), the Cotacachi-Pichamba family, off the main plaza behind the church, sells beautiful tapestries, finished with tassels and loops, ready to hang. At the entrance to Peguche is **Galería Peguche Huasi**, an interesting museum about the native way of life and weaving tradition. In **Ilumán** (east of the Panamericana, north of the turn-off for Cotacachi), the Conterón-de la Torre family of Artesanías Inti Chumbi, on the northeast corner of the plaza, gives backstrap loom-weaving demonstrations and sells crafts. There are also many felt

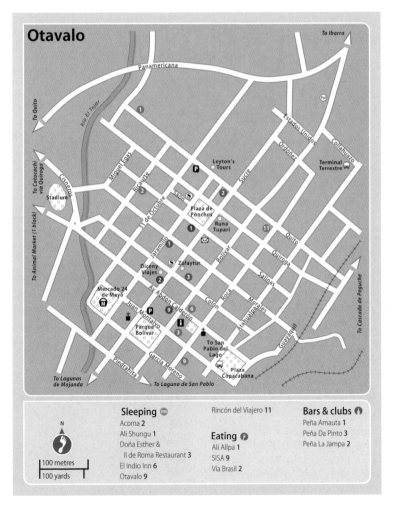

Otavalo

Sleeping 😴
Acoma **2**
Ali Shungu **1**
Doña Esther &
  Il de Roma Restaurant **3**
El Indio Inn **6**
Otavalo **9**

Rincón del Viajero **11**

Eating 🍴
Ali Allpa **1**
SISA **9**
Vía Brasil **2**

Bars & clubs 🍸
Peña Amauta **1**
Peña Da Pinto **3**
Peña La Jampa **2**

100 metres
100 yards

hatmakers in town who will make hats to order. In **Agato** (northeast of Otavalo), the Andrango-Chiza family of Tahuantinsuyo Weaving Workshop gives weaving demonstrations and sells textiles. In **Carabuela** (west of the Panamericana, just south of the road to Cotacachi) many homes sell crafts including wool sweaters. Carlos de la Torre, a backstrap weaver, can be found above the Evangelist Church.

To the southeast of Otavalo, at the foot of Cerro Imbabura and just off the Panamericana is the scenic **Lago San Pablo**, the largest natural lake in the country. A secondary road circumnavigates the lake. Along it are several native villages and a number of upmarket places to stay (see box on page 349). San Pablo is a popular weekend destination for wealthier Ecuadoreans, looking for water sports, good food, or just a place to get away. There is a network of old roads and trails between Otavalo and the Lago San Pablo area, none of which takes more than an hour or two to explore. Boats can be hired to explore the lake itself.

Sleeping

Otavalo *p346, map p347*
A Ali Shungu, Quito y Miguel Egas, T06-292 0750, www.alishungu.com. Nicely decorated hotel with lovely garden, nice comfortable rooms, good restaurant with live music on weekends, parking, no smoking, safe deposit boxes, can arrange transport from Quito, credit cards only accepted over the internet using Paypal, surcharge for credit cards and TCs, US run.
B El Indio Inn, Bolívar 904 y Calderón, T06-292 2922, hindioinn@andinanet.net. Attractive hotel, includes breakfast, restaurant, parking, carpeted rooms and suites, spotlessly clean, refurbished in 2004.
B Hotel Otavalo, Roca 504 y J Montalvo, T06-292 3712, www.hotelotavalo.com.ec. Refurbished colonial house, good breakfast included, pricey restaurant, large rooms, patio, good service, helpful.
B-D Acoma, Salinas 07-57 y 31 de Octubre, T06-292 6570. A lovely modern hotel built in colonial style, includes breakfast, cafeteria, cheaper with shared bath, parking, nice comfortable rooms, some with balcony, one room with bathtub, one suite with kitchenette in A range, good value.
C Doña Esther, Montalvo 4-44 y Bolívar, T06-292 0739, www.otavalohotel.com. Nicely restored colonial house, good pizzeria downstairs, simple rooms with nice wooden floors, colourful décor.

D Rincón del Viajero, Roca 11-07 y Quiroga, T06-292 1741, rincondelviajero@hotmail.com. Very pleasant hostel and meeting place. Simple but nicely decorated rooms, includes a choice of nice breakfasts, cheaper with shared bath, laundry facilities, parking, rooftop hammocks, sitting room with fireplace, US-Ecuadorean run, friendly.

Around Otavalo *p346*
B La Casa de Hacienda, Entrance at Panamericana Norte Km 3, then 300 m east, T06-292 3105, www.casadehacienda.com. Tasteful cabins with fireplace, includes breakfast,

Otavaleños in traditional dress.

Budget busters

LL **Casa Mojanda**, Vía Mojanda Km 3.5, T06-292 2986, www.casamojanda.com Beautiful setting on 7 ha of farmland and forested gorge. Includes breakfast and tasty dinner prepared with ingredients from their own organic garden, comfortable adobe cabins each one decorated with its own elegant touch. Traditional hot tub with great views, quiet, good library, horse riding.

L **Hacienda Pinsaquí**, Panamericana Norte Km 5, 300 m north of the turn-off for Cotacachi, T06-294 6116, www.haciendapinsaqui.com. Converted hacienda with 23 suites, includes breakfast, restaurant with lovely dining room, lounge with fireplace, beautiful antiques, colonial ambience, gardens, horse riding.

L **Hacienda Cusín**, by the village of San Pablo del Lago to the southeast of the lake, T06-291 8013, www.haciendacusin.com A converted 17th century hacienda with lovely courtyard and garden, includes breakfast, fine expensive restaurant, 25 rooms with fireplaces, sports (pool, horses, mountain bikes, squash court, games room), library, book in advance, British run, English and German spoken.

restaurant serves Ecuadorean and international food, parking, advance reservations required for horse riding.
C **Aya Huma**, on the railway line in Peguche, T06-292 2663, www.ayahuma.com. In a country setting between the unused rail tracks and the river. Restaurant, cheaper in annex with cooking facilieties, quiet, pleasant atmosphere, live music Sat night, Dutch run, popular.
D **La Luna de Mojanda**, On a side-road going south off the Mojanda road at Km 4, T09-9737415, lalunaecuador @yahoo.co.uk. Pleasant country hostel in nice surroundings, restaurant, cheaper in dorm, parking, some rooms with fireplace and private bath, others shared, terrace with hammocks, pleasant dining room-lounge, camping possible, taxi from Otavalo US$3 or take Punyaro city bus, excursions arranged, popular.

Eating

Otavalo *p346, map p347*
Il de Roma, J Montalvo 4-44 at Hotel Doña Esther. Good pizza and pasta, warm atmosphere.

Via Brasil, Sucre y Abdón Calderón, second floor, Wed-Sun 1200-2200. Brazilian rodizio with a variety of meat choices and nice salad bar, feijoada, caipirinha, nicely decorated, authentic, Brazilian-Ecuadorean run.
SISA, Abdón Calderón 4-09 y Sucre, daily 0700-2200. Cultural centre, restaurant on second floor serve excellent setmeals and à la carte, coffee shop with capuccino, slow service, also bookstore, weekly international films, live music Fri-Sun.
Ali Allpa, Salinas 509 at Plaza de Ponchos. Good value set meals and à la carte, trout, vegetarian, meat dishes.

Bars and clubs

Otavalo *p346, map p347*
Most peñas are open Fri and Sat from 2000, entrance US$2. During festivals, there are nightlife tours on a chiva (open-sided bus with a musical group on board), it stops at the Plaza de Ponchos.
Peña Amauta, Morales 5-11 y Jaramillo, T06-292 2475. Good local bands, varied music, friendly and welcoming, popular with foreigners.
Peña Da Pinto, Colón 4-10 y Bolívar, T09-4188438, www.dapinto.com.

Colourfully decorated, live Latin music on weekends, drinks and snacks.

Peña la Jampa, Jaramillo y Quiroga, T06-292 2988, Fri-Sat 1930-0300. Andean and dancing music, popular with Ecuadoreans and foreigners.

✹ Festivals and events

If you wish to visit fiestas in the local villages, ask the musicians in the tourist restaurants, they may invite you; outsiders are not always welcome. The music is good and there is a lot of drinking, but transport back to Otavalo is hard to find. **Inti Raymi** celebrations of the summer solstice (**21 Jun**) are combined with the **Fiesta de San Juan** (**24 Jun**) and the **Fiesta de San Pedro y San Pablo** (**29 Jun**). There are bullfights in the plaza and regattas on Lago San Pablo, 4 km away (see Around Otavalo below for transport). These combined festivities are known as **Los San Juanes** and participants are mostly indigenous. Most of the action takes place in the smaller communities surrounding Otavalo. Groups of musicians and dancers compete with each other as they make their way from one village to another over the course of the week. The **Fiesta del Yamor** and **Colla Raimi** (fall equinox or festival of the moon) are held during the first 2 weeks of **Sep**. This is the largest festivity in the province of Imbabura, it takes place in several cities and is mainly a mestizo celebration.

○ Shopping

Otavalo *p346, map p347*
Otavalo can seem like a giant souvenir shop at times. As well as the market, there are countless shops selling sweaters, tapestries and other souvenirs
The Book Market, Jaramillo 6-28 y Salinas, for buying, selling or exchanging books in English, French, German and other languages at cheap prices. Also guidebooks, maps, postcards, CDs and cassettes, handicrafts

Galeria de Arte Quipus, Sucre y Morales, paintings with native motifs.
Galeria Inti Ñan, Salinas 509 y Sucre, Plaza de Ponchos, also has a nice selection of paintings with native themes.
Palos de Lluvia, Morales 506 y Sucre, rain sticks and other crafts.
Tagua Muyu, Sucre 10-11 y Colón, tagua (vegetable ivory) carvings.

▲▲ Activities and tours

Otavalo *p346, map p347*
Tour operators
All agencies offer similar tours and prices. One-day tours with English-speaking guides to artisans' homes and villages, which usually provide opportunities to buy handicrafts cheaper than in the market, cost US$20 per person. Horse-riding tours around Otavalo: 5 hrs to Tangali thermal springs or El Lechero lookout US$20; full day to Cuicocha crater lake US$30-35.
Diceny Viajes, Sucre 10-11 y Colón, T06-292 1217, zulayviajes@hotmail.com. Run by Zulay Sarabino, an indigenous Otavaleña, English and French spoken, native guides knowledgeable about the area and culture, climbing trips to Cotacachi volcano.
Runa Tupari, Sucre y Quiroga, Plaza de Ponchos T/F06-292 5985, nativetravel@runatupari.com. Trips to community inns in the Cotacachi area, US$20 per person per day, half board, includes transport (see Cotacachi below), also the usual tours at higher-than-average prices, English and French spoken.
Suni Tours, no store-front at this time, contact owner Iván Suárez through Hostal Valle del Amanecer or T06-292 3383, T09-9933148, www.geocities.com /sunitour. Interesting itineraries, trekking and horse-riding tours, climbing, cycling, also rafting on the Río Intag. English spoken, guides carry radios. Note that in early 2005 this agency was in the process of expanding and will operate with a new name later in the year.

Balsa wood parrots on sale in Otavalo.

Zulaytur, Sucre y Colón, p2, T06-292 1176, F06-292 2969. Run by Rodrigo Mora. English spoken, information, map of town, slide show, horse riding, interesting day trip to local artisan communities.

⊖ Transport

Otavalo *p346, map p347*
Bus From Quito, Terminal Terrestre, every 10 mins, US$2, 2 hrs. Take a **Cooperativa Otavalo** or **Cooperativa Los Lagos** bus, as they are the only ones which go into Otavalo; other companies bound for points further north will drop you off on the highway, which is far from the centre and not safe after dark.
Taxi A fast and efficient alternative is shared taxis with **Supertaxis Los Lagos** (in Quito at Asunción 3-82, T06-256 5992; in Otavalo at Roca 8-04, T06-292 3203) who will pick you up at your hotel (in the New City only); hourly Mon-Fri 0700-1900, Sat 0700-1600, Sun 0800-1800, 2 hrs, US$7.50 per person, buy ticket at their office the day before travelling. A regular taxi costs US$50 one way, US$80 return with 3 hours wait.

Around Otavalo *p346*
To **Peguche** take a city bus along Av Atahualpa, these stop outside the bus terminal and Plaza Copacabana (Atahualpa y Montalvo), every 15 mins, US$0.18. You can also take a taxi or go with a tour. Buses to **San Pablo del Lago** from Otavalo terminal every 30 minutes, more often on Saturday, US$0.18. A taxi costs US$4.

❶ Directory

Otavalo *p346, map p347*
Banks Banco del Pacífico, Bolívar 614 y García Moreno. Banco del Pichincha, Bolívar y Piedrahita. **Casa de Cambio**, Sucre 11-05 y Colón. TCs 3% commission, also change Euros and other currencies, poor rates. **Vaz Corp**, Jaramillo y Saona, Plaza de Ponchos, T06-292 2926, Tue-Sat 0900-1700. TCs 1.80-2% commission, also change Euros, reasonable rates.
Internet Many in town especially along C Sucre, US$1 per hr. **Language schools** Instituto Superior de Español, Sucre 11-10 y Morales, p 2, T06-299 2414, www.instituto-superior.net (see also Language schools, Quito, p344). **Mundo Andino Internacional**, Salinas 509, p 3, at Plaza de Ponchos T/F06-292 5478, mundoandinoinn@hotmail.com Dancing and cooking classes at no extra cost. **Post office** Sucre y Salinas esquina at Plaza de Ponchos, p 1, entrance on Sucre.

Central Sierra

South from Quito is some of the loveliest mountain scenery in Ecuador. This part of the country was named the 'Avenue of the Volcanoes', by the German explorer, Alexander Von Humboldt, and it is easy to see why. An impressive roll call of towering peaks lines the route south: Cotopaxi, the Ilinizas, Carihuayrazo and Chimborazo, to name but a few. This area attracts its fair share of trekkers and climbers, while the less active tourist can browse through the many colourful markets and colonial towns that nestle among the high volcanic cones. Baños, named and famed for its thermal baths, is a popular spa on the main road from the Central Highlands to the Oriente jungle. It is the base for activities ranging from mountain biking to café lounging, as well as volcano watching.

Getting there Frequent buses from Quito and other towns. Baños is a main gateway to the Oriente.

Getting around Plenty of buses or private transport arranged with tour agencies.

Time required 7-10 days.

Weather Rainy season Oct-May, in Baños Jun-Sep. Cold nights on Quilotoa circuit.

Sleeping Several *haciendas* and interesting places through countryside. Many hotels in Baños.

Eating Huge variety in Baños, several options in Riobamba.

Activities and tours Mountain biking, climbing, hiking, volcano watching, train ride over the Devil's Nose.

★ **Don't miss...** the Chimborazo Vicuña reserve ›› *p360.*

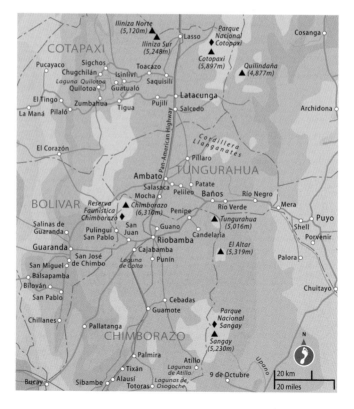

Latacunga & Quilotoa Circuit ⊖❷❶❀⊙▲❸❸ ⊁ *pp360-372*

Gateway to the popular Quilotoa Circuit, a loop through several colourful villages in the Cotopaxi countryside, is Latacunga, a thoroughly authentic highland town which has preserved its colonial character. Cotopaxi is 29 km away and dominates the city; while many other mountains can also be seen on a clear day. The Panamericana goes by the western side of town, the Terminal Terrestre is just along it. A few simple hotels and restaurants are dotted along the highway, with better quality and more selection in the centre. The town centre is compact and quite pleasant to walk around and the Terminal is a 10 minute walk away.

Getting there and around Latacunga is well served by buses along the Panamericana from the north and south as well as from Quevedo. Getting from one town to another along the Quilotoa circuit can at times be difficult, as the bus routes go from Latacunga to each individual town. To get from one town to another it may be necessary to transfer buses an the schedules can be inconvenient. It is all do-able and worthwhile but allow enough time. Note that buses returning from the communities to Latacunga often leave very early, before dawn. Alternative ways to explore the Quilotoa Circuit are cycling and walking. The area lends itself to trekking or cycling from town to town. ⊖ ⊁ *p370*.

Tourist information The **Oficina de Turismo** is at the Terminal Terrestre in Latacunga, second floor ⓘ *Mon-Fri 0900-1200, 1330-1800, Sat 0900-1600, Sun 0900-1400*. It is staffed by high school students from the tourism program at the local college.

Quilotoa Circuit

This is a popular route with visitors, yet preserves an authentic feel in the many small villages and vast expanses of open countryside. You could easily spend a few days or more hiking, horse riding, cycling, visiting indigenous markets or just relaxing. The scenery is both magnificent and varied, ranging from the immense Río Toachi Canyon, through patchwork fields and high páramo to cloud forest. The emerald crater lake of Quilotoa is not to be missed.

A recommended round trip is from Latacunga to Pujilí, Tigua, Zumbahua, Quilotoa, Chugchilán, Sigchos, Isinliví, Toacazo, Saquisilí, and back to Latacunga, which can be done in two to three days by bus. Some enjoy riding on the roof for the views and thrills, but hang on

Laguna Quilotoa, one of the highlights of the Central Sierra.

Quito & the Highlands Central Sierra

tight and wrap up well. The whole loop is around 200 km and can be covered in a car or by taxi in 7-8 hours of non-stop driving, but it is a long, hard trip. A better idea is to break it up into two to three days or more. Accommodation is available in all the villages listed. Be prepared for cold temperatures; many places along the loop are above 3,000 m.

Some 15 km along the paved road west from Latacunga is **Pujilí**, which has a beautiful church (but it's closed most of the time). There is some local ceramic work, a good market on Sunday, and a smaller one on Wednesday. From Pujilí the road climbs steeply to cross the western cordillera. Beyond the pass, it gradually descends through high rolling country with some lovely views. Ten kilometres from Pujilí is the Tigua area where the local people produce interesting crafts, such as primitivist paintings on leather (a form of art that started here and has spread to other parts of Cotopaxi), hand-carved wooden masks and baskets. The best artists are the Toaquiza family, now regarded as the most accomplished of the Tigua painters, with exhibitions in the USA and Europe. In the village of Tigua-Chimbacucho, by the side of the road is a community-run hotel and a large art gallery where the local work can be admired and bought. You may meet some of the artists here. Visits to artisans' workshops are possible with advance notice. There are several walking trails in the area including one to Quilotoa.

Zumbahua is a small indigenous village 500 m north of the main Latacunga road, 65 km from Pujilí. It is quite sleepy for most of the week, but comes alive on weekends, festivals and market day, Saturday. The market starts at 0600, and is only for local produce and animals, interesting and best before 1000. Friday nights involve much dancing and drinking.

Zumbahua is the point to turn off to continue along the Quilotoa Circuit and to visit **Quilotoa**, a volcanic crater filled by a beautiful emerald lake. The crater is reached by a paved road which runs north from Zumbahua. It's about 12 km and takes 3-5 hours to walk, or 30

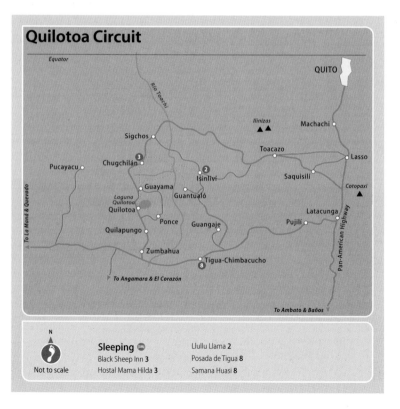

Quilotoa Circuit

Equator

QUITO

Río Toachi

Ilinizas ▲ ▲   Machachi

Sigchos

Toacazo

Chugchilán **3**   Lasso

Pucayacu   Isinliví **2**   Saquisilí

Guayama   Cotopaxi ▲

Laguna Quilotoa   Guantualó

Quilotoa   Latacunga

Ponce   Guangaje   Pujilí

Quilapungo   Pan-American Highway

To La Maná & Quevedo   Zumbahua

Tigua-Chimbacucho **8**

To Angamara & El Corazón

To Ambato & Baños

N   **Sleeping** ⊜   Llullu Llama **2**
Not to scale   Black Sheep Inn **3**   Posada de Tigua **8**
Hostal Mama Hilda **3**   Samana Huasi **8**

Saquisilí market is one of the best in the region, if not the whole country.

minutes by car. Along the access road to the rim of the crater the small community of **Lago Verde Quilotoa**, which caters to visitors, has sprung up. A number of the houses are basic *residenciales*. Everyone in the village tries to sell the famous naïve Tigua pictures and carved wooden masks. Try to spread your business as people in this area are very poor (the community charges a US$1 entry fee to Quilotoa). From the rim of the crater several snowcapped volcanoes can be seen in the distance. During the wet season, the best views are in the early morning. There's a 300-m drop down from the crater rim to the water. The hike down takes about 30 minutes (an hour or more to climb back up). The trail starts to the left of the parking area down a steep, canyon-like cut. You can hire a mule to ride up from the bottom of the crater, but arrange it before heading down. Bring drinking water as there's none at the top of the crater and the water in the lake is salty and sulphurous.

Beyond Quilotoa the road is unpaved and can be quite poor at times. It is 22 km from the Quilotoa crater to **Chugchilán**, a small, poor, mainly indigenous village in a beautiful setting. The area offers good trekking, horse riding and cycling. Horses with a guide for a trip to Quilotoa are available at US$20 per horse. Continuing north from Chugchilán the road runs through **Sigchos**, a somewhat larger town along this circuit. There are beautiful views of both Iliniza peaks from here, and a Sunday market. Sigchos is the main starting point for hiking in the Río Toachi Canyon, but this can also be done from other towns along the loop.

From Chugchilán a cobbled road runs east to the town of **Toacazo** from where there are paved roads to Saquisilí and to the Panamericana near Lasso. An alternative route heads southeast from Sigchos along secondary roads to **Isinliví**, a pleasant town populated mainly by mestizos. There are some spectacular hikes and bike rides in the area and several *pucarás* (hill fortresses) to explore.

Some 16 km south of Lasso and 6 km west of the Panamericana, is **Saquisilí**, a small but very important market town. Its Thursday market (0700-1400) is famous throughout Ecuador for the way in which its seven plazas and most of its streets become jam-packed with people, the great majority of them indigenous locals with red ponchos and narrow-brimmed felt hats. The best time to visit the market is between 0900 and 1200. The animal market is a little way out of the village and it's best to be there before 0700. There is accommodation in town and a few simple *comedores*, but you will find a much better selection of places to eat in Latacunga.

Baños and around ⊜❶❻❻❀❍▲❷❸❻ ⊸ *pp360-372*

The town of Baños, with its beautiful setting and pleasant sub-tropical climate, is a major holiday resort, bursting at the seams with hotels, *residenciales*, restaurants and tour agencies. The sidewalks of the main street, Calle Ambato, are lined with outdoor cafés and teem with visitors on a Saturday night. Ecuadoreans flock here on weekends and holidays for a dip in the hot springs and to escape the Andean chill. Foreign visitors are also frequent; using Baños as a base for trekking, organizing a visit to the jungle, making local day-trips on horseback or by mountain bike, or just plain hanging out. The Río Pastaza rushes past Baños to the Agoyán waterfalls 10 km further down the valley, nearly dry now because of the construction of a hydroelectric dam. Beyond, many beautiful waterfalls can be seen tumbling into the Pastaza in an area well suited for excursions. The whole area has a relaxing sub-tropical climate , but it can be cool during the rainy season, usually June to September.

Ins and outs

Getting there Baños is reached from Ambato or Puyo. The road from Riobamba to Baños remains closed due to landslides and volcanic activity. The bus station is on the Ambato-Puyo road (Avenida Amazonas) a short way from the centre. ⊜ ⊸ *p372.*

Getting around Baños is an easy place to get around, with most hotels centrally located. A unique feature is the presence of sidewalk ramps, which make the centre of town wheelchair accessible. City buses run throughout the day from Alfaro y Martínez east to Agoyán and from Rocafuerte by the market, west to El Salado and the zoo.

Information **iTur** ⓘ *at the Municipio, Halflants y Rocafuerte, opposite the Parque Central, Mon-Fri 0830-1230, 1400-1700, Sat-Sun 0800-1600.* Helpful, with colourful maps of the area, some English spoken. There are also several private 'tourist information offices' run by travel agencies near the bus station. The latter offer high-pressure tour sales, maps and pamphlets.

Sights

The thermal baths which gave Baños its name are a popular attraction and well worth trying. Six sets of baths are located in and around town. On holidays and weekends they can get very crowded (but note that the brown colour of the water is due to its high mineral content). All charge US$1 unless otherwise noted.

The town of Baños makes the ideal break between the highlands and eastern jungles.

Top tips

Climbing Cotopaxi

If you only climb one of Ecuador's many volcanoes, then it should probably be the beautiful snow-capped cone of **Volcán Cotopaxi** (5,897 m). Because of the altitude and weather conditions, Cotopaxi is a serious climb; equipment and experience are required. Agencies in Quito and throughout the Central Highlands offer Cotopaxi climbing trips (as well as biking trips in Cotopaxi National Park). The best season is December to April. The climb to the summit of Cotopaxi is a steep one, takes 5-8 hours and the snow and ice section is heavily crevassed. You start climbing at 0100, as the snow deteriorates in the sun, and if you're lucky, you'll be illuminated by a full moon, a practical and magical experience.

The **Baños de la Virgen** ⓘ *open 0430-1700 and 1800-2200, US$1.25*, are by the waterfall opposite the Hotel Sangay. The water in the hot pools is changed daily, and the cold pool is chlorinated. It's best to visit very early in the morning before the crowds. Two small hot pools are open in the evenings only and their water is also changed daily. The **Piscinas Modernas**, with a water slide, are next door and are open weekends and holidays only (0800-1700).

The **El Salado** baths (several hot pools with water changed daily, plus icy-cold river water) are 1½ km from the centre, off the Ambato road (0430-1700). If walking from town, take a trail that starts at the west end of Martínez and crosses the Bascún river; the baths are at the top of the road on the west side of the river. Be warned that this is a high risk area during volcanic activity.

To go along with the medicinal baths, there is a growing number of spas. Several hotels ranging from luxurious to more modest establishments have spas and there are also independent spa centres and massage therapists. These offer a combination of sauna, steam bath (Turkish or box), jacuzzi, clay and other types of baths, a variety of massage techniques (shiatsu, reiki, Scandinavian) and more. ▲▲ ▸▸ *p368*.

East of Baños

The road from Baños to Puyo (58 km) is very scenic, with many waterfalls tumbling down to the Pastaza. It has been dubbed 'The Avenue of the Waterfalls'. It is paved and goes through seven tunnels between Baños and Río Negro. The area has excellent opportunities for walking and nature observation and the route is popular for cycling. ▲▲ ▸▸ *p367*.

Background

Tungurahua, south of Baños

Baños is nestled between the Río Pastaza and the Tungurahua volcano, only 8 km from its crater. After over 80 years of inactivity, Tungurahua began venting steam and ash in 1999 and the town was evacuated because of the threat of a major eruption between October and December of that year. Volcanic activity gradually diminished during 2000, former residents and tourists returned, and Baños recovered its wonderful resort atmosphere. The positive side of the reactivation of Tungurahua is that the Baños area has acquired an important new attraction: volcano watching, which can be enjoyed from Baños, Patate, Pelileo and several other nearby locations. With clear weather and a little luck, you can experience the unforgettable sight of mushroom clouds being expelled from the crater by day, and occasionally even red-hot boulders tumbling down the flanks of the volcano at night. In town, you can see the volcano from a small bridge over the Río Bascún, accessed from the top (west) end of Calle Ambato. Several operators in town offer volcano-watching tours, both day and night, which take you to viewing spots outside town.

The first town you reach beyond the Agoyán generating station is **Rio Blanco**, beyond which is the hamlet of La Merced with a lookout and a trail with a swingbridge over the Pastaza going to the base of the lovely **Manto de La Novia** waterfall, on the Río Chinchín Chico. About one kilometre beyond is the *tarabita*, a cable car crossing the Pastaza to the village of San Pedro; it is powered by an old lorry engine, US$1. From the cable car you have nice views of the Pastaza and the **San Pedro** waterfall on the river of the same name. Several other *tarabitas* are being installed along this road.

About 3 km beyond and 17 km from Baños is the town of **Río Verde** at the junction of the Verde and Pastaza rivers, with several snack bars, simple restaurants and a few places to stay. The Río Verde has crystalline green water and it is nice for bathing. Before joining the Pastaza, the Río Verde tumbles down several falls, the most spectacular of which is **El Pailón del Diablo** (the devil's cauldron). Cross the Río Verde on the old road and take the path to the right after the church, then follow the trail down towards the suspension bridge over the Pastaza, for about 20 minutes. Just before the bridge take a side trail to the right (signposted) which leads you to Paradero del Pailón, a viewing platform above the falls; there is a kiosk selling drinks and snacks (they maintain the lookout, a contribution is expected). There are excellent hiking opportunities up the Rio Verde. The trail on the west side of the river begins at the town park and makes a good day trip. There is basic lodging three hours up the trail; ask about Angel's cabins at the store just east of the town square.

Riobamba and around ●●●●●●▲●● ›› pp360-372

Riobamba is a pleasant friendly city, if somewhat chilly due to the breeze blowing down from Chimborazo. The centre has many nice colonial buildings and churches, and magnificent views of five of the great volcanic peaks. Riobamba is not only the heartland of Ecuador, but it is at the heart of a beautiful and interesting region. Located at the foot of the magnificent Chimborazo, the highest mountain in the country, and surrounded by other impressive

peaks such as El Altar, Tungurahua, Carihuayrazo and Sangay, it is the perfect base from
which to explore Parque Nacional Sangay and the Reserva Chimborazo. The famous Devil's
Nose train ride also runs through this area. The city is the commercial centre for the Province
of Chimborazo and an important centre of highland culture. There are a number of markets
worth visiting and on market days (Wednesday and especially Saturday), the city lights up
with the bright ponchos and shawls worn by the native people.

Ins and outs

Getting there Buses from Quito and Cuenca arrive at the well-run Riobamba Terminal
Terrestre on Epiclachima y Av Daniel León Borja. Buses from Baños and the Oriente arrive at
the Terminal Oriental, at Espejo y Cordovez. Buses to smaller towns within the province leave
from specific street corners throughout the city. A taxi between terminals costs US$1. The
railway station remains a central landmark, but is used only for tourist rides (see The Devil's
Nose train ride below). ◖ ▸▸ *p370.*

Getting around The city centre is compact and easy to walk around. City buses and taxis
are available out to the Terminal Terrestre, about 1 km from the centre. A taxi ride within the
city costs US$1. There is frequent bus service to the larger towns within the region. Some
more out-of-the-way communities will usually have one or two buses per day and more
transport on market days. Riobamba tour operators offer tours or just transport to the
attractions in the area.

Information Ministerio de Turismo ⓘ *Av Daniel León Borja y Pasaje Municipal, in the
Centro de Arte y Cultura, T/F03-294 1213. Open Monday-Friday 0830-1300, 1430-1800.* They are
very helpful and knowledgeable and speak English.

Sights

The one real sight in the city, the **Convento de la Concepción** ⓘ *entrance to the museum at
Argentinos y J Larrea, T03-296 5212. Tue-Sat 0900-1200, 1500-1800. US$2,* has been carefully
restored and functions as a religious art museum. It is a veritable treasure chest of
18th-century religious art. The priceless gold monstrance, *Custodia de Riobamba Antigua,* is
the museum's greatest treasure, one of the richest of its kind in South America. The museum
is well worth a visit. The guides are friendly and knowledgeable (tip expected).

Chimborazo, Ecuador's highest peak, is easily accessed from Riobamba.

Riobamba is an important market centre where indigenous people from many communities congregate. Saturday is the main market day when the city fills with colourfully dressed *indigenas* from many different parts of the province of Chimborazo, each wearing their distinctive costume. Trading overflows the markets and buying and selling go on all over town. Wednesday is a smaller market day. The 'tourist' market is in the small **Plaza de la Concepción** or **Plaza Roja**, on Orozco y Colón, south of the Convento de la Concepción. It is a good place to buy local handicrafts and authentic Indian clothing (Saturday and Wednesday only, 0800-1500). The wholesale **Mercado Mayorista** is to the south of the centre, near the turnoff for Chambo, with busiest trading on Friday. Nearby is the animal market with trade on Saturday morning. In town the main produce market is **San Alfonso** (Argentinos y 5 de Junio) which on Saturday spills over into the nearby streets and also sells clothing, ceramics, baskets and hats. Other markets in the colonial centre are **La Condamine** (Carabobo y Colombia) open daily, largest market on Friday, **San Francisco** and **La Merced**, near the churches of the same name, both open daily.

Devil's Nose train ride

Riding the rails from Riobamba over the Devil's Nose (La Nariz del Diablo) is extremely popular and makes a great day-trip. The train leaves Riobamba on Wednesday, Friday and Sunday at 0700, arrives in Alausí around 1100, reaches Sibambe about 1130-1200, and returns to Alausí by 1330-1400. It stops for a lunch break and returns to Riobamba by about 1700. From Riobamba to Sibambe and back to Alausí costs US$11; Alausí-Sibambe-Alausí US$7; Alausí back to Riobamba US$3.40. Tickets are sold the day before departure, or the same morning starting around 0600 (passport is required to purchase tickets). Seats are not numbered, so it's best to arrive early. Riding on the roof is fun, but hang on tight and remember that it is very chilly early in the morning. It's also a good idea to rent a cushion, and sit away from the engines to avoid getting covered in oil from the exhaust. Since the train changes directions, sit in the middle. The best views going are on the right. The train service is subject to frequent disruptions and timetables are often changing, best enquire locally about current schedules. The railway administration office is on Espejo, next to the post office, where information is available during office hours, T03-296 0115, or at the station T03-296 1909. At times when there have been heavy rains and minor landslides, a motorized rail-car (*autoferro*) runs instead of the longer train.

Reserva Faunística Chimborazo

Chimborazo, a beautiful massive (inactive) snow-capped volcano, the highest peak in Ecuador (6,310 m), and Carihuayrazo also striking, but dwarfed by its neighbour (5,020 m), are the most outstanding features of this reserve, created to protect the vicuñas, alpacas and llamas which were re-introduced here. Day visitors can enjoy lovely views, a glimpse of the handsome vicuñas and the rarefied air above 4,800 m. There are great opportunities for trekking in the area and, of course, for climbing Ecuador's highest peak and its neighbour (from where there are great views of Chimborazo). Chimboarzo is a difficult climb owing to the altitude and no one without mountaineering experience should attempt it. Horse-riding tours are offered along the Mocha Valley between the two peaks and downhill cycling from Chimborazo is a popular activity. Many Riobamba tour agencies run tours here. ▲▲ ▶▶ *p367.*

● Sleeping

Latacunga *p353*

C **Makroz**, Valencia 8-56 y Quito, T03-280 0907, F03-280 7274. Modern hotel with nicely decorated comfortable rooms, restaurant serves economical meals (closed Sun), parking.

D **Tilipulo**, Guayaquil y Belisario Quevedo, T03-281 0611. Comfortable hotel, cafeteria, ample rooms, popular, very helpful owner.

Budget buster

A night with the Incas

Care to sleep in the Inca's room and dine at his table? **San Agustín de Callo** (near Cotopaxi National Park, www.incahacienda.com) is a hacienda built on Inca foundations and has two complete Inca rooms within the main buildings. Alongside other historic haciendas, it has opened its doors to a few discerning and well heeled guests. These are truly ancestral homes and a gateway to the country's past, to a time when hacendados (wealthy landowners) ruled supreme in their own little fiefdoms. Their descendants remain among Ecuador's economic and social élite and, even today, they and their servants welcome outsiders with the slightest hint of aloof condescension. Mignon Plaza, proprietor of San Agustín de Callo and granddaughter of former president Leonidas Plaza, encouraged archaeologists to excavate the foundations and placed lighting and window panes to display what was uncovered. Evening meals are served by candlelight in the principal Inca room. An ordinary double room (not the Inca's) costs around US$230. For more information about haciendas in Ecuador see page 28.

Quilotoa Circuit *p353, map p354*

AL-B The Black Sheep Inn, a few mins below the village of Chugchilán, on the way to Sigchos, T03-281 4587, www.blacksheepinn.com A lovely eco-friendly inn built on a hillside. Nice private rooms with fireplace or cheaper in dorm, includes excellent vegetarian dinner and breakfast, also drinking water and hot drinks all day, composting toilets, book exchange, organic garden, sauna, discount for ISIC, seniors or SAE members, llama treks, horse riding arranged, reservations advised.

B Posada de Tigua, 3 km east of Tigua-Chimbacucho, 400 m north of the road, T03-281 3682, laposadadetigua@latinmail.com Refurbished hacienda house, part of a working dairy ranch. Five rooms, wood-burning stove, includes 3 tasty home cooked meals, shared bath, pleasant family atmosphere, horses for riding, trails to river and forest, nice views.

C-D Samana Huasi, In the village of Tigua-Chimbacucho, Km 53 from Latacunga, T03-281 4868 or T02-2563175 (Quito), www.tigua.org A nice community-run lodge, includes breakfast and dinner, shared composting toilets, some rooms with fireplace or wood burning stove, cheaper in dorm, nice views.

D Hostal Mama Hilda, 100 m from centre of Chugchilán, T03-281 4814. A pleasant family run hostel, homey sitting room with stove, large rooms, includes good dinner and breakfast, shared bath, parking, warm atmosphere, arrange horse-riding and walking trips. Good value.

D-E Llullu Llama, Isinliví, T03-281 4790, www.isinlivi.safari.com.ec Name means baby llama (pronounced zhu-zhu-zhama), nicely refurbished house, cosy sitting room with woodburning stove, good hardy meals available, shared composting toilet with great views, abundant hot water, private, semi-private and dorm (cheaper) accommodations, nicely decorated rooms (some are a bit small), organic herb garden, warm and relaxing atmosphere, a lovely spot.

LL **Luna Runtún**, Caserío Runtún Km 6, T03-274 0882, www.lunaruntun.com. A classy hotel in a beautiful setting overlooking Baños. All-inclusive packages with meals, spa and adventure tours. Very comfortable rooms with balconies and superb views, lovely gardens. Excellent service, English, French and German spoken, hiking, horse riding and biking tours, nanny service available.

A **Finca Chamanapamba**, outside town, a 20 min walk from Ulba on the east shore of the Río Ulba, T03-274 2671, chamanapamba@hotmail.com. Two nicely finished wooden cabins in a spectacular location overlooking the Río Ulba and just next to the Chamanapamba

waterfalls, very good café-restaurant serves German food.

A-B **Sangay**, Plazoleta Isidro Ayora 101, next to waterfall and thermal baths, T03-274 0490, www.sangayhotel.com. A comfortable hotel and spa with 3 types of rooms, includes buffet breakfast, good restaurant specializes in Ecuadorean food, pool and spa open to non-residents 1600-2000 (US$5), parking, tennis and squash courts, games room, car hire, attentive service, British-Ecuadorean run.

B **Pequeño Paraíso**, 1½ km east of Río Verde, west of Machay, T09-9819756, www.geocities.com/pequeno_paraiso/. Comfortable cabins in lovely surroundings. Includes breakfast and dinner, small pool, nicely furnished,

Baños

To ❶, Río Blanco, Río Verde & Puyo

Puente San Francisco

Sleeping 🛏
El Oro & Jireh **22** *B1*
Isla de Baños **6** *C2*
La Floresta **7** *C2*
La Petite Auberge &
  Le Petit Restaurant **8** *C2*
Llanovientos **12** *C1*
Luna Runtún **1** *A3*
Plantas y Blanco **13** *C3*
Posada del Arte **4** *C3*

Princesa María **15** *B1*
Sangay **17** *C3*
Villa Gertrudis **21** *C2*

Eating 🍴
Café Blah Blah **1** *B2*
Casa Hood **3** *C2*
Mariane **11** *B2*
Pancho Villa **25** *C2*
Pizzería de Paolo **9** *B3*

Rincón de Suiza **5** *C2*

Bars & clubs 🍸
Bamboos **1** *B3*
Buena Vista **2** *B2*
Jack Rock **3** *B2*

200 metres
200 yards

abundant hot water, tasty vegetarian meals with homemade bread, climbing wall, camping possible. Swiss-run.

B-C Isla de Baños, Halflants 1-31 y Montalvo, T/F03-274 0609, islabanos@andinanet.net. Nicely decorated hotel, includes European breakfast, internet, glass-enclosed spa open when there are enough people, nice atmosphere, pleasant garden.

B-C Posada del Arte, Pasaje Velasco Ibarra y Montalvo, T03-274 0083, www.posadadelarte.com. Nice cosy inn, includes breakfast, restaurant, pleasant sitting room, more expensive rooms have fireplace.

B-D La Petite Auberge, 16 de Diciembre y Montalvo, T/F03-274 0936, lepetitbanos@yahoo.com. Pleasant hotel. Rooms, some with fireplace, around a patio, includes breakfast, good French restaurant, parking, quiet, French run.

C La Floresta, Halflants y Montalvo, T03-274 1824, la_floresta_hospedaje @hotmail.com. Nice hotel with large comfortable rooms set around a lovely garden, includes excellent breakfast, other meals available on request, parking, friendly service.

C Villa Gertrudis, Montalvo 2975, T03-274 0441, F03-274 0442. Classic old resort, includes breakfast, pool open to non-residents (US$1.50), parking, lovely garden, reserve in advance.

D El Oro, Ambato y JL Mera. With bath, T03-274 0736, elorohostal@hotmail.com. Includes breakfast, laundry and cooking facilities, good value, popular.

D-E Llanovientos, Martínez 1126 y Sebastián Baño, T03-274 0682, gvieirah@hotmail.com. A modern breezy hostel with wonderful views. Comfortable rooms, cafeteria, plenty of hot water, cooking facilities, parking, very clean, nice garden.

D-E Plantas y Blanco, 12 de Noviembre y Martínez, T/F03-274 0044, option3@hotmail.com. Pleasant hostel in a multi-storey building decorated with plants, a variety of rooms and prices,

cheaper with shared bath and in dorm, internet, excellent breakfast and fruit salads in rooftop cafeteria, steam bath 0730-1100 (US$3), French run, good value.

E Princesa María, Rocafuerte y Mera, T03-274 1035. Clean spacious rooms, private bath, hot water, laundry and cooking facilities, budget travellers' meeting place, popular. Good value.

Riobamba *p358, map p364*

A La Andaluza, 16 km north of Riobamba along the Panamericana, T03-294 9370, www.hosteria-andaluza.com. An old hacienda with modern facilities, good restaurant, parking, nice rooms with heaters and roaring fireplaces, lovely views, good walking in the area.

B Rincón Alemán, Remigio Romero y Alfredo Pareja, Ciudadela Arupos del Norte, T03-260 3540, arupo@gmx.de. Family-run hotel in a quiet residential area. Includes breakfast, laundry and cooking facilities, parking, garden, sauna, fitness room, fireplace. German spoken.

B Zeus, Av Daniel L Borja 41-29, T03-296 8036, www.hotelzeus.com.ec. Restaurant, parking, modern, comfortable and pleasant. Bathtubs with views of Chimborazo.

B-C Montecarlo, Av 10 de Agosto 25-41 entre García Moreno y España, T03-296 0557, montecarlo@laserinter.net. Includes breakfast, restaurant, parking, colonial style house, central location.

D La Estación, Unidad Nacional 2915 y Carabobo, T03-295 5226. A nicely refurbished building, coveniently located near the train station. Nice restaurant, good beds, several sitting rooms, wooden floors, terrace with hammocks and good views. Good value.

D Tren Dorado, Carabobo 22-35 y 10 de Agosto, T/F03-296 4890, htrendorado@hotmail.com. Conveniently located near the train station, early breakfast available in time to catch the train, restaurant serves good vegetarian lunch, reliable hot water, modern, nice large rooms, friendly, very good value.

Quito & the Highlands Central Sierra Listings

🍴 Eating

Latacunga *p353*

🍴 **Rodelú**, Quito 16-31 at the hotel, closed Sun. Good breakfasts, steaks and pizzas, popular with travellers.

🍴 **Pizzería Buon Giorno**, Sánchez de Orellana y Maldonado esquina, Mon-Sat 1300-2300. Great pizzas and lasagne, large selection.

🍴 **Café Precolombino**, Belisario Quevedo 6-31 y Padre Salcedo, Mon-Sat 0800-1400, 1500-2200. Breakfast, snacks such as humitas, empanadas and Mexican tacos, desserts and sweets, pleasant atmosphere.

Baños *p356, map p362*

🍴 **Le Petit Restaurant**, 16 de Diciembre y Montalvo, T03-274 0936, Tue-Sun 0800-1500, 1800-2200. Very good French cuisine, their onion soup is particularly recommended, also vegetarian dishes, fondue, great atmosphere, Parisian owner.

🍴 **Mariane**, Halflants y Rocafuerte, daily 1800-2300. Excellent authentic Provençal cuisine, large portions, nice atmosphere, good value and attentive service.

🍴 **Pancho Villa**, Montalvo y 16 de Diciembre, Mon-Sat 1230-2130. Very good quality Mexican food, good service.

🍴 **Pizzería de Paolo**, Rocafuerte at Parque de la Basílica. Good pizza, pasta and salads.

🍴 **Casa Hood**, Martínez between Halflants and Alfaro, closed Wed. Largely vegetarian, but also serve some meat dishes, economical set lunches, juices, good desserts, varied menu including Indonesian and Thai dishes. Travel books and maps sold, book exchange, repertory cinema, very popular.

Cafés

Ali Cumba, Maldonado opposite Parque Central, daily 0700-1800. Excellent breakfasts, fruit salads, filtered coffee, espresso, muffins, large sandwiches. Pricey but good, Danish-Ecuadorean run.

Café Blah Blah, Halflants 620 y Ambato, open 0900-2100. Cosy café. Very good breakfast, good coffee, snacks and juices. Popular, friendly meeting place.

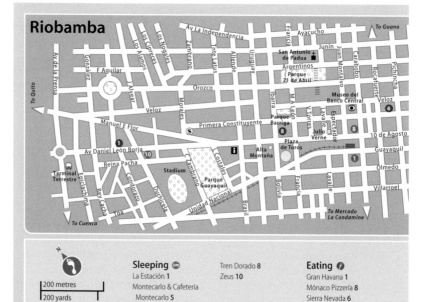

Riobamba

200 metres
200 yards

Sleeping 🛏
La Estación **1**
Montecarlo & Cafetería
Montecarlo **5**

Tren Dorado **8**
Zeus **10**

Eating 🍴
Gran Havana **1**
Mónaco Pizzería **8**
Sierra Nevada **6**

Rincón de Suiza, Martínez y Halflants, Tue-Sun 0900-0000. Snacks, drinks, good coffee, capuccino, best cakes and pastries in town. Pleasant atmosphere, books, games, pool table, table tennis. Swiss-Ecuadorean run.

Riobamba *p358, map p364*

† **Cafetería Montecarlo**, 10 de Agosto 25-45 y García Moreno, daily 0700-1200, 1600-2200 (0500 breakfast can be arranged before train ride). Ecuadorean and international, good breakfasts, snacks and complete meals, pleasant.

† **La Gran Havana**, Daniel León Borja 42-52 y Duchicela, daily 1100-2300. Economical set lunch, very good Cuban and international food à la carte.

†-† **Mónaco Pizzería**, Diego Ibarra y Daniel León Borja, Mon-Fri 1400-2200, Sat-Sun 1200-2300. Delicious pizza and pasta, nice salads, very good food, service and value.

† **Sierra Nevada**, Primera Constituyente y Rocafuerte, Mon-Sat 0800-2200, Sun 0800-1600. Excellent value set lunch, vegetarian on request. Nice atmosphere.

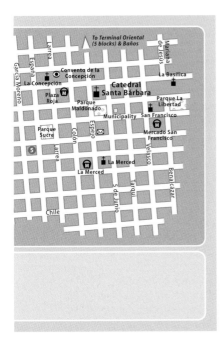

Bars and clubs

Baños *p356, map p362*
Many bars are along Eloy Alfaro between Ambato and Oriente. Córdova Tours (see Tour operators below) has a chiva (open sided bus) cruising town, playing music, it will take you to different night spots.
Bamboos Bar, on a small street at the east end of town near C Oriente, popular for salsa, live on weekends.
Buena Vista, Alfaro y Oriente. A good place for salsa and other Latin music.
Jack Rock Café, Alfaro y Ambato, a favourite travellers' hangout, fantastic piña colada and juices.

Riobamba *p358, map p364*
Gens-Chop Bar, Av Daniel León Borja 42-17 y Duchicela. Bar, good music and sport videos, open daily, popular.
Romeo Bar, Vargas Torres y Av Daniel León Borja, US$2 cover. Popular, nice bar and club, with pleasant sitting area on the second floor. A variety of music from Latin to Rythm and Blues.

Entertainment

Baños *p356, map p362*
Cinema
Casa Hood, Martínez y Eloy Alfaro. Shows interesting films.
Mini Cine, Oriente y Halflants. Has an extensive selection of films and screens to view, US$1.

Festivals and events

Latacunga *p353*
Fiesta de la Mama Negra the most important festival in Latacunga is held on **23-25 Sep** and on the weekend before **11 Nov**, the Fiestas de Latacunga, in homage to the Vírgen de las Mercedes and the Santísima Tragedia. There is a very well attended parade in which a man dressed as a black woman, the 'Mama Negra' is the focus of the

celebrations. There is dancing in the streets with colourful costumes, head-dresses and masks. Market vendors are among the most enthusiastic participants in the Sep event which is open to all, while all the elected officials of the Municipio participate in the civic festival in Nov.

Quilotoa Circuit *p353, map p354*

Festivals in all the villages are quite lively. Life in these small villages can be very quiet, so people really come alive during their festivals, which are genuine and in no way designed to entertain tourists. These include **Año Nuevo** (New Year), **Domingo de Ramos** (Palm Sunday), **Carnaval** (Mardi Gras), **Semana Santa** (Easter Week), **Corpus Cristi**, **Mama Negra**, and **Finados** (Day of the Dead). Very colourful celebrations are held in Pujilí for **Corpus Christi** (Thu after Trinity Sun and on to the weekend) with parades featuring masked dancers (*danzantes*), fireworks, parties, and *castillos*, 5-20 m high poles which people climb to get prizes suspended from the top (including sacks of potatoes and live sheep!). Saquisilí also has colourful **Corpus Christi** processions.

Baños *p356, map p362*

Fiestas de Nuestra Señora de Agua Santa are held throughout **Oct** with several daily processions, bands, fireworks, sporting events and general partying. **Fiestas de Baños** are week long celebrations ending **16 Dec**, the town's anniversary, with parades, fairs, sports and cultural events and much partying. On the evening of **15 Dec** are the *verbenas* when each barrio hires a band and there are many street parties.

Riobamba *p358, map p364*

Fiesta del Niño Rey de Reyes culminates on **6 Jan** a period of Pases del Niño, parades in honour of the baby Jesus, which are carried out throughout Dec and the first week of Jan. On the eve

there are fireworks and parties and on the 6th a street parade with floats which gathers thousands of people dressed up in costumes. **Semana Santa**, on the Tue of Holy Week, an impressive, well attended, solemn procession is held in honour of El Señor del Buen Suceso. **Fiestas de Abril**, Riobamba's independence day is **21 Apr**, celebrated for several days with lively parades, concerts, bullfights and drinking. Hotel prices rise and rooms may be difficult to find during this period. **Fiestas Patronales**, in honour of San Pedro are held on **29 Jun** with street parties; the daring jump over bonfires. **Fiestas del 11 de Noviembre** are festivals to celebrate the first attempt at independence from Spain take place for several days around **11 Nov** with cultural events.

○ Shopping

Latacunga *p353*

There is a Sat market on the **Plaza de San Sebastián** at Juan Abel Echeverría. Goods for sale include shigras (finely stitched colourful straw bags), reed mats, and homespun wool and cotton yarn.

Baños *p356, map p362*

Camping gear
Varoxi, Maldonado 651 y Oriente, quality backpacks, repairs luggage. Recommended.

Handicrafts
There are craft stalls at Pasaje Ermita de la Virgen, between C Ambato and Rocafuerte, by the market.
Las Orquídeas, Ambato y Maldonado, also at Halflants y Montalvo (Hotel La Floresta), has a large selection of nice crafts from the area and throughout Ecuador.
La Tienda de Mercedes, 12 de Noviembre y Ambato, good quality handicrafts and T-shirts, reasonable prices.

Recuerdos, at the south end of Maldonado. For painted balsa-wood birds.

Riobamba *p358, map p364*
Camping gear
Hobby Sport, 10 de Agosto y Rocafuerte, sleeping bags, tents, fishing supplies. Directly opposite is a store which also has some camping supplies, including Camping Gaz. Julio Verne tour operator also sells Camping Gaz.

Handicrafts
Crafts are sold Wed and Sat, 0800-1500, at Plaza Roja.
Almacén Cacha, Orozco next to the Plaza Roja, closed Sun-Mon. Cooperative of native people from the Cacha area, sells good value woven bags, wool sweaters and other crafts, also excellent honey.
Alta Montaña, Av Daniel León Borja y Diego Ibarra. Nice tagua carvings and other crafts, you can also see how the tagua is carved.
Artesanías Ecuador, Carabobo y 10 de Agosto. Good selection of crafts, ceramics, wood, tagua, straw.

▲ Activities and tours

Latacunga *p353*
All operators and some hotels offer day-trips to Cotopaxi and Quilotoa (US$35 per person, includes lunch and a visit to a market town if on Thu or Sat); prices for 3 or more people. Enquire about the service they offer and compare; there have been reports of some tours being little more than transport to the site. Climbing trips to Cotopaxi cost US$120-130 per person for 2 days (includes equipment, park entrance fee, meals, refuge fees), minimum 2 people.

Tour operators
Ruta de los Volcanes, Padre Salcedo 4-55 y Quito, T03-281 2452. Day trips, tour to Cotopaxi follows a secondary road through interesting country, instead of the Panamericana.
Selvanieve, Padre Salcedo 4-38, 2895, selvanieve1@hotmail.com. Various tours, climbing, also has an agency in Baños, runs tours throughout Ecuador.
Tovar Expediciones, Guayaquil 5-38 y Quito, T03-281 1333. Climbing and trekking, helpful service. Fernando Tovar is a qualified mountain guide.

Baños *p356, map p362*
Biking
A very nice, popular ride is along the scenic road east toward the jungle as far as Río Verde or even Puyo (see East of Baños). Note that cyclists have to go through the first tunnel at Agoyan, but not the following tunnels where you stay along the old road at the river's edge; the views are magnificent and you get away from the traffic for those streches. At Río Verde you can leave your bike at one of the snack bars (a tip is expected), while you visit the falls. You can continue to Puyo (4-5 hours from Baños); at any point along the route you can get on a bus to return to Baños, the bike goes on the roof. The countryside around Baños is well suited for cycling; several tour operators and independent guides offer tours.
Hotel Isla de Baños runs cycling tours with good equipment.
Adrián Carrillo, 12 de Noviembre y Martínez, rents mountain bikes and motorcycles (reliable machines with helmets). Many other places rent bikes but the quality is variable; check brakes and tyres, find out who has to pay for repairs, and insist on a helmet, puncture repair kit and pump. Bicycles cost from US$4 per day; moped US$5 per hr; motorcycles US$10 per hr.

Climbing and trekking
Baños operators offer climbing and trekking tours to several destinations. Note that due to the reactivation of the volcano, Tungurahua has been officially

→ **Adrenaline rush**

Background

A number of potentially hazardous activities are currently in vogue in Baños, including old favourites such as mountaineering and whitewater rafting, as well as more recent adrenaline sports like canyoning and bridge jumps. Canyoning involves rappelling down steep river gorges, above and in the water. Many agencies offer this sport, rates US$25-35. Franco at **Pequeño Paraiso**, Rio Verde, T09-9819756, is experienced in canyoning. Puenting, or bridge jumps, are like bungee jumping, but it is done with a harness attached to the torso and supported by three ropes. In a **swing jump** you jump outwards, head first, and you sway back and forth in a pendular movement. A different jump involves jumping straight down, feet first and bobbing up and down. The jumps are done from different bridges around Baños, all of different heights. Many agencies offer jumps, quality and safety varies. US$10-15 per jump. You should be aware that safety standards for these sports vary greatly from agency to agency, and may be completely different from standards in other parts of the world. Be sure to ascertain the quality of equipment and the qualifications of guides.

closed to climbers since 1999. Unless volcanic activity has completely ceased, do not be talked into climbing to the refugio, crater or summit.
Expediciones Amazónicas, Oriente 11-68 y Halflants, T03-274 0506, www.amazonicas.banios.com. Run by Hernán and Dosto Varela, the latter is a recommended mountain guide.
Willie Navarrete, at Café Higuerón, T03-274 1482, T09-932411, is a highly recommended climbing guide.

Health and beauty
El Refugio, a couple of blocks north of the Baños-Puyo road, access opposite the Santa Ana baths. Steam baths, massage, a variety of therapeutic media, meditation, and more. US$5 for a basic set of services and add from there.
Massage and Body Work, Alfaro y Martínez, T03-274 1071. Swedish and Thai massage, very good, US$20 per hr.
Stay in Touch, Martínez entre Alfaro y 16 de Diciembre, T09-9208000 (mob). Various techniques, US$20 per hr.

Horse riding
The countryside around Baños is well suited for riding, several tour operators and independent riding guides offer tours. Rates average US$5 per hr, a 3 day tour about US$45 per day.
Angel Aldaz, Montalvo y JL Mera (on the road to the statue of the Virgin).
Hotel Isla de Baños, horses for rent; 3½ hrs with a guide and jeep transport costs US$25 per person, English and German spoken.
Ringo Horses, 12 de Noviembre y Martínez (Pizzeria El Napolitano), nice horses, very well looked after.

Rafting
Note that the Chambo, Patate and Pastaza rivers are all polluted. Fatal rafting accidents have taken place here, but not with the operators listed.
Geotours, Ambato y Thomas Halflants, T03-2741344, geotours@hotmail.com. Has merged with Río Loco, an operator which for many years ran rafting tours. Half-day US$35, US$60 for full day (rapids and calm water in jungle).

Tour operators

There are many tour agencies in town, some with several offices, as well as 'independent' guides who seek out tourists on the street, or in hotels and restaurants. The latter are generally not recommended. Quality varies considerably; to obtain a qualified guide and avoid unscrupulous operators, it is best to seek advice from other travellers who have recently returned from a tour. We have received some critical reports of tours out of Baños, but there are also highly respected and qualified operators here. In all cases, insist on a written contract and, if possible, try to pay only half the fare up-front. Most agencies and guides offer trips to the jungle (US$30-$50 per person per day in 2005) and 2-day climbing trips to Cotopaxi (about US$130 per person) and Chimborazo (about US$140 per person). There are also volcano-watching, trekking and horse tours, in addition to the day-trips and sports mentioned above.

Córdova Tours, Maldonado y Espejo esquina, T03-274 0923, www.cordovatours.banios.com. Tours on board their *chiva Mocambo*, an open-sided bus (reserve ahead): waterfall tour, along the Puyo road to Río Verde, 0930-1430; Tour to Puyo 0930-1830, Baños and environs, 1400-1600; night tour with music and volcano watching, 2100-2300 (they will drop you off at the nightclub of your choice).

Deep Forest Adventure, no storefront, contact T09-8374530, deepforest adventure@hotmail.com. Eloy Torres, speaks German, English and French, jungle and trekking tours, goes to off-the-beaten-path destinations.

Huilla Cuna, there are 2 agencies of the same name: at Ambato y Halflants, T03-274 1292, huilacuna@yahoo.es. Marcelo Mazo organizes jungle trips; and at Rafael Vieira y Montalvo, T03-274 0187, Luis Guevara runs jungle and mountain trips.

Rainforestur, Ambato 800 y Maldonado, T/F03-274 0743, www.rainforestur.com.ec. Run by Santiago Herrera, guides are knowledgeable and environmentally conscious.

Vasco Tours, Alfaro entre Martínez y Montalvo, T03-274 1017, vascotours@andinanet.net. Run by Juan Medina a very experienced guide who speaks English.

Riobamba *p358, map p364*

Riobamba is an excellent starting point for trips to Chimborazo, Carihuayrazo, Altar, Tungurahua, Sangay and the Inca Trail to Ingapirca. Most companies offer climbing trips (from US$150 per person for 2 days), trekking (from US$50 per person per day) and cycling tours, including a downhill ride from Chimborazo (from US$10 per day for rentals, from US$35 per day for a tour including transport, guide, meal). Many hotels also offer tours, but note that not all are run by qualified guides.

Alta Montaña, Av Daniel León Borja 35-17 y Diego Ibarra, T03-294 2215, aventurag@ch.pro.ec. Trekking, climbing, cycling, birdwatching, photography and horse-riding tours in the highlands, logistic support for expeditions, transport, equipment rental, English spoken.

Andes Trek, Rocafuerte 22-66 y 10 de Agosto, T03-294 0964, www.andes-trek.com. Climbing, trekking and mountain-biking tours, transport, equipment rental, run by Marcelo Puruncajas a known climber, English and German spoken.

Expediciones Andinas, Vía a Guano, Km 3, across from Hotel Abraspungo, T03-296 4915, www.expediciones-andinas.com. Climbing expeditions, operate Chimborazo Base Camp on south flank of mountain. Cater to groups, contact well in advance, run by Marco Cruz a well known climber and certified guide of the German Alpine Club, German spoken.

Background

Rail days

As you climb aboard for the Devil's Nose, consider the rich history of the train you are about to ride. What is today an exhilarating tourist excursion was once the country's pride and joy, and its construction was an internationally acclaimed achievement.

A spectacular 464 km railway line (1.067 m gauge), which ran from Durán up to Riobamba, was opened in 1908. It passed through 87 km of delta lands and then, in another 80 km, climbed to 3,238 m. The highest point (3,619 m) was reached at Urbina, between Riobamba and Ambato. It then rose and fell before reaching the Quito plateau at 2,857 m.

This was one of the great railway journeys of the world and a fantastic piece of engineering, with a maximum gradient of 5.5%. Rail lines also ran from Riobamba south to Cuenca, and from Quito north to Ibarra, then down to the coast at San Lorenzo. There were even more ambitious plans, never achieved, to push the railhead deep into the Oriente jungle, from Ambato as far as Leticia (then Ecuador, today Colombia).

Sadly, time and neglect have taken their toll and today only a few short rail segments remain in service as tourist rides: from Ibarra to Tulquizán, from Quito to Parque Nacional Cotopaxi, and from Riobamba to Alausí and over the Devil's Nose to Sibambe. There has often been talk of reviving the Ecuadorean railway, and such talk persists. As time passes however, the tracks rust and the ties rot, that seems like an ever more remote possibility. Which is a great shame because a working railroad could serve Ecuador today as much as, if not more than, it did in the past.

Julio Verne, El Espectador 22-25 y Av Daniel León Borja, 2 blocks from the train station, T/F03-296 3436, www.julioverne-travel.com. Climbing, trekking, cycling, jungle and Galápagos trips, river rafting, transport to mountains, good equipment rental, Ecuadorean-Dutch run, uses official guides, English spoken.

Pro Bici, Primera Constituyente 23-40 or 23-51 y Larrea (if the bike shop is closed, try at the clothing shop across the street), T03-295 1759, www.probici.com. Run by guide and mechanic, Galo Brito, bike trips and rental, guided tours with support vehicle, full equipment (use Cannondale ATBs).

Veloz Coronado, Chile 33-21 y Francia, T/F03-296 0916, best reached after 1900.

Enrique Veloz Coronado is a known climber, his sons are also guides and work with him on climbing and trekking expeditions.

⊖ Transport

Latacunga p353

Note that on Thu many buses to nearby small communities leave from the Saquisilí market instead of Latacunga. Buses to **Quito** and all regional destinations leave from the **Terminal Terrestre** on the Panamericana. Long distance interprovincial buses which pass through Latacunga, such as Quito-Cuenca, Quito-Riobamba, etc do not go into the terminal. During the day (0600-1700) they go along a bypass road

Devil's Nose train ride.

called Av Eloy Alfaro, to the west of the Panamericana. To try to get on one of these buses during daytime you have to ask for the Puente de San Felipe, 4 blocks from the terminal. The bus terminal has some shops, a bakery, cafeteria, restaurant and a tourist information office on the second floor. **Cooperativa Santa**, has its own terminal at Eloy Alfaro 28-57 y Vargas Torres, 3 blocks north of the Terminal Terrestre along the Panamericana, T2811659; they have buses **Cuenca** and **Loja** via Riobamba.

Quilotoa Circuit *p353, map p354*
All bus times quoted are approximate; buses sometimes wait to fill before leaving and they can be late owing to the rough roads or too many requests for photo stops.

To **Zumbahua** from **Latacunga** there are frequent buses 0500-1900, 2 hrs, US$2. The noon bus continues up to **Laguna Quilotoa**. Buses on Sat are packed full; ride on roof for best views and buy ticket the day before. A **pick-up** truck can be hired from Zumbahua to Quilotoa for US$5; also to Chugchilán for US$30. On Sat mornings there are many trucks leaving the Zumbahua market for Chugchilán which pass Quilotoa. A **taxi** day-trip to Zumbahua and Quilotoa and back to Latacunga is US$40.

To **Quilotoa** from **Latacunga** with **Trans Vivero** daily at 1000, 1100, 1200 and 1300, US$2.50, 2½ hrs. Return bus to **Latacunga** around 1230 and 1330. Buses returning around 1430 and 1530 go only as far as **Zumbahua**, from where you can catch a Latacunga bound bus at the highway. Note also that in addition to the above, buses going through **Zumbahua** bound for **Chugchilán** will drop you at the turnoff, 5 mins from the Quilotoa crater, where you can also pick them up on their way to Zumbahua and Latacunga.

To **Chugchilán** from **Latacunga**, daily at 1130 (except Thu) via Sigchos, at 1200 via Zumbahua; on Thu from **Saquisilí** market via **Sigchos** around 1130 (US$2.50, 3½-4 hrs). Buses return to Latacunga daily at 0300 via Sigchos, at 0400 via Zumbahua. On Sun there are 2 extra buses to Latacunga leaving 0900-1000. There are extra buses going as far as **Zumbahua** Wed 0500, Fri 0600 and Sun between 0900-1000; these continue towards the coast. Milk truck from **Chugchilán** to **Sigchos** around

0900-1000. On Sat also pick-ups going to/from market in **Zumbahua** and **Latacunga**. **Taxi** from Latacunga to **Chugchilán,** US$60.

To **Sigchos** from **Latacunga** there's a frequent daily service US$1.50, 2-2½ hrs. From **Quito** direct service on Fri and Sun, US$3, 3 hrs.

To **Saquisilí** from **Latacunga** every 10 min, US$0.30, 20 mins. From **Quito**, frequent service 0530-1300, US$2, 2 hrs. Bus tours to **Saquisilí** from Quito cost about US$45 per person, **taxis** charge about US$60, with 2 hrs wait at market.

Baños *p356, map p362*
To **Riobamba**, note that the direct Baños-Riobamba road is closed, buses go via Ambato. To **Puyo**, Puyo-bound buses stop at the corner of Av Amazonas (highway) and Maldonado, across Maldonado from the terminal. Some continue from Puyo to Tena or Macas. From **Baños** to **Rio Verde**, take any of the buses bound for Puyo from the corner of Amazonas (main highway) y Maldonado, across from the bus terminal, US$0.50, 20 minutes. **Córdova Tours** offer a tour to Río Verde, stopping at several sites along the way, on a *chiva* (see Tour operators above). For a thrill, ride on the roof.

Riobamba *p358, map p364*
To **Quito** and **Cuenca**, frequent buses from the Terminal Terrestre. To **Baños** and the **Oriente**, from the **Terminal Oriental**. Note that because the direct road is closed, buses go via Ambato.

ⓘ Directory

Latacunga *p353*
Banks Banco de Guayaquil, General Maldonado 720 y Sánchez de Orellana, for TCs, Visa and MC. **Medical services** Hospital Provincial General, at southern end of Amazonas y Hermanas Páez, T03-281 2505, good service.

Baños *p356, map p362*
Banks Banco del Pacífico, Halflants y Rocafuerte by the Parque Central, Mon-Fri 0845-1600. TCs, Visa and Mastercard cash advances, minimum US$200, and Mastercard ATM, but there have been reports of international cards being rejected. Banco del Pichincha, Ambato y Halflants, Visa and Mastercard advances, Mon-Fri 0900-1300. **Cooperativa de Ahorros Ambato**, Maldonado y Espejo. TCs, 2% comission. Mon-Fri 0900-1700.
Car hire Córdova Tours, Maldonado y Espejo, hires 4WD vehicles with driver, US$80 a day. **Internet** Many in town, US$2 per hour. Note that this is a much higher rate than in most places in Ecuador. **Language schools** Baños Spanish Center, Oriente 820 y Julio Cañar, esquina, T/F03-274 0632, elizbasc@uio.satnet.net Elizabeth Barrionuevo, English and German speaking, flexible, salsa lessons. From US$4.50-5 per hr. **Laundry** Many laundromats in town, US$0.80-1 per kg, but there is a minimum value per load.
Post office Halflants y Ambato across from Parque Central.

Riobamba *p358, map p364*
Banks Banco del Pacífico, Av Daniel León Borja y Zambrano, esquina. Banco del Pichincha, Primera Constituyente y García Moreno. Banco de Guayaquil, Primera Constituyente 2626 y García Moreno. **Laundry** Donini, Villarroel entre España y Larrea, Mon- Sat 0830-1230, 1500-1800, US$0.40/lb.
Medical services Metropolitano Hospital, Junín, entre España y García Moreno, T03-294 1930. **Post office** 10 de Agosto y Espejo, esquina.

Cuenca and the Southern Highlands

Ecuador's Southern Highlands are home to many of the country's treasures but are only now beginning to attract tourists in large numbers, as they form the safest and most convenient overland route to and from neighbouring Peru. Cuenca, the focal point, boasts some of the country's finest colonial architecture and the surrounding area is a major *artesanía* centre, producing ceramics, baskets, gold and silver jewellery, textiles and the famous Panama hat. In addition to the cultural attractions, a pleasant climate and magnificent scenery make the Southern Highlands ideal walking country. Vilcabamba, south of Loja, is a suitable base for trekking and horseback excursions, with nearby undisturbed *páramo* and cloud forest which are home to many birds and other wildlife.

Getting there Daily flights from Quito to Cuenca and Loja. Good bus connections and buses from Loja to Piura, Peru.

Getting around Frequent buses between most towns.

Time required 7-10 days.

Weather Rainy season Oct-May. Vilcabamba is warm and dry most of the year.

Sleeping Cuenca has a good selection in all categories. Vilcabamba is more limited.

Eating Cuenca has a good range, Vilcabamba has a few excellent places to eat.

Activities and tours Trips to Ingapirca. Horse riding and trekking from Vilcabamba into Podocarpus National Park.

★ Don't miss... Cuenca's huge cathedral ▸▸ *p374*.

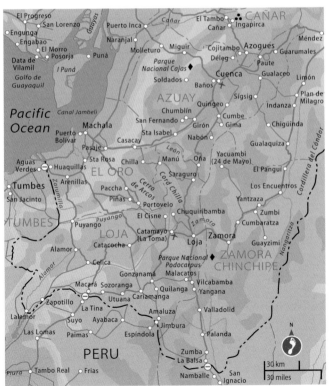

Cuenca and around ⊖🝑🝑⊛🝑🝑⊖🝑 » *pp377-387*

Cuenca, the third largest city in Ecuador, has preserved much of its colonial air. Most Ecuadoreans consider this their finest city and few would disagree. Its cobblestone streets, flowering plazas and whitewashed buildings with old wooden doors and ironwork balconies make it a pleasure to explore. In 1999 Cuenca was designated a UNESCO World Heritage Site.

Ins and outs

Getting there The **Terminal Terrestre** is on Avenida Expaña, 20 minutes' walk northwest of the centre, T284 2023. The **airport** is five minutes' walk from the Terminal Terrestre, T07-286 2203. Both can be reached by city bus. The **terminal for local buses** in the province is at the Feria Libre on Avenida Las Américas. Many city buses pass here. ⊖ » *p386*.

Getting around The old centre is fairly compact and flat, making it easy to get around on foot. The Río Tomebamba separates the colonial heart from the newer districts to the south. Avenida Las Américas is a ring road around the city and the new multi-lane highway bypasses the city to the south.

Tourist offices Ministerio de Turismo ⓘ *Sucre y Benigno Malo, on Parque Calderón next to the municipio, T07-284 1139, helpful, Mon-Fri 0830-1700,* has a list of trained guides, *guías carnetizados* (head office is at Presidente Córdova y Benigno Malo, T07-282 2058, mtouraustro@ec-gov.net). **Cámara de Turismo** ⓘ *at the Terminal Terrestre, T07-286 8482, Mon-Fri 0700-2100, Sat 0800-2000, Sun 0800-1300.*

Sights

On the main plaza, **Parque Abdón Calderón**, are the Old Cathedral, **El Sagrario**, begun in 1557, and the immense 'New' **Catedral de la Inmaculada**, started in 1885. It contains a famous crowned image of the Virgin, a beautiful altar and an exceptional play of light and shade through modern stained glass. The church of **El Carmen de la Asunción**, close to the southwest corner of La Inmaculada, has a flower market in the tiny **Plazoleta El Carmen** in front. There is a colourful daily market in **Plaza Rotary** where pottery, clothes, guinea pigs and local produce, especially baskets, are sold. Thursday is the busiest.

Rooftop view of Cuenca's New Cathedral.

Temple of Sun, Ingapirca.

The **Banco Central 'Pumapungo'** museum complex ⓘ *C Larga y Huayna Capac*, on the edge of the colonial city is at the actual site of Tomebamba excavations. The **Museo Arqueológico** section ⓘ *entrance is on the far left of the building, T07-283 1255, Mon-Fri 0900-1800, Sat 0900-1300, US$2*, contains all the Cañari and Inca remains and artifacts found at this site. There are also book and music libraries, free cultural videos and music events. About 300 m from Pumapungo, there are excavations at the **Todos Los Santos** site ⓘ *C Larga 287, Mon-Fri 0900-1300, 1500-1800, Sat 0900-1300, US$0.25*, which reveal traces of Inca and Cañari civilizations and show how the Spanish reused the stonework. Further along the river is the **Instituto Azuayo de Folklore**, better known as **CIDAP** ⓘ *Escalinata 303 y C Larga, extension of Hermano Miguel, Mon-Fri 0930-1300, 1430-1800, Sat 100-1300, free*. It has an exhibition of popular art and a library and supports research and promotes sales for artisan workers. It also has a recommended craft shop and good information.

There are sulphur baths at **Baños**, with a domed, blue church in a delightful landscape, 5 km southwest of Cuenca. These are the hottest commercial baths in Ecuador. There are four separate complexes of warm baths, *Marchan, Rodas, Familiar* and *Durán*. The latter two are by far the largest and best maintained, with numerous hot pools, tubs and steam baths.

Ingapirca
ⓘ *Between Cuenca and Alausí, 8½ km east of Cañar, daily 0800-1800, US$6, including museum and guided tour in Spanish. Café serves cheap set lunches.*
Ecuador's most important Inca ruin lies at 3,160 m. Access is from Cañar or El Tambo. The Inca Huayna Capac took over the site from the conquered Cañaris when his empire expanded north into Ecuador in the third quarter of the 15th century. Ingapirca was strategically placed on the Royal Highway that ran from Cusco to Quito and soldiers may have been stationed there. The site shows typical imperial Cusco-style architecture, such as tightly fitting stonework and trapezoidal doorways. The central structure may have been a solar observatory. Nearby is a throne cut into the rock, the **Sillón del Inga** (Inca's Chair) and the **Ingachugana**, a large rock with carved channels. A 10-minute walk away from the site is the **Cara del Inca**, or 'face of the Inca', an immense natural formation in the rock looking over the landscape. On Friday there is an interesting Indian market at Ingapirca. There is a good co-operative craft shop next to the church. There is a beautiful four-hour, 16-km walk from Ingapirca to Cañar. The start of the road is signposted, along the main street; take water.

South of Cuenca ⬤𝕚▲⬛❶ ›› *pp377-372*

From Cuenca various routes go to the Peruvian border, fanning out from the pleasant city of Loja. Due south of Loja is Vilcabamba, famous for its invigorating climate, lovely countryside and the extraordinary longevity of its people (see page 379) . The road between Cuenca and Loja can be rough after heavy rains but is one of the most beautiful and breathtaking in Ecuador.

Loja

This friendly highland city, encircled by hills, is a traditional gateway between the highlands and southern Amazonia. It was founded on its present site in 1548, having been moved from La Toma, and was rebuilt twice after earthquakes, the last of which occurred in the 1880s. There is an airport at **La Toma**, 35 km west of Loja. ⬤ ›› *p386.*

The **Museo de la Historia y Culturas Lojanas del Banco Central** ⓘ *on the main plaza, 0800-1600,* has exhibits of local art, archaeology, folklore and history. **Mercado Centro Comercial Loja** (Mercado Modelo) ⓘ *10 de Agosto y 18 de Noviembre, Mon-Sat (the main market day) 0600-1630, Sun 0600-1330,* rebuilt in 1991, is worth a visit. It is efficient and the cleanest in Ecuador. Tourist information is available at the **Ministerio de Turismo** ⓘ *Sucre y Eguiguren, edif Banco de Fomento, p 4, T257 2964, miturgfs@impsat.net.ec, Mon-Fri 0830-1300, 1430-1730.* **Parque Educacional Ambiental y Recreacional de Argelia** ⓘ *0830-1700 except Tue and Wed, take a city bus marked 'Argelia,* is superb, with trails through the forest to the *páramo.* It is 500 m before the police checkpoint on the road south to Vilcabamba.

Vilcabamba

Once an isolated village, Vilcabamba has become increasingly popular with foreign travellers, an established stop along the gringo trail between Ecuador and Peru. The whole area is beautiful and very relaxing, with an agreeable climate (17°C minimum, 26°C maximum). There are many places to stay and several good restaurants. There are also many good walks in the Río Yambala valley and on the Mandango mountain trail (exposed and slippery in parts).

Ecuador to Peru

An alternative to the Huaquillas border crossing is the quieter and more scenic route from Loja to Piura, via Macará. The road is fully paved and winds its way through stunning countryside and beautiful little towns until it descends through forests to the border town of Macará. There is a choice of accommodation here (see page 381) and good road connections to Piura in Peru (see page 387).

Ecuadorean immigration is open 24 hours. Formalities last about 30 minutes. During the day there are money changers dealing in soles at the international bridge and in Macará at the park where taxis leave for the border. The international bridge over the Río Macará is 2½ km from town. There is a taxi and pick-up service (US$0.30 shared, US$1.25 private). For details of buses from Loja or Macará to Piura, in Peru, see page 386.

An alternative route to Peru offers the chance to travel from Vilcabamba to Chachapoyas (see page 190) in just 2 days. Take a bus (several daily) from Loja or Vilcabamba to **Zumba** (see page 386), 112 km south of Vilcabamba (several basic places to stay and eat). It is then a 3-hr rough ride by *ranchera* (open-sided bus, 0800, 1430, US$1.65) from Zumba to **La Balsa**, where there is an immigration post. A bridge crosses the river to the Peruvian border post and on the Peruvian side a minibus service runs to **Namballe**, 15 minutes away. Another minibus goes to **San Ignacio** (Peru) when full, 2 hours, from where there is transport to **Jaén** and from there to Chachapoyas.

Vilcabamba is famous as Ecuador's gringo capital and for the remarkable longevity of its residents.

● Sleeping

Cuenca *p374, map p378*
Prices in Cuenca are a bit higher than elsewhere in Ecuador.
AL Santa Lucía, Borrero 8-44 y Sucre, T07-282 8000, www.santaluciahotel.com. A luxurious, elegantly restored colonial house with 20 comfortable rooms around a patio, includes breakfast, Italian restaurant in the central courtyard, fridge, safe deposit box.
A Victoria, C Larga 6-93 y Borrero, T07-282 7401, www.grupo-santaana.com. Elegant refurbished hotel overlooking the river, includes breakfast, excellent expensive restaurant, comfortable modern rooms, nice views, friendly service.
B El Príncipe, J Jaramillo 7-82 y Luis Cordero, T07-284 7287, htprince@etapaonline.net.ec. A refurbished 3-storey colonial house in the centre of town. Comfortable rooms around a nice patio with plants, includes breakfast, restaurant serves lunch.
B Posada del Angel, Bolívar 14-11 y Estévez de Toral, T07-284 0695, www.hostalposadadelangel.com. A nicely restored colonial house, includes breakfast, internet, parking, comfortable rooms, sitting area in patio with plants.
C Chordeleg, Gran Colombia 11-15 y Gral Torres, T07-282 2536, hostalfm @etapaonline.net.ec. Charming house with courtyard and fountain, includes breakfast, cafeteria, carpeted rooms.
C La Castellana, Luis Cordero 10-47 y Gran Colombia, T/F07-282 7293, castelho@etapaonline.net.ec. Elegant refurbished colonial house in the centre of town, includes breakfast, restaurant, carpeted rooms, a couple of sitting areas, good service.
C-D Macondo, Tarqui 11-64 y Lamar, T07-284 0697, www.hostalmacondo.com. Lovely, restored colonial house, includes breakfast, cheaper with shared bath, cooking facilities, pleasant patio with plants, garden, very popular, US run.
D Casa Naranja, Lamar 10-38 y Padre Aguirre, T07-282 5415, www.casanaranja.galeon.com. Restored colonial house, breakfast available weekdays, cheaper with shared bath or in dorm, cooking facilities, motorcycle parking, 2 inner patios, storage room, long stay discounts.
D Posada Todos Santos, C Larga 3-42 y Tomás Ordóñez, near the Todos Santos

Church, T07-282 4247. Nice clean and tranquil hostel, includes breakfast, very good, friendly service.

D-E Tinku, Honorato Vázquez 5-66 y Hermano Miguel, T09-7245696, tinkuenca@yahoo.es. A friendly popular hostel, most rooms with shared bath, cheaper in dorm, internet, cooking facilities, very clean, sitting room with videos and games, book exchange, helpful.

E Pichincha, Gral Torres 8-82 y Bolívar, T07-282 3868, karolina @etapaonline.net.ec. Shared bath, hot water, cooking facilities, spacious rooms but a little noisy on the street side, helpful.

Ingapirca *p375*

A Posada Ingapirca, 500 m uphill from the archaeologic site, T07-221 5116, T07-283 8508 (Cuenca), www.grupo-santaana.com. A nice

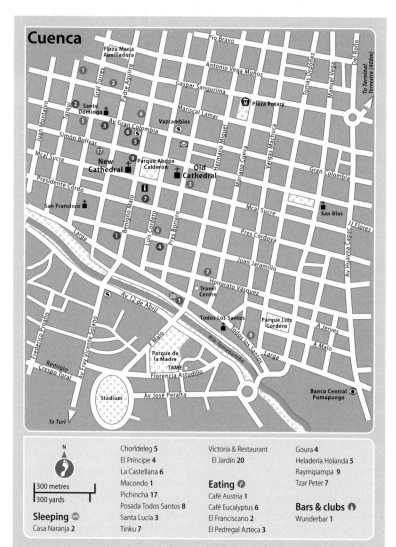

Cuenca

Sleeping

Casa Naranja 2
Chorldeleg 5
El Príncipe 4
La Castellana 6
Macondo 1
Pichincha 17
Posada Todos Santos 8
Santa Lucía 3
Tinku 7

Victoria & Restaurant
El Jardín 20

Eating
Café Austria 1
Café Eucalyptus 6
El Franciscano 2
El Pedregal Azteca 3
Goura 4
Heladería Holanda 5
Raymipampa 9
Tzar Peter 7

Bars & clubs
Wunderbar 1

300 metres
300 yards

Background

→ **Live forever**

The isolated and little known village of Vilcabamba was thrust into the limelight in the 1960s when doctors announced that it was home to one of the oldest living populations in the world. It was said that people here often lived to well over 100 years old, some as old as 135. Fame, though, turned to infamy when it was revealed that researchers had been working with parish records which corresponded to the subjects' parents. However, given that first children are often born to parents in their teenage years, this still means that there are some very old people living in these parts. There is also a high incidence of healthy, active elders. It's not unusual to find people in their 70s and 80s toiling in the fields and covering several miles a day to get there. Such longevity and vitality is not only down to the area's famously healthy climate. Other factors at play are physical exercise, strong family ties, a balanced diet low in animal fats and a lack of stress. In recent years, a number of outsiders – both Ecuadoreans and foreigners – have settled in the area, no doubt attracted by the promise of a long and healthy old age.

converted hacienda with superb views, includes typical breakfast with dishes such as *mote pillo* and *morocho*, good expensive restaurant and well-stocked bar, good service.

Loja *p376*
L-AL La Casa Lojana, París 00-08 y Zoilo Rodríguez, T07-258 5984, casalojanahotel@utpl.edu.ec. A refurbished residence elaborately decorated in colonial style. Rooms are plain compared to the opulent common areas. Includes breakfast, elegant dinning room, lovely grounds and views of the city. Run by the Universidad Particular de Loja and staffed by their Hotel School students.
A-B Bombuscaro, 10 de Agosto y Av Universitaria, T07-257 7021, www.bombuscaro.com.ec. Comfortable rooms and suites, includes buffet breakfast, restaurant, internet, airport transfers, car rental, good service.
C Aguilera Internacional, Sucre 01-08 y Emiliano Ortega, T07-257 2894, F07-258 4660. Comfortable hotel to the

north of the centre. Nice rooms, includes breakfast, restaurant and bar, parking, gym, steam bath and sauna.
E Londres, Sucre 7-51 y 10 de Agosto, T07-256 1936. Hostel in a well maintained old house, shared bath, hot water, basic but clean, good value.

Vilcabamba *p, map p380*
AL-C Madre Tierra, 2 km north on road to Loja, then follow signs west, T07-2580269, www.madretierra1.com. A variety of rooms from elaborate suites to simple cabins and dorms, each one nicely decorated with its own character. Includes breakfast and dinner, superb home cooking, vegetarian to order, non-residents must reserve meals a day in advance. Cheaper in dorm, nice grounds, pool, spa (extra charge), videos, games, under new US management, English and French spoken, popular.
C-D Izhcayluma, 2 km south on road to Zumba, T07-2580895, www.izhcayluma.com. Comfortable cabins with terrace and hammocks. Includes a very good breakfast available

all day, excellent restaurant with European specialties. Cheaper with shared bath, parking, nice grounds, pool, dining area with wonderful views of Vilcabamba. Pleasant bar, billards, table tennis and other games. English and German spoken, friendly and helpful. A bit out of the way but includes use of bikes to get to town.

D Cabañas Río Yambala, Yamburara Alto, 4 km east of town, www.vilcabamba.cwc.net. Cabins in a beautiful setting on the shores of the Río Yambala. Some with kitchen facilities, meals also available. Cheaper with shared bath, one simple cabin across the river with kitchen facilities is

in the **F** range, access to Las Palmas private nature reserve, good birdwatching. English spoken, owners Charlie and Sarah are very friendly and also run Las Palmas nature reserve.

D El Jardín Escondido (Hidden Garden), Sucre y Diego Vaca de Vega, T07-2580281, www.vilcabamba.org/jardinescondido.html. A nicely refurbished old house around a lovely patio. Brightly decorated comfortable rooms, includes very good and generous breakfast, excellent restaurant, small pool, jacuzzi extra, parking for small vehicle, luggage storage.

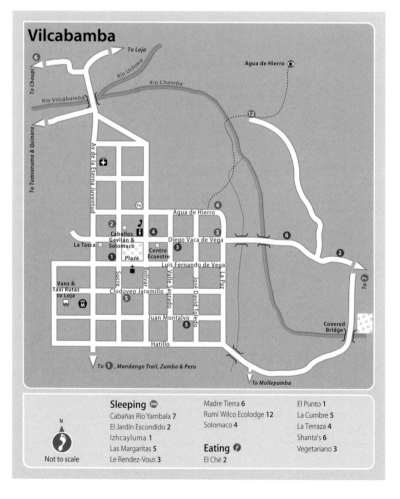

Sleeping
Cabañas Río Yambala 7
El Jardín Escondido 2
Izhcayluma 1
Las Margaritas 5
Le Rendez-Vous 3

Madre Tierra 6
Rumi Wilco Ecolodge 12
Solomaco 4

Eating
El Ché 2

El Punto 1
La Cumbre 5
La Terraza 4
Shanta's 6
Vegetariano 3

N
Not to scale

D **Las Margaritas**, Sucre y Clodoveo Jaramillo esquina, www.vilcabamba.org /lasmargaritas.html. Small family-run hotel with very comfortable and nicely-furnished rooms, includes good breakfast, small pool, parking, solar heated water, nice garden. Good value.

D **Le Rendez-Vous**, Diego Vaca de Vega 06-43 y La Paz, rendezvousecuador @yahoo.com. Very nice adobe cabins with terrace and hammocks around a lovely garden. Comfortable modern rooms, includes breakfast, pleasant atmosphere, friendly service, French run by Isabelle and Serge, English also spoken.

D **Solomaco**, Agua del Hierro y La Paz, at northeast end of town, T07-2580904, martinesolomaco@yahoo.fr. A large house on a quiet corner by the stream, away from the centre. Includes good breakfast, most rooms with private bath, parking, nice wooden floors and ceilings. Under new French management in 2005, some English spoken, good friendly service, runs tours.

D-E **Rumi Wilco Ecolodge**, 10-min walk northeast of town, follow Agua de Hierro to La Paz and turn left, follow the signs from there, http://koberpress.home. mindspring.com/vilcabamba/ Nice adobe cabins and a wooden one on stilts (the 'Pole House') located in a 40 ha private nature reserve with walking trails. Lovely setting on the shores of the river, very tranquil, cheaper with shared bath, laundry facilities, fully furnished kitchens, discounts for long stays, friendly owners: Orlando and Alicia.

Macará *p376*

D **El Conquistador**, Bolívar y Calderón, T07-269 4057. Includes breakfast, hot water, fan, parking, modern and comfortable.

D **Santigyn**, Bolívar y Rengel, T07-269 5035. Hot water, fan, some rooms with fridge, modern, comfortable.

● Eating

Cuenca *p374, map p378*

††† **El Franciscano**, Gran Colombia 11-80 y Tarqui, T07-285 0513. Very elegant restaurant in the centre of the city, excellent international food.

††† **El Jardín**, in Hotel Victoria, C Larga 6-93, T07-282 7401, closed Sun-Mon. Lovely elegant restaurant overlooking the river. Good international food and service.

†† **Café Austria**, Benigno Malo 5-99 y J Jaramillo, 1100-2200. A traditional Cuenca café, under new management and refurbished in 2004, now also serves international food. Pastries are very good.

†† **Café Eucalyptus**, Gran Colombia 9-41 y Benigno Malo, Mon-Fri 1700-2300, Sat 1900-late. A pleasant restaurant, café and bar in an elegantly decorated 2 storey house. Large menu with dishes from all over the world, varied tapas (try their Vietnamese shrimp) and drinks. Ladies night on Thu, Salsa and dancing on Sat. Good service, pleasant atmosphere, popular, reserve in advance for the couch by the fireplace. British-American run.

†† **El Pedregal Azteca**, Gran Colombia 10-29 y Padre Aguirre. Very good Mexican food. In the Casa Azul, a refurbished colonial house with nice patios, live music in the evenings.

†† **Raymipampa**, Benigno Malo 8-59, at Parque Calderón. Very good international food in a nice central location. Fast service, popular, at times it is hard to get a table.

††-† **Tzar Peter**, Presidente Córdova 8-34 y Luis Cordero. Formally decorated restaurant-bar, serves very good international and Russian specialties, also set lunches Mon-Fri 1200-1500. Happy hour 1800-2100.

† **Goura**, Juan Jaramillo 7-27 y Borrero. Very good vegetarian restaurant. Nice economical set lunches, tasty pizza, great fruit salad, good choice of à la carte dinners with some Indian dishes.

Heladería Holanda, Benigno Malo 9-51, open from 0930. Yoghurt for breakfast, good ice-cream, fruit salads, cream cakes. Popular.

The English Café and Bookshop, C Larga 6-69 y Borrero, closed Wed. Pleasant small café, serves good breakfast all day, juices, snacks and sandwiches. Nice atmosphere, British-Ecuadorean run. English books for sale and trade.

Loja *p376*

♉ **José Antonio's**, José Antonio Eguiguren 12-24 y Olmedo, 2nd floor, daily 1000-2200. Excellent French and other international food. Enthusiastic chef.

♉ **Casa Sol**, 24 de Mayo 07-04 y José Antonio Eguiguren, daily 0900-0000. Economical set meals and à la carte. Pleasant seating on a balcony overlooking the small Parque Cristóbal Ojeda.

♉ **Diego's**, Colón 14-88 y Sucre, 2nd floor, Mon-Sat 0800-2130, Sun 0800-1530. Pleasant restaurant in the second floor of a colonial house, seating on balconies around a courtyard. Good filling set lunches and international à la carte dishes, very popular.

♉ **Pizzería Forno di Fango**, Bolívar 10-98 y Azuay, Tue-Sun 1200-2230. Excellent wood-oven pizza, salads and lasagne. Large portions, friendly service and good value.

Cafés

Topoli, Bolívar 13-78 y Riofrío esquina, Mon-Fri 0800-2100, Sat 0800-2000. Best coffee and yoghurt in town, good for breakfast, sandwiches, snacks, nice sweets. Very popular with young and old, can get crowded and noisy.

Vilcabamba *p, map p380*

♉♉ **El Jardín**, Sucre y Agua de Hierro, at Jardín Escondido hotel, 0800-2000. Excellent authentic Mexican food and drinks (Mexican chef), also international dishes and very good breakfasts. Pleasant

atmosphere in a garden setting, attentive service, live music some Sat nights.

♉♉ **Izhcayluma**, At Hostería Izhcayluma south of town (don´t confuse with El Molino de Izhcayluma next door), Mon 1700-2000, Tue-Sun 0800-2000. Excellent international dishes with some German specialties, also serve nice breakfasts. Lovely terrace dining room with wonderful views.

♉♉ **Shanta's**, 800 m from town on the road to Yamburara. Good international food with specialties such as trout and frog legs, tasty pizza. Nicely decorated rustic setting just outside town, pleasant atmosphere, friendly service.

♉♉-♉ **La Terraza**, D Vaca de Vega y Bolívar, esquina, daily 1000-2100. Popular restaurant with sidewalk seating, right at the main park. A variety of international dishes, good fajitas.

♉ **El Ché**, In Yamburara, next to Craig's Book exchange, 1½ km from town. Terrace restaurant serving Argentine specialties. Tasty meat, pasta and pizza, good quality and generous portions, friendly owner.

♉ **La Cumbre**, J Montalvo 07-36 y J D Toledo, Sun-Tue 1200-11800, Wed-Fri 1200-2200, Sat 1200-0100. At the cultural centre and language school, Ecuadorean and international cuisine in a covered patio setting. Films shown some Wed evenings, dancing on Sat night if not booked for private events.

♉ **Vegetariano**, Valle Sagrado y Diego Vaca de Vega esquina, daily 0830-2030. Small vegetarian restaurant in a nice garden setting. Very good 3 course set meals and a few à la carte dishes, also breakfasts.

Cafés

El Punto, Sucre y Luis Fernando de Vega, esquina, 0800-2100, closed Tue. A pleasant sidewalk café on the main park. Breakfast, snacks, pizza, sandwiches on home-made bread, sweets, coffee and drinks.

⊙ Bars and clubs

Cuenca *p374, map p378*
Café del Tranquilo, Borrero 7-47 y Presidente Córdova. Pleasant popular bar, live music, US$3 cover.
La Mesa Salsoteca, Gran Colombia 3-36 entre Vargas Machuca y Tomás Ordóñez, no sign. Latin music, very popular among locals and travellers, young crowd.
Wunderbar, C Larga 3-43 y Hermano Miguel, T07-283 1274. A café-bar-restaurant, drinks, good coffee and food including some vegetarian dishes. Nice atmosphere, a popular travellers' hangout, games, German magazines, book exhchange, German-run.

⊛ Festivals and events

Cuenca *p374, map p378*
On **24 Dec** there is an outstanding parade: **Pase del Niño Viajero**, probably the largest and finest Christmas parade in all Ecuador. Children and adults from all the *barrios* and surrounding villages decorate donkeys, horses, cars and trucks with symbols of abundance. Little children in colourful Indian costumes or dressed up as Biblical figures ride through the streets accompanied by musicians. The parade starts at about 1000 at San Sebastián, proceeds along C Simón Bolívar and ends at San Blas about 5 hrs later. On **Good Friday** there is a fine procession through the town to the Mirador Turi. On **3 Nov** is **Independence of Cuenca**, with street theatre, art exhibitions and night-time dances all over the city.

⊙ Shopping

Cuenca *p374, map p378*
Good souvenirs are carvings, leather, basketwork, painted wood, onyx, ceramics, woven stuffs, embroidered shirts, jewellery and, of course, the Panama hat, Ecuador's most famous

export. Cuenca is the main export centre and countless shops here sell the *sombreros de paja toquilla*, as they are known locally. There are craftware shops along Gran Colombia and on Benigno Malo. There are several good leather shops in the arcade off Bolívar between Benigno Malo and Luis Cordero.
Arte Artesanías y Antigüedades at Borrero y Córdova. Textiles, jewellery and antiques.
Galería Claudio Maldonado, Bolívar 7-75. Unique pre-Columbian designs in silver and precious stones.
Joyería Turismo owned by Leonardo Crespo, at Gran Colombia 9-31. He will let wholesale buyers tour his factory.
Exportadora Cuenca, Mcal Lamar 3-80. Jaime Ortega Ramírez and his wife, Tania, will make Panama hats to order.
Homero Ortega P e Hijos, Av Gil Ramírez Dávalos 3-86, T07-280 9000, www.homero ortega.com. Highest quality Panama hats. He will show you his factory opposite bus station, open 0900-1200, 1500-1800 for visits.
Kurt Dorfzaun, Gil Ramírez Dávalos 4-34, T07-280 7563, www.kdorfzaun.com. Good prices and display of the complete Panama hat making process.

⛰ Activities and tours

Cuenca *p374, map p378*
Ecotrek, C Larga 7-108 y Luis Cordero, T07-2842531, ecotrek@az.pro.ec. Contact Juan Gabriel Carrasco. Trips to Kapawi Ecological Reserve, excellent, experienced guides and great adventure travel, monthly departures, specialize in Shaman trips.
Enmotur, Gran Colombia 10-45. Bus tours to Ingapirca, US$35-45 pp.
Travel Center, Hermano Miguel 4-46 y C Larga, T07-2823782, www.terradiversa.com. Houses 3 tour operators: **Biketa**, for mountain biking; **Montaruna Tours**, T07-F2846395, www.montaruna.ch, horse riding, treks, German and English spoken, helpful;

Whale watching on the coast

If you have time, the Ecuadorean coast is well worth a detour.
Puerto López is a pleasant little fishing town, set on a horseshoe
bay with a broad sweep of beach enclosed by headlands to the
north and south. Visitors flock here every year during 'whale
season'. Lying offshore is **Isla de la Plata**, an island with nesting
colonies of waved albatross, frigates and three different booby
species. A small colony of sea lions also makes its home here and
whales can be seen from June to September. As in Galápagos, it is
easy to see the bird life, you will walk just by their nests. The island
is visited in a day trip from Puerto López. Another top attraction
around Puerto López is the magnificent beach of **Los Frailes**, one
of the nicest on the entire coast, 11 km north of the town. Another
recommended trip is to **San Sebastián**, 9 km from Agua Blanca up
in tropical moist forest (altitude 800 m), for sightings of orchids
and possibly howler monkeys. All of these sights are part of the
Parque Nacional Machalilla, and can easily be visited on a tour
from Puerto López.

The whale-watching season runs from June to September/
October. All agencies offer the same tours for the same price. In
high season: US$30 per person for whale watching, Isla de la Plata
and snorkelling, including a snack and drinks, US$25 for whale
watching only. In low season tours to Isla de la Plata and
snorkelling cost US$25 per person, US$20 for whale watching only.
Trips start about 0800 and return around 1700. Agencies also offer
tours to the mainland sites of the national park from US$25 per
person. These rates don't include the National Park fee of US$20,
payable at the park office next to the market in Puerto López (open
0700-1800) or directly to the park rangers (insist on a receipt). The
ticket is valid for several days so you can visit the different areas.
During high season book your tour and accommodation in
advance and with a reputable agency.

Tour operators
Bosque Marino, on the highway, near the bus stop, T09-9173556
(mob). Experienced guides, some of whom speak English. They also
offer hikes through the forest and birdwatching tours for US$20 per
day for groups of 2-3.
Machalilla Tours, on Malecón next to *Viña del Mar* restaurant,
T05-604 206. They also offer horse-riding, surfing and fishing tours;
all cost US$25 per person for a day trip.

Terra Diversa Team, T07-2823782,
info@terradiversa.com, jungle tours, well
informed, very helpful.

Loja *p376*
Aratinga Aventuras, Lourdes 14-80 y
Sucre, T07-2582434, jatavent
@cue.satnet.net. Specializes in
birdwatching tours, overnight trips to

Manta Raya, on Malecón Norte, T05-604 233. They have a comfortable and spacious boat. They also have diving equipment and charge US$100 per person, all inclusive.

Sleeping
The best place to stay by far is **B-C Hostería Alandaluz**, T05-278 0686, F05-278 0690, T/F02-254 3042 (Quito), alandalu@interactive.net.ec. Part of an ecological centre, accommodation is in a variety of cabins ranging from bamboo with palm-leaf thatched roofs and compost toilets to more luxurious with flush toilets, all with private bath. It is a very peaceful place, with a clean beach and stunning organic vegetable and flower gardens in the middle of a desert. Good homemade organic food, vegetarian or seafood, at mid-range prices, and there's a bar. Expensive tours in the area are also offered. Reservations are necessary as it is popular.

In Puerto López itself is **C Mandala**, on the Malecón beyond fish market, at the north end of the beach, T/F05-230 0181. It has cabins with screened windows, lovely grounds, a good restaurant, and is Swiss-Italian run (English spoken), friendly and helpful.

Getting there
Bus to Quito with Carlos Aray at 0500, 0900, 1830, from Quito at 1010 and 1900, US$8, 11 hrs.

cloud forest. Pablo Andrade is a knowledgeable guide.
Biotours, Eguiguren y Olmedo, T07-2578398, biotours@loja.telconet.net. City, regional and jungle tours, airline tickets.

Vilcabamba *p376*
Caballos Gavilán, Sucre y Diego Vaca de Vega, T07-2580281, gavilanhorse @yahoo.com. Run by New Zealander Gavin Moore, good, experienced horseman.

Caminatas Andes Sureños, Bolívar by the plaza, T07-2673147, jorgeluis222@latinmail.com. Run by Jorge Mendieta, knowledgeable.

Centro Ecuestre, Diego Vaca de Vega y Bolívar, T07-2673183, centroecuestre@hotmail.com. A group of local guides, helpful.

Orlando Falco is an experienced English-speaking guide. Contact through *Rumi Wilco Ecolodge* (see Sleeping above) or *Primavera* craft shop on plaza.

La Tasca, Diego Vaca de Vega y Sucre, T07-2580888, latascatours@yahoo.fr. Riding tours to Los Helechos Reserve, guide René León.

Solomaco, Sucre y Diego Vaca de Vega, T07-2673186, solomaco@hotmail.com. French-run by Bernard and Martine, friendly and helpful.

⊖ Transport

Cuenca *p374, map p378*
Air
Airport is 5 mins walk beyond the bus terminal. No ticket reservations at the airport. To **Quito** US$63, with **TAME** and **Icaro**. Schedules change often so ask. Reconfirm all flights. Arrive at least 1 hr before departure.

Bus
Terminal for local services is at the Feria Libre on Av Las Américas. Many city buses pass here. City buses US$0.25. Local buses to **Baños** leave to and from every 5-10 mins, 0600-2330, US$0.25, they pass the front of the Terminal Terrestre. The long distance Terminal Terrestre is on Av España, northeast of centre, 20 mins walk, or take a minibus or taxi. It is well-organized and policed. To **Riobamba**, 6 hrs, US$6.25. To **Quito**, 10 hrs, US$12. To **Loja**, 5 hrs, US$7.50. To **Baños**, US$5.

Taxi
US$1 for short journey; US$1.40 to airport or bus station.

Ingapirca *p375*
Transportes Cañar has 2 direct buses daily from Cuenca to Ingapirca, at 0900 and 1300, returning 1300 and 1600, US$2.50, 2 hrs. Agencies in Cuenca offer day tours to Ingapirca for US$35-45, including visits to other nearby sites.

Loja *p376*
Air
The airport is at La Toma (Catamayo), 35 km west, shared taxi US$3 pp. There are **TAME** and **Icaro** flights to Quito direct (US$63). Flights are often cancelled due to strong winds and the airport is sometimes closed by 1000. The **TAME** office is at 24 de Mayo y E Ortega, T07-573030, Mon-Fri 0830-1600. **Icaro** is at Eguiguren y Olmedo, T07-578416.

Bus
All buses leave from the Terminal Terrestre at the north of town, some companies also have ticket offices in the centre. Taxi from centre, US$1.25. To **Cuenca**, 5-6 hrs, 7 a day, US$7.50. To **Quito**, US$15, 16 hrs. **Panamericana Internacional**, office at *Grand Hotel Loja* (Iberoamérica y Rocafuerte), luxury service to Quito (US$18.75). To **Macará**, 5 hrs, US$6.25. To **Vilcabamba**, a spectacular 1½-hour bus ride; **Sur Oriente** leave hourly from the bus terminal, US$0.75; **Taxiruta** (shared taxis) along Av Iberoamérica, US$1.25, 1 hr (US$6.25 to have the car to yourself); **Vilcabaturis** vans, from the bus terminal, every 30 minutes, US$1.25, 1 hr. To **Piura (Peru)**, luxury coach service with **Loja Internacional**, at 0700, 1300 and 2130 daily, 8 hrs including border formalities, US$10 (reservations can be made in Vilcabamba with *Vilcabaturis*). Also with the Peruvian bus company **Civa**, at 2130 daily. To **Zumba** (for Chachapoyas in Peru, see p376) via Vilcabamba with **Sur Oriente** at 0800, 1730 and 2130 daily, also **Unión Cariamanga** at 0530, 0900, 1200 and 1600, 7 hrs, US$6. It's a rough route and prone to landslides after heavy rain.

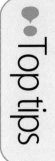

Top tips

Vilcabamba syndrome

Vilcabamba has become famous among travellers for its locally-produced hallucinogenic cactus juice called San Pedrillo. In addition to being illegal, it is more dangerous than it may seem because of flashbacks which can occur months or years after use. The resulting medical condition has been named the 'Vilcabamba Syndrome' and can affect sufferers for the rest of their lives. Tourist demand for San Pedrillo and other drugs is a problem in Vilcabamba and it's probably best not to get involved.

Vilcabamba *p376, map p380*

Regular buses, vans and shared taxis and from Loja, US$0.75, 1-1½ hrs. Vans and taxis leave from behind the market, buses pass along the highway. The Loja-Zumba bus passes through about 1-1½hrs after leaving Loja (see above for times).

Macará *p376*

Bus Coop Loja and Cariamanga have frequent buses, daily from Macará to **Loja**; 5-6 hrs, US$6.25. **Loja Internacional** buses, which have direct service Loja-**Piura**, 3 daily, can also be boarded in Macará. They pass through at 0330, 1300 and 1830; US$4.25 to Piura, 3 hrs. **Coop Loja** also has service to **Quito**, US$17.50, 17 hrs.

● Directory

Cuenca *p374, map p378*

Airline offices TAME, Benigno Malo 508 y C Larga, T07-2843222. **Icaro**, Av España 1114, T07-280 2700, F07-280 8261. **Banks** Banco del Pacífico, Benigno Malo 9-75. TCs only. Banco del Austro, Sucre y Borrero. Visa ATM. Banco de Guayaquil, Sucre entre Hermano Miguel y Borrero. For Visa, MC and TCs. Banco del Pichincha, Av Solano y 12 de Abril, no commission on TCs (this is subject to change), also Visa. **Vaz Cambios**, Gran Colombia 7-98 y Cordero. Open on Sat morning, efficient. No Peruvian currency is available in Cuenca. **Car rental** Inter, Av España, opposite the airport, T07-2801892.

Internet Rates US$0.70-1 per hr. Many to choose from. **Medical services** Clínica Los Andes, Mariano Cueva 14-68 y Pío Bravo, T07-2842942. Excellent care, clean, 24 hr service. **Farmacia Botica Internacional**, Gran Colombia 7-20 y Borrero. Experienced staff, wide selection. **Post offices** On corner of Gran Colombia and Borrero, helpful. **Telephones** ETAPA, Benigno Malo 7-27y Sucre, access to internet Mon-Fri 0800-2200.

Loja *p376*

Banks Banco de Guayaquil, Eguiguren y Valdivieso, TCs and Mastercard. Banco del Austro, Eguiguren 14-12 y Bolívar, Visa. Mutualista Pichincha, on plaza, Mastercard. There is nowhere to change Peruvian currency. **Embassies and consulates** Peru, Sucre y Azuay, T07-2571668. **Internet** Many internet cafés in town, price about US$1.50 per hr. **Post office** Colón y Sucre; no good for sending parcels. **Telephones** Pacifictel:, Eguiguren entre Olmedo y Valdivieso. **Useful addresses** Immigration: Bolivia y Argentina, T07-2573600.

Vilcabamba *p376, map p380*

Internet Service is scarce, slow and expensive, about US$3 per hr. Better to do your email in Loja. **Telephones** Pacifictel, Bolívar near the park, poor service, long queues.

Canopy walkway in the Oriente

COLOMBIA

CARCHI

SUCUMBIOS

NAPO

ORELLANA

PASTAZA

MORONA
SANTIAGO

ECUADOR

PERU

Chiles

Tulcán

El Angel
San
Gabriel
Bolívar
Gruta de
La Paz
La Bonita
Salinas

Ibarra
San Francisco
de Sigsigpamba
Gral Farfán
Tetetes
Puerto El
Carmen de
Putumayo
Putumayo
Zuleta
Puerto Libre
Lumbaquí
Reserva
Faunística
Cuyabeno
Equator
Olmedo
Cayambe
Lago Agrio
(Nuevo Loja)
Tarapoa
Güeppi
Güeppi
Cayambe
(5,790m)
Reventador
Shushifindi
Cuyabeno
Reventador
(3,562m)
Coca
Aguarico

Sta Rosa de Chicos
Pañacocha
El Chaco
Coca
(Pto Francisco
De Orellana)
La Joya de
los Sachas
Napo
Zancudo
Papallacta
ntisana
5,758m)
Borja
Pan de Azucár
Pompeya
Tiputini
Tiputini
Baeza
Sumaco
(3,732m)
Nuevo
Rocafuerte
e Nacional
topaxi
Cosanga
Parque
Nacional
Yasuní
topaxi
897m)
Cordillera Galeras
Loreto
Pante
Archidona
Chontapunta
Shiripuno
Nashiño
Tena
Misahuallí
Napo
Ahuano
HUA
Puerto Napo
Tiguino
Cononaco
Río Negro
Arajuno
Villano
Mera
Curaray
Cononaco
Shell
Puyo
Curaray
Cononaco
Palora
Porvenir
Canelos
Pavacachi
Pintoyacu
ltar
Sarayacu
19m)
Conambo
Bobonaza
Chuitayo
e Nacional
angay
Montalvo
Conambo
230m)
Pastaza
Macas
Taisha
Río
Corientes
cúa
Morona
San Jacinto
ño
Patuca
Andoas
Yaupi
Morona
eonidas
rrez)
Puerto Morona
nora
Santiago
Morona

N

30 km

30 miles

Don't miss...

⭐1 A visit to one of the local
indigenous communities
around Tena ▶▶ *p392.*

⭐2 Exploring the lagoons of the
Cuyabeno Wildlife Reserve by
canoe ▶▶ *p395.*

⭐3 **A guided night safari in the
jungle** ▶▶ *p399.*

⭐4 The chance to spend a few nights
in the **Kapawi Eco-Lodge** ▶▶ *p400.*

⭐5 **Whitewater rafting from Tena**
▶▶ *p401.*

East of the Andes the hills fall away to the vast green carpet of the Oriente, Ecuador's Amazon Basin. Some of this beautiful wilderness remains unspoiled and sparsely populated, with indigenous settlements along the tributaries of the Amazon. Additionally, the Ecuadorean jungle has the advantage of being relatively accessible and tourist infrastructure here is well developed.

The eastern foothills of the Andes, where the jungle begins, offer the easiest access and a good introduction to the rainforest for those with limited time, money, or interest. Further east lie the remaining large tracts of primary rainforest. Here are two vast national parks, Cuyabeno and Yasuní, as well as the Huaorani Reserve. Many excellent (and expensive) lodges offer an unforgettable immersion into life in the jungle. This is Ecuadorean jungle tourism at its best. Despite all the lip-service paid to conservation and ecotourism here, the eastern jungle is also under severe threat from petroleum development and colonization. It is hoped that sustainable tourism can help tip the economic balance in favour of conserving the rainforest and its people.

Southern Oriente is as yet less developed for tourism or other activities, and is not covered in any detail here.

Introduction

Oriente

Ratings

Culture
★★★

Landscape
★★★★★

Wildlife
★★★★★

Activities
★★★★

Chillin'
★★★

Costs
$$$$

Oriente

The beauty of visiting the jungle in Ecuador, as opposed to its larger neighbours, is the relative ease of access. There are scheduled commercial flights from Quito to Lago Agrio and Coca. Much of western Oriente is also accessible by roads which wind their way down from the highlands. Baños to Puyo is fully paved, and Quito to Tena is in reasonable shape. The remainder are mostly narrow and tortuous, subject to landslides in the rainy season. Nonetheless, all have regular if rough bus service. Most of these roads can also be attempted in an ordinary car with good ground clearance, but 4WD is an asset. Deeper into the rainforest, motorized canoes provide the only alternative to air travel.

⊘ **Getting there** Flights from Quito to Lago Agrio and Coca. Buses from Quito and Baños.
⊖ **Getting around** Slow buses on rough roads. Light aircraft and motorized canoe.
⊖ **Time required** 5-10 days.
◗ **Weather** Hot and wet. Oct-Feb it can rain every day, Mar-Sep it can rain all day.
⊖ **Sleeping** Jungle lodges; a few good hotels in Lago Agrio, Coca, Tena and Puyo, otherwise basic.
⊙ **Eating** Not much choice, only a few good simple places.
▲ **Activities and tours** Whitewater rafting, ethnotourism and medicinal plants.
★ **Don't miss...** the jungle by night ›› *p401*.

Tena ⊜⊙▲⊜⊙ ›› *pp396-403*

Tena is the capital of Napo Province. Once an important early colonial missionary and trading posts of the Amazon, it is now a relaxed and friendly town on a hill above the confluence of the Ríos Tena and Napo. In recent years, it has become an important centre for whitewater rafting and ethnotourism.

Ins and outs

The road from the north passes the airstrip and market and heads through the town centre as Avenida 15 de Noviembre on its way to the bus station, nearly 1 km south of the river. Tena is quite spread out. There is a pedestrian bridge and a vehicle bridge which link the two halves of the town. ⊖ ›› *p401*.

Information Tourist information offices ① *García Moreno between Calderón and JL Mera, near the river, T2886536, Mon-Fri 0800-1230, 1330-1700.*

Excursions

The **Jumandí caves** ① *T06-2889185, daily 0900-1700, US$2,* are 15 km north of Tena. The main cave has electric lights (take a torch anyway), and a recreation complex with pools and waterslides has been built at the entrance. It gets crowded at weekends. **Comunidad Capirona** is one hour by bus, then three hours on foot from Tena. Visits can be arranged here or to nine other communities in the area. This is part of a highly regarded project which combines eco/ethnotourism and community development. There are also opportunities for volunteers. Contact the **Red Indigena de las Comunidades del Alto Napo para la Convivencia Intercultural y El Ecoturismo** (Ricancie) ① *15 de Noviembre 722, T06-2887072, http://ricancie.nativeweb.org*

Misahuallí ⊜❼▲⊜ ↠ pp396-403

This small port at the junction of the Napo and Misahuallí rivers was once the westernmost access for navigation on the Río Napo and very important because of the lack of roads. Its decline as a port began with the opening of the Loreto road to Coca, and tourism has since replaced transport as the town's major activity. Today, it is a particularly pleasant and peaceful little place, well suited to those in no hurry. A local curiosity is the troop of mischievous capuchin monkeys who live in the park.

Misahuallí is perhaps the best place in Ecuador from which to visit the **'near Oriente'**, but your expectations should be realistic. The area has been colonized for many years and there is no virgin rainforest nearby (except at Jatun Sacha, see below). Access is very easy however, prices are reasonable, and while you will not encounter large animals in the wild, you can still see birds, butterflies and exuberant vegetation – enough to get a taste for the jungle. Some Misahuallí operators also offer tours deeper into the jungle, past Coca.

Sights

There is a **mariposario** (butterfly farm) in Misahuallí, two blocks from the plaza. Several colourful species can be observed and photographed close up. Interesting and worthwhile. Make arrangements through **Ecoselva** (see Tour operators, page 401), entry US$1.50. About 8 km downriver from Misahuallí, reached by road or river, is the **Jatun Sacha Biological Station** ('big forest' in Quichua), a reserve set aside for environmental education, field research, community extension and ecotourism. The biological station and the adjacent Aliñahui project together conserve 1,300 ha of tropical wet forest. So far, 507 birds, 2,500 plants and 765 butterfly species have been identified at Jatun Sacha. They offer excursions with good views and walking on a well-developed trail system.

Puyo ⊜❼❶⊙▲⊜❻ ↠ pp396-403

The capital of the province of Pastaza is the largest urban centre in the whole of Oriente. It feels more like a small lowland city anywhere, rather than a typical jungle town. Visits can nonetheless be made to nearby forest reserves and tours deeper into the jungle can also be arranged from Puyo. Sangay and Altar volcanoes can occasionally be seen from town.

Canoe is often the only way to navigate around the further reaches of the Oriente.

Top tips

Taking a jungle tour

Jungle tours can be divided into three basic types: lodges, guided tours, and indigenous ecotourism. Staying in a lodge usually involves the purchase of an all-inclusive package in Quito or from your home country. Tour companies and guides are mainly concentrated in Quito, Baños, Puyo, Tena, Misahuallí, Coca and Lago Agrio where travellers tend to congregate to form or join groups and arrange a jungle tour, usually of between one and seven days. A number of indigenous communities and families offer ecotourism programmes in their territories. A growing number of independent indigenous guides are working out of Puyo, Tena, Coca and Misahuallí. Accommodation is typically in simple native shelters of varying quality.

⊘ There may be a shortage of tourists for group travel outside the months of July and August and travellers may find that in the off-season it will take several days to assemble a reasonably sized group. It may be easier to form a group in Quito or Baños, before heading for the Oriente.

⊘ When shopping around for a guided tour ensure that the guide or agency specifies the details of the programme, the services to be provided and whether park fees and payments to indigenous communities are involved.

⊘ A common misconception is that it is easy to find a cheap jungle tour in Coca. In fact, the majority of tours out of Coca are booked through agencies in Quito (see Quito tour operators, page 339) and other tourist centres. There are not many tour operators left in Coca itself.

⊘ There are frequent military checkpoints in the Oriente, so always have your passport handy.

⊘ A yellow fever vaccination is required. Anti-malaria tablets are recommended and be sure to take an effective insect repellent. A mosquito net may be helpful if you are travelling independently.

Getting there Puyo is the junction for road travel into the northern and southern Oriente, and for traffic heading to or from the highlands via Baños. The road from Puyo to Baños is fully paved and offers a journey with superb views of the Pastaza valley and a plethora of waterfalls.

Information Ministerio de Turismo ① *Francisco de Orellana y 24 de Mayo, Mon-Fri 0830-1700*. **Consejo Provincial** ① *Orellana 145 y 27 de Febrero, ground floor*.

Sights

The **Museo Etno-Arqueológico**, Atahualpa y 9 de Octubre, third floor, has displays of the traditional dwellings of various cultures of the province of Pastaza. **Omaere** ① *daily 0800-1700. US$3, www.omaere.net*, is a 15.6-ha ethnobotanical reserve located 2 km north of Puyo on the road to Tena. It has three trails with a variety of plants, an orchidarium and traditional native homes. There are other small private reserves of varying quality in the Puyo

The Baños-Puyo road is one of the more comfortable land routes to the Oriente.

area and visits are arranged by local tour operators (see below). You cannot however expect to see large tracts of undisturbed primary jungle here or many wild animals. Sites include: **Criadero de Vida Silvestre Fátima**, 9 km north on the road to Tena, which attempts to 'rehabilitate' captive jungle animals (entry US$2); **Jadín Botánico La Orquideas**, 3 km south on the road to Macas, with orchids and other tropical plants (entry US$5), and **Fundación Ecologica Hola Vida**, 27 km from Puyo near **Porvenir**, which offers rustic accommodation in the forest, and a 30-minute canoe trip.

Lago Agrio ⊜❼⚠⊜❺ →→ pp396-393

Lago Agrio is first and foremost an old oil town. It has grown in recent years and the infrastructure is adequate, but it remains very much on the frontier. It is the capital of the province of Sucumbíos. The town's official name is Nueva Loja, owing to the fact that the majority of the first colonizers were from the southern province of Loja. The name Lago Agrio comes from Sour Lake, the US headquarters of Texaco, the first oil company to exploit the crude reserves beneath Ecuador's rainforest. Avenida Quito is the main street where many hotels and restaurants are located, but there are no street signs.

Lago Agrio is among the places in Ecuador that has been most severely affected by the armed conflict in neighbouring Colombia. Enquire about safety before travelling here and enquire again in Lago Agrio before visiting outlying regions of the province of Sucumbíos. Due to the risk of bus holdups, do not travel to Lago Agrio overnight. For information try the **Camara de Turismo de Sucumbíos**, at Avenida Quito y Pasaje Gonzanamá, T06-2832502.

Reserva Faunística Cuyabeno

This large tract of pristine rainforest, covering 602,000 ha, is located about 100 km east of Lago Agrio. The extensive jungle area is along the Río Cuyabeno, which eventually drains into the Aguarico. In the reserve are many lagoons and a great variety of wildlife, including river dolphins, tapirs, capybaras, five species of caiman, ocelots, 15 species of monkey and over 500 species of birds.

Cuyabeno is among the best places in Ecuador to see jungle animals and the reserve is very popular with visitors. Access to Cuyabeno is either by road from Lago Agrio, or by river along the Río Aguarico. Within the reserve, transport is mainly by canoe. In order to see as many animals as possible and minimally impact their habitat, look for a small tour group (eight people or less) which scrupulously adheres to responsible tourism practices. The reserve entrance fee is US$20. ▲▲ ▶▶ *p401*.

Coca ⬤🌐👤▲⬛● ▶▶ *pp396-403*

Officially named Puerto Francisco de Orellana, Coca is a hot, bustling and sprawling oil town at the junction of the Ríos Payamino and Napo, just upstream from the confluence of the Coca and Napo. As a tourist centre, however, Coca offers few attractions other than being closer to undisturbed primary rainforest than the larger jungle towns further west. Hotel and restaurant provision is adequate and there are plenty of bars and discos, usually filled with oil workers. Electricity and water supply are erratic, better hotels have reserve tanks and generators. Ironically, the petroleum production capital of Ecuador also suffers from occasional gasoline shortages.

⬤ Sleeping

Tena *p392*
B **Los Yutzos**, Augusto Rueda 190 y 15 de Noviembre, T06-2886458, www.geocities.com/losyutzos. Comfortable rooms and beautiful grounds overlooking the Río Pano, quiet and family-run. Includes breakfast, a/c, cheaper with fan, parking, clean and simple annex next door is cheaper.
C **Establo de Tomás**, in Muyuna village, 5 km from Tena on the road to San Antonio, T09-8778709, paorivade @hotmail.com. Cabins in a pleasant setting with river bathing nearby. Meals available on request, solar hot water, parking, nice but can get busy on weekends.
D **Traveler's Lodging**, 15 de Noviembre 438, T06-2888204, amarongachitours @yahoo.com. Restaurant and tour agency, fan, some rooms have fridge, several different kinds of rooms, better ones are on second floor.
D **Villa Belén**, on Baeza road (Av Jumandy) just north of town, T06-2886228, F06-2888091. Fan, laundry and cooking facilities, parking, excellent rooms, quiet.
E **Limoncocha**, Sangay 533, Sector Corazón de Jesús, on a hillside 4 blocks from the bus station, ask for directions, T06-288 7583, limoncocha @andinanet.net. Concrete house with terrace and hammocks. Cafeteria, cheaper with shared bath, hot water, fan, internet, laundry and cooking facilities, parking, German-Ecuadorean run, enthusiastic owners organize tours, pleasant atmosphere. Out of the way in a humble neighbourhood, sometimes noisy but nice views and good value.

Misahuallí *p393*
A **Misahuallí Jungle Hotel**, across the river from town, T06-2890063, www.misahuallijungle.com. Includes breakfast, restaurant, electric shower, fan, pool, cabins for up to 6, nice setting.
E **El Paisano**, Rivadeneyra y Tandalia, T06-2890027. Restaurant, private bath, hot water, simple rooms, friendly owner, pleasant atmosphere and good value.
E **Shaw**, Santander on Plaza, T06-2890019, ecoselva@yahoo.es. Café downstairs, private bath, hot water, simple clean rooms, operate their own tours, English spoken, very friendly and knowledgeable. Good value.

Puyo *p393*
A **Flor de Canela**, Paseo Turístico, Barrio Obrero, T03-2885265, F03-2886083. Includes breakfast, restaurant and bar, pool (US$1.50 for non-residents), comfortable cabins, pleasant location but a bit out of the way.

Jungle lodges near Misahualli

L **Yachana Lodge**, is based in the indigenous village of Mondaña, 2 hrs downstream from Misahuallí. All proceeds from the lodge go towards supporting community development projects. The lodge is comfortable, has 10 double rooms and family cabins and solar power. Yachana offers highly recommended packages which include river transport, all meals, lodging and guides; US$336 per person for 4 days (3 nights). Quito T02-2523777, www.yachana.com

L **Cabañas Aliñahui**, 8 cabins with 2 bedrooms and bath, lush tropical garden, rainforest and nature trails. Includes 3 delicious meals in the dining hall. Profits contribute to conservation of the area's rainforest. Quito office: Fundación Jatun Sacha, Pasaje Eugenio de Santillán N34-248 y Maurian, T02-432246, F02-453583, www.jatunsacha.org.

A-B **Hostería Safari**, outside town at km 5 on the road to Tena, T03-2885465, www.hosteriasafari.com. Includes breakfast, restaurant, pool, parking, ample grounds, peaceful and out of the way.

B **Turingia**, Ceslao Marín 294, T03-2885180, www.hosteriaturingia.com. Restaurant, fan, small pool, parking, comfortable rooms, nice garden.

D **Colibrí**, C Manabí entre Bolívar y Galápagos, T03-288 3054, cascadayanarumi@yahoo.es. Parking, away from centre, modern, friendly, good value.

Lago Agrio *p395*

AL-A **Arazá**, Quito 610 y Narváez, T06-283 0223, arazahot@uio.satnet.net. Quiet location away from centre. Includes breakfast, restaurant, a/c, pool (US$5 for non-residents), fridge, parking, comfortable, clean and nice. Best in town.

B **El Cofán**, 12 de Febrero 2-12 y Av Quito, T06-283 0526, F06-283 2409. Includes breakfast, restaurant, a/c, fridge, parking, well cared-for and nice.

B **Gran Hostal de Lago**, Km 1½ Vía Quito, T06-283 2415. Includes breakfast, restaurant, a/c, pool, internet, parking, cabins, nice gardens, quiet.

C **D'Mario**, Quito 171, T06-283 0172, F06-283 0456. Set meals and pizza in the evening, cheaper with cold water, a/c,

small pool, some rooms have fridge, clean place, helpful owner.

D **Machala 2**, Colombia entre Quito y Añazco, T06-283 0673. Good restaurant, cold water, fan, parking, refurbished in 2003, friendly.

Coca *p396*

A-C **El Auca**, Napo entre Rocafuerte y García Moreno, T06-288 0600, www.interactive.net.ec/hotel-auca. Restaurant, disco on weekends, a/c, cheaper with fan, parking, a variety of different rooms and mini-suites. Comfortable, nice garden with hammocks, manager speaks English. Popular and centrally located but can get noisy.

B **La Misión**, by riverfront 100 m downriver from the bridge, T06-288 0260, F06-288 0263. Restaurant and disco, a/c and fridge, cheaper with fan, pool and water-slide, internet, parking, upscale for where it is, nice location by the river, English spoken, arranges tours.

B **Puerto Orellana**, Av Alejandro Labaka, at the entrance to town from Lago Agrio, T06-288 0129, jesseniabrito @andinanet.net. Electric shower, a/c, parking, out of the way but modern and very nice. Popular, best book in advance.

B-C **Amazonas**, 12 de Febrero y Espejo, T06-288 0444. Nice relaxed setting by the

Staying in a lodge, though expensive, ensures more comfort and fewer unwanted creatures.

river, away from centre, restaurant, a/c, cheaper with fan, parking, quiet, friendly and good.

C-D San Fermín, Bolívar Y Quito, T06-288 0802. A/c, cheaper with fan and cold water, parking, modern and comfortable, good value.

Jungle lodges near Coca

Note that all Napo area lodges count travel days as part of their package, which means that often a '3-day tour' spends only 1 day actually in the forest. Also, keep in mind that the return trip must start before dawn if it is to connect to that day's Coca-Quito flight; if it starts later it will be necessary to spend the night in Coca. Most lodges have fixed departure days from Coca (eg Mon and Fri) and it is very expensive to get a special departure on another day. Bookings can usually be made on the Internet and through most Quito agencies. The prices given below include accommodation, 3 meals and guiding, but do not include transport to Coca or national park fees. They are all subject to change.

AL Yuturi is 5 hrs downstream from Coca. Birdwatching is excellent, and there are some species (eg Black-necked Red Cotinga) that are difficult to find at other lodges. There is a wide variety of habitats here, and wildlife is good. The guides are usually local people accompanied by translators. Five-days/4-nights cost US$350 per person. Itineraries can combine visits here and to Yarina, see above. Quito office: Amazonas N24-240 y Colón, T/F02-250 4037, www.yuturilodge.com.

AL Tiputini Biodiversity Station, on the Río Tiputini, is far from any settlement and has experienced very little hunting, not even by native people. The result is the best site in Ecuador for observing the full range of Amazonian wildlife and birds. Facilities are extremely well designed and merge into the forest; the canopy tower and canopy walkway are exceptional. Food is good. It is a scientific station, not a tourist facility, and potential visitors must form or join an educational group and receive approval in advance; services are oriented towards scientists. Spider monkeys, curassows, large macaws, large raptors and other threatened wildlife are more common and more confiding here than at most other sites, and this is the best place in Ecuador for jaguar (but you still have to be lucky to see one). If you would like to join an educational workshop contact Carol Walton, USA T1-512-2630830, http://tiputini.usfq.edu.ec.

Budget busters

Jungle lodges near Coca

LL Sacha is an upmarket lodge 2½ hrs downstream from Coca. Cabins are very comfortable, with private bath and hot water, and meals are excellent. The bird list is outstanding, and they have a local bird expert, Oscar Tapuy (T06-2881486), who can be requested in advance by birders. Guides are generally knowledgeable. Boardwalks through swamp habitats allow access to some species that are difficult to see at other lodges, and nearby river islands provide another distinct habitat. Five-days/4-nights cost US$750 per person. Quito office: Julio Zaldumbide 397 y Valladolid, T2566090, www.sachalodge.com.

LL La Selva is also an upmarket lodge, 2½ hrs downstream from Coca and close to Sacha. It is professionally run and situated on a picturesque lake surrounded by excellent forest. Bird and animal life is exceptionally diverse. A total of 580 bird species can be found here, one of the highest totals in the world for a site at a single elevation, and some of the local guides (eg José) are very good at finding them. There is a biological station on the grounds (the Neotropical Field Biology Institute) as well as a butterfly farm. Cabins have private bath and hot water. Meals are excellent. Usually the guides are biologists, and in general the guiding is of very high quality. A new canopy tower was completed in 2004. Five-days/4-nights cost US$756 per person. Quito office: San Salvador E7-85 y Martín Carrión, T02-255 0995, www.laselvajunglelodge.com.

LL Napo Wildlife Center is operated by and for the local Añangu community, across the Río Napo from La Selva, 2½ hrs downstream from Coca. This area of hilly forest is rather different from the low flat forest of some other sites, and the diversity is slightly higher. There are big caimans, good mammals, including Giant Otters, and the birding is excellent. The local guide, Giovanny Rivadeneyra, is one of the most knowledgeable birders in the Oriente. Five days/4 nights costs US$705 per person. Contact their Quito office, T02-289 7316, www.ecoecuador.org.

🍴 Eating

Tena *p392*

🍴🍴 **Chuquitos**, García Moreno by Plaza. Good food, à la carte only, seating on a balcony overlooking the river. Pleasant atmosphere and nice views. Popular.

🍴🍴 **Pizzería La Massilia**, Malecón y 9 de Octubre, by the river, open from 1700 onwards. Really good pizza.

🍴 **Cositas Ricas**, 15 de Noviembre, next to Hostal Traveler's Lodging. Tasty set meals, vegetarian available, good fruit juices.

🍴 **Heladería Italiana**, 9 de Octubre y Tarqui, daily 0930-2130. Excellent ice-cream made fresh on the premises.

Misahuallí *p393*

🍴 **Doña Gloria**, Arteaga y Rivadeneyra by corner of plaza, daily 0730-2030. Very good set meals.

🍴 **Ecocafé**, At Hotel Shaw, on the plaza. Good breakfast, à la carte dishes and cappuccino.

Budget buster

Jungle lodges in southern Oriente

LL **Kapawi** is a top-of-the-line jungle lodge located on the Río Capahuari not far from the Peruvian border. It is accessible only by small aircraft and motor canoe, vistors are usually flown in through Coca. The lodge was built in partnership with the Achuar indigenous organization **OINAE** and built according to the Achuar concept of architecture, using typical materials, and emphasizes environmentally friendly methods such as solar energy, biodegradable soaps and rubbish recycling. It is in a zone rich in biodiversity, with many opportunities for seeing the forest and its inhabitants. Five-days/4-nights cost US$835 per person, plus US$200 for transport to and from Quito. The location, indigenous participation, quality of service, cabin accommodation, and food have all been highly recommended. Operated by Canodros, Guayaquil T04-2285711, www.kapawi.com Or book through agencies in Quito or abroad.

Puyo *p393*

♀♀ **El Alcázar**, 10 de Agosto 936 y Sucre, Mon-Sat 0900-2300, Sun 0900-1600. Very good restaurant with an unexpectedly Spanish-European flavour in the Ecuadorean Amazon. Good value set meals and varied à la carte.

♀♀ **El Jardín**, On the Paseo Turístico in Barrio Obrero, Tue-Sun 1200-2200. Pleasant setting and atmosphere, international food, meat and pasta are specialties.

♀♀-♀ **Pizzería Buon Giorno**, Orellana entre Villamil y 27 de Febrero, Mon-Sat 1200-2300. Good pizza, lasagne and salads, pleasant atmosphere, very popular.

Lago Agrio *p395*

♀ There are decent restaurants at the better hotels. Those at D'Marios and **Machala** are recommended. There are also a great many very cheap and basic comedores, all along Av Quito between Manabí and Colombia.

Coca *p396*

♀♀ **Parrilladas Argentinas**, Cuenca e Inés Arango. Argentine style grill.

♀♀-♀ **Pizza Choza**, Rocafuerte y Napo, daily 1700-2200. Good pizza, English spoken.
♀ **Ocaso**, Eloy Alfaro between Napo and Amazonas. Good value set meals and à la carte.

🍷 Bars and clubs

Tena *p392*
Araña Bar, García Moreno by the plaza and near the riverfront, open from 1700. Nice place.

Puyo *p393*
At Barrio Obrero, along the river on the road north to Tena, are several bars and discos in a pleasant setting.

Coca *p396*
Pappa Dan's, Napo y Chimborazo by the river, open from around 1600 hrs, pleasant location. There are a many others in town.

🛍 Shopping

Puyo *p393*
Amazonía Touring, Atahualpa y 9 de Octubre, has a good selection of local crafts.

⛰ Activities and tours

Tena *p392*
Ríos Ecuador / Yacu Amu, 15 de Noviembre y 9 de Octubre, on the Malecón between the footbridges, T06-288 6346, www.riosecuador.com. Highly recommended white-water rafting and kayak trips and a 4-day kayak school. See also Rafting, page .

Misahuallí *p393*
There are guides available to take parties into the jungle for trips of one to 10 days, all involving canoeing and varying amounts of hiking. The going rate is US$25-$40 per person per day, depending on the season, size of group and length of trip. This should include food and rubber boots, which are absolutely essential. Tours can also be arranged by most hotels.
Ecoselva, Santander on the plaza, T06-289 0019, ecoselva@yahoo.es. Recommended guide Pepe Tapia speaks English and has a biology background. Trips from 1-6 days. Well organized and reliable.

Puyo *p393*
Prices range from US$25-50 per person per day.
Entsa Tours, T09-8016642. Mentor Marino is helpful and knowledgeable.
Papangu Tours, 27 de Febrero y Sucre, T03-288 7684, papangu@andinanet.net. Operated by the Organización de Pueblos Indígenas de Pastaza (OPIP).

Lago Agrio *p395*
Most Cuyabeno tours are booked through agencies in Quito. These include **Neotropic Turis**, T02-2521212, www.neotropicturis.com, which operates the Cuyabeno Lodge, cabins with private or shared baths, US$295 per person for 4 days/3 nights, including all meals and bilingual guides, but excluding transport to and from Lago Agrio and the park entry fee, and **Ecuador Verde Pais**,

T02-2220614, www.cabanasjamu.com, which operates Jamu Lodge, 4 days/3 nights cost US$180 per person plus transport and park fees.

Coca *p396*
Prices here start at around US$40 per person per day.
River Dolphin Expeditions, Ramiro Viteri, no storefront, contact T09-4603087 rde4amazon@yahoo.com, or through Hotel El Auca.
Wymper Torres, no storefront, contact T06-2880336, ronoboa@latinmail.com. He specializes in the Río Shiripuno and Pañacocha areas, Spanish only.

⊖ Transport

Tena *p392*
To **Misahuallí**, hourly, US$1, 45 mins, buses leave from the local bus station not the long distance terminal.

Misahuallí *p393*
Buses to **Tena**, every 45 mins 0745-1800, US$1, 45 min. Make long distance connections in Tena. To **Quito**, one direct bus a day at 0830, US$6, 6 hrs.

Puyo *p393*
The Terminal Terrestre is on the outskirts of town, on the Shell and Baños road in the southwest, a 10-15 min walk from the centre or take a taxi (US$1).

Lago Agrio *p395*
Air
The airport is 5 km southeast of the centre. TAME and Icaro fly to **Quito**, daily except Sun, US$60 one way. It's best to book 1-2 days in advance, and reconfirm often. If there is no space available to **Lago Agrio** then you can fly to **Coca** instead, from where it is only 2 hours by bus on a good road.

Bus
The Terminal Terrestre is located in the north of town, but buses for **Coca** leave

❝

Travellers' tales

Keeping your head in the jungle

In a bid to be more adventurous, I had endured a gruelling 24-hour bus trip from Macas to the remote 'village' of Morona, in the southern Ecuadorean Oriente. But as I stepped down off the bus and stared in disbelief at two wooden shacks standing self-consciously by the riverbank, adventurous wasn't what I was feeling. Criminally naïve would have been closer to the mark. As I tried to work out what I was going to do next the bus driver asked me if I was meeting someone. "Er, no," I confessed. He then informed me that this bus wasn't returning to Cuenca for a week, but there was a Shuar family who were taking the canoe up river to their house and who might let me stay with them. Shuar? Weren't they the ones who, until a mere few decades ago, used to shrink the heads of their enemies?

I was introduced to Pedro, the head of the family, so to speak. He seemed genuinely keen to have me as a guest for a few days and act as a guide, in exchange for me paying the cost of the canoe trip upriver to the family 'finca', or farmstead. Two hours later we pulled into the side of the river and disembarked. After an hour's hike through the dense undergrowth we reached a clearing, in the centre of which stood Pedro's house - a simple circular wooden structure with a thatch roof. After a dinner of fish soup and boiled bananas, we arranged the following day's 'guided tour'. I then turned in for the night and lay in my sleeping bag listening to the sounds of Pedro and his brother-in-law, Wilson, sharpening their machetes and discussing, as far as I could make out, the value of the contents of my backpack. I silently prayed that if anyone should fall ill, they wouldn't blame me.

Next morning I awoke to heavy rain. After breakfast of fish soup and boiled bananas, we set off, Pedro and Wilson carrying ancient flintlock rifles, bow and arrows and a fishing line. After a two-hour slog through knee-deep mud and across numerous log bridges - most of which I managed to fall off - we came to a clearing where a dugout canoe was moored to a tree at the side of a large lake. As we paddled our way across the lake, Wilson pointed to a caiman in the water; "Quick! Shoot!" I grabbed my camera. "No, with this!" he rebuked, handing me his rifle. But by the time I'd worked out how to fire the damned thing, the caiman had disappeared. Wilson snatched his rifle back and glared at me. I stroked my neck nervously. No caiman on the menu this evening, but at least we did manage to hook a fish. A very big fish. And a very heavy one, as I found out while lugging it back to the house. A few rain-soaked days later, suffering from exhaustion, mud overload, and becoming ever more fearful that I might outstay my welcome, we agreed that I should leave. Back in Morona I felt like I'd arrived in a bustling Metropolis. And I only had to wait two days for a return bus. Now I really did feel adventurous. *Alan Murphy*

66 99 They passed the snow-covered peak of Chimborazo, cold in the moonlight and the constant wind of the high Andes. The view from the high mountain pass seemed another, larger planet than Earth. *William Burroughs*

from the market area on Orellana, 3 blocks south of Av Quito. There are 2 routes from Lago Agrio to **Quito**, both with bus service. Although slower, the southern route through Coca and Loreto may be somewhat safer from holdups than the northern one through El Dorado de Cascales and Lumbaqui. Do not travel to or from Lago Agrio overnight.

Coca *p396*
Air
The airport is in the north of town. To/from **Quito**, 3-4 flights daily Mon-Sat, only 1 on Sun, with **TAME** and **Icaro**. Mon-Sat US$60 one way; reserve as far in advance as possible and always reconfirm. Flights in and out of **Coca** are heavily booked, oil workers may have priority. **Icaro** office is in Hotel La Misión, T06-288 0546. **TAME** office is at Napo y Rocafuerte, T/F06-288 1078, Mon-Fri 0800-1200, 1300-1700.

Bus
Long distance buses depart from company offices in town (see map); local destinations, including **Lago Agrio**, are served from the terminal a little to the north.

🅘 Directory

Tena *p392*
Banks TCs can be difficult to change in Tena. In a pinch, try **Hostal Limoncocha**. Otherwise **Banco del Pichincha**, Amazonas y JL Mera and **Banco del Austro**, 15 de Noviembre y Diaz de Pineda.

Puyo *p393*
Banks Casa de Cambios Puyo, Atahualpa y 9 de Octubre, T/F03-288 3064. 3% commission for Amex US$ TCs. Helpful, friendly and recommended. **Banco del Austro**, Atahualpa entre 10 de Agosto y Dávila.

Lago Agrio *p395*
There are no reliable ATMs in Lago Agrio and TCs are very difficult to use or exchange, try **Hotel Americano** if you are stuck. Credit cards are only accepted at the best hotels.

Coca *p396*
Banks Banco de Pichincha, Bolívar y 9 de Octubre. **Cambiaria Ramírez**, Napo y García Moreno, T06-288 1229, Mon-Sat 0800-2000, sometimes changes TCa for 4% commission. Does not change Peruvian soles. **Internet** Prices around US$2 per hr.

Galápagos Islands

Blue-footed booby

↑ Don't miss...

1 A horse ride to the rim of a volcanic crater ▶▶ *p415*.

2 Snorkelling with rays, turtles and sharks ▶▶ *p417*.

3 A walk through mangroves to see nesting boobies and frigates ▶▶ *p417*.

4 Swimming with sea lion pups ▶▶ *p418*.

5 A meal at Angermeyer Point ▶▶ *p422*.

Introduction

Lying on the Equator, 970 km west of the Ecuadorean coast, the Galápagos are Ecuador's tourist trump card. These islands have never been connected with the continent. Gradually, over many hundreds of thousands of years, animals and plants from over the sea somehow migrated there and as time went by they adapted themselves to Galápagos conditions and came to differ more and more from their continental ancestors. Much of the flora and fauna is unique and, in many cases, different forms have evolved on the different islands. Charles Darwin recognized this speciation within the archipelago when he visited the Galápagos in 1835 and his observations played a substantial part in his formulation of the theory of evolution. One of the extraordinary features of the Galápagos is the tameness of the animals. They were uninhabited when they were discovered in 1535 and the animals still have little instinctive fear of man. This lack of fear enables visitors the opportunity to snorkel with penguins and sea-lions, watch giant 200 kg tortoises lumbering through cactus forest and enjoy the courtship display of the blue-footed booby and frigatebird, all in startling close up.

Ratings
Culture
★★
Landscape
★★★
Wildlife
★★★★★
Activities
★★★★★
Chillin'
★★★
Costs
$$$$$

The Galápagos Islands have been declared a World Heritage Site by UNESCO and 97% of the land area and 100% of the surrounding ocean are now part of the Galápagos National Park and Marine Reserve. Within the area of the park there are some 60 landing sites, each with defined trails, so the impact of visitors to this fragile environment is minimized. The number of visitors to the islands is, in principle, controlled by the authorities to protect the environment. A visit to the islands doesn't come cheap. The return flight from Quito and national park fee add up to almost US$500; plus a bare minimum of US$70 per person per day for sailing on the most basic boat, when you can find space at this price. Top-end luxury cruises cost up to US$4,000 for eight days. Land-based and independent travel on the populated islands are both viable alternatives, but there is, at present, simply no way to enjoy Galápagos on a shoestring. The once-in-a-lifetime Galápagos experience is well worth saving for, however, and at the same time, these high prices are one way of keeping the number of visitors within reasonable levels in order to limit impact on the islands and their wildlife.

✈ **Getting there** Several daily flights from Quito.
🚌 **Getting around** About 80 tourist vessels ranging in capacity from 8 to 110 passengers.
⏱ **Time required** 4-8 days, a week is highly recommended.
☔ **Weather** Jan-Apr have warm air and water, afternoon showers, and best underwater visibility; cold water and some mist May-Dec.
🛏 **Sleeping** Cruise vessels range from functional to opulent. There are some top-end hotels in Puerto Ayora alongside a good selection of more modest establishments. There are also several comfortable and very interesting places to stay in Puerto Baquerizo Moreno, Puerto Villamil, and Floreana.
🍴 **Eating** Cooking on cruises caters to international tastes. There are a couple of good local places in the towns.
▲ **Activities and tours** Enjoying the greatest wildlife show on earth.
★ **Don't miss...** swimming with sea-lion pups ▶ *p422*.

Ins and outs

Getting there

There are no international flights to Galápagos; all flights originate in Quito. There are two airports which receive flights from mainland Ecuador. The most frequently used airport is at Baltra (South Seymour), across a narrow strait from Santa Cruz, the other at Puerto Baquerizo Moreno, on San Cristóbal. **TAME** has two flights daily to Baltra and operates Monday, Wednesday and Saturday to San Cristóbal. **AeroGal** flies daily to Baltra, and Monday, Thursday, Saturday and Sunday to San Cristóbal. These schedules are subject to change. The return fare in high season (1 November-30 April and 15 June-14 September) is US$390. The low season fare is US$334. The same prices apply regardless of whether you fly to San Cristóbal or Baltra; you can arrive at one and return from the other. The ticket is valid for 21 days from the date of departure. Independent travellers should always reconfirm their bookings, especially in high season. On both **TAME** and **AeroGal**, a 15% discount off the high season fare applies to students with an ISIC card.

Two buses meet flights from the mainland at Baltra: one runs to the port or muelle (10 minutes, no charge) where the cruise boats wait; the other goes to Canal de Itabaca, the narrow channel which separates Baltra from Santa Cruz. It is 15 minutes to the Canal, then you cross on a small ferry for US$0.75, another bus waits on the Santa Cruz side to take you

The delicate ecological balance of the Galápagos Islands is ensured by strict limitations on visitor numbers.

to Puerto Ayora in 45 minutes, US$1.80. If you arrive at Baltra on one of the local inter-island flights (see below) then you have to wait until the next flight from the mainland for the bus service, or you might be able to hire a taxi (US$15). For the return trip to the airport, buses leave from opposite the two companies offices near the pier in Puerto Ayora (see map, page 421) to meet flights at Baltra (enquire locally for current schedules). The airport on San Cristóbal is within walking distance of Puerto Baquerizo Moreno town, but those on prearranged tours will be met by transport. Pick-up trucks can be hired if you are on your own and have have lots of gear (US$1).

Getting around

Emetebe Avionetas ⓘ *Avenida Charles Darwin opposite the port, 3rd floor, in Puerto Ayora, T05-2526177, emetebe@ecua.net.ec,* operates inter-island flights between San Cristóbal, Baltra and Isabel. There is no fixed schedule but flights usually operate in the morning Monday-Saturday. There is also boat service between Puerto Ayora, Puerto Baquerizo Moreno, Puerto Villamil and occasionally Floreana island: contact **INGALA** in San Cristóbal, T05-2520133 for details.

Entry tax

Every foreign visitor to Galápagos must pay a National Park Tax of US$100 on arrival, cash only. Be sure to have your passport to hand. Do not lose your park tax receipt; boat captains need to record it. A 50% reduction on the national park fee is available to children under 12, but only those foreigners who are enrolled in an Ecuadorean university are entitled to the reduced fee for students.

Information

Ministerio de Turismo ⓘ *Avenida Charles Darwin y Tomas de Berlanga, T05-252 6174, mturgal@ec-gov.net, Mon-Fri 0800-1200, 1400-1700,* has general information and maps for all of Galápagos. The **Dirección Municipal de Turismo**, on the same premises, T05-252 6613, has information about Puerto Ayora and Santa Cruz Island.

Touring in Galápagos

There are two main ways to travel around the islands: a cruise (also called 'tour navegable'), where you sleep on the boat, or slightly less expensive land-based tours where you sleep ashore at night and travel during the day. On the former you travel at night, arriving at a new landing site each day, with more time ashore. On the latter you spend less time ashore, cover less ground and cannot visit the more distant islands. A third option is independent travel on the populated islands. Although neither cheap nor a substitute for either of the above, it can be done and allows those with plenty of time to explore a small part of the archipelago at their leisure. All tours begin with a morning flight from the mainland on the first day and end on the last day with a midday flight back to the mainland. Prices are somewhat cheaper in the low season and you will have more options available.

Cruises

It is not possible to generalize about exactly what you will find on the boat in which you cruise around the Galápagos Islands. The standard of facilities varies from one craft to another and you basically get what you pay for in terms of comfort, service and food. Once on shore at the visitor sites, no matter what price you have paid, each visitor is shown the same things because of the strict park rules on limited access. Note however that smaller and cheaper boats may not visit as many or as distant sites. On the other hand, larger vessels may not be allowed to take passengers to some of the more fragile landings such as Daphne Major.

The less expensive boats are normally smaller and less powerful so you see less and spend more time travelling; also the guiding may be in Spanish only. The more expensive boats will probably have air conditioning, hot water and private baths, all of which add to the comfort factor but are not critically important.

Each day starts early and schedules are usually full. If you are sailing overnight, your boat will probably have reached its destination before breakfast. After eating, you disembark for a morning on the island. The usual time for snorkelling is between the morning excursion and lunch. The midday meal is taken on board because no food is allowed on the islands. If the island requires two visits (for example Genovesa/ Tower, or Española/Hood), you will return to shore after lunch, otherwise part of the afternoon may be taken up with a sea voyage. After the day's activities, there is time to clean up, have a drink and relax before the briefing for the next day and supper.

Price categories

The least expensive boats (called economy class) cost about US$70-100 per person per day; they are usually small and slow. For around US$100-150 per day (tourist and tourist superior class) you will be on a faster small boat which can travel more quickly between visitor sites, leaving more time to spend ashore. US$150-200 per day (first class) is the price of the majority of better boats. Over US$200 per day is entering the luxury bracket, with far more comfortable and spacious cabins, as well as a superior level of service and cuisine. No boat may sail without a park-trained guide.

Note however, that the above classification is somewhat arbitrary and involves considerable overlap. An excellent Galápagos experience can be had on even the cheapest boats if you are willing to rough it a little. Almost all visitors are thoroughly satisfied, but there is the occasional complaint. Remember that all boats look good in brochures and websites, and nothing is more valuable than a personal recommendation by a recent passenger if you can find one. Note that Footprint has received repeated complaints about the vessel *Free Enterprise*.

Booking a cruise

You can book a Galápagos cruise in several different ways: 1) over the the internet; 2) from either a travel agency or directly though a Galápagos wholesaler in your home country; 3) from one of the very many agencies found throughout Ecuador, especially in Quito but also in Guayaquil; or 4) from agencies in Puerto Ayora but not Puerto Baquerizo Moreno. The trade-off is always between time and money: booking from home is most efficient and expensive, Puerto Ayora cheapest and most time-consuming, while arranging a tour from Quito is somewhere between the two. Prices for a given category of boat do not vary all that much, however, and it is not possible to obtain discounts or make last-minute arrangements in high season. Those who attempt to do so in July, August or over Christmas/New Year often spend several very frustrating weeks in Puerto Ayora without ever sailing around the islands. For recommended agencies and operators abroad see p 46. For agencies in Quito, see page 339.

Many, if not most, Galápagos tours are now sold on-line. English or multilingual sites specializing in tours to the Islands include www.galapagosislands.com and www.galapagosdiscover.com. Multilingual background and scientific information about Galápagos is provided by the Charles Darwin Foundation at www.darwinfoundation.org.

To arrange last-minute tours from Puerto Ayora, a recommended contact is the Moonrise travel agency (see Puerto Ayora Tour operators, page 424). Especially for cheaper boats, try to get a personal recommendation from someone who has recently taken a tour and check carefully about what is and is not included (for example drinking water, snorkelling equipment and so on).

Top tips

Getting the most out of the islands

✓ Always bring some US$ cash, no other currencies are accepted. There is only one bank and ATM system on Galápagos, which may not work with all cards. Although the more expensive establishments accept credit cards and TCs, tourists frequently find themselves strapped for cash.

✓ A remedy for seasickness is recommended. A good supply of sun block and skin cream to prevent windburn and chapped lips is essential, as are a hat and sunglasses. You should be prepared for dry and wet landings. The latter involves wading ashore.

✓ Take plenty of memory cards or film with you. The animals are so tame that you will use far more than you expected. A telephoto lens is not essential, but bring it if you have one. Take filters suitable for strong sunlight. An underwater camera is also an excellent idea.

✓ Never miss the opportunity to go snorkelling. There is plenty of underwater life to see, including rays, turtles, sharks, sea lions, penguins and many spectacular fish and invertebrates. Few of the cheaper boats provide equipment and those that do may not have good snorkelling gear. If in doubt, bring your own, rent in Puerto Ayora, or buy it in Quito. It may be possible to sell it afterwards either on the islands or back in Quito.

✓ Most items can generally can be purchased on the islands, but cost up to twice as much as the mainland.

✓ The islands get very busy in July and August, when it is impossible to make last minute cruise arrangements.

✓ On most cruises a ship's crew and guides are usually tipped separately. The amount is a very personal matter; you may be guided by suggestions made onboard or in the agency's brochures, but the key factors should always be the quality of service received and – of course – your own resources.

✗ Never touch any of the animals, birds or plants. Do not transfer sand, seeds or soil from one island to another. Do not leave litter anywhere – it is highly undesirable in a National Park and is a safety and health hazard for wildlife – and do not take food on to the islands.

✗ Boats with over 18 passengers take quite a time to disembark and re-embark people, while the smaller boats have a more lively motion, which is important if you are prone to seasickness.

✗ There may be limitations for vegetarians on the cheaper boats, best to enquire in advance.

Climate

The Galápagos climate can be divided into a hot season (January to April), when the sea temperature rises and there is a possibility of brief heavy showers, and the cool, or *garúa*, season (May to December), when the ocean is cooler and days generally are more cloudy with some mist or light drizzle. During July and August the southeast trade winds can be very strong. At night, temperatures can fall below 15°C, particularly at sea. The underwater visibility is best from January to March. Ocean temperatures are usually higher to the east and lower at the western end of the archipelago. Despite all these variations, conditions are generally favourable for visiting Galápagos throughout the year.

Santa Cruz » *pp420-425*

This is the main inhabited island. Most of the 11,400 inhabitants live in and around **Puerto Ayora**, the economic centre of the Galápagos with a wide range of hotels, restaurants and tour operators. If you choose to arrange a tour from here rather than the mainland, it's a pleasant place to spend a few days.

Sights and landing sites

Every cruise visits Puerto Ayora for one day anchoring at Academy Bay to do some shopping, make phone calls and to visit the **Charles Darwin Research Station** ⓘ *station offices Mon-Fri 0700-1600, visitor areas daily 0600-1800*, at Academy Bay, a 20-minute walk from the dock at Puerto Ayora. A visit to the station is a good introduction to the islands, as it provides a lot of information. Collections of several of the rare sub-species of giant tortoise are maintained on the station as breeding nuclei, though, sadly, no mating partner has yet been found for Lonesome George, the sole remaining member of the Isla Pinta sub-species. There is also a tortoise-rearing area where the young can be seen.

There are a number of sights worth visiting in the interior which are included in the itineraries of many island cruises. Tour operators in Puerto Ayora (see page 424) also run excursions to the highland sites for about US$20-30 per person, depending on the number of sites visited and the size of the group. The main sights include **Los Gemelos**, a pair of twin sinkholes, formed by a collapse of the ground above a fault. The sinkholes straddle the road to Baltra, beyond Santa Rosa. You can take a *camioneta* all the way, otherwise take a bus to Santa Rosa, then walk. It's a good place to see the Galápagos hawk and barn owl.

There are several **lava tubes** (natural tunnels) on the island. Some are at **El Mirador**, 3 km from Puerto Ayora on the road to Bellavista. Barn owls can be seen here. Two more lava tubes are 1 km from Bellavista. They are on private land, it costs US$1.50 to enter the tunnels (bring a torch) and it takes about 30 minutes to walk through the tunnels. Tours to the lava tubes can be arranged in Puerto Ayora.

Marine iguana.

Another worthwhile trip is to the **El Chato Tortoise Reserve**, where giant tortoises can be seen in the wild, during the dry season. There are many trails in the reserve itself and it is easy to get lost, so take food and water. It's best to go with a guide if you have no hiking experience; tours can be arranged in Puerto Ayora. Near the reserve is the **Butterfly Ranch** (Hacienda Mariposa) ⓘ *US$3, including a cup of hierba luisa tea, or juice*, where you can see giant tortoises in the pastures (but only in the dry season; in the wet season the tortoises are breeding down in the arid zone). Vermillion flycatchers can be seen here also. The ranch is beyond Bellavista on the road to Santa Rosa (the bus passes the turn-off).

San Cristóbal ⊖🚍🚶▲⊡🚌 ▸▸ *pp420-425*

San Cristóbal is the easternmost island of Galápagos and one of the oldest. The principal town is **Puerto Baquerizo Moreno** which is the capital of the province of Galápagos. It is a pleasant tranquil place which sees its share of tourism, but far less than Puerto Ayora. Always take food, plenty of water, and a compass or GPS when hiking on your own on San Cristóbal. There are many crisscrossing animal trails and it is easy to get lost. Also watch out for the large-spined opuntia cactus and the poisonwood tree (manzanillo), which is a relative of poison ivy and can cause severe skin reactions.

Sights and landing sites

There are good beaches near the town, an interesting National Park visitors' centre and worthwhile excursions to the highlands. The **municipal tourist office** ⓘ *by the muelle turístico, T05-2521166, www.sancristobalgalapagos.com, Mon-Fri 0730-1230, 1400-1700*, has local information. To the north of town, opposite Playa Mann, is the Galápagos National Park visitors' centre or **Centro de Interpretación** ⓘ *daily 0700-1800, free, T05-2520138 (ext 102)*. It has an excellent display of the natural and human history of the islands and is highly recommended.

There are a few good beaches near the town, such as the small **Playa Mann** (follow Avenida Northía to the north), and **Playa de Oro**, where some hotels are located. Right in the centre of town, along the sand by the tidal pool, sea lions can be seen (be careful with the male who 'owns' the beach). Further afield to the northeast and reached by boat (15 minutes) is **Puerto Ochoa**, another beach popular with locals. To the south of town, 20 minutes' walk past the airport, is **La Lobería,** a rocky bay with shore birds, sea lions and marine iguanas. You can continue along the cliff to see tortoises and rays, but do not leave the trail.

There are five buses a day inland from Puerto Baquerizo Moreno to **El Progreso** (6 km, 15 minutes, US$0.20), then it's a 2½ hour walk to **El Junco lake**, the largest body of fresh water in Galápagos. You can also take a tour to El Junco which costs US$15, or US$40 including a visit to the beaches at **Puerto Chino** on the other side of the island past **La Galapaguera** – a man-made tortoise area. Prices are for a return trip and include waiting time. The road through the highlands was under construction and in poor shape in early 2005. At El Junco there is a path to walk around the lake in 20 minutes. The views are lovely in clear weather but it is cool and wet in the *garúa* season, so take adequate clothing.

It's a three-hour hike from the landing site at **Caleta Tortuga**, on the northwest shore of the island, to **La Galapaguera Natural** where you can see tortoises in the wild. **Isla Lobos** is an islet with a sea lion colony and nesting site for sea birds northeast of Puerto Baquerizo Moreno.

Kicker Rock (León Dormido), the basalt remains of a crater, is not strictly speaking a landing site, but the rock is split by a narrow channel and is navigable to the smaller yachts. It is home to a large colony of many seabirds, including masked and blue-footed boobies, nesting in the cliffs rising vertically from the channel. **Punta Pitt**, in the far northeast of the island, is a tuff formation which serves as a nesting site for many sea birds, including all three boobies. Up the coast is **Cerro Brujo** beach with sea lions, birds and crabs, though not in any abundance.

Sally Lightfoot crab.

Isabela ⬟🖐🏔🛏🍴 ▸▸ *pp420-425*

The largest of the Galápagos Islands, Isabela is slowly developing for tourism. The extensive lava flows from the six volcanoes – Ecuador, Wolf, Darwin, Alcedo, Seirra Negra and Cerro Azul, from north to south – joined together and formed Isabela. Five of the six volcanoes are active and each have (or had) their own separate sub-species of giant tortoise. Northern and southern sections of the island are separated by the narrow Perry Isthmus.

Sights and landing sites

If you have a few days to spare and are looking for peace and quiet, it is worthwhile spending some time here. Isabela fits most people's image of a South Pacific island: coconut palms, azure ocean, white sand beaches, rocky inlets, mangroves, and a wonderfully laid-back feeling. In the main settlement, **Villamil**, there is a reasonable selection of accommodation, many little restaurants and a couple of bars. The **Municipal Tourist Office** ⓘ *T05-2529191, Mon-Fri 0730-1200, 1330-1700*, is at the pier at the foot of Calle Las Fragatas.

There are several lovely beaches right by the town, but mind the strong undertow and enquire locally about the best spots for swimming. It is 2½ hours walk west to **Muro de las Lágrimas**, a gruesome place built by convict labour under hideous conditions. It gets very hot, so start early and take plenty of water. Along the same road, 30 minutes from town, is the **Centro de Crianza**, a man-made breeding centre for giant tortoises surrounded by lagoons with flamingos and other birds, and pleasant walking trails. In the opposite direction, 30 minutes east toward the *embarcadero* (fishing pier) is **Concha Perla Lagoon**, with a nice access trail through mangroves and a little dock from which you can go swimming with sea lions and other creatures. Fishermen can take you to **Las Grietas,** a set of small *isletas* in the harbour where *tintoreras* (white-tipped reef sharks) may be seen in the still crystalline water; there may also be penguins. A trip costs about US$10 per boat, negotiate in advance.

Tours can be arranged to visit **Sierra Negra Volcano,** which has the largest basaltic caldera in the world, 7½ x 12 km. It is 18 km (1 hour) by pickup truck to a spot called El Cura, where you switch to horses for the 1½ hour beautiful ride to the crater rim at 980 m. It is a further 1½ hrs walk along bare brittle lava rock to **Volcán Chico**, with several fumaroles and

Background

→ **Talking about evolution**

Without doubt, the most famous visitor to the islands is Charles Darwin. His short stay in the archipelago proved hugely significant for science and for the study of evolution.

In September 1835, Darwin sailed into Galápagos waters on board the *HMS Beagle*, captained by the aristocratic Robert FitzRoy whose job was to chart lesser known parts of the world. FitzRoy had wanted on board a companion of his own social status and a naturalist to study the strange new animals and plants they would find en route. He chose Charles Darwin to fill both roles.

During the five weeks that the *Beagle* spent in the Galápagos, Darwin went ashore to collect plants, rocks, insects and birds. The unusual life forms and their adaptations to the harsh surroundings made a deep impression on him and eventually inspired his revolutionary theory on the evolution of species. The Galápagos provided a kind of model of the world in miniature. Darwin realized that these recently created volcanoes were young in comparison with the age of the Earth, and that life on the islands showed special adaptations. Yet the plants and animals also showed similarities to those from the South American mainland, where he guessed they had originally come from.

Darwin concluded that the life on the islands had probably arrived there by chance drifting, swimming or flying from the mainland and had not been created on the spot. Once the plants and animals had arrived, they evolved into forms better suited to the strange environment in which they found themselves. Darwin also noted that the animals were extremely tame, because of the lack of predatory mammals. The islands' isolation also meant that the giant tortoises did not face competition from agile mammals and could survive.

On his return to England, Darwin, in effect, spent the rest of his life publishing the findings of his voyage and developing the ideas it inspired. It was, however, only when another scientist, Alfred Russell Wallace, arrived at a similar conclusion to his own that he dared to publish a paper on his theory of evolution. Then followed his all-embracing *The Origin of the Species by means of Natural Selection*, in 1859. It was to cause a major storm of controversy and to earn Darwin recognition as the man who did much of the groundwork for the entire structure of modern biology.

more stunning views. The round trip takes a full day but there are only two buses a day along the road, no water, and it is easy to get lost; so going on your own is not advised. Tours can be arranged by most hotels. Contact Antonio Gil at **Hotel San Vicente**, T05-2529140; about US$20 per person, minimum 4 people.

66 99 The natural history of this archipelago
is very remarkable: it seems
to be a little world within itself. *Charles Darwin*

A visit to **Punta Moreno**, on the southwest part of Isabela, starts with a dinghy ride along the beautiful rocky shores where penguins and shore birds are usually seen. After a dry landing there is a hike through sharp lava rocks. **Elizabeth Bay**, on the west coast, is home to a small colony of penguins living on a series of small rocky islets and visited by dinghy.

Floreana ⊜⊜ ▶ *pp420-425*

Floreana is the island with the richest human history. Most of its inhabitants live in **Puerto Velasco Ibarra**, by Black Beach. Among those born on the island are a former director of the National Park, a boat owner, several naturalist guides and captains. There is electricity for a few hours each day, telephones and one small shop with very basic supplies, but you should be a self-sufficient as possible.

One of the original families to settle Floreana were the Wittmers, who arrived in 1932. Margret Wittmer, who experienced their arrival on the island, died in 2000 at age 95, but you can meet her daughter Floreanita, and granddaughter Erica. They are congenial hosts and staying with them is delightful. The pace of life is gentle and locally produced food is very good, but you will not be entertained. Unless you come with one of the few cruise boats which land at Black Beach for a few hours, or make special advance arrangements, it is difficult to get to Floreana and even more difficult to leave. The Cruz family, also descendants of early settlers, can organize local excursions by land and sea.

Sights and landing sites
Among the main visitor sites on Floreana is **Devil's Crown**, an almost completely submerged volcano that forms a dramatic snorkelling site to the north of Punta Cormorant. Erosion has transformed the cone into a series of jagged peaks with the resulting look of a crown. There is usually a wide selection of fish, sharks and turtles easily visible in about 6 m of water. **Punta Cormorant** is on the northern part of Floreana. The landing is on a beach of green sand coloured by olivine crystals, volcanic-derived silicates of magnesium and iron. The trail leads to a lake normally inhabited by flamingos and other shore birds and continues to a beach of fine white sand particles known as Flour Beach, an important nesting site for turtles.

Post Office Bay is west of Punta Cormorant. It gets its name from the Post Office barrel which was used in the late 18th century by English whaling vessels and later by the American whalers. It is the custom for visitors to place unstamped letters and cards in the barrel, and to deliver, free of charge, any addressed to their own destinations. There is a short walk to look at the remains of a Norwegian commercial fish drying and canning operation that was started in 1926 and abandoned after a couple of years. A lava tube that extends to the sea is also visited.

Other islands

Just north of Baltra (South Seymour), **Seymour Norte** is home to sea lions, marine iguanas, swallow-tailed gulls, frigatebirds and blue-footed boobies. The tourist trail leads through mangroves in one of the main nesting sites for blue-footed boobies and frigates in this part of

Giant tortoise, Santa Cruz island.

the archipelago. West of Baltra, **Daphne island** has a very rich birdlife, in particular the nesting boobies. Because of the possible problems of erosion, only small boats may land here and are limited to one visit each month.

One of the closest islands to Puerto Ayora is **Plaza Sur**. It's an example of a geological uplift and the southern part of the island has formed cliffs with spectacular views. It has a combination of both dry and coastal vegetation zones. Walking along the sea cliffs is a pleasant experience as the swallowtail gull, shearwaters and red billed tropic birds nest here. This is the home of the Men's Club, a rather sad looking colony of bachelor sea lions who are too old to mate and who get together to console each other. There are also lots of blue-footed boobies and a large population of land iguanas.

Santa Fe is in the southeastern part of Galápagos, between Santa Cruz and San Cristóbal, and was formed by volcanic uplift. The lagoon is home to a large colony of sea lions who are happy to join you for a swim. From the beach, the trail goes inland through a semi-arid landscape of cactus. This little island has its own sub-species of land iguana.

Española is the southernmost island of the Galápagos and, following a successful programme to remove all the feral species, is now the most pristine of the islands with many migrant, resident and endemic sea birds. **Gardner Bay**, on the northeastern coast, is a beautiful white sand beach with excellent swimming and snorkelling. **Punta Suárez**, on the western tip of the island, has a trail through a rookery. As well as a wide range of sea birds (including blue-footed and masked boobies) there is a great selection of wildlife including sea lions, the largest and most colourful marine iguanas of the Galápagos and the original home of the waved albatrosses.

Fernandina is the youngest of the islands, about 700,000 years old. It is also the most volcanically active, with eruptions every few years. **Punta Espinosa** is on the northeast coast of Fernandina. The trail from the landing site goes up through a sandy nesting site for huge colonies of marine iguanas. The nests appear as small hollows in the sand. You can also see flightless cormorants and go snorkelling in the bay.

Santiago, also known as James, is northwest of Santa Cruz. It has a volcanic landscape full of cliffs and pinnacles, home to several species of marine birds. This island has a large population of goats, one of the four species of animals introduced in the early 1800s. **James Bay** is on the western side of the island, where there is a wet landing on the dark sands of **Puerto Egas**. The trail leads to the remains of an unsuccessful salt mining operation. Fur seals are seen nearby. **Espumilla Beach** is another famous visitor site. After landing on a large beach, walk through a mangrove forest that leads to a lake usually inhabited by flamingos, pintail ducks and stilts. There are nesting and feeding sites for flamingos. Sea turtles dig their nests at the edge of the mangroves. **Buccaneer Cove**, on the northwest part of the island, was a haven for pirates during the 1600s and 1700s. **Sullivan Bay** is on the eastern coast of Santiago, opposite Bartolomé Island. The visitor trail leads across an impressive lunar landscape of lava fields formed in eruptions in 1890.

Bartolomé is probably the most easily recognized – the most visited and most photographed – of the islands in the Galápagos with its distinctive **Pinnacle Rock**. It is a small island located in Sullivan Bay off the eastern shore of Santiago. The trail leads steeply up to the summit, taking 30-40 minutes, from where there are panoramic views. At the second landing site on the island there is a lovely beach from which you can snorkel or swim and see the penguins.

Rábida is just to the south of Santiago. The trail leads to a salt water lagoon, occasionally home to flamingos. There is an area of mangroves near the lagoon where brown pelicans nest. This island is said to have the most diversified volcanic rocks of all the islands. You can snorkel and swim from the beach.

Sombrero Chino is just off the southeastern tip of Santiago, or James, and its name refers to its shape. It is most noted for the volcanic landscape including sharp outcroppings, cracked lava formations, lava tubes and volcanic rubble. This site is only available to yachts of less than 12 passengers capacity.

Genovesa, at the northeast part of the archipelago, is an outpost for many sea birds. It is an 8-10 hour all-night sail from Puerto Ayora. Like Fernandina, Genovesa is best visited on longer cruises or ships with larger range. One of the most famous sites is **Prince Phillip's Steps**, an

Frigate bird, North Seymour Island.

amazing walk through a seabird rookery that is full of life. You will see tropic birds, all three boobies, frigates, petrels, swallow-tailed and lava gulls, and many others. There is also good snorkelling at the foot of the steps, with lots of marine iguanas. The entrance to **Darwin Bay**, on the eastern side of the island, is very narrow and shallow and the anchorage in the lagoon is surrounded by mangroves, home to a large breeding colony of frigates and other seabirds.

● Sleeping

Puerto Ayora *p413, map p421*
LL-L Red Mangrove Inn, Darwin y las Fragatas, on the way to the research station, T05-2527011, www.redmangrove.com. A beautiful hotel with loads of character. Includes breakfast, restaurant, jacuzzi, deck bar and lovely dining room. Very tasteful rooms all overlooking the water, ample bathrooms. Owner Polo Navaro offers day tours and diving.
AL Las Ninfas, Los Colonos y Berlanga, T05-2526127, galaven@pa.ga.pro.ec. Modern and comfortable but bathrooms are small. Includes breakfast, good restaurant, a/c, large terrace and pool, fridge, full range of services, has its own boat for day trips, helpful with arrangements.
AL-C Lobo de Mar, 12 de Febrero y Darwin, T05-2526188, www.lobodemar.com.ec. Modern building with balconies and rooftop terrace, great views over the harbour. Includes breakfast, a/c, cheaper with fan, small pool, the new section is modern and comfortable, older rooms are simpler but good value. Friendly and attentive service.
A-B Sol y Mar, Darwin y Binford, T05-2526281, F05-2527015. Right in town but with an exceptionally pleasant location. Fan, offers a variety of rooms, each one is a little different. Lovely terrace on the water, attentive owners. Renovations planned in 2005.
B-C Castro, Los Colonos y Malecón, T05-2526113, F05-2526508. Modern and pleasant. Restaurant, a/c, cheaper with fan, owner Miguel Castro arranges day tours on his own motor launch, he is an authority on wildlife.

D España, Berlanga y Naveda, T05-2526101. Cold water, fan, spacious rooms, small sitting area with hammocks, good value.
D Salinas, Naveda y Berlanga, T05-2526107. Cheaper with cold water, fan, clean, pleasant and good value.

Puerto Baquerizo Moreno (San Cristóbal) *p414*
B Alojamiento en Hogares. This is an association of community bed & breakfasts offering accomodation in private homes. Includes breakfast, airport transfers, the use of kitchen and laundry facilities. Long stays also available. For information and bookings contact Berenice Norris, T05-2520258 (Mob T09-4148924), berenicenorris@gmail.com.
C Mar Azul, Northía y Esmeraldas, T05-2520139, F05-2520384. A/c, cheaper with fan, clean and pleasant, nice gardens, friendly and good value.
D Cabañas Don Jorge, above Playa Mann, T05-2520208. Fan, simple cabins in a quiet setting overlooking the ocean, shared kitchen, very friendly propietor.

Puerto Villamil (Isabella) *p415*
AL La Casa de Marita, at east end of beach, T05-2529238, www.galapagosisabela.com. Definitely upscale, even chic, for its location. Includes breakfast, other meals on request, a/c and fridge, right on the beach, very comfortable, each room is a bit different and some have balconies. A hidden gem.
B-C Ballena Azul and Isabela del Mar, Conocarpus y Opuntia, T05-2529030, www.hosteriaisabela.com.ec. An older wooden building next to modern cabins, both are very nice. Solar hot water, fan, large balcony, common area and dining room. Swiss run, friendly and helpful.

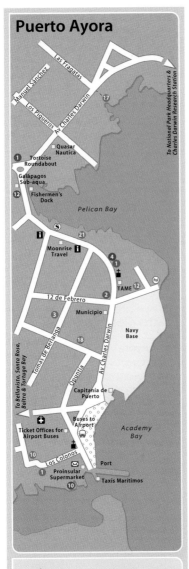

Puerto Ayora

Eating ⓪
Capricho 1
La Garrapata 4
Salvavidas 10
Tikki Takka 12
Tratoria de Pipo 12

50 metres
50 yards

Sleeping ⬡
Castro 1
España 3
Las Ninfas 10
Lobo de Mar 12
Red Mangrove Inn 17
Salinas 18
Sol y Mar 21

Bars & clubs ⓿
La Panga & Bongo 1
Limon y Café 2

p417

L **Pensión Wittmer**, right on Black Beach, T05-2529506. Includes 3 delicious meals, fan (when there is electricity), simple and comfortable, a very special place.

⓪ Eating

Puerto Ayora *p413, map p421*

♥♥♥ **La Garrapata**, Charles Darwin between 12 de Febrero and Tomás de Berlanga, closed Sun. Good food, attractive setting and good music, juice bar and sandwiches during the day, choice of 2 set meals at lunch, and la carte at night.

♥♥ **Trattoria de Pippo**, Charles Darwin entre Indefatigable y Isla Floreana, second location called 'El Patio' at Charles Darwin entre Naveda y 12 de Febrero, 1700-2200 daily. Italian and seafood, pleasant atmosphere, attentive owner.

♥ **Capricho**, Charles Darwin y Isla Floreana by the tortoise roundabout, daily 0630-2200, Mon to 1700. Good vegetarian food, salads and juices, breakfast.

♥ **Salvavidas**, On the waterfront overlooking the activity at the pier. Good set lunch, breakfast and seafood. Good value.

♥ Along Charles Binford, between Padre J Herrera and General Rodríguez Lara are many kiosks selling traditional food, including good seafood at economical prices; **Tía Juanita** cooks well, as does **William** with Esmeraldeño specialties. All the kiosks have simple outdoor seating and a lively pleasant atmosphere, popular with locals and busy at night.

♥ **Tikki Takka**, Charles Binford y Charles Darwin, Mon-Sat 0800-2000. For breakfast and snacks, excellent bread flown in from Cyrano bakery in Quito, plus pastries.

Puerto Baquerizo Moreno (San Cristóbal) *p414*

♥♥♥ **La Playa**, Av de la Armada Nacional, by the navy base. Varied menu, nice location, popular.

Galápagos Islands Listings

It's easy to bust your budget in Galápagos and there are more wonderfully lavish cruises here than we can recommend. But those who stay a couple of days in Puerto Ayora, either on a land-based tour or to book a last minute cruise, can still indulge themselves with a meal at ♈♈♈ **Angermeyer Point**, T05-252 6452, Tue-Sat 1900-2200, Sun brunch 1100-1600. Located across the bay from town, take a *taxi marítimo* (water-taxi) and go a little early to enjoy the sunset (take insect repellent). This is the former home of Galápagos pioneer and artist Carl Angermeyer, with his works on display, and it has a gorgeous setting over the water. The menu is innovative, varied and excellent, and the service very attentive. A meal costs about US$15, without drinks.

♈♈-♈ **Rosita**, Ignacio de Hernández y General Villamil. Set meals and varied à la carte, old-time yachtie hangout.
♈ **Barracuda**, Charles Darwin y 12 de Febrero. Tasty grilled meat, fish, and menestras.
♈ **Panadería Fragata**, Northía y Rocafuerte. Excellent bread and pastries.

Puerto Villamil (Isabela) *p415*
♈♈♈ **El Encanto de la Pepa**, Conocarpus y Pinzón Artesano. Lots of character, good food, attractive setting, friendly and pleasant.

🌙 Bars and clubs

Puerto Ayora *p413, map p421*
Limón y Café, Charles Darwin y 12 de Febrero. Evenings only, good snacks and drinks, lots of music, pool table, popular.
La Panga, Av Charles Darwin y Berlanga and **Bar Bongo**, upstairs at the same location; both are popular.

Puerto Baquerizo Moreno (San Cristóbal) *p414*
El Barquero, Hernández y Manuel J Cobos. Bar and peña. Open daily.
Neptuno, Charles Darwin y Herman Melville. Disco with young crowd, Tue-Sat 2030-0300. There are a couple of other bars along Av de la Armada Nacional towards the waterfront.

Puerto Villamil (Isabela) *p415*
Beto's Beach Bar, Antonio Gil y Los Flamencos. Pleasant location, irregular hours, very relaxed.

▲ Activities and tours

Puerto Ayora *p413, map p421*
Scuba diving
There are several diving agencies in Puerto Ayora offering courses, equipment rental, dives within Academy Bay (2 dives for about US$90), dives to other central islands (2 dives, US$140), daily tours for 1 week in the central islands and several-day live-aboard tours. Note that the waters around the Galápagos islands are for experienced and hardy divers only. Cold seas and strong currents mean that novices will struggle and even experienced divers may only manage one or two dives a day.
Galápagos Sub-Aqua, Av Charles Darwin by Pelican Bay, T05-252 6633, www.galapagos-sub-aqua.com. (Quito: Pinto 439 y Amazonas, office 101, T02-256 5294). Open 0800-1230, 1430-1830. Instructor Fernando Zambrano offers full certificate courses up to divemaster level (PADI or NAUI).
Scuba Iguana is a long-time reliable and recommended dive operator who was changing premises and telephones at the close of this edition. Check their website (www.scubaiguana.com) for information.

Galápagos Islands Listings

Bay excursions in glass-bottom boats visit sites near Puerto Ayora such as Isla Caamaño, Punta Estrada, Las Grietas, Franklin Bay and Playa de los Perros. It involves some walking and you are likely to see sea lions, birds, marine iguanas and marine life including sharks. Snorkelling can be part of the tour. Full-day tours (0900-1600) are around US$25 per person and can be arranged through tour operators listed below. Reservations are strongly recommended in the high season. Discounts may be available in low season.

Tour operators

Touts sometimes approach tourists at the airport or in the street, claiming to represent well-known agencies and offering cheap tours. As elsewhere, their services are generally not recommended.

Moonrise Travel Agency, Av Charles Darwin entre Charles Binford y Tomás de Berlanga, opposite Banco del Pacífico, T05-2526348, sdivine@pa.ga.pro.ec. Last-minute cruise bookings, day-tours to different islands, bay tours, highland tours, airline reservations. Knowledgeable, helpful and reliable.

Puerto Baquerizo Moreno (San Cristóbal) *p414*

Chalo Tours, Malecón Charles Darwin y Villamil, T05-252 0953. Bay tours to Kicker Rock and Isla de los Lobos, boat tours to the north end of the island, highland tours to El Junco and Puerto Chino beach, diving tours, bike rentals, snorkelling gear, surf boards, book exchange.

→ The Galápagos Affair

One of the more bizarre and notorious periods in the islands' human history began in 1929 with the arrival of German doctor, Friedrich Ritter, and his mistress, Dore Strauch. Three years later, the Wittmer family also decided to settle on the island, and Floreana soon became so fashionable that luxury yachts used to call in. One of these visitors was Baroness von Wagner de Bosquet, an Austrian woman who settled on the island with her two lovers and grandiose plans to build a hotel for millionaires. Soon after landing in 1932 the Baroness proclaimed herself Empress of Floreana, which was not to the liking of Dr Ritter or the Wittmer family, and tensions rose. There followed several years of mysterious and unsavoury goings-on, during which everyone died or disappeared, except Dore Strauch and the Wittmer family. The longest survivor of this still unexplained drama was Margret Wittmer, who lived at Black Beach on Floreana until her death in 2000, at age 95. Her account of life there, entitled *Floreana, Poste Restante*, was published in 1961 and became a bestseller. Also see *The Galápagos Affair*, by John Treherne.

⊖ Transport

See also Getting there, p408 and Getting around, p409 for buses to and from the airports, flights and boats between islands. In Puerto Ayora, **water taxis** (*taxis marítimos*) run from the pier to anchored boats, Punta Estrada and nearby beaches, US$1.

⊙ Directory

Puerto Ayora *p413, map p421*
Banks Banco del Pacífico, Av Charles Darwin y Charles Binford, T05-2526282, Mon-Fri 0800-1530, Sat 0930-1230. US$5 commission per transaction to change TCs, maximum US$500 a day. ATM works with MasterCard only, cash advances from tellers on some Visa and MasterCards.
Internet There are several cyber cafés throughout town, US$1.50-$3/hr.
Medical services The local hospital on Padre J Herrera provides first aid and basic care. For anything more serious, locals usually fly to the mainland. **Hyperbaric Chamber**, 12 de Noviembre y Rodríguez Lara, T05-2526911, sss@puertoayora.com, www.sssnetwork.com. Also has a private

medical clinic. Hyperbaric treatment costs US$850/hr, unless you or your dive operator are covered by insurance. **Post** By the port, often runs out of stamps.

Puerto Baquerizo Moreno (San Cristóbal) *p414*
Banks Banco del Pacífico, Charles Darwin entre Española y Melville. Same services as in Puerto Ayora. Open Mon-Fri 0800-1530, Sat 1000-1200. **Internet** Several cyber cafés in town, US$1.50-$3/hr.
Medical services The local hospital at Av Northía y Quito offers only basic care. **Dr David Basantes**, Av Northía opposite Hotel Mar Azul, T05-252 0126, is a helpful general practitioner. **Farmacia San Cristóbal**, Villamil y Hernández, is the best stocked pharmacy in town. **Post** Charles Darwin y 12 de Febrero.

Puerto Villamil (Isabela) *p415*
Banks There are no banks on Isabela, no ATMs, and nowhere to use credit cards or change TCs. You must bring US$ cash. If you are stuck, ask at **Hotel Marita**.
Internet There are one or two slow and expensive cyber cafés in town.

Index

Index

Advertisers' index

Map index

Advertisers' & map index

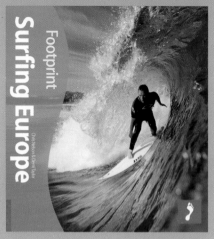

Credits

Footprint credits
Editor: Alan Murphy
Deputy editor: Angus Dawson
Map editor: Sarah Sorensen
Picture editor: Robert Lunn

Publisher: Patrick Dawson
Editorial: Sophie Blacksell, Sarah Thorowgood, Claire Boobbyer, Felicity Laughton, Laura Dixon, Nicola Jones
Cartography: Robert Lunn, Claire Benison, Kevin Feeney, Angus Dawson, Esther Monzón, Thom Wickes
Cover design: Robert Lunn
Advertising: Debbie Wylde
Finance and administration: Sharon Hughes, Elizabeth Taylor, Lindsay Dytham

Photography credits
Front cover: Powerstock (Traditional dress)
Inside: Robert Lunn, Jamie Marshall, Powerstock, Julius Honnor, Alex Robinson, Nature PL, Photolibrary, Alamy, South American Pictures (Tony Morrison, Kathy Jarvis, Kimball Morrison, Britt Dyer, Hilary Bradt, Danny Aeberhard, Sue Mann, Steve Harrison, Katie Moore, Luke Peters, Chris Sharp)
Back cover: Jamie Marshall (Children playing on Taquile Island)

Print
Manufactured in Italy by Printer Trento
Pulp from sustainable forests

Every effort has been made to ensure that the facts in this guidebook are accurate. However, travellers should still obtain advice from consulates, airlines etc about travel and visa requirements before travelling. The authors and publishers cannot accept responsibility for any loss, injury or inconvenience however caused.

Publishing information
Footprint Peru, Bolivia and Ecuador
1st edition
© Footprint Handbooks Ltd
May 2005
ISBN 1 904777 34 1
CIP DATA: A catalogue record for this book is available from the British Library
® Footprint Handbooks and the Footprint mark are a registered trademark of Footprint Handbooks Ltd

Published by Footprint
6 Riverside Court
Lower Bristol Road
Bath BA2 3DZ, UK
T +44 (0)1225 469141
F +44 (0)1225 469461
discover@footprintbooks.com
www.footprintbooks.com

Distributed in the USA by
Publishers Group West

Neither the black and white nor colour maps are intended to have any political significance.

Hotel and restaurant price codes should only be taken as a guide to the prices and facilities offered by the establishment. It is at the owner's discretion to vary from them from time to time.

The South American Handbook: 1924-2005

It was 1921

Ireland had just been partitioned, the British miners were striking for more pay and the federation of British industry had an idea. Exports were booming in South America – how about a Handbook for businessmen trading in that far away continent? The *Anglo-South American Handbook* was born that year, written by W Koebel, the most prolific writer on Latin America of his day.

1924

Two editions later the book was 'privatized' and in 1924, in the hands of Royal Mail, the steamship company for South America, became *The South American Handbook*, subtitled 'South America in a nutshell'. This annual publication became the 'bible' for generations of travellers to South America and remains so to this day. In the early days travel was by sea and the Handbook gave all the details needed for the long voyage from Europe. What to wear for dinner; how to arrange a cricket match with the Cable & Wireless staff on the Cape Verde Islands and a full account of the journey from Liverpool up the Amazon to Manaus: 5898 miles without changing cabin!

1939

As the continent opened up, *The South American Handbook* reported the new Pan Am flying boat services, and the fortnightly airship service from Rio to Europe on the Graf Zeppelin. For reasons still unclear but with extraordinary determination, the annual editions continued through the Second World War.

1970s

From the 1970s, jet aircraft transformed travel. Many more people discovered South America and the backpacking trail started to develop. All the while the Handbook was gathering fans, including literary vagabonds such as Paul Theroux and Graham Greene (who once sent some updates addressed to **"The publishers of the best travel guide in the world, Bath, England"**.)

1990s

During the 1990s Patrick and James Dawson, the publishers of *The South American Handbook* set about developing a new travel guide series using this legendary title as the flagship. By 1997 there were over a dozen guides in the series and the Footprint imprint was launched.

2000s

In 2003, Footprint launched a new series of pocket format guides focusing on short-break European cities. The series grew quickly so that at the end of 2004 there were over 100 Footprint travel guides covering more than 150 destinations around the world. In January 2004, *The South American Handbook* reached another milestone: 80 annual editions. A memorable birthday party was held at Stanfords in London to celebrate.

The future

There are many more guides and pocket guides in the pipeline. A Lifestyle series was launched in 2004 with *Surfing Europe*, packed with 500 full-colour photographs and 70 maps and charts and the Backpacker series is set to grow with new titles in 2005. To keep up-to-date with new releases check out the Footprint website for all the latest news and information, **www.footprintbooks.com**.